The Official Guide

PhotoImpact 7

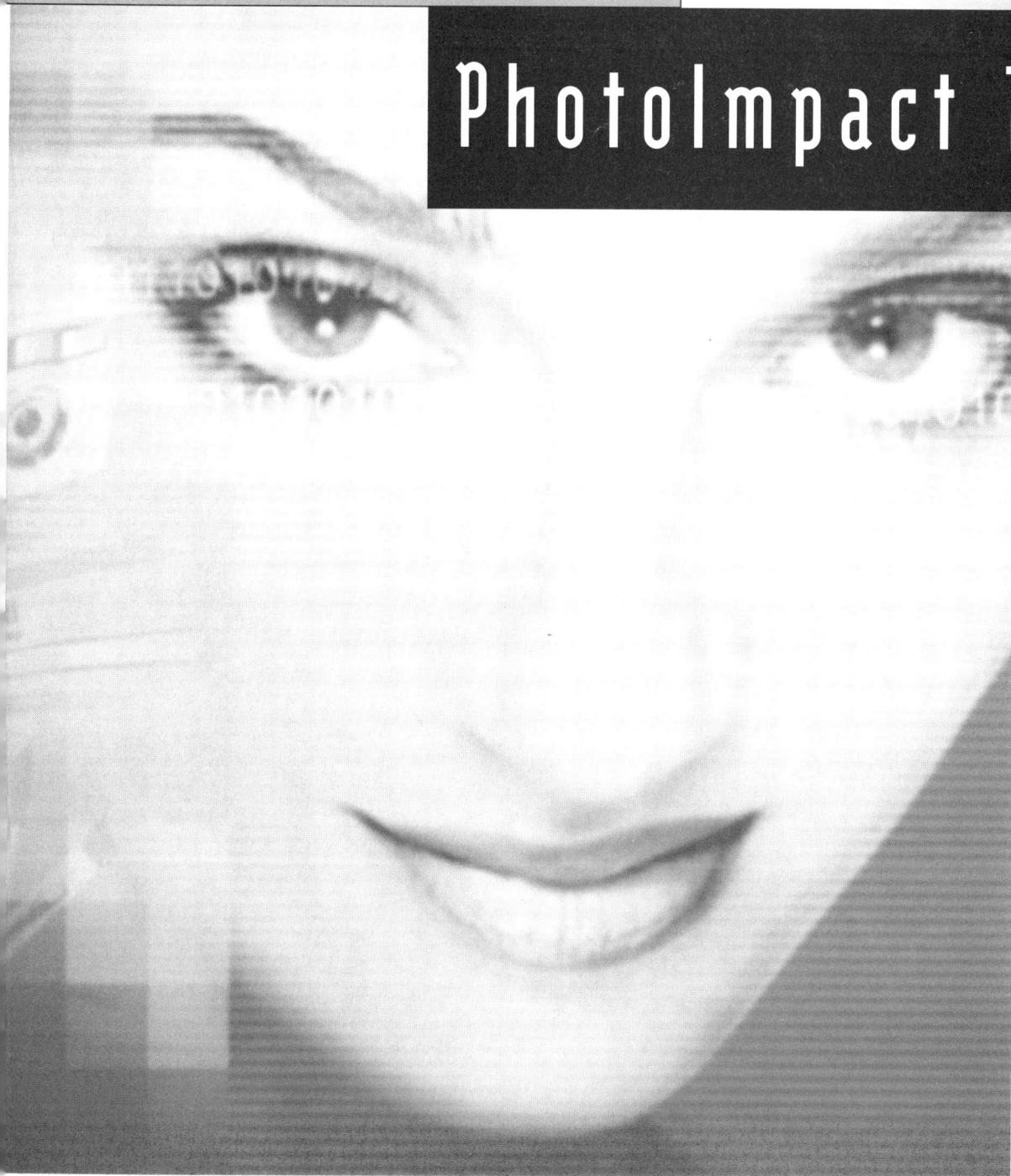

The Official Guide

PhotoImpact 7

Michael Meadhra
with Anthony L. Celeste

McGraw-Hill/Osborne

New York   Chicago   San Francisco
Lisbon   London   Madrid   Mexico City   Milan
New Delhi   San Juan   Seoul   Singapore   Sydney   Toronto

McGraw-Hill/Osborne
2600 Tenth Street
Berkeley, California 94710
U.S.A.

To arrange bulk purchase discounts for sales promotions, premiums, or fund-raisers, please contact **McGraw-Hill**/Osborne at the above address. For information on translations or book distributors outside the U.S.A., please see the International Contact Information page immediately following the index of this book.

PhotoImpact® 7: The Official Guide

1234567890 FGR FGR 0198765432

Book p/n 0-07-219406-5 and CD p/n 0-07-219407-3
parts of
ISBN 0-07-219405-7

Publisher: Brandon A. Nordin
Vice President & Associate Publisher: Scott Rogers
Acquisitions Editor: Megg Bonar
Project Editor: Monika Faltiss
Acquisitions Coordinator: Tana Diminyatz
Technical Editors: Colwin Chan, Jesse Stewart
Consulting Editor: Anthony L. Celeste
Copy Editor: Marilyn Smith
Production: Apollo Publishing Services
Illustrators: Michael Mueller, Lyssa Wald
Series Design: Mickey Galicia, Peter F. Hancik
Cover Illustrator: Cristina Deh-Lee

This book was composed with Corel VENTURA™ Publisher.

About the Author

Michael Meadhra is an author, consultant, and web designer. After working as a photographer, graphic designer, media producer, and manager for a number of years, he discovered that his best efforts were directed toward writing and teaching others how to use the computer technology that figured so prominently in all of those occupations. So, he turned to writing as a full-time career, first as a writer/editor of technical journals, then as a freelance book author. To date, Michael has written or contributed to more than 30 computer books and countless articles on topics such as graphics, presentation, and publishing software. He is the author of *How To Do Everything with Dreamweaver 4*, also published by McGraw-Hill/Osborne.

About the Contributing Writers

Anthony L. Celeste is a writer, designer, and programmer who specializes in interface design, animation, and special effects. He owns acdesigns.com, a company focusing on web and multimedia design. Anthony is a frequent contributor to web and print magazines and to Ulead's Learning Center, located at http://www.ulead.com/learning/learning.htm.

Rowena White is an independent web application developer and graphic artist. She has been a contributing author for several computer books and illustration technique magazines. Having written for over 20 years, she has authored more than 50 technical references and over 30 computer-related articles.

When she's not writing computer books and raising her four children, she airbrushes wildlife portraits that she donates to local zoos. Teaching others how to paint and write creatively is something she enjoys volunteering her time toward. To her, creative expression is the doorway to one's soul.

Contents at a Glance

Contents

Acknowledgments

This book would not exist without the contributions of a lot of different people. I'm glad that tradition allows me this opportunity to acknowledge some of those people for their efforts.

Thanks to Megg Bonar, acquisitions editor for Osborne/McGraw-Hill, for pulling this book project together and for giving me the opportunity to write it. Tana Diminyatz, acquisitions coordinator, and Monika Faltiss, project editor, were my regular contacts and they've both been a pleasure to work with. Jesse Stewart, the technical editor, helped ensure the accuracy of the text and offered many suggestions that enriched and improved the book. Marilyn Smith, the copy editor, saw to it that my prose was readable. I didn't have much direct contact with the rest of the Osborne/McGraw-Hill staff working on this book, but their contributions are appreciated nonetheless. My thanks to all of you!

This book would not be possible without the active participation of the PhotoImpact developers, Ulead Systems. Thanks to Colwin Chan and the rest of the folks at Ulead for their help with beta software, reviewing manuscripts, and answering questions. Special thanks are due to Joyce in Ulead's Taiwan office for her help with the CD.

It's nearly impossible for one author to write a book like this from scratch in the limited time between the availability of beta software and a press date that gets the book out before the software is ready for its next update. But a team of authors can do what a single author cannot. In this case, the supporting team members are Tony Celeste, Rowena White, and Winston Steward. Thanks to all of you guys!

And finally, I wish to thank my agent, David Fugate, Waterside Productions, for getting me this gig and for his continued support and help to make it a reality.

—Michael Meadhra

I've been using PhotoImpact since it was first released in 1996. I've always found it to be an exceptional program, so I was very pleased with the opportunity to co-author PhotoImpact's first Official Guide. I extend my thanks to the entire Ulead team and Ulead user community, along with a special thanks to Michelle Gallina, Ulead's marketing communications manager, and to Colwin Chan, PhotoImpact's product manager and one of this book's technical editors. I also want to take a moment to thank my family, and my many friends, both online and off, for constantly being such a positive part of my life.

—Anthony L. Celeste

Introduction

Film is dead!

This headline and others like it are showing up with increasing regularity. It's an acknowledgement of the accelerating trend of digital cameras replacing traditional film-based still cameras. All those digital cameras, along with the increasingly common scanners, are producing a lot of digital images. And there are plenty of uses for those digital images, too, what with the prevalence of inexpensive color printers for hardcopy output and the growing hunger for digital images and graphics for the web and for use in other programs.

As the prevalence of digital images rises in all areas of personal computing, so does the need for capable and easy to use image-editing software. Unfortunately, the simplistic entry-level paint programs are inadequate for all but the most basic uses, and the high-end professional image editors are outrageously expensive and hard to use.

Ulead Systems has been a leader in providing an image editor—PhotoImpact— that is a lot more robust and capable than the entry-level programs and yet is still much easier to use and far less expensive than the high-priced programs designed for graphics professionals. In fact, PhotoImpact, and its companion program GIF Animator, can produce some effects that are difficult to match with the most advanced software, and it does so with ease and speed. As a result, PhotoImpact gives you professional caliber results without the high price and steep learning curve that is usually associated with such power. PhotoImpact's outstanding capabilities and modest price have even earned it a place in many professional artists' computer toolbox.

PhotoImpact is an excellent tool for editing digital images of all kinds. You can use it to color correct and retouch images, create new images by assembling components, and add an impressive assortment of special effects. You can also use PhotoImpact to create original images and graphics from scratch, or use the built-in tools that make creating buttons, backgrounds, and other web components a snap. The GIF Animator program (included with PhotoImpact and covered in this book) is a leading tool for producing banners and other animated graphics for web sites. Another companion program, PhotoImpact Album, helps you tackle the chore of organizing your collection of digital images.

Who Is This Book For?

This book is for anyone wanting to learn how to use Ulead PhotoImpact 7 and its companion programs, GIF Animator and PhotoImpact Album. It's targeted primarily toward beginning to intermediate PhotoImpact users and assumes no prior experience with the software. Also, readers who have used other image editing software (including older versions of PhotoImpact) will find this book a good way to get up to speed with PhotoImpact 7.

In writing this book, the authors made a few assumptions about you, the reader. We presume that the reader is an intelligent and interested adult with basic computer skills and at least a beginner's understanding of image editing. This book shows you how to use PhotoImpact to edit images produced by your scanner or digital camera, but it doesn't attempt to cover how to use the scanner or camera. Similarly, the book shows you how to use PhotoImpact's features to produce graphics and animations for use on a web site, but doesn't cover web site design and development.

What's in This Book?

This book is neither an introductory tutorial that gives a brief overview of the program at the expense of omitting important details, nor a dry reference that provides a comprehensive description of every feature and setting without showing you how to use them. Instead, it strives to find the middle ground between these two extremes with clear descriptions of features and step-by-step instructions that describe the options you'll encounter at each step so you'll have the information you need to apply those instructions to your own images.

The book is organized into five major parts that correspond to the kinds of things you may want to do with PhotoImpact. Similarly, each part is divided into chapters, and each chapter is divided into sections to organize the coverage of PhotoImpact into logical chunks. We don't necessarily expect you to read the entire book from cover to cover in sequence. Instead, you'll probably want to select the combination of parts, chapters, and sections that apply to the way you intend to use PhotoImpact and then read those sections in the order that makes sense to you for the way you work. You can always go back and read additional chapters and sections later when you want to expand your knowledge of PhotoImpact and what you can do with the program.

Part I: Use the PhotoImpact Tools

Chapter 1 provides a get acquainted tour of the PhotoImpact user interface—the windows, panels, and toolbars that make up the PhotoImpact application. Chapter 2 continues the program orientation with an introduction to the various tools such as the Paintbrush and the Retouch tools.

Part II: Acquire and Manage Images

Chapter 3 covers opening and saving image files, creating a new image document, and acquiring images from scanners and digital cameras. Chapter 4 is about image management and covers topics such as converting images from one file format to another, sharing images on the web or via e-mail, and using the PhotoImpact Album program to build albums of digital images.

Part III: Create and Edit Images

This part starts off with Chapter 5, which covers PhotoImpact's tools for correcting image flaws with tools such as brightness and contrast adjustment and color correction. Chapter 6 continues the theme with coverage of effect filters, shadows, and other image enhancements. Chapter 7 shows you how to create an image by assembling image objects and working with objects, selections, and layers. Chapter 8 adds to your graphics skills with instructions on how to use PhotoImpact's text tools and effects. Chapter 9 wraps up this part with an exploration of fills and PhotoImpact's more specialized filters and effects.

Part IV: Create Web Components and Pages

Part IV shows you how to use PhotoImpact's features for producing graphics for the web. It starts (in Chapter 10) with how to optimize and slice images and proceeds (in Chapter 11) to give instructions for creating web components such as buttons and backgrounds. Chapter 12 covers PhotoImpact's ability to produce complete web pages.

Part V: Build Animations

This part is focused on animation. Chapter 13 starts with the some basic animation in PhotoImpact and how to prepare base images for animation in another program. Chapter 14 introduces the GIF Animator program that ships with PhotoImpact. GIF Animator is a leading application in its own right. It's designed specifically for producing compact and efficient animated GIF files for use on the web and in presentations.

Part VI: Online Bonus: Advanced Techniques

In addition to the fourteen chapters printed in this book, there are three bonus chapters available online. Chapter 15 covers how to use some of the more advanced features of GIF Animator. Chapter 16 includes instructions on using features such as the Batch Convert tool and Quick Command panel to automate common tasks in PhotoImpact. Chapter 17 covers the many preference settings that enable you to customize PhotoImpact to suit your working style. Chapters 15, 16, and 17 are available in PDF format on the Osborne site at www.osborne.com.

Conventions Used in This Book

The design of this book includes special icons that help call out certain bits of information and make them more accessible. Among them are the following:

- **Tip**   A time-saving alternative
- **Note**   Supplemental information
- **Caution**   Something to watch out for
- **New to PhotoImpact 7**   A new or substantially changed feature of PhotoImpact 7

Another important convention is the way we give instructions for choosing commands from the PhotoImpact menus. The individual menu commands are separated with vertical bars (|). For example, "choose File | Open" means to choose File from the Menu bar and then choose Open from the File menu that appears.

About This Book's CD-ROM

You undoubtedly noticed that this book includes a CD-ROM disk. The CD is much more than a stiffener for the back cover. It includes a free demo version of PhotoImpact 7, including the Ulead companion program GIF Animator. You get these two programs, and several other Ulead products to try out, plus an assortment of sample images from the book's chapters that you can use to get started experimenting with PhotoImpact and its capabilities. The software is fully functional, but it will expire after a 30-day trial period. You can convert the trial software to unlimited use by purchasing a license from the Ulead web site at http://www.ulead.com. (See the installation instructions and license agreement on the CD for full details.)

Also on the CD, you will find color versions of many of the figures and illustrations that appear in the book. That way, you can open the images to see what the images really look like instead of relying solely on the black-and-white illustrations on the book pages. The images are located on the CD in a folder called PhotoImpact Official Guide and are organized into subfolders according to chapter.

Talk to Us

Do you have some comments you'd like to make about the book? If so, we'd like to hear from you. You can send the authors an e-mail at pi7tog@meadhra.com. You'll get an immediate acknowledgment from our mail robot. And although we can't promise to respond to every message, the authors *will* read your messages and respond to as many as possible.

PART I

Use the PhotoImpact Tools

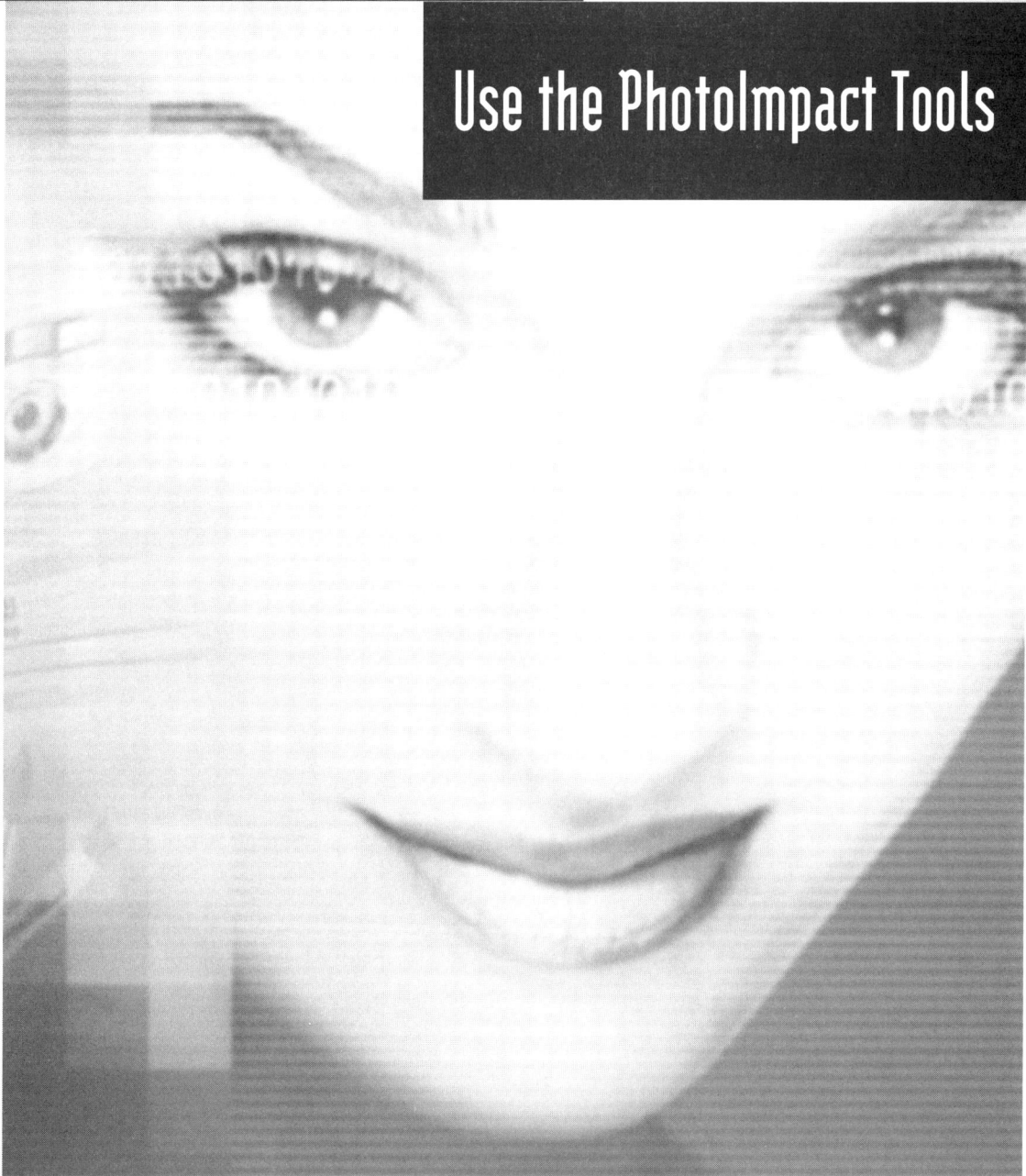

CHAPTER 1

Get to Know the PhotoImpact User Interface

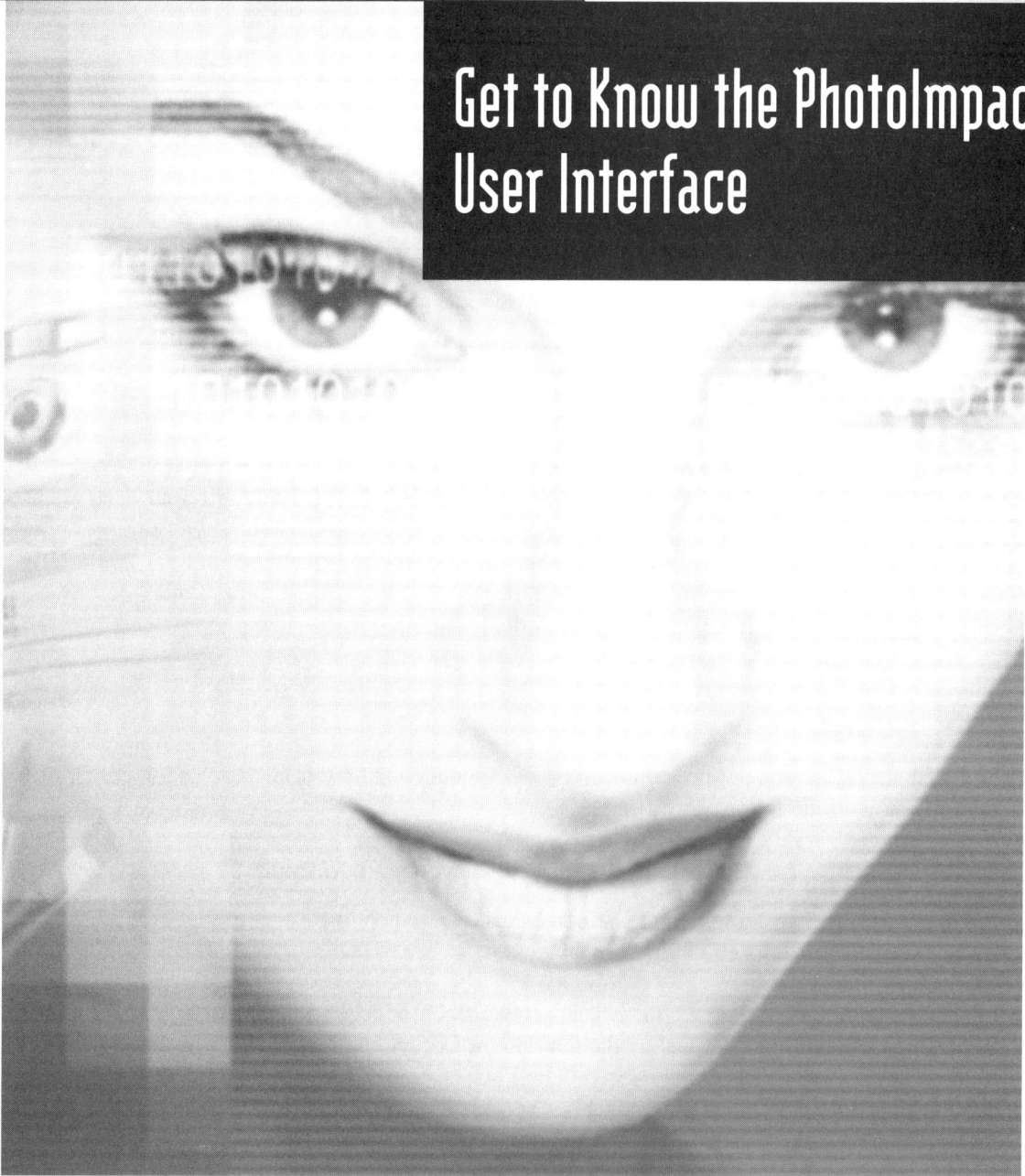

PhotoImpact 7 is the latest version of the premier image-editing program from Ulead Systems, a worldwide leader in developing graphics, video, and animation software. Each new version of PhotoImpact increases in power and versatility with the addition of new features and utilities. Over the years, the program has grown from a simple image editor to a sophisticated graphics tool that includes text and vector-drawing capabilities, effects filters, and the ability to generate web components and pages. To add even more versatility, the program ships with two utility programs: PhotoImpact Album, for image cataloging and management, and Ulead GIF Animator, for creating animated graphics.

This chapter introduces you to the PhotoImpact user interface—the collection of windows, menus, toolbars, panels, palettes, and buttons that you will use to interact with the PhotoImpact program. It's intended to be a roadmap to help you identify and locate the major components of the PhotoImpact program. Later chapters show you how to use those components to do something useful, such as create and edit images.

If you're new to PhotoImpact, or to image editors in general, you'll want to study this chapter carefully, since the PhotoImpact user interface is quite different from applications such as word processors and spreadsheet programs. Even if you're already acquainted with other versions of PhotoImpact, you'll probably want to at least skim this chapter to familiarize yourself with the numerous additions and refinements introduced in the new version of the program.

Launch PhotoImpact

The first step in getting to know PhotoImpact is to launch the program. You can do that in one of the following ways:

PhotoImpact 7

- Double-click the PhotoImpact 7 shortcut icon on your desktop.

- Click the Start button on the Windows taskbar and choose Programs | Ulead PhotoImpact 7 | PhotoImpact 7.

When you launch PhotoImpact, the splash screen (the product logo and copyright notice) appears briefly, followed by the main PhotoImpact application window and an assortment of auxiliary windows and dialog boxes. One of those dialog boxes is the Tip of the Day. By default, this dialog box appears each time you start the program. After reading the tip, you can close the Tip of the Day dialog box by clicking the Close button.

1

| TIP | *If you don't want to see the Tip of the Day dialog box each time you launch PhotoImpact, simply uncheck the Show Tips On Startup checkbox at the bottom of the dialog box before closing it. You can always view a tip any time you want by choosing Help | Tip of the Day from the PhotoImpact menu bar.* |

Each time you launch PhotoImpact, the program automatically checks the status of the Ulead web site. If PhotoImpact finds any new information posted since you last ran the program, it displays the PhotoImpact News dialog box alerting you to the fact. Simply click the highlighted web address to open your web browser and view the site. Click the Close button to close the PhotoImpact News dialog box.

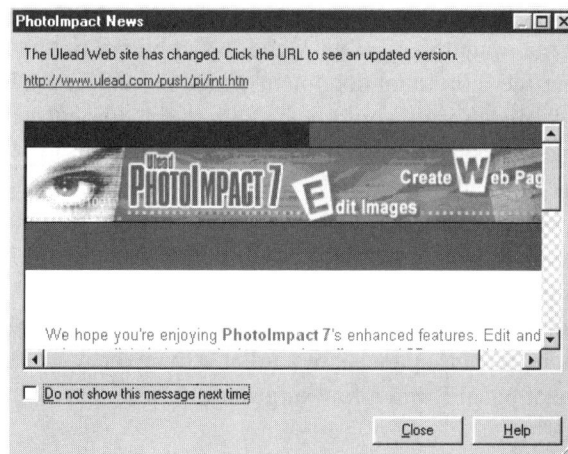

This handy feature helps to keep you informed of the availability of add-ons and other news about PhotoImpact. It takes only a couple of seconds to check the Ulead web site if you have an always-on broadband connection to the Internet. If there is no Internet connection available, PhotoImpact skips this step. However, if you have a dial-up Internet connection, it may take a little longer for PhotoImpact to complete its check for PhotoImpact News. Be patient; the program will load momentarily.

TIP

To prevent the PhotoImpact News dialog box from appearing when you launch the program, click the Don't Show This Next Time checkbox before closing the dialog box. Disabling the dialog box also prevents PhotoImpact from automatically attempting to access the Internet when you launch the program. You can also configure PhotoImpact to check the Ulead web site periodically instead of every time you launch the program. Choose File | Preferences | General to open the Preferences dialog box and then select the PhotoImpact category. Adjust the Check Ulead Web Site... setting to control how often PhotoImpact checks for news.

Get Acquainted with the PhotoImpact Window

The PhotoImpact program is composed of the main application window and several auxiliary windows, as shown in Figure 1-1. The application window includes the usual title bar, menu bar, toolbars, and status bar, as well as a large work area where you can open and edit image documents in their own document windows.

You can minimize, maximize, move, resize, and close the PhotoImpact window just as you would manipulate any other Windows application window. Similarly, you can manipulate the individual document windows within the PhotoImpact application window just as you would work with the document windows within a typical word processor or spreadsheet application that supports the Windows multiple document interface.

The auxiliary windows, called *floating panels*, provide easy access to some of PhotoImpact's most-used features. Each panel is a separate window that you can move and resize independently of the main PhotoImpact application window. Floating panels, sometimes called *palettes*, are a common feature of many graphics programs, and PhotoImpact's panels are similar. However, you'll probably find that the PhotoImpact panels hold a few surprises.

PhotoImpact
application window

Attribute toolbar

Menu bar   Standard toolbar   EasyPalette panel

Tools
panel

Panel
Manager

Access
panel

Status bar   Quick Command panel

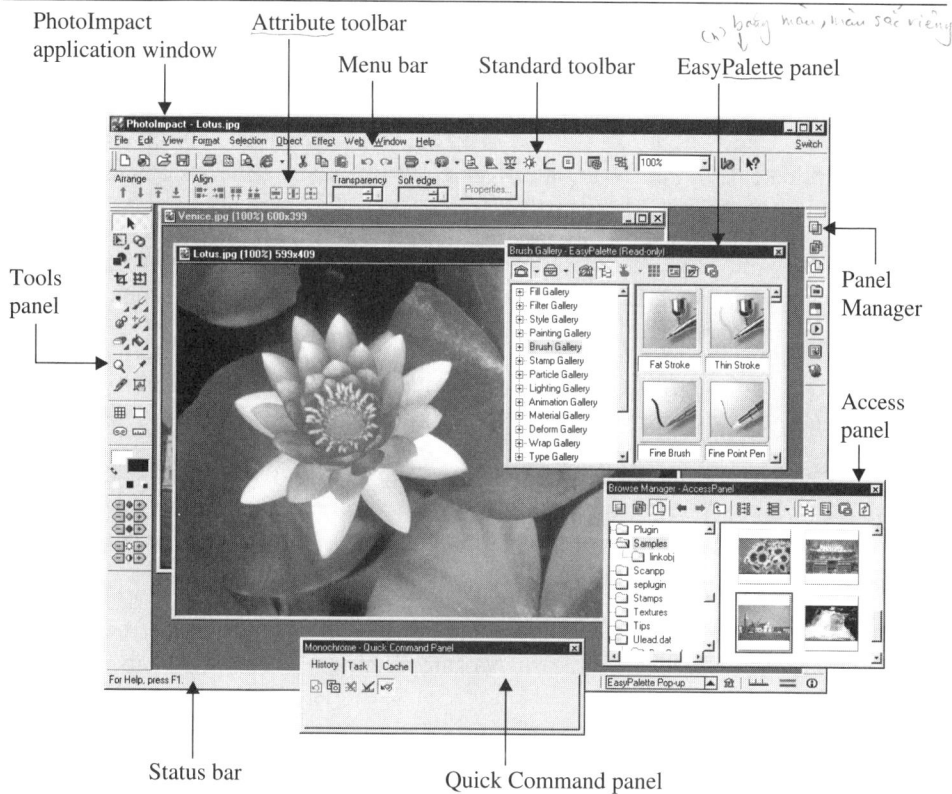

FIGURE 1-1   The PhotoImpact program window with a typical assortment of panels

In addition to the floating panels that appear in their own windows, some panels (such as the Tool panel) can be attached to the edges of the PhotoImpact application window, making them look more like toolbars than separate windows.

The following sections explore each at the major components of the PhotoImpact user interface in more detail.

Choose Options from PhotoImpact's Menus

Selecting options from the PhotoImpact menu bar works just like making menu selections in any other Windows program. The following list provides a brief summary of the commands on each of the PhotoImpact menus.

- **File**   Commands that allow you to create, open, save, print, import, and export image documents; access to program preferences; and the Exit command.

- **Edit**   Undo and Redo commands; Cut, Copy, and Paste commands; Crop, Duplicate, Fill, Fade Out, and Rotate & Flip; Stage and Trace; and Mask Mode.

- **View**   View and zoom controls, and commands that allow you to show or hide on-screen elements such as toolbars, panels, marquees, object boxes, image map areas, ruler, and guidelines.

- **Format**   Commands that affect the overall image, such as Color Balance, Brightness & Contrast, Image Size, Expand Canvas, and Data Type.

- **Object**   Commands that enable you to work with objects, such as Merge, Edit Object, Wrap, Convert Object Type, Group, Align, Arrange, Import Object, and Export Object; and the Shadow, Split Shadow, and Properties commands.

- **Effect**   Access to PhotoImpact's many effects filters such as Add Noise, Charcoal, Despeckle, Emboss, Mosaic, Sharpen, Turnpage, Warping, and many more.

- **Web**   Commands for creating and manipulating web objects, such as HTML Text Object, Link Object, Component Designer, Background Designer, Button Designer, Web Properties, and Image Optimizer.

- **Window**   Commands to control the document windows, including standard commands such as Cascade and Tile Horizontally, as well as Batch Manager, Tile with Album, and Tile with EasyPalette commands.

- **Help**   Access to the standard PhotoImpact help files, plus quick links to the online resources and online registration.

- **Switch**   Quick access to PhotoImpact's companion programs, PhotoImpact Album and Ulead GIF Animator.

You could easily overlook the Switch menu, which is tucked away at the right end of the menu bar. Also note that many menu items (and some entire menus) are not visible when you first launch PhotoImpact. They appear only after you open an image document.

1

The simplest way to see all of the individual menu commands available on the PhotoImpact menus is to open each menu in turn. That's the best way to familiarize yourself with the locations of all the various commands. Instructions on how to use specific commands will be covered in context with the related tasks throughout this book.

Access Features with PhotoImpact's Toolbars

You're probably already familiar with the concept of a *toolbar*—a collection of buttons that provide one-click access to many of the program's most-used commands and tools. Toolbars are a common feature of most Windows programs today. Generally, the toolbar buttons provide a more convenient alternative to using the program's menus for accessing the same feature, although a few features may be accessible only from the toolbar.

Toolbar buttons are fast and easy to use. Simply click a toolbar button to issue the command or activate the feature the button represents. The hard part of using toolbar buttons is learning to identify the buttons by their (sometimes cryptic) icons. A few button icons have become standardized over the years—such as a floppy disk for the File | Save command and a pair of scissors for the Edit | Cut command— but most button icons are unique to the individual program or software developer.

TIP *To identify a toolbar button, point to the button and let the mouse pointer hover over the button for a few seconds without clicking. PhotoImpact will display a small tool-tip box showing the name of the button under the pointer. A brief description of the toolbar button appears in the status bar at the bottom of the PhotoImpact window.*

The PhotoImpact toolbars aren't locked in their default positions. You can move them by clicking and dragging the toolbar border. You can rearrange the order of the toolbars at the top of the PhotoImpact window, or drag one or both toolbars to the bottom of the window, above the status bar. You can also drag a toolbar into the PhotoImpact work area to transform it into a panel-like floating window, complete with a title bar.

The following sections provide an overview of PhotoImpact's Standard toolbar and Attribute toolbar. Instructions on how to use specific toolbar buttons will be covered in context with the related tasks throughout this book.

Standard Toolbar

The PhotoImpact Standard toolbar contains 26 buttons representing a wide
assortment of frequently used program commands and features.

	New image
	New Web Page
	Open (image)
	Save
	Print
	Print Multiple
	Print Preview
	Preview in Browser
	Cut
	Copy
	Paste
	Undo
	Redo
	Scanner

	Digital Camera
	Post-processing Wizard
	Color Enhancer
	Color Balance
	Brightness & Contrast
	Highlight Midtone Shadow
	Frame & Shadow
	Start/Stop Capture
	Layout
100%	Zoom
	Ulead Homepage
	Help

TIP   *You can customize the PhotoImpact Standard toolbar to display buttons for the commands and features you use the most. Right-click the toolbar and choose Options to open the Options dialog box; then click Customize to open the Customize Standard Toolbar dialog box. Select a button in the Available Buttons list and click Add to add that button to the toolbar. Select a button in the Selected Buttons list and click Remove to remove the button from the toolbar. Click OK to update the toolbar.*

Attribute Toolbar

The PhotoImpact Attribute toolbar provides a convenient place to see and control the attributes of the selected object or the tool in use. The Attribute toolbar is more than a collection of buttons; it's an interactive control panel that displays the attributes of the currently active selection or tool and enables you to adjust those attributes.

The buttons, list boxes, and other options that appear on the Attribute toolbar change depending on what you're currently doing in the program. For example, if you're working with the Paintbrush tool, the Attribute toolbar looks like this:

If you're selecting a portion of an image with the Standard Selection tool, you'll see the following Attribute toolbar.

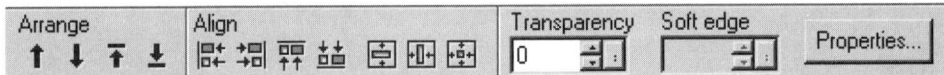

And if you're creating a text object, the Attribute toolbar includes a different set of tools for controlling fonts and other text attributes, as shown here.

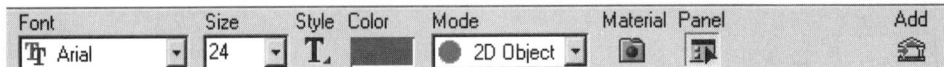

Get Information and Access Features from the Status Bar

Most Windows applications include a status bar at the bottom of the application window, and PhotoImpact is no exception.

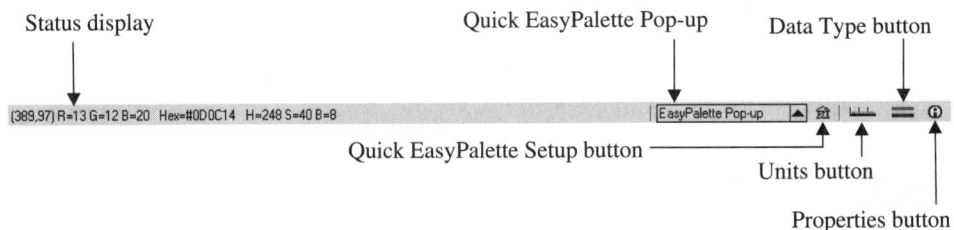

The changing status message at the left end of the status bar displays information about whatever is under the mouse pointer at the time. For example, if you point to an image with the Paintbrush tool selected, the status bar displays the x-y coordinates of the pointer, plus information about the color of the pixels at that location. If you point to a toolbar button, the status bar displays a description of that button.

TIP	*The information displayed in the status bar can be very useful. Get in the habit of checking the status bar often as you work.*

PhotoImpact loads the status bar with other handy features in addition to the status display. The largest feature is the Quick EasyPalette Pop-up, but there are also three handy buttons that provide convenient access to features that would otherwise require digging into various menus and dialog boxes.

Quick EasyPalette Pop-up

New to
PhotoImpact 7

Clicking the Quick EasyPalette Pop-up button causes PhotoImpact to open a sort of graphical menu displaying the content from one of PhotoImpact's many galleries or libraries as a set of thumbnail images.

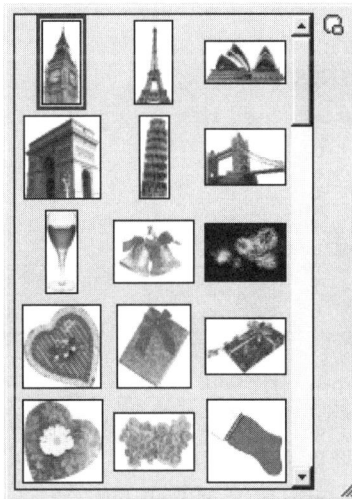

When the Quick EasyPalette appears, you can simply click a thumbnail image to apply the corresponding fill, filter, style, or other gallery effect to your image. The Quick EasyPalette disappears automatically after you make your selection.

You can define any number of Quick EasyPalettes so your favorite PhotoImpact gallery effects are always just a couple of mouse clicks away. If you have more than one Quick EasyPalette defined, you can click the arrow button at the right end of the Quick EasyPalette Pop-up to display a menu of the available palettes. Selecting a palette from the list displays that palette name in the Quick EasyPalette Pop-up. Clicking the Quick EasyPalette Pop-up button opens the palette named on the button.

New to
PhotoImpact 7

Quick EasyPalette Setup

Clicking the Quick EasyPalette Setup button opens the Quick EasyPalette Pop-up dialog box. You use this dialog box to define the palettes that are available in the Quick EasyPalette Pop-up.

To add a palette to the Quick EasyPalette Pop-up in the PhotoImpact status bar, follow these steps:

1. Click the Quick EasyPalette Setup button. PhotoImpact opens the Setup EasyPalette Pop-up dialog box.

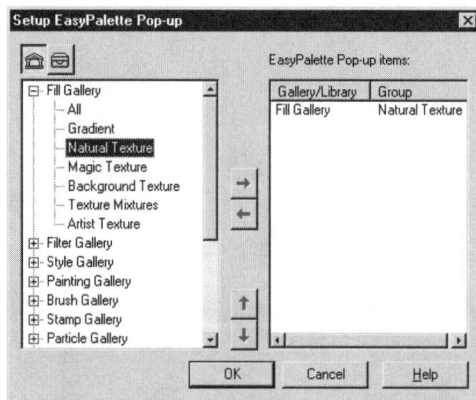

2. Select a gallery or library from the list on the left. Clicking one of the buttons above the list selects galleries or libraries, and clicking the plus box beside a gallery or library name expands the list to show all the subsets of the gallery or library that are available for selection.

3. Click the right arrow button between the list boxes to add the selected item to the list on the right.

4. Repeat steps 2 and 3 as needed to add more galleries and libraries to the list of EasyPalette pop-up items. You can also select an item in the list on the right and click the left arrow button to remove the selected item from the list.

5. Click OK to close the dialog box and update the palettes available on the Quick EasyPalette Pop-up.

Units Options

Clicking the Units button displays a menu of options related to PhotoImpact's ruler, guidelines, and grid features.

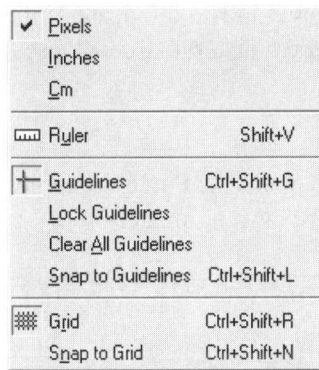

You can use the Units menu options turn the features on and off, change the units of measure displayed on the ruler, activate or deactivate the snap feature for guidelines and grids, and lock or clear guidelines. All of the options on the Units menu are available on other menus and dialog boxes, but the Units menu brings them together in one convenient location.

Data Type Option

Clicking the Data Type button displays a menu that enables you to change the data type (color depth) of the current image.

Black & White...	(1-bit)
Grayscale	(8-bit)
Optimized Indexed 16-Color	(4-bit)
Optimized Indexed 256-Color	(8-bit)
Web Optimized	(8-bit)
RGB True Color	(24-bit)
Indexed 16-Color...	(4-bit)
Indexed 256-Color...	(8-bit)
16-bit Grayscale	(16-bit)
48-bit RGB True Color	(48-bit)
✓ Create New Image	
Split to CMYK	
Combine from CMYK	

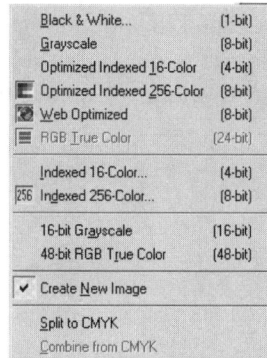

The Data Type menu is essentially a duplicate of the Data Type submenu of the Format menu, but it's a little quicker to access these options from the status bar.

Properties

Clicking the Properties button opens the Photo Properties dialog box which displays essential information about the current image.

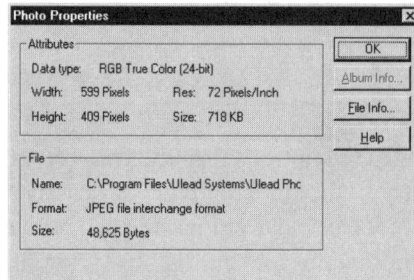

Photo Properties

Attributes
Data type: RGB True Color (24-bit)
Width: 599 Pixels   Res: 72 Pixels/Inch
Height: 409 Pixels   Size: 718 KB

File
Name: C:\Program Files\Ulead Systems\Ulead Phc
Format: JPEG file interchange format
Size: 48,625 Bytes

OK
Album Info...
File Info...
Help

If you do not have an image document open in PhotoImpact, the System Properties dialog box appears instead. The System Properties dialog box displays information such as the amount of memory and disk space available on your computer.

Use the Tools on the Attached Panels

By default, both the Tool panel and the Panel Manager appear attached to the borders of the PhotoImpact application window (see Figure 1-1, earlier in this chapter). In that configuration, they look like a couple of toolbars attached to the sides instead of the top of the PhotoImpact window.

The Tool panel and Panel Manager contain a very toolbar-like assortment of buttons, but the official name for these PhotoImpact features is *panels*. If you click and drag the border of the Tool panel or Panel Manager, you can move it off the side of the PhotoImpact window, and a more panel-like title bar will appear. Then you can position the panel anywhere you want. However, the default locations for these two panels seem to work well for many users.

Tool Panel

The Tool panel contains PhotoImpact's selection and drawing tools, all grouped together in one convenient location.

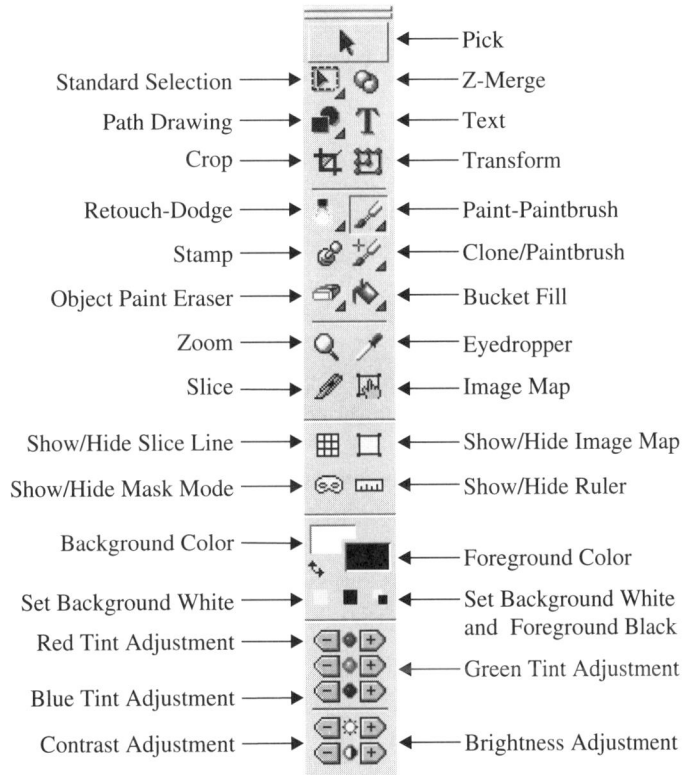

These are the tools you use to select portions of an image, draw objects, paint and manipulate images at the pixel level, adjust color and brightness, and more. Chapter 2 covers the basics of how to use most of the tools on the Tool panel. The applications of individual tools to accomplish tasks are covered in context throughout this book.

PhotoImpact actually has many more tools available than will fit on the Tool panel. To provide access to all those tools, several of the tool buttons can be expanded to reveal a subpanel of related tools. You can identify the buttons that are linked to subpanels by the small arrowhead symbol in the lower-right corner of the button. If you click and hold the mouse pointer on a button with an arrow, the subpanel appears. You can then select a tool from the subpanel. That tool becomes active, and its icon appears on the Tool panel as the default selection from that group. Let's take a quick tour of the tool-specific subpanels.

Selection Tool Panel   The Selection tool panel contains four tools for selecting portions of an image for editing. The Bezier Curve tool is a bit of a surprise addition, since that technology is more commonly seen as an object-drawing tool in illustration programs.

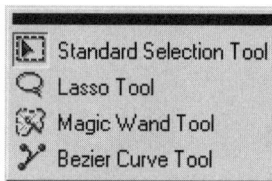

> Standard Selection Tool
> Lasso Tool
> Magic Wand Tool
> Bezier Curve Tool

Path Tool Panel   The Path tool panel also contains four tools. Three are for drawing objects, and one is for editing points on those objects.

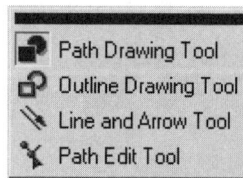

> Path Drawing Tool
> Outline Drawing Tool
> Line and Arrow Tool
> Path Edit Tool

Eraser Tool Panel   The Eraser tool panel consists of just two tools, the Object Paint Eraser tool and the Object Magic Eraser tool. The Eraser tools may be few in number, but they are versatile.

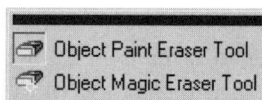

> Object Paint Eraser Tool
> Object Magic Eraser Tool

Retouch Tool Panel   The Retouch tool panel is the largest of the individual tool panels, with 14 separate tools. The tools range from the standard Dodge and Burn tools, to specialized tools for removing red-eye and scratches from photos.

	Dodge
	Burn
	Blur
	Sharpen
	Tonal Adjustment
	Smudge
	Saturation
	Warping
	Bristle Smear
	Remove Red Eye
	Remove Scratch
	Remove Noise
	Color Transform Pen
	Colorize Pen

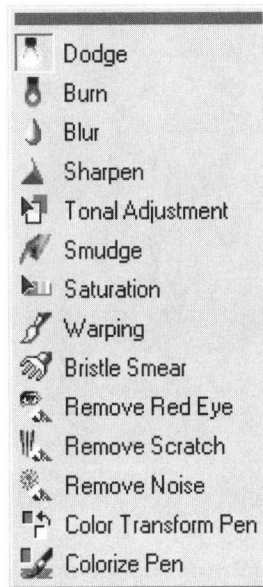

Paint Tool Panel   The Paint tool panel is home to the basic Paintbrush tool and 11 other painting tools that enable you to imitate drawing and painting with various media, such as crayons, markers, and oil paint.

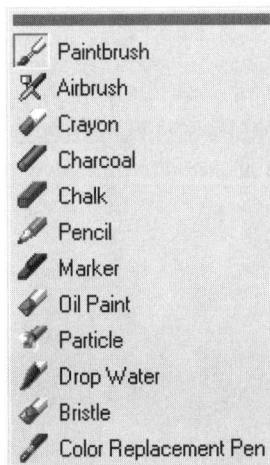

	Paintbrush
	Airbrush
	Crayon
	Charcoal
	Chalk
	Pencil
	Marker
	Oil Paint
	Particle
	Drop Water
	Bristle
	Color Replacement Pen

Clone Tool Panel   The tools on the Clone tool panel duplicate most of the brush and media effects of the Paint tools. The difference between the Paint tools and the Clone tools is that the Clone tools paint by applying a clone of the current image, rather than a specific color.

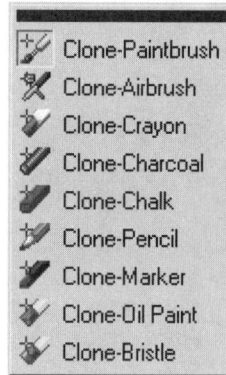

```
Clone-Paintbrush
Clone-Airbrush
Clone-Crayon
Clone-Charcoal
Clone-Chalk
Clone-Pencil
Clone-Marker
Clone-Oil Paint
Clone-Bristle
```

Fill Tool Panel   The Fill tools enable you to fill an area with a solid color or with one of three different gradients.

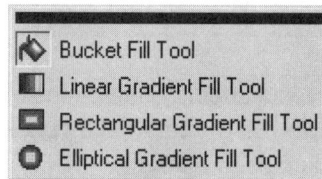

```
Bucket Fill Tool
Linear Gradient Fill Tool
Rectangular Gradient Fill Tool
Elliptical Gradient Fill Tool
```

New to PhotoImpact 7

Panel Manager

The other attached panel, the Panel Manager, is much smaller than the Tool panel. Its default location is attached to the right side of the PhotoImpact window. The buttons on the Panel Manager enable you to quickly open or close the floating panels.

Show/Hide Document Manager ⟶

Show/Hide EasyPalette ⟶

Show/Hide Quick Command Panel ⟶

GIF Animator ⟶

⟵ Show/Hide Layer Manager

⟵ Show/Hide Browse Manager

⟵ Show/Hide Color Panel

⟵ PhotoImpact Album

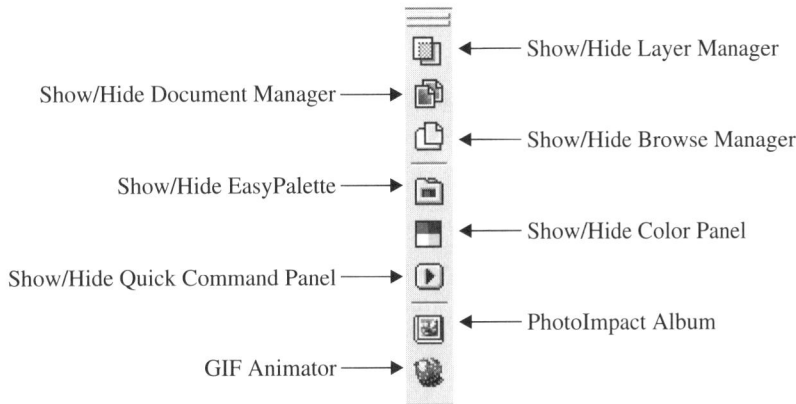

Just click the button once to open the associated panel. Click it again to close the panel. The "bonus" buttons at the bottom of the Panel Manager provide one-click access to other Ulead programs, such as PhotoImpact's companion programs PhotoImpact Album and Ulead GIF Animator.

Access PhotoImact Features from the Floating Panels

Floating panels appear as separate auxiliary windows that "float" in front of the PhotoImpact application window and document windows. They provide easy access to a group of related settings (such as in the Color panel) or display thumbnail images to show the contents of a PhotoImpact gallery or library (such as in the EasyPalette panel).

In some respects, panels are much like dialog boxes in that they present options and features for your selection and you can move them around on top of the PhotoImpact application and document windows. But PhotoImpact's panels have some features that set them apart from dialog boxes:

- ■ You can resize floating panels. You can't minimize or maximize panels, but you can resize them by dragging the window border.

- ■ The selections you make from a panel take effect immediately; there's no need to click a separate OK or Apply button.

- ■ Panels remain open on your desktop after you make a selection.

Having a panel open doesn't pause or otherwise interfere with your work. As a result, you can keep a panel open so that its contents are immediately available and you can make multiple selections from a panel without needing to reopen the panel each time. To close a panel, simply click the close (X) button at the right end of the panel's title bar.

TIP	*You can collapse a panel so that only its title bar remains visible by double-clicking the title bar. This is sometimes called the "window shade" or "roll up" effect. To expand the panel to its previous size, double-click the title bar again.*

Color Panel

New to PhotoImpact 7

The Color panel provides detailed control over the fill and brush colors. You can select a color by clicking in the spectrum band at the bottom of the Color tab or adjust the RGB/HSB values "by the numbers."

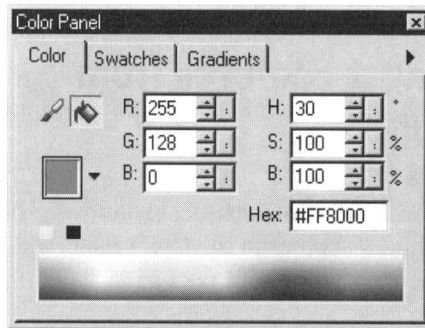

The Swatches tab gives you access to a palette of predefined color swatches. The Gradients tab presents an assortment of two-color and multicolor gradients for your selection. You can also define your own swatches and gradients. Clicking the small arrowhead in the upper-right corner of the panel opens a context-sensitive menu of configuration options for the panel, such as options to select color or grayscale mode on the Color tab.

EasyPalette

The EasyPalette panel makes PhotoImpact's many effect and style galleries and object libraries accessible and easy to use by presenting them as collections of thumbnail images. The thumbnail images create a visual index of the contents of the galleries and libraries.

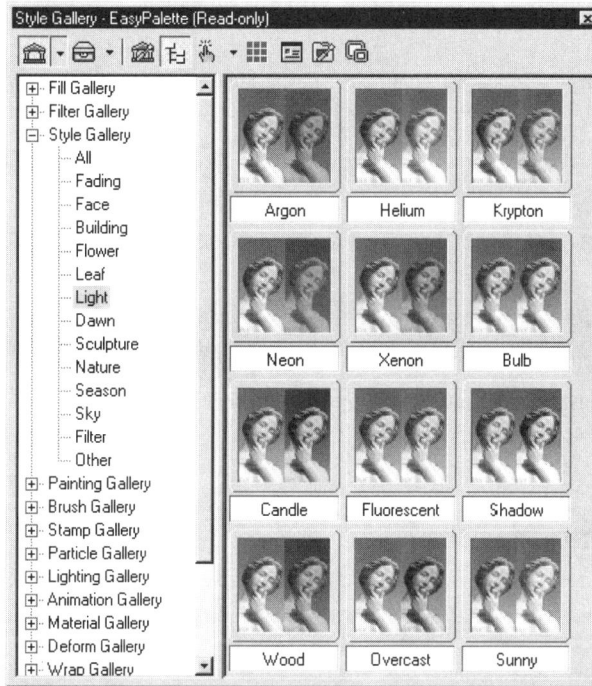

You can quickly scroll through the thumbnails in the EasyPalette panel and see a sample of the styles, effects, and objects. Then you can select and apply an effect or style by double-clicking the thumbnail in the EasyPalette panel or by dragging the thumbnail from the EasyPalette panel and dropping it on your image. If you want to fine tune an effect before applying it your image, you can right-click the thumbnail and choose Modify Properties and Apply to open a dialog box where you can adjust settings for the effect before applying it to your image.

The buttons across the top of the EasyPalette perform the following functions, from left to right:

Displays a list of PhotoImpact galleries in the tree view. The arrow opens a menu listing all the galleries you can select for display in the EasyPalette.

Switches the tree view to display the list of PhotoImpact libraries. The arrow opens a menu listing all the libraries you can select for display in the EasyPalette.

Opens the Setup EasyPalette Pop-up dialog box, where you can configure the EasyPalette pop-ups that are available from the status bar.

Toggles on or off the display of the gallery/library list on the left side of the panel.

Replaces the standard thumbnail image with the image (or selected area or object) from the document window.

Opens the Variations dialog box showing a preview of varying degrees of the selected effect.

Displays a menu of options related to the thumbnail images in the EasyPalette panel.

Opens a menu of view options for the EasyPalette, including various ways to tile the EasyPalette panel with the document window.

Opens a menu offering a choice of thumbnail image sizes.

Quick Command Panel

The Quick Command panel is aptly named, because it provides quick access to lists of your favorite and recently used commands. Using this panel, you can even create and play back sequences of commands that PhotoImpact calls *tasks*.

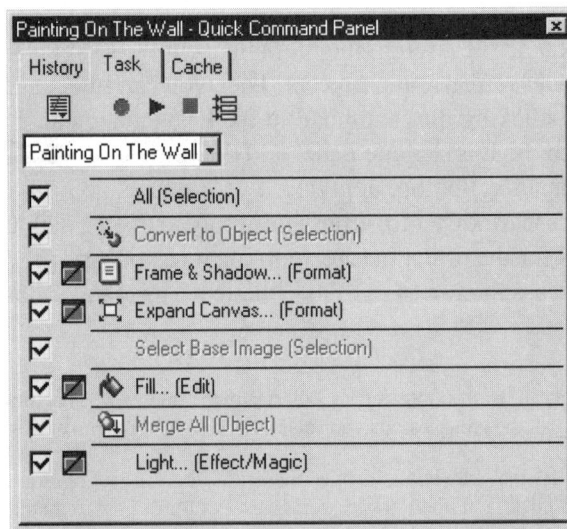

The Quick Command panel has three tabs:

- **History**   Lists the last several commands issued (how many depends on the Undo level setting). Drag the slider up or down the list to undo/redo commands. Like the Edit | Undo Before command, the History tab allows you to cancel the effect of recent actions and revert your image to its previous state; or like the Edit | Redo To command, reverse the effect of the Undo command and reinstate actions that were undone. However, the History tab is a big improvement over the Undo and Redo commands, because you can see the list of commands in sequence and quickly undo/redo multiple commands.

- **Cache**   Similar to the History tab in that it records up to 32 recently used commands. The difference is that you can lock favorite commands so they stay on the list, and you can select and apply any command on the list.

- **Task**   Allows you to record a sequence of commands and define them as a named task. Then you can select the task and click Play to apply the sequence of commands to another image. This feature is called a *macro recorder* in some other software. PhotoImpact ships with several predefined tasks, such as Apply Fadeout Effect and Make Button.

Using the Quick Command panel is covered in detail in Chapter 16, which is available online at www.osborne.com.

Access Panel

The Access panel is a new feature of PhotoImpact 7. It combines a mini file browser with a tool for managing open document windows, and another tool for managing layers on your image. All three tools reside within the same panel window.

Browse Manager   The Browse Manager, shown in Figure 1-2, puts a miniature version of the Windows Explorer in the Access panel and adds a few PhotoImpact enhancements. The left side of the Browse Manager shows your computer's folder structure in a tree display. The right side of the Browse Manager shows thumbnails of any image files located in the folder that is selected in the tree display. The buttons across the top of the Browse Manager enable you to navigate to other folders, batch-process selected images, sort images, and so on.

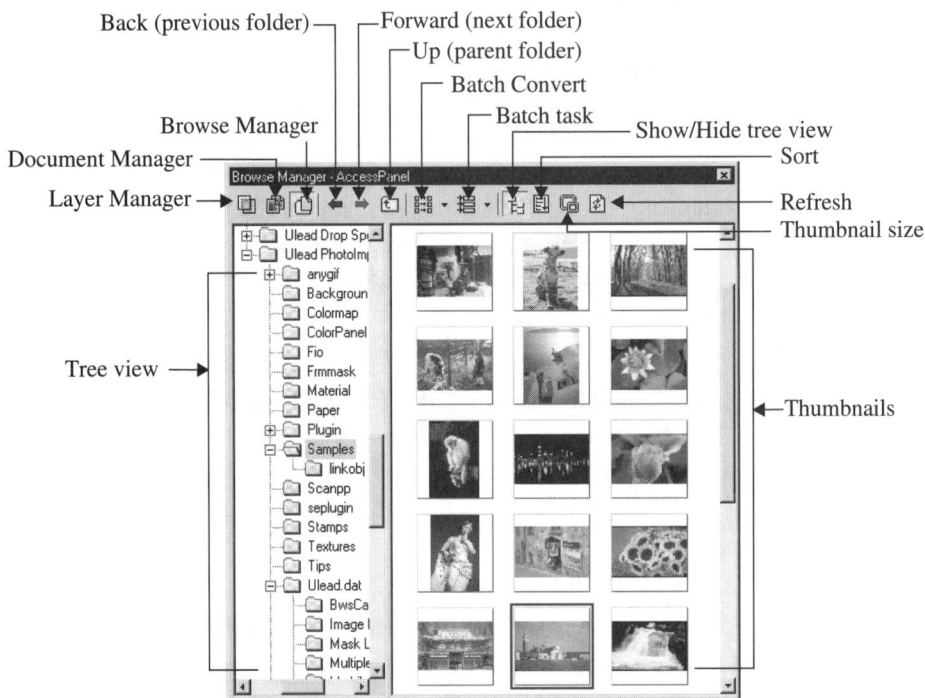

Back (previous folder)
Forward (next folder)
Up (parent folder)
Batch Convert
Browse Manager
Batch task
Document Manager
Show/Hide tree view
Layer Manager
Sort
Refresh
Thumbnail size
Tree view
Thumbnails

FIGURE 1-2   The Access panel in Browse Manager mode

Document Manager   The Access panel's Document Manager mode, shown in Figure 1-3, enables you to quickly access any open document in PhotoImpact, regardless of whether that document window is minimized or hidden behind other document windows in the PhotoImpact workspace. Of course, you can always use the Window menu to access any document window, but the Document Manager's thumbnail images are much easier to identify than the often cryptic filenames that label the document windows in the menus.

The Quick Command Manager and Batch Manager buttons allow you to select a document thumbnail and apply a command or batch operation to that document, directly from the Document Manager. Another nice touch is the Global Viewer thumbnail at the bottom of the panel. You can use the zoom in and zoom out icons and the zoom ratio slider to quickly zoom (enlarge or reduce the display of) the selected document to any size you want. And if the zoomed image is bigger than its document window, you can drag a rectangle around on the Global Viewer thumbnail to select which part of the image is visible in the document window.

New to PhotoImpact 7

Global Viewer button

Quick Command Manager

Browse Manager

Batch Manager

Sort

Document Manager - AccessPanel

Layer Manager

Thumbnail size

Document Manager

Document thumbnails

Desk.jpg   Forest.JPG   Girl.jpg

Lotus.jpg   Monkey.jpg

Global Viewer

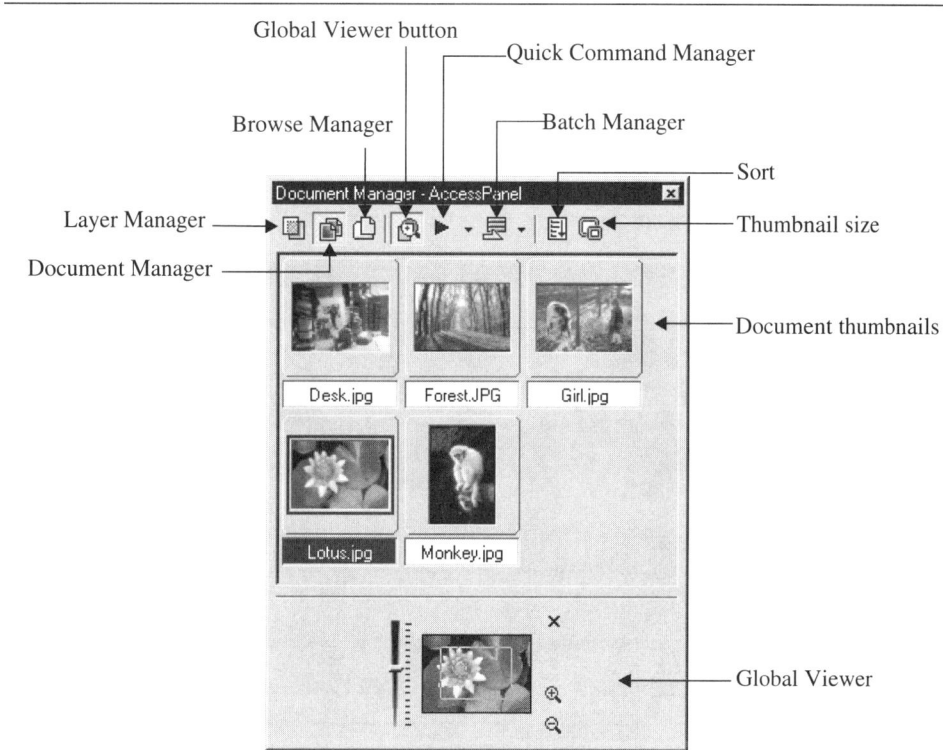

FIGURE 1-3   The Document Manager in the Access panel

New to PhotoImpact 7   **Layer Manager**   The Layer Manager, shown in Figure 1-4 is the third component of the Access panel. Just as the Document Manager helps you work with multiple document windows in PhotoImpact, the Layer Manager helps you keep track of and work with the multiple layers that might exist in the current document. And since PhotoImpact creates a separate layer for each object you import, paste, or draw, you can quickly accumulate a sizable inventory of layers in an image. See Chapter 7 for more information on working with objects and layers.

Brush, Path, and Text Panels

The Brush panel opens automatically when you select one of the painting tools (any of the Retouch, Paint, Clone, or Erase tools). The options available in the Brush panel enable you to monitor and control all the attributes of the selected painting tool. In addition to obvious brush attributes such as the size, shape, and

Display groups

Thumbnail display

Global Viewer button

Browse Manager

Show/Hide base image

Delete selected object

Thumbnail menu commands

Layer Manager options

Layer Manager

Document Manager

Merge

Thumbnail size

Transparency

Object thumbnail

Show/Hide object

Lock/Unlock object

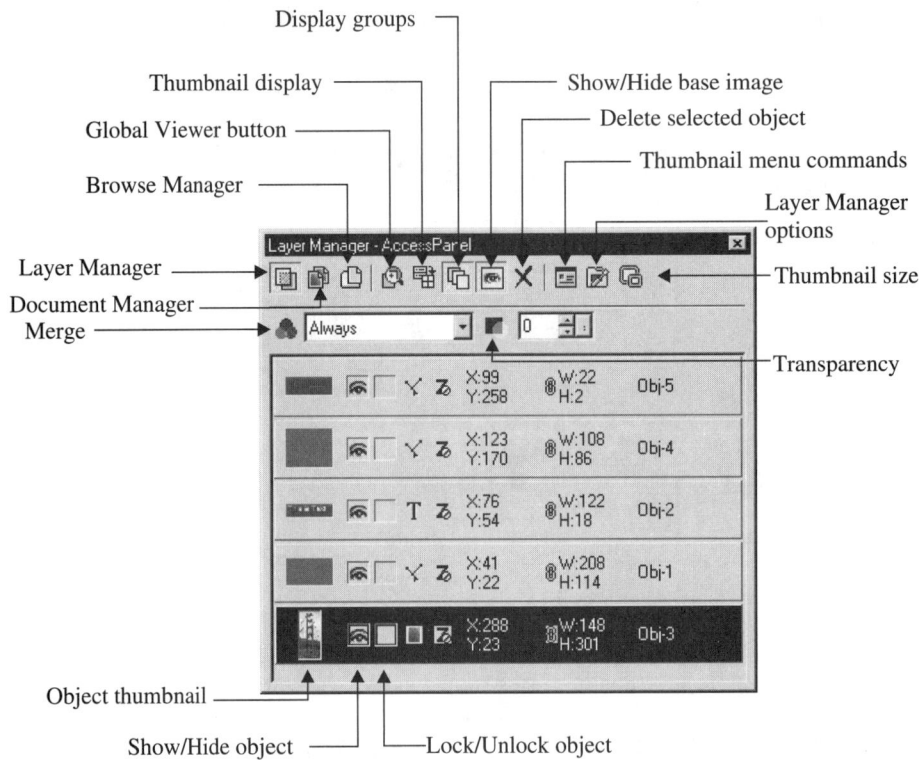

FIGURE 1-4   The Access panel in Layer Manager mode

color of the brush, you can adjust the transparency, texture, merge method, and pressure options.

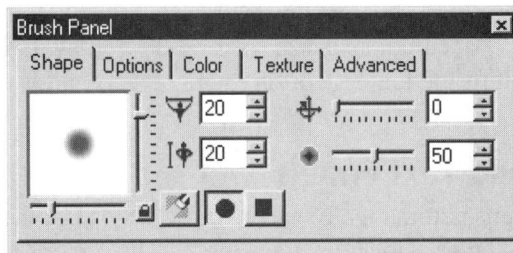

Just as the Brush panel appears when you select a painting tool, the Path panel appears when you select a path-drawing tool, and the Text panel appears when you select the Text tool. Like the Brush panel, the Path panel and Text panel contain all the attribute options for their respective object types.

Control Which Tools Appear

As you've seen, when you first launch PhotoImpact, the program appears with an assortment of toolbars and floating panels arranged in and around the main application window. However, as you work with the program, you'll probably find that you prefer to have a different selection of toolbars and panels. Fortunately, you're not locked into the default selection. You can open, close, and rearrange the various PhotoImpact tools to suit your own working style and preferences. The next time you launch PhotoImpact, all the toolbars and panels will reappear where they were the last time you used the program.

The View | Toolbars & Panels submenu is your master control center for determining which of PhotoImpact's toolbars and panels are open and available. All the toolbars and panels are listed on this menu, including individual tool panels such as the Paint tool panel. To open a panel (or a toolbar), choose View | Toolbars & Panels | *panelname.* You can also close an open toolbar or panel by repeating the same command.

Use the Document Window

The PhotoImpact document window is where you actually work with the image that you are creating or editing. Each open image document appears in its own document window, as shown in Figure 1-5. Unlike the panel windows, the document window must remain within the workspace of the main PhotoImpact application window.

Manage Document Windows

PhotoImpact document windows follow the same rules as their counterparts in most word processors, spreadsheets, and other Windows programs that support working with multiple documents. For example, you can move a document window by dragging its title bar and resize it by dragging the window border. If the document window isn't big enough to display the entire image, scroll bars appear along the

Inactive document window   Active document window

Minimized document window

FIGURE 1-5   A PhotoImpact window with several document windows open

right and bottom sides of the document window to allow you to bring different parts of the image into view.

The buttons in the upper-right corner of the document window enable you to minimize, maximize, and close the window. When you minimize a document window, only its title bar is visible, positioned at the bottom edge of the PhotoImpact workspace, just above the status bar. When you maximize a document window, that document occupies the entire PhotoImpact workspace. In a maximized document window, the title bar disappears, and the document's minimize, restore, and close buttons appear at the right end of the PhotoImpact menu bar, just below the corresponding buttons for the PhotoImpact window.

NOTE   *If you maximize one document window, PhotoImpact automatically maximizes all the other document windows as well. All the maximized document windows are stacked on top of each other in the PhotoImpact workspace, but only the top (active) document is visible.*

1

Although you can have multiple documents open simultaneously in PhotoImpact, you can work with only one document at a time. The document window for the active document always appears in the foreground, on top of any other document windows in the PhotoImpact workspace. You can use any of the following techniques to select a document and bring its window to the foreground for editing:

■ Click the document window's title bar.

■ Choose Window I *documentname*.

■ Click the document's thumbnail in the Document Manager Access panel.

■ Press CTRL-TAB to switch the focus to the next document window in sequence. Repeat as needed to step through the open documents until you reach the correct one.

Create a New Document

To create a new image document in PhotoImpact, you can use any of the following techniques:

■ Choose File I New I New Image.

■ Press CTRL-N.

■ Click the New button on the Standard toolbar.

PhotoImpact displays the New Image dialog box, shown in Figure 1-6, where you can set the initial properties of the image, such as its data type (color depth), background color, image size, and resolution. Adjust the settings as needed, and then click OK to close the dialog box and create the new document.

The new image document appears in a document window labeled "Untitled." The image doesn't get a name until you save the file.

NOTE   *PhotoImpact displays the current zoom percentage and image size (in pixels) in the document window title bar along with the document's file name.*

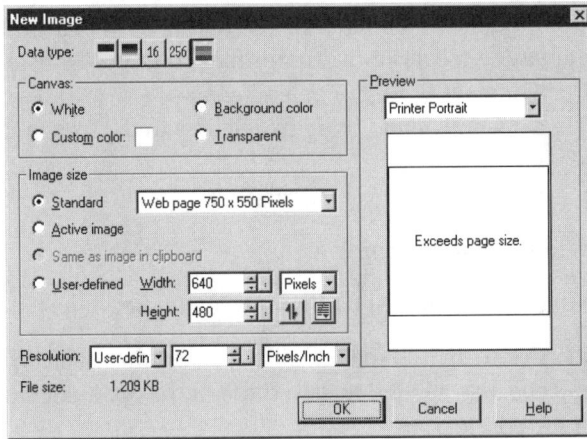

FIGURE 1-6   New Image dialog box

Use the Ruler, Grid, and Guidelines

A PhotoImpact document window is more than a simple container for an image document. It also includes some optional aids to assist you as you work with the image, including the ruler, grid, and guidelines.

The Ruler

You can choose to display the ruler along the top and left side of the document window, as shown in Figure 1-7. The ruler provides a constant size reference, regardless of the zoom level at which you are viewing the image. PhotoImpact displays a hash mark on each ruler scale to indicate the horizontal and vertical position of the pointer. You can use this feature to measure and align objects in the image.

You can use any of the following techniques to activate or deactivate the ruler display on the current document window:

- Choose View | Ruler.

- Press SHIFT-V.

- Click the Ruler button in the Tool panel.

FIGURE 1-7   A PhotoImpact document window with the ruler along the top and left side

■   Click the Units button on the status bar and choose Ruler from the menu that appears.

The ruler can display measurements in inches, centimeters, or pixels. The simplest way to change the ruler measurement units is to click the Units button in the status bar and choose the desired unit from the menu that appears. You can also set the units in the Preferences dialog box. Choose File | Preferences | General to open the dialog box, then change the measurement unit option in the PhotoImpact category.

The Grid

The grid is a series of evenly spaced horizontal and vertical lines superimposed on the image in the document window, as shown in Figure 1-8. The gridlines do not become part of the image, but exist only as a visual aid to assist you in positioning objects on the image.

You can turn the grid display on or off using any of the following techniques:

■   Choose View | Guidelines & Grid | Grid.

■   Press CTRL-SHIFT-R.

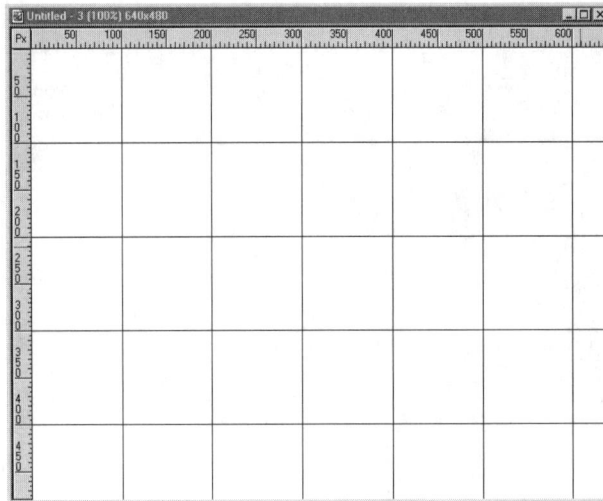

FIGURE 1-8   A document window with gridlines displayed

- Click the Units button on the status bar and choose Grid from the menu that appears

The gridlines are handy as a visual reference in the document window, but aligning objects precisely with the gridlines can be challenging when you're trying to do it freehand. PhotoImpact includes a Snap to Grid feature to solve this problem. When the Snap to Grid option is active, if you click within a few pixels of a gridline, PhotoImpact automatically aligns the object or point precisely with the grid. You can use any of the following methods to toggle the Snap to Grid option on or off:

- Choose View | Guidelines & Grid | Snap to Grid.

- Press CTRL-SHIFT-N.

- Click the Units button on the status bar and choose Snap to Grid from the menu that appears.

NOTE   *The Snap to Grid option is available only when the grid is active. This means that PhotoImpact won't unexpectedly move an object in an attempt to align it with an invisible grid, as sometimes happens in other programs.*

1

By default, the spacing between the horizontal and vertical gridlines is 100 pixels and the gridlines are black. See Chapter 17 for information on changing the preference settings for the grid.

Guidelines

Guidelines are similar to the grid. They are horizontal and vertical lines superimposed on the image in the document window to assist you in positioning and aligning objects and points as you work with the image. The difference is that you position guidelines wherever you need them, instead of having PhotoImpact position the gridlines at fixed intervals. Notice the spacing and position of the guidelines in Figure 1-9 compared with the uniform spacing of the gridlines in Figure 1-8.

To activate the guidelines, you can use any of the following methods:

- Choose View | Guidelines & Grid | Guidelines.

- Press CTRL-SHIFT-G.

- Click the Units button on the status bar and choose Guidelines from the menu that appears.

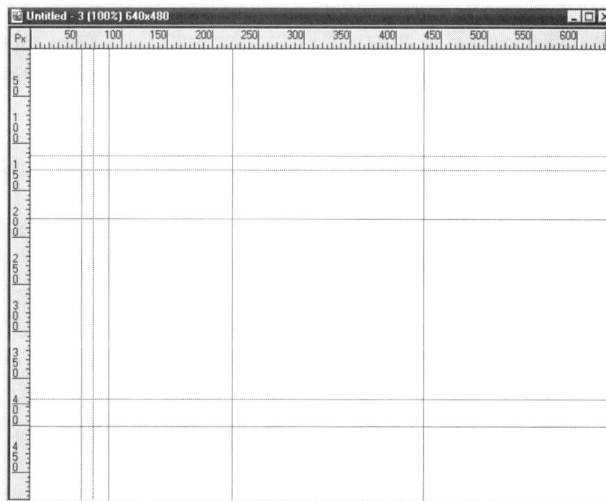

FIGURE 1-9   A document window with guidelines

Like the grid, the guidelines can optionally work with the Snap to Guidelines feature, so that PhotoImpact automatically aligns objects and points that you place within a few pixels of a guideline. To activate or deactivate the Snap to Guidelines feature, you can use any of the following methods:

- Choose View | Guidelines & Grid | Snap to Guidelines.

- Press CTRL- SHIFT-L.

- Click the Units button on the status bar and choose Snap to Guidelines from the menu that appears.

Unlike the grid, no lines appear in the document window when you activate the guidelines. Guidelines don't exist until you create them. Since guidelines are a bit more versatile than the grid, there are a few more techniques involved in using them. The following list summarizes those techniques:

- To create a vertical guideline, click the ruler on the left side of the document window and drag to the right. PhotoImpact displays a vertical line in the document window as you drag. Release the mouse button to drop the guideline at the desired position.

- To create a horizontal guideline, click and drag the guideline down from the top ruler.

- To move a guideline, click the Pick tool in the Tool panel, then click and drag the guideline.

- To lock all guidelines in place so that they can't be moved accidentally, choose View | Guidelines & Grids | Lock Guidelines or click the Units button on the status bar and choose Lock Guidelines from the menu that appears.

- To delete all the existing guidelines in a document window so you can create new ones, choose View | Guidelines & Grids | Clear All Guidelines or click the Units button on the status bar and choose Clear All Guidelines from the menu that appears.

By default, the guidelines appear as solid blue lines. Choose File | Preferences | General to open the Preferences dialog box and then select the Guidelines & Grid category. You can adjust the color and style of both the guidelines and grid lines.

View Images

PhotoImpact provides a long list of options for viewing image documents. Many of those options are variations on the Zoom feature, which controls the magnification of the image. Other options enable you to do things like show or hide slice lines and image map areas.

Use Zoom

PhotoImpact's Zoom commands provide a variety of ways to view your images at actual size, magnified size, or reduced size.

View at Actual Size   To display an image at its actual size, use one of the following methods:

- Choose View | Actual View.

- Press CTRL-0 (that's a zero, not the letter *O*).

- Click the Actual Size button on Attribute toolbar.

- Choose Actual View in the Zoom drop-down on the Standard toolbar.

> **TIP** *To maximize the current document window and also display the image at its actual size, choose View | Maximize at Actual View or press* CTRL-M.

Enlarge the View   To zoom in on (enlarge) the current image, use one of the following techniques:

- Choose View | Zoom | Zoom In.

- Press the plus key (+) on the keyboard.

- Select the Zoom tool from the Tool panel, then click the document.

To zoom in an image to the largest size that will fit in the document window, use one of these techniques:

- Choose View | Fit in Window.

■ Press CTRL-SHIFT-0 (zero).

■ Click the Fit in Window button on the Attribute toolbar.

■ Choose Fit In Window in the Zoom drop-down on the Standard toolbar.

Reduce the View   Use one of the following methods to zoom out from (reduce) the current document:

■ Choose View | Zoom | Zoom Out.

■ Press the minus key (–) on the keyboard.

■ Select the Zoom tool from the Tool panel, and then SHIFT-click or right-click the document.

Set a Zoom Level   To select a specific zoom level for a document, use one of these methods:

■ Choose View | Zoom | *percent* (a zoom level between 1 and 1600 percent).

■ In the zoom level box on the Attribute toolbar or the Standard toolbar, select the zoom level or type a number.

■ To quickly change the zoom level of a document, drag the pointer on the zoom level slider in the Attribute toolbar.

Choose Document View Options

PhotoImpact offers several options for viewing the document window:

■ To temporarily enlarge the active document window to fill your entire computer screen, choose View | Full Screen or press CTRL- U. Press ESC to return to normal view.

■ To maximize the PhotoImpact application window and hide the title bar and menu bar, choose View | Remove Menu Bar. Press ESC to return to normal view.

1

■ To open a new document window displaying the same image as the current document window, choose View | Add a View or press CTRL- I.

TIP *Using the View | Add a View command enables you to have two document windows open showing different views of the same image. For example, one window could show an extreme close-up zoom, while the other displays the image at actual size.*

Show or Hide Elements

When you are working with your images, you may want to show or hide certain elements to facilitate your current task. PhotoImpact lets you turn on and off the display of the background, slices, and other elements, as follows:

■ To show or hide the base image (background), choose View | Base Image or press CTRL-F5.

■ To show or hide a dashed line around the perimeter of the selected object, choose View | Show Marquee or press CTRL-F8.

■ To show or hide a dashed rectangle around each of the objects in a document, choose View | Show Box Around Objects or press CTRL-F7.

■ To show or hide the slices used to optimize an image for the web, click the Show/Hide Slice Line button in the Tool panel, choose View | Slice Line, or press SHIFT-F7.

■ To show or hide the hotspot areas in web image maps, click the Show/Hide Image Map button in the Tool panel, choose View | Image Map, or press SHIFT-F8.

NOTE *See Chapter 11 for information on working with slices and image maps.*

Save a File

One of the fundamental tasks in any program is to save the current document in a file. PhotoImpact offers many options for saving files in various file formats, and

Chapter 4 covers those options in detail. However, simply saving a file in PhotoImpact's default format is a straightforward procedure:

1. Choose File | Save As or press CTRL-SHIFT-S. PhotoImpact opens the Save As dialog box.

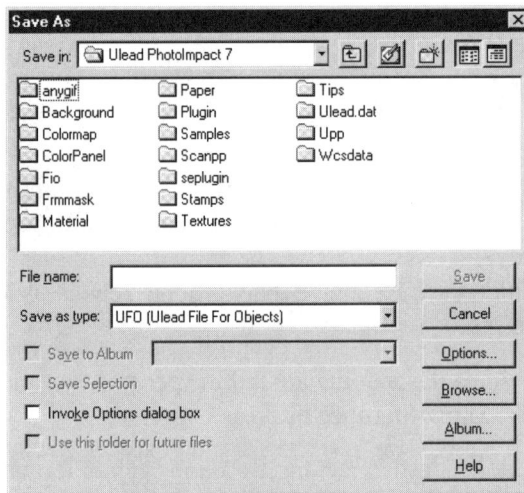

2. Navigate to the folder where you want to save the file. Use the Save In list box to select the correct drive, then drill down to the folder by clicking icons in the folder list box.

3. Type a filename in the File Name text box and select the file format from the Save As Type list box. PhotoImpact's default file format, UFO (Ulead File for Objects), preserves objects as well as image data.

4. Click Save to close the dialog box and save the file.

After you save an image document for the first time, you don't need to repeat the entire process of typing a filename and selecting a folder each time you save the file. To save the file using the same settings, simply choose File | Save or press CTRL-S.

Get Help

Like most modern software, PhotoImpact includes an online help system to provide you with convenient access to information about program features. To access the help system, choose Help | Ulead PhotoImpact Help or press F1. PhotoImpact opens the Ulead PhotoImpact Help window, shown in Figure 1-10.

To locate a topic in the Help window, click the Contents tab in the left panel of the window. Drill down to the topic that interests you by clicking the plus signs to expand categories and display individual help articles. Click an article name in the Contents list to display that article in the right side of the window.

You can also use the Index and Search tabs to locate help articles. Click the Index tab to display an alphabetized list of help articles. You can scroll down the list to

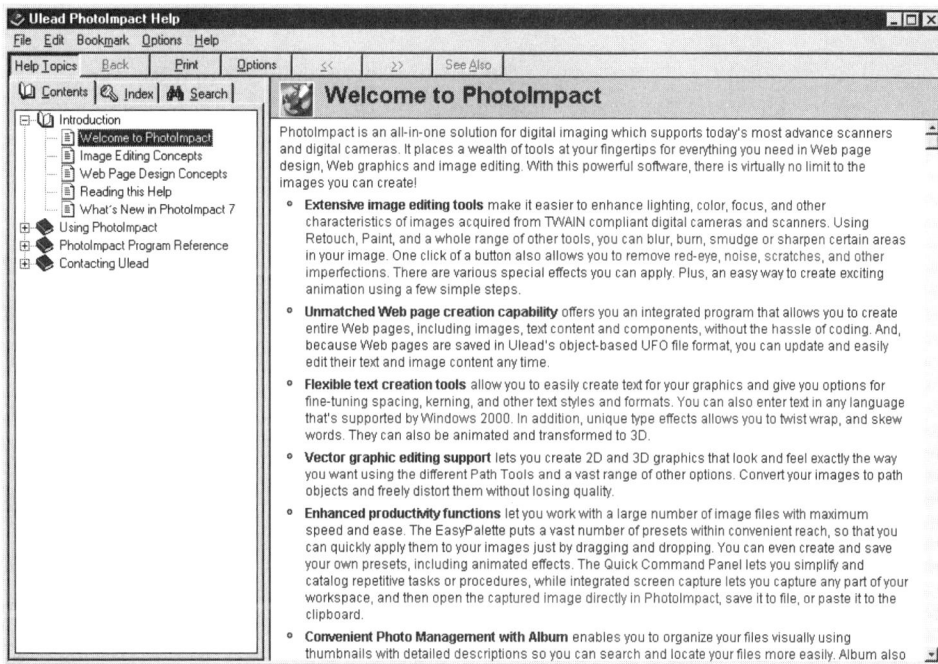

FIGURE 1-10   The Ulead PhotoImpact Help window

find the topic you need or type the topic in the box at the top of the list to jump to that topic. The Search tab enables you to enter a search term. The help system will attempt to locate the search term in the text of the help articles, instead of just checking article titles and keywords as the Index tab does.

The following list summarizes some of the other help options available in PhotoImpact:

- ■ To display a dialog box containing a random tip, choose Help | Tip of the Day.

- ■ To open the Ulead PhotoImpact Help window to the page listing all the PhotoImpact shortcut keys, choose Help | PhotoImpact Shortcut Keys.

- ■ To open your web browser to the Ulead home page, choose Help | Ulead on the Web | Ulead Homepage.

- ■ To open your web browser to the PhotoImpact home page, choose Help | Ulead on the Web | PhotoImpact Homepage.

- ■ To open your web browser to the Ulead technical support page, choose Help | Ulead on the Web | Technical Support.

- ■ To display a message box showing the PhotoImpact copyright information and your serial number, choose Help | About PhotoImpact.

CHAPTER 2

Use the Editing and Drawing Tools

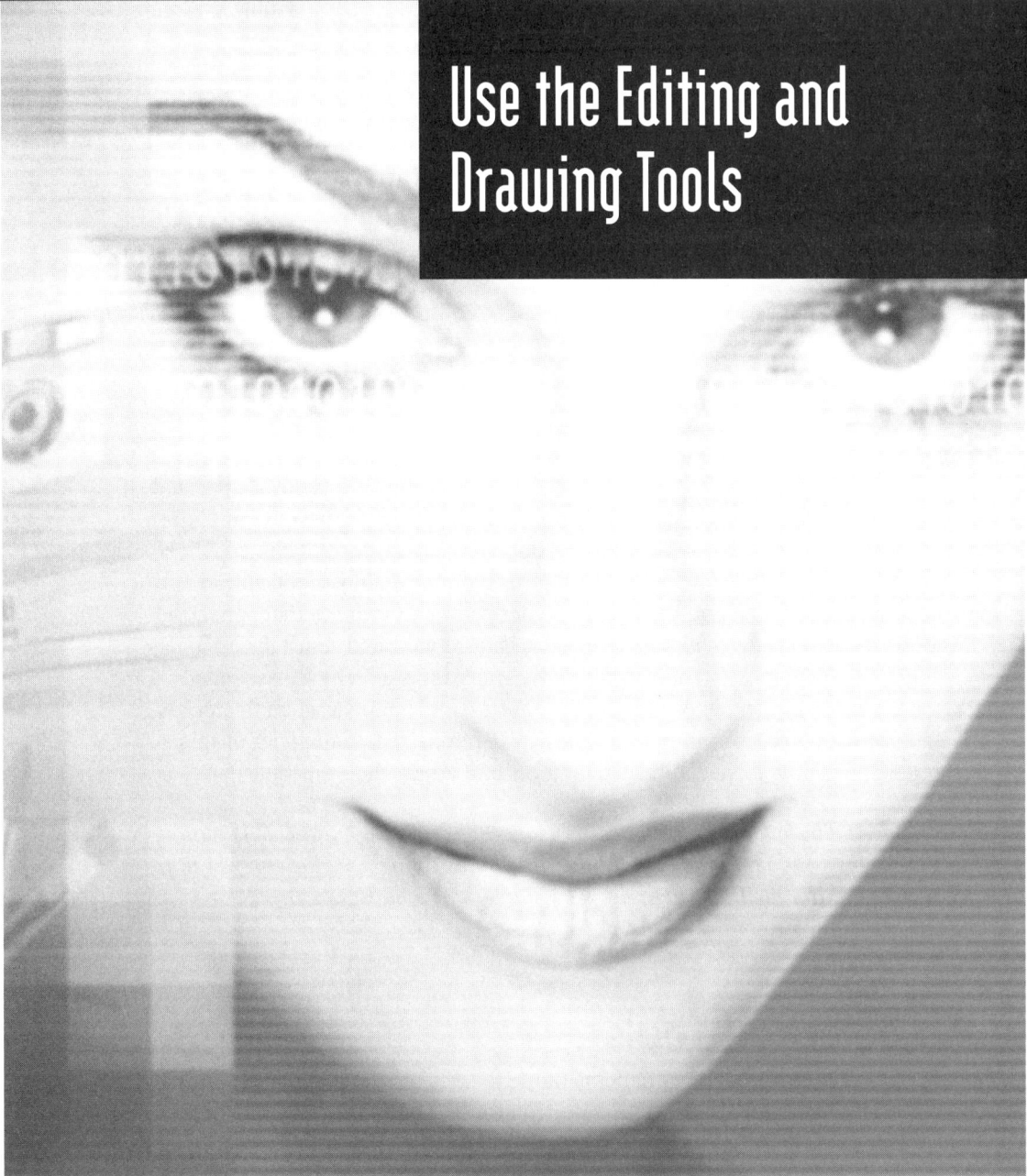

This chapter continues the introduction to the PhotoImpact 7 user interface that started in Chapter 1, which introduced the various windows, toolbars, and panels. This chapter concentrates on the specific image drawing and editing tools PhotoImpact provides.

The goal of this chapter is to familiarize you with the tools. It explains how to identify, access, and adjust options for the individual tools. Other chapters of this book cover using those tools, along with other PhotoImpact features, to create, edit, and manipulate images.

Select Tools and Attributes

Almost all the tools covered in this chapter are located in the Tool panel. The default location for the toolbar-like Tool panel is on the left side of the PhotoImpact application window, as shown in Figure 2-1. You access a given PhotoImpact tool by clicking the associated button in the Tool panel.

In many cases, several related tools share a position in the Tool panel as indicated by a small arrow in the lower-right corner of the tool button. If the specific tool that you want to use doesn't appear in the Tool panel as the current choice, click and hold the mouse button on the tool that appears in the Tool panel position until the tool subpanel appears, and then click the desired tool button in that panel.

The Attribute toolbar provides the primary means to view and adjust the attributes of each PhotoImpact tool as you work with it. Many tools also have associated panels, such as the Brush panel shown in Figure 2-1, that appear when the tool is active and provide access to more attributes and options. The remainder of this chapter describes how to select individual tools and adjust their attributes.

> **NOTE**   *The Attribute toolbar for many tools includes an Add button. This button enables you to add the current tool attributes to the EasyPalette for future use. For detailed instructions, see Chapter 17, which is available at www.osborne.com.*

Use the Selection Tools

The top of the PhotoImpact Tool panel is home to some of the most-used tools in the program—the Pick tool and the selection tools. These tools enable you to

Attribute toolbar

Tool panel

Brush panel

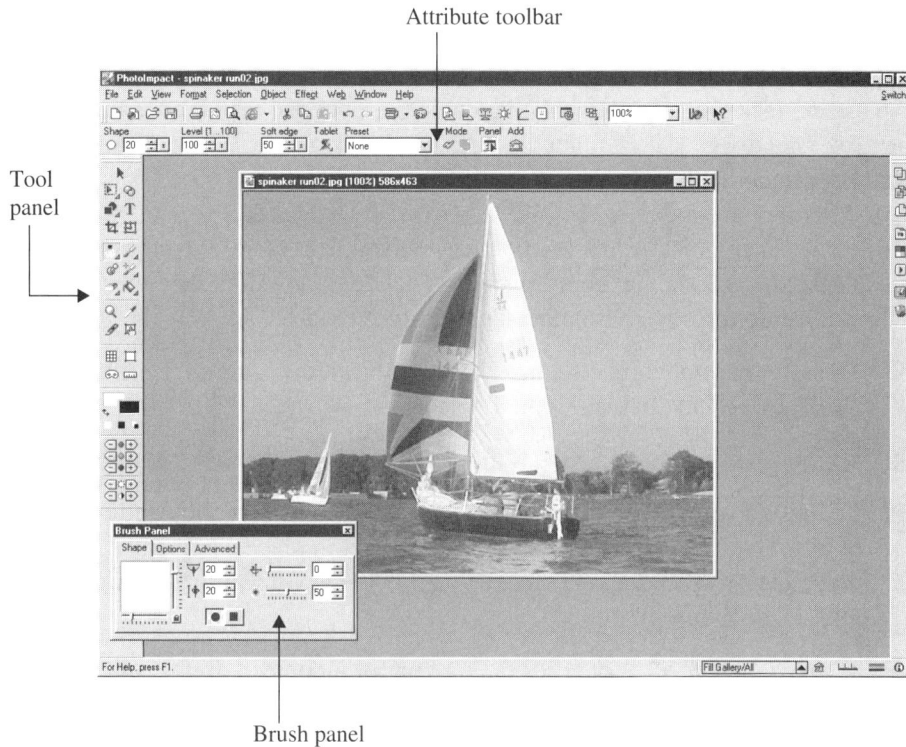

FIGURE 2-1   The Tool panel and Attribute toolbar enable you to select and control the PhotoImpact tools.

select objects and areas of an image, and then move or manipulate the selected object or area.

Use the Pick Tool

The Pick tool is the large arrow button at the top of the Tool panel. You use the Pick tool to select and move objects in a PhotoImpact image. Since the Pick tool manipulates objects, you rarely use it when working with a single, simple image. The base image is always selected by default, so clicking the base image with the Pick tool has no effect. Instead, the Pick tool is used to select and manipulate various objects you draw on an image such as path objects (filled shapes, lines and arrows, and outlines that you draw with the Path Drawing tools), image objects (pixel-based image data that you select with a Selection tool), and text objects (text that you create with the Text tool).

To use the Pick tool, simply click the tool in the Tool panel and move the mouse pointer over the image. The pointer changes to a black arrow. With the Pick tool active, you can do the following:

- To select an object, click the pointer on the object. After the object is selected, you can change its attributes, delete it, or manipulate the object in a variety of ways with other PhotoImpact tools.

- To select multiple objects, click the first object, then press the SHIFT or CTRL key as you click additional objects.

- To move an object, click and drag the object to the desired location.

- To make a copy of an object, press the CTRL key as you click and drag an object. PhotoImpact leaves the original object in place and creates a copy that moves as you drag and is deposited in the new location when you release the mouse button.

- To open the Object Properties dialog box for an object, double-click the object.

- To move an image area selection *marquee* (dashed line) without moving the image data, click and drag the selection marquee with the Pick tool pointer.

Unlike many of the other tools in the PhotoImpact Tool panel, the Pick tool doesn't have attributes of its own or create objects and impart attributes to those objects. As a result, the Attribute toolbar doesn't display the attributes of the Pick tool as you use the tool. Instead, the Attribute toolbar displays alignment options that you can use to align selected objects to each other or to the image. (See Chapter 8 for more information about using the alignment options.) You can also adjust the transparency and soft edge effect of selected objects using settings in the Attribute toolbar.

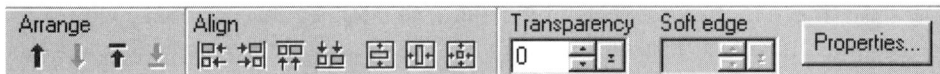

Select Image Areas

There are many reasons why you might want to select a portion of an image and manipulate it separately from the rest of that image. The PhotoImpact selection tools enable you to do just that. Depending on which of the selection tools you use, you can select a rectangular area, draw an irregular-shaped area, define an area with precise curves, or let PhotoImpact help you select areas based on color similarity.

After you select an image area, you can cut, copy, paste, and manipulate the selection in a variety of ways, including applying the many PhotoImpact effects and filters. (See Chapter 7 for more information about working with selected areas of an image.) When you create a selection and manipulate it, the selected image data becomes an image object, which you can move and manipulate separately from the rest of the image.

> **TIP** *Any filters and other effects that you apply while a selection is active affect only the selected image area, not other areas of the base image.*

Select Areas with the Standard Selection Tool

The Standard Selection tool enables you to quickly and easily select a portion of the image based on one of four standard shapes: rectangle, square, circle, or ellipse. To use the Standard Selection tool, follow these steps:

1. Click the Standard Selection tool in the Tool panel.

2. Select the desired shape from the Shape list in the Attribute toolbar. You can choose a rectangle, square, ellipse, or circle.

3. Click and drag on the image to define the size and location of the selection. Start by positioning the pointer at one corner of an imaginary box around the shape you want to define, and then drag the pointer diagonally toward the opposite corner. PhotoImpact draws a marquee around the selection area, and adjusts the size and position of the marquee in real time as you drag the pointer. Release the mouse button when the marquee surrounds the desired selection area.

Figure 2-2 shows an image with a rectangular selection defined. Note the marquee delineating the edges of the selection.

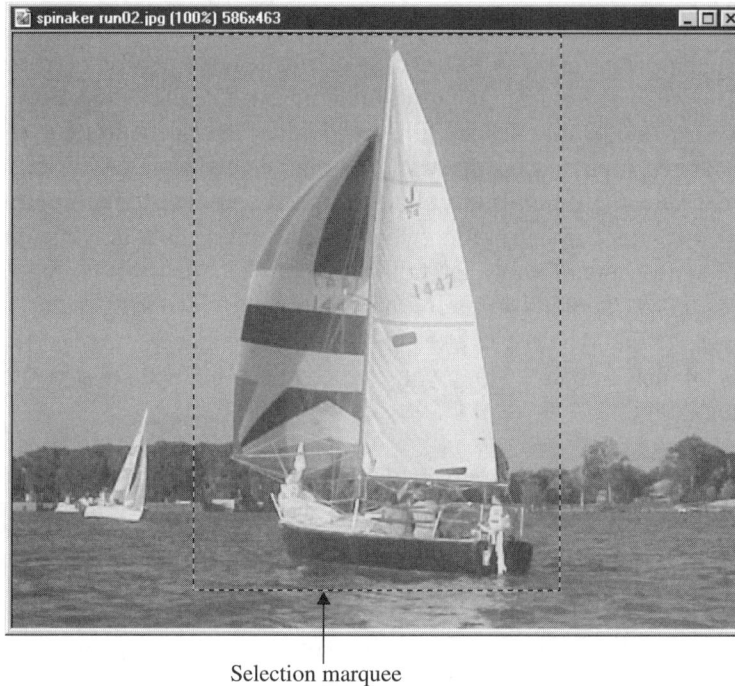

Selection marquee

FIGURE 2-2   An image with a rectangular selection marquee

Set Standard Selection Tool Attributes   The options on the Attribute toolbar enable you to change the selection and the selection process in some interesting ways.

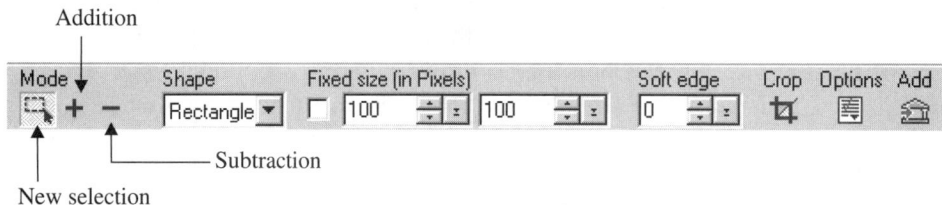

- To create new selection areas, click the New Selection button and drag the selection pointer on the image. PhotoImpact creates a new selection as you drag; any existing selection area is automatically deselected.

■ To expand an existing selection, click the Addition (+) button and drag the selection pointer on the image. The new selection area will be added to the existing selection.

■ To subtract from an existing selection, click the Subtraction (–) button and drag the selection pointer on the image. The selection area you define is subtracted from the existing selection.

■ To create a selection of a predefined size, click the Fixed Size checkbox and then set the horizontal and vertical size of the selection in the adjacent spin boxes. Simply click the image to place a selection box of that size on the image. There is no need to drag the pointer to define the size of the selection when using the Fixed Size option.

■ To create a selection area with a soft (*feathered*) edge, set the size (in pixels) of the edge softness in the Soft Edge spin box. Set the Soft Edge box to 0 to create a crisp edge.

■ To crop the image to the current selection, define a selection and then click the Crop button on the Attribute toolbar. PhotoImpact immediately crops the image to the current selection.

Set Standard Selection Tool Options   To change the Standard Selection tool options, click the Options button on the Attribute toolbar and choose an option from the menu that appears. The menu choices toggle the options on or off:

■ Draw from Center enables you to draw shapes by dragging from the center out to a corner instead of dragging from one corner to another.

■ Preserve Base Image causes the selection to be duplicated so you can manipulate it without corrupting the base image.

■ Anti-aliasing uses dithering to smooth the edge of the selection.

Use the Lasso Tool

With the Standard Selection tool, you can select portions of an image in one of four standard geometric shapes. The Lasso tool enables you to select irregular shapes by drawing a selection outline around the desired area. The Lasso tool is usually the selection tool of choice for defining a *knock-out* or *outline* selection around a foreground object (such as a person, car, or product) in a photograph so you can separate the foreground object from the background.

To use the Lasso tool to make a selection, follow these steps:

1. Click the Lasso tool in the Tool panel.

2. Click and drag on the image to define the selection area. Start by positioning the pointer at a point along the edge of the area you want to select. Work your way around the perimeter of the selection area using a combination of clicks and drags to draw straight and freehand lines to define the edge of the selection.

   - To draw a straight-line segment, click at one corner, then move the pointer to the next corner and click again. PhotoImpact joins the two click points with a straight-line segment.

   - To draw a freehand-line segment, click at the beginning point and drag the pointer along the path you want to define as the edge of the selection. PhotoImpact traces the pointer's path with a freehand-line segment.

3. Click the starting point to complete the selection shape. (You can also double-click to have PhotoImpact automatically close the selection shape with a straight line from the click point to the starting point.) PhotoImpact encloses the selection with the cyan dashed line that indicates a selection marquee.

Set Lasso Tool Attributes   The New Selection, Addition (+), and Subtraction (–) buttons and the Soft Edge option on the Lasso tool Attribute toolbar work in the same way as their counterparts on the Attribute toolbar for the Standard Selection tool.

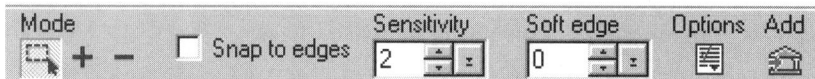

The Snap to Edges option allows you to automatically trace the edge of an area of a particular color. When you use the Lasso tool to draw straight-line segments with the Snap to Edges attribute active, PhotoImpact tries to detect and follow the edge between different colors that is in the path of the line segment you are creating. The Sensitivity setting enables you to control the extent to which PhotoImpact ignores minor color variations as it determines the edge between color areas. Lower settings ignore minor variations and detect the edge based on big color changes (such as a light foreground object compared to a dark background). Higher sensitivity settings will detect the edges between subtle shades of similar colors.

Set Lasso Tool Options   To change the Lasso tool options, click the Options button and choose an option from the menu that appears:

- Preserve Base Image causes the selection to be duplicated so you can manipulate it without corrupting the base image.

- Anti-aliasing uses dithering to smooth the edge of the selection.

Use the Magic Wand Tool

The Magic Wand tool enables you to simply click a spot on an image to instruct PhotoImpact to automatically create a selection composed of all the pixels that match the color of the spot where you click. The Magic Wand tool provides a fast and easy way to select areas of similar color anywhere on your image. For example, you can use the Magic Wand tool to quickly select the blue sky in a landscape.

Follow these steps to make a selection with the Magic Wand tool:

1. Click the Magic Wand tool in the Tool panel.

2. Click the pointer on a sample of the color you want to select. You can click a single spot or drag to create a line or area of sample color. PhotoImpact instantly selects other areas of the image that match the sample color and surrounds those areas with the selection marquee.

Set Magic Wand Tool Attributes   You can use the options on the Attribute toolbar for the Magic Wand tool to control how close the color match must be between the sample you designate and the image areas PhotoImpact selects.

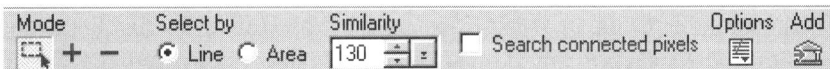

Adjust the setting in the Similarity spin box to control how closely other pixels must match the sample color in order to be included in the selection. A zero (0) in the Similarity box means that PhotoImpact will select only pixels that match the sample color exactly. Increasing the Similarity setting allows PhotoImpact to select pixels that are similar, but don't match exactly. The higher the Similarity setting, the broader the range of color difference that is included in the selection.

You often need to experiment with different Similarity settings to get the selection you want with the Magic Wand tool. A Similarity setting of 35 is usually a good starting point. Make a selection with that setting and see what PhotoImpact selects. Then you can press CTRL-Z to undo the selection, adjust the Similarity setting, and try again.

The New Selection, Addition (+), and Subtraction (–) buttons work in the same way as their counterparts on the Attribute toolbar for the Standard Selection tool. The other attributes work as follows:

- Click the Select by Line radio button and drag on the image to select pixels that match any of the pixels you drag the pointer through.

- Click the Select by Area radio button and drag on the image to select pixels that match any of the pixels inside a sample area you define by dragging the pointer.

- Check the Search Connected Pixels option to instruct PhotoImpact to select only pixels that are adjacent to the sample you designate with the Magic Wand tool. If you clear this checkbox, PhotoImpact selects matching pixels anywhere in your image.

> TIP
>
> *Often, you must fine-tune your Magic Wand selections by adding or subtracting areas from the selection. Try selecting an area with the Magic Wand tool and then fine tuning your selection with the Lasso tool*

Set Magic Wand Tool Options   To change the Magic Wand tool options, click the Options button on the Attribute toolbar and choose an option from the menu that appears:

- Choose either Compare by RGB or Compare by HSB to instruct PhotoImpact to make its selection based on similarity of colors expressed as RGB (Red, Green, Blue) values or HSB (Hue, Saturation, Brightness) numbers. The two different color models frequently produce slightly different results.

- Preserve Base Image causes the selection to be duplicated so you can manipulate it without corrupting the base image.

- Anti-aliasing uses dithering to smooth the edge of the selection.

Another way to make a selection based on similarity is to start by making a selection using any of the selection tools, and then right-click within the selection and choose Similar from the pop-up menu that appears. PhotoImpact displays the Similar dialog box. Adjust the Similarity setting, check the Expand from Current Selection option, and click OK. PhotoImpact adds to the selection using the same criteria as the Magic Wand tool, which selects adjacent pixels based on their similarity to the pixels in the current selection.

Use the Bezier Curve Tool

The Bezier Curve tool lets you define selection areas with great precision. It uses the same Bezier curve drawing techniques as the Path Drawing tool in Bezier/Polygon mode (introduced in the "Draw Solid Paths" section later in this chapter) to draw straight lines and smooth curves. The difference is that the Bezier Curve selection tool draws a selection area instead of a path object (a filled or outlined shape).

The Bezier Curve tool works with two different kinds of points: nodes and control points. A *node* is a point through which the edge of the shape must pass. A node is a vertices or corner for a straight-line segment and an apex or plot point for a curve segment. Nodes appear as small squares on the edge of the path. A *control point* is located at the end of a control handle line and serves as a "magnet" that pulls the curve in a given direction but doesn't lie on the path of the curve.

To use the Bezier Curve selection tool to make a selection, follow these steps:

1. Click the Bezier Curve selection tool in the Tool panel.

2. Select a shape from the Shape drop-down list box in the Attribute toolbar. You can select one of four predefined shapes (Rectangle, Square, Ellipse, Circle) or Free Path. The default, Free Path, is the choice you'll use most often, since the Standard Selection tool can produce the other shapes.

If you select one of the predefined shapes to create a selection area of the designated shape, you can then edit that shape by moving the Bezier Curve control points to create a new shape.

3. Click and drag on the image to define the selection area. Start by positioning the pointer at a point along the edge of the area you want to select and click to place a node at that location. Work your way around the perimeter of the

selection area using a combination of clicks and drags to create straight-line and curved segments to define the edge of the selection.

■ To define a straight-line segment, click at one corner to place a node there, then move the pointer to the next corner and click again to place another node. PhotoImpact joins the nodes with a straight-line segment.

■ To define a Bezier curve segment, click at the node and drag to create a control handle that will influence the curve. Release the mouse button to place the control point at the end of the control handle line, and then click at the next node. PhotoImpact draws a curved-line segment from one node to the next, with the curve arching toward the control point.

■ To draw one of the predefined shapes, click and drag diagonally to define the opposite corners of a box surrounding the desired shape. The process is identical to drawing the corresponding shapes with the Standard Selection tool. When working with predefined shapes, you can skip step 4.

4. Double-click the starting node to complete the selection shape. (You can also double-click the last node you place to have PhotoImpact automatically close the selection shape with a straight line from the last node to the starting node.) PhotoImpact encloses the selection with the solid line. At this point, the shape is a path object, not a selection.

5. Click the Edit Existing Path radio button on the Attribute toolbar to switch into path-editing mode. You can click and drag any of the nodes or control points to edit and refine the shape. When you click a node, the control handles and control points affecting the adjacent line segments appear, as shown in the example below. Edit the path as necessary to achieve the desired shape.

Control handle

Node

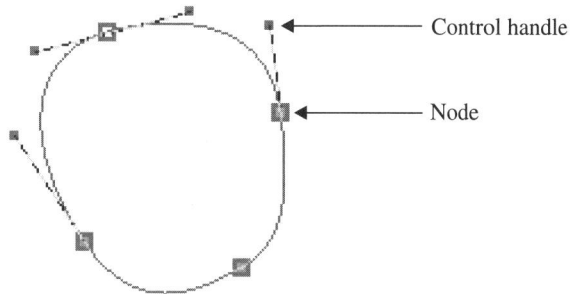

6. Click the Toggle button in the Attribute toolbar to convert the path to a selection area. PhotoImpact replaces the solid line around the perimeter of the path with the cyan dashed line that indicates a selection marquee.

Set Bezier Curve Tool Attributes   The options on the Attribute toolbar for the Bezier Curve selection tool are quite different from those of the other selection tools.

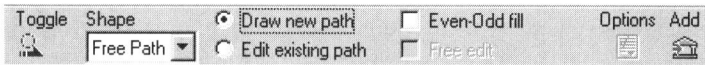

Toggle	Shape				Options	Add
	Free Path ▼	⦿ Draw new path ○ Edit existing path	☐ Even-Odd fill ☐ Free edit			

■ To convert a Bezier Curve path to a selection area (or vice versa) click the Toggle button. The button is only available after you complete a path or when you are in edit mode.

■ To select a shape before you start drawing with the Bezier Curve selection tool, choose an option from the Shape drop-down list box.

■ To draw a new shape with the Bezier Curve selection tool, click the Draw New Path radio button.

■ To edit an existing shape, click the Edit Existing Path radio button.

■ Check the Even-Odd Fill checkbox to allow overlapping lines to create voids in the selection. Uncheck the option to create a selection based on the outer perimeter of the path, without regard to any overlapping lines. Here's an example of selecting the same shape with Even-Odd Fill enabled and disabled:

Even-odd fill enabled   Even-odd fill disabled

■ Check the Free Edit checkbox to enable you to edit each of the control handle lines radiating from a node independently, which allows you to change the angle at which the line segments intersect at the node. When the Free Edit option is cleared, both control lines attached to a node move together, thus ensuring a smooth curve going through the node. Here's an example of selecting the same shape with Free Edit enabled and disabled:

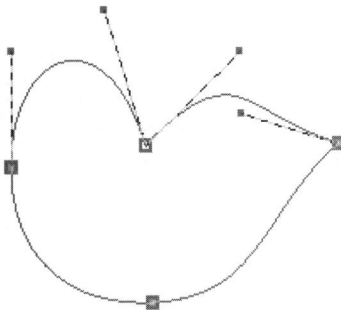

Free edit enabled   Free edit disabled

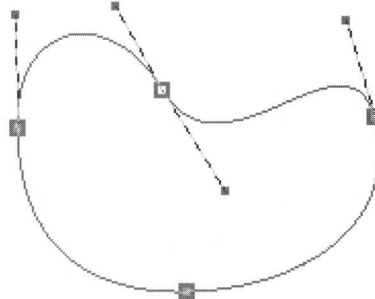

Set Bezier Curve Tool Options   Click the Options button to display a pop-up menu of options for editing a path. Different options appear depending on whether you have one or multiple paths selected for editing and on whether a specific line segment or node is selected:

■ When a single path is active for editing, you can delete or duplicate the path.

- When multiple paths are active (SHIFT-click each path), the menu includes an assortment of group and align options.

- When a node or line segment is active (click a node or double-click a line segment), menu options enable you to add and delete nodes and convert a curve to a straight line or a line to a curve.

More Selection Techniques

Here are some techniques that apply to all of the selection tools:

- To cancel a selection in progress, press the ESC key.

- To cancel a selection, use the Pick tool to click the base image anywhere outside the selection. You can also choose Selection | None or press SHIFT-G.

- To add to or expand an existing selection, press and hold the A key as you drag with any of the selection tools.

- To subtract from or contract an existing selection, press and hold the S key as you drag with any of the selection tools.

NOTE *The A and S keyboard shortcuts work the same as the + and – buttons in the Attribute toolbar.*

There can be only one selection area active in the document window at a time. You can expand and contract the selection area using combinations of selection tools, but when you start a new selection with any selection tool, you automatically deselect any previously existing selection.

Use the Zoom Tool

The Zoom tool enables you to change the magnification of the image as you view it in PhotoImpact. You can make the image larger to see more detail, or make it smaller to see an overview or simulate viewing the image from a distance. The Zoom tool is unusual in that it doesn't actually change the image you're working on in PhotoImpact; it changes only your view of that image in the PhotoImpact document window.

To use the Zoom tool, simply click the tool in the Tool panel, and then do one of the following:

■ Click the image to zoom in to the next higher magnification. PhotoImpact centers the document window on the point where you click.

■ Click at one corner of an imaginary rectangle and drag toward the opposite corner to define a box around a portion of the image you want to magnify. PhotoImpact zooms in so that the selected area fills the document window.

■ Right-click (or SHIFT-click) the image to zoom out to the next lower magnification.

Set Zoom Tool Attributes   When you select the Zoom tool, the Attribute toolbar displays a number of handy zoom options that you can use to change the image magnification.

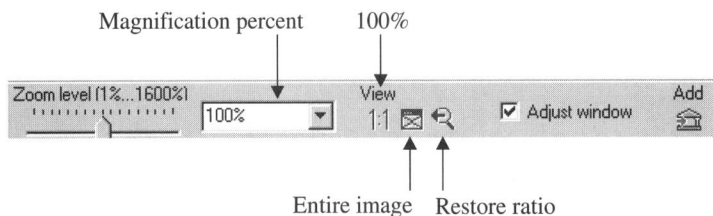

The Attribute toolbar options adjust the magnification as follows:

■ Drag the Zoom Level slider left or right to adjust the image magnification. This is the quickest way to make very large magnification changes.

■ Select a magnification percentage from the drop-down list box. The box displays the zoom level as a percent of the image's actual size. You can also type in a number to instantly change the zoom level to any desired magnification, including intermediate percentages between the preset zoom levels.

■ Click the 1:1 button to set the zoom level to 100% (view the image at its actual size).

■ Click the Entire Image button to zoom the image to the largest size that will allow the entire image to fit in the document window.

■ Click the Restore Ratio button to revert to the previous zoom level.

■ Check the Adjust Window checkbox to allow PhotoImpact to automatically resize the document window to accommodate changes in the total image size (up to the maximum document window size that will fit within the PhotoImpact application window, of course).

Adjust and Select Colors

PhotoImpact includes several tools for working with colors. There are tools for the quick adjustment of image brightness, contrast, and color tint; and there are color pickers for specifying foreground, background, and tool colors that you use with the drawing, painting, and retouching tools.

Adjust Image Tint and Brightness

PhotoImpact makes adjusting the brightness, contrast, and color tint of an image fast and easy with tools located on the Tool panel. There are also other, more powerful and flexible, tools available elsewhere in the program. However, the simplicity and accessibility of the color and brightness adjustment tools on the Tool panel guarantees that you will use these tools first and resort to the other image-adjustment features (covered in Chapter 5) only when special circumstances require.

Adjust Image Color

PhotoImpact provides a set of color-tint adjustments that mimic those found on most color television sets. This tool set is located near the bottom of the Tool panel:

The color-adjustment tools enable you to separately increase or decrease the three primary color (Red, Green, or Blue) components of the image. As a result of the television color control metaphor, most users will intuitively know how to adjust the tint of an image using the tools. Simply click the plus (+) button next to the red, green, or blue button to make the image more red, green, or blue. Click the minus (–) button next to the color dot to make the image less of that color.

When you click a color-adjustment button, PhotoImpact immediately changes the image and displays a color level pop-up across the bottom of the image, as shown below. The yellow marker in the center of the pop-up shows the image's starting level of the color. The red marker shows the current color level. The color level pop-up disappears after a second or two.

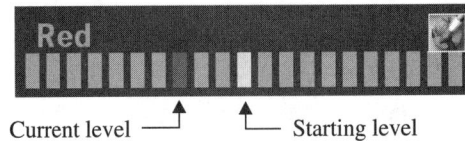

Current level ⎯⎯⌐   ⌐⎯ Starting level

Adjust Image Brightness and Contrast

In addition to adjusting the color tint of the image, you can also adjust brightness and contrast with buttons on the Tool panel. These two tools appear at the bottom of the Tool panel.

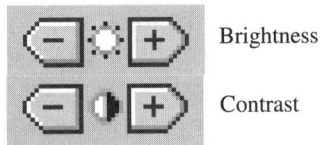

Brightness

Contrast

The Brightness and Contrast adjustment buttons work the same as the color tint buttons described in the previous section. To make the image lighter or darker, click the plus (+) or minus (−) button beside the Brightness icon. To increase or decrease the contrast of the image, click the plus (+) or minus (−) button beside the Contrast icon. When you adjust the brightness or contrast of your image, PhotoImpact displays a pop-up window showing the Brightness or Contrast level, just as it does when you adjust the color tint.

Select Painting Colors

PhotoImpact provides a variety of color-selection tools. Perhaps the most obvious are the Foreground and Background color swatches on the Tool panel. The Eyedropper tool on the Tool panel provides a convenient way to select an existing color from an image. PhotoImpact also includes dialog boxes and pop-up menus that you can use in various combinations to specify colors for use with the assorted painting and drawing tools.

Set Foreground and Background Colors

The Foreground and Background color swatches and related buttons appear on the Tool panel just above the color-tint adjustment buttons.

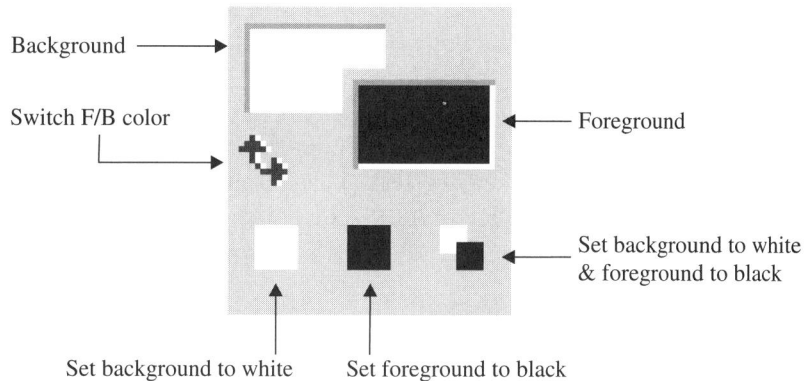

Background →

Switch F/B color

Foreground

Set background to white & foreground to black

Set background to white   Set foreground to black

The Background color swatch sits above and behind the Foreground color swatch. You can use the two swatches in the Tool panel as a reminder of what the current background and foreground colors are and to change those colors. The foreground and background colors you select affect the colors of the painting tools, but not the fill, drawing, or text tools.

The default background color is white, and the default foreground color is black. You can change either of those colors by clicking the corresponding swatch and selecting another color from the Ulead Color Picker dialog box that appears. The other small buttons below the Foreground and Background color swatches enable you to make common standard color selections very quickly:

- Click the Switch F/B Color button to swap the current foreground and background colors.

- Click the small, white rectangle button to set the background color back to the default white.

- Click the small, black rectangle button to set the foreground to the default black.

- Click the small, black and white rectangles button to set the foreground and background colors to their default values (black foreground and white background)

Use the Eyedropper Tool

The Eyedropper tool enables you to set the foreground or background color to match an existing color in your image. There's no need to visually match colors or go through the tedious process of sampling a color, noting its color values, and then laboriously entering those values in a dialog box to duplicate the color. You simply click the Eyedropper tool on your image, and PhotoImpact does all the sampling and color matching for you.

To set the foreground color, click the Eyedropper tool in the Tool panel, and then click the sample color in your image. PhotoImpact adjusts the foreground color to match the sample you clicked. To set the background color, the procedure is the same, except that you right-click or SHIFT-click on the sample color.

Use the Ulead Color Picker

The Ulead Color Picker dialog box, shown in Figure 2-3, provides enough variety to satisfy the pickiest of color pickers. You can choose a color by clicking one of hundreds of sample swatches, selecting from a spectrum display, or by entering values (RGB, HSB, or hexadecimal code).

NOTE *Some other programs use HSV (Hue, Saturation, Value) or HSL (Hue, Saturation, Lightness) in place of HSB (Hue, Saturation, Brightness). The terms are synonymous and all refer to the same basic color model.*

The Ulead Color Picker dialog box appears when you click a color swatch box almost anywhere in PhotoImpact. That includes either the Foreground or Background color swatches in the Tool panel, the color swatch box that appears in the Attribute toolbar when a drawing or painting tool is selected, and color swatches in many dialog boxes and panels throughout the program. You can select a color in any of the following ways:

- **RGB**   Type a number or use the spin box controls to enter a value for each of the RGB (Red, Green, Blue) components of a color in the RGB spin boxes on the right side of the dialog box.

Web Palette tab

Brightness tab ———

————Color tabs

Gray tab

Hue tab ———→

RGB spin boxes

Standard color
swatches

HSB spin boxes

RGB/HSB readouts ———

Hexadecimal
code box

Web Safe checkbox

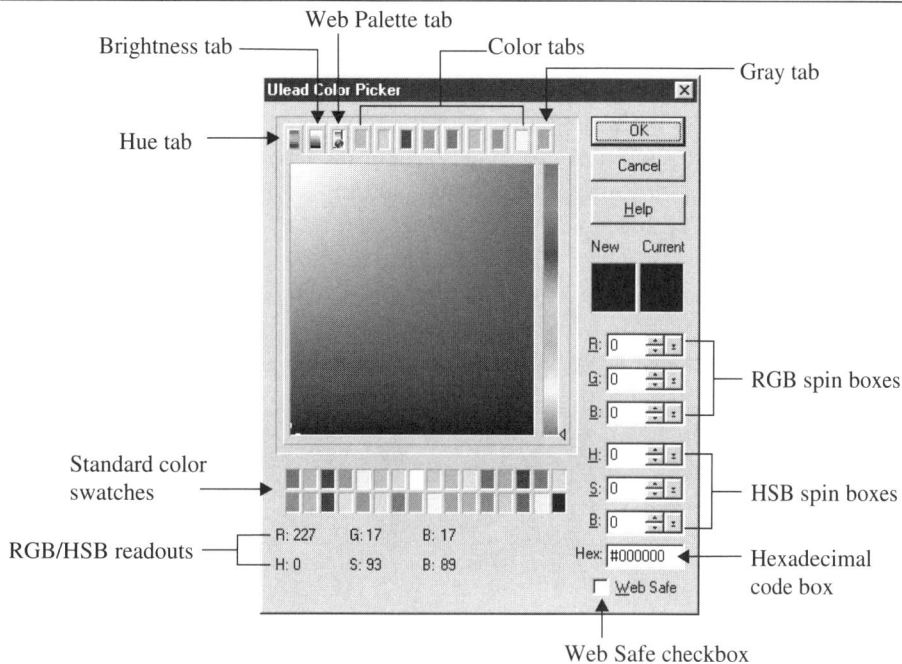

FIGURE 2-3 The Ulead Color Picker dialog box

- **HSB** Type a number or use the spin box controls to enter a value for each of the HSB (Hue, Saturation, Brightness) components of a color in the HSB spin boxes on the right side of the dialog box.

- **Hexadecimal code** Type in the Hexadecimal code for a color in the Hex text box in the lower-right portion of the dialog box.

- **Standard color swatches** Click any one of the 32 standard color swatches across the lower part of the dialog box.

- **Web Safe** Click the Web Safe checkbox to restrict all the tabs and color swatches to show only the 216 web-safe colors. When this option is active, the large color boxes and spectrums take on a banded or blocky appearance, and you can only choose web-safe colors.

You can also click a tab in the Ulead Color Picker dialog box to choose colors based on hue, brightness, the web-safe palette, a color, or shades of gray.

Hue Tab   The Hue tab displays a large color box that shows a range of shades of a given color. A spectrum slider sits just to the right of the large color box. First, select a base hue by adjusting the slider up or down, and then click in the large color box to select the shade of that hue.

Brightness Tab   The Brightness tab is similar to the Hue tab, with a large color box occupying most of the tab and a slider on the right. The difference is that the color box contains a color spectrum and the slider controls brightness. First, select the color from the large box, and then adjust the slider to control the brightness.

Web Palette Tab   The Web Palette tab displays a grid of color swatches showing all 216 web-safe colors. Click a swatch to select that color.

Color Tabs   There are eight separate color tabs that each show a grid of 88 variations on the basic color. Click a tab to select the base color range, and then click a swatch to select the specific color.

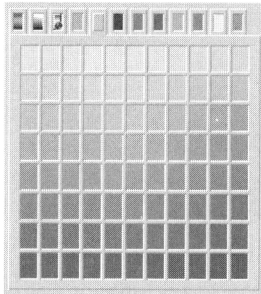

Gray Tab   The Gray tab is just like the eight color tabs except that it shows a range of grays instead of color variations. Click a swatch to select a gray value.

Color Selection   When you select a color in the Ulead Color Picker dialog box, PhotoImpact displays the selected color in the New box on the right side of the dialog box, next to the Current color swatch for easy comparison. Your color selection is also automatically reflected in all displays in the dialog box, which means you can select a color from a swatch or spectrum display and see its RGB values displayed in the RGB spin boxes or vice versa.

In addition, the RGB and HSB readouts below the standard color swatches show the RGB and HSB values for any color sample under the pointer, so you can see those values for a color without selecting it. You can fine-tune your color selection as much as you want. When the color selection is correct, click OK to close the Ulead Color Picker dialog box and record the color selection in the color swatch box from which you opened the dialog box.

Use the Color Pop-up Menu

Just as the Ulead Color Picker dialog box appears when you click a color swatch box in the Tool panel and elsewhere in PhotoImpact, the Color pop-up menu appears when you right-click any of those same color swatch boxes.

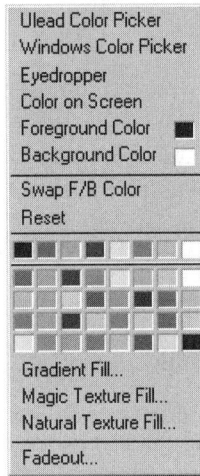

```
Ulead Color Picker
Windows Color Picker
Eyedropper
Color on Screen
Foreground Color   ■
Background Color   □

Swap F/B Color
Reset

[color swatches]

Gradient Fill...
Magic Texture Fill...
Natural Texture Fill...

Fadeout...
```

The Color pop-up menu provides quick access to a variety of color-selection options, including a few that aren't available anywhere else. As you can see, the pop-up menu includes two sets of standard color swatches. You can just click a swatch to select that color. The other options work as described in the following sections.

Ulead Color Picker   The Ulead Color Picker option opens the Ulead Color Picker dialog box described in the previous section.

Windows Color Picker   The Windows Color Picker option opens the standard Windows Color dialog box, which is the same one you use to select colors for Windows desktop items, as shown in Figure 2-4. You can then use the Color dialog box to specify a color for PhotoImpact.

Eyedropper   The Eyedropper option on the Color pop-up menu opens the Eyedropper dialog box, which contains a preview box showing the current image, as shown in Figure 2-5. Use the buttons below the image to zoom the image and the scrollbars to move around. Click the image to sample a color, and then click OK to record that color in the color swatch box from which you launched the

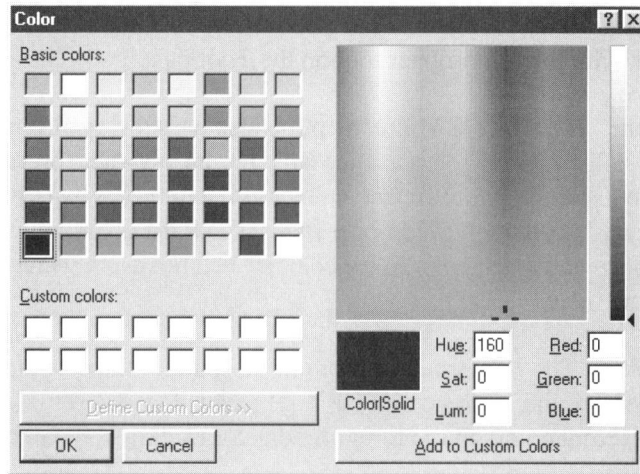

FIGURE 2-4   The Windows Color dialog box

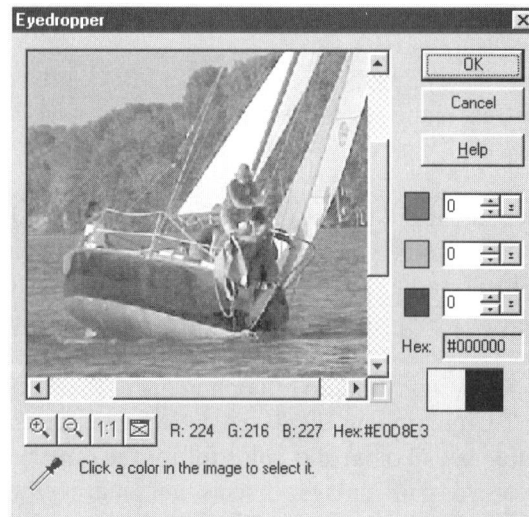

FIGURE 2-5   The Eyedropper dialog box

Eyedropper dialog box. This option enables you to use the "eyedropper" color-sampling technique to specify colors for path objects, fills, and other color boxes that don't work with the Eyedropper tool on the Tool panel.

Color On Screen   The Color On Screen option also uses the eyedropper sampling technique, but it allows you to select a color sample from anywhere on your Windows desktop, even outside the PhotoImpact application window. When you choose this option, the pointer becomes an eyedropper shape. Click the color you want to match, and PhotoImpact records that color in the color swatch box from which you opened the Color pop-up menu.

Foreground Color   The Foreground Color option changes the current color swatch to match the Foreground color box on the Tool panel. This is useful for matching drawing and text tool colors to the foreground color used by the painting tools.

Background Color   The Background Color option changes the current color swatch to match the Background color box on the Tool panel. Again, this is useful for matching drawing and text tool colors to the colors used by the painting tools.

Swap F/B Color   The Swap F/B Color option swaps the foreground and background colors in the Tool panel. The effect is the same as clicking the Swap F/B Color button on the Tool panel.

Reset   The Reset option returns the Foreground and Background colors to their default colors. The effect is the same as clicking the small black and white button on the Tool panel.

Gradient Fill   The Gradient Fill option opens the Gradient Fill dialog box, shown in Figure 2-6. In this dialog box, you can define a graduated fill pattern for the object instead of a solid color. Available only when specifying colors for path and text objects, not painting tools.

Magic Texture Fill   The Magic Texture Fill option opens the Texture Library dialog box with the Magic Texture options displayed. Select a texture sample and click OK to use that texture instead of a solid-color fill for the object. Available only when specifying colors for path and text objects, not painting tools.

Natural Texture Fill   The Natural Texture Fill option opens the same Texture Library dialog box as does the Magic Texture Fill option except with the Natural

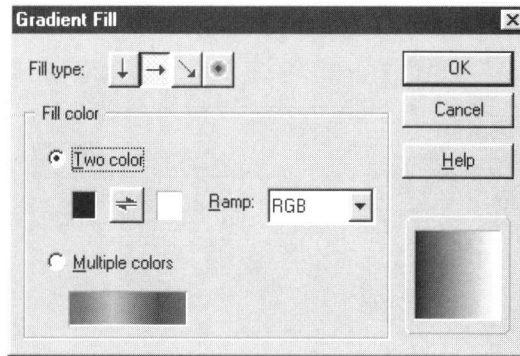

The Gradient Fill dialog box

Texture options displayed as shown in Figure 2-7. It's also available only when specifying colors for path and text objects, not painting tools.

Fadeout   The last option on the Color pop-up menu, Fadeout, opens the Fadeout dialog box, shown in Figure 2-8. In this dialog box, you can specify how you want

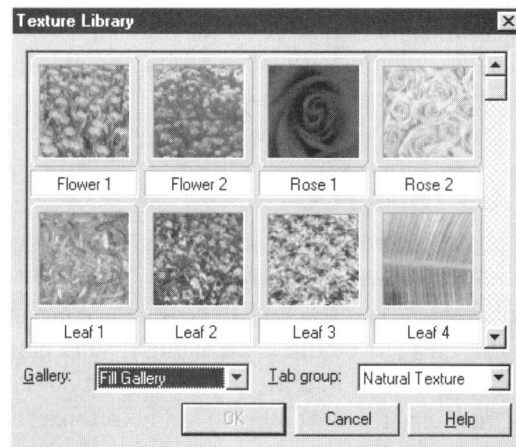

The Texture Library dialog box

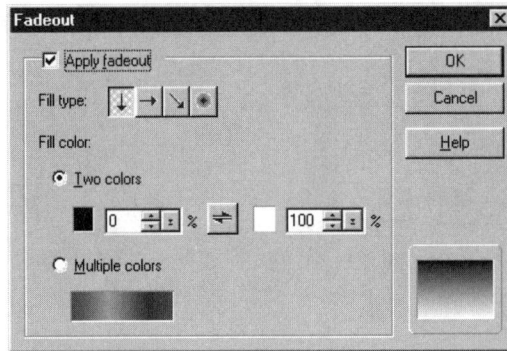

FIGURE 2-8   The Fadeout dialog box

the object to fade into the background. Like the Fill options, the Fadeout option is available only when specifying colors for path and text objects, not painting tools.

Use the Painting Tools

PhotoImpact includes a rich assortment of painting tools that you can use to modify an existing image or to create a new image from scratch. These are the tools that you use to manipulate pixels in your image. The pixel-based orientation of the painting tools sets them apart from the drawing tools that you use to create path objects and text. The painting tools include the various paintbrushes, plus the retouching tools, cloning tools, erasers, fill tools, and the Stamp tool.

Paint with the Paint Tools

When you think of painting tools in PhotoImpact and other image editors, the Paintbrush tool is the first to come to mind, and no wonder. The basic operation of the Paintbrush tool is easy to understand since it's the electronic counterpart of its real-world namesake. Just as you dip a real paintbrush in paint and then drag its bristles across the painting surface to leave a trail of paint on the paper or canvas, you select a color for your electronic paintbrush in PhotoImpact and drag the pointer across your electronic canvas to leave a trail of color on the image.

PhotoImpact starts with this simple concept of an electronic paintbrush and adds many variations of attributes such as brush size, shape, and pattern. The result is an impressive assortment of tools that simulate the effect of drawing and painting with different media such as pencil, crayon, airbrush, and oil paint.

PhotoImpact provides a full dozen Paint tools to simulate different drawing and painting media. You can select the desired tool from the Tool panel. Just click the button to use the default brush. To select one of the alternate Paint tools, click and hold the pointer on the brush tool button until the Paint Tool panel appears, and then click the desired tool button in that panel.

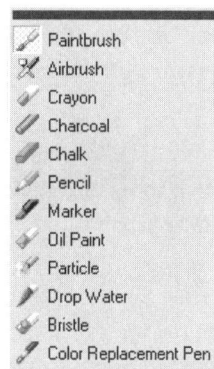

You can select any of the following from the Paint Tools panel:

- The Paintbrush tool simulates a watercolor brush with solid-color coverage.

- The Airbrush tool simulates the fine-spray pattern of an airbrush.

- The Crayon tool simulates a crayon on rough paper with flecks of darker and lighter color.

- The Charcoal tool simulates charcoal by allowing some background to show through a random paper texture.

- The Chalk tool is similar to the Charcoal tool, but it allows more of the background to show through.

- The Pencil tool simulates a pencil line by drawing a nearly opaque line with a slight soft edge.

- The Marker tool simulates a felt marker by drawing a smooth, semi-transparent line.

■ The Oil Paint tool simulates an oil painter's brush with a hint of bristle texture.

■ The Particle tool creates multicolor "droplets."

■ The Drop Water tool simulates the effect of using a brush wet with clear water on a watercolor painting. This tool doesn't add any color to the image (so there is no color option on the Attribute toolbar). Instead, it blurs and smears the existing image colors in its path.

■ The Bristle tool simulates a "dry brush" technique with a stiff-bristle brush. A lot of background shows through the bristle texture.

■ The Color Replacement Pen tool replaces one color with another.

Despite the variety of different brush tools, almost all of them work the same way. To paint on your image with the Paintbrush tool (or any of its variations), follow these steps:

1. Click the Paintbrush tool button in the Tool panel. Just click the button to use the default brush. The Attribute toolbar displays the settings for the selected tool. The Brush panel may also open to provide access to even more options.

2. Select a color for the brush. By default, PhotoImpact uses the Foreground color shown in the Tool panel. To specify another color, click the Foreground color swatch (or the color box in the Attribute toolbar or on the Color tab of the Brush panel) and select a color in the Ulead Color Picker dialog box. (See the previous section for details on selecting colors.)

3. Adjust settings in the Attribute toolbar and/or Brush panel as needed to control the size, shape, transparency, and other characteristics of the tool.

4. Click and drag on the image in the document window. As you drag the pointer, PhotoImpact traces its path with a trail of color.

The color, thickness, transparency, and other characteristics of the color trail that you paint depend on the attributes of the Paint tool you selected. (If you have a pressure-sensitive graphics tablet, you can vary the line thickness with the pressure of the pen tip on the tablet.) Figure 2-9 shows several paintbrush effects.

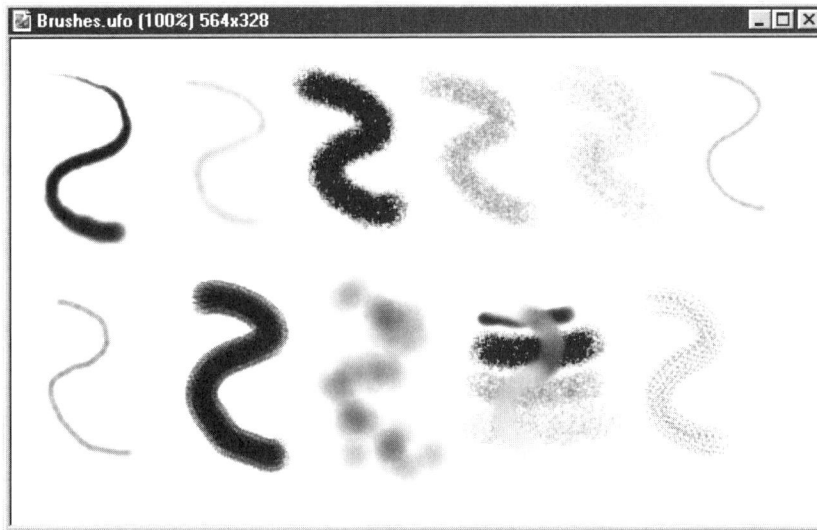

Brushes.ufo (100%) 564x328

FIGURE 2-9   PhotoImpact's various paintbrush tools produce different effects.

Select Paint Tool Attributes

When you select one of the Paint tools, the Attribute toolbar contains many options for determining how the tool works.

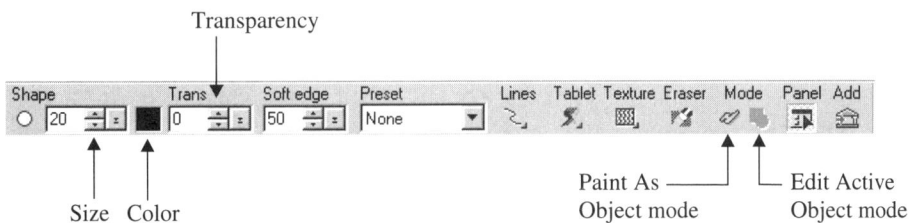

Transparency

Shape   Trans   Soft edge   Preset   Lines   Tablet   Texture   Eraser   Mode   Panel   Add

Size   Color

Paint As ———   ⌐— Edit Active
Object mode   Object mode

These attributes work as follows:

■   Click the Shape button to select one of six standard shapes or a custom shape that you define in the Brush panel. The standard shapes are square, circle, horizontal line, vertical line, and two diagonal lines.

■ Adjust the brush size (in pixels) in the Size spin box.

■ Click the color box to set the brush color, which also changes the Foreground color swatch in the Tool panel.

■ Adjust the degree of transparency (how much of the background image shows through the brush line) in the Trans (Transparency) spin box. Valid values are 0 to 99. Set Transparency to 0 for an opaque brush.

■ Adjust the degree of softness around the edge of the brush in the Soft Edge spin box. Set Soft Edge to 0 for a hard-edged line and 100 for maximum softness or blur around edges. (This option doesn't appear when tools such as the Crayon and Pencil are selected.)

■ Select one of the Preset options to instantly adjust the other attributes to preset values. Presets include Fine Brush, Wide Marker, and Chinese Calligraphy, among others.

■ Click the Lines button to display a menu of line types. Freehand enables unconstrained drawing on the canvas—simply drag to draw a freehand line. Straight draws single, straight-line segments—click to start the line and click again to end it. Connected draws a series of connected straight-line segments—click to start the line, click again to draw a segment, click again to add another segment, and so on.

■ Click the Tablet button to display a menu of options for linking a brush attribute to the pen pressure of a pressure-sensitive graphics tablet. The choices are None, Size, Transparency, or Size and Transparency.

■ Click the Texture button to display a menu of options for adding texture to the selected brush. Select Texture opens a dialog box where you can choose one of several standard textures. Add Texture opens a dialog box where you can select an image file to use as a texture. Delete Texture enables you to remove a custom texture from the Select Texture dialog box.

■ Click the Eraser button to reverse the action of the brush so that it removes painting from the image instead of adding to the image. Click the Eraser button again to revert to normal painting mode.

New to PhotoImpact 7

■ Click the Paint As Object Mode button to paint on a separate transparent overlay layer, so painting strokes can be manipulated like objects. (See

Chapter 7 for information on working with objects.) Toggle this button off to paint directly onto the base image.

2

■ Click the Edit Active Object Mode button to enable that mode, which makes all objects except the currently active object semi-transparent. This makes it easier to see and work with an object when other objects overlap it. You can also enable this mode by choosing Edit | Edit Active Objects Only or by pressing SHIFT-Z.

■ Click the Panel button to open or close the Brush panel, described in the next section.

Set Brush Panel Options

The options available in the Attribute toolbar enable you to control most characteristics of each Paint tool. However, for an added measure of control, you can turn to the options in the Brush panel, shown in Figure 2-10.

The Brush panel has five tabs of options:

■ **Shape**   Options to control the shape of the brush tip. You can adjust the height, width, angle, soft edge, shape, and eraser mode.

■ **Options**   Settings include the application method, transparency, and buttons to select freehand, straight, or connected lines.

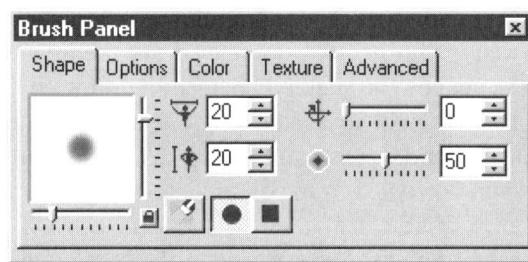

FIGURE 2-10   The Brush panel offers more painting options.

- ■ **Color**   In addition to a single color, you can choose a multicolor mode and specify the hue, saturation, and brightness delta (difference) between the colors.

- ■ **Texture**   Select a texture or click the X button for no texture.

- ■ **Advanced**   Set pressure options, spacing, and fade in/out options.

Replace Colors

The Color Replacement Pen tool works differently from the other painting tools, since its purpose is to replace one color with another. You specify the "color from" and "color to," and then drag the tool across your image. As you drag the tool across your image, it changes the old color to the new color but leaves all other colors unaffected.

Because of the special requirements of the Color Replacement Pen tool, the Attribute toolbar and Brush panel contain different options when you select the tool. The Attribute toolbar gets two color boxes (From Color and To Color), and a Similarity box replaces the usual Transparency and Soft Edge boxes so you can control how exact the color match must be for the replacement to take place. Also, the Texture and Mode buttons are not available, since those options don't apply.

Use the Clone Tools

Cloning is a computer-painting technique that is almost impossible to duplicate in the real world. Instead of painting with a solid color, cloning paints with a cloned duplicate of a patch of pixels from elsewhere in the same image. It's a sort of copy-and-paste operation that copies pixels from one part of the image and pastes them into another part of the image. The slick part is that PhotoImpact performs the copy/paste automatically and continuously as you drag one of the Clone tools across your image. You can use the Clone tools to do things like cover facial blemishes and wrinkles with flesh tones borrowed from adjacent areas of a portrait.

The Clone tools are available in a variety of brush shapes and textures that mirror the characteristics of their Paint tool counterparts. To select one of the Clone tools, click and hold the pointer on the Clone tool button until the Clone tool subpanel appears, and then click the desired tool button in that panel.

2

Clone-Paintbrush
Clone-Airbrush
Clone-Crayon
Clone-Charcoal
Clone-Chalk
Clone-Pencil
Clone-Marker
Clone-Oil Paint
Clone-Bristle

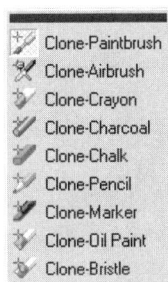

You can adjust all the same attributes of a Clone tool as you can a Paint tool, except color. Instead of selecting a color as you do with a Paint tool, you specify a sample area of the image from which you want to begin cloning.

To use a Clone tool, follow these steps:

1. Click the Clone tool button in the Tool panel. Just click the button to use the default brush. As with the Paint tools, the Attribute toolbar displays the settings for the selected tool, and the Brush panel may also open to provide access to even more options.

2. Adjust settings in the Attribute toolbar and/or Brush panel as needed to control the size, shape, transparency, and other characteristics of the tool. (The attribute settings are the same as for the Paint tools, except for the absence of the color attribute.)

3. SHIFT-click your image to designate the area you want to begin cloning. Normally, this is a spot just off to one side of the spot where you want to begin painting with the Clone tool, but it can be anywhere on the image.

4. Click and drag on the image in the document window. As you drag the pointer, PhotoImpact copies image data from the clone source spot and pastes it into the path of the Clone tool. As you move the Clone tool, the clone source moves to maintain a consistent offset from the Clone tool.

Figure 2-11 shows an exaggerated example of the Clone tool in action. The figure was created by selecting an area near the top of the left half of the image as the clone source, and then dragging the Clone tool down the middle of the blank right half of the image. A very large tool size makes it easy to see how the tool cloned image details from the source and deposited them into the path of the tool.

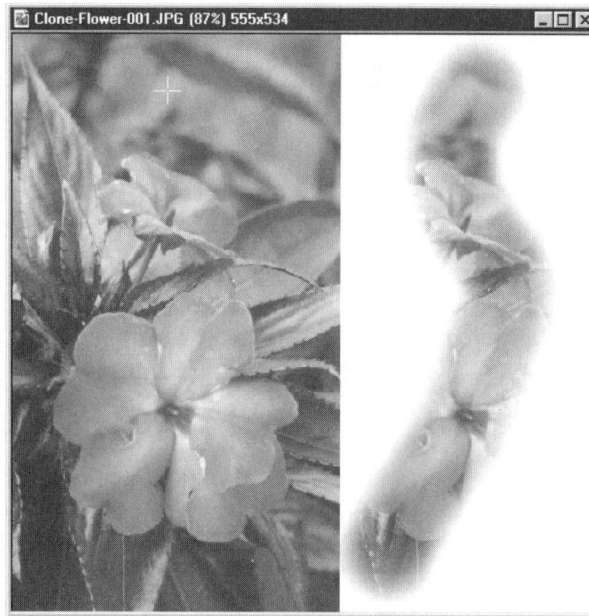

FIGURE 2-11   The Clone tool in action

Use the Retouch Tools

The PhotoImpact Retouch tools let you to selectively edit and manipulate detailed areas of your image. Various Retouch tools have the ability to lighten, darken, smudge, smear, or sharpen the image areas they touch. There are even specialized Retouch tools for removing red-eye and scratches from photos.

In some respects, the Retouch tools are similar to the Paint tools. You select a Retouch tool, adjust its attributes, and drag it across your image in much the same way you use Paint tools such as the Paintbrush. However, there is a very significant difference between the Paint tools and the Retouch tools. When you drag a Paint tool across your image, the tool leaves a trail of color in its wake that is added to the image. When you drag a Retouch tool across the image, the tool modifies the existing image instead of adding to it. Depending on which Retouch tool you use, it may lighten, darken, or distort the image where you drag the tool.

As with the other tools, if the Retouch tool that you want to use doesn't appear on the Tool panel, click and hold the pointer on the Retouch tool button until the Retouch Tool panel appears, and then click the desired tool button in that panel.

```
  ▪   Dodge
  ▲   Burn
  )   Blur
  ▲   Sharpen
  ▣   Tonal Adjustment
  ∧   Smudge
  ▶   Saturation
  ✐   Warping
  ✍   Bristle Smear
  ✎   Remove Red Eye
  ✎   Remove Scratch
  ✦   Remove Noise
  ✏   Color Transform Pen
  ✐   Colorize Pen
```

Here's a list of the Retouch tools and what they do:

- The Dodge tool lightens the image, like *dodging* (casting a shadow to reduce the exposure in an area) to lighten a portion of a photographic print.

- The Burn tool darkens the image, like *burning* (giving an area extra exposure) to darken a portion of a photographic print.

- The Blur tool blurs or blends the image, similar to the Drop Water painting tool.

- The Sharpen tool adds contrast to accentuate the difference between adjacent colors, thus enhancing the sharpness of edges.

- The Tonal Adjustment tool darkens and intensifies colors.

- The Smudge tool blurs and also drags colors in the direction you drag the tool. It simulates dragging your finger through wet paint.

- The Saturation tool intensifies the color saturation without making the color significantly darker.

- The Warping tool drags colors along the direction you drag the tool, but without the blurring that the Smudge tool creates.

- The Bristle Smear tool drags colors along in the direction you drag the tool like the Warping tool, but does so in an uneven pattern to simulate smearing with a coarse-bristled brush.

- The Remove Red Eye tool replaces red with black. If a photographic subject's eyes exhibit the bright red-eye effect that results from taking a flash photo in a darkened room, just drag this tool across the eyes to get rid of the red and make the eyes look natural.

- The Remove Scratch tool fills thin lines with surrounding colors to disguise or eliminate scratches in photos

- The Remove Noise tool blends colors to eliminate pixels that differ significantly from the average color of surrounding pixels.

- The Color Transform Pen tool replaces one color with another, similar to the Color Replacement Pen in the Paint tools. When you select this tool, the Attribute toolbar includes two color boxes, where you specify the color from and color to for the transformation.

- The Colorize Pen tool changes the color (but not the value) of the image where you drag the tool. This is the tool to use when the client decides that the red car in the picture should be blue. The tool changes the hue to blue but keeps intact the shading that gives the car its three-dimensional shape. When you select this tool, the Attribute toolbar includes a color box where you select the desired color you want to apply with the tool.

The Attribute toolbar displays the same set of options for almost all the Retouch tools. In fact, most of the options are the same as those for the Paint tools. The differences are that the Level spin box replaces the Transparency box to provide a way to set the strength of the Retouch tool effect, and the Texture and Eraser buttons don't appear on the Attribute toolbar for Retouch tools.

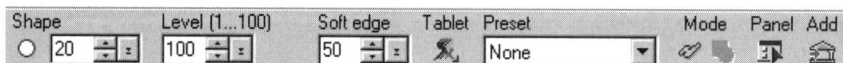

Shape	Level (1...100)	Soft edge	Tablet	Preset		Mode	Panel	Add
○ 20	100	50	𝒳	None	▼			

Remove Effects with the Eraser Tools

After you make changes to your image with the various painting tools, you might want to selectively remove or erase some of those changes. That's the job of the PhotoImpact eraser tools.

The eraser tools work like a painting tool in that you select the tool and drag it across your image to affect the image along the path of the tool. However, the eraser tools don't deposit color on the image like the Paint tools, clone image areas like the Clone tools, or alter image areas like the Retouch tools. Instead, the eraser tools remove or reverse the effects of those other painting tools.

> CAUTION
>
> *At first, using the eraser tools may seem a little like playing a rock, paper, scissors game in which you don't know the rules. Each eraser tool affects portions of your image that were created by certain painting tools and not others. Furthermore, you need to select the correct layer for the Object Eraser tools to work as expected. It can be confusing at first, but you'll get the hang of it as you gain experience using the tools.*

Use Paint Tools as Erasers

One kind of eraser that is available in PhotoImpact isn't a separate eraser tool, but an attribute of a Paint tool. The Eraser button is available on the Attribute toolbar for most of the Paint tools, such as the Paintbrush. When you select the Paint tool and click the Eraser button, the tool reverses its normal action and erases, instead of depositing color.

When used as an eraser, a Paint tool can erase what you painted with any of the Paint tools, Clone tools, or Retouch tools, provided the painting hasn't yet been merged into the base image by switching to another tool or selecting another object. The Paint tool in Erase mode also cannot erase painting done in Paint As Object mode. Anything you create in Paint As Object mode must be erased with the Object Paint Eraser tool.

> NOTE
>
> *None of the eraser tools or attributes have any effect on the base image itself or anything merged into the base image. They also have no effect on path or text objects.*

Use the Object Paint Eraser

When you use a painting tool in Paint As Object mode, the results are placed on a separate layer, where they can be selected and manipulated in much the same way as a path object. It's a separate object composed of pixel-based image data that you created with a paint tool, so you could call it an *image object* or a *paint object*. You cannot edit such paint objects with the normal Eraser attribute of a Paint tool, so PhotoImpact provides a special tool, called the Object Paint Eraser tool, just for erasing paint objects.

To use the Object Paint Eraser tool, follow these steps:

1. Select the paint object you want to erase. Either click the paint object with the Pick tool or click the object's layer in the Access panel's Layer Manager. It's important to select the paint object *before* you use the Object Paint Eraser tool. If you attempt to use the Object Paint Eraser without a paint object selected, the pointer takes the shape of the classic "Prohibited" symbol (a circle with a diagonal slash), and PhotoImpact displays an error message.

2. Click the Object Paint Eraser tool button in the Tool panel. The Attribute toolbar displays the settings for the selected tool, and the Brush panel may also open to provide more options.

3. Adjust settings in the Attribute toolbar and/or Brush panel as needed to control the size, shape, transparency, and other characteristics of the tool.

4. Click and drag on the image in the document window. As you drag the pointer across a selected paint object, PhotoImpact erases the corresponding portions of that paint object.

Use the Object Magic Eraser

Like the Object Paint Eraser, the Object Magic Eraser works on paint objects. The difference between the two eraser tools is that the Object Paint Eraser tool erases the portions of the paint object that you touch with the tool, whereas the Object Magic Eraser automatically erases all portions of the paint object that match the color you click with the tool. The tool acts like the Magic Wand selection tool in the way it selects similar colors to delete, except that the Object Magic Eraser tool affects only the currently active paint object.

To use the Object Magic Eraser tool, follow these steps:

1. Select the paint object you want to erase. Either click the paint object with the Pick tool or click the object's layer in the Access panel's Layer Manager.

2. Click the Object Magic Eraser tool in the Tool panel. The Attribute toolbar displays the settings for the selected tool. The Brush panel may also open to provide access to even more options.

Shape	Trans	Soft edge	Preset	Lines	Tablet	Texture	Mode	Panel	Add
○ 100	0	50	None ▼						

3. Adjust the settings in the Attribute toolbar as needed. You can set color similarity options as you do with the Magic Wand selection tool, and you can also set a transparency option as with other painting tools to effectively erase all or only part of the selected color.

4. Click the pointer on a sample of the color you want to select. You can click a single spot or drag to create a line or area of sample color within the paint object. PhotoImpact instantly deletes other areas of the paint object that match the sample color within the tolerances set in the Attribute toolbar.

> **TIP** *You can use the Object Paint Eraser and Object Magic Eraser on path and text objects, provided that you first convert those objects to paint objects. See Chapter 7 for information about converting objects.*

Fill Areas with the Fill Tools

The Fill tools enable you to fill an area of your image with a color. These are the tools for changing large areas of color, such as a sky or background.

Depending on which of the Fill tools you use, the fill color can be a solid color or one of three different kinds of gradient fill. (*Gradient fills* produce a graduated color change across the filled area.) Unlike the other painting tools, the Fill tools don't share the same foreground and background colors with the other tools. Instead, you specify fill colors in the Attribute toolbar, and these colors are independent of those used by any other tool.

Fill tools work on areas of the base image and on the currently selected image object, but not on path or text objects.

Use the Bucket Fill Tool

The simplest of the Fill tools is the Bucket Fill tool. This tool is probably familiar to anyone who has ever used a paint program or image editor of any kind (including the simplistic Windows Paint applet). Not surprisingly, the PhotoImpact version behaves in much the same way as its counterparts in other programs. The Bucket Fill tool applies the tool's color to the image where you click the tool and spreads out the color to fill adjacent areas of the image that match the color of the spot you click.

To use the Bucket Fill tool, follow these steps:

1. Click the Bucket Fill tool button in the Tool panel.

2. Select the fill color in the Attribute toolbar. Adjust the other attribute settings as needed.

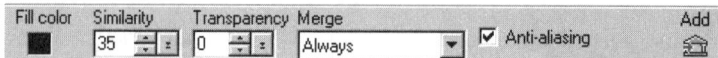

Fill color	Similarity	Transparency	Merge			Add
■	35	0	Always ▼	✔ Anti-aliasing		🏠

3. Click the pointer on your image. Be sure to click a sample of the color you want to replace with the fill color. PhotoImpact applies the fill color to that area of your image and to all adjacent areas of similar color.

Use Gradient Fills

The fill color you apply with the Fill tools doesn't need to be a single solid color. You can also apply a gradient fill that transitions from one color to another. In other words, the gradient fills apply a color shading to the filled area instead of the solid color. For example, you can create a gradient fill that transitions smoothly from black, through the full range of grays, to white.

Unlike the Bucket Fill tool, which selectively replaces colors in your image, the gradient fills spread over the entire image or selection. You can create gradient fills in three different patterns: linear, rectangular, and elliptical. From the Fill tool subpanel, choose the appropriate tool for the pattern you want to use.

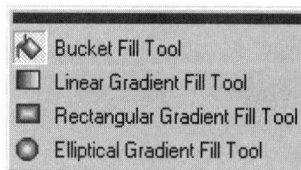

◇ Bucket Fill Tool
▦ Linear Gradient Fill Tool
▢ Rectangular Gradient Fill Tool
○ Elliptical Gradient Fill Tool

The three gradient fills are essentially the same except for the fill pattern:

- The Linear Gradient Fill tool uses a pattern in which the color gradient progresses along and parallel to a straight line.

- The Rectangular Gradient Fill tool uses a pattern in which the color gradient radiates out from the center to the edges of a rectangle.

- The Elliptical Gradient Fill tool uses a pattern in which the color gradient radiates out from the center to the edges of an ellipse.

Figure 2-12 illustrates the fill patterns created by each tool.

To use a Gradient Fill tool, follow these steps:

1. Click the Linear Gradient Fill tool button (or the Rectangular or Elliptical Gradient Fill button) in the Tool panel.

2. Select the beginning and ending fill color in the Attribute toolbar. Adjust the other attribute settings as needed.

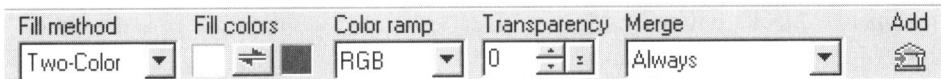

Fill method	Fill colors	Color ramp	Transparency	Merge		Add
Two-Color ▼	⬜ ⇌ ⬛	RGB ▼	0 ⬍ ⋮	Always	▼	🏛

3. Click and drag the pointer on your image. Drag starting at the point where you want the transition to begin with the beginning fill color, through the area where the color gradient should appear, and release the mouse button where you want the ending fill color to appear. PhotoImpact applies the gradient fill to your image.

By dragging the pointer, you specify the location and length of the color gradient. PhotoImpact extends the beginning and ending fill colors to fill the rest of the image beyond the ends of the drag. If you use the Linear Gradient Fill tool, you drag to create a line, and PhotoImpact extends the gradient parallel to that line.

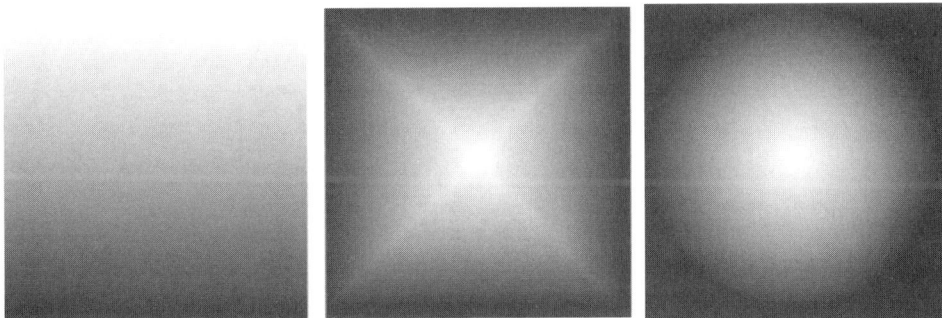

Linear gradient fill   Rectangular gradient fill   Elliptical gradient fill

FIGURE 2-12   The Gradient Fill tools create different fill patterns.

Figure 2-13 shows an example of using the Linear Gradient Fill tool to fill the background of an image. With the Rectangular Gradient Fill tool, you drag from the center to one corner of a rectangle. With the Elliptical Gradient Fill tool, you drag from the center to the edge of an ellipse.

Use the Stamp Tool

The Stamp tool is a strange, but fun, painting tool. The Stamp tool enables you to instantly paste a copy of a predefined image object anywhere you click your image document. Select a butterfly stamp, and start clicking; soon, you'll have an entire flock of butterflies on your image.

> **NOTE** *Some other image-editing programs use a rubber stamp icon to represent their cloning feature. If you've used one of these programs, you may be quite surprised by what happens when you use the PhotoImpact Stamp tool. If you're looking for the PhotoImpact counterpart to the Rubber Stamp tool in another program, check out the Clone tools described previously in this chapter.*

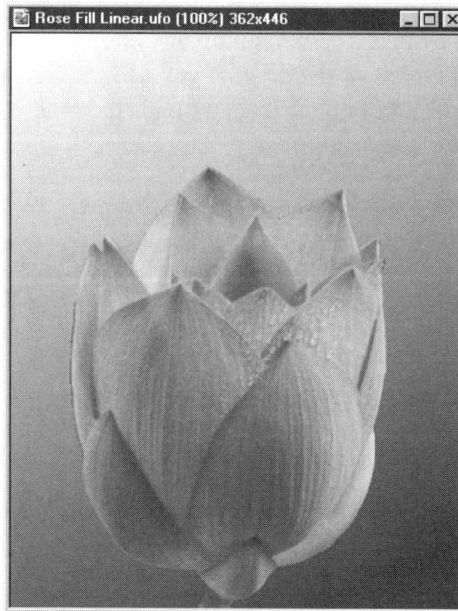

FIGURE 2-13   A linear gradient fill applied to the background of an image

To use the Stamp tool, follow these steps:

1. Click the Stamp tool in the Tool panel. PhotoImpact displays the options for the Stamp tool in the Attribute toolbar.

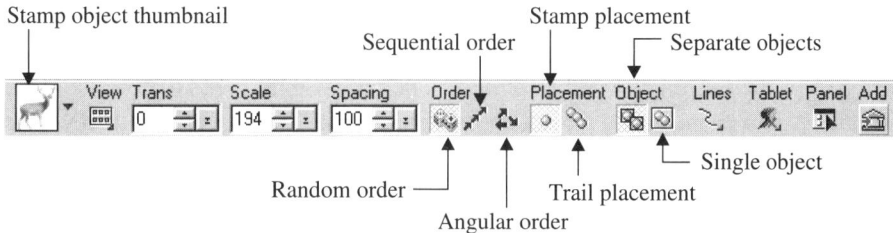

Stamp object thumbnail

Sequential order

Stamp placement

Separate objects

View Trans   Scale   Spacing   Order   Placement Object   Lines Tablet Panel Add

Random order

Angular order

Trail placement

Single object

2. Click the stamp thumbnail in the Attributes toolbar. PhotoImpact opens a dialog box showing thumbnail images representing the available files of stamp images.

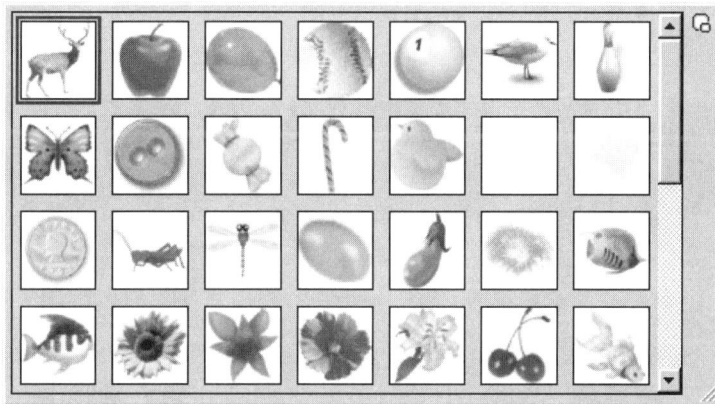

3. Click the stamp thumbnail in the selection box. PhotoImpact closes the dialog box and shows the selected stamp in the Attribute toolbar.

4. Adjust the other settings in the Attribute toolbar as needed.

5. Click (or click and drag) on your image. PhotoImpact places a copy of the stamp object at the location where you click. If you click and drag, PhotoImpact places multiple copies of the stamp object on your image along the path of the pointer.

Figure 2-14 shows the effect of using the Stamp tool to place multiple stamp objects (in this case, butterflies) on an image. One of the cool things about using the Stamp tool is that you don't necessarily get an identical object each time you click the tool. Actually, a stamp file usually contains multiple images that PhotoImpact accesses randomly (or sequentially) when you click the Stamp tool. For example, the flock of butterflies shown in Figure 2-14 are all part of the same stamp file.

When you click the Stamp tool, PhotoImpact displays the tool's attributes in the Attribute toolbar. Along with the stamp thumbnail, which opens the dialog box of available stamp files, there are options for controlling the appearance of the stamp objects:

■ Click the View button to open a box showing thumbnails of all the individual image objects in the stamp. Click again to close the box.

■ Adjust the value in the Trans (Transparency) spin box to set the transparency of the image objects.

■ Adjust the value in the Scale spin box to specify the size of the image objects, as a percent of their original size.

FIGURE 2-14   The Stamp tool and a single stamp object created this flock of butterflies.

2

■ Adjust the value in the Spacing spin box to set the spacing between image objects when you drag the Stamp tool to deposit a stream of objects.

■ Click the Random Order button to place images from the stamp in random order.

■ Click the Stamp Placement button to place a single image with each click of the stamp tool (disabling the drag option).

■ Click the Separate Objects button to make each image placed by the Stamp tool a separate image object that you can move independently.

■ Click the Lines button to display a menu of line-drawing modes. Your choices are Freehand, Straight, and Connected, and they are the same as their counterparts in the painting tools. Freehand is the default choice, and you'll rarely need to use the others.

■ Click the Tablet button to display a menu of options for pressure-sensitive tablets. Select what effect changes in pen pressure will have. Your choices are None and Transparency.

■ Click the Panel button to show or hide the Brush panel, where you can access the same attributes that are available in the Attribute toolbar, plus a few more, such as the source file for the stamp.

Use the Path-Drawing Tools

The PhotoImpact path-drawing tools are fundamentally different from the painting tools. The painting tools create and manipulate images composed of pixels. The path-drawing tools create and manipulate vector-based objects. The Path tools are the kind of drawing tools normally found in graphics programs such as Adobe Illustrator, Corel Draw, and Macromedia Freehand. PhotoImpact makes these tools available in an image-editing program.

Each vector/path object is really a mathematical formula for producing a shape, curve, or line, along with the data describing the attributes of the object, such as its color. When you edit a path object, PhotoImpact works behind the scenes to edit the formula describing the object. This is in contrast to the painting tools, which edit your image by changing the color of various pixels. As a result, you can edit, enlarge, and distort path objects in ways that you can't manipulate a pixel-based image; and you can do so without getting the jagged edges that often characterize enlarged or distorted images.

Chapter 7 covers how to use the path-drawing tools and how to work with the objects they create. This section merely acquaints you with the location of the tools and their various options.

Draw Solid Paths

The Path Drawing tool enables you to draw various solid-filled shapes. You can create predefined shapes such as squares and circles, as well as polygons and free-form curved shapes. You can fill the shapes with a solid color, color gradations, textures, and even image files.

When you draw a solid path object, you start by clicking the Path Drawing tool in the Tool panel. Next, you select the desired shape from the Shape list in the Attribute toolbar.

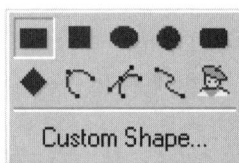

You can select one of the following shapes:

- Rectangle

- Square

- Ellipse

- Circle

- Rounded Rectangle

- Diamond

- Spline

- Bezier/Polygon

- Freehand

- Custom Shape

2

The first six options (rectangle through diamond) let you draw standard shapes quickly and easily. In addition, the three irregular shape modes—Spline, Bezier/ Polygon, Freehand—enable you to draw polygons and shapes composed of smooth curves. The Custom Shape choice opens the Custom Shape dialog box displaying PhotoImpact's Shape Library. Click a shape thumbnail in the dialog box, and then click OK to close the dialog box and begin drawing that shape.

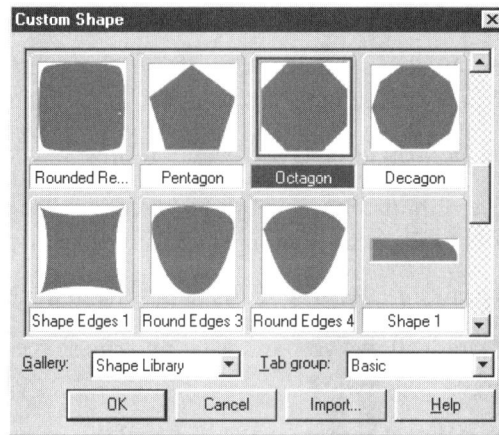

The drawing technique varies somewhat depending on the shape you use. However, all of the shapes offer the same attribute options.

When you're using the Path Drawing tool (or the Outline Drawing tool or Line and Arrow tool), PhotoImpact displays these options in the Attribute toolbar. You must select the shape before you draw the path object. The other attributes can be set before you draw the shape or changed afterward.

- ■ From the Shape list, select the shape to draw.

- ■ Click the Color box to select the color for the path object.

- ■ Select the drawing mode from the Mode drop-down list box. You can choose one of the following modes:

  - ■ 2D Object creates a flat, two-dimensional shape.

- 3D Round creates a shape with a three-dimensional rounded border.

- 3D Chisel creates a shape with a three-dimensional chiseled border.

- 3D Trim creates a shape that appears to be cut out and wrapped around a larger three-dimensional shape.

- 3D Pipe creates a three-dimensional pipe or tube effect around the perimeter of the shape.

- 3D Custom creates a shape with a custom three-dimensional effect applied. You can alter the Custom effect in the Materials dialog box.

- Horizontal Deform distorts the path object horizontally

- Vertical Deform distorts the object vertically. (The deform options are used only to edit an existing shape, not for initial drawing.)

- Selection draws a selection marquee instead of a path object.

- Continue Draw allows you to create multiple shapes that are grouped together as a single object.

- Click the Material button to open the Material dialog box, where you can specify a broad range of attributes and effects such as color and textures, shading, shadow, 3D effects, image-mapping effects, and more. (See Chapter 9 for more information about Material effects.)

- Click the Panel button to show or hide the Path panel, where you can adjust all the attributes in the Attribute toolbar, plus a few more.

- Click the Editing button to switch to Path Edit mode.

Draw Standard Shapes

The Path Drawing tool can create a number of standard shapes such as rectangles and circles. To draw one of the standard shapes, you first click the Path Drawing tool button in the Tool panel. Next, you select the desired shape from the Shape list in the Attribute toolbar and adjust other settings in the Attribute toolbar as needed. Then, you click and drag on the image to define the size and location of the shape.

Start by positioning the pointer at one corner of an imaginary box around the shape you want to define and drag the pointer diagonally toward the opposite corner.

PhotoImpact draws an outline of the shape and adjusts its size and position in real time as you drag the pointer. Release the mouse button when the outline is the correct size and proportion. PhotoImpact draws the completed shape, filled with color.

Figure 2-15 shows several different path objects, drawn with different attribute settings ranging from simple two-dimensional shapes to shapes with three-dimensional effects.

Draw a Spline Shape

To draw a path object with smooth curved sides, you select the Spline shape from the Attribute toolbar.

Then, to draw the object on your image, start by clicking to place the first node (or plotting point) along the edge of the shape. Continue to click to place more nodes to define the edge of the desires shape. PhotoImpact joins each new node to the previous node with a smooth spline curve, as shown in the example on the next page.

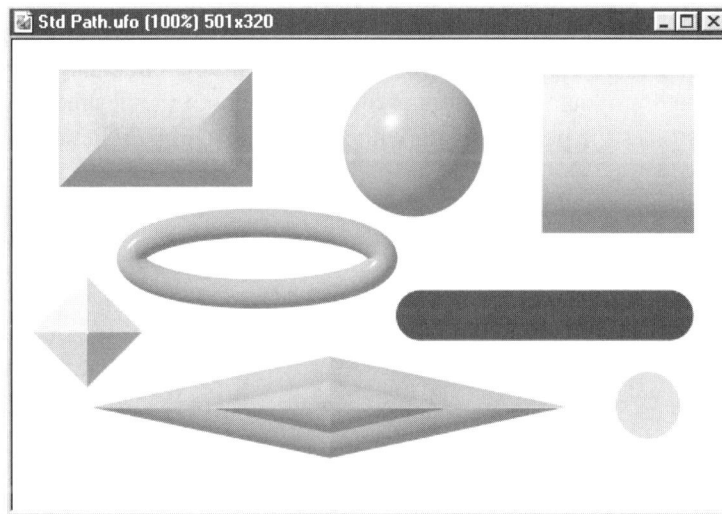

FIGURE 2-15   Path objects drawn using basic shapes

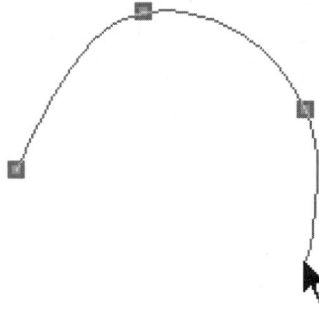

Finally, double-click to link the last node to the starting node and enclose the shape. PhotoImpact fills the shape with the color, texture, or 3D effect you specified in the Attribute toolbar.

Create a Freehand Shape

Perhaps the fastest way to draw an irregularly shaped path object is to select the Freehand shape from the Attribute toolbar.

To draw a path object with the Freehand shape, simply click and drag on your image. As you drag your mouse pointer along the edge of the desired shape, PhotoImpact traces the pointer's path with a thin line, as shown here.

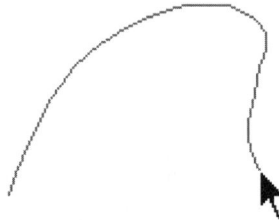

When you release the mouse button, PhotoImpact closes the shape and fills it with the color, texture, or 3D effect you specified in the Attribute toolbar.

Draw a Bezier/Polygon Shape

The Bezier/Polygon shape enables you to draw path objects composed of straight-line segments, precisely controlled curved segments, or any combination of the two.

When you draw a path object using the Bezier/Polygon shape, you create either a straight-line segment or a curve, depending on how you click and drag your mouse pointer. Like the Bezier Curve selection tool, Bezier/Polygon path drawing tool works with nodes and control points, as shown here. A *node* is a point through which the edge of the shape must pass. A node is a vertices or corner for a straight line segment and an apex or plot point for a curve segment. A *control point* is located at the end of a control handle line and serves as a "magnet" that pulls the curve in a given direction but doesn't lie on the path of the curve.

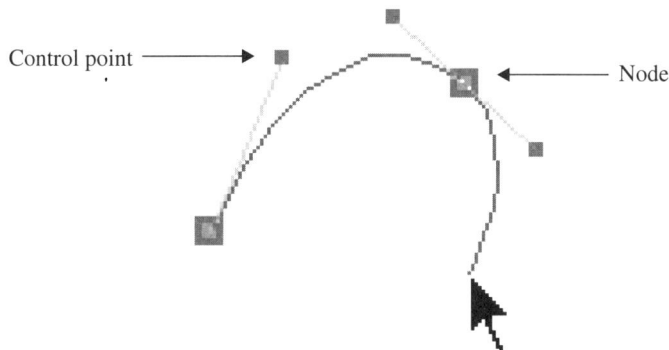

Control point ⟶ ◼   ◻ ⟵ Node

To define a straight-line segment, click at one corner to place a node there, then move the pointer to the next corner and click again to place another node. PhotoImpact joins the nodes with a straight-line segment.

To define a Bezier curve segment, click at the node and drag to create a control handle that will influence the curve. Release the mouse button to place the control point at the end of the control handle line, and then click at the next node. PhotoImpact draws a curved-line segment from one node to the next, with the curve arching toward the control point.

Continue to add straight and/or curve segments to define the shape of the path object. Double-click the starting node to close the shape by connecting the first and last nodes. PhotoImpact fills the path object with the color, texture, or 3D effect you specified in the Attribute toolbar.

Draw Outlines

The Outline Drawing tool creates path objects just like the Path Drawing tool. The difference between the two tools is that the Path Drawing tool creates solid-filled shapes and the Outline Drawing tool creates shapes with outlines, as shown in Figure 2-16.

The techniques for drawing path objects with the Outline Drawing tool are the same as for the Path Drawing tool. You have the same choices of shapes and attributes for both tools.

Draw Lines and Arrows

As its name implies, the Lines and Arrows tool enables you to draw path objects that are lines and arrows. The path objects you create with this tool share the same vector-object characteristics of the objects you create with the Path Drawing tool and Outline Drawing tool. About the only difference is that the Lines and Arrows tool draws open lines instead of closed shapes.

Drawing a path object with the Lines and Arrows tool is essentially the same as drawing a shape with the Path Drawing tool, except when you double-click the

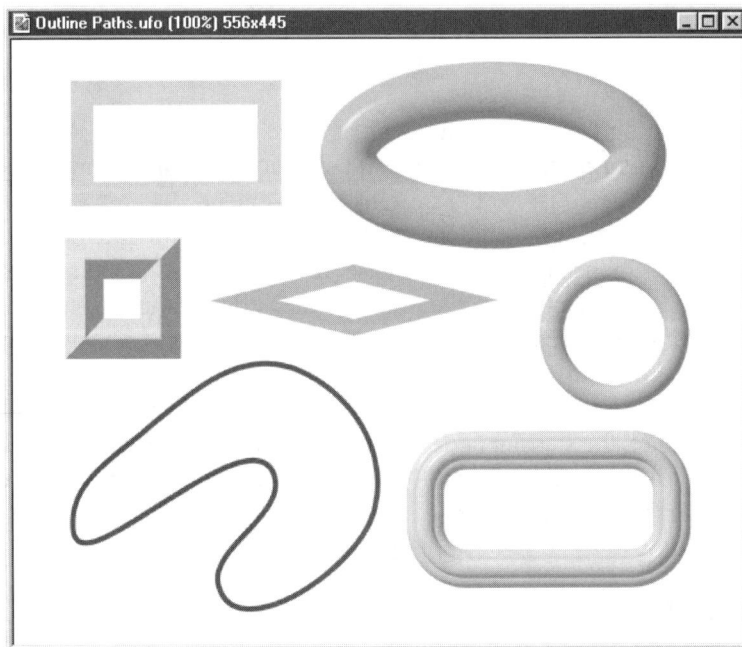

FIGURE 2-16   Path objects created with the Outline Drawing tool

last point, PhotoImpact simply ends the object instead of adding a line segment to close the shape.

When you draw with the Lines and Arrows tool, the Shape list is missing the standard and custom shapes, since those are all closed shapes that don't apply to the Lines and Arrows tool. The available shapes include the Spline, Bezier, and Freehand shapes, which are like their counterparts in the Path Drawing tool. There is also a Line/Arrow choice, which draws a single straight-line segment with an arrowhead. Figure 2-17 shows some examples of path objects drawn with the Lines and Arrows tool.

Some of the significant attributes of path objects drawn with the Lines and Arrows tool are not available on the Attribute toolbar. Instead, they are in the Path panel. To open the Path panel, click the Panel button on the Attribute toolbar.

The Line Style and Arrow attributes are found only on the Outline tab of the Path panel, as shown here. To change the line style, select the desired dash pattern from the Style drop-down list box. To change the line ending, make a selection from the Arrow drop-down list box. You can choose from an assortment of arrowheads, dots, and diamonds on one or both ends of the line.

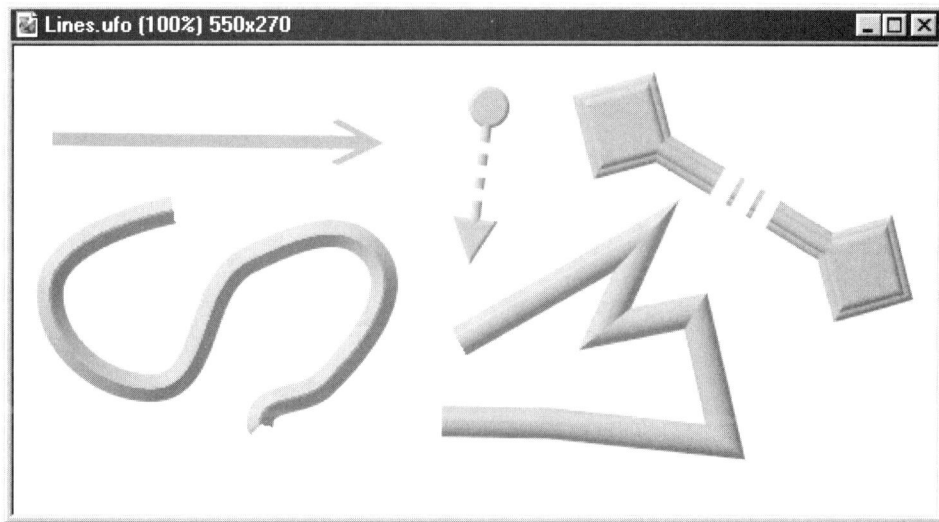

FIGURE 2-17   An assortment of path objects drawn with the Lines and Arrows tool

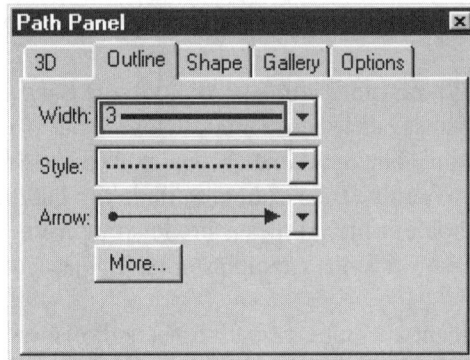

If the Arrow drop-down list, doesn't contain the combination you need, click the More button to open the Color & Line dialog box, shown in Figure 2-18. In this dialog box, you can specify each end of the line independently and adjust the size of the ending symbol.

Use the Path Edit Tool

One of the biggest advantages of path objects is that you can edit the objects extensively and with great precision. You can do some of that editing by selecting a path object and adjusting its attributes in the Attribute toolbar or the Path panel,

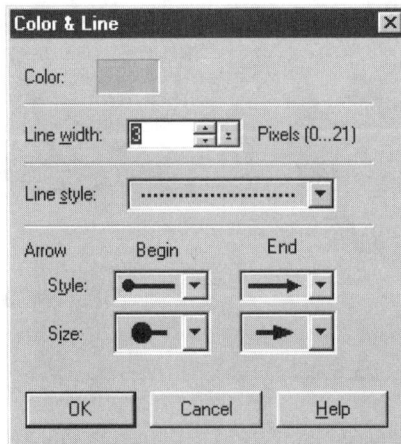

FIGURE 2-18   The Color & Line dialog box

but for editing the shape itself, PhotoImpact provides another tool, called the Path Edit tool. You can use it to add, delete, and move the individual nodes and control points; convert straight-line segments to curves and curves to lines; and duplicate, delete, align, and group objects.

To edit a path object with the Path Edit tool, click the Path Edit tool button in the Tool panel. PhotoImpact displays the Attribute toolbar for the Path Edit tool.

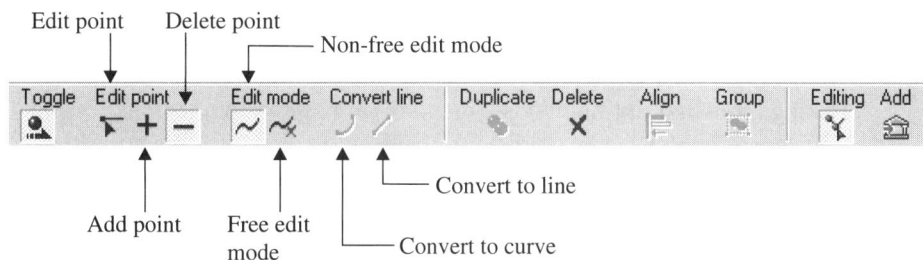

2

Edit point   Delete point
                         Non-free edit mode

| Toggle | Edit point ▼ | Edit mode | Convert line | Duplicate | Delete | Align | Group | Editing | Add |

                                                  Convert to line

Add point   Free edit
               mode   Convert to curve

You can adjust path objects using their nodes and control points. Nodes appear as small squares on the edge of the path. When you click a node, the control handles and control points affecting the adjacent line segments appear.

Chapter 7 provides detailed instructions on editing path objects with the Path Edit tool. The following list summarizes the use of the options available on the Attribute toolbar:

■ Click the path object you wish to edit and then click the Toggle button to switch between displaying the path object and edit outlines for that object.

■ The Edit Point choices determine how nodes are affected. While in the normal editing mode, Edit Point, enables you to edit nodes and control points by dragging them to new locations. To add a node to the path, click the Add Point (+) option, and then click where you want to add the node. To delete a node, click the Delete Point (−) option, and then click the node you wish to remove.

■ The Edit Mode options affect how you can manipulate control handle lines attached to nodes. In Non-free Edit Mode, both control lines attached to a node move together, thus ensuring a smooth curve going through the node. In Free Edit Mode, you can edit each of the control lines independently, which allows you to change the angle at which the line segments intersect at the node.

- The Convert Lines buttons allow you to convert a line to a curve or a curve to a line. Select a straight-line segment and click the Convert to Curve button to convert the line to a curve and add control handles that you can move to reshape the curve. Select a curved-line segment and click the Convert to Line button to convert the curve to a straight-line segment.

- Click the Duplicate button to duplicate the current path object.

- Click the Delete button to delete the current path object.

- When you're working with a path object that contains multiple shapes, clicking the Align option opens a menu of alignment options that you can choose to align the shapes with each other. (CTRL-click to select multiple shapes.)

- Click the Group button to group one or more shapes together so you can move and manipulate them as one. (CTRL-click to select multiple shapes.)

- Click the Editing button to switch between the Path tool used to create the path object (so you can edit the fill color and other attributes) and the Path Edit tool.

Add Type with the Text Tool

Text is an important part of many of the images and graphics you create with PhotoImpact. So, naturally, PhotoImpact includes a capable tool for creating and editing text. This section introduces the Text tool and outlines its primary options. Chapter 8 covers using the Text tool in detail.

The Text tool produces vector-based objects much like the Path tools. As a result, you can select, move, resize, and edit text objects with a degree of flexibility and precision that isn't possible with pixel-based image objects.

To create a text object with the Text tool, follow these steps:

1. Click the Text tool in the Tool panel. The Attribute toolbar displays the options for the Text tool, and the pointer changes to an arrow beside an I-beam insertion point icon.

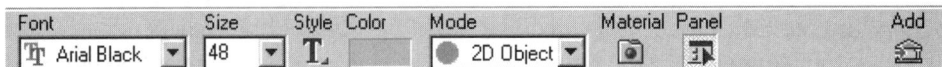

Font	Size	Style	Color	Mode	Material Panel	Add
Arial Black	48	T		2D Object		

2

2. Click the pointer on your image at the location where you want the text object to appear. PhotoImpact opens the Text Entry Box dialog box, as shown in Figure 2-19.

3. Adjust the font, size, style, and other text attributes in the Text Entry Box as needed. Most of the options available in the Text Entry Box are clearly labeled or familiar to users from working with word processor programs.

4. Type the desired text in the large text box at the bottom of the Text Entry Box. The box scrolls automatically to accommodate longer lines of text. Press ENTER to create a new line of text.

5. Click OK to close the Text Entry Box and display the text object on your image.

Figure 2-20 shows several text objects with different formatting. They range from simple text to more elaborate text treatments with 3D effects and shadows.

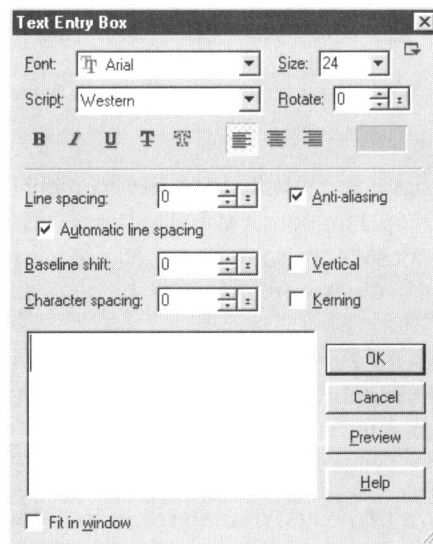

FIGURE 2-19   The Text Entry Box

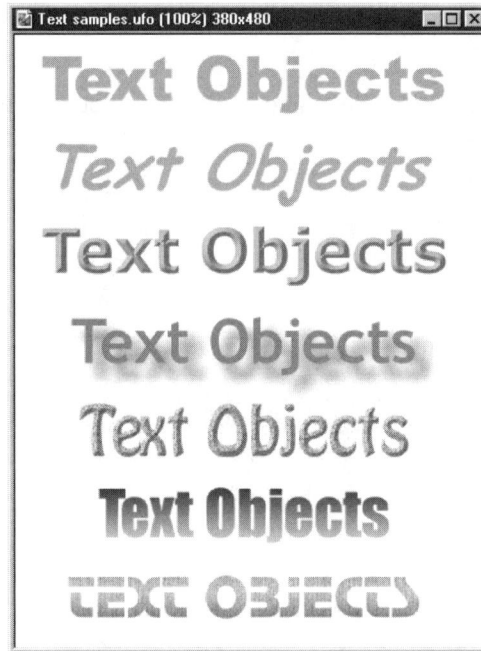

FIGURE 2-20   An assortment of text objects with different formatting and effects

You can use the options on the Attribute toolbar to apply these and other effects to a text object without reopening the Text Entry Box. You'll notice that many of the Attribute toolbar options are the same ones you use with path objects. Here's a rundown on the Attribute toolbar options and what they do:

■ Select a font from the Font drop-down list. This list gives you access to the full range of fonts installed on your Windows system. PhotoImpact adds a nice touch by displaying a preview box to the right of the font list that shows a word or two from your text object in the highlighted font.

■ Select the text size (in points) from the Size drop-down list.

■ Click the Style button to display a menu of style options such as Bold and Italic, alignment options, plus some other options such as access to Galleries and Shadow effects.

2

- Click the Color button to display the Color pop-up menu, including options that lead to gradient fill and texture fills.

- From the Mode drop-down list, select a drawing mode option, such as a 3D effects. (This list offers the same drawing mode options as its counterpart on the Path Drawing tool's Attribute toolbar.)

- Click the Material button to open the Material dialog box, where you can specify a broad range of attributes and effects such as color and textures, shading, shadow, 3D effects, image mapping effects, and more.

- Click the Panel button to shows or hide the Text panel, which includes still more options, such as the ability to split the text object into separate words or characters.

| NOTE | *The text you create with the Text tool becomes a part of the image, much like a path object. To create web pages, you need to handle text separately from any graphics on the page because web browsers render text and graphics differently. PhotoImpact includes a separate HTML Text feature just for that purpose. See Chapter 12 for information on using HTML Text.* |

Quick Access to Web-Optimization Tools

In addition to all the other tools for creating and editing images, PhotoImpact includes tools designed specifically for adapting and optimizing those images for use on web sites. Most of the web-specific tools in PhotoImpact are located on the web menu. However, two of the tools are located on the Tool panel for convenient access as you work with your images:

- The Slice tool enables you to divide your image into multiple smaller pieces that you can save in separately optimized files. PhotoImpact can automatically generate the individual files and an HTML file containing the code necessary to reassemble the slices into the full image.

- The Hotspot tool enables you to define and edit hotspots for use in web image maps. After defining hotspots that are hyperlinked to other web resources, you can save your image and have PhotoImpact generate the HTML code that makes the image map work.

Chapter 10 covers the web-optimization tools in detail.

Use the Crop Tool

The ability to crop pictures is an essential feature in an image-editing program. The PhotoImpact Crop tool handles the task in a simple and straightforward manner. To crop an image, follow these steps:

1. Click the Crop tool in the Tool panel. The pointer assumes the shape of the crop icon.

2. Click and. drag on your image to define the area you want to crop. Click at one corner of the crop area and then drag toward the opposite corner. Release the mouse button when the rectangular cropping area is the correct size. PhotoImpact displays a cropping box consisting of a rectangular outline with adjustment handles (small boxes) at each corner and in the middle of each side.

3. Fine-tune the cropping box by dragging a handle to move a side or by dragging the center of the box to move the entire cropping box.

4. Click the Crop button in the Attribute toolbar or press ENTER to complete the crop. PhotoImpact trims the image to the edges of the cropping box.

Any portion of the image outside the cropping box is discarded, and the document window automatically resizes to fit the new dimensions of the image. Figure 2-21 shows an example of an image before and after cropping.

Use the Transform Tool

The Transform tool is an image-manipulation tool that can work on the entire image or on a selected object. You can use it to resize, rotate, slant, or distort an image. To use the Transform tool to resize or distort an image, follow these steps:

1. Click the Transform tool in the Tool panel.

2. Click the object in your image that you want to manipulate. To select the base image, click part of the background.

3. Select a transformation mode by clicking the button at the left end of the Attribute toolbar and choosing one of the modes from the menu that appears.

Cropping box with handles   After cropping

FIGURE 2-21   Cropping an image

After you choose one of the following modes, PhotoImpact displays a box around the selected object with control handles (small squares) at the corners.

- Resize makes the image or object larger or smaller.

- Slant slants the image or object to one side.

- Distort stretches and distorts the image.

- Perspective applies distortions that simulate the tilt and size change of a perspective view.

4. Click and drag a handle. PhotoImpact adjusts the transform box according to the handle movement and the transform mode you chose in the previous step. When you release the mouse button, PhotoImpact instantly applies the change to your image or object.

Figure 2-22 shows an example of a text object transformed using the Perspective mode of the Transform tool.

The Transform tool can do a lot of other cool stuff. You can rotate your image in several different ways, flip the image horizontally or vertically, and perform a virtual 3D rotation.

Transform box with handles   Perspective transformation

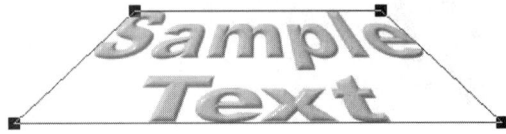

FIGURE 2-22   Transforming a text object

Position 3D Objects with the Z-Merge Tool

New to PhotoImpact 7

The Z-Merge tool enables you to control how objects in your image overlap and interact with each other by controlling their position along a Z axis, which represents depth or elevation. This is different from the layer-stacking order that you control with the Layer Manager. Layers enable you to place objects in front of or behind other objects. The Z-Merge tool allows you to position 3D objects so they share the same space, with their 3D projections merging and poking through each other.

The following steps can get you started experimenting with this fun tool.

1. Start with two or more path objects and/or text objects with 3D effects applied. Position them on the image so that they overlap.

2. Click the Z-Merge tool in the Tool panel. PhotoImpact displays the Z-Merge options in the Attribute toolbar.

3. Click one of the path or text objects to select it.

4. Click the Z-Merge checkbox in the Attribute toolbar to enable Z-Merge for the selected object and adjust the Z-Elevation setting to specify the depth of the object.

5. Repeat steps 3 and 4 for each of the other objects.

6. Drag the objects and/or adjust their Z-Elevation settings and observe the effect.

Figure 2-23 shows the effect of using the Z-Merge tool on some 3D path objects. The original objects appear on the left, and the merged objects are on the right.

NOTE *The Z-Merge tool is designed to work with path objects and text objects that have 3D effects applied. Using the Z-Merge tool with regular two-dimensional objects produces unexpected results.*

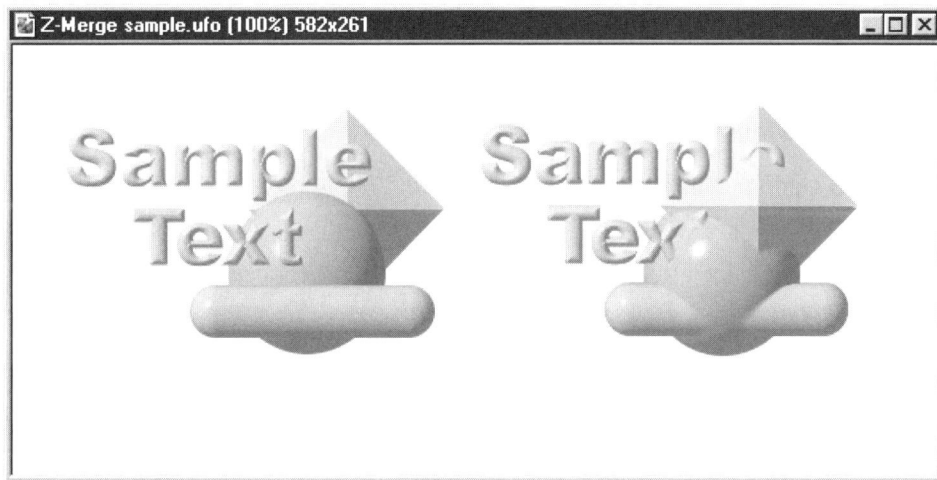

Original objects   Z-merged objects

FIGURE 2-23 Objects before and after being merged with the Z-Merge tool

Correct Errors with Undo and Redo

Most users are probably familiar with Undo and Redo commands, since they are common features of most computer programs. The Undo command cancels the last action and returns the document to its state immediately before that action was taken. The Redo command reverses the effect of the Undo command and reinstates the document changes resulting from an action that was undone.

PhotoImpact expands on the typical Undo capability by providing the ability to keep track of up to 99 actions in its Undo/Redo list. (By default, PhotoImpact tracks 20 levels of Undo. To change that setting, choose File | Preferences | General to open the Preferences dialog box and select the PhotoImpact category. You can set PhotoImpact to track 1–99 undo levels.) Tracking multiple undo levels isn't too unusual, but PhotoImpact includes a nice feature that allows you to select any of those undo levels from its menu and restore the document to that state immediately instead of needing to repeatedly issue the Undo command to step back through the various levels one by one.

Here are the various ways to use Undo and Redo:

- To restore your image to its condition before a specific action or command, choose Edit | Undo Before | *Command*.

- To Undo the last command, click the Undo button on the Standard toolbar or press CTRL-Z.

- To reverse the effect of one or more undo steps, choose Edit | Redo To | *Command*.

- To redo the effect of the last Undo command, click the Redo button on the Standard toolbar or press CTRL-Y.

NOTE *You can also Undo and Redo actions using the History tab of the Quick Command panel. See Chapter 16, which is available at www.osborne.com.*

Although PhotoImpact's Undo and Redo commands aren't represented by buttons on the Tool panel as are the rest of the tools described in this chapter, you'll probably use the Undo and Redo commands at least as often (if not more frequently) than you use the Tool panel tools.

PART II

Acquire and Manage Images

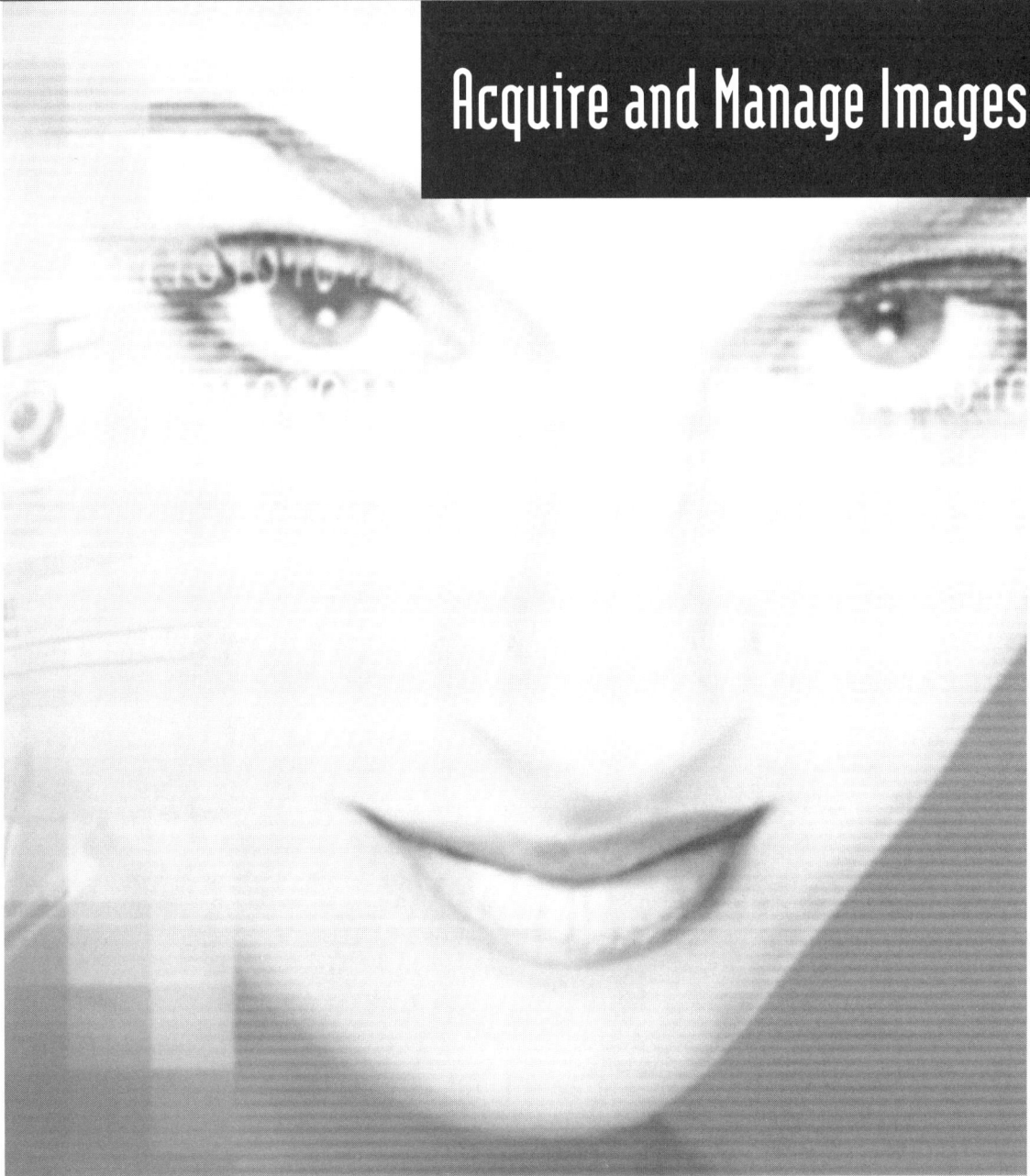

CHAPTER 3

Acquire, Import, and Export Images

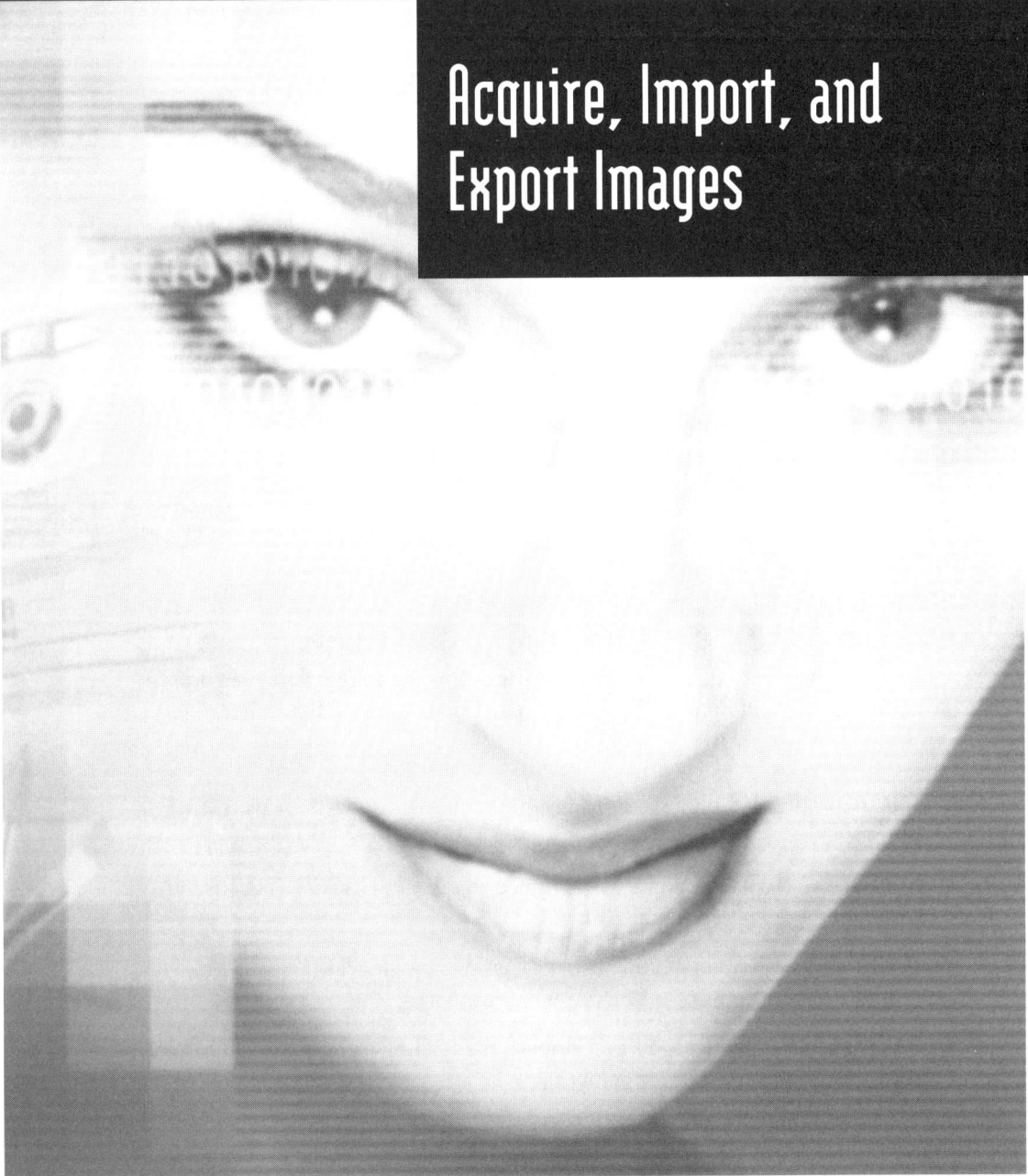

One of PhotoImpact's greatest strengths is its ability to open and edit image files from a wide variety of sources and in a large assortment of file formats. This chapter covers the various techniques for opening, importing, and exporting image files. It also covers how to acquire images from scanners and digital cameras, and even how to capture images of your computer screen.

Open Image Files

Before you can edit or work with an image in PhotoImpact, you need to open that image document in a PhotoImpact document window. PhotoImpact gives you several options for opening image documents. In addition to opening a file through the standard File | Open command and Windows filename extension associations, you can use PhotoImpact's Visual Open utility, which enables you to preview images before you open them.

> **NOTE**   *PhotoImpact also offers a few of other options for opening image files. One is the Browse Manager in the Access panel. Another is to use PhotoImpact Album to preview and open images. PhotoImpact Album is covered in Chapter 4.*

What File Formats Can PhotoImpact Open?

One of the more impressive features of PhotoImpact is the long list of file formats the program supports. Of course, PhotoImpact can open the standard image file formats such as the following:

- **GIF** (Graphics Interchange Format), the reigning standard for web graphics.

- **JPG/JPEG** (Joint Photographic Engineering Group), the leading format for compressed photographic images.

- **PNG** (Portable Network Graphics), an aspiring new standard for web graphics (and the native format for Macromedia Fireworks).

- **TIF/TIFF** (Tagged Image File Format), the leading cross-platform format for lossless, high-resolution images.

In addition, PhotoImpact can open image files stored in a wide range of other file formats, ranging from Windows bitmaps to the native file formats of other image editors such as Adobe Photoshop and Jasc Paint Shop Pro. In fact, when it opens a Photoshop PSD file, it even includes layer data in addition to the pixel-based image. Table 3-1 shows the full list.

File Extension	Format Type
001	Hayes JT Fax
BMP/RLE/UPI	Windows bitmap
CLP	Windows clipboard
CUR	Windows cursor
DCS	DCS file format
DCX	Intel SatisFAXion
EPS	Encapsulated PostScript
FAX	Generic FAX
GIF	Graphics Interchange Format
ICO	Windows icon
IFF	Amiga LBM
IMG	GEM image
JP2	JPEG 2000 with metadata
JPC	JPEG 2000
JPG/JPEG	Joint Photographic Engineering Group
MAC	MacPaint
MSP	Windows Paint
PBM	Portable Bitmap
PCD	Kodak Photo CD
PCT/PICT	Mac Picture File Format
PCX	PC Paintbrush
PGM	Portable Graymap
PIC	Lotus Picture
PNG	Portable Network Graphics
PPM	Portable Pixel Map
PSD	Adobe Photoshop

TABLE 3-1   File Formats PhotoImage Can Open

File Extension	Format Type
PSP	Jasc Paint Shop Pro
PXR	Pixar
RAS	Sun Raster
SCI	SciFAX
SCT	Scitex CT
SHG	Segmented Hypergraph
TGA	Targa
TIF/TIFF	Tagged Image File Format
UFO	Ulead File for Objects
WBM/WBMP	Wireless Bitmap
WMF	Windows Metafile

TABLE 3-1   File Formats PhotoImage Can Open *(continued)*

The following list provides important notes about a few of the file formats:

- **EPS**   Encapsulated PostScript — PhotoImpact reads raster images stored in the EPS format but doesn't interpret PostScript text and vector graphics from an EPS file.

- **PSD**   Adobe Photoshop; includes layer data in addition to the pixel-based image.

- **PSP**   Jasc Paint Shop Pro; also includes layer data in addition to the pixel-based image.

- **UFO**   Ulead File Object — the native file format for PhotoImpact, which includes full support for text, path, and image objects stored separately from the base image.

- **WMF**   Windows Metafile — This is another file format that can include both raster images and vector graphics. PhotoImpact can read both components of a WMF file and display both the raster image and the text and vector graphics components.

In addition to the file formats that you can open with PhotoImpact using the Open dialog box, you can import images in any of these formats as image objects (as described in the "Insert Image Objects" section later in this chapter), and you can import images in the RAW file format using the File | Import | RAW Import command (as described in the "Import and Export RAW Format Files" section later in this chapter).

It's not uncommon for an image editor (or other program) to be able to open files stored in a number of different file formats. However, the list of formats that a typical program supports for saving edited documents is usually much shorter. PhotoImpact is unusual in that it can also save files in almost all the same formats it can read, which means that you can open, edit, and save an image file without changing its file format.

TIP	*You can convert images from one file format to another by simply opening the file in PhotoImpact and then saving it in another format. See Chapter 4 for more details.*

Open Files with the Open Dialog Box

Perhaps the most straightforward technique for opening files is to use the standard techniques that PhotoImpact shares with most other Windows programs. PhotoImpact's Open dialog box, shown in Figure 3-1, is a typical Windows program file-open dialog box.

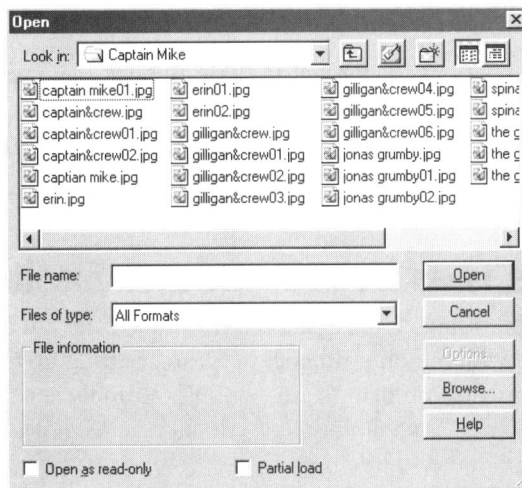

FIGURE 3-1   The PhotoImpact Open dialog box

Here are the steps for accessing and using the PhotoImpact Open dialog box:

1. Click the Open button on the Standard toolbar, choose File | Open, or press CTRL-O. PhotoImpact opens the Open dialog box.

2. Navigate to the drive and folder where your image file is stored. Select the correct storage device and folder in the Look In list box and/or use the Up One Level button to move up the folder tree, and double-click folder icons in the file list box.

3. Select the file format of the file you're looking for in the Files of Type list box. By default, PhotoImpact lists all the image file formats it can open, but you can select a specific file format if you need to filter the list to show only a particular file format.

4. Select the file you want to open by clicking its icon.

5. Click Open to close the Open dialog box and load the selected file in PhotoImpact. The image appears as the base image in a new document window in the PhotoImpact work area.

> **NOTE** *It sometimes takes PhotoImpact a moment or so to load a large image file. If you'll need to wait, you'll see a black bar moving across the status bar to indicate the progress of the load operation.*

When you open an image document in PhotoImpact, the image appears at its actual size if there is room in the PhotoImpact workspace for a document window of that size. Otherwise, PhotoImpact zooms the image down to the largest standard magnification that will fit in the window.

Open Image Files from Windows Explorer

When you install PhotoImpact, the installation routine offers to associate certain filename extensions with the PhotoImpact program. Setting up these associations for the image file formats you plan to edit with PhotoImpact enables you to launch PhotoImpact and load files from the Windows desktop, a Windows Explorer window, or anywhere else within the Explorer shell.

In a Windows Explorer window, locate a file that you want to open with PhotoImpact. Double-click the file icon in Windows Explorer. Windows automatically launches PhotoImpact (if it isn't already running), and then loads the selected image file into a document window in PhotoImpact.

New to PhotoImpact 7

Use Visual Open

One of the perpetual problems with locating and opening the correct image file is identifying which one of the many image files on your disk is the one you want. Even long filenames aren't enough to describe the typical image, especially when you have several images of a similar subject or event. For example, if you have a bunch of images with similar names (such as Regatta01.jpg and Regatta02.jpg), you might end up opening several different files before finding the correct one.

To address this problem, PhotoImpact includes a built-in file-opening utility, named Visual Open, that shows thumbnail representations of your image files. The Visual Open window is shown in Figure 3-2. Notice the folder tree display on the left. It looks (and works) just like its counterpart in Windows Explorer.

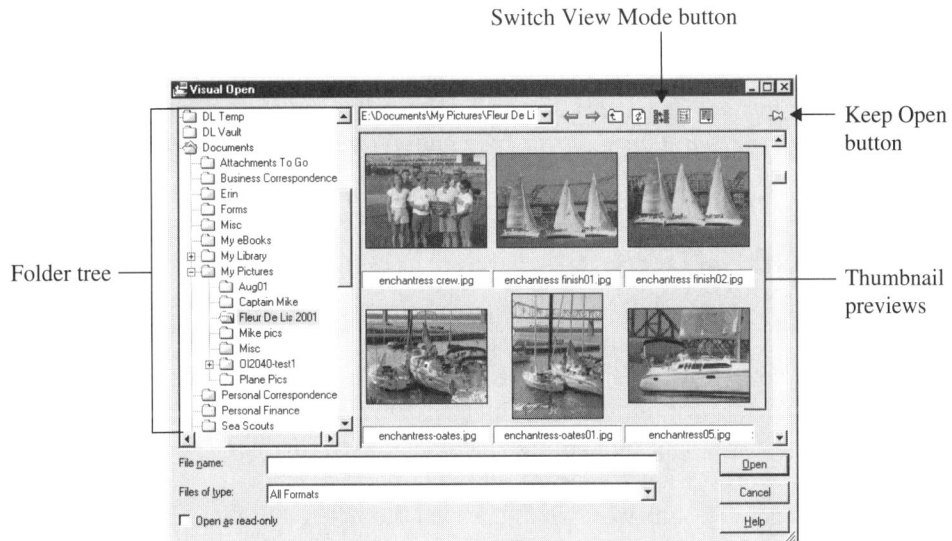

FIGURE 3-2   The Visual Open window

Using Visual Open, you can easily locate, identify, and open image files. Here's how it works:

1. Choose File | Visual Open or press SHIFT-O. PhotoImpact opens the Visual Open window (see Figure 3-2).

> **TIP**   *You can instruct PhotoImpact to use Visual Open in place of the regular Open dialog box when you issue the File | Open command or click the Open button on the toolbar. Choose File | Preferences | General to open the Preferences dialog box. You'll find the option under the Open & Save category.*

2. Select a folder in the folder tree display. Visual Open displays thumbnails of the images in that folder in the large box on the right. You can switch the display to a list of filenames and details by clicking the Switch View Mode button. Click the button again to switch back to thumbnails.

3. Scroll through the thumbnails. Click a thumbnail to select it. PhotoImpact highlights the selected thumbnail with a blue outline.

4. Click Open to close the Visual Open window and open the selected image in a PhotoImpact document window, ready for editing.

> **NOTE**   *The PhotoImpact Visual Open window looks and functions like a typical dialog box, but it's really an application window for a separate utility program. Visual Open gets its own button on the Windows taskbar.*

Insert Image Objects

In addition to opening an image file as the base image in its own document window, you can also insert an image into an existing document. One very important consequence of this technique is that the inserted image becomes an object that you can select, move, edit, filter, resize, and manipulate independently of the base image or background of the document. (See Chapter 7 for more information on working with objects.)

There are many reasons why you might want to insert an image object into an existing document, and most of them involve creating a composite image of some sort. For example, you might want to combine an image with some graphic elements on a background. In this case, you will need to be able to move the image object around on the background to position it properly.

The file format of the image you insert as an image object does *not* need to match the file format of the base image in the document window. You can mix and match any file formats supported by PhotoImpact. All the image data will be converted to a common file format when you save the image file.

To insert an image object into a document, follow these steps:

1. Open the document window into which you want to insert the image object. It can be a new, blank document or an existing document with a base image or other elements already in place.

2. Choose Object | Insert Image Object | From File. PhotoImpact displays the Open dialog box (the same one that appears when you issue the File | Open command).

3. Select the image file you want to insert. Navigate to the correct folder, and then click the file's icon in the Open dialog box.

4. Click Open to complete the file selection. PhotoImpact closes the Open dialog box and loads the image into the current document window.

Unlike the base image, the inserted image object is a separate object, floating above the background on its own layer. Figure 3-3 shows the initial result of inserting an image object of a sailboat into an image of an art gallery.

You can select the image object and manipulate it like a path object or other independent element. For example, you can resize and distort the image object with the Transform tool and apply effects from the Effects menu, without affecting the base image. In Figure 3-4, the sailboat image inserted in Figure 3-3 was manipulated with the Transform tool to make it fit onto the picture frame, and a fadeout effect simulates glare on glass over the picture.

Import and Export Images

PhotoImpact's Import and Export commands let you transfer image data to and from certain scientific applications using the RAW format. In addition to RAW import and export, PhotoImpact also offers export options that enable you to create Scalable Vector Graphics files, send images via e-mail, and post images to the web.

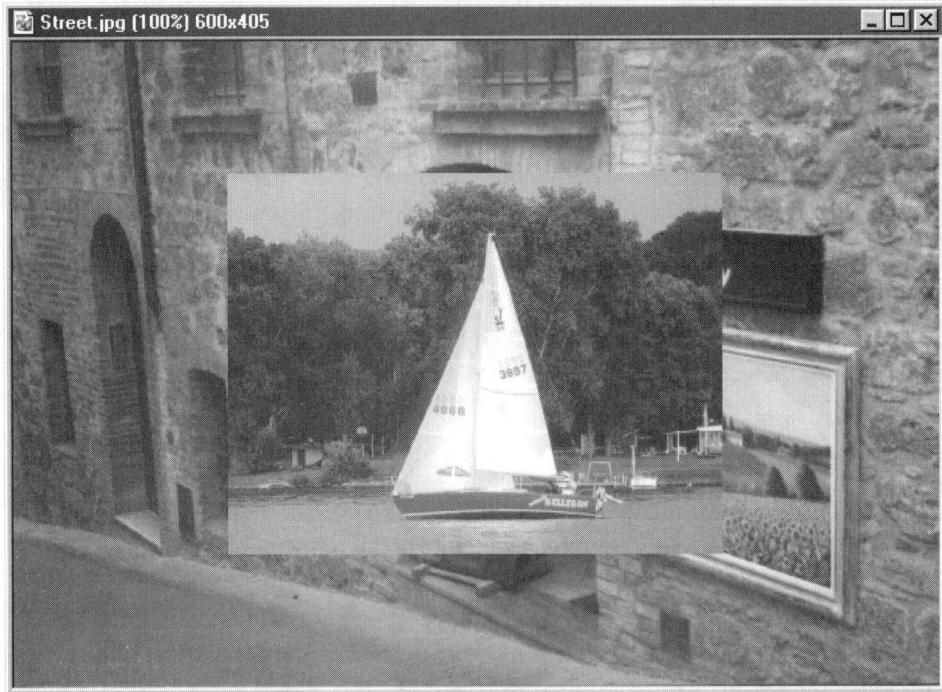

FIGURE 3-3   An inserted image object floats above the background in its own layer.

Import and Export RAW Format Files

The RAW format differs from standard file formats in that you can specify several details of the way the image is recorded in the file in order to match the peculiar needs of another program with which you want to exchange images. The downside of this versatility is that you must "get your hands dirty" dealing with these details in order to achieve a successful image transfer to or from the other program.

Before you export an image to a RAW file, you need to know what settings to use for successful import into the target program. Similarly, you need to know what settings were used to export a RAW file from another program before attempting to import that file into PhotoImpact.

The actual import and export techniques for RAW files are similar to those for opening or saving other file types, but they involve the extra step of specify the settings to use.

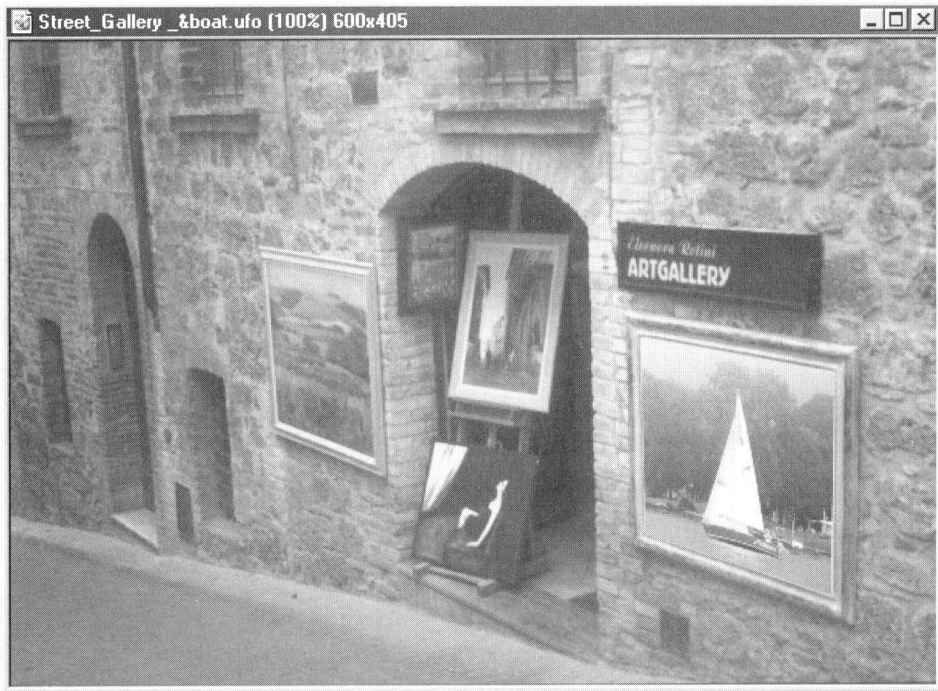

FIGURE 3-4 The sailboat image is a separate image object inserted into the base image of the picture frame on the wall.

Export a RAW File

Here's the procedure for exporting a RAW file:

1. Open the image document you want to export. Make sure it's the active document window in PhotoImpact.

2. Choose File | Export | RAW Export. PhotoImpact displays the Save As dialog box with the Save As Type box preset to RAW Files (*.raw).

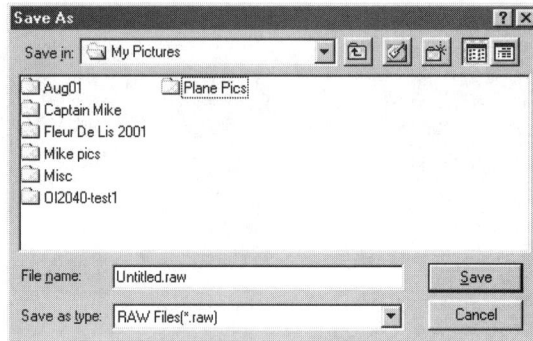

3. Navigate to the correct folder, type a filename in the File Name box, and then click Save. PhotoImpact closes the Save As dialog box and opens the Export RAW File dialog box.

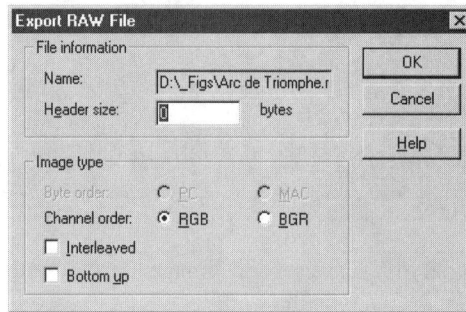

4. Fill in the header size and select image type options as appropriate for the needs of the target program.

5. Click OK. PhotoImpact closes the Export RAW File dialog box and creates the file according to your specifications.

Import a RAW File

To import a RAW file into PhotoImpact, follow these steps:

1. Choose File | Import | RAW Import. PhotoImpact displays the Open dialog box with RAW Files (*.raw) preselected in the Files of Type box.

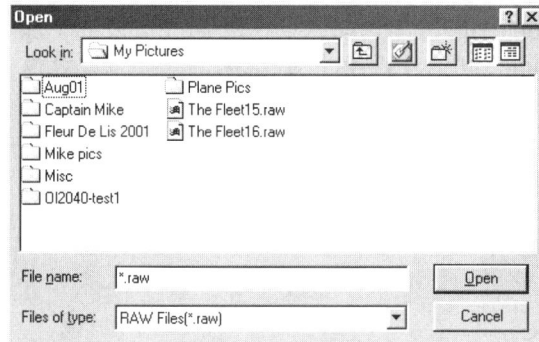

2. Navigate to the correct folder and click the icon for the file you want to import, then click Open. PhotoImpact closes the Open dialog box and displays the Import RAW File dialog box.

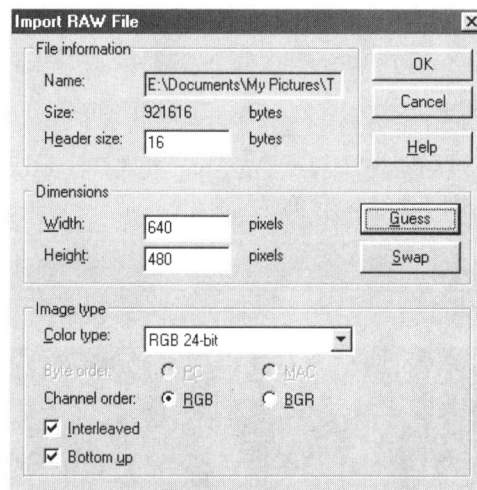

3. Fill in the header size and dimensions in the corresponding boxes and select the image type options to match the specifications of the file you want to import.

4. Click OK. PhotoImpact closes the Import RAW Files dialog box, opens a new document window and loads the selected file into it.

If your file specification settings matched the imported file, it should appear as a normal image, ready for editing in PhotoImpact. However, if the settings weren't correct, the document window displays a distorted image or a series of streaks, similar to the example shown in Figure 3-5. When that happens, you need to close the document window and try the import again with different settings.

Export Images

In addition to the RAW import and export features described in the previous section, PhotoImpact offers the following export options:

- SVG Export
- Send
- Post to Web
- Post to iMira
- Web Album
- Web Slide Show

The Web and iMira options are covered in Chapter 4. The other two export options are discussed in the following sections.

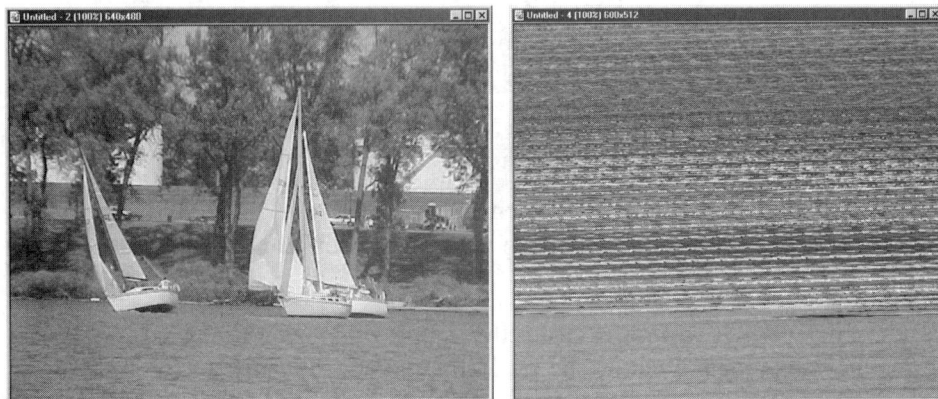

FIGURE 3-5   A successful RAW import and an unsuccessful RAW import

Export As an SVG File

The SVG Export option enables you to create Scalable Vector Graphics (SVG) files from your PhotoImpact image documents. This file format is based on the XML (eXtensible Markup Language) standard and is designed for storing vector graphics for display in web browsers and elsewhere.

The SVG format features small file sizes and the ability to zoom in on an image without sacrificing image quality. It's primarily useful for graphic images composed of path and text objects, not pixel-based images and image objects. However, the SVG file format is capable of recording raster image information in the JPEG format, along with its vector graphics data.

To create an SVG file from your PhotoImpact image, follow these steps:

1. Open the image document you want to export. Make sure it's the active document window in PhotoImpact.

2. Choose File | Export | SVG Export. PhotoImpact displays the Save As dialog box with the Save as Type box preset to Scalable Vector Graphics (*.svg).

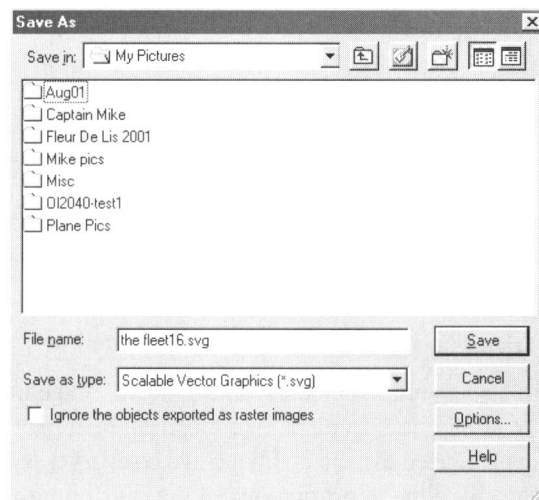

3. Navigate to the correct folder and type a filename in the File Name box. (PhotoImpact supplies a suggested filename based on the name of the image you are exporting.)

4. Check or clear the Ignore the Objects Exported As Raster Images checkbox. Checking this option causes PhotoImpact to export only vector objects, such as path and text objects. Clearing the option causes PhotoImpact to export pixel-based images as well as vector objects.

5. Click Options to open the SVG Export Options dialog box.

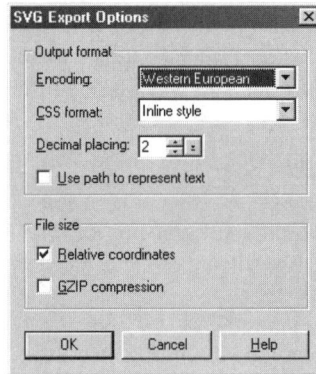

6. Adjust the option settings as needed. (If you need an explanation of the options, click Help to display a box with a description of each option.) Then click OK to close the SVG Export Options dialog box and return to the Save As dialog box.

7. Click Save. PhotoImpact closes the Save As dialog box and creates the SVG file according to your specifications. If you opted to include raster data in addition to vector graphics data, PhotoImpact creates a second file (BACKGROUND.JPG) that contains the pixel-based image data.

Send Images via E-mail

How many times have you found yourself working on an image in PhotoImpact that you need to e-mail to someone? If you're like most PhotoImpact users, it probably happens a lot. Perhaps you need to send an image to a co-worker or client for approval, or maybe you want to share the latest pictures of the kids with their grandparents.

3

The normal procedure for sending images by e-mail is to manually save your image, open your e-mail program, create and compose a new message, locate and attach the saved image file, send the message, and then close the e-mail program. PhotoImpact saves you a few steps by allowing you to send the e-mail message from within PhotoImpact. PhotoImpact actually uses your default e-mail program to send the message, but does so without opening the e-mail program window.

The first time you use the Send command, PhotoImpact displays a message box giving you directions on how to configure some common e-mail programs as the default MAPI service. In most cases, that configuration was done automatically when you installed your e-mail program, so you can simply click OK to close the message and display the Send dialog box.

The three options in this dialog box work as follows:

- **Web Page**   Attaches a self-extracting archive file to the e-mail message. The archive contains a web page and associated files for viewing with a web browser.

- **Image File**   Attaches an image file to the e-mail message. This produces the same as using the manual procedure to attach the file to a message in your e-mail program.

- **Smart Send**   Automatically creates a compressed JPEG file of the image. If you clear this checkbox, the File Name box is grayed out and PhotoImpact sends the file in its current format (or displays the Save As dialog box for you to specify another file format if you haven't yet saved the image).

| CAUTION | *The Web Page option is not recommended because the self-extracting archive it creates is an executable file. Safe-computing practices dictate not running any executable file that arrives as an e-mail attachment. In fact, some e-mail programs automatically delete executable files from e-mail messages as an antivirus protection measure. So the odds are that your intended recipient cannot or will not view an image sent in this way.* |

Follow these steps to send an image via e-mail:

1. Choose File | Export | Send. PhotoImpact opens the Send dialog box.

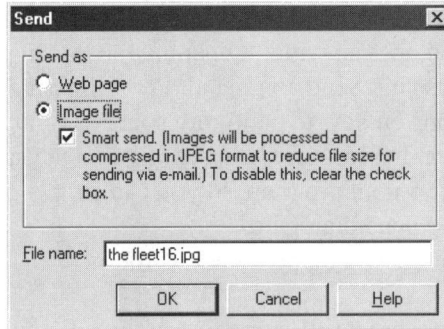

2. Select Image File and check the Smart Send option (these are the default settings). Type a new name in the File Name box if desired.

3. Click OK. PhotoImpact closes the Send dialog box and opens a new message window with the image file already attached.

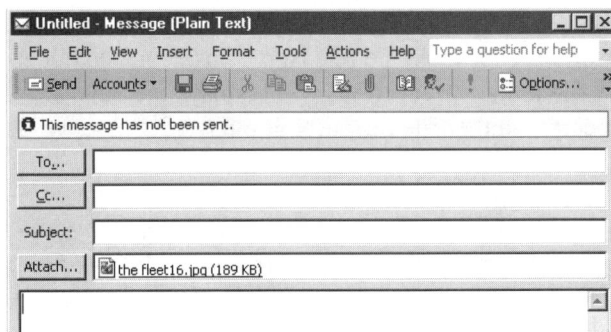

4. Fill in the address, subject, and the text of your message.

5. Click Send. The message is on its way.

Depending on your e-mail program and Internet connection, the message may be sent immediately or stored in the e-mail program's outbox, awaiting the next Internet connection and mail-processing session.

Acquire Images from a Scanner or Digital Camera

Not only can PhotoImpact open, import, and insert images stored as files on your various disk drives and network, the program can also acquire images directly from a scanner or digital camera. PhotoImpact is capable of interfacing with most TWAIN-compatible scanners and cameras to facilitate the process of opening and then manipulating or printing scanned or digital camera images.

Usually, a scanner's or digital camera's TWAIN control software is a streamlined version of the device's regular control software. For example, the TWAIN version of the software for my scanner omits the file output options, since the scanned output is destined for another program (PhotoImpact) instead of a file.

Set Up Your Scanner or Camera

Before you can use your scanner or digital camera with PhotoImpact, you need to configure the program to recognize your imaging device. Of course, the scanner or camera software must be properly installed before you attempt to configure PhotoImpact to work with that software.

To set up a scanner or digital camera for use in PhotoImpact, follow these steps:

1. Choose File | Scanner | Select Source to configure a TWAIN-compatible scanner. Choose File | Digital Camera | Select Source to configure a TWAIN-compatible camera. PhotoImpact opens the Select Source dialog box showing a list of the available TWAIN devices installed on your system.

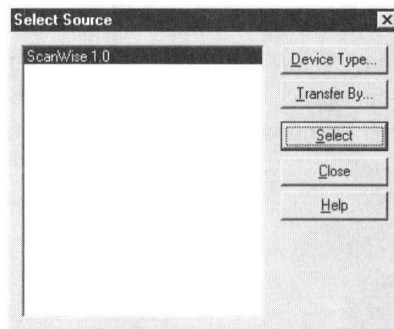

2. Select the scanner or camera from the list.

3. If necessary, set the Device Type option for the selected device. Click Device Type to open the Device Type dialog box. Select the device type (Flatbed Scanner, Sheetfed Scanner, Digital Camera, or Other) and click OK to close the dialog box and record the setting.

4. If necessary, set the Transfer By option for the selected device. Click Transfer By to open the TWAIN Transfer Mechanism dialog box. Select the transfer mode (Automatic, Memory, DIB, or a file type) and click OK to close the dialog box and record the setting.

5. Click Select to close the Select Source dialog box and record the settings in PhotoImpact.

Now PhotoImpact will recognize your scanner or digital camera, and you'll be able to acquire images from that device.

Acquire an Image from Your Scanner or Digital Camera

After you set up PhotoImpact to recognize your scanner or digital camera, the process for transferring an image from the scanner or digital camera to PhotoImpact is fairly straightforward.

Here are the steps for acquiring a scanner or digital camera image:

1. Choose File | Scanner | *Scanner Name* (With Post Processing) or File | Digital Camera | *Camera Name* (With Post Processing) to initiate a scan or transfer from a camera with automatic post processing options in PhotoImpact. PhotoImpact opens the Acquire Image dialog box. Alternatively, you can choose File | Scanner | *Scanner Name* or File | Digital Camera | *Camera Name* to skip the post processing options, in which case, PhotoImpact activates the scanner or digital camera control software immediately, so you can skip the next step.

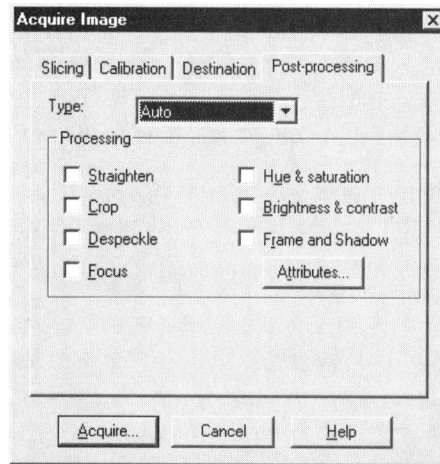

2. If you select the With Post Processing option, you will see the Acquire Image dialog box when you choose your scanner or camera. This dialog box offers settings on four tabs. Adjust the settings on each of the Acquire Image dialog box tabs as needed.

   ■ **Slicing**   If you include multiple images in a scan, the options on the Slicing tab enable you to split the scan into individual image documents in PhotoImpact.

   ■ **Calibration**   Check the Apply Calibration Scheme option and select your scanner from the Scheme list box to have PhotoImpact automatically optimize the image based on the scanner's characteristics.

   ■ **Destination**   Select any combination of New Image, File, Printer, and Fax/Mail for the output of the scan. The New Image option creates a new, untitled document window in the PhotoImpact workspace. The buttons beside the other options enable you to specify a filename and type, select a printer, and so on.

   ■ **Post-processing**   Select post-processing options. This tab enables you to select which (if any) post-processing options you want PhotoImpact to apply to the scanned image.See Chapter 5 for information on the automatic and manual processing options PhotoImpact makes available.

3. Click Acquire. PhotoImpact opens the scanner's TWAIN control software.

4. Preview the scan and adjust the scanning area and other settings as needed, and then click Scan or Import (or whatever command initiates the scan in your scanner control software or the transfer in your digital camera software). The software does its thing and sends the results to PhotoImpact.

5. Switch to the PhotoImpact window. The scanned or digital camera image appears in a new, untitled document window in the PhotoImpact workspace ready for editing. If you selected post-processing options, PhotoImpact performs the specified tasks.

> **NOTE** *Depending on the settings in the Acquire Image dialog box, the image could be sent to a printer or file instead of the PhotoImpact workspace. Various processing steps might be completed automatically, or PhotoImpact might launch the Post-processing Wizard.*

After you get the image from the scanner or digital camera into PhotoImpact, you can edit, retouch, and manipulate it like any other image. (See Chapter 5 for information on image editing and retouching techniques.)

> **TIP** *Choose File | Scanner | Troubleshooting to open a Help window where you can browse several pages of tips and troubleshooting advice to help you make the most of your scans and digital camera images.*

Work with non-TWAIN Devices

Not every scanner or digital camera comes with control software that is compatible with the TWAIN standard, but that doesn't mean that you can't use the device to create images to open in PhotoImpact. It just means that you'll need to take a couple of extra steps to get the scanner or camera output into PhotoImpact.

Save Scans or Camera Images As Files

Basically, all you need to do to create images for use in PhotoImpact is use the software that came with your scanner or camera to save the scans or camera images as files on your hard disk. Then you can open those files with PhotoImpact. Since PhotoImpact can open so many different file formats, there is rarely any problem accessing the output of a scanner or camera.

You will need to launch the scanner/camera software manually and you must go through an extra step to open the resulting file in PhotoImpact instead of having it appear automatically, but the results are usually just as good—as long as you use appropriate file types and settings when you save the scanner or camera output.

For the best results when scanning or saving digital camera images, save the images in a lossless format such as TIF or PNG and use image resolution and color depth settings at or higher than you need in the final image. Use a lossy format such as JPEG only if no other format is available, and if you must use JPEG, choose the minimum compression level. Apply compression, color reduction, and resizing in PhotoImpact before saving the final image, not when doing the scan or shooting the picture. That way, PhotoImpact has the best possible image to work with.

Transfer Images Directly from a Digital Camera

Many of the newer digital cameras allow you to forgo using any proprietary software to transfer images from the camera to your computer. If you have the proper device drivers installed and your camera supports the new "storage-class USB device" specification, you can simply plug the cable from the camera into your computer's USB port, and the computer sees the camera's image-storage memory as if it were another file-storage device. You can then access image files on the camera with Windows Explorer or any other file manager.

Normally, you will use Windows Explorer to drag and drop files from the camera to your hard disk and then open the image files in PhotoImpact from there. However, it is also possible to use PhotoImpact's Open dialog box to access and open an image file directly from the camera's memory.

Capture Computer Screens

One interesting source of images for PhotoImpact is your computer screen. PhotoImpact includes a screen-capture feature that enables you to grab almost anything on your screen and bring it into PhotoImpact, where you can work with it like any other image. You can capture screen images and then cut and paste them into other documents, print the screen images, or save them as separate files.

Obviously, capturing screen images to illustrate documents is something authors of computer books do all the time. It's also a feature that might be used by anyone who needs to prepare a set of instructions on how to use a computer program—

whether those instructions are intended for publication in a book, a web site, or a memo for co-workers or students. You can also use PhotoImpact's screen-capture facility as a solution of last resort if you can't find any other way to export a graph, diagram, or image from one program that you need to insert into a document in another program. If you can display the image on your screen, you can capture it with PhotoImpact and save it to a file that you can then insert into the target program.

> **TIP** *Capturing and printing a screen is also a quick and easy way to record configuration settings for future reference.*

When you set up PhotoImpact's screen-capture feature (by choosing File | Capture | Setup), the Capture Setup dialog box appears. This dialog box offers several options for the capture process:

- **Source**   Choose the portion of the screen you want to capture. You can capture the active window or workspace, the full screen, the selected object or area of the screen, or just the menu under the pointer.

- **Destination**   Choose any combination of the PhotoImpact workspace, the Windows clipboard, or a file. If you choose File, PhotoImpact opens the Save As dialog box, where you can specify the filename, location, and file type.

- **Activation**   Select a hotkey to trigger the screen capture. By default, the hotkey is F11. Depending on the source selection, you can also specify the Delay setting (a pause after you press the hotkey that allows you time to open a menu or highlight some text) or the AutoScroll option (scrolls the window to capture the entire contents).

- **Pointer**   Select whether or not to include the pointer in the screen capture. If you choose to include the pointer, you can also select a pointer shape.

- **Post-processing**   Click the Change button to open the Post-processing dialog box, where you can specify a different color depth or resolution for the captured image.

To capture a computer screen with PhotoImpact, follow these steps:

1. Choose File | Capture | Setup. PhotoImpact displays the Capture Setup dialog box.

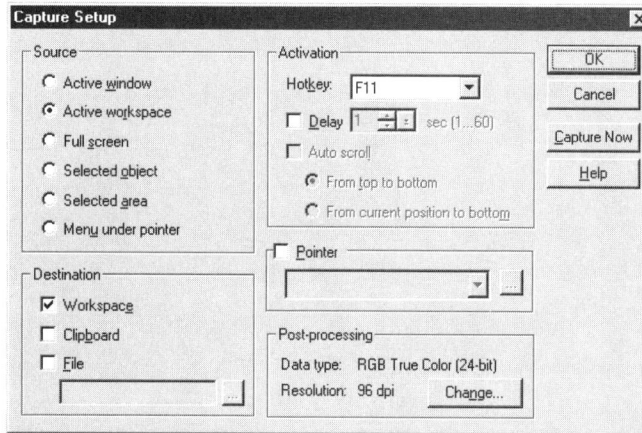

2. Adjust the capture options as needed.

3. Click the Capture Now button. PhotoImpact closes the Capture Setup dialog box, records the settings, and activates the capture mode. (Despite the name of the button, clicking Capture Now does not capture the current screen; it only activates the screen-capture feature.)

4. Arrange your computer desktop to show the window(s) you want to capture.

5. Press F11 (or the capture hotkey you specified in step 2). If you selected a predefined screen area (such as full screen or active window) as the source, the capture occurs immediately. If you selected the Select Object or Selected Area options, you'll need to click the object or drag to define the area. As soon as the source is defined, PhotoImpact captures the screen and sends it to your selected destination: a file, the Windows clipboard, or the PhotoImpact workspace. If the destination includes the PhotoImpact workspace, the screen capture appears in a new document window, ready for editing.

    To capture another screen using the same settings, simply press F11 when the windows you want to capture are on your screen. You only need to go through the full procedure when you want to change the settings in the Capture Setup dialog box.

    After you configure the Capture Setup dialog box, you can activate or deactivate the capture mode by choosing File | Capture | Start or by clicking the Start/Stop Capture button on the toolbar.

CHAPTER 4

Manage, Share, and Print Images

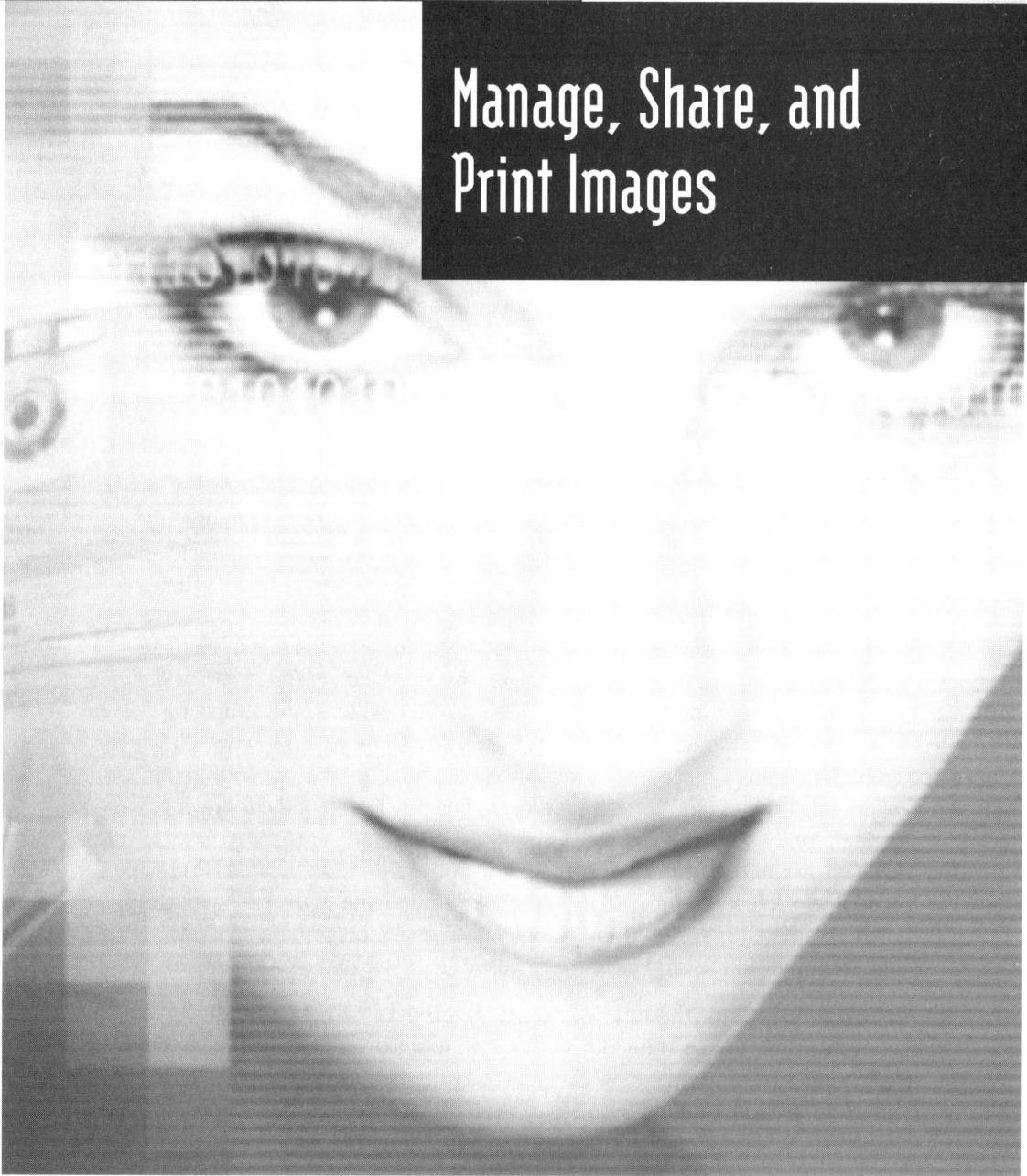

Photolmpact offers so many choices for creating and modifying images that you're sure to build a sizable image collection if you didn't already have one. This chapter is about using the tools PhotoImpact provides for managing those images and putting them to use.

This chapter shows you how to quickly create duplicate images so you can experiment with image variations. It also covers how to convert images into the formats you need for use in reports, presentations, and other applications; as well as how to use PhotoImpact's EasyPalette libraries to save and reuse your favorite images. In this chapter, you'll also find coverage of PhotoImpact printing and instructions for how to use PhotoImpact's Post to Web and Post to iMira features to share images online.

And that's not all. This chapter also introduces PhotoImpact Album, a utility that ships with PhotoImpact 7. Using Album, you can build and manage electronic image albums.

Duplicate Images

Making a duplicate copy of your image is a basic technique that you'll probably use frequently as you work in PhotoImpact. It's always safer to work on a duplicate image as you experiment with various retouching and manipulation effects. That way, if your experiments take an unwanted turn, you can simply delete the duplicate you were working on, and then start over with a new duplicate image that you create almost instantly from the pristine original image. This approach is faster and easier than stepping back through multiple levels of undo. And besides, PhotoImpact's Duplicate command offers some handy merge options that allow you to kill two birds with one stone—merging objects and duplicating the image in one combined step.

To duplicate the image in the current document window, do one of the following:

- **Make a duplicate of the entire image** Choose Edit | Duplicate | Base Image With Objects or press CTRL-D to make a duplicate of the entire image, including any path, text, and image objects. The objects remain separate, editable entities in the duplicate image, just as they are in the original image.

- **Make a duplicate of the image and merge objects** Choose Edit | Duplicate | Base Image With Objects Merged to make a duplicate image with all the path, text, and image objects merged into the base image. This is the equivalent of duplicating the image with all the objects and then choosing

Object | Merge All. After merging, the path, text, and image objects in the duplicate image are fully integrated into the base image and cannot be edited separately.

■ **Make a duplicate of the base image only**   Choose Edit | Duplicate | Base Image Only to create a duplicate image that consists of just the base image, without any of the path, text, or image objects floating on separate layers on top of the base image in the original.

No matter which version of the Edit | Duplicate command you use, the result is that the duplicate image appears in a new, untitled document window in the PhotoImpact workspace, while the original image remains untouched in a separate document window, as illustrated in Figure 4-1.

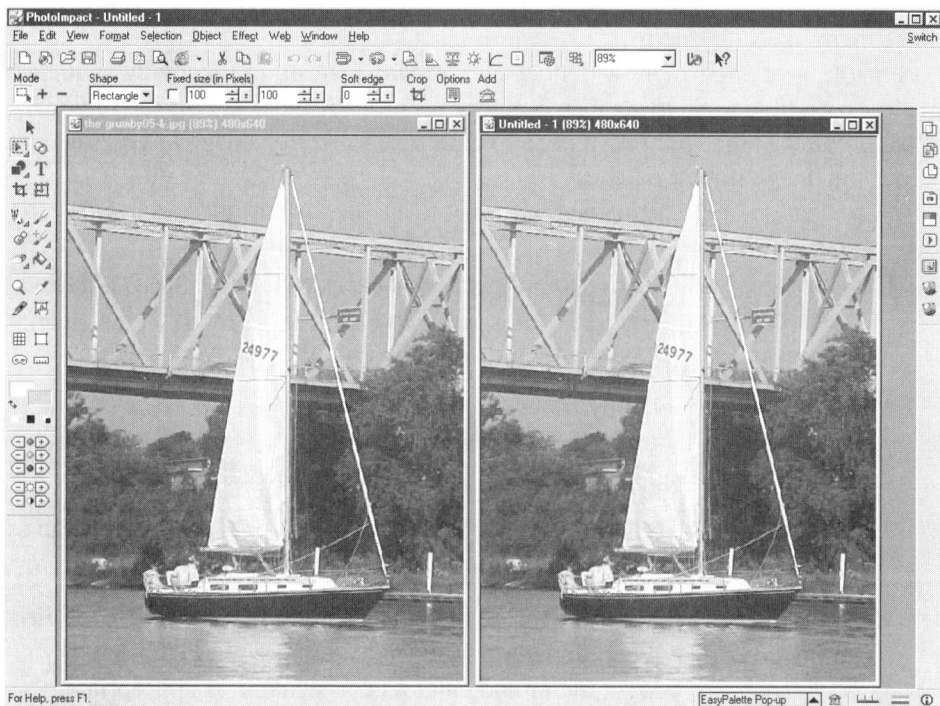

FIGURE 4-1   A duplicate image appears in an "Untitled" document window.

> TIP   *The File | Restore command provides another way to reverse changes to your image and return to its original condition. Just choose File | Restore to reload the image from the original disk file, and overwrite the image in the document with a fresh, unadulterated, copy.*

Convert Image Formats

One of PhotoImpact's more impressive features is its ability to convert image files to and from a large assortment of file formats. The ability to both open and save files in so many different file formats enables PhotoImpact to serve as a translator between otherwise incompatible applications and files.

You can use PhotoImpact to convert a file created in an older specialty program so it can be used on the web or in a report or presentation that you're preparing in modern office suite software. Or you might need to move an image in the other direction, starting with an image file in a standard format and converting it to one of the many specialty file formats PhotoImpact supports.

PhotoImpact offers more with image conversion than simply changing an image file from one file format to another. You can also change the data type (color depth) as well. For example, you might need to convert a full-color image to grayscale or reduce the image's color palette.

To convert an image from one file format to another, follow these general steps:

1. Open the original file in PhotoImpact. (You can use the File | Open command, the Visual Open utility, or any other technique to open the file.) The image appears in a new document window in the PhotoImpact workspace.

2. Change the data type by choosing Format | Data Type | *data type* (see the next section of this chapter for descriptions of the data type options). Perform any other edits and image manipulations that are needed.

3. Choose File | Save As to open the Save As dialog box. (It's the same Save As dialog box you use to save any PhotoImpact image.)

4. Select the new target file format in the Save As Type list box (see the "Select an Image Format" section, which follows the discussion of data types). Navigate to the correct folder and enter a new filename as appropriate.

5. Click the Options button, if it's available for the selected file type, to open the Save Options dialog box. (Some file formats don't offer any user-selectable options, so the Options button will be grayed out.) The contents

of the Save Options dialog box vary depending on the file format selected. The following illustration shows the options for the TIF format:

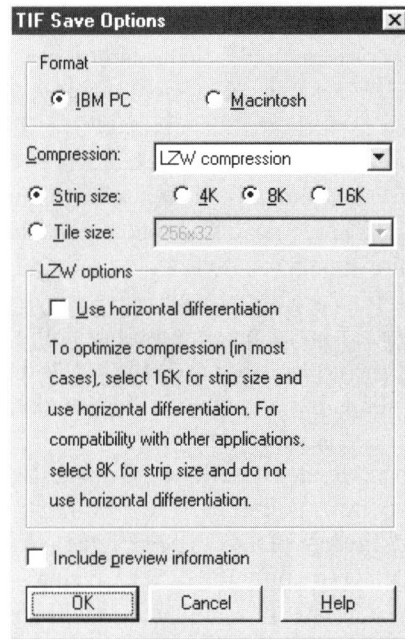

6. Adjust the settings in the Save Options dialog as needed and click OK to close the dialog box and set the options.

7. Click the Save button to close the Save As dialog box and save the image in the selected file format.

TIP *If you need to convert several image files, PhotoImpact offers a special Batch Convert feature to automate the process so you don't need to open and save each file individually. For information on Batch Convert see Chapter 16, which is available online at www.osborne.com.*

Change the Data Type

Often, as you convert an image file from one file format to another, you also need to change the data type (also called *color depth*) of the image. Typically, any change in data type goes in the direction of reducing the color depth of a full-color image to use a restricted color palette, so that it will be compatible with a different file format and/or to reduce file size. Sometimes you need to convert a color image to grayscale for output on a black-and-white printer. Occasionally the data type change goes in the other direction to increase the color depth of an image that is being converted to a more robust file format.

Although PhotoImpact automatically takes care of any color reduction or expansion that is required by the new file format when you save a file, you will often find it appropriate to perform this data type conversion separately. When you change the data type of an image manually, you have more control and more options than PhotoImpact provides automatically. You also have the advantage of seeing the result of the data type change so you can fine-tune the resulting image. For example, after converting a full-color image to grayscale, you might want to increase the brightness and contrast to produce a more attractive grayscale image.

To change the data type of an image, choose Format | Data Type | *data type,* where *data type* is one of the types listed in Table 4-1. Alternatively, click the Data Type button on the status bar and choose the new data type from the pop-up menu that appears.

By default, PhotoImpact creates a new image using the selected data type and displays it in an untitled document window. The existing image remains unchanged. However, you can choose Format | Data Type | Create New Image to disable that option and force PhotoImpact to apply the data type change to the image in the existing document window. Choose the command again to toggle the option back on.

Select an Image Format

When it comes to converting image files from one format to another, the conversion procedure itself is relatively simple. You just open the existing image file in PhotoImpact and use the File | Save As command to save it in another file format. The potentially confusing part is trying to decide which of the many file formats to use for a particular purpose.

Often, you won't have any choice in the selection of a file format. If you are submitting an image for publication or for use in another department's project, the publisher or department usually dictates which kind of image files it will accept. You just need to match PhotoImpact's Save As options to those specifications. With PhotoImpact's long list of supported file types and options, that's easy to do.

The challenge comes when you do not have a predefined set of file specifications to follow, so you need to select a file format on your own. That's when it helps to

Data Type	Description
Black & White	Reduces the image to pure black and white, without color or shades of gray. A dialog box appears, giving you the option of simulating gray shades with one of several halftone screens.
Grayscale	Converts a color image to 8-bit grayscale (256 shades of gray).
Optimized Indexed 16-color	Converts an image to a 4-bit indexed color palette of 16 colors. The palette colors are optimized to best represent the colors in the original image. Dithering simulates colors from the original that aren't available in the indexed color palette.
Optimized Indexed 256-color	Converts an image to an 8-bit indexed color palette of 256 colors. The palette colors are optimized to best represent the colors in the original image. There is little or no dithering.
Web Optimized	Converts an image to an indexed color palette composed of the 216 web-safe colors. Dithering simulates colors from the original that aren't available in the indexed color palette.
RGB True Color	Converts an image to 24-bit color.
Indexed 16-color	Converts an image to a 4-bit indexed color palette of 16 colors. A dialog box offers palette optimization and dithering options.
Indexed 256-color	Converts an image to an 8-bit indexed color palette of 256 standard colors. A dialog box offers palette optimization and dithering options.
16-bit Grayscale	Converts an image to an expanded 16-bit grayscale with millions of shades of gray. This is a nonstandard format, but it can be useful as an intermediary data type to maintain maximum quality while manipulating an image in PhotoImpact. You normally convert the image to the standard 8-bit grayscale before saving it in a final file format.
48-bit True Color	Converts an image to the special, expanded, 48-bit color model. This is another non-standard format that is useful for maintaining maximum quality while manipulating an image in PhotoImpact. Although the TIF file format can record 48-bit color, you normally convert the image to the standard 24-bit True Color data type before saving it in a final file format.
Split to CMYK	Converts a standard RGB (Red, Green, Blue) image to the CMYK (Cyan, Magenta, Yellow, Black) color scheme used in four-color printing processes.
Combine from CMYK	Converts a CMYK image to the RGB color scheme used by computer displays and printers.

TABLE 4-1   PhotoImpact Data Type Options

know a little about the various file formats. Table 4-2 provides a brief description of each of the available file types.

File Type	Description
001	Stores fax images for Hayes fax modems (and compatible units). Rarely used.
BMP/RLE/UPI	Windows bitmap, a simple, but ubiquitous standard for pixel-based images and the native format for the Windows Paint program. BMP is the most widely used, but it doesn't include any compression, so the files are quite large. RLE and UPI are compressed variations, but they aren't widely supported by other programs. Other file formats are more efficient and should be used if supported, but BMP is the format that works when all else fails. There is an OS/2 version of BMP that is rarely used.
CLP	Format for saving the contents of the Windows clipboard.
CUR	Specialized format for storing Windows cursors.
DCS	Desktop Color Separation (DCS) file format.
DCX	Another fax image format, this one for Intel SatisFAXion fax modems.
EPS	Encapsulated PostScript, a special variation of the PostScript page-description language that combines PostScript code for text and graphics with the ability to store high-resolution pixel-based images as well as a low-resolution preview image. PhotoImpact ignores the PostScript code in an EPS file and deals with the pixel-based images. Used primarily by desktop publishing programs and other output intended for PostScript printers.
FAX	Generic fax image format.
GIF	Graphics Interchange Format, the reigning standard for web graphics. The key features of this format are a limited color palette (256 colors max), good compression, the ability to designate part of the image as transparent, and multiple frames in one file for animation effects. The preferred format for pixel-based images of text and graphics.
ICO	Windows icon.
IFF	Native format for Amiga LBM image editor. Rarely used.
IMG	Native image format for the old GEM program environment. Rarely used.
JP2	JPEG 2000 with metadata, a new extension to the JPEG format that adds the ability to store vector data as well as pixel-based images.
JPC	JPEG 2000, a new extension to the JPEG format that adds transparency and other refinements.
JPG/JPEG	Joint Photographic Engineering Group, the leading format for compressed photographic images. Features variable compression and a full range of colors. Works well for photographs and other images with lots of subtle color, but doesn't work as well as GIF for hard-edged graphics and text. Lossy compression sacrifices image detail to achieve small file sizes. Image quality remains good at moderate compression ratios but suffers noticeably as compression ratios increase.

TABLE 4-2   PhotoImpact File Type Options

File Type	Description
MAC	Native format for the MacPaint program and a de facto standard on Macintosh computers.
MSP	Native format for the original Windows Paint program. Replaced by BMP.
PBM	Portable Bitmap, a generic format for bitmap images. Popular on Unix systems.
PCD	Native format for Kodak Photo CD images.
PCT/PICT	Standard Macintosh Picture file format. The format supports vector data as well as pixel data, but PhotoImpact works with only the pixel-based image data.
PCX	Native format for PC Paintbrush software. Widely used as a de facto standard for pixel-based graphics outside the web.
PGM	Portable Graymap, a generic format for grayscale images. Popular on Unix systems.
PIC	Lotus Picture, native format for Lotus 1-2-3 spreadsheet graphics.
PNG	Portable Network Graphics, an aspiring new standard for web graphics. Native format for Macromedia Fireworks. Attempts to combine the features of GIF and JPG. Supports full color rendering like JPG or indexed color palettes like GIF. The file format has provisions for supporting objects/layers and vector graphics in addition to pixel-based images, but PhotoImpact merges all objects into the base image before saving as PNG. Several compression options. A very versatile format, but it doesn't usually produce the smallest or most efficient files.
PPM	Portable Pixel Map, a generic format for bitmap images. Popular on Unix systems. Similar to PBM.
PSD	Native format for Adobe Photoshop and a de facto standard among image editors and other graphics programs. Includes layer data in addition to the pixel-based image.
PSP	Native format for Jasc Paint Shop Pro. Also supports layer data in addition to pixel-based image data.
PXR	Native format for Pixar software.
RAS	Sun Raster file format. Widely used on Unix systems.
SCI	SciFAX, yet another fax image format.
SCT	Native format for Scitex software.
SHG	Segmented Hypergraph.
TGA	Native format for Targa software and other video-frame capture programs.
TIF/TIFF	Tagged Image File Format, the leading cross-platform format for lossless, high-resolution images. The standard format for high-quality images in desktop publishing, printing, and elsewhere. This format enjoys almost universal support, although there can be problems with PC/Mac variations and some compression options. About the only place the TIF format isn't used much is on the web.
UFO	Ulead File for Object, the native file format for PhotoImpact. Includes full support for text, path, and image objects stored separately from the base image.

TABLE 4-2   PhotoImpact File Type Options *(continued)*

File Type	Description
WBM/WBMP	Wireless Bitmap, a relatively new format designed for sending bitmap images to wireless devices such as cell phones and handheld computers.
WMF	Windows Metafile, a generic format intended for all Windows programs. Supports both vector graphics and pixel-based images in the same file (which PhotoImpact can read and display). However, all objects are merged into the base image before an image is saved as a WMF file. Although not well known, it can be a useful fallback if one of the standard formats don't work.

TABLE 4-2   PhotoImpact File Type Options *(continued)*

The UFO file format is an excellent file format for your PhotoImpact images, but it isn't usually a good choice for transferring images to other programs or for other applications. You'll probably want to save your working copy of an image in the UFO format in order to keep all the selections and objects fully editable, and then save a copy of the image in another format for compatibility with another program.

The Big Three Image Formats

After considering the long list of file formats supported by PhotoImpact, you may be wondering which one to use for your image. Often, it comes down to a choice of one of the big three image formats: GIF, JPEG, or TIF. These three file formats are widely recognized and supported standards. It's likely that any program that imports or otherwise works with images will support all three. As a result, you can usually pick whichever one of the three best suits the needs of the image and the desired file size.

GIF   Use the GIF format for hard-edged graphics and text with a limited color palette, as well as for web animation (animated GIFs are covered in Chapters 13 and 14). The key features of this format are a limited color palette (256 colors maximum), good compression, the ability to designate part of the image as transparent, and multiple frames in one file for animation effects. Generally, this format produces the smallest files with good image quality, provided you don't need a full range of subtle colors.

JPG/JPEG   Use JPEG for photographs and other images that contain a lot of subtle colors and need to be stored in a small file. The lossy compression of JPEGs produces very compact files, but this compression can degrade sharp-edged details in text and similar graphics. Lossy compression sacrifices image detail to achieve small file sizes. Image quality remains good at moderate compression ratios, but it suffers noticeably as compression ratios increase. Use the GIF format instead to preserve quality in hard-edged graphics and text.

TIF   The TIF format provides the best quality in high-resolution images intended for desktop publishing and printing. TIF is probably the most widely supported format for moving images across computer platforms and programs, although there can be problems with PC/Mac variations and some compression options. TIF files are not widely used on the web, because they tend to be larger than the same images stored in GIF or JPEG format.

The Second-Tier Image Formats

If, for some reason, one of the "big three" formats isn't appropriate, you can try one of the "second-tier" image formats: PNG, BMP, or EPS. Like the big three, these formats are all industry standards. However, they're not as widely used because the format is relatively new (PNG), inefficient (BMP), or specialized (EPS).

PNG   PNG attempts to combine the features of GIF and JPEG. It supports full-color rendering like JPEG or indexed color palettes like GIF. The file format has provisions for supporting objects/layers and vector graphics in addition to pixel-based images, but PhotoImpact merges all objects into the base image before saving a file in PNG format. PNG offers several compression options and is a very versatile format, but it usually doesn't produce the smallest or most efficient files.

BMP   Since the BMP format is a standard of the Windows operating system, it's almost universally recognized by all Windows programs and many programs running on other systems as well. However, the standard version of BMP doesn't include compression, so the files are quite large. Other file formats are more efficient and should be used if supported, but BMP is the format that works when all else fails.

EPS   The EPS format is used primarily by desktop publishing programs and other output intended for PostScript printers. It's a special variation on the PostScript page description language that uses PostScript code as a container for an image or graphics. PhotoImpact ignores the PostScript code in an EPS file and deals with the pixel-based images.

Specialized File Formats

Finally, you get down to the long list of specialized file formats that PhotoImpact supports. Generally, you will convert an image file into one of these formats only when you have a specific need, such as targeting a particular program or computer platform. For example, you might choose the PSD format if you're targeting a Photoshop user. If you need to send an image to someone who works on a Unix-based computer, PBM might be a good choice. And if you're sending a file to a Macintosh user, the MAC or PICT formats are good alternatives.

Work with an Image Library

As you work with images in PhotoImpact, you'll probably find that there are images that you use frequently as components of other images. For example, you might add a corporate logo to your designs, or place a full moon on your night sky backgrounds.

Of course, you can always open those images in PhotoImpact, just like any other image file, or you can insert the image into another document using the Object | Insert Image Object | From File command (see Chapter 3 for details). But for images that you use frequently, PhotoImpact offers a special feature, called a *library*, that keeps selected images close at hand for convenient access.

Use Images from the Object Library

The Object Library is housed in the EasyPalette panel and houses collections of objects and complete images. Adding an image from the Object Library in the EasyPalette panel to the active image document in the PhotoImpact workspace is a simple process.

NOTE *To open the EasyPalette panel, press* F2, *choose View | Toolbars & Panels | EasyPalette, or click the Show/Hide EasyPalette button in the Panel Manager panel.*

In the EasyPalette panel, click the Object Libraries button, and then click Image Library in the tree display to display thumbnail previews of the image library in the right side of the EasyPalette, as shown in Figure 4-2.

Browse through the image thumbnails and select the one you want. You can use any of the following techniques to add the selected image to your document:

- Double-click the thumbnail in the EasyPalette panel.

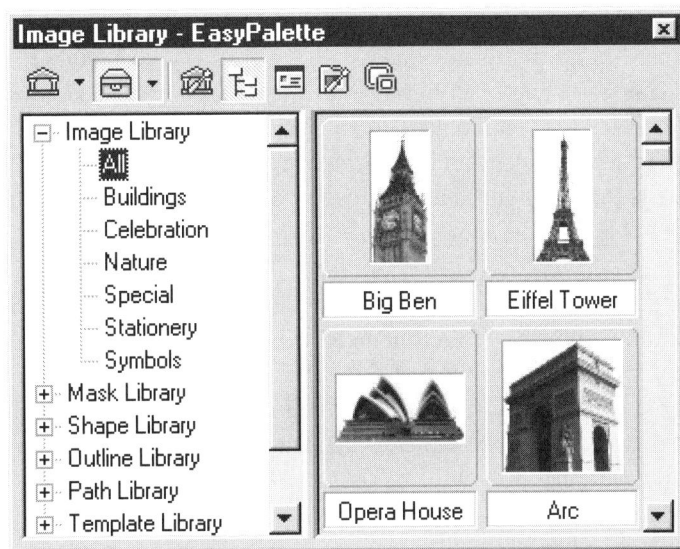

FIGURE 4-2 Use the EasyPalette to access the Image Library.

- Drag the thumbnail from the EasyPalette panel and drop it on your image document.

- Right-click the thumbnail and choose Copy Object to Image.

- Right-click the thumbnail and choose Copy Object to New Document.

PhotoImpact inserts the library image into the document as an image object, which means that the library image is an object, floating on top of the base image on a separate layer. You can select, move, edit, and manipulate the image object separately from the base image.

Add an Image to the Library

PhotoImpact comes with a selection of sample images in the Object Library. They give you something to experiment with as you learn to use the feature. However, it's only when you add your own images to the EasyPalette libraries that they really become useful.

The sample images in the standard Object Library are locked, so adding images to the Object Library requires extra steps. However, PhotoImpact's EasyPalette contains another library that is designed specifically for your images, called My Library. You can store almost any image in this library—from a small selection of a larger image, to a text or path object, to an entire image file. Using an image from My Library is the same as using an image from one of the other Object Libraries. The only difference is that it's your image instead of a sample image supplied by Ulead.

Here's how you can add an image to My Library:

1. Open the image file you want to add to the library. Optionally, if you want to add only a portion of the image to the library, select the desired portion of the image and delete the rest. To delete the unwanted portion of the image, select the portion you want with a selection tool, choose Selection | Invert to select everything else, press DELETE, and then choose Selection | None to get rid of the selection outline. The result is essentially the same as adding an image object to the library. Here's an example of a portion of an image, ready to be added to the library:

2. Open the EasyPalette (press F2) and click the Object Libraries button to display the list of libraries.

3. Right-click a thumbnail and choose Add Current Document As Thumbnail. PhotoImpact opens the Add to EasyPalette dialog box.

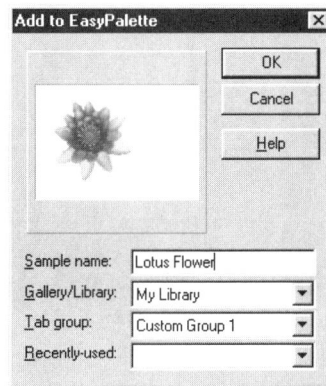

4. Type a name in the Sample Name box.

5. Choose My Library in the Gallery/Library box and any desired option in the Tab Group box.

6. Click OK to close the Add to EasyPalette dialog box and add your image to My Library in the EasyPalette panel. PhotoImpact automatically saves the image to a special folder and displays the newly added thumbnail in the EasyPalette panel, as shown in Figure 4-3.

TIP *If you want to add an entire image to My Library in the EasyPalette panel, you don't have to open the image in a PhotoImpact document window first. Just right-click a thumbnail in an EasyPalette library, choose Add Image File As Thumbnail, and then select the desired image file in the Open dialog box that appears. The image file appears in the Add to EasyPalette dialog box, and you can continue the procedure as described.*

NOTE *To delete an image that you no longer need from My Library in the EasyPalette panel, right-click the thumbnail in the EasyPalette and choose Delete from the pop-up menu that appears.*

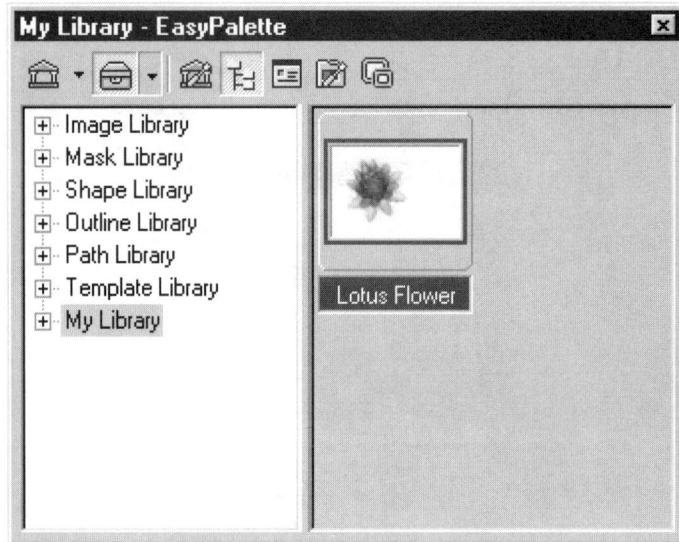

FIGURE 4-3   Adding an image to My Library

Print Images

No matter how nice your images look on your screen, sooner or later you'll want to print at least a few of them. When that time comes, PhotoImpact stands ready to meet your needs. In addition to the standard printing capability that allows you to print individual images, PhotoImpact 7 includes a new Print Multiple feature to facilitate printing multiple images and working with special papers and labels.

Print the Active Image Document

PhotoImpact's standard print feature does exactly what you would expect: It prints the active image document on the selected system printer.

1. Open the image file you want to print and make sure it is the active document window in the PhotoImpact workspace.

2. Choose File | Print, press CTRL-P, or click the Print button in the toolbar. PhotoImpact opens the Print dialog box.

4

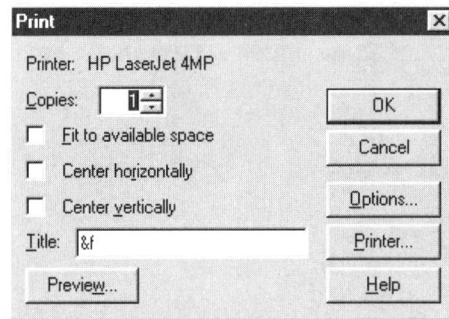

3. Click the Options button to open the Options dialog box if you need to exercise precise control over the gamma curve or halftone screens used to print your image. Adjust settings on the Calibration and Halftone tabs and click OK to close the Options dialog box and return to the Print dialog box.

4. Click the Preview button. PhotoImpact opens the print preview window, as shown in Figure 4-4. In fact, you can bypass the Print dialog box and go directly to the print preview window by clicking the Print Preview toolbar button.

5. Move or resize the image and adjust settings in the print preview window as needed. You can modify any of the options on the left side of the window, as follows:

- In the Printer Name drop-down list, select a printer from the Printer Name list box. Click the button to the right of the Printer Name box to open the standard Windows properties dialog box for the selected printer.

- In the Paper Size drop-down list, select a paper size.

- For Orientation, select Portrait (tall) or Landscape (wide).

- Check the Title box to print a title, and then type the title into the adjacent text box. The default setting (&f) automatically inserts the filename.

- Check the Fit to Available Space box to size the image as large as possible in the available print area.

- Check the Center Horizontally box to center the image horizontally on the page.

- Check the Center Vertically box to center the image vertically on the page.

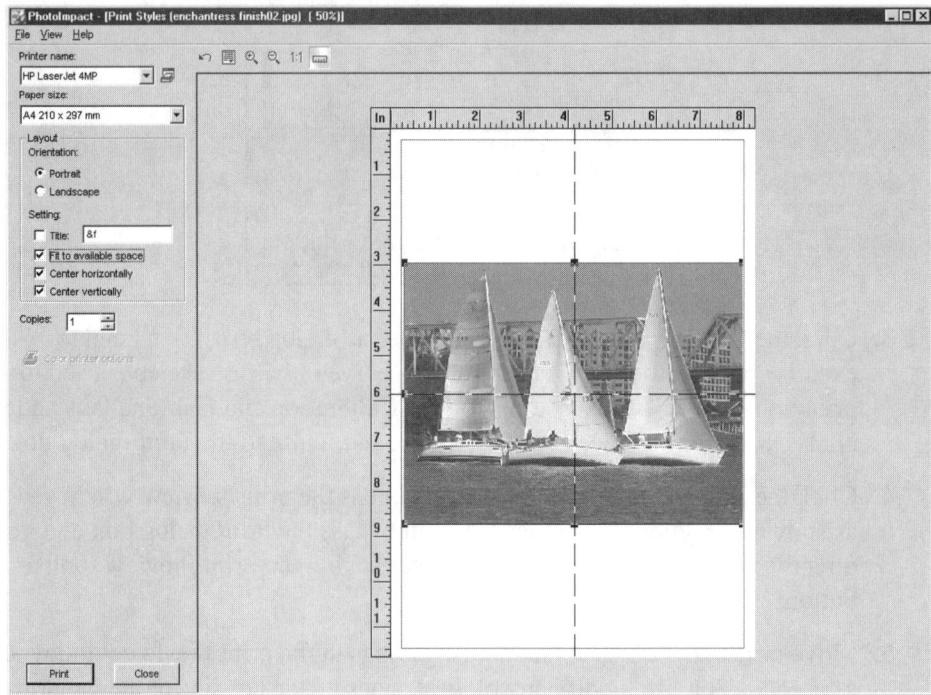

FIGURE 4-4 PhotoImpact previews the print job in a special window

- In the Copies box, type or select the number of copies you want to print.

- Click and drag the image to move the image on the page.

- To resize the image, drag one of the sizing handles (black squares) on the perimeter of the image. Press and hold the SHIFT key as you drag to avoid distorting the image proportions.

CAUTION *Be careful about resizing your image on the printer page. Enlarging the image can significantly reduce print quality. Consider resizing the image in the document window in PhotoImpact rather than resizing the image in the print preview window.*

6. Click the Print button to begin printing. PhotoImpact prints your image on the selected printer.

7. Click the Close button to close the print preview window and return to the PhotoImpact application window.

Print Multiple Images on a Page

You may need to print multiple copies of a single image or print several different images on the same page. Furthermore, when you print on label stock or special photographic paper, you need to precisely position and align those images to fit into predefined locations on the page.

PhotoImpact's new Print Multiple feature is designed to meet these specialized printing needs. It supports a large assortment of label stock and specialty papers from Avery and Kodak, as well as generic page layouts for disk labels and various arrangements of multiple images on a single page (see Figure 4-5).

4

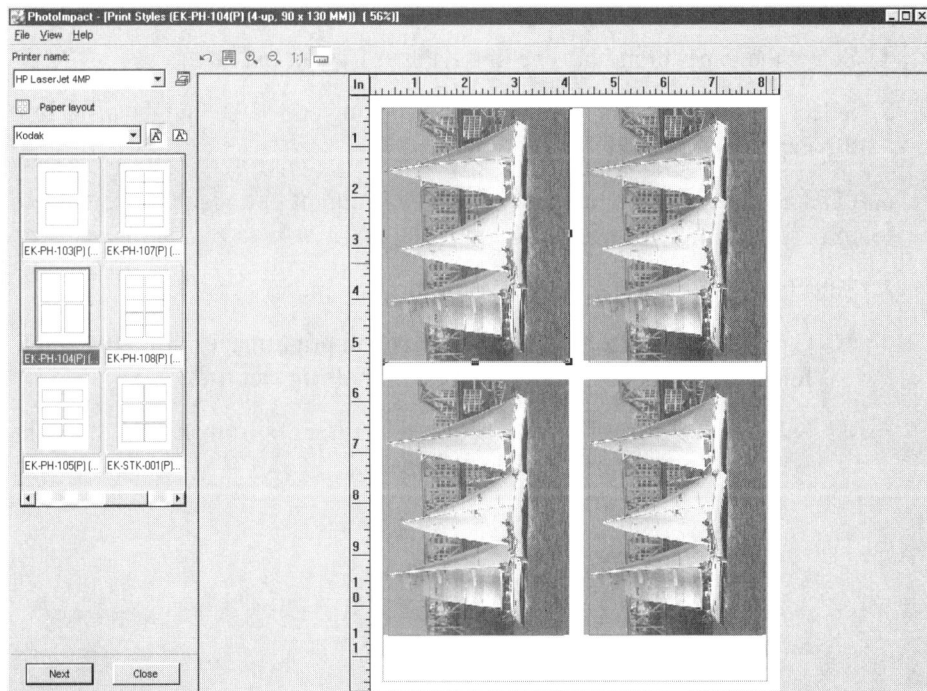

FIGURE 4-5   The Print Multiple window

The Print Multiple feature can print image files directly from a folder without opening them in PhotoImpact. However, you'll probably want to open the images so you can preview them and make any needed adjustments before printing.

To use the Print Multiple feature, follow these steps:

1. Open the image or images you want to print so that they appear in individual document windows in the PhotoImpact workspace.

2. Choose File | Print Multiple, press CTRL-SHIFT-P, or click the Print Multiple button in the toolbar. PhotoImpact opens the Print Multiple preview window (see Figure 4-5). Initially, the image from the active document window appears in the preview pane, duplicated as many times as needed to fill all the available print areas (designated by red outline boxes) on the selected page layout.

3. Select the printer in the Printer Name list box on the left side of the preview window.

4. Select the paper brand or type in the Paper Layout list box.

5. Select the specific paper stock layout by clicking one of the thumbnails below the Paper Layout box.

6. Click the Next button to display the next group of options in the left side of the Print Multiple preview window.

7. Select the source of the images you want to print.

   ■ Choose Open It from Folder to select and print images directly from a folder without opening the images in PhotoImpact first.

   ■ Select Open It from Workspace to select images from among those that are open in the PhotoImpact workspace.

4

Please select the source target
or keep the currently selected
files.

Source target:

    ⦿ Open it from folder

    ○ Open it from workspace

You can change any of the
images to print by dragging and
dropping a new image file from

8. Click the Next button. PhotoImpact displays another set of options on the left side of the Print Multiple preview window. The options vary slightly depending on your selection in the previous step. The next illustration shows the options for printing from a folder. If you chose to print from the PhotoImpact workspace, the Currently Browsed Folder box is missing, and the thumbnails show the images open in the PhotoImpact workspace.

Select the file you want to put
into the page.

Currently browsed folder:

PHOTOIMPACT 7\Sa ▾

Thumbnail sorting

Bridge.jpg

Dog.jpg

Building.jpg

Forest.JPG

Desk.jpg

Girl.jpg

9. If you chose to print from a folder, select the folder containing the files you want to print from the Currently Browsed Folder list box. When you click the arrow button to expand the list box, it shows a tree display of your drives and folders like the left pane of the Windows Explorer window. Thumbnails of the image files in the selected folder appear below the list box.

10. Drag an image from the thumbnail preview box and drop it into a print area in the page preview to select that image for printing. Repeat as needed to select all the images you want to print on this page. PhotoImpact automatically rotates and sizes each image to fit the print area, but you may need to fine-tune some of the images. You can move an image by dragging it and resize an image by dragging one of the handles on the outer edge of the image. To remove the image from a print area, click the image and then press DELETE.

> **TIP** *There is no undo capability in the Print Multiple window, so you can't undo a mistake such as distorting an image. However, you can simply replace the image with a fresh copy by dragging the image from the thumbnail to the page preview. You can also go back to a previous set of options by clicking the Back arrow button beside the Next button at the bottom of the window.*

11. Click the Next button. PhotoImpact displays the final options on the left side of the Print Multiple preview window.

12. Select the number of copies you want to print in the Copies box.

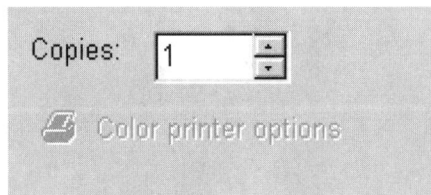

Copies: 1

Color printer options

13. Click the Print button. PhotoImpact prints the page of images.

14. Click the Close button to close the Print Multiple preview window and return to the PhotoImpact application window.

Share Images Online with Friends and Family

With nearly everyone able to surf the web these days, what better way to share your photos with family and friends than to post your images on a web site? Instead of attempting the nearly impossible task of printing and mailing photos to family members scattered across the country and around the globe, you can simply post your images on a web site. Send an e-mail message to anyone who might be interested to inform them of the web site address, and they can view your images at their own convenience—all they need is a web browser.

Posting images on a web site isn't an exceptionally difficult task. PhotoImpact includes the tools you need to do it manually, as well as a couple of options for automating the process. With the web export options, even people with little or no knowledge of web design procedures can share their images on the web.

NOTE *If you're interested in creating web pages manually, see Chapters 10 through 12 for information on PhotoImpact's web page production capabilities.*

PhotoImpact offers two web export options: Post to Web and Post to iMira. Which one you use will depend on whether you have access to a personal web site.

NOTE *Another way to share images with family and friends is to send an image file as an attachment to an e-mail message. See Chapter 3 for instructions.*

Post Images to a Personal Web Site

The Post to Web option is for PhotoImpact users who want to post images to a personal web site. With many Internet service providers including a personal web page with every Internet access account, it's quite likely that you have one.

NOTE *Before you attempt to use the Post to Web option in PhotoImpact, your web site needs to be active and you need to configure the Microsoft Web Publishing Wizard to access the site. Check with the system administrator from your web hosting service for the settings you need to configure the Web Publishing Wizard.*

To post an image to the web, follow these steps:

1. Open the image you want to post to the web. Make any needed adjustments to the image and make sure the image is the active document window in the PhotoImpact workspace.

2. Choose File | Export | Post to Web. PhotoImpact opens the Post to Web dialog box.

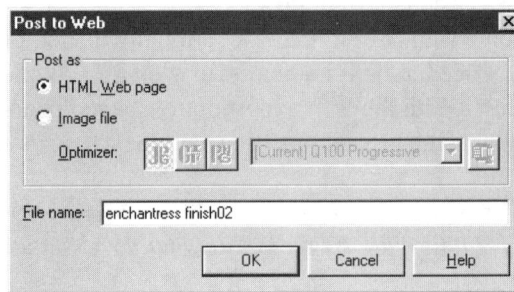

3. Select a posting option.

   ■ Choose HTML Web Page to create a JPEG image file and also a web page to display that image.

   ■ Choose Image File to create an image file without an accompanying web page.

4. If you selected the image file posting option, click a button on the Optimizer line to select JPG, GIF, or PNG as the file type for your image, and then select a compression/optimization option from the list box.

NOTE	*See Chapter 10 for more information about optimizing images for the web.*

5. Type a filename in the File Name box.

6. Click the OK button. PhotoImpact closes the Post to Web dialog box, creates the necessary image and web page files, and launches the Web Publishing Wizard.

7. Follow the prompts in the Web Publishing Wizard dialog box to post the image to your web server. Windows connects to the Internet and transfers the files that PhotoImpact created to the web server.

The Post to Web option simply creates an image file (and maybe a web page) for an image and transfers the files to your web server. In order to make such an image accessible to visitors to your web site, you'll need to manually edit your site's home page to add links to the image file.

Post Images to the iMira Web Site

The Post to iMira option is for PhotoImpact users who don't have their own web space. The option ties into the iMira.com web site, where Ulead allows registered users of the site to create, share, and view online image albums.

Create an iMira Account

Before you use the Post to iMira option, you need to create an account on the iMira.com web site. Here's the simplest way to do that:

Ulead Drop Spot

1. Click the Ulead Drop Spot shortcut that the PhotoImpact installation placed on your desktop. PhotoImpact opens the small Ulead Drop Spot window.

2. Click the Create New Account on the Web button to launch your web browser and go to the Sign Up page on the iMira site.

3. Follow the prompts to create an account.

CAUTION | *Be sure you read the entire iMira Member Agreement before you post any images on the iMira service! Do not post any of your images on the iMira site unless you fully understand and agree to accept the terms in that agreement!*

Send an Image to iMira

After you create an iMira account, you can send images from PhotoImpact to your iMira album by following these steps:

1. Open the image you want to post on the iMira web site. Make any needed adjustments to the image and make sure the image is the active document window in the PhotoImpact workspace.

2. Choose File | Export | Post to iMira. PhotoImpact opens the Post to iMira dialog box.

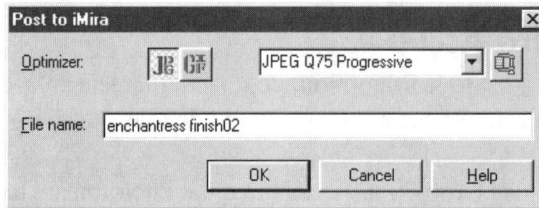

3. Click the JPG or GIF button to select the file type for your image, and then select a compression/optimization option from the list box.

4. Type a filename in the File Name box.

5. Click the OK button. PhotoImpact closes the Post to iMira dialog box, creates the necessary image and web page files, connects to the iMira.com web site, and then opens the Share Images on the Web dialog box.

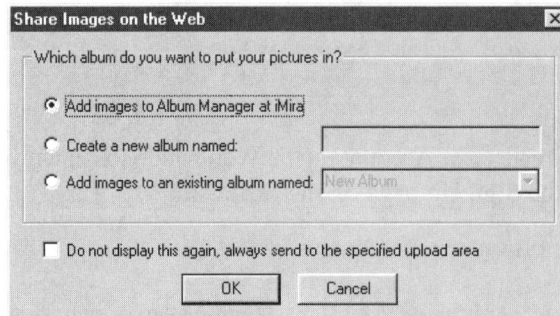

6. Select the iMira album into which you want to place the image, and then click OK. PhotoImpact uploads the image to the iMira web site and displays the status of the transfer in the Post to iMira message box.

4

7. When the upload is complete, click OK to close the Post to iMira message box and automatically launch your web browser to display your My Photo Albums page at the iMira.com site.

At the iMira web site, you can view and modify your albums and the images they contain. Figure 4-6 shows an example of a My Photo Albums page. You can elect to keep your album private, share it with specific friends, or publish it in one of the many public galleries at iMira. And you can do it all from within your web browser.

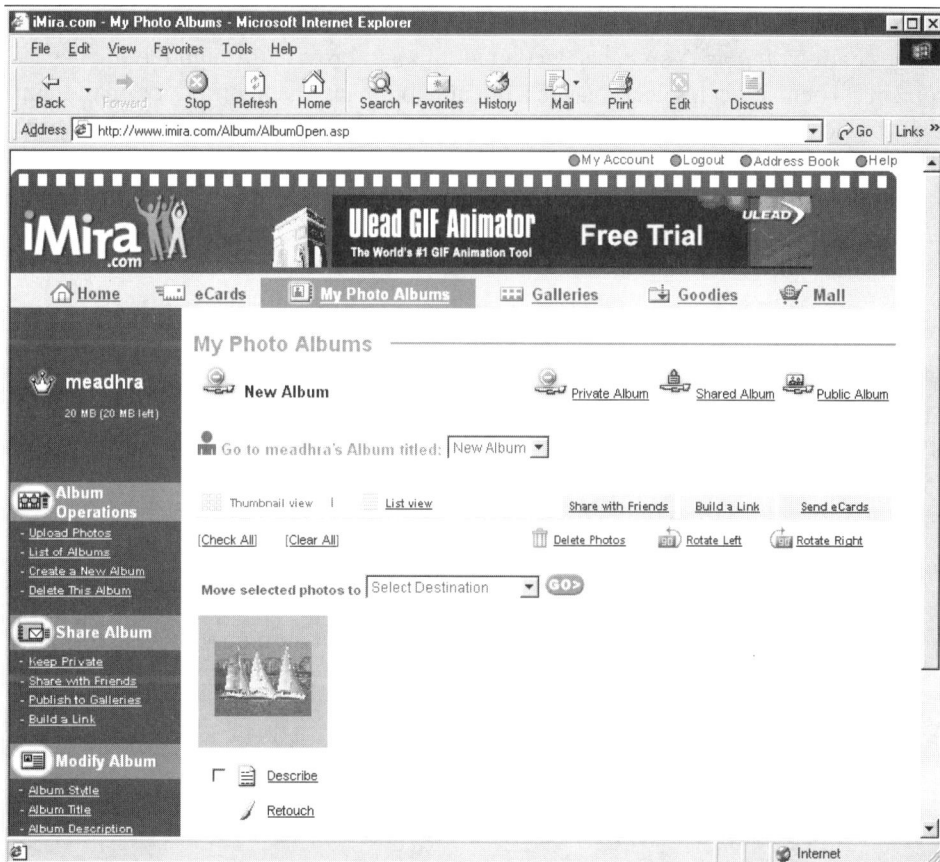

FIGURE 4-6 You can share your images at the iMira web site

Build Image Albums

If you're like most PhotoImpact users, you have more than a few image files stored on your hard drive and various disks. Keeping track of all those images can be quite a challenge.

In the paper-based world, a popular way to address the challenge of how to organize your images is to compile collections of related images in photo albums. Then, when you need to find a particular image (or just want to browse through the images), you can open an album and start leafing through the pages to view the images.

PhotoImpact Album, an image management program that ships with PhotoImpact 7, creates an electronic counterpart to the traditional photo album. This program is installed when you install PhotoImpact.

You can use PhotoImpact Album to create, maintain, and view collections of images called *albums*. You can select an album and browse through the images it contains. Then you can select images from an album and open, print, or e-mail them. You can post an image album to the web, and you can view images in an on-screen slide show.

Album has a long list of features and capabilities—too long to cover completely on these pages. However, a quick look at some of the program's highlights will demonstrate their usefulness.

Launch PhotoImpact Album

PhotoImpact Album is a separate program that you can launch and run independently. It's *not* an integral part of the PhotoImpact image editor. You can use any of the following techniques to launch Album:

PhotoImpact
Album 7

- Click the Start button on the Windows taskbar and choose Programs | Ulead PhotoImpact 7 | PhotoImpact Album 7.

- Double-click the PhotoImpact Album 7 shortcut icon on your desktop.

- Choose Switch | PhotoImpact Album in the PhotoImpact image editor or in GIF Animator

The PhotoImpact Album Window

The normal PhotoImpact Album window, shown in Figure 4-7, consists of the usual menu bar and toolbar across the top. It also includes the following components:

Export Web Album

Send mail

Print

Tool panel

Album panel

Album thumbnail

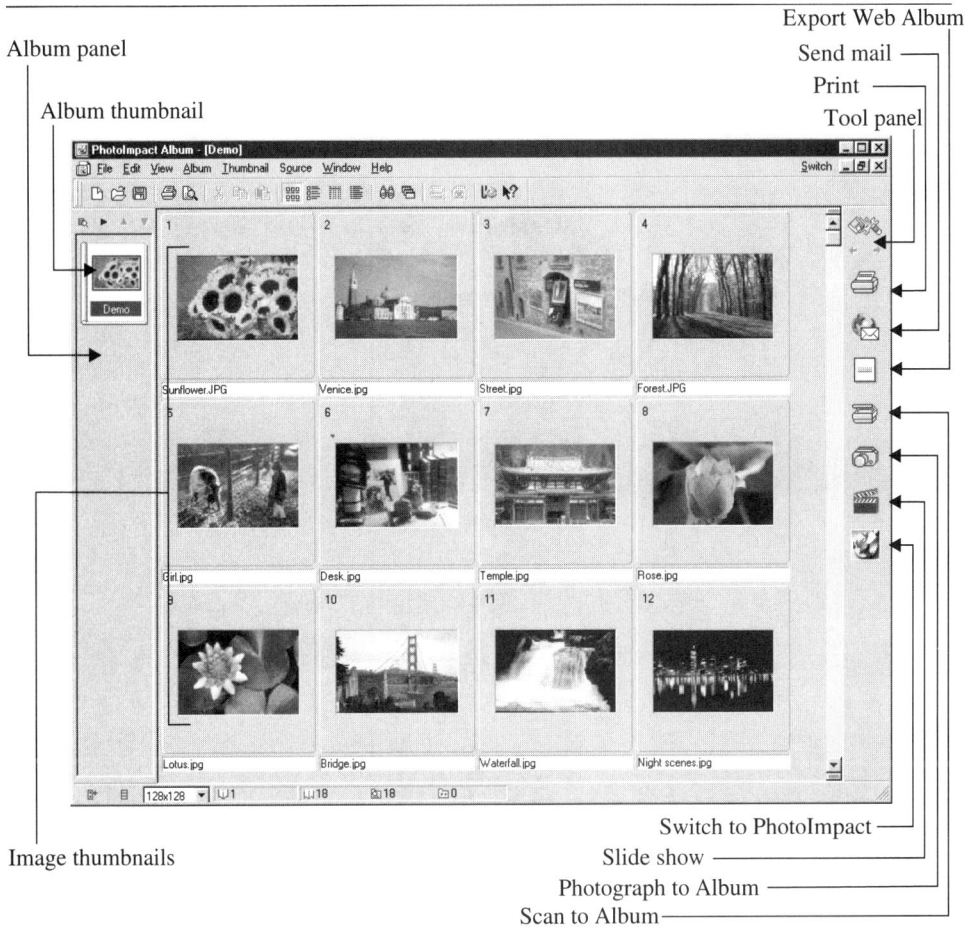

Image thumbnails

Switch to PhotoImpact

Slide show

Photograph to Album

Scan to Album

The Album window in Normal mode

- An Album panel on the left side that shows thumbnails representing albums.

- The Tool panel on the right, containing a series of buttons for various tasks, such as e-mailing the images or displaying them in a slide show.

- The main workspace in the middle, where thumbnails of individual images in the selected album appear.

Album Compact Mode

PhotoImpact Album can also run in Compact mode, which reduces the Album window to a narrow vertical slit without the usual menus, toolbar, and panels. Choose View | Compact Mode to switch to this mode.

Compact mode is useful for positioning the Album window tiled alongside a larger PhotoImpact window. This configuration allows you to use Album as a supercharged Visual Open–type feature for PhotoImpact. A quick way to set up this configuration is to click the Quick Album icon located in the system tray at the right end of the Windows taskbar. This opens Album in Compact mode, tiled with the previously active application window.

With the normal menu bar hidden in Compact mode, you must rely on the alternate pop-up menu to control the program. Click the Display Menu button in the status bar at the bottom of the Album window to display the pop-up menu, which contains all of the normal Album menu commands arranged in cascading menus.

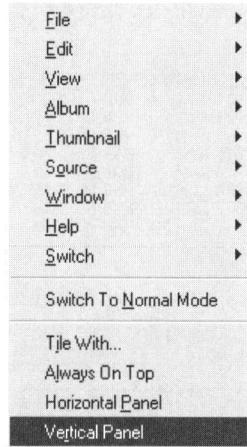

Viewing Modes

In addition to the Normal and Compact window modes, you can choose View | Mode | *mode* commands (or click toolbar buttons) to select different viewing modes for the album contents in the main work area:

- **Thumbnail mode**   Displays thumbnail previews of all the images in the album, arranged in rows and columns. This is the default mode.

- **Attribute mode**   Displays a single column of thumbnails with the attributes of each image listed to the right of its thumbnail. Here's an example of the display for one thumbnail:

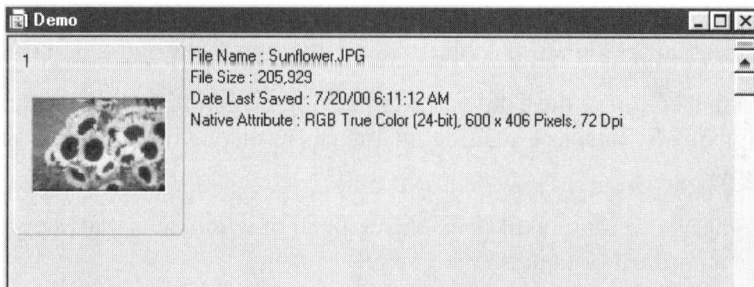

■ **File Name mode**   Displays a list of the filenames and other pertinent data for the image files in the album. This is a text-only display.

■ **Data Entry mode**   Displays a single thumbnail and a series of text boxes where you can enter a description and other information for the image.

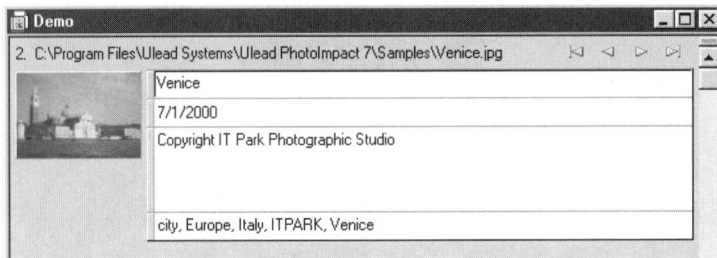

Work with Album and Image Thumbnails

Basic operations in Album are straightforward:

■ Click an album's thumbnail in the Album panel to display the contents of that album in the main workspace.

■ Click an image thumbnail to select it. CTRL-click image thumbnails to select multiple images. A blue outline highlights selected thumbnails.

■ Click a button in the Tool panel to perform an action on the selected thumbnails, such as e-mailing the images or displaying them in a slide show.

■ Right-click a thumbnail to display a menu of commands that apply to the thumbnail or to its source image.

■ Double-click a thumbnail to view a full-sized version of the image in its own window.

TIP *Right-click a thumbnail and choose Open from the pop-up menu to open the image in PhotoImpact.*

4

Create an Album

The Demo album that appears when you first open PhotoImpact Album contains some nice pictures, but the whole purpose of the Album program is to enable you to create and maintain your own albums.

Here's how to create a new album:

1. Choose File | New, press CTRL-N, or click the New button in the toolbar. Album opens the New dialog box.

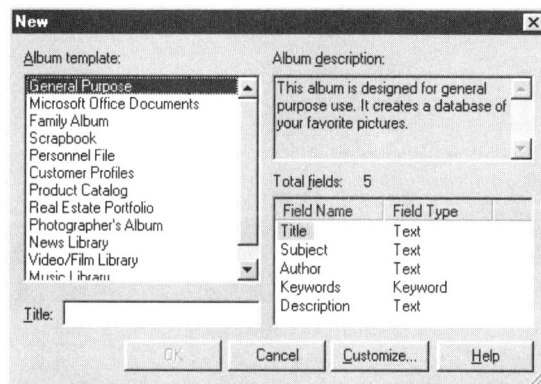

2. Select an album template and enter a title. The Album Template setting controls what information about each image is stored in the album file along with the images themselves. If all you're interested in is the images and their file names, then any template will do.

3. Click the OK button. Album closes the New dialog box and creates the new album. A document window appears in the workspace for the new album, and a thumbnail representing the album appears in the Album panel. Album opens the Insert dialog box to start the process of adding images to the new album.

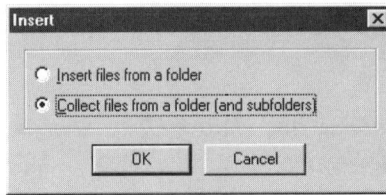

4. Select the Collect Files from a Folder (and Subfolder) option to populate your new album with all the image files from an entire folder. Optionally, you could also select the Insert Files from a Folder option to select individual files for addition to the album. (See the next section, "Add Images to an Album," for details on inserting individual files.) Album opens the Collect Files dialog box.

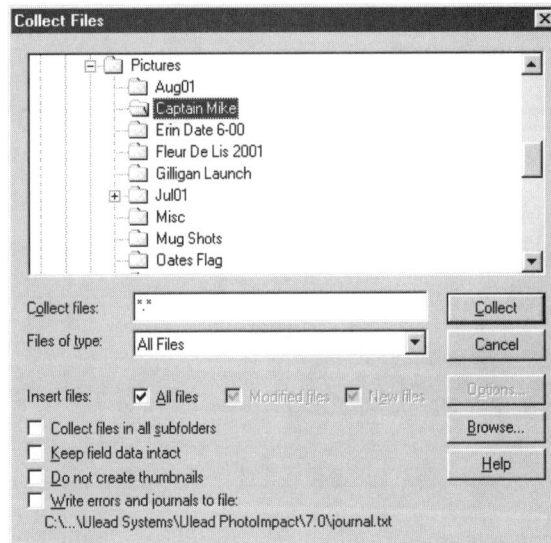

5. Select the folder containing the image files you want in the Album. Adjust the other options and settings in the Collect Files dialog box as needed.

6. Click the Collect button. Album closes the Collect Files dialog box, scans the selected folder for image files, and adds thumbnails of those images to the album. The thumbnails appear in the album window.

TIP   *To delete an album, right-click its thumbnail in the Album panel and choose Delete from the pop-up menu that appears.*

Add Images to an Album

Album automatically prompts you to add images to a new album when you create it. After you've set up an album, you can insert new images into that album at any time. Here's how:

1. Select the album to which you want to add images.

2. Choose Thumbnail | Insert. Album opens the Insert dialog box (the same one that appears when you create a new album).

3. Select Insert Files from a Folder or Collect Files from a Folder (and Subfolder). The procedure for collecting files from a folder was covered in the previous section. When you select Insert Files from a Folder, the Insert Files dialog box appears.

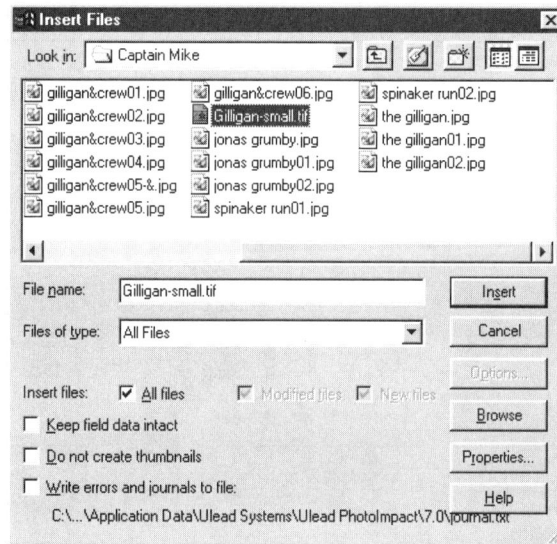

4. Navigate to the folder containing the image(s) you want to add to the album and select the image file by clicking its icon. (You can CTRL-click to select multiple files.) Adjust the other settings in the Insert Files dialog box as needed.

5. Click the Insert button. Album adds the selected image files to the current album.

6. Repeat steps 4 and 5 to add more images if desired.

7. Click the Close button to close the Insert Files dialog box.

TIP *To delete a thumbnail from an album, right-click the thumbnail and choose Clear from the pop-up menu that appears.*

If you have trouble identifying the images you want to add to your album based on their filenames, you can try another option for adding images to an album. Choose Thumbnail | Visual Insert to open the Visual Insert dialog box, shown in Figure 4-8.

Use the folder tree display in the left pane of the dialog box to navigate to the folder containing the images you want to add to the album, and then select the images by clicking the thumbnails that appear in the right pane. Click the Open button to close the dialog box and add the selected images to your album.

FIGURE 4-8   The Visual Insert dialog box shows thumbnails of your images.

NOTE   *The albums you create with PhotoImpact Album consist of thumbnail images and links to the source image files, which remain in their original location. If you move a source image file after creating the album, you will need to use the Thumbnail | Relink command to update the link between the thumbnail in the album and the image file in its new location.*

Print an Album

One useful feature of Album is the ability to print an album as pages of thumbnails. This creates a printed "contact sheet" that is very convenient as an index or printed reference. Here's how you can print your album:

1. Open the album containing the images you want to print.

2. Select the thumbnails you want to include in the printed album. CTRL-click to select multiple thumbnails. To quickly select all the thumbnails in an album, press CTRL-A.

3. Choose File | Print Preview or click the Print Preview button in the Tool panel. Album opens the print preview window, as shown in Figure 4-9. (Alternatively, you can choose File | Print to bypass the print preview window and go directly to the Print dialog box.)

4. Click the Print button. Album closes the print preview window and opens the Print dialog box.

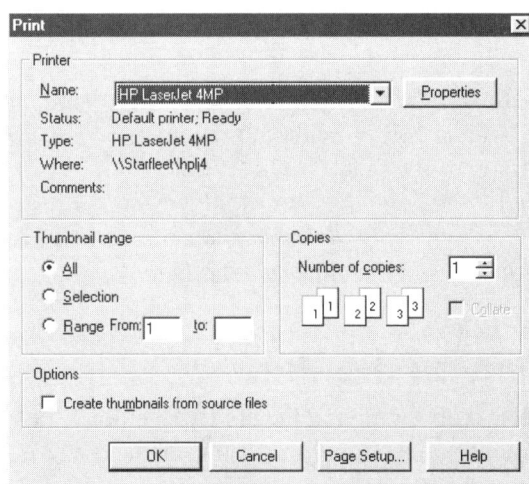

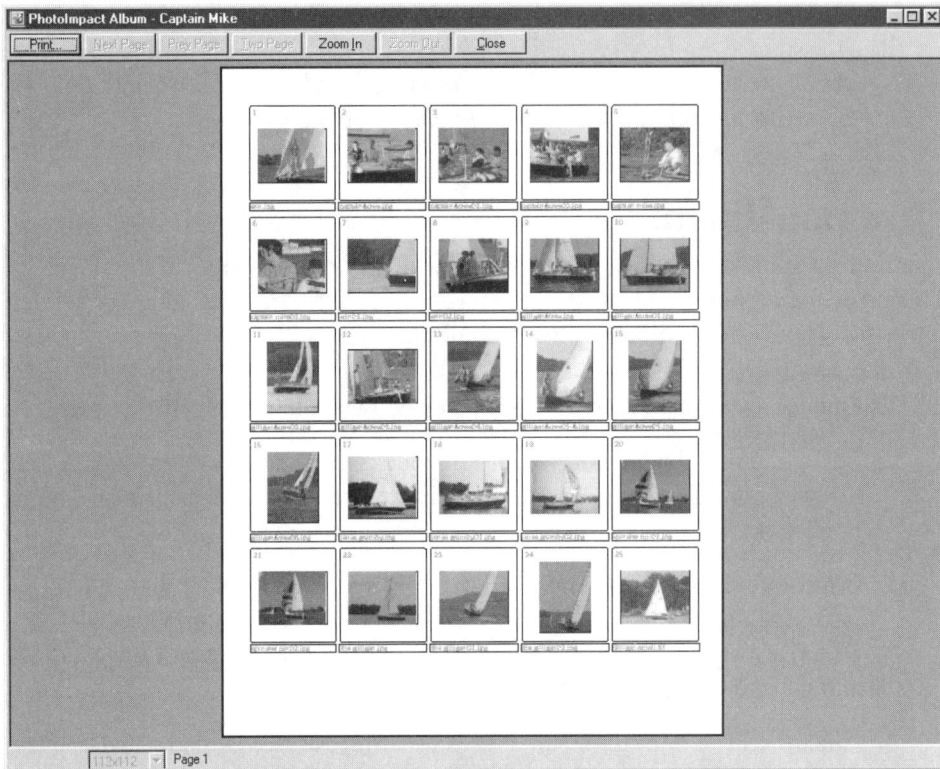

FIGURE 4-9   PhotoImpact Album's print preview window

5. Adjust the settings in the Print dialog box if necessary, and then click the Print button. Album prints the thumbnail images.

> **TIP**   *Choose File | Page Setup to open the Page Setup dialog box. Adjust the settings in the Page Setup dialog box to change the page margins and add header and footer text to your printed album pages.*

Post an Album on the Web

If you have access to a web server and the ability to upload files to that server, you can use Album to produce all the files you need to create a web-based image album. The online album features a thumbnail index, individual pages for each image, and navigation links to facilitate browsing through the images. Album produces all the web pages and image files automatically. The only part you need to do manually is upload the files to your web server.

Here's the procedure for setting up your web album:

1. Open the album containing the images you want in the web album.

2. Select the thumbnails you want to include. CTRL-click to select multiple thumbnails.

3. Choose Thumbnail | Export | Web Album or click the Export Web Album button in the Tool panel. Album opens the Export to Web Album dialog box.

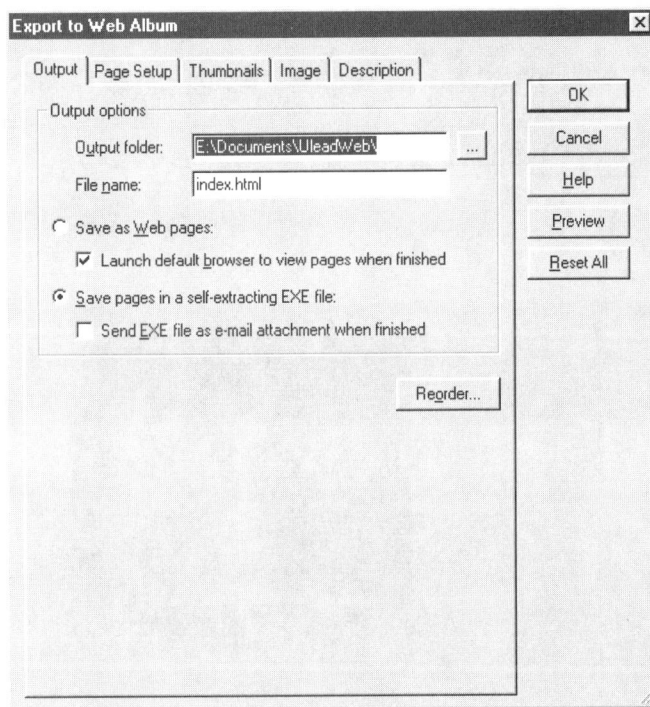

Export to Web Album

Output | Page Setup | Thumbnails | Image | Description |

Output options

Output folder: E:\Documents\UleadWeb\   ...

File name: index.html

○ Save as Web pages:
   ☑ Launch default browser to view pages when finished

● Save pages in a self-extracting EXE file:
   ☐ Send EXE file as e-mail attachment when finished

Reorder...

OK
Cancel
Help
Preview
Reset All

4. Adjust the settings on each tab of the Export to Web Album dialog box to match your needs and preferences. Most of the settings are strictly a matter of preference, so feel free to experiment. If you want to create a real web page, be sure to select Save As Web Pages on the Output tab.

> **CAUTION**   *Using the Save EXE File as E-mail Attachment When Finished option on the Output tab of the Export to Web Album dialog box is not recommended. Many e-mail systems automatically strip EXE files from e-mail attachments as an antivirus precaution. The chances are good that the intended recipient cannot or will not run an EXE file arriving attached to an e-mail message.*

5. Click the OK button. Album creates the necessary files for your web album and stores them in the folder you specified on the Output tab. If you selected the Launch Default Brower to View Pages When Finished option in the Export to Web Album dialog box, Album launches your web browser so you can view the resulting web pages, as shown in Figure 4-10.

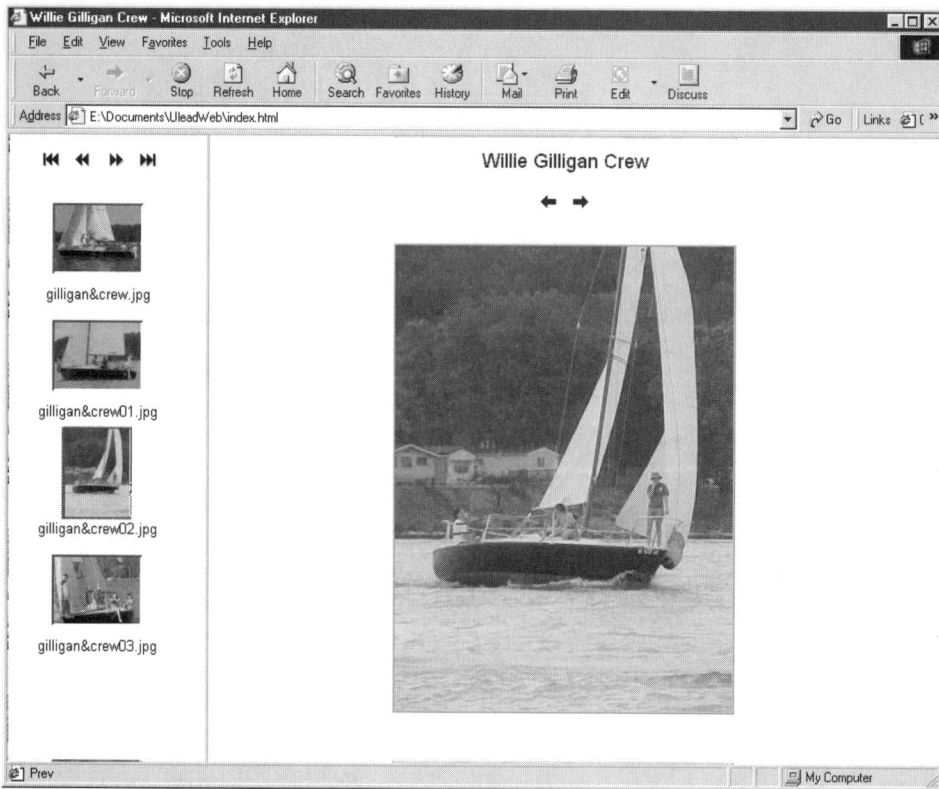

FIGURE 4-10   Previewing a web album created automatically by PhotoImpact Album

6. Transfer all the files created in the previous step to your web server. You can use the Web Publishing Wizard (Start | Programs | Accessories | Internet Tools | Web Publishing Wizard), your favorite FTP program, any other suitable Internet file transfer technique to post the files on your web site.

TIP   *You can also e-mail individual images from an album. Select the thumbnail of the image you want to e-mail, and then choose File | Send or click the Send Mail button in the Tool panel. Album uses your default e-mail client to open a new message window with the image(s) attached. Address the message, type in the subject and the message text, and then click Send to send it on its way.*

4

View a Slide Show

Another way to view images from an album is as an on-screen slide show. In its basic form, a slide show simply displays selected images on your screen one at a time. However, you slide show doesn't need to remain basic. Album supports a variety of transition effects, audio annotations, and music.

To create a basic slide show, follow these steps:

1. Open the album containing the images you want in your slide show.

2. Select the thumbnails you want to include in the slide show. CTRL-click to select multiple thumbnails.

3. Click the Slide Show button in the Tool panel. Album opens the Slide Show dialog box.

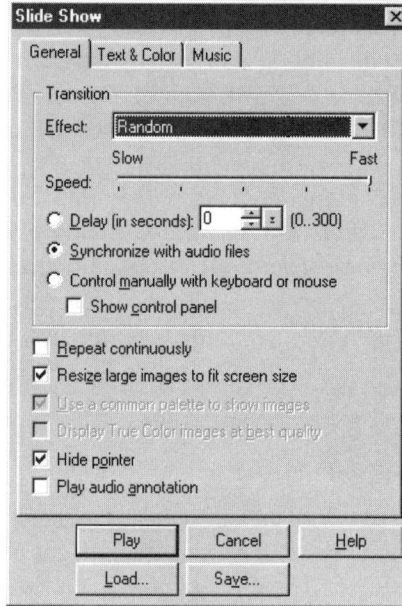

4. Adjust the settings in the Slide Show dialog box as needed. If you don't select the Control Manually with Keyboard or Mouse option (on the General tab), be sure to increase the Delay setting. Otherwise, the images will blink by too fast to see.

5. Click the Play button. Album closes the Slide Show dialog box and begins displaying the selected images in the slide show. The images and their background occupy the full screen, obscuring the Windows desktop and all its icons and windows.

TIP   *To control a slide show from the keyboard press the right arrow key to move forward and the left arrow key to move back. Press ESC to cancel the slide show and return to the normal Windows desktop.*

Copy an Album

One of the more useful features of Album is the ability to quickly replicate an album and all its source files in another folder. You can use this feature to create an album comprised of images drawn from a variety of folders scattered around your hard disk, and then copy all those images (and the album file, too) to a single folder or removable disk in one convenient operation. Copying all those files from their scattered locations manually would be a tedious process.

Album provides the Package Album feature for copying albums. To use this feature, open the album containing the images you want copy and choose Album | Package. Album opens the Package Album dialog box, shown in Figure 4-11.

In the Package Album dialog box, navigate to the folder to which you want to copy the album and its contents and click the OK button. Album closes the Package Album dialog box and copies the album files and all the image source files to the destination folder.

4

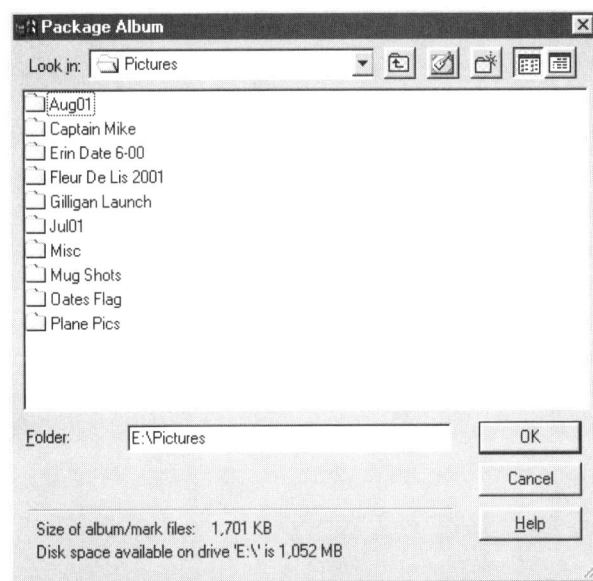

FIGURE 4-11   Album's Package Album dialog box

PART III

Create & Edit Images

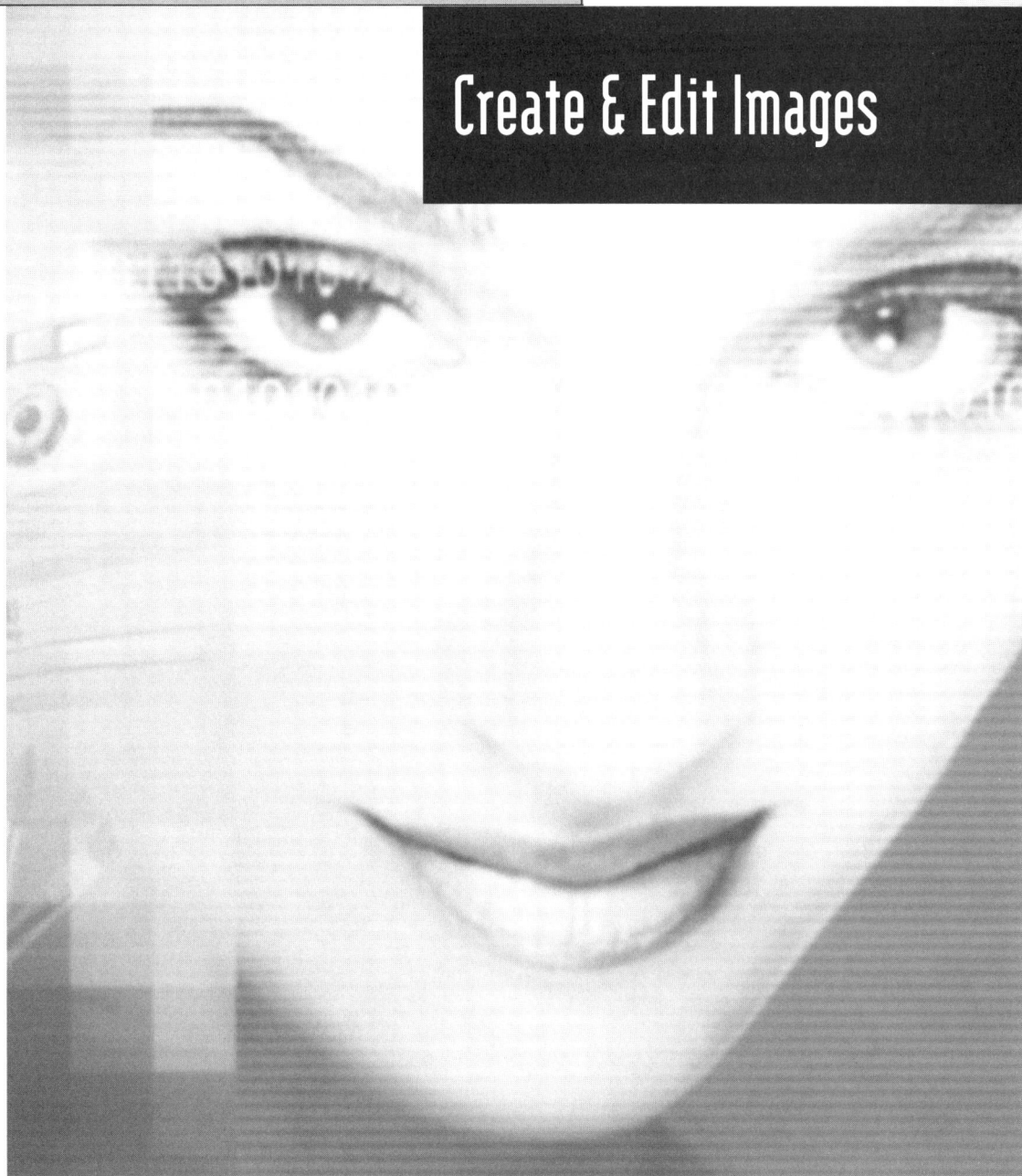

CHAPTER 5

Retouch and Enhance Photos

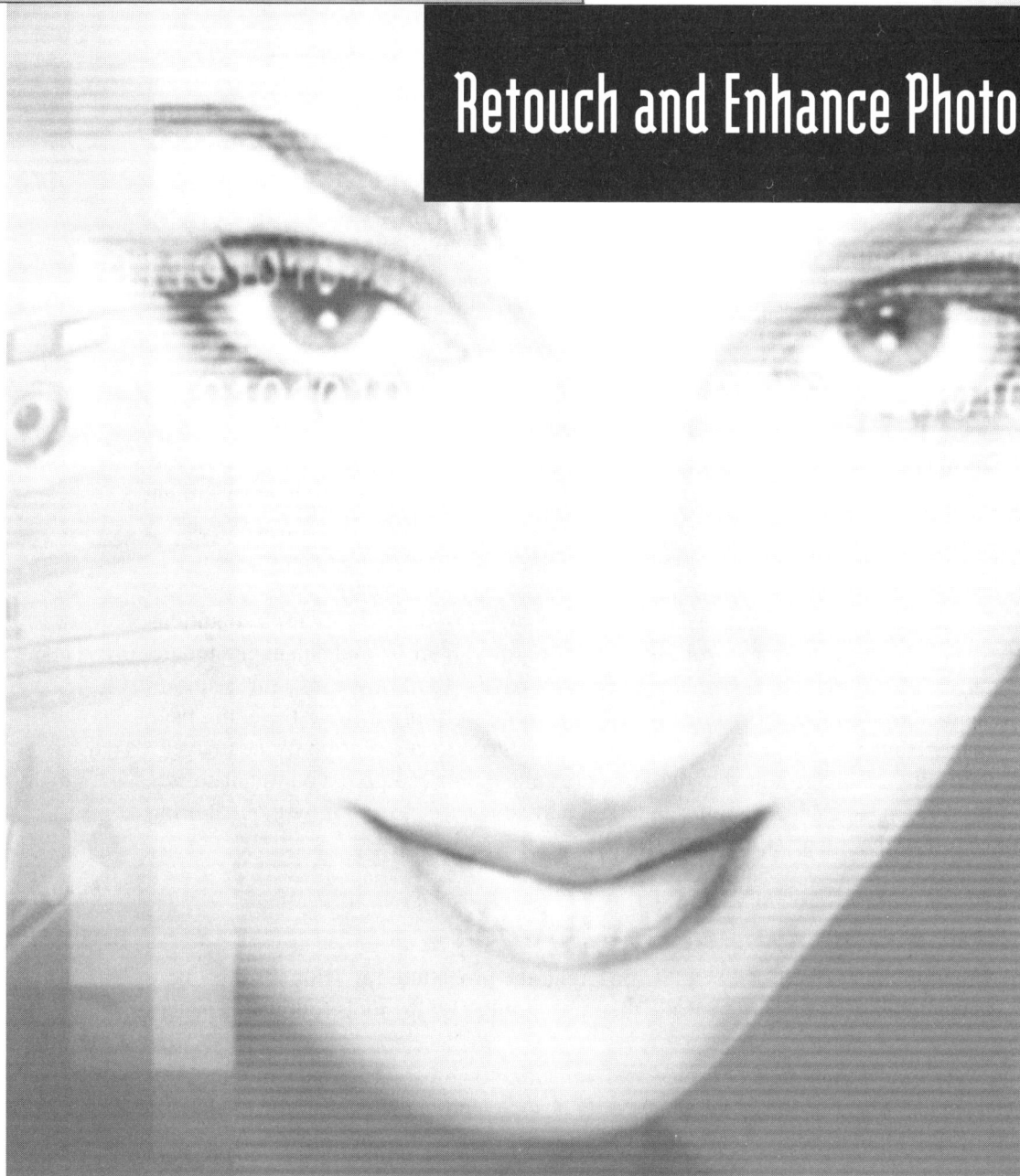

Photographs, whether scanned or shot with a digital camera, are rarely perfect in their raw state. They may be a little dark, off-color, or crooked; or they may have flaws such as scratches, dust spots, and the dreaded red-eye. That's why one of the most common uses of image-editing software such as PhotoImpact is to serve as a digital darkroom, where you can correct and repair such flaws. But you're not restricted to repairing obvious flaws in an image—you can use the same tools to enhance and improve your images.

This chapter covers how to enhance images with PhotoImpact's color, brightness, and focus controls; adjust the size and resolution of images; rotate and flip images; and use PhotoImpact's automatic enhancement tools. It also covers how to retouch images to repair and enhance local areas.

Enhance and Correct Images

One of the most common problems with a newly acquired image is that its overall brightness, contrast, or color balance may not be what it should be. The image might be too dark, lack contrast, or be off-color. Or perhaps the image itself is a reasonably good representation of the original scene, but you need to change the image to achieve a particular effect. For example, you might want to darken an image and give it a color cast to simulate a different time of day or different lighting conditions.

PhotoImpact includes a robust set of tools for correcting and enhancing tonal range, color, and other image characteristics. All the tools covered in this section can be found on the Format menu, and you normally apply them to the entire base image. However, you can use the selection tools to select a portion of the image and apply the image adjustment to that area alone. For example, you might select the sky in a landscape so you can darken and adjust the sky color, without altering the rest of the image at the same time.

Use the Image-Adjustment Tools

Although their effects can be quite different, the procedure for using most of the image-adjustment tools is basically the same. Almost all the tools follow this pattern:

1. Select the image or image area you want to adjust. Use a selection tool to select a portion of the image or choose Selection | None and then Selection | All to cancel any previous selection and select the entire image.

2. Open the Format menu and choose the command to perform the adjustment you want to make to your image. PhotoImpact opens a dialog box where you can adjust settings to control factors such as the strength of the effect and preview the effect with a thumbnail image.

3. Adjust the settings as needed to achieve the desired effect.

4. Click the OK button. PhotoImpact closes the dialog box and applies the image adjustment to your image or selection.

| NOTE | *Objects are not affected by the image-adjustment tools when you apply them to the base image or to a selected portion of the base image. However, you can use the Pick tool to select one or more objects and then apply an image adjustment to those objects.* |

Work with Image-Adjustment Thumbnails

Some of the dialog boxes for the image-adjustment commands present various option settings along with Before and After thumbnails to preview the change in your image as a result of the settings. In this kind of dialog box, you can adjust a setting and observe its effect on the After thumbnail.

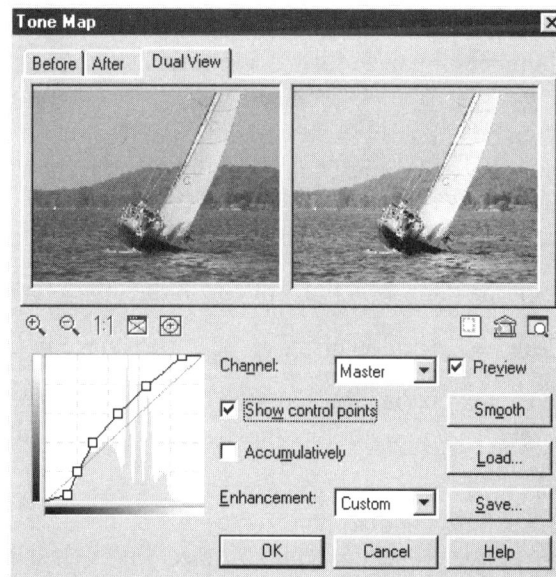

Other image-adjustment dialog boxes present an array of thumbnails representing an assortment of preset effects. Just click a thumbnail to select a preset or click the Options button to open another dialog box where you can manually set levels and other options for the chosen command.

When one or more thumbnails appear in a PhotoImpact dialog box, the thumbnail starts out showing the entire image. However, in most of those dialog boxes, you have the option to select which portion of the image appears in the thumbnail. Since the thumbnail is small, you may need to zoom in to enlarge the image in order to preview the effect adequately or to see the effect on a particular part of the image.

To adjust the thumbnail image, follow these steps.

1. Click the Thumbnail button or the Select Image Region for Preview Window icon. PhotoImpact opens the Thumbnail dialog box, shown in Figure 5-1. The larger thumbnail shows the entire image from which you can select a portion to display. The smaller thumbnail shows the result of your selection.

2. Choose one of the three selection options in the lower-right corner:

   ■ The Entire Image option displays the entire image in the thumbnail.

   ■ The Preset Box option places a small box on the larger image, which you drag to select a portion of the image for the thumbnail. The size of the box is preset.

   ■ The Drag to Select option lets you drag diagonally on the larger thumbnail to designate the corners of a box to select the enclosed portion of the image for the thumbnail. It's just like dragging to draw a rectangular selection area or path object.

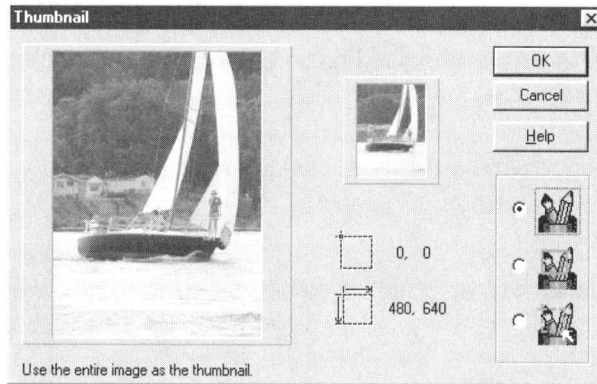

FIGURE 5-1 The Thumbnail dialog box allows you to adjust the thumbnail image.

3. Drag on the larger thumbnail to select a portion of the image.

4. Click the OK button to close the Thumbnail dialog box and return to the image-adjustment dialog box. PhotoImpact displays the selected portion of the image as the thumbnails in that dialog box.

Preview Image Adjustments and Other Effects

PhotoImpact provides several ways to preview changes to your image before they take effect. Thumbnail previews appear in most dialog boxes, and you often have the option to display a real-time preview in the document window as well. However, even with the real-time preview activated, it's sometimes hard to anticipate the full effect on your image until you close the dialog box and view the document window unobstructed. That's exactly what the Preview button allows you to do.

When you see the Preview button in a dialog box, you can click it to apply the current settings to your document temporarily. The Optimization Preview icon that appears below Before and After preview windows does the same thing. PhotoImpact replaces the dialog box you were using by a much smaller dialog box of the same name, as in this example:

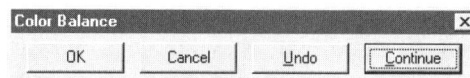

The preview dialog box contains just four buttons:

- Click OK to close the dialog box and make the changes permanent.

- Click Cancel to close the dialog box and abort the changes.

- Click Undo to remove the changes from the image in the document window. When you do, the button changes to Redo, and you can click it to reapply the changes.

- Click Continue to reopen the full dialog box so you can make further changes.

Adjust Tonal Range

Perhaps the most used of the image-adjustment commands are those that control the *tonal range*, or brightness and contrast, of your images. These are the tools you turn to when you need to lighten a dark image, darken a light image, or make adjustments to bring out the detail in highlights (lighter shades), midtones (middle shades), or shadows (darker shades).

The Brightness and Contrast quick-adjustment buttons on the Tool panel provide yet another way to make an image lighter or darker and to increase or decrease its contrast. While the quick-adjustment buttons are handy for fast, general brightness and contrast adjustments, the image-adjustment commands offer much more precision and flexibility.

At first, it may seem confusing to have multiple commands that do essentially the same thing: make the image lighter or darker. However, each of the commands differs in the way that changes you make to one part of the image (such as the midtones) affect other parts of the image (such as the shadows). Those differences make one command better suited to achieving certain effects and another command better suited to working with other images.

Brightness & Contrast

The Brightness & Contrast command enables you to precisely adjust the brightness, contrast, and gamma (tonal range of the target output device) of an image. Choose Format | Brightness & Contrast or press CTRL-B to open the Brightness & Contrast dialog box, shown in Figure 5-2.

The dialog box contains an array of nine thumbnail preview images, showing preset combinations of brightness and contrast settings. A tenth thumbnail in the upper-right corner shows the original image for reference. The thumbnail in the

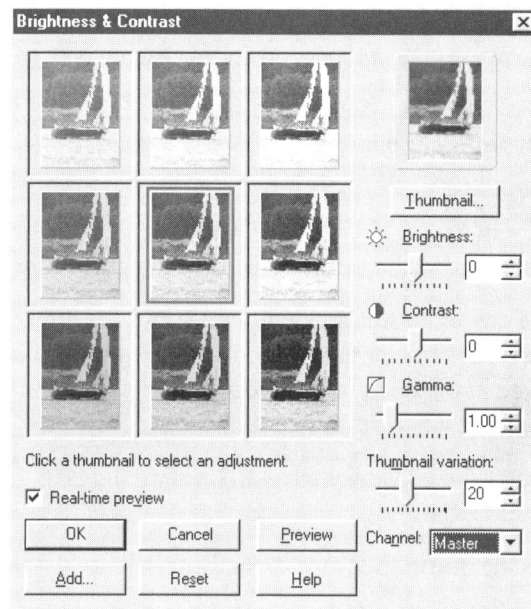

FIGURE 5-2   The Brightness & Contrast dialog box

center of the preview images shows the current settings. Changes in brightness are shown in the vertical axis of the array, and changes in contrast are shown horizontally.

Click one of the preview images to transfer settings to the center thumbnail and adjust the other preview images to show variations on those settings. The preview images are also interactive with the sliders and text boxes on the right side of the dialog box. The Brightness and Contrast settings reflect the values from the thumbnail at the center of the preview images and vice versa.

The Brightness & Contrast dialog box offers the following settings and options:

- **Thumbnail**   Displays the Thumbnail dialog box (see Figure 5-1), where you can change the portion of the image shown in the thumbnails, as described in the previous section.

- **Brightness**   Changes overall lightness/darkness. Higher numbers lighten the image.

- **Contrast**   Exaggerates or subdues the differences between midtone values. Higher numbers increase contrast.

- **Gamma** Changes the relationship of midtones in the image. Decreasing the gamma reduces the number of shades between black and white. Increasing the gamma increases the number and visual spacing between midtone shades.

- **Thumbnail Variation** Sets the amount of brightness/contrast change between adjacent thumbnails in the preview images.

- **Channel** Sets the color channel (Red, Green, Blue, or Master) to which the adjustments will apply. Normally, this setting remains on Master to apply brightness and contrast adjustments across the entire color spectrum evenly.

- **Real-Time Preview** Automatically previews the effects of your dialog box selections in the document window. With this option unchecked, the original image in the document window remains unchanged until you exit the dialog box.

- **Reset** Returns the preview images and other settings to their original values so you can start over.

- **Add** Adds the current settings to the EasyPalette.

- **Preview** Previews the changes in the document window with the option of accepting the changes or returning to the Brightness & Contrast dialog box.

Histogram

The Histogram command displays a graph that charts the distribution of color and tonal values in your image or in the selected portion of your image. You can't use this dialog box to adjust your image, but it can provide some useful information about your image, especially if you examine the histogram before using one of the commands (Tone Map or Highlight Midtone Shadow) that employs a scaled-down version of the histogram graph in its dialog box.

Choose Format | Histogram to open the Histogram dialog box, shown in Figure 5-3. Your only options are to select the color channel and whether to graph the values for the entire image or the currently selected area. The graph shows the relative distribution of image data across the tonal range, with black at the left end of the graph and white at the right end of the graph. Click the Close button to close the Histogram dialog box after examining its contents.

Highlight Midtone Shadow

The Highlight Midtone Shadow command enables you to quickly redistribute image tones. It's the quickest and simplest way to expand the range of an exceptionally dark image that lacks highlights or a washed-out image that lacks shadows. Choose Format | Highlight Midtone Shadow or press CTRL-SHIFT-H to open the Highlight Midtone Shadow dialog box.

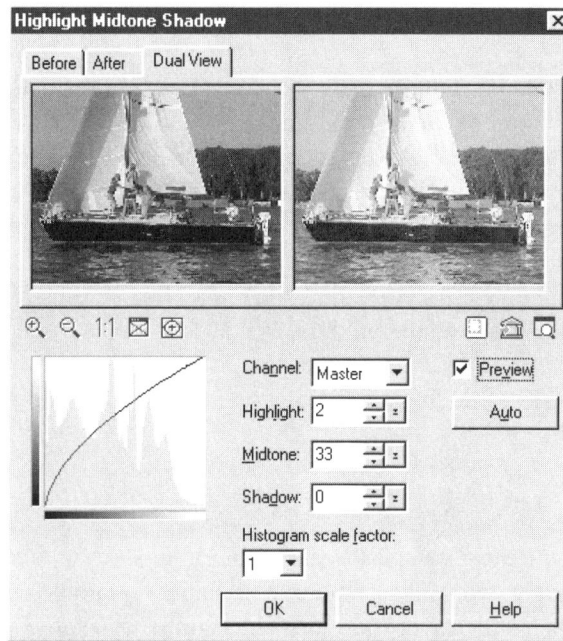

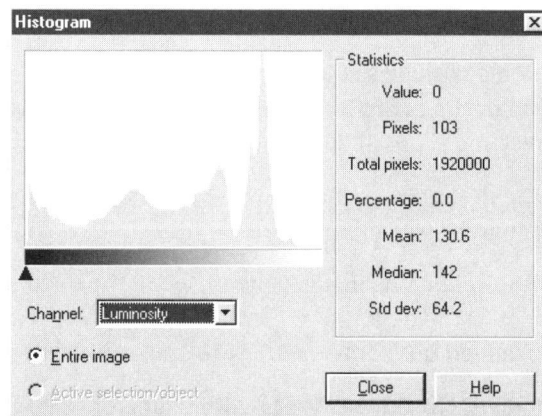

The Histogram dialog box

The Highlight Midtone Shadow dialog box features a set of preview box tabs at the top. You can click a tab to select the Before image, the After image, or Dual View to show side-by-side Before and After thumbnails. The icons below the preview box enable you to zoom the preview image, center it, select an image area to show in the thumbnails, add settings from the dialog box to the EasyPalette, or preview the effect.

The lower-left quadrant of the dialog box displays a mini-histogram graph showing the distribution of tones in the image. Superimposed on the histogram is a line that plots how tones will be remapped from the original image when you apply the command. The horizontal axis represents the current image tones, and the vertical axis represents the altered image tones. When the mapping line appears as a straight diagonal line from the lower-left corner to the upper-right corner, it indicates no change in the image tones. As you adjust the dialog box settings, you can see the mapping line change in the histogram box, as well as observe the effect on the image in the preview box.

The Highlight Midtone Shadow dialog box includes the following settings and options:

- **Channel**   Sets the color channel (Red, Green, Blue, or Master) to adjust.

- **Highlight**   Remaps shades at the highlight end of the tonal range (moves the upper-right end of the graph line in the histogram box). Basically, it redefines the white level and redistributes other tones from there.

- **Midtone**   Remaps midtones in the image (arches the middle of the graph line on the histogram box up or down). Positive number settings make the image lighter, negative number settings make the image darker.

- **Shadow**   Remaps shades at the shadow end of the tonal range (moves the lower-left end of the graph line in the histogram box). Shadow redefines the black level and redistributes other tones from there.

- **Histogram Scale Factor**   Increases the scale of the histogram graph to make the histogram plot more visible.

- **Preview**   Automatically changes the image in the document window to reflect changes in the dialog box. Uncheck Preview to leave the document window unchanged until you click OK to apply the dialog box settings.

- **Auto**   Automatically adjusts the Highlight and/or Shadow settings to use the range of shades in the histogram for the current image.

Tone Map

The Tone Map command is another way to redistribute image tones. It's similar to the Highlight Midtone Shadow command in some ways, but it offers more detailed control over image tones at the expense of being more tedious to use. Choose Format | Tone Map or press CTRL-SHIFT-T to open the Tone Map dialog box, shown in Figure 5-4.

The preview box tabs at the top of the Tone Map dialog box and the icons beneath the preview box work just like their counterparts in the Highlight Midtone Shadow dialog box. The histogram box in the lower-left quadrant of the dialog box is the main feature of the Tone Map dialog box. It's similar to one in the Highlight Midtone Shadow dialog box and displays the same information. The difference is that in the Tone Map dialog box you manipulate the mapping line in the histogram box directly, instead of adjusting settings elsewhere in the dialog box and observing their effect on the mapping line.

To adjust the distribution of tones in your image, simply drag the pointer in the histogram box to change the shape of the mapping line. The thumbnails in the preview box show the results of your tonal manipulations. The concept is simple, and it enables you to exercise control over any portion of the tonal range of your

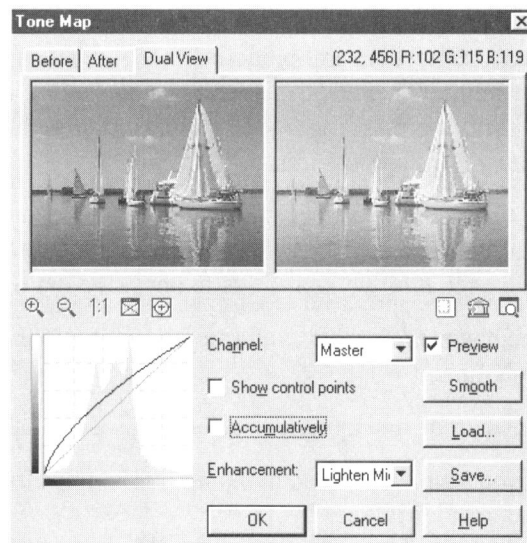

FIGURE 5-4   The Tone Map dialog box

image, not just the ends and the middle of the tonal range, as in the Highlight Midtone Shadow dialog box.

> **NOTE**   *Making precise adjustments to the mapping line in the histogram box can be a challenge, especially if you use a traditional mouse or a touch pad. You'll have better luck with this command if you have a steady hand and use a graphics tablet and pen stylus as your pointing device.*

In addition to dragging the mapping line in the histogram box, you can choose the following settings and options in the Tone Map dialog box:

- **Channel**   Sets the color channel (Red, Green, Blue, or Master) to adjust.

- **Show Control Points**   Adds handles (six small square boxes) to the mapping line. Manipulating the mapping line is significantly easier using the control points. You can just drag a handle to distort a section of the mapping line with no need to trace the entire section of the line with your pointer.

- **Accumulatively**   Causes each new change to the mapping line to accumulate and compound the effect of previous changes instead of referencing the original image.

- **Enhancement**   Offers several predefined mapping curves that you can apply to your image. There is also a Reset Curve setting in this drop-down list, which returns the mapping line to its original straight line so you can start over with your manipulations.

- **Preview**   Automatically changes the image in the document window to reflect changes in the dialog box. Uncheck Preview to leave the document window unchanged until you click OK to apply the dialog box settings.

- **Smooth**   Removes the handles and smoothes out minor bumps and dips in the mapping line.

- **Load**   Lets you load and apply a previously saved mapping line.

- **Save**   Lets you save the current mapping line settings to a file so you can apply them to another image.

Equalize

The Equalize command attempts to adjust automatically an image that is too dark. When you choose Format | Equalize, PhotoImpact instantly adjusts brightness, contrast, and color saturation to bring the image into a normal tonal range. No dialog box appears, and there are no settings you can adjust. If you don't like the effect, press CTRL-Z or choose Edit | Undo Before | Equalize to return your image to its previous state. This command works wonders on some images and fails miserably with others, but it's worth a try when you need to correct a dark image.

Adjust Colors

The next group of image-adjustment commands enables you to manipulate the color of your image. You can use these commands to correct an off-color image, add a color tint as a creative effect, create the look of a color negative, or posterize the image.

Color Balance

The Color Balance command adjusts all the colors in your image based on your color selections in the Color Balance dialog box. Typically, you use the Color Balance command to shift the image color slightly to compensate for an off-color image, much like adding a color filter when shooting a photograph. However, you can also use the Color Balance dialog box to create a major color shift by replacing one color in the image with another color.

Choose Format | Color Balance or press CTRL-L to open the Color Balance dialog box. By default, the Color Balance dialog box appears with the Preset tab active, as shown in Figure 5-5. (To see this dialog box in color, open ColorBalPre.tif in the CH05 folder on the CD.)

Add Colors   The Preset tab features an array of nine thumbnails. A tenth thumbnail in the upper-right corner of the dialog box shows the original image as a reference. The central thumbnail shows the current color balance setting, and the eight surrounding thumbnails show variations on that setting that result from adding a preset amount of different colors to the central image. Listed below are the colors added by each thumbnail, arranged to correspond to their position in the dialog box:

Green	Green and yellow	Yellow
Cyan	Current color setting	Red
Blue	Blue and magenta	Magenta

To adjust the color balance of your image, simply click one of the thumbnails. PhotoImpact moves the color settings from that thumbnail to the center position

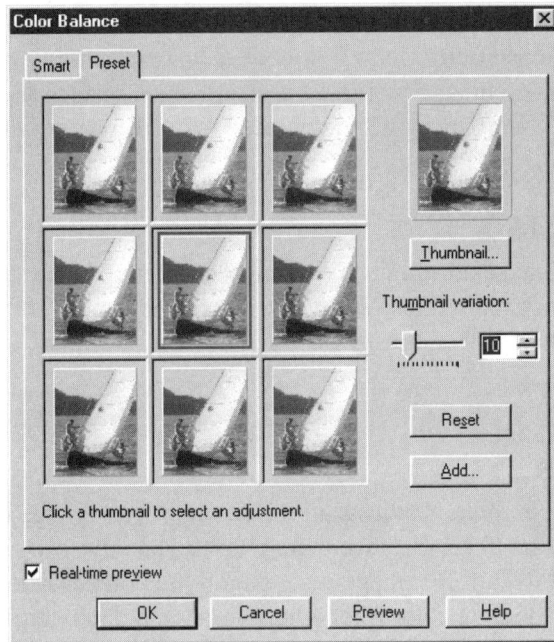

FIGURE 5-5   The Preset tab of the Color Balance dialog box

and displays a new set of variations. Repeat the process of clicking thumbnails until the center thumbnail shows the desired color balance, and then click OK to apply the settings to your image. The Preset tab also offers the following options:

- **Thumbnail**   Displays the Thumbnail dialog box, where you can change the portion of the image shown in the thumbnails. See the "Work with Image-Adjustment Thumbnails" section earlier in the chapter for details.

- **Thumbnail Variation**   Controls the amount of change from the central thumbnail to any one of the variations. Increase this value to make big changes; reduce the number to fine-tune the color.

- **Reset**   Returns the preview images and other settings to their original values, so you can start over.

- **Add**   Adds the current settings to the EasyPalette.

■ **Real-time Preview**   Automatically previews the effects of your dialog box selections in the document window. With this option unchecked the original image in the document window remains unchanged until you exit the dialog box.

■ **Preview**   Displays a preview of the changes in the document window with the option of accepting the changes or returning to the Color Balance dialog box.

Replace Colors   The Smart tab of the Color Balance dialog box, shown in Figure 5-6, allows you to select a color from your image and replace it with another color. The rest of the original image also shifts toward the selected replacement color. The result can be subtle if you choose a replacement color that is very close to the current color, or it can be quite dramatic if the replacement color is substantially different. (To see a color version of this dialog box, open ColorBalSmart.tif in the Ch05 folder on the CD.)

FIGURE 5-6   The Smart tab of the Color Balance dialog box

The Smart tab is dominated by a large box showing a portion of your original image. Use the scroll bars to view different areas of the image and the buttons below the image box to zoom in or out. The thumbnail image in the upper-right corner of the Smart tab previews the effect. Click the large image box to select the color you want to replace. PhotoImpact displays that color in the Current Color box. Then click the Desired Color color box to open the Ulead Color Picker dialog box, where you can select the replacement color.

Hue & Saturation

The Hue & Saturation command provides another way to adjust the color of an image. The Hue & Saturation dialog box controls enable you to adjust the hue (color), saturation (color intensity), and lightness (brightness) of the image (see Figure 5-7). The unique features of this command are its ability to shift the color of a selected portion of the spectrum without affecting other colors and to increase or decrease the intensity of the colors. You can also *colorize* the image—change it to a monochromatic image composed of shades of one color.

Choose Format | Hue & Saturation or press CTRL-E to open the Hue & Saturation dialog box. (To see a color version of this dialog box, open Hue&Sat.tif in the Ch05 folder on the CD.) This dialog box features Before and After thumbnails, similar to the Tone Map dialog box.

You can manipulate the image with the following controls:

- **Hue**   Shifts colors up and down the spectrum.

- **Saturation**   Increases or decreases the intensity of colors. Decreasing saturation removes color from the image, leaving more of a grayscale image. Increasing saturation makes colors more intense and garish.

- **Lightness**   Makes the image darker or lighter. You probably won't use this much, since the various tonal adjustments are more effective at adjusting image brightness. It's included here because lightness is part of the color model.

- **Master**   Applies color changes to the entire spectrum uniformly.

- **Range**   Allows you to select which part of the color spectrum is affected by the Hue, Saturation, and Lightness sliders. Four sliders appear between the color bars. Drag the sliders to select a range of colors to be affected. The dark-gray area between the color bars gets the full effect; the light-gray areas change less; and the white areas of the color spectrum are unaffected.

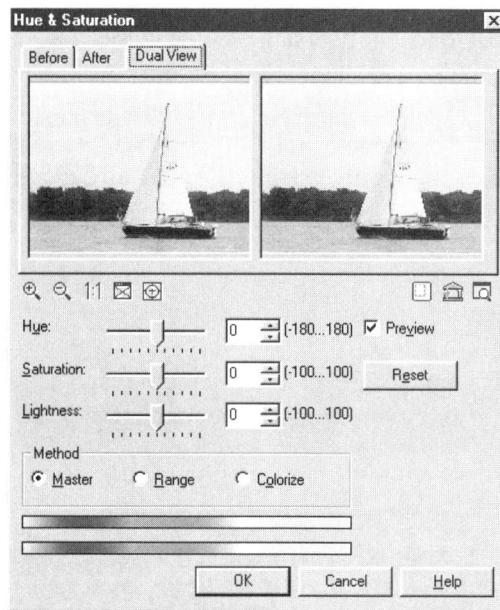

FIGURE 5-7   The Hue & Saturation dialog box

- **Colorize**   Changes colors to shades of the color you select. The bottom color bar becomes a solid color, and all colors in the image change to shades of that color. Drag the Hue slider to select the color of the bottom color bar.

- **Preview**   Automatically previews the effects of your dialog box selections in the document window. With this option unchecked the original image in the document window remains unchanged until you exit the dialog box.

- **Reset**   Returns the preview images and other settings to their original values so you can start over.

The top color spectrum bar at the bottom of the dialog box represents the colors in the current image. The bottom color bar represents the new colors. As you adjust the Hue, Saturation, and Lightness sliders, you can observe the way colors from the top bar will become colors in the bottom bar.

Invert

Choose Format | Invert to instantly change all the colors and shades in your image to the complementary color and shade. Reds become cyan; blues become yellow; darks become light; and lights become dark. This simulates the appearance of a photographic negative (without the orange tint of the typical color film base).

This command takes effect immediately. There is no dialog box that appears and no options that you can adjust. Figure 5-8 shows an example of using the Invert command.

Level

The Level command is more of a special-effect tool than a color-correction or enhancement tool. It enables you to adjust the number of *levels*, or shades, of

FIGURE 5-8   The Invert command creates an image the looks like a photographic negative.

each color that appears in the image. Typically, you use the Level command to drastically reduce the color levels and produce an abstracted, posterization effect.

Choose Format | Level to open the Level dialog box, shown in Figure 5-9. This dialog box contains an array of nine thumbnail previews, showing an assortment of preset level settings. To select one of the presets, simply click the thumbnail, and then click the OK button.

To exercise more control over the Level command, click the Options button. PhotoImpact opens another version of the Level dialog box, as shown in Figure 5-10. This dialog box has Before and After thumbnails at the top. You can adjust the Level and Channel controls to achieve the desired effect:

5

- **Level**   Sets the number of levels or shades of each color in the image. Reduce the number to create sharp bands and areas of color. Increase the number to create many subtle color divisions.

- **Channel**   Lets you select the color channel (Red, Green, Blue, or Master) you want to adjust.

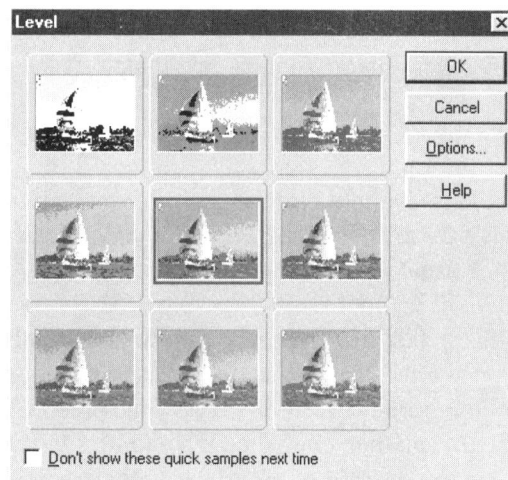

FIGURE 5-9   The Level dialog box with preset level adjustments

FIGURE 5-10   The Level dialog box with options

Other Image Enhancements

In addition to the brightness and color control commands, PhotoImpact offers a couple of other image-adjustment commands that are worth noting. The Focus command affects the apparent sharpness of your image. The Calculation command allows you to combine several images into a new image.

Focus

The Focus command enables you to blur the image or make it appear sharper. It's essentially an alternate way to apply the Blur and Sharpen effects. (More on filters in Chapter 6). Choose Format | Focus or press CTRL-SHIFT-F to open the Focus dialog box.

When the Focus dialog box first appears, it shows six thumbnails representing three levels of the sharpen effect across the top and three levels of blur effect across the bottom, as shown in Figure 5-11. To use one of the presets, simply click the corresponding thumbnail, and then click the OK button.

To exercise more control over the focus effects (and get a slightly better preview of the effect), click the Options button to open another version of the Focus dialog box, as shown in Figure 5-12. This dialog box includes Before and After thumbnails and option controls.

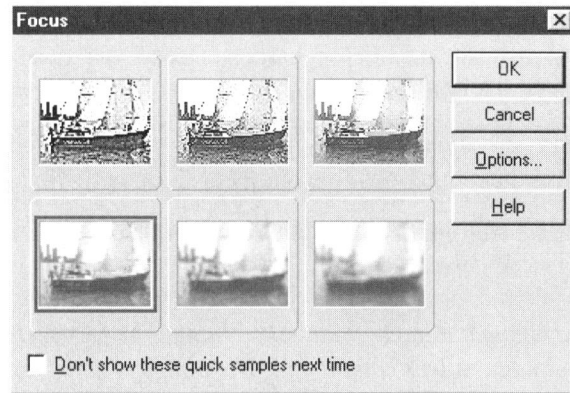

FIGURE 5-11 The Focus dialog box with preset sharpen and blur effects

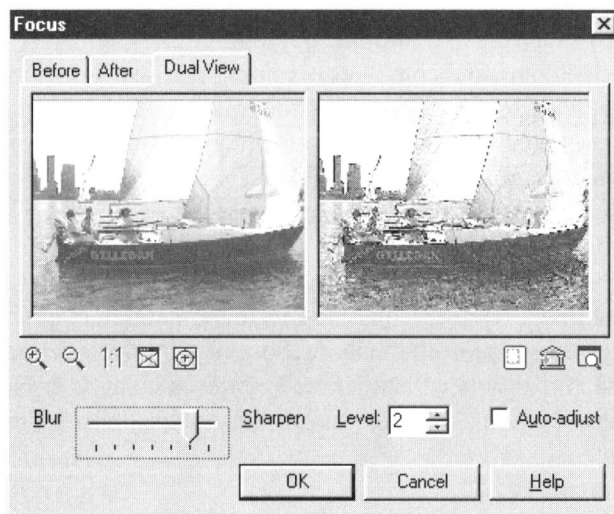

FIGURE 5-12 The Focus dialog box with options

The three controls in the options version of the dialog box work as follows:

- **Blur/Sharpen**   Sets the blur or sharpen effect. Drag the slider to the left to blur the image. Drag to the right to sharpen it.

- **Level**   Lets you adjust the blur/sharpen effect with a Level value. Negative numbers blur the image; positive numbers sharpen the image.

- **Auto-adjust**   Automatically applies the blur/sharpen setting PhotoImpact determines to be correct.

NOTE	*The Focus command doesn't actually change the focus of the image. Only the original camera lens can do that. The blur and sharpen settings simulate changes in focus by diffusing the image for a blur effect and enhancing edge contrast to simulate sharper focus.*

Calculation

The Calculation command is a special effect that allows you to overlay or superimpose two images to create a new, merged image. The result simulates a sandwich negative or a double-exposure effect in traditional photography.

The Calculation command combines two (or sometimes three) images and creates a new, separate image as a result. Consequently, the procedure for using the Calculation command is different from the image adjustment commands that alter the image in the active document window.

Before using the Calculation command, open each of the images you want to combine. The images must be exactly the same size and each image must be open in its own document window in PhotoImpact. Make any needed image adjustments to the component images before using the Calculation command. If the component images contain objects, you need to merge those objects with their respective base image; otherwise, the objects will be ignored by the calculation operation.

When you have both images open, follow these steps to merge them with the Calculation command:

1. Choose Format | Calculation. PhotoImpact opens the Calculation dialog. The dialog box contains four thumbnails: Foreground, Mask, Background, and a results preview.

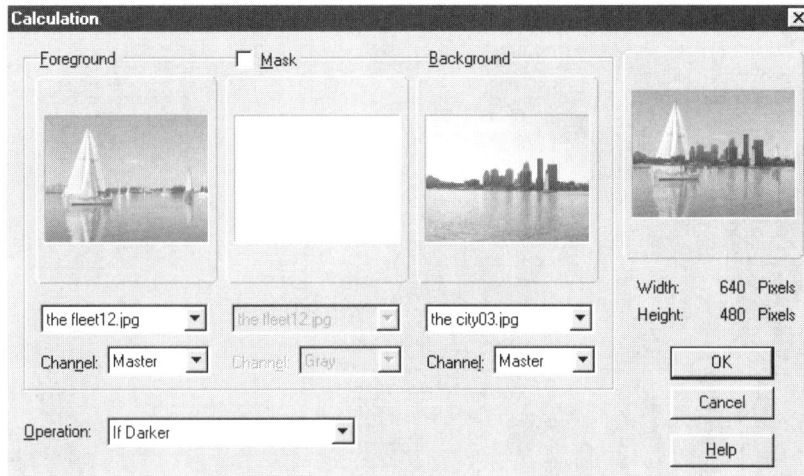

2. Select a filename in the drop-down list box below the Background thumbnail. This becomes the base image for the new image that will be created. Select a color channel in the Channel list box if desired.

3. Select a filename in the drop-down list box below the Foreground thumbnail. This image will be combined with the background image to produce a new image. Select a color channel in the Channel list box if desired.

4. Optionally, click the Mask checkbox and select a filename in the drop-down list box below the Mask thumbnail. The image you choose becomes a mask (a filter applied to the foreground image). Select a color channel in the Channel list box.

5. Select an option from the Operation list box to determine how the foreground image combines with the background image. Experiment with the various settings (start with Multiply) and observe their effect on the preview thumbnail.

6. Click the OK button. PhotoImpact closes the Calculation dialog box, creates a new image by combining image data from the foreground and background images, and displays the new image in a new document window in the PhotoImpact workspace. The original images remain unchanged in their respective document windows.

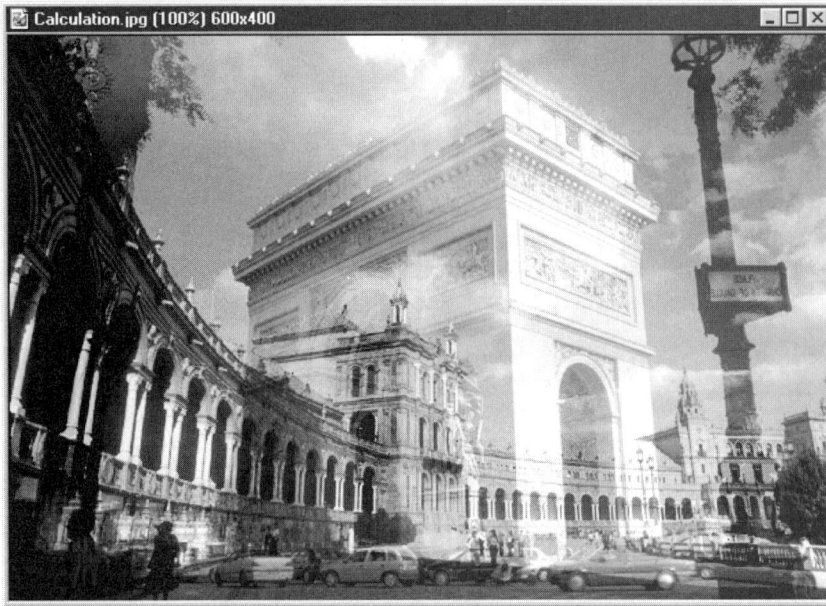

FIGURE 5-13   The Calculation command creates a new image by combining two
existing images.

Figure 5-13 shows an example of an image created with the Calculation
command.

Adjust Image Size and Resolution

As you work with your images in PhotoImpact, you will undoubtedly need to change
the image size and resolution from time to time. Although image size and resolution
may seem irrelevant when most programs allow you to resize any image by dragging
its borders, the appropriate size and resolution settings can eliminate the need to
resize an image in a target application. Image size and resolution settings can also
be important factors in optimizing the files you create in PhotoImpact for specific
uses, such as web page graphics or printed illustrations.

Adjust Image Resolution

The image-resolution setting in the image file tells a printer or program how big the image is supposed to be. It does this by defining the preferred spacing between pixels, which is expressed as a number of pixels per inch. Setting the correct resolution for an image before saving the image file can help ensure that the image displays and prints at the correct size when you import that image file into another application, such as a desktop publishing program. Since image resolution primarily affects printed output, it's an important consideration in desktop publishing and other applications where images are printed as hard copy, but image resolution is rarely a factor for web graphics.

5

You can change the image resolution without changing the file size or adversely affecting the image data, because you aren't changing any of the pixels that make up the image but only a setting that instructs the printer how to distribute pixels on a page.

To adjust the image size, follow these steps:

1. Choose Format | Resolution. PhotoImpact opens the Resolution dialog box.

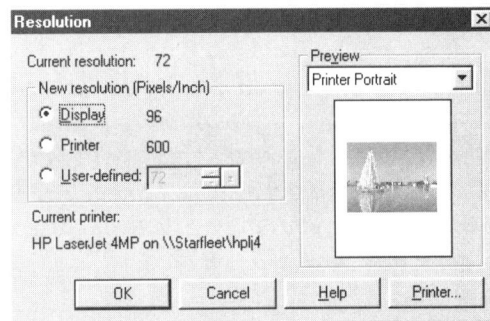

2. Select a paper or screen size from the Preview list box. The thumbnail preview shows the approximate size of the image on the selected output device at the resolution setting.

3. Select the desired resolution in the New Resolution area:

   ■ Click Display to select 96 pixels per inch (a common display resolution).

   ■ Click Printer to select 600 pixels per inch.

■ Click User Defined and select or enter the desired resolution in the adjacent spin box.

4. Click the OK button. PhotoImpact closes the Resolution dialog box and sets the desired resolution in the current image. This is the resolution that will be recorded into the image file when you save the image.

Adjust Image Size

The image size settings control the number of pixels used to record the image data. Unlike changing the image resolution, changing the image size significantly alters the image data by increasing or decreasing the total number of pixels in the image. When you change image size, PhotoImpact must resample the existing image and interpolate (guess) the correct color for each new pixel based on the image data for the surrounding pixels in the original image. The result is a new image that uses more or fewer pixels to approximate the appearance of the original image.

When you reduce the size of an image, PhotoImpact discards some image data to record the image as depicted with fewer pixels. This reduces the size of the image file. When you increase the size of an image, PhotoImpact must add pixels to the image, and the image file grows accordingly.

NOTE
It's important that web pages load and display as fast as possible. Because the download time for web graphics is directly proportional to the size of the image file, it's essential that web graphics files are as small as possible. Therefore, setting the correct image size for web is crucial. Create (or resize) web graphics to be exactly the size needed by the web page layout—not a pixel larger or smaller.

To resize an image, follow these steps:

1. Choose Format | Image Size or press CTRL-G. PhotoImpact opens the Image Size dialog box. In the upper-left corner, you see the dimensions and resolution of the original image.

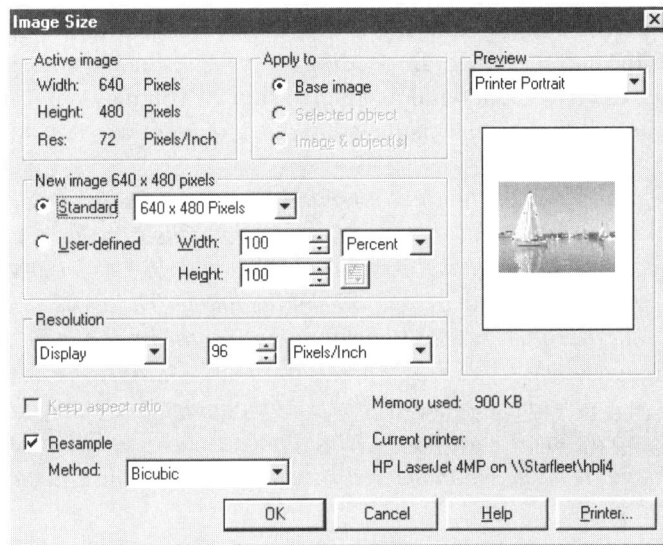

2. Adjust the settings in the Image Size dialog box as needed. As you make changes in the settings, the Memory Used readout shows the approximate size of the resized image file. You can adjust the following:

- **Apply to** Sets the part of the image you want to resize. You can choose Base Image, Selected Object, or Image & Objects.

- **New Image** Specifies the new size for the image. You can select one of several standard image sizes from the Standard drop-down list box. Alternatively, click User Defined and enter the Width and Height values measured in pixels, inches, or centimeters, or select a percentage of the original size.

- **Resolution** Sets the image resolution. Select one of the standard printer or display resolutions.

- **Keep Aspect Ratio** Prevents distortion of the image when setting the new image size.

- **Resample Method** Sets one of three methods for PhotoImpact to use when resampling the image to determine what each new pixel should be. The Nearest Neighbor method usually works best for very small images and for hard-edged graphics. The Bicubic and Bilinear methods are preferred for most photographic images.

3. Click the OK button. PhotoImpact closes the Image Size dialog box and resizes the current image. Depending on the size change you specified, you may see the document window change size, or you may only see a change in the image dimensions displayed in the document window's title bar.

> **TIP** *Unlike web graphics, images intended for printed output produce the best results if they are slightly oversized compared to their final output dimensions. The rule of thumb is that the image should contain 1.5–2.0 pixels for each dot in the halftone screen used to print the image. Therefore, if you're using a 150-line-per-inch screen to print an image, the optimum image size for that image would be 225–300 pixels per inch. Multiply the desired pixel count per inch times the desired size of the image to get the image size in pixels. So a 3-inch-wide image would need to be 675–900 pixels wide. An image that is bigger than needed is unnecessarily slow and cumbersome to work with.*

Flip, Flop, and Turn

How many times have you opened an image file only to discover that the image was upside down, lying on its side, or crooked? It happens to everyone from time to time. PhotoImpact includes commands to correct these (and other) orientation errors quickly and easily.

One common orientation problem is an image that is rotated out of its correct orientation. This happens most frequently when you hold the camera on end as you shoot in order to frame the image in a vertical (portrait) orientation instead of the normal horizontal (landscape) orientation. A few digital cameras can compensate for this orientation change, but most do not, and the resulting image looks as if lying on its side. Another variation of the same orientation problem is a scanned image that was scanned upside down or rotated, either accidentally or because the original wouldn't fit onto the scanner in the preferred orientation.

PhotoImpact gives you the option of making several standard orientation changes with simple menu commands. In addition to the rotation options you can also flip an image (create a mirror image). To change the orientation of an image, simply select the image or object you need to rotate, choose Edit | Rotate & Flip, and then choose the appropriate command from the submenu:

- The Rotate Left 90° command rotates the image counter-clockwise 90°.

- The Rotate Right 90° command rotates the image clockwise 90°.

- The Rotate 180° command rotates the image 180°, turning it upside down.

- The Flip Horizontally command creates a mirror image in which right becomes left.

- The Flip Vertically command creates a mirror image in which top becomes bottom.

- The Use Transform Tool command selects the Transform tool, which you can use to rotate, flip, or distort your image.

TIP *You can use the Transform tool to rotate an image freely, which comes in handy if you need to straighten an image that is slightly crooked.*

Automate the Process

PhotoImpact offers a wealth of image-adjustment tools. This chapter has covered some of the image-adjustment commands; others, such as the Crop and Transform tools, are covered elsewhere. You can use any of these tools individually to correct and enhance your images. However, PhotoImpact strives to make the process of enhancing images faster and easier by providing alternate ways to accomplish some of the same image adjustments. These alternatives automate or combine steps to simplify the image enhancement tasks you perform most frequently. This section covers two commonly used automated image-enhancement features: the Auto-process commands and the Post-processing Wizard. (Chapter 16, which is available online at www.osborne.com, covers styles, batch commands, and other more advanced automation features.)

Use Auto-process Commands

The Auto-process commands automatically apply common image adjustments such as brightness and contrast, hue and saturation, and focus to the current image. Using the Auto-process commands is fast and easy because they are automatic and preset.

Apply Automatic Image Adjustments

To adjust an image with an Auto-process command, choose Format | Auto-process and then choose an appropriate command from the submenu:

- The Brightness & Contrast command automatically adjusts image brightness and contrast, similar to using the Brightness & Contrast dialog box.

- The Hue & Saturation command automatically adjusts image color, similar to using the Color Balance dialog box. This command works best on images that are off-color as a result of being shot indoors without a flash or on images that have similar color shifts.

- The Focus command automatically sharpens or blurs the image, similar to using the Focus dialog box.

- The Straighten command automatically detects a straight line and attempts to make it horizontal or vertical.

- The Crop command automatically crops the image to eliminate large areas of solid color around the edges.

New to
PhotoImpact 7

- The Enhance command automatically applies the Format | Enhance command to lighten an image that is too dark.

Run Multiple Automatic Image Adjustments

The Batch command on the Auto-process submenu (Format | Auto-process | Batch) opens the Auto-process dialog box, where you can select multiple Auto-process commands to apply to an image. The Auto-process dialog box is shown in Figure 5-14.

This dialog box contains Before and After thumbnails and a row of buttons for the Auto-process commands. In addition to the commands that appear on the Auto-process menu, you have two other options:

- **Remove Moiré**   Removes the interference patterns caused by scanning pictures containing a halftone screen.

- **Despeckle**   Removes small spots and speckles.

Click a button to apply the command to the image. The row of icons at the bottom of the dialog box shows which commands are selected and the order in which they will be applied. Click OK to close the Auto-process dialog box and execute the selected commands.

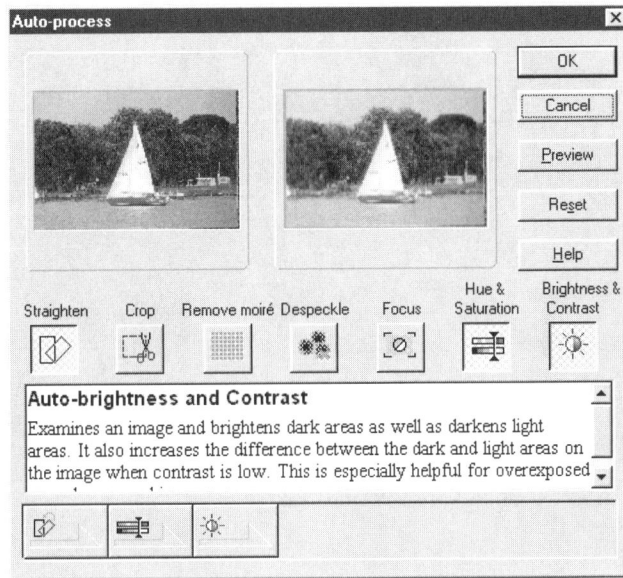

FIGURE 5-14   The Auto-process dialog box

Use the Post-processing Wizard

The Post-processing Wizard is designed specifically for addressing typical problems with scanned images. Its adjustments include straightening and cropping the image; adjusting focus, brightness, and color balance; removing red-eye; and even adding an optional frame and shadow. As the name implies, the Post-processing Wizard leads you step by step through the process, so you can control each adjustment.

The Post-processing Wizard is invoked automatically when you acquire an image from a scanner. You can also launch the wizard manually to apply its adjustments to an image from any source. Just choose Format | Post-processing Wizard or press F9 to start the Post-processing Wizard, as shown in Figure 5-15.

In the Post-processing Wizard dialog boxes, click the Next button to move to the next step or the Back button to return to the previous step. Click the Finish button to close the dialog box and skip the remaining steps. Each wizard page (except the first and last pages) also includes a button for a processing step. Clicking that button opens another dialog box, where you select the settings for that step in the process. Then click the OK button to close the dialog box, apply the image adjustment, and return to the Post-processing Wizard.

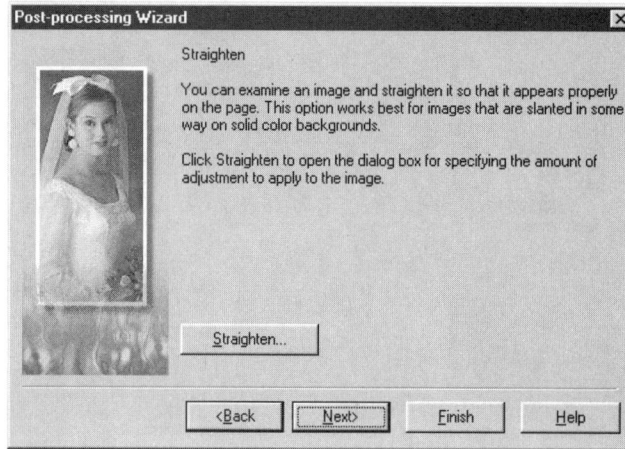

FIGURE 5-15   Starting the Post-processing Wizard

The Post-processing Wizard leads you through the following options:

■ **Straighten**   Opens the Straighten dialog box. Select Horizontal or Vertical to determine the orientation of the control line superimposed on the large thumbnail. Drag the handles at each end of the control line to align it with a picture element that should be horizontal or vertical.

- **Crop**   Opens the Crop dialog box. Drag on the preview thumbnail to define a rectangle outlining image area you want to keep. This creates a selection box with handles at the corners and sides. Drag the handles to fine-tune the selection box. Click the button with the scissors icon to preview the effect.

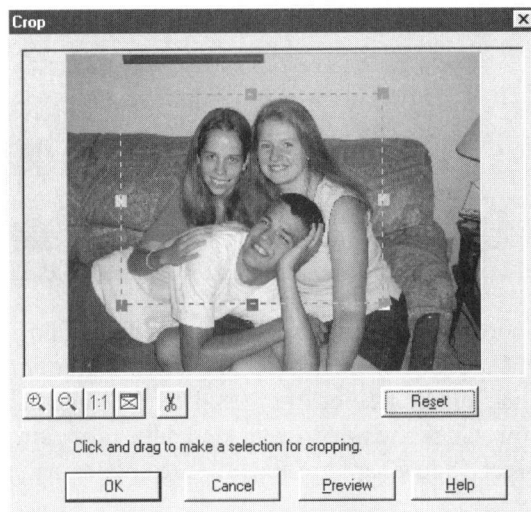

- **Focus**   Opens the Focus dialog box—the same one that appears when you choose the Format | Focus command (see Figure 5-11). Click a preset thumbnail to select the sharpen or blur effect or click the Options button to open another dialog box with more detailed option settings (see Figure 5-12).

- **Brightness**   Opens the Brightness dialog box—a slightly simplified version of the dialog box that appears when you choose the Format | Brightness & Contrast command. Click a preset thumbnail to select the brightness adjustment or click the Advanced button to open the full Brightness & Contrast dialog box with more detailed option settings (see Figure 5-2).

- **Color Balance**   Opens the Color Balance dialog box—the same one that appears when you choose the Format | Color Balance command (see Figure 5-5). Click a preset thumbnail to select the desired color adjustment.

- **Remove Red Eye**   Opens the Remove Red Eye dialog box. Adjust the selections in the in the Select Area for Filtering area to control the number and size of the selection circles in the left thumbnail. The red-eye filtering occurs only within these circles. Drag the circle(s) onto the subject's eyes. Adjust the color boxes and the Red Tolerance and Effect Level sliders if needed.

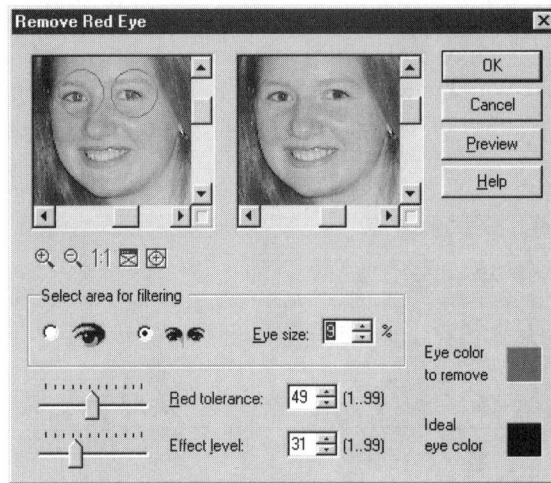

- **Frame & Shadow** Opens the Frame & Shadow dialog box, shown in Figure 5-16. On the Frame tab, select a general frame style from the Style drop-down list, and then select the specific frame and adjust its options in the area below. Click the Shadow tab and adjust the settings there to define a shadow effect. (See Chapter 6 for full instructions on using frames and shadow effects.)

Retouch Photos

Image adjustments—such as brightness, contrast, and color balance changes—are almost always applied to the entire image or to relatively large areas of the image. They are important tools for enhancing your images, but they don't address the need for the more localized enhancements that many images need. Perhaps you need to lighten a shadowed face to bring out the detail, or darken a distracting highlight. A scanned image might be marred by scratches and dust spots, or a portrait disfigured by red-eye and exaggerated wrinkles and blemishes. To correct these and other problems, you need to edit the image on the pixel level.

PhotoImpact's tools provide unlimited capability to draw, redraw, retouch, and edit pixels in any image. (See Chapter 2 for basic coverage of how to use the various tools.) You can use any of the Paint tools, the Clone tools, and the Retouch tools in a variety of mundane or imaginative ways to alter existing images or to create new ones. However, there are a few tools and techniques that are particularly well suited to

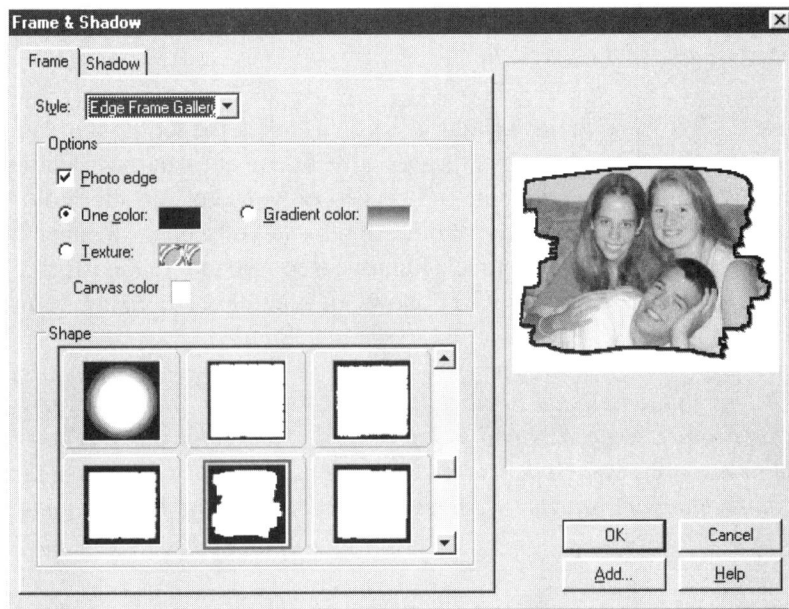

FIGURE 5-16   The Frame and Shadow dialog box

dealing with common image flaws. The following sections describe the ones you're likely to use most often.

Remove Red Eye

The red-eye effect is an unfortunately common side effect of flash photography. When a photographic subject looks directly at the camera lens, light from the flash can travel into the subject's eye, reflect off the blood-red retina, and then be focused back into the camera by the lens of the subject's eye. The result is a bright red spot where the pupil of the subject's eye should be. Red eye can give the most angelic child a demonic appearance.

Removing red eye is actually fairly simple. You just replace the bright red spot in the subject's eye with black to give the pupil of the eye a more natural appearance. It's simple in theory, but not so simple to do with a tool like the Paintbrush, because you need to work precisely to accurately touch up a very small spot. You could work at extreme magnification, but PhotoImpact provides a special tool, appropriately named the Remove Red Eye tool, to make the job easier.

> **TIP**   *Another way to remove red-eye is to use the Remove Red Eye dialog box. Choose Effect | Camera Lens | Remove Red Eye to open the dialog box. See Chapter 6 for full details.*

To use the Retouch-Remove Red Eye tool, just click the tool in the Tool panel and then click or drag on the subject's eye in the document window. PhotoImpact automatically replaces red with black. If necessary, you can adjust the colors, tolerance, and strength of the effect on the Options tab of the Brush panel. You can also adjust the size of the Retouch-Remove Red Eye tool in the Brush panel or in the Attribute toolbar. Figure 5-17 shows an example of an image before and after using the Retouch Red-Eye tool.

> **TIP**   *Although the Retouch-Remove Red Eye tool's name implies a very specific application, you can actually use it to replace any color with any other color. For example, you could use it to change the color of a logo in a photo by making the appropriate changes to the settings in the Brush panel.*

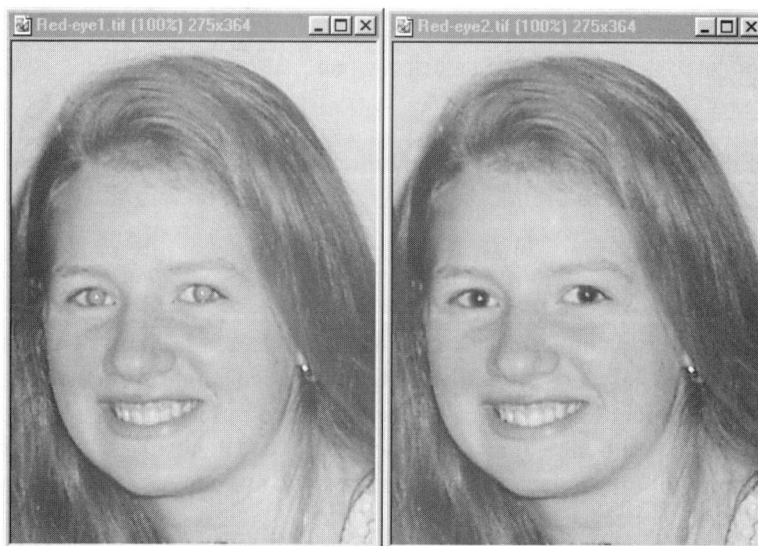

FIGURE 5-17   The Retouch-Remove Red Eye tool quickly repairs the glaring red eyes that often appear in flash photos.

Soften Blemishes

Another problem you might encounter in photographs of people is emphasized flaws, such as wrinkles or blemishes. You can try using the Retouch-Blur tool to soften these imperfections. The Retouch-Blur tool enables you to selectively soften some blemishes without overcorrecting other areas and thus making your corrections look too artificial.

> **TIP** *Check out the Beautify Skin effect filter if you need to smooth skin tones throughout an image. See Chapter 6 for details.*

Remove Scratches and Noise

Another common problem with many images is scratches or other unwanted lines. Dust spots and scratches usually appear as hard-edged spots and lines. Again, you could use a variety of different painting tools to carefully touch up the scratches, but PhotoImpact includes a special tool, called Retouch-Remove Scratch, for just this purpose. This tool works best on hard-edged spots and lines that contrast strongly with their surroundings.

To use the Retouch-Remove Scratch tool, click the tool in the Tool panel, and then click or drag on the scratch or dust spot in the document window. PhotoImpact fills in the scratch with a blend of colors from the surrounding pixels. You can adjust the size of the tool and other options in the Brush panel and in the Attribute toolbar.

> **TIP** *Use the Retouch-Remove Scratch tool to tone down or eliminate distracting specular highlights and reflections.*

You can also use the Retouch-Remove Noise tool to remove spots, dots, and specks in your image. As you drag the tool on your image, it detects clumps of pixels that differ significantly from the surrounding pixels and replaces them with an average color from the surroundings. The effect is similar to using the Retouch-Remove Scratch tool.

Lighten and Darken Areas

The Dodge and Burn tools enable you to selectively lighten and darken areas of your image. These tools are named after traditional photographic printing techniques.

In a photographic darkroom, the photographer can use a tool called a dodger to cast a shadow on an area of the photographic paper during part of the time while it is being exposed under the enlarger, thus reducing the exposure that area receives and making it lighter on the finished print. To make an area of the photographic print darker, a piece of cardboard with a hole in it is held over the photographic paper during an extra exposure, thus allowing extra light to "burn" into a selected portion of the image to make it darker.

Use the Retouch-Dodge tool to lighten and the Retouch-Burn tool to darken, as follows:

- **Dodge**   To make an area of your image lighter, click the Retouch-Dodge tool button in the Tool panel, and then drag the tool on the image in the document window. To increase the effect, drag the pointer back and forth over the area you want to lighten. You can adjust the size of the tool and other options in the Attribute toolbar or in the Brush panel.

- **Burn**   To make an area of your image darker, click the Retouch-Burn tool button in the Tool panel, and then drag the tool on the image in the document window. Like the Dodge tool, the effect is additive, so you can drag back and forth over the area to increase the effect. Options for the Burn tool are available in the Attribute toolbar and in the Brush panel.

Both the Retouch-Dodge and Retouch-Burn tools make subtle changes in your image. Plan on making several passes back and forth over the area to achieve the desired effect.

Use a fairly large brush size with a large, soft edge setting with the Dodge and Burn tools to help blend the effects into the surrounding image areas. If you need a sharp edge to a dodged or blended area, first select the area you want to manipulate and then apply the tool. The selection edge will protect adjacent image areas from the effect of the tool.

Replace Distracting Elements

You can use the Clone-Paintbrush tool to remove distracting elements and replace them with samples of the surrounding image. Removing powerlines from a sky is a classic application of this tool. The powerlines and tower shown in the left image in Figure 5-18 were too indistinct to respond to the Retouch-Remove Scratch tool,

FIGURE 5-18 The Clone-Paintbrush removes unwanted powerlines by painting over them with pixels copied from another part of the sky.

but the Clone-Paintbrush obliterated them easily. The same tool, combined with some careful selections, removed the bridge pier from behind the sail.

To make the other changes shown in Figure 5-18, the Retouch-Remove Scratch tool was used on the distracting white line across the bridge. A few passes with the Retouch-Dodge tool lightened the side of the boat to make the name more visible.

Of course, the tools mentioned in this chapter aren't the only ones you can use to fix flaws in your images. You can use any and all of the various pixel-editing tools, including all of the Paint, Retouch, and Clone brushes, as well as the selection and eraser tools, to edit and enhance images. All the basic pixel editing tools are covered in Chapter 2.

CHAPTER 6

Edit Images with Effect Filters

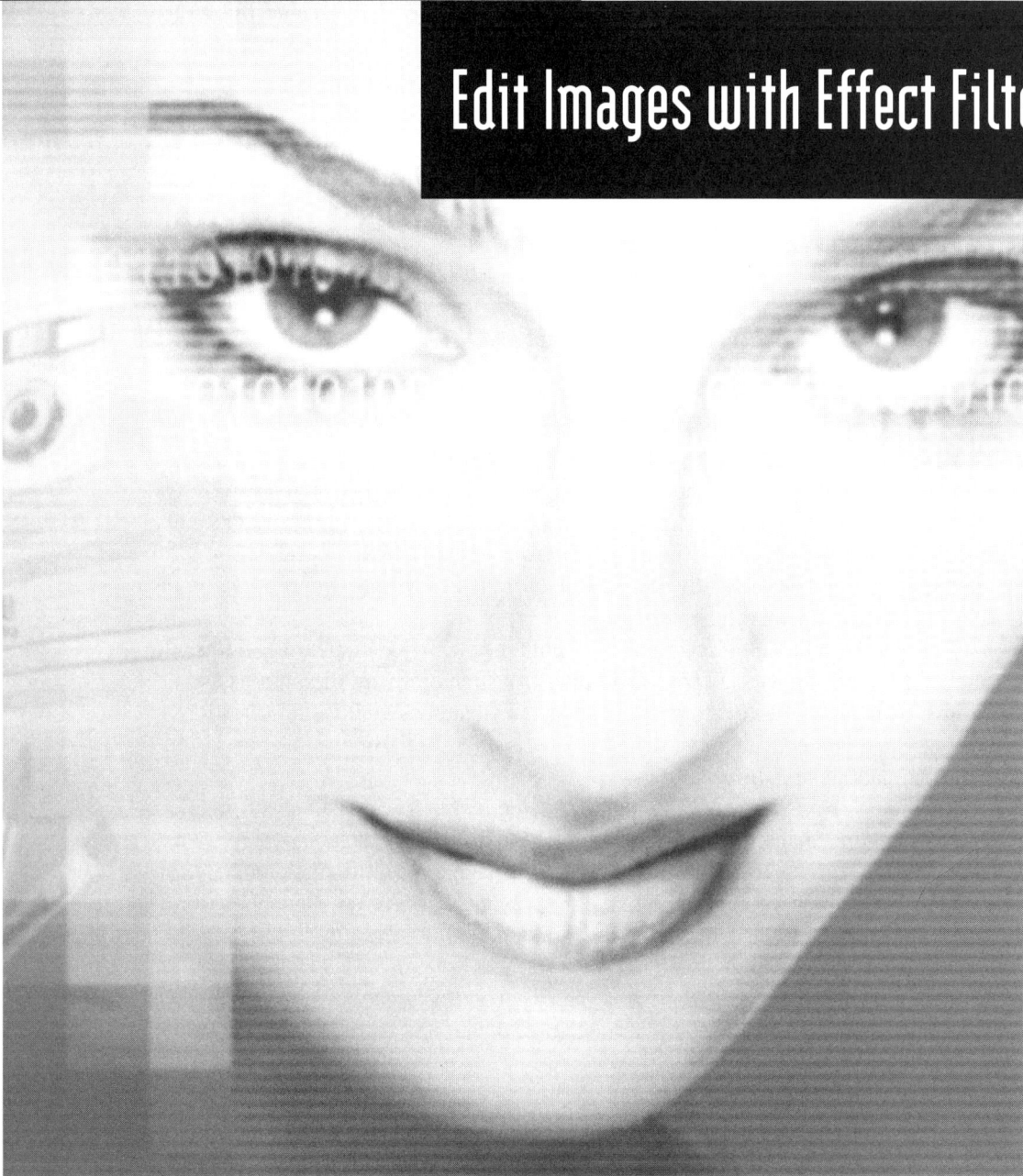

This chapter continues the trend started in the last chapter of describing PhotoImpact's tools for editing and manipulating images. While the last chapter focused primarily on tools for correcting common problems in images, this chapter focuses on tools for enhancing images and adding artistic pizzazz and special effects.

This is fun stuff! The various filters and other effects are fast and easy to use (and just as fast and easy to undo), which helps to encourage experimentation. And the variety of effects available in PhotoImpact means that you have a lot of possibilities to explore.

This chapter doesn't attempt to be a comprehensive survey of all the effect filters available in PhotoImpact. While it covers all of the "standard" effect filters, plus the Fadeout feature and the Frames & Shadows features, several of the special-purpose filters and plugins are reserved for later chapters.

Apply Effect Filters

Effect filters enable you to alter and enhance images in all sorts of interesting ways. You can sharpen or blur an image, simulate camera lens distortions and motion streaks, or create a ripple effect that makes your image look like a reflection on rippling water. You can distort your image or transform it into an oil or watercolor painting. And that's just the beginning.

The list of available effect filters is a long one, with 40 "standard" effects and another 17 special-purpose effects and plugins. Then there are the options and settings that can change a filter's effect on your image, as well as the variations you get when you combine two or more effects on a single image. The variations and permutations are almost endless.

As with the Format menu commands covered in the previous chapter, the effects described in this chapter are normally applied to an entire image. However, you can also apply effects to a selected area of the image or to an image object. Most of the effects can be applied to path and text objects as well, but since they don't usually have much effect on solid colors and small areas, there's seldom any point in doing so.

The effect filters on the Effects menu share another trait with the Format commands: The basic procedure for applying almost all of the effects is essentially the same.

The results of different effect filters may differ greatly, but the steps for applying almost all the effects follow this pattern:

1. Select the image or image area you want to adjust. Use a selection tool to select a portion of the image or choose Selection | None and then Selection | All to cancel any previous selection and select the entire image.

2. From the Effect menu, choose the category of the filter you wish to apply, and then choose the specific effect filter from the submenu that appears. In most cases, PhotoImpact opens a dialog box with a selection of preset thumbnails. Some of the effect filters skip this dialog box and go directly to the options dialog box (step 4).

3. If you like one of the preset thumbnails, click it to select the preset option settings for the effect filter. Otherwise, click the Options button to display another version of the effect's dialog box, where you can manually set levels and other options for the chosen effect and preview the result in Before and After thumbnails. Some of the effect filters skip this step and go directly to the options dialog box without showing the preset thumbnails.

4. Select or adjust the settings as needed to achieve the desired effect. As you adjust a setting, you can observe its effect on the After thumbnail.

5. Click the OK button. PhotoImpact closes the dialog box and applies the effect filter to your image or selection.

Because there are so many effect filters available in PhotoImpact, the available effects are arranged into a series of submenus in the Effect menu. The following sections of this chapter group the effect descriptions according to the same submenu groupings that PhotoImpact uses on the Effect menu.

| TIP | *As if the built-in effects filters that come with PhotoImpact aren't enough, the program can also use Photoshop-compatible plugins available from a variety of sources to expand the list of available filters. Choose File | Preferences | General to open the Preferences dialog box and select the Plugins category to specify the locations of the plugin files. For more details, see Chapter 17, which is available at the Osborne online site (www.osborne.com).* |

Use Blur & Sharpen Effects

The Blur & Sharpen submenu contains a selection of seven effect filters that enable you to blur or diffuse an image, make an image appear sharper, or detect and accentuate edges.

Blur Effect

The Blur filter produces an out-of-focus effect. It's useful for producing a soft, romantic mood or for subduing blemishes and wrinkles in a portrait.

When you choose Effect | Blur & Sharpen | Blur, the initial dialog box offers thumbnails for three presets. Clicking the Options button displays a larger Blur dialog box that still only offers a choice of three levels of blurring, but the larger Before and After preview thumbnails give you a better preview of the effect. To see an example of the Blur effect, see Blur&Sharp_Before.tif and Blur_After.tif in the Ch06 folder on the CD.

Average Effect

The Average effect filter produces a stronger blurring effect than the Blur filter. It softens the image by changing each pixel to make it closer to the average of the surrounding pixels. The larger the group of pixels PhotoImpact uses for its averaging calculations, the stronger the effect.

Choosing Effect | Blur & Sharpen | Average displays an initial dialog box giving you a choice of seven preset thumbnails. Click the Options button to display a larger Average dialog box, where you can adjust the size of the averaging zone directly and preview the effect in the Before and After thumbnails. To see an example of the Average effect, see Blur&Sharp_Before.tif and Average_After.tif in the Ch06 folder on the CD.

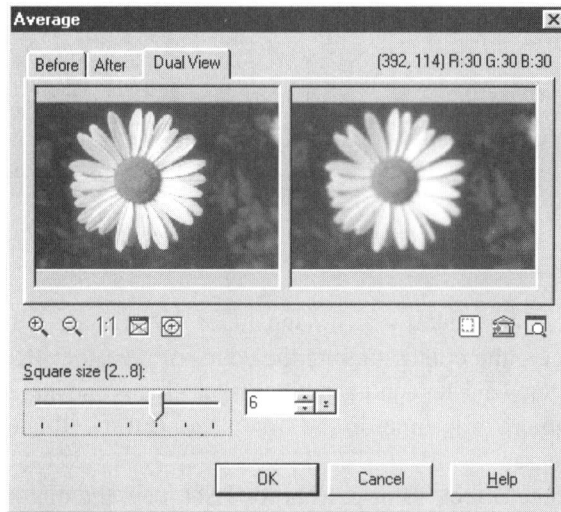

Gaussian Blur Effect

The Gaussian Blur filter is the strongest of the blur effects. You can vary the effect across a range from gentle diffusion (much like the Blur effect) to a total blur that renders your image as an unrecognizable blend of colors.

Like the other Blur effects, choosing Effect | Blur & Sharpen | Gaussian Blur displays a dialog box of preset thumbnails. Select one of the nine presets or click the Options button to display the full Gaussian Blur dialog box, where you can specify the blur level with the Variance box. To see an example of the Gaussian Blur effect, see Blur&Sharp_Before.tif and Gaussian_After.tif in the Ch06 folder on the CD.

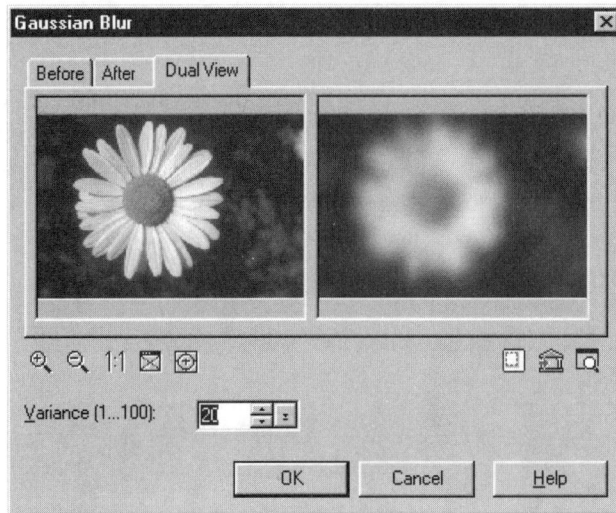

Sharpen Effect

The Sharpen effect filter makes your image appear to be sharper and more crisply focused by enhancing the contrast along the edges of areas of different colors and shades. It's an illusion—a filter can't actually sharpen focus and add detail that wasn't captured by the camera or scanner in the first place. But the illusion can be very effective in some cases.

When you choose Effect | Blur & Sharpen | Sharpen, the dialog box initially presents five preset thumbnails for your selection. Click the Options button to display the full Sharpen dialog box. The Level slider still gives you a choice of only five intensities for the effect, but the Before and After thumbnails provide a better preview than the presets. To see an example of the Sharpen effect, see Blur&Sharp_Before.tif and Sharpen_After.tif in the Ch06 folder on the CD.

Unsharp Mask Effect

Despite its name, the Unsharp Mask effect filter actually increases the apparent sharpness of an image. It does so by increasing the contrast of adjacent pixels along edges of areas of different brightness. It's basically a supercharged version of the Sharpen effect filter that offers a greater range of the effect and more control over the settings.

When you choose Effect | Blur & Sharpen | Unsharp Mask, the initial dialog box contains nine preset thumbnails. Select one of the presets or click the Options button to open the main Unsharp Mask dialog box.

In the main dialog box, you can adjust two settings: the Sharpen Factor and the Aperture Radius.

- **Sharpen Factor** Determines the degree of contrast change. Higher values increase contrast.

- **Aperture Radius** Determines the size of the circle of pixels PhotoImpact uses to calculate changes in the image. Increase the setting to apply the contrast change to larger areas of the image, and decrease it to accentuate details and texture.

> **NOTE** *To see an example of the Unsharp effect, see Blur&Sharp_Before.tif and Unsharp_After.tif in the Ch06 folder on the CD.*

Emphasize Edges Effect

The Emphasize Edges effect filter detects the edges of areas of differing brightness and enhances them by exaggerating the contrast of adjacent pixels. If you're thinking that this sounds like what the Sharpen and Unsharp Mask filters do, you're right. The difference is that the Emphasize Edges filter produces a more exaggerated effect. In fact, the lowest setting of the Emphasize Edges filter produces results similar to the Unsharp Mask filter set to the highest Sharpen Factor setting and the lowest Aperture Radius setting.

When you choose Effect | Blur & Sharpen | Emphasize Edges, the dialog box initially presents five preset thumbnails for your selection. Click the Options button to display the full Emphasize Edges dialog box. The Level slider still gives you a choice of only five intensities for the effect, but the Before and After thumbnails provide a better preview than the presets. To see an example of the Emphasize Edges effect, see Blur&Sharp_Before.tif and EmphEdges_After.tif in the Ch06 folder on the CD.

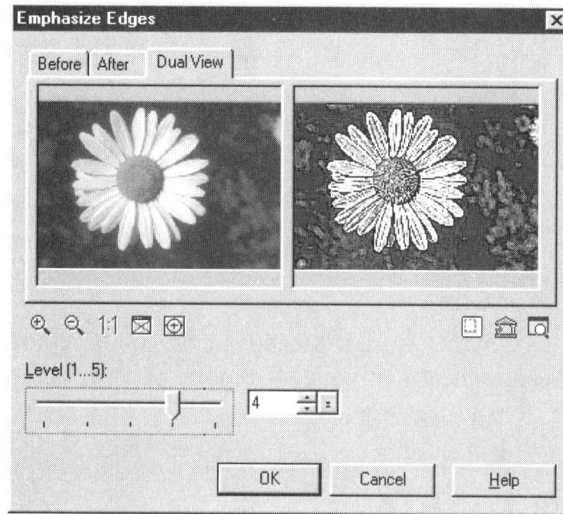

Find Edges Effect

The Find Edges effect filter is a little different from the others in the Blur & Sharpen group. It detects the edges of areas of different brightness and creates an outline around those areas. The result is a black background with white (sometimes colored) lines where PhotoImpact detected edges.

The Find Edges effect filter has no options or settings to adjust, so no dialog box appears when you choose Effect I Blur & Sharpen I Fine Edges; the image changes immediately. If you don't like the effect, choose Edit | Undo Before | Find Edges or press CTRL-Z to revert to your unchanged image.

> **TIP** *To produce an image composed of black lines on a white background, first apply the Find Edges effect filter, and then choose Format | Invert to reverse the foreground/background colors.*

Use Noise Effects

The three effect filters on the Noise submenu enable you to remove or add visual noise (random dots and specks) or reduce the moiré patterns that often result from scanning an image from a magazine.

Despeckle Effect

The Despeckle effect filter removes the random dots and specks that so often appear in images, especially when the image is dithered to reduce colors or exhibits artifacts from compression. When you choose Effect | Noise | Despeckle, PhotoImpact applies the effect filter immediately—there are no options or settings. The effect of the Despeckle filter is subtle, but you can apply it multiple times to achieve a stronger effect.

> **CAUTION** *The Despeckle effect can't tell the difference between undesirable spots and specks in your image and the kind of small highlights that help define textures and patterns that belong in the image. Using the Despeckle effect can blur or even obliterate some textures and patterns in your image.*

Remove Moiré Effect

The Remove Moiré effect filter attempts to improve the appearance of images that exhibit a moiré pattern (usually a result of interference between the image pixels and the halftone dots of printed illustrations or the pattern of dots in a dithered image). The filter smooths and blends the image in an effort to reduce or eliminate the moiré.

> **CAUTION** *If you need to use the Remove Moiré effect filter on an image, you might want to reconsider whether you should be using the image in the first place. Moiré patterns typically occur when you scan an image that contains halftone dots, such as images printed in magazines, newspapers, and books. Such published images are almost always copyrighted. You need permission from the copyright owner before you can use any copyrighted material.*

Like the Despeckle effect, the Remove Moiré effect filter has no options or settings for you to adjust. PhotoImpact applies the filter to your image immediately. The effect is a little stronger that that of the Despeckle filter, but it's still rather subtle. You can apply the Remove Moiré effect more than once to achieve a stronger effect, but use caution, because the blurring side effect builds rapidly.

The Despeckle effect and the Remove Moiré effect are very similar but have distinctly different effects. The Despeckle filter tends to darken random light spots. The Remove Moiré filter tends to lighten and blend dark spots.

Add Noise Effect

The Add Noise effect filter does exactly what its name implies: It adds visual noise to your image by scattering random speckles across the image. The result often looks like the "snow" that is typical of poor television reception. And like the television snow, the Add Noise filter's effect on your image can range from a subtle softening of the image to such strong interference that only vague suggestions of the original image remain.

When you choose Effect | Noise | Add Noise, the initial dialog box contains nine preset thumbnails. Select one of the presets or click the Options button to open the main Add Noise dialog box. In the main dialog box, you can select either Uniform or Varied for the noise-distribution pattern. You can also adjust the Variance setting to control the strength of the Add Noise effect. The higher the Variance setting, the more noise PhotoImpact adds to your image. To see an example of the Add Noise effect, see Addnoise_Before.tif and Addnoise_After.tif in the Ch06 folder on the CD.

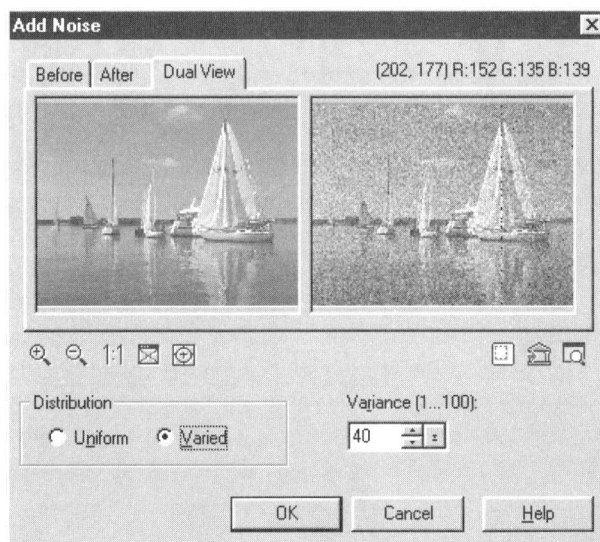

Use Camera Lens Effects

The Camera Lens submenu is home to an assortment of 11 different effect filters. The common theme is that the filters produce effects that simulate those produced by photographic camera lenses and lens attachments. The effects range from color shifts, to fractured images, to distortions, to subject or lens movement simulations, and more.

Cool and Warm Effects

The Cool and Warm effect filters tint the image with a color, like adding a color filter to the camera lens. The Cool filter adds varying amounts of cyan or blue. The Warm filter adds red or yellow. The two filters are alike in their operation; the only difference is the color choices.

When you choose Effect | Camera Lens | Cool, the dialog box initially presents nine preset thumbnails for your selection. Select one of the presets or click the Options button to display the full Cool dialog box. You can select either Blue or Cyan and control the strength of the color with the Level setting. Higher Level values produce stronger effects. The Warm dialog box works in the same way, except that you have a choice of Red or Yellow instead of Blue or Cyan.

Facet Effect

The Facet effect filter simulates the effect of viewing the image through cut glass. It achieves this effect by fracturing the image into squares and shifting them to simulate the diffraction caused by facets in the cut glass.

When you choose Effect | Camera Lens | Facet, the initial dialog box contains nine preset thumbnails. Select one of the presets or click the Options button to open the main Facet dialog box. In the main dialog box, you can set the Square Size and Shift Value options. Higher values create a stronger effect with larger facets. Click the Random button to try moving the facets to slightly different positions on the image. To see an example of the Facet effect, see Facet_Before.tif and Facet_After.tif in the Ch06 folder on the CD.

6

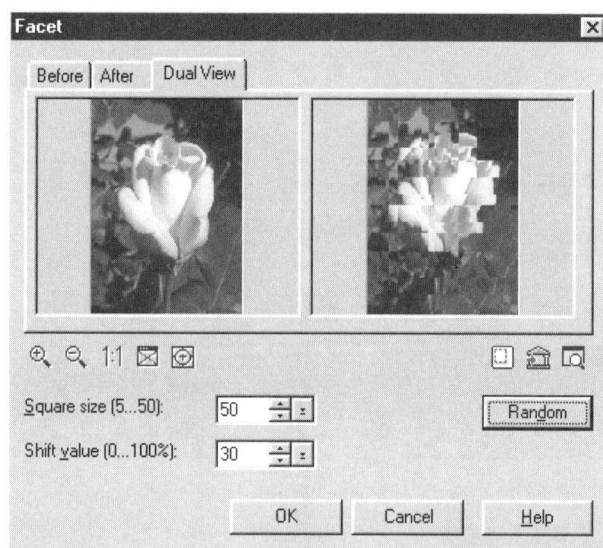

Mosaic Effect

Like the Facet effect, the Mosaic effect filter breaks your image into blocks. However, the Mosaic filter further abstracts the image by averaging all the pixels in each block so that each block is a single color. The result is supposed to simulate a mosaic composed of square tiles. However, most PhotoImpact users will probably think of the result as being similar to the pixelization that occurs when you enlarge an image too much or examine it under extreme magnification.

When you choose Effect | Camera Lens | Mosaic, the initial dialog box contains nine preset thumbnails. Select one of the presets or click the Options button to open the main Mosaic dialog box. In the main dialog box, you can set the X-Axis Size and Y-Axis Size options to control the horizontal and vertical size of the mosaic squares, respectively. Higher settings make the squares larger, resulting in more loss of detail and abstraction of the image. Check the Square option to force the X and Y Axis settings to remain the same. Then you can adjust only one of the settings, and the other changes automatically. To see an example of the Mosaic effect, see Mosaic_Before.tif and Mosaic_After.tif in the Ch06 folder on the CD.

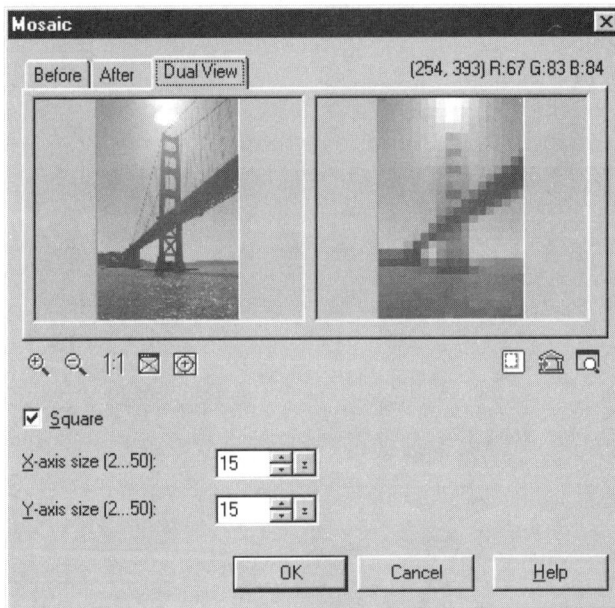

Fat and Thin Effects

The Fat and Thin effect filters simulate lens distortion that makes the subject look fatter or thinner. The Fat filter stretches the center of the image and compresses the sides to make the central part of the image expand horizontally, which make it look "fatter." The Thin filter does just the opposite: It compresses the central part of the image, making anything in the center of the image look "thinner."

When you choose Effect | Camera Lens | Fat, the initial dialog box contains the usual nine preset thumbnails. Select one of the presets or click the Options button to open the main Fat dialog box. In the main dialog box, you can set the Level value to control the strength of the effect. Higher values produce a stronger distortion of the image. The Thin effect filter works in the same way, but the effect is reversed.

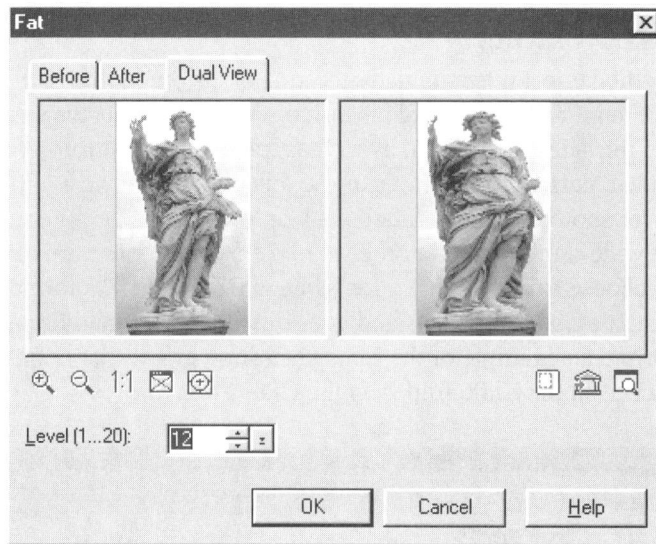

The illustration below shows an original image and the same image after applying the Fat and Thin filters.

Lens Distortion Effect

The Lens Distortion effect filter simulates the kind of distortion that is often introduced by a wide-angle lens. You can control pincushion (squeezing in at the sides) or barrel (bulging out at the sides) distortion, as well as trapezoidal distortion (converging lines that simulate perspective). You can use this effect to make a normal image look as if it were shot with a wide-angle lens or to compensate for some of the lens distortion in a wide-angle photo in order to make it look more normal.

When you choose Effect | Camera Lens | Lens Distortion, PhotoImpact dispenses with the usual dialog box of presets and goes directly to the main Lens Distortion dialog box. To see an example of the Lens Distortion effect, see Lens_Before.tif and Lens_After.tif in the Ch06 folder on the CD.

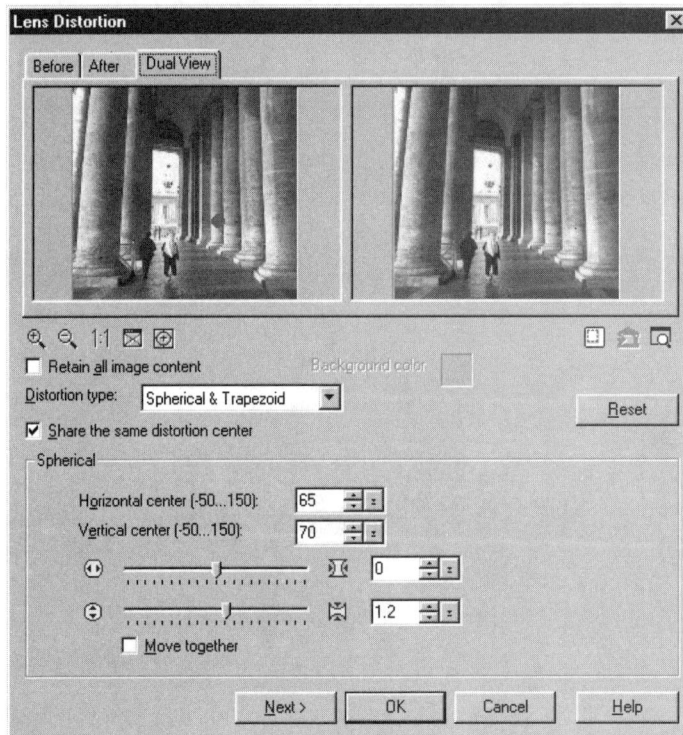

You can adjust a number of settings to control the effect:

- **Retain All Image Content** Check this option to show the entire image, right out to the distorted edges of the frame. Otherwise, PhotoImpact automatically crops the image to keep the edges from showing.

- **Background Color** Specify a background color to fill around the outer edges of the image if you chose the Retain All Image Content option.

- **Distortion Type** Select Spherical distortion (pincushion and barrel), Trapezoidal distortion (perspective), or Spherical & Trapezoidal (both).

- **Share the Same Distortion Center** Check this box if you selected Spherical & Trapezoidal distortion and want both to share the same center point.

- **Horizontal Center** Specify the horizontal center of distortion.

- **Vertical Center** Specify the vertical center of distortion.

- **Horizontal Distortion** Specify the strength of the horizontal distortion. The center position on the slider (value of 0) represents no distortion. Drag the slider left or right to increase the distortion.

- **Vertical Distortion** Specify the strength of the vertical distortion. The center position on the slider (value of 0) represents no distortion. Drag the slider left or right to increase the distortion.

- **Move Together** Check this option to move the horizontal and vertical distortion together. (This option is more appropriate with spherical distortion than with trapezoidal distortion.)

TIP	*Instead of entering numerical values for the horizontal and vertical center of distortion, you can drag the red crosshair or dot on the Before thumbnail to position the center of distortion visually.*

Motion Blur Effect

The Motion Blur effect filter simulates the blurring effect of a fast-moving subject or a fast pan of the camera.

When you choose Effect | Camera Lens | Motion Blur, the initial dialog box contains nine preset thumbnails. Select a preset or click the Options button to display the main Motion Blur dialog box. To see an example of the Motion Blur effect, see MotionBlur_Before.tif and MotionBlur_After.tif in the Ch06 folder on the CD.

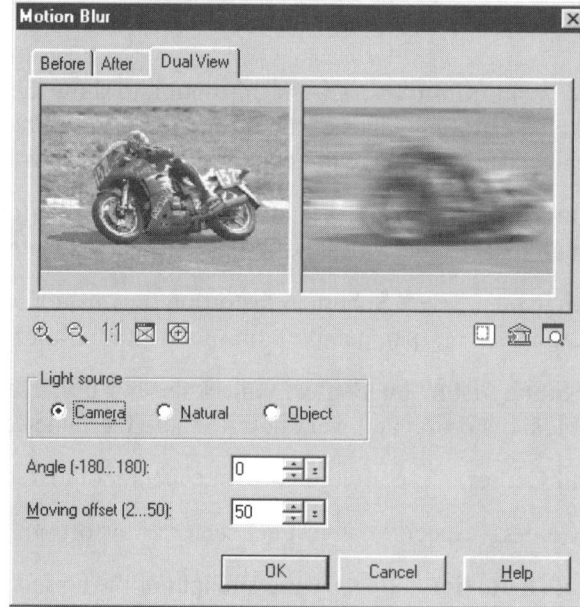

In the main dialog box, you can adjust the following settings:

- **Camera**   Creates a general blur to simulate camera motion.

- **Natural**   Keeps the leading edge sharp and creates a blurred trail to simulate movement of the light source. Light areas tend to expand out into dark areas.

- **Object**   Keeps the trailing edge sharp and creates a blurred trail to simulate movement of the object. Dark areas tend to encroach on light areas.

- **Angle**   Sets the angle for the simulated motion. A zero (0) value simulates motion to the left, leaving a trail to the right.

- **Moving Offset**   Sets the length of the simulated motion.

Zoom Blur Effect

New to
PhotoImpact 7

The Zoom Blur effect filter simulates the effect of zooming a camera lens during an exposure. The central portion of the image remains sharp, while the surrounding areas of the image are streaked and blurred. The electronic effect is far more versatile than the actual camera lens zoom, because you can reposition the center point and preview the effect in ways that aren't possible with a camera lens.

When you choose Effect | Camera Lens | Zoom Blur, PhotoImpact goes directly to the main Zoom Blur dialog box instead of showing an assortment of preset thumbnails.

You can adjust the following settings to control the effect:

- **Zoom Type**   Sets the type of zoom effect. Zoom In and Zoom Out create straight-line streaks toward or away from the central spot. Clockwise and Counterclockwise create swirling streaks.

- **Unblurred Area Radius**   Sets the size of the circle around the center point where the image remains sharp.

- **Inward Blur Extent**   Adjusts the size of the transition area between the sharp center ring and the thoroughly blurred outer area.

- **Surrounding Blur Extent**   Adjusts the strength of the blurring effect outside the central area.

- **Twist Extent**   Sets the strength of the twisting effect when you choose Clockwise or Counterclockwise as the zoom type.

Along with setting these options, you can drag the red dot and bulls-eye rings on the Before thumbnail to position the center point of the zoom effect.

> **TIP** *When you use Clockwise or Counterclockwise zoom types, the Surrounding Blur Extent and Twist Extent settings compound each other. Start with both set to low values. Otherwise, the surrounding image area will be so strongly blurred that it will be completely obscured.*

The following illustration shows an image before and after applying the Zoom Blur effect filter.

Beautify Skin Effect

New to PhotoImpact 7

The Beautify Skin effect filter is a retouching tool that removes blemishes and wrinkles by smoothing and blending skin tones. The filter is unusual in that it is not designed to apply to your entire image or a selection from your image. Instead, it singles out certain colors in the image and applies its effects to those colors alone.

When you choose Effect I Camera Lens I Beautify Skin, PhotoImpact opens the main Beautify Skin dialog box. To apply the effect filter to your image, click in the Before thumbnail to select a sample of the skin color you want to blend. The Skin Tone box will show the skin tone to be smoothed by the effect. Use the Level spin box to set the strength of the blending effect applied to the selected skin tone. Optionally, you can select one of five complexion changes (such as Pale or Sunburn) to apply to the selected skin tone and set the level for the complexion change. To view color versions of the Beautify Skin images, open Skin_before.jpg and Skin_after.jpg in the Ch06 folder on the CD.

Beautify Skin

Before | After | Dual View

(226, 513) R:206 G:202 B:222

Click in the image to select a skin tone

Skin softening settings

Skin tone

Level (1...10) : 8

Style

Complexion : None

Level (1...10) : 5

OK   Cancel   Help

6

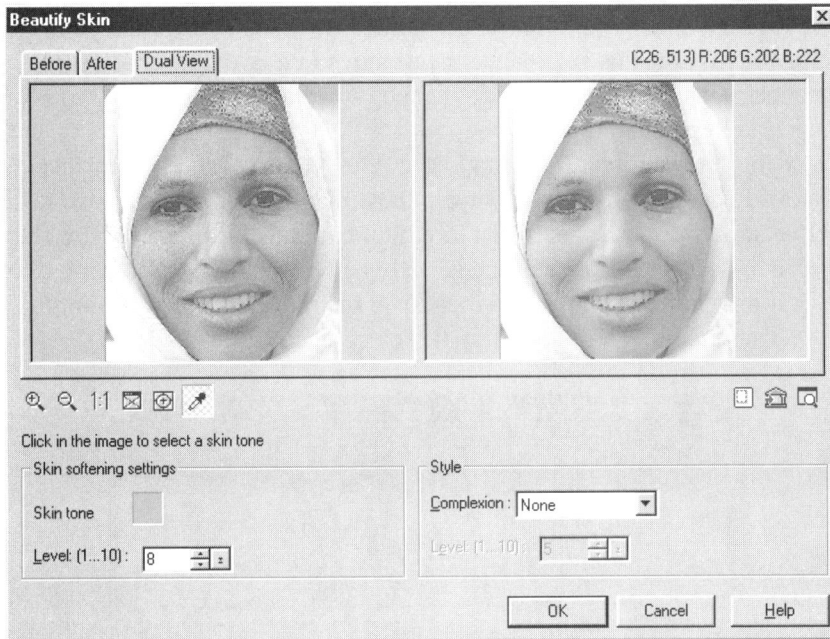

- **Level**   Sets the strength of the blending effect applied to the selected skin tone.

- **Complexion**   Select one of five complexion changes (such as Pale or Sunburn) to apply to the selected skin tone.

- **Level**   Sets the strength of the complexion change.

TIP   *Often, a single skin tone selection isn't enough to smooth all the flesh tones in a picture. You can make multiple skin tone selections without closing the Beautify Skin dialog box. Each new skin tone selection is additive—it doesn't cancel the smoothing already accomplished by the previous skin tone selection.*

Remove Red Eye Effect

The Remove Red-Eye effect filter is another retouching tool. It's designed specifically for the task of correcting the red-eye effect that commonly afflicts flash photos of people. Like the Beautify Skin filter, the Remove Red Eye filter is not designed to apply to your entire image, or even a selection that you make before opening the

Remove Red Eye dialog box. Instead, it works on a specific area that you select in the dialog box. Within that small area, the Remove Red Eye filter replaces the bright red that appears in the eyes of flash photography subjects with black to give the pupils of the eyes a more natural appearance.

When you choose Effect | Camera Lens | Remove Red Eye, PhotoImpact opens the Remove Red Eye dialog box. To apply the effect, select one eye or two to create one or two selection circles on the Before thumbnail. Adjust the Eye Size setting to increase or decrease the size of the selection circles. Drag the selection circles on the Before thumbnail to position them over the eye(s) where you want to apply the filter. The filter only works within the selection circles.

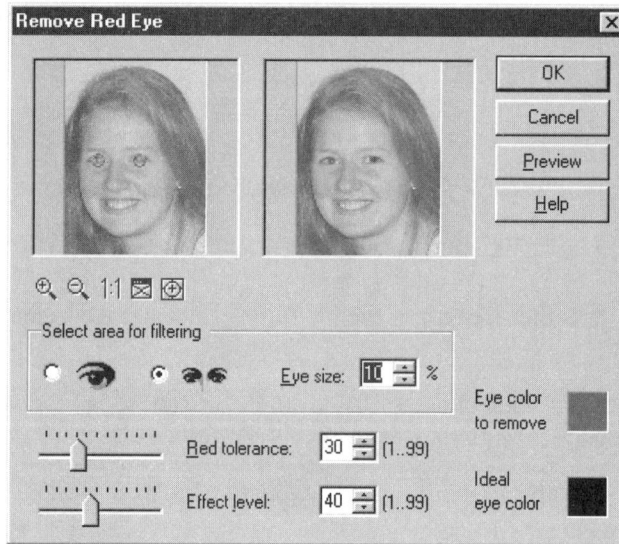

You can also adjust the following settings:

- **Red Tolerance**   Controls how closely the red in the image must match the Eye Color to Remove sample.

- **Effect Level**   Controls the strength of the color replacement effect.

- **Eye Color to Remove**   Shows a sample of the color that the Remove Red Eye filter will replace.

- **Ideal Eye Color**   Shows a sample of the color that the filter will insert into your image in place of the red that is removed.

| TIP | *The default color in the Eye Color to Remove box may not match the eye color you're trying to correct in your image. You can easily replace the default color with a sample from your image. Just right-click the Eye Color to Remove box and choose Eyedropper from the pop-up menu that appears. (See Chapter 2 for instructions on using the Eyedropper dialog box.)* |

The following illustration shows a flash photograph of a person before and after applying the Remove Red Eye filter effect.

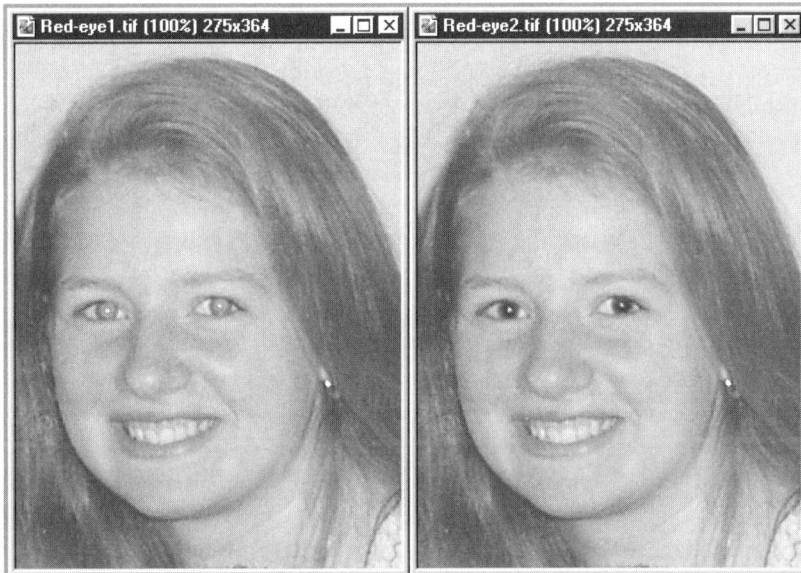

Apply 2D Effects

The 2D submenu offers a couple of interesting special-effect filters that simulate distortions caused by water surface effects. The submenu gets its name from the fact that the image is distorted in two dimensions.

Ripple Effect

The Ripple effect filter simulates ripples or small waves on the surface of water and the image distortions that would result from viewing your image through that water.

When you choose Effect | 2D | Ripple, PhotoImpact opens a dialog box containing the usual nine preset thumbnails. Select one of the presets or click the Options button to open the main Ripple dialog box.

You can control the Ripple effect by adjusting the following settings in the dialog box:

- **Direction**   Controls the direction of the ripples. Select Center to create ripples in concentric circles, simulating a pebble dropped into water. Select Edge to create ripples running diagonally across the entire image.

- **Frequency**   Sets the spacing of the ripples. Low creates fewer ripples, spaced farther apart. High creates more ripples, spaced closer together.

- **Amplitude**   Sets the size of the ripples. Higher numbers create a stronger effect.

The following illustration shows a sample image before and after applying the Ripple effect filter.

Whirlpool Effect

The Whirlpool effect filter distorts your image in a swirling pattern that simulates a whirlpool.

When you choose Effect | 2D | Whirlpool, PhotoImpact opens a dialog box containing nine preset thumbnails. Select one of the presets or click the Options button to display the full Whirlpool dialog box. The Whirlpool filter controls are straightforward. You can choose Clockwise or Counterclockwise for the swirl direction, and you can control the amount of distortion with the Twist Degrees setting. To see an example of the Whirlpool effect, see Whirl_Before.tif and Whirl_After.tif in the Ch06 folder on the CD.

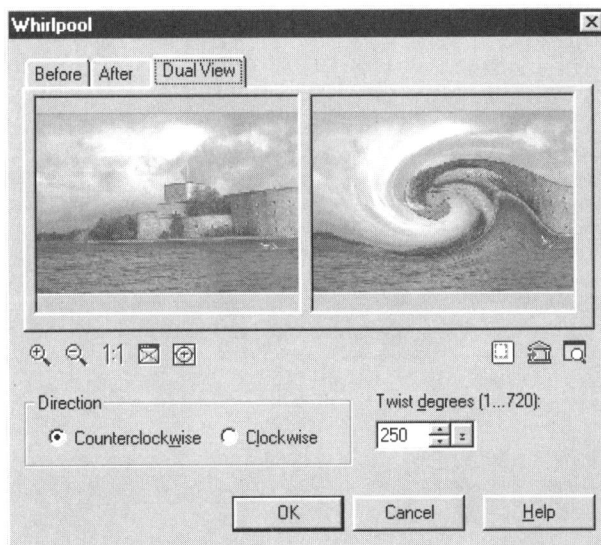

Apply 3D Effects

The 3D submenu includes three effect filters that distort images in such a way that they appear to have three-dimensional bulges or depressions.

Pinch and Punch Effects

The Pinch effect filter simulates a depression in the center of the image by shrinking the center of the image and pulling adjacent image data in toward the center. The Punch effect filter is the opposite of the Pinch filter. It expands the center of the image to simulate a bulge that extends out from the image plane toward the viewer.

When you choose Effect | 3D | Pinch, PhotoImpact opens a dialog box containing nine preset thumbnails. Select one of the presets or click the Options button to display the full Pinch dialog box. You can adjust the Power setting to control the strength of the effect. The Punch effect filter works the same way but produces the opposite effect.

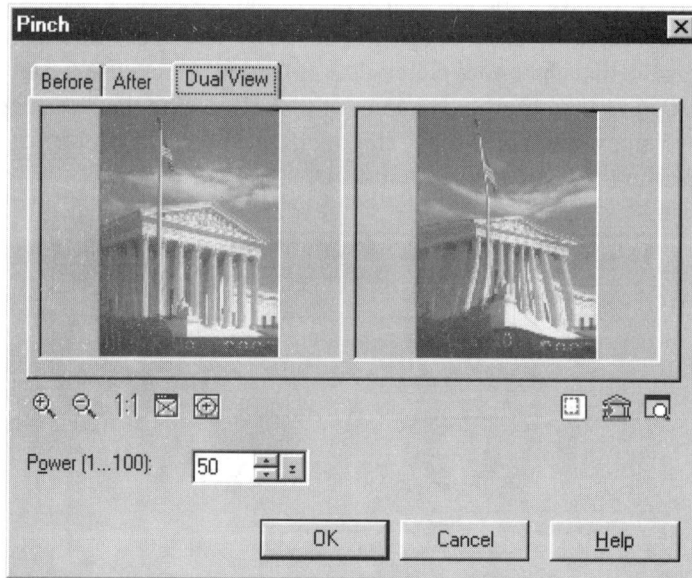

The following illustration shows a sample image after applying the Pinch and Punch effect filters.

Sphere Effect

The Sphere effect filter simulates the distortion you would see if the image were on the surface of a sphere rather than in a flat plane.

When you choose Effect | 3D | Sphere, PhotoImpact first opens a small dialog box containing three preset thumbnails. Select one of the presets or click the Options button to display the full Sphere dialog box. In this dialog box you can select one of three Light Direction settings, which change shading added to the image to simulate lighting on the three-dimensional sphere. To see an example of the Sphere effect, see 3D_Before.tif and Sphere.tif in the Ch06 folder on the CD.

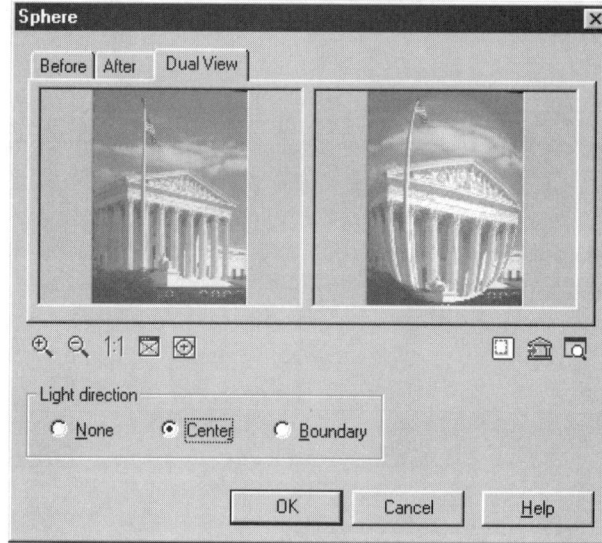

Apply Natural Painting Effects

The Natural Painting submenu offers an assortment of effect filters that simulate an artist's brush strokes and other artist media. These filters can give your image the look of a watercolor painting or a drawing done with colored pencils or pens. In the process, the filters simplify the image by subduing fine details.

> **TIP**   *To achieve a stronger effect from the Natural Painting effect filters, reduce the image size of high-resolution images before applying the effect filter. This has the added benefit of making the images faster and easier to work with.*

Watercolor Effect

The Watercolor effect filter simulates the effect of painting the image with watercolors. When you choose Effect | Natural Painting | Watercolor, PhotoImpact opens a dialog box containing nine preset thumbnails. Select one of the presets or click the Options button to display the full Watercolor dialog box. In this dialog box, you can select Large or Small brush strokes. You can also set the Moisture Level value, which is supposed to simulate varying the moisture content of the paint, but actually seems to strengthen the effect by increasing contrast. To see an example of the Watercolor effect, see NaturalPaint_before.tif and Watercolor_after.tif in the Ch06 folder on the CD.

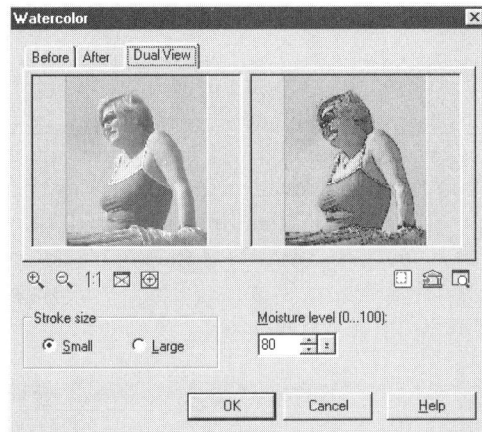

Oil Paint Effect

The Oil Paint effect filter simulates the effect of painting the image with oil paints or acrylics. The effect is similar to the Watercolor filter, but you have more control over the size of the brush strokes and the edges of the brush strokes blend more together.

When you choose Effect | Natural Painting | Oil Paint, PhotoImpact opens a dialog box with the usual nine preset thumbnails. Select one of the presets or click the Options button to display the full Oil Paint dialog box. This dialog box contains sliders for Stroke Detail and Level. Higher Stroke Detail settings obliterate more of the original image by replacing it with simulated brush strokes. Higher Level settings allow less of the original image to show through. To see an example of the Oil Paint effect, see NaturalPaint_before.tif and Oilpaint_after.tif in the Ch06 folder on the CD.

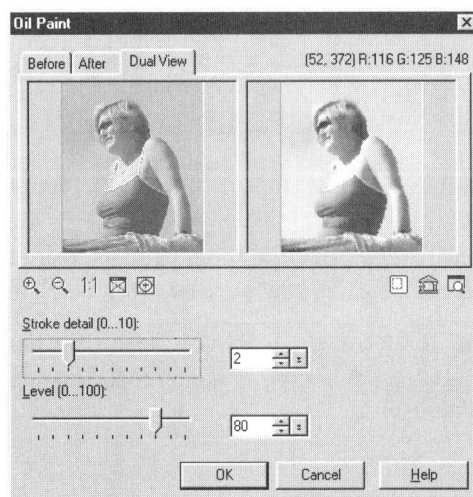

Charcoal Effect

The Charcoal effect filter is supposed to simulate drawing the image with charcoal. However, it comes closer to simulating artist's pastels or colored chalk rather than a pure charcoal drawing (which would be all black, white, and gray), because some of the original image color remains, even at the highest level settings.

When you choose Effect | Natural Painting | Charcoal, PhotoImpact skips the usual dialog box of presets and goes directly to the main Charcoal dialog box. To see an example of the Charcoal effect, see NaturalPaint_before.tif and Charcoal_after.tif in the Ch06 folder on the CD.

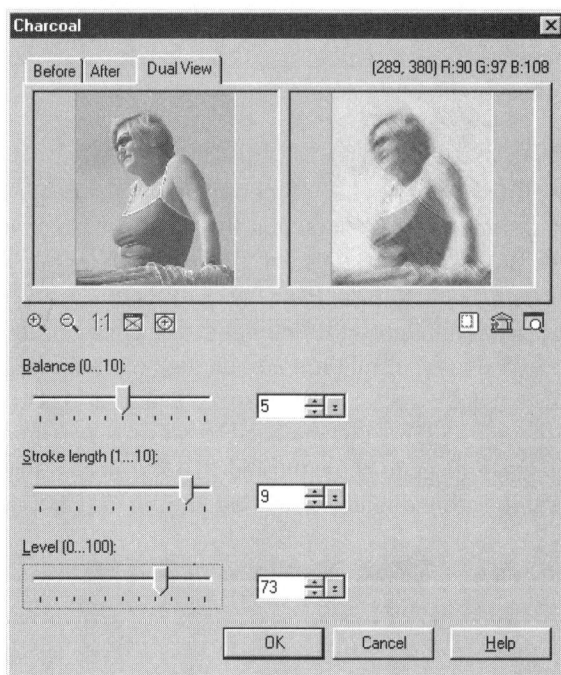

You can adjust the following settings to control the Charcoal filter:

■ **Balance**   Controls how much of the image is covered by the black of the simulated charcoal. Higher values create more black areas on the image.

■ **Stroke Length**   Controls the length of the streaks that simulate the sketchy lines and cross-hatching of a charcoal drawing. Higher values create longer lines.

■ **Level**   Controls the strength of the effect. Higher values let less of the original image show through.

Colored Pen Effect

The Colored Pen effect filter simulates a line drawing using colored pencils or pens. The filter detects and enhances edges in the original image to create outlines, and then washes out much of the fill color in solid areas and replaces it with a light cross-hatch pattern in a pale version of the color.

When you choose Effect | Natural Painting | Colored Pen, PhotoImpact goes directly to the main Colored Pen dialog box. There is only one adjustment available in the Colored Pen dialog box: the Level setting, which controls how much of the original image shows through. Higher settings create a stronger effect. To see an example of the Colored Pen effect, see NaturalPaint_before.tif and Colorpen_after.tif in the Ch06 folder on the CD.

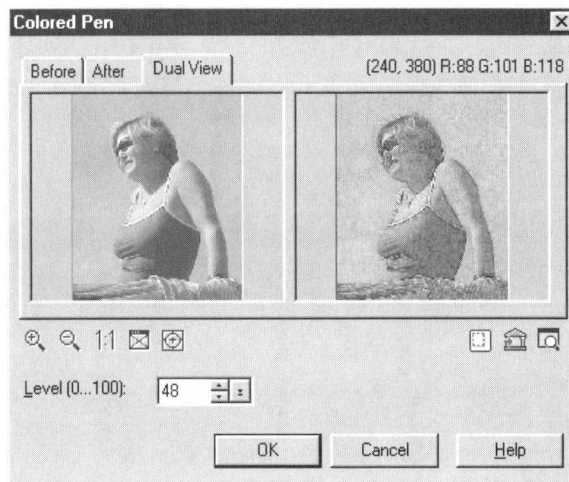

Apply Special Effects

The Special submenu is home to an assortment of eight miscellaneous effects filters. There are wind effects, tile effects, an emboss effect, and more.

Wind and Blast Effects

The Wind effect filter adds white streaks to the image to evoke the feeling of a strong wind blowing on the subject. The streaks start at the leading edges of the subject and gradually fade as they trail away. Blast creates the same kind of streaking effect as the Wind filter, but the streaks are stronger and harder-edged, and there are more of them.

When you choose Effect | Special | Wind, PhotoImpact opens a dialog box showing nine preset thumbnails. Select one of the presets or click the Options button to display the full Wind dialog box. In this dialog box, you can choose the wind direction (to the left or right) and set the Moving Offset value (the length of the wind streaks). Click the Random button to cycle through alternate positions for the wind streaks. The Blast effect filter works the same as the Wind filter, and the Blast dialog box contains the same options. To see an example of the Wind and Blast effects, see Wind&Blast_before.tif, Wind_after.tif and Blast_after.tif in the Ch06 folder on the CD.

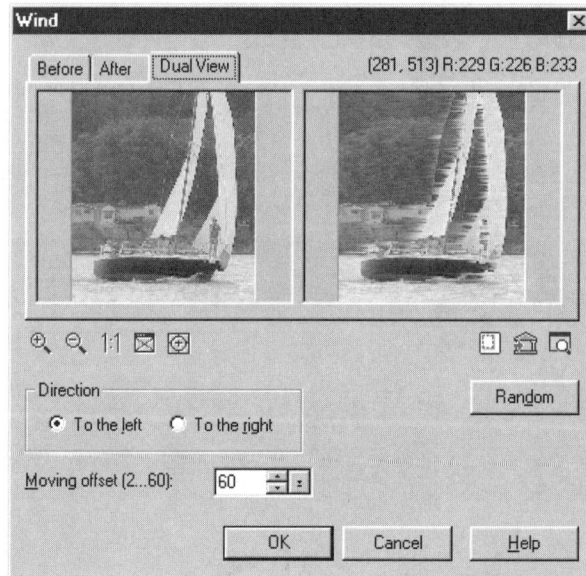

The Stagger Effect

The Stagger effect filter evokes a feeling that is similar to the Wind filter, but it accomplishes the effect in a different way. The Wind filter adds white and light-colored streaks to the image. The Stagger filter streaks the colors of the image itself.

When you choose Effect | Special | Stagger, PhotoImpact skips the usual preset thumbnails and goes straight to the main Stagger dialog box. Here, you can choose the direction (to the left or right) for the streaks. Click the Random button to cycle through alternate positions for the stagger streaks. To see an example of the Stagger effect, see Stagger_before.tif and Stagger_after.tif in the Ch06 folder on the CD.

Puzzle Effect

The Puzzle effect filter breaks your image into square blocks, and then rearranges those blocks out of sequence. The result looks like a puzzle that must be solved by sliding blocks around to maneuver them into their correct position. It's an interesting effect, but one that has limited application, because it renders most images unrecognizable.

When you choose Effect | Special | Puzzle, PhotoImpact displays the usual array of nine preset thumbnails. Select one of the presets or click the Options button to go to the main Puzzle dialog box. In this dialog box, you can set the Square Size value of the puzzle blocks (in pixels) and the background color used for the separating lines between the blocks. Click the Random button to cycle through alternate positions for the puzzle blocks. To see an example of the Puzzle effect, see PuzzleTile_before.tif and Puzzle_after.tif in the Ch06 folder on the CD.

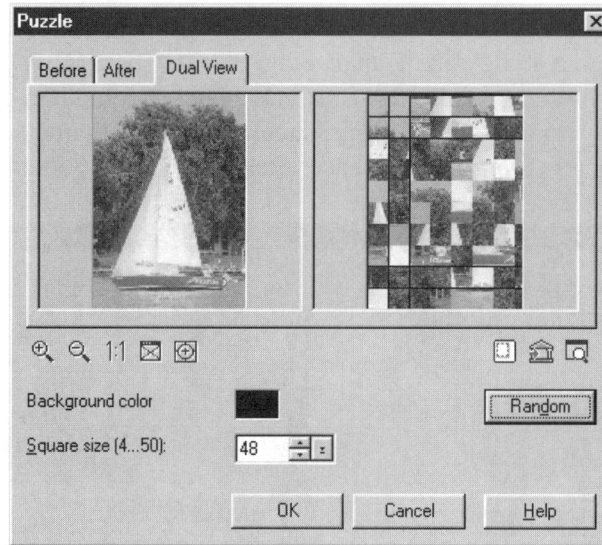

Tile Effect

The Tile effect filter breaks your image into square blocks, much like the Puzzle filter, but the Tile filter doesn't rearrange the blocks randomly. The blocks remain in proper sequence, but they are shifted slightly to produce random variations in the spaces between blocks.

When you choose Effect | Special | Tile, PhotoImpact opens a dialog box containing nine preset thumbnails. Select one of the presets or click the Options button to open the main Tile dialog box. In this dialog box, you can set the tile size and background color for the lines and spaces between tiles. You can also specify a Shift Value setting to control the maximum percentage of the block size that a tile can move out of position. Click the Random button to cycle through alternate positions for the tile blocks. To see an example of the Tile effect, see PuzzleTile_before.tif and Tile_after.tif in the Ch06 folder on the CD.

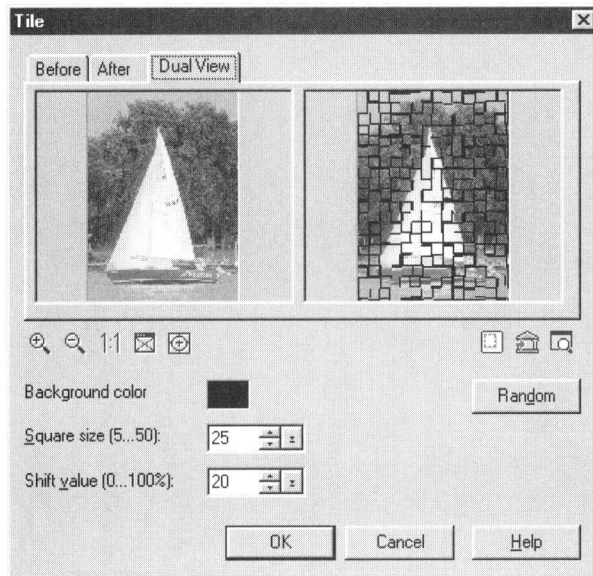

> **TIP**   *If setting the Square Size option to the maximum value of 50 produces tiles that are still too small, try reducing the image size before applying the Tile filter effect.*

Emboss Effect

The Emboss effect filter simulates converting your image to bas-relief sculpture, like the images embossed onto the face of coins. The filter removes all color from your image and replaces it with a single, solid color. Edges and shading differences in your image are represented by simulated highlights and shadows. Depending on the settings you choose, the result can look a little like a rubbing, a block print, or embossed metal.

When you choose Effect | Special | Emboss, PhotoImpact displays eight preset thumbnails in a dialog box. Select one of the presets or click the Options button to open the main Emboss dialog box. You can select a coating color, specify the depth of the relief effect (the thickness of the edge effects), and select a light source. To see an example of the Emboss effect, see PuzzleTile_before.tif and Emboss_after.tif in the Ch06 folder on the CD.

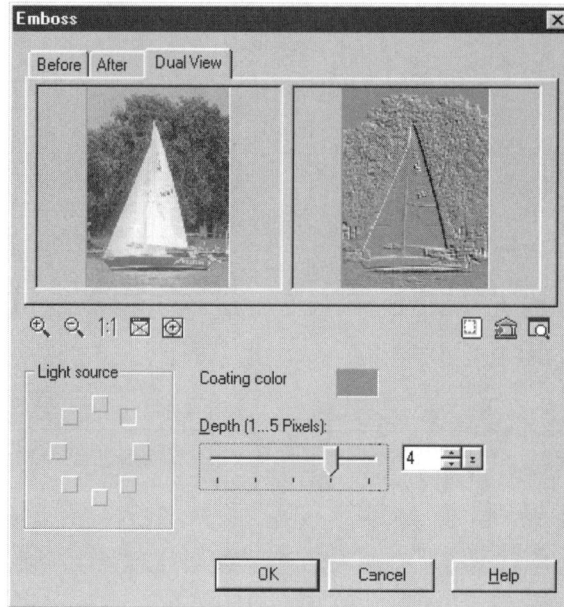

Monochrome Effect

The Monochrome effect filter changes your full-color image into a grayscale image. The result looks the same as applying the Format | Data Type | Grayscale command. However, there is one very important difference: When you use the Monochrome effect filter, the image retains its 24-bit RGB data type, which means that you can paint on the image, create path and text objects, and import image objects in full color without having them converted to grayscale.

When you choose Effect | Special | Monochrome, PhotoImpact applies the effect immediately. There are no options for the Monochrome effect filter, so no dialog boxes appear.

Two-Color Effect

The Two-Color effect filter transforms your full-color image into a *duotone*, which is basically a grayscale image that is rendered with two different colors: one for the darker midtones and shadows and another for the lighter midtones and highlights. You can use this filter to produce effects that are reminiscent of old sepia-toned photographs and grayscale pictures printed with colored inks.

When you choose Effect | Special | Two-Color, PhotoImpact skips the usual preset thumbnails and goes straight to the main Two-Color dialog box. In this dialog box, you can specify the two colors to use for the effect and adjust the way the colors are applied to the tonal range in the image. Click a color box to select a color. (The left color box controls the darker midtones and shadows and the right color box controls the lighter midtones and highlights.) Drag the two sliders under the horizontal color bar to control which part of the tonal range each color sample applies to.

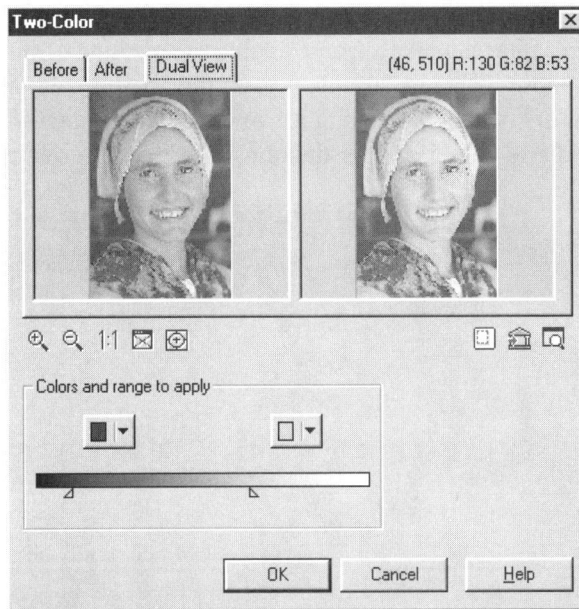

Apply Video Effects

The two effect filters on the Video submenu color-correct images so that the colors all fall within the range that can be reproduced on a television screen. The two filters are Adjust for NTSC and Adjust for PAL. Using these filters helps avoid surprises caused by unanticipated color shifts when you use an image in a video production.

The Adjust for NTSC effect filter color-corrects the image for compliance with the television broadcast standard in the United States. There are no options to set, so no dialog box appears when you choose Effect | Video | Adjust for NTSC. PhotoImpact immediately adjusts the image and displays the results in the document window. For most images, the change is very subtle (if it's visible at all).

The Adjust for PAL effect filter works just like the Adjust for NTSC filter, except that it color corrects to the slightly different PAL broadcast television standard, which is used in most of Europe and the British Commonwealth.

Apply the Warping Effect

The Warping effect filter is in a class by itself. It allows you to apply freeform distortions to an image.

Imagine your image printed on a sheet of rubber or Silly Putty and held in a frame. It starts out looking like the original image, but you can grab spots on the image and drag them around, distorting that part of the image but leaving other areas untouched. The Warping effect filter is the electronic analog of that kind of distortion.

You simply choose Effect | Warping to open the Warping dialog box, without going through any submenus or pausing to view preset thumbnails. PhotoImpact superimposes a red grid onto the larger thumbnail image in the Warping dialog box.

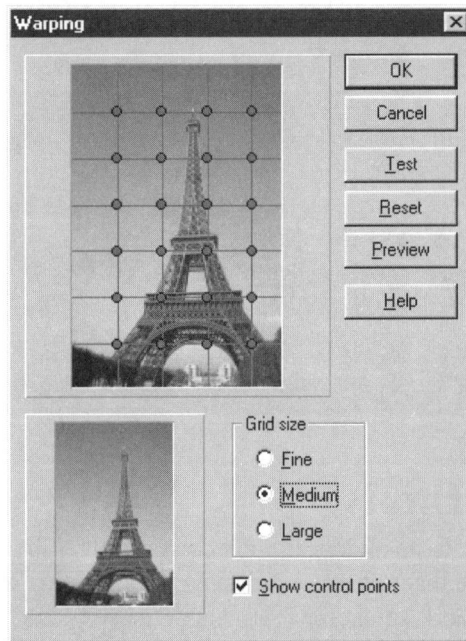

You control the image distortion by dragging the grid intersections. You can select one of three grid sizes to create more or fewer grid intersections, and you can make the intersections easier to see by checking the Show Control Points option. Click the Test button to show the results of your distortions in the smaller thumbnail at the bottom of the dialog box. Click Reset to return the grid to its original, straight-line condition so you can start over.

The following illustration shows a sample image before and after applying the Warping effect filter.

Use the Fadeout Feature

The Fadeout feature allows you to vary the transparency of objects and selections in such a way that the object gradually fades into its background. The effect is similar to what you would achieve if you could apply a linear gradient to an object or selection, except that the gradation goes from opaque to transparent, instead of from one color to another. It's a nice effect that greatly enhances the versatility of objects and selections as illustration tools.

The Fadeout feature isn't an effect filter. It's more like a color attribute for objects and selections. However, it produces a result that is similar to the results of using effect filters and plugins in other programs.

NOTE   *The Fadeout feature is available only when working with images in True Color and Grayscale modes.*

The Fadeout feature can be applied to text and path objects, image objects, selections, and base images. To use the Fadeout feature, first select the object to which you want to apply the fadeout effect. (You can use the Pick tool or the Layer Manager to select an object, a selection tool to select a portion of the image, or choose Selection | None to cancel all other selections in order to select the base image.) Then follow these steps:

1. Choose Edit | Fadeout or press CTRL-H. PhotoImpact opens the Fadeout dialog box.

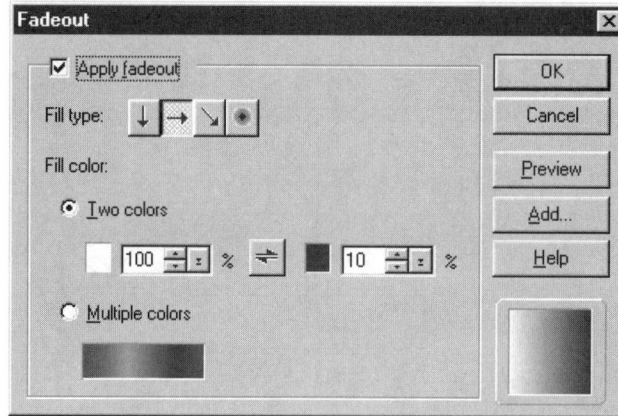

TIP *You can also open the Fadeout dialog box by right-clicking a color swatch box for a selected object and choosing Fadeout from the pop-up menu that appears.*

2. Check the Apply Fadeout checkbox to activate the other options in the dialog box. (This option isn't available or necessary if you're working with an image or image object.)

3. Click one of the Fill Type buttons to select the direction of the gradation.

4. Select a fill color pattern. You can choose a pattern composed of two colors or multiple colors. Click the color swatches to control the fadeout gradation. Black represents a complete fadeout (completely transparent), white represents full object/selection color (completely opaque), and the various shades of gray represent varying degrees of transparency. If you click the Multiple Colors swatch, PhotoImpact opens the Palette Ramp Editor dialog box. Select one of the preset rings from the samples at the bottom of the dialog box, or create your own ramp by editing the large ring in the upper-left side of the dialog box. Click anywhere on the ring to open a Ulead Color Picker dialog box and specify the color for that spot on the ring. Drag the handles around

the ring to redistribute the colors around the ring. Click the OK button to close the Palette Ramp Editor dialog box and apply the selected ramp to the Fadeout feature.

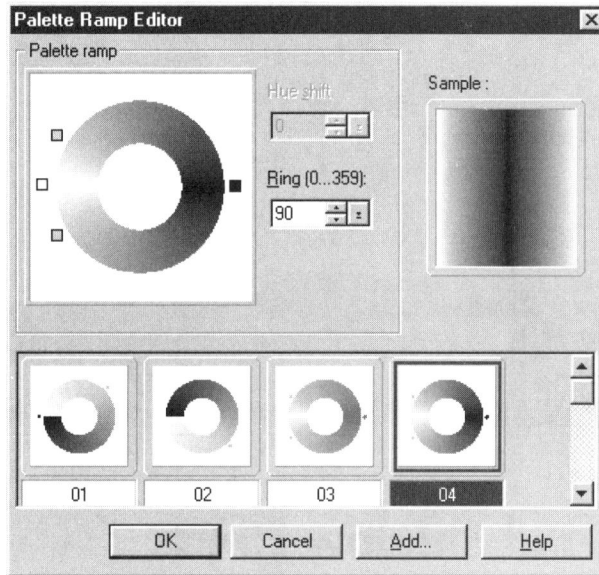

5. Click the OK button to close the Fadeout dialog box and apply the effect to the selected object or selection. If you want to preview the effect first, click the Preview button to reduce the Fadeout dialog box to a set of buttons and display the Fadeout effect in the document window. Then click OK to apply the effect, or click Continue to reopen the full Fadeout dialog box so you can adjust the settings.

NOTE *When you apply the Fadeout effect to the base image or a selected portion of the base image, you may not see the results immediately. That's because the Fadeout command creates the Fadeout effect in a selection that sits atop a complementary Fadeout effect in the base image. The two fades effectively neutralize each other as long as they remain perfectly aligned. But if you move or delete the selection, you'll see the Fadeout effect in the base image and in the selection.*

The following illustration shows an example of the Fadeout effect applied to several objects in an image.

Add Frame and Shadow Effects

PhotoImpact combines two very different visual effects into the same menu command and dialog box. The Frame & Shadow command allows you to add a simulated picture frame surrounding your image. The same command allows you to create drop shadow effects behind your image or any object or selection in your image. The Shadow command is also available separately on some pop-up menus.

> **NOTE** *Actually, from a programmer's perspective, the Frame and Shadow effects have a great deal in common: They both expand the image or selection and add to its edges. So there is some logic in combining the effects into a single command after all.*

Add Drop Shadow Effects

Drop shadow effects are immensely popular in all sorts of graphics and illustrations. A drop shadow effect creates the illusion that a graphic element is floating above a background or casting a shadow onto that background. The drop shadow effect adds an illusion of depth to your image, which isn't a factor with photographic images but is often a major enhancement to otherwise flat-looking graphics. And since the drop shadow is usually soft-edged, it also tends to soften the look of hard-edged graphics and text.

The Frame & Shadow command enables you to add a shadow quickly and easily to any text or path object in your image. However, shadows are not restricted to text and path objects alone. You can also add shadows to image objects, selections, or the entire image. When you add a shadow to the entire image, PhotoImpact automatically expands the canvas to create a background on which to cast the shadow.

Add a Shadow to an Image or Selection

To add a shadow to your image or to a selection within your image, follow these steps:

1. Select the image or the selection to which you want to add a shadow. You can use a selection tool to select a portion of the image, or you can choose Selection | None to cancel all other selections in order to select the base image.

2. Choose Format | Frame & Shadow or press SHIFT-F. PhotoImpact opens the Frame & Shadow dialog box.

3. Select None in the Style box on the Frame tab, and then click the Shadow tab to display the Shadow options.

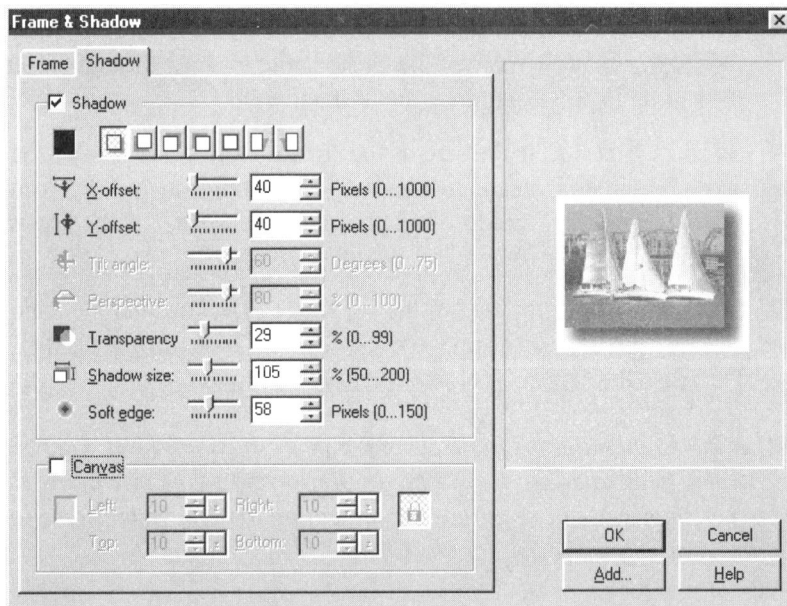

4. Click the Shadow checkbox near the top of the Shadow tab. PhotoImpact activates the options on the rest of the Shadow tab.

5. Adjust the Shadow options as needed to define the shadow effect you want to create. You can adjust the following settings:

- **Shadow color**   Sets the color of the shadow. Click the color swatch box to display the Ulead Color Picker dialog box, where you can select the shadow color. Normally, the shadow color is black, but you can select other colors for special effects.

- **Shadow style**   Sets the style and direction of the shadow. Click one of the seven buttons. The first four buttons create drop shadows cast up or down and to one side. The fifth button creates a shadow cast straight back behind the selection. The last two buttons create perspective shadows cast back from the base of the selection.

- **X-Offset**   Sets the horizontal offset for drop shadows.

- **Y-Offset**   Sets the vertical offset for drop shadows.

- **Tilt Angle**   Sets the tilt angle for perspective shadows.

- **Perspective**   Sets the length of perspective shadows.

- **Transparency**   Sets the transparency level for the shadow. Increase the setting to allow more of the background to show through. Decrease the setting to create a more opaque shadow.

- **Shadow Size**   Sets the size of the shadow as a percent of the selection size. (Be sure to increase the Shadow Size setting above 100 percent if you select the fifth shadow style button; otherwise, the shadow will be completely hidden behind the selection.)

- **Soft Edge**   Sets the size of the soft-edge effect around the edge of the shadow. Increase the setting to create a softer, more diffuse shadow effect. Decrease the setting to create a crisper shadow.

NOTE   *The Soft Edge setting is in pixels, not a percentage of the shadow size. You may need to adjust the setting in proportion to the size of the shadow. Larger shadows will require a higher setting to achieve the same look as a lower setting on a smaller shadow.*

6. If you are adding a shadow to the entire image, you can click the Canvas checkbox and manually adjust the settings below it to control the canvas expansion that is needed to accommodate the shadow added to the outside of the image. You can specify the background color and the amount of canvas added to each side of the image. This step is optional. If you don't specify the canvas expansion yourself, PhotoImpact automatically expands the canvas, using the current background color from the Tool panel.

7. Click the OK button to close the Frame & Shadow dialog box and create the shadow behind the image or selection in the document window. The following illustration shows the result of adding a drop shadow to an image. Note the expanded canvas, which automatically added background area around the outside edge of the image.

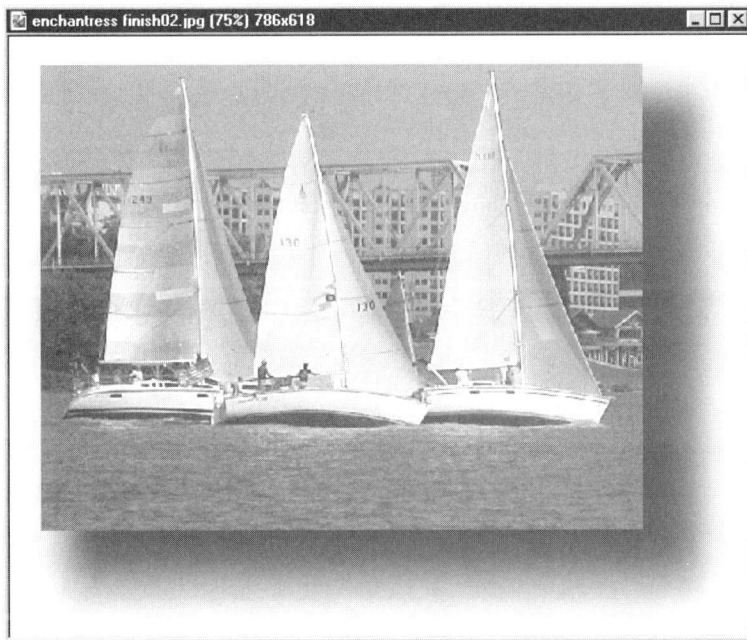

Add a Shadow to an Object

To add a shadow to an object instead of an image or selection, start by using the Pick tool to select the object or objects to which you want to add a shadow. Then right-click the selected object and choose Shadow from the pop-up menu that appears (or press SHIFT-S) to open the Shadow dialog box. As you can see, the Shadow dialog box has the same options as the Shadow tab of the Frame & Shadow dialog box, which are described in the previous section. It's just missing the Canvas options, because they don't apply to an object.

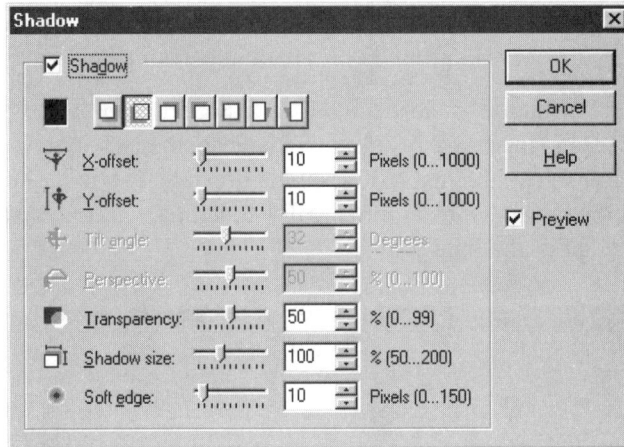

The following illustration shows the result of adding different kinds of shadows to text objects.

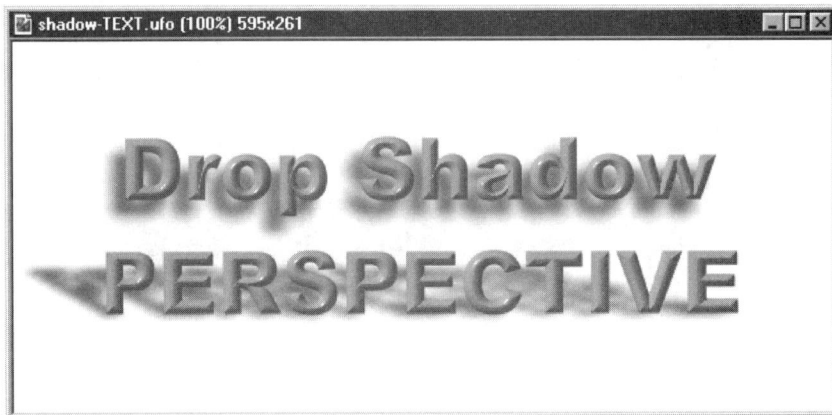

Separate a Shadow from an Object or Selection

When you add a shadow to an object or selection, the shadow is linked to the selection and moves with it when you move, resize, delete, or otherwise manipulate the object or selection. However, on occasion, you might want to manipulate the shadow separately from the object or selection. In that case, simply right-click the object or selection to which the shadow is attached, and then choose Split Shadow from the pop-up menu that appears. PhotoImpact splits the original object and the shadow into two separately selectable objects.

You can use the Pick tool to select and move the shadow independently from the original object or selection. You can move, resize, delete, or otherwise manipulate either the original object or the shadow without affecting the other.

Add a Picture Frame Around Your Image

One of the "cute" effects built into PhotoImpact is its ability to add a simulated picture frame around your image. With a few mouse clicks, you can make your image look like it's sitting in an ornate picture frame, add a graphic border around your image, or apply any one of a variety of edge effects that can accent or blend the edges of your image. There are a lot of frames and effects to choose from, and you can add color and texture options to many of them to create almost endless variations.

To add a frame or edge effect to your image, first select the image or selection to which you want to add a frame effect. (The frame effect is not available for path and text objects.) Then follow these steps:

1. Choose Format | Frame & Shadow or press SHIFT-F. PhotoImpact opens the Frame & Shadow dialog box.

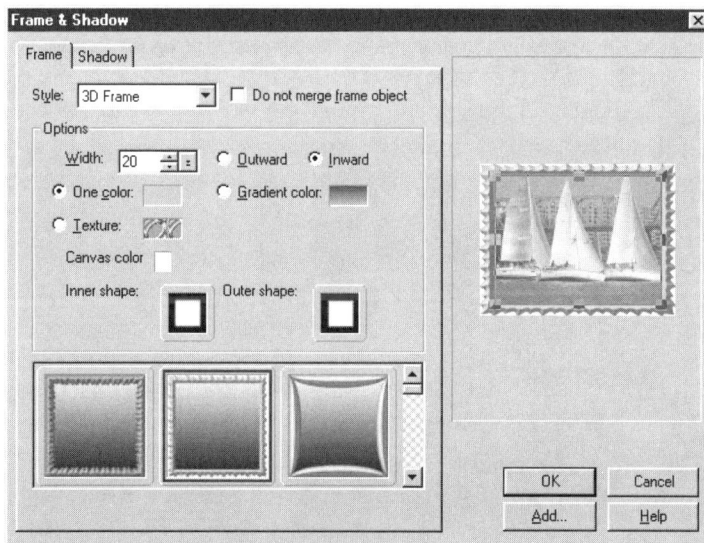

2. Select the frame style from the Style box. Each general frame style includes a variety of frame effects, which are displayed as thumbnails in the list box at the bottom of the dialog box. PhotoImpact changes the options shown in the middle of the dialog box to reflect those available for the frame style you select.

3. Select a specific frame effect by clicking one of the thumbnails at the bottom of the dialog box.

4. Adjust the option settings as needed to achieve the effect you desire. The options that are available will vary depending on the frame style you selected. There are no options for the Classic Frame effects. There are limited options available for a few effects in the Edge Frame Gallery. For most of the other frame effects, you can set options such as the frame thickness and color. The thumbnail image at the right side of the dialog box previews the effect.

5. If necessary, click the Shadow tab and adjust the settings to control the shadow effect for your image. If you don't want a shadow added to your image, uncheck the Shadow checkbox.

6. Click the OK button to close the Frame & Shadow dialog box and apply the frame effect to your image. The following illustration shows the result of adding a frame effect to an image in a PhotoImpact document window. This example shows one of the Classic Frames, but there are many other frame and edge effects available.

CHAPTER 7

Assemble and Create Images

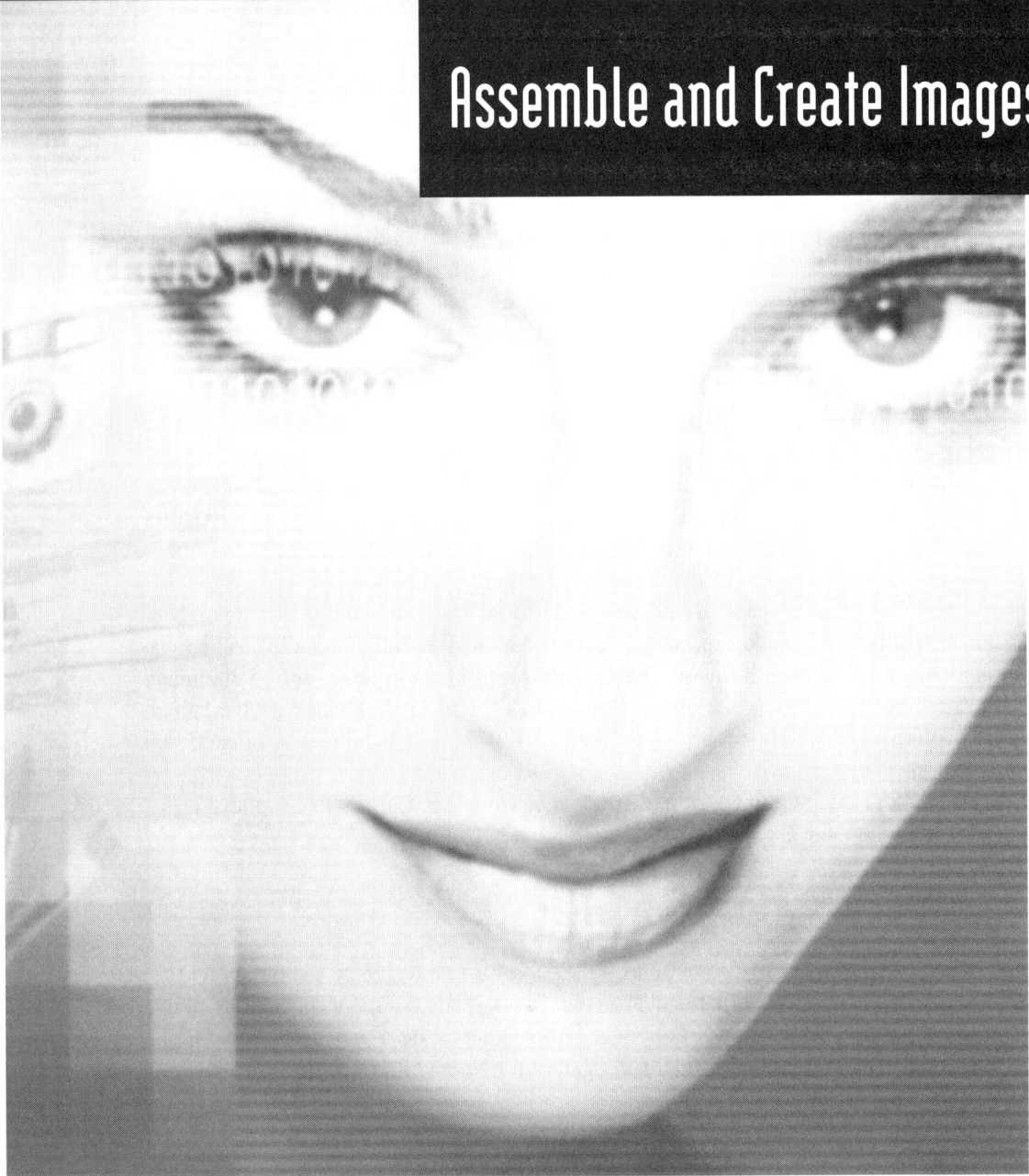

The previous chapters covered how to acquire images and how to retouch and enhance those images. But what if you would prefer to create a new image, rather than using an existing one? With PhotoImpact, you can assemble a new image by combining image elements from multiple sources, or you can create a new image from scratch using the drawing, painting, and Text tools.

In this chapter, you'll find coverage of the tools that PhotoImpact provides for assembling and creating new images. First, there are instructions on resizing the canvas to accommodate your new images and using cut, copy, and paste to assemble images. Then there's a discussion on how to work with objects, masks, selections, paths, and layers. Finally, the chapter concludes with coverage of PhotoImpact's Stitch feature, which allows you to stitch together multiple images to create a panorama.

Resize the Canvas

When you create a new image in PhotoImpact (File | New | New Image), you create a background on which to build your image. Similarly, when you open an existing image file in PhotoImpact, that image sits on a background that matches the image dimensions. PhotoImpact refers to this background as the *canvas*.

As you work with your image, you may find that you need to make the canvas larger or smaller than you originally planned. An artist working on a physical canvas might need to start over if the original canvas doesn't have room to add to the image the artist is creating. Fortunately, in PhotoImpact, you're not stuck with the canvas size you originally defined when you created your image document or opened your image file.

You can crop the image to make the canvas smaller. Using the Crop tool is covered in Chapter 2.

Expand the Canvas

If you are running out of room, you can expand the canvas. When you expand the canvas of a PhotoImpact document, you add blank space to one or more sides of the existing image, as shown in Figure 7-1. This increases the dimensions of the image document without enlarging any of the existing image components.

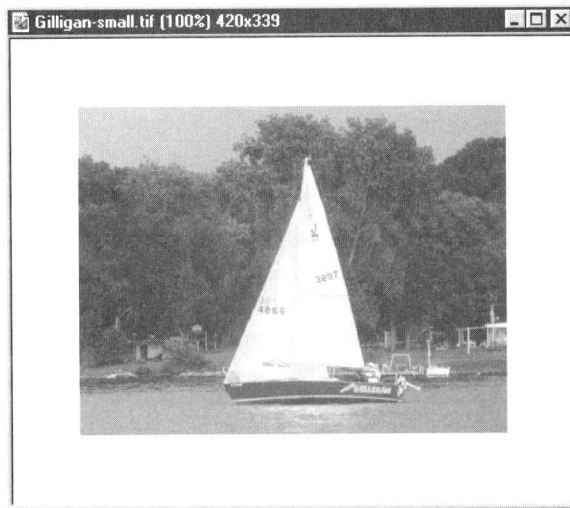

FIGURE 7-1   Expanding the canvas of an existing image

7

NOTE   *Expanding the canvas is distinctly different from changing the image size (Format | Image Size), which makes the image document larger or smaller by enlarging or reducing the entire existing image.*

To enlarge an existing image document by expanding the canvas, follow these steps:

1. Choose Format | Expand Canvas. The Expand Canvas dialog box appears.

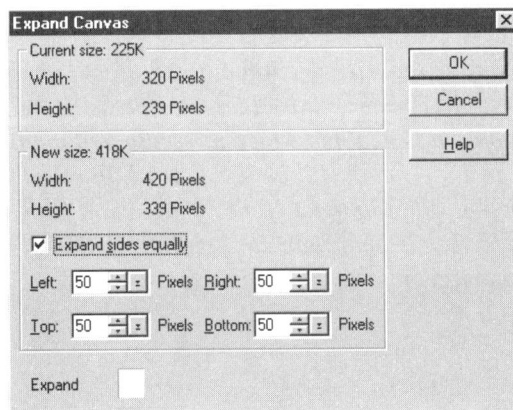

2. Type a number in the Left, Right, Top, and Bottom boxes to specify the number of pixels by which you want to increase the canvas. To increase all sides by an equal pixel amount, click the Expand Sides Equally checkbox and type a number into any one of the boxes. The values in the other three boxes will change to match.

3. Pick a color for the image's new background by clicking the Expand color box and choosing a new color in the Ulead Color Picker dialog box that appears.

4. Click the OK button to close the Expand Canvas dialog box. PhotoImpact enlarges the image in the active document window, adding blank space around the existing image according to your specifications.

> **NOTE** *After expanding the background, you may want to reposition the original image you started with. When doing so, you'll find that moving the image leaves a telltale rectangle of the original background color where the image used to be, as in the example shown in Figure 7-2. To avoid "canvas holes," before you expand your canvas, make sure your new background color is the same as the original, which is usually white. PhotoImpact makes it very easy to select or insert a new background image later.*

Cut, Copy, and Paste

You may want to cut, copy and paste image selections in PhotoImpact 7 to remove or duplicate a portion of the image or use an image portion in another document. The basic steps for cutting and pasting are the same in PhotoImpact as in any other Windows-based application. You select an area of an image and cut or copy it to the clipboard.

> **TIP** *When you want to make a selection but not affect the underlying image, choose Selection | Preserve Base Image or press F5. When the Preserve Base Image option is enabled, you can create and manipulate selections, and the image underneath will be unchanged. In other words, when you make a selection, PhotoImpact copies image data from the base image to create the selection, rather than cutting that portion of the base image out to create the image object.*

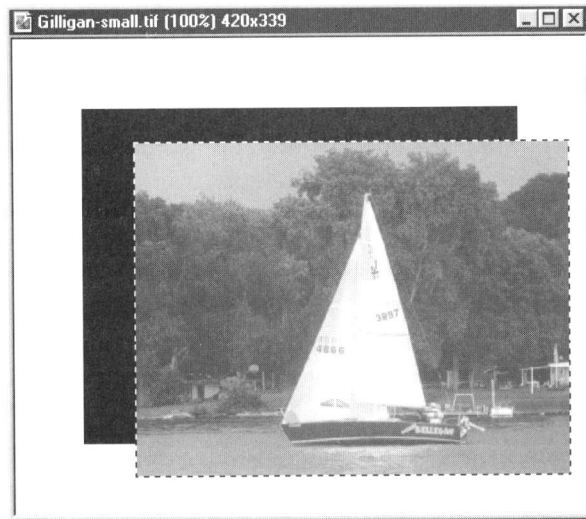

FIGURE 7-2   If you've used a background color different from the image's original background color, moving your original image can leave a telltale outline.

Cut or Copy Image Selections

To cut or copy a portion of an image, first use one of the selection tools to select an area of your image. (See Chapter 2 for instructions on using the selection tools.) Then use one of the following commands:

- Choose Edit | Cut (or press CTRL-X) to remove the selected image area from the canvas.

- Choose Edit | Copy (or press CTRL-C) to copy the selected image area while leaving the original untouched.

PhotoImpact stores the selected image data in the clipboard, where it becomes available for pasting into any image you open in PhotoImpact.

Use Image Data from the Clipboard

Once image data is copied to the clipboard, PhotoImpact provides several ways that you can paste from the clipboard into the active document window:

- To paste the selection into an image as an image object, choose Edit | Paste | Paste As Object (or press CTRL-V). The pasted selection appears in the upper-left corner of the document window, surrounded by a selection marquee. Use the Pick tool to move the image object to the desired location.

- ■ To paste the selection into an image and move it to a new position in one step, choose Edit | Paste | Under Pointer. When you choose this option, the pasted selection appears under your mouse pointer and follows your cursor position until you click the mouse button.

- ■ To paste the selection from the clipboard into an existing selection marquee in an image, choose Edit | Paste | Paste into Selection. This option works much like the Under Pointer option, except that you can move the pasted image data only within the confines of the active selection area. When the selection is positioned where you want it, click the mouse button, and the pasted selection merges with the image data in the selection area.

- ■ To paste the selection from the clipboard into an active selection area and automatically resize it to fit that selection, choose Edit | Paste | Fit into Selection. PhotoImpact resizes the pasted image data as needed to fit the active selection.

Work with Objects

In PhotoImpact, any item that needs to be moved freely around an image, resized, treated with effects, or otherwise edited independently of the base image is an *object*. For example, you can select any portion of an image and with a click of the mouse, transform that portion into an independent object. This process is similar to cutting a portion of a picture out of a magazine and pasting it into a collage.

Once you separate a selection from the surrounding image, it becomes an independent object with its own characteristics. You can edit and manipulate the object, without affecting the rest of the image document. You can also cut, copy, and paste it into a different image.

Objects don't need to be composed of image data selected from existing images. You can create new objects from scratch with the painting tools, path-drawing tools, and Text tool, among others.

Types of Objects

PhotoImpact supports three basic object types:

- **Image object**   An object composed of pixel-based image data. You normally create an image object by selecting a portion of an existing image and then separating it from the base image for manipulation. However, you can also create image objects by importing image files into a document, copying an object from the EasyPalette, and using other techniques.

- **Path object**   An object that you create with PhotoImpact's path-drawing tools. A path object differs from an image object, in that it contains vector graphics instead of pixel-based image data.

- **Text object**   An object containing type characters that you create with PhotoImpact's Text tool. Like a path object, a text object contains vector graphics instead of pixel-based image data. The distinguishing characteristic of a text object is that it contains editable text.

As you work with PhotoImpact, you may see references to other kinds of objects, but they are really just variations on these three object types. For example, a *stamp object* is just convenient shorthand terminology for an image object that you create with the PhotoImpact Stamp tool. Similarly, a *paint object* is an image object that you create by using one of PhotoImpact's painting tools in Paint As Object mode. A *Web component object* (or Web object) is a combination of path, image, and text objects merged together into a single object that you can use as a button or other Web page component.

As objects, the images or image portions you create will be freely editable and mobile. Image objects can be used, for example, to create a collage of a family event or a photo catalog. Your composite image need not be made up exclusively of image objects cut and pasted from other images. You can draw graphics with path objects and add type for titles and labels with text objects as well.

Create Objects

Objects come from many sources. Selections, imported images, and paths are all examples of objects. Once you create an object, it can be edited and reshaped with all the object-editing tools. The following sections describe the various methods for creating objects.

Create an Object from a Selection

Manipulating a selection is the most common method for creating image objects. Using this method, any portion of your image can be reshaped, recolored, or edited with a filter. To create an object from a selection, simply create a selection, and then choose Selection | Convert to Object. PhotoImpact converts the selected image area into an image object.

In most cases, you don't need to explicitly issue the Convert to Object command. As soon as you move or otherwise manipulate a selection, PhotoImpact automatically converts the selection into an image object.

> **NOTE** *Clicking and dragging a newly created selection marquee with the Pick tool does not convert the selection into an image object. Doing so moves the selection marquee without moving any of the image data with it. You move the image data in a selection by dragging the selection with the Selection tool, which does automatically convert it to an image object.*

Import an Image As an Object

Importing an image as an object is one of the easiest and fastest methods for creating composite images. With an existing image open, choose Object | Insert Image Object | From File. PhotoImpact displays the Open dialog box. Select the image file you want to import and click Open.

PhotoImpact closes the dialog box, and the imported image appears in the active document window as an image object. The selection marquee around the imported image object shows that it's the active object, ready for you to move, resize, or manipulate it in any way you like. Figure 7-3 shows an exmaple of an image imported as an object.

You can also import image objects from the Image Library in the EasyPalette panel. Just open the EasyPalette and display any of the Image Library categories. Click the thumbnail of the image you want to import from the EasyPalette, and then drag and drop it on the document window. PhotoImpact imports the selected image as an image object. You can use the same technique to import objects from the Shape, Paths, and Outline Libraries as path objects. You can even save your own text objects to the EasyPalette and then import them into your image. They will appear as fully editable text objects.

Paint an Object

Normally, when you use a painting tool, any strokes of color and other painting effects automatically merge into the base image as soon as you click on a non-

FIGURE 7-3   An imported image object

painting tool or select another object in your image document. However, PhotoImpact gives you the option to keep your painting strokes separate from the base image in an independent image object.

The paint object (as such an image object is sometimes called) allows you to select and edit the painting strokes separately from the base image, even after selecting other objects and using other tools. The paint object remains a separate object indefinitely; it doesn't merge into the base image until you manually issue the Merge command.

You can use most any painting tool or combination of tools to create a paint object. This includes all of the Retouch and Clone tools, as well as all the Paint tool brushes, except the Color Replacement Pen tool.

To create a paint object, follow these steps:

1. Choose any painting tool from the Tool panel. PhotoImpact displays the associated options in the Attribute toolbar.

2. Click the Paint As Object button under Mode. When the button is depressed, Paint As Object mode is active.

3. Paint with the selected tool. PhotoImpact places your painting strokes in a separate image object instead of directly onto the base image.

4. Add to your paint object by painting with other colors and other tools as needed to achieve the desired effect. All your painting is part of the same object until you end the object by selecting a non-painting tool.

5. Click the Pick tool. PhotoImpact displays a message saying that you are leaving Paint As Object mode.

6. Click Yes. PhotoImpact closes the dialog box and outlines your paint image with a selection marquee, showing that the paint strokes are selected as an object. The paint object acts just like any other image object.

Figure 7-4 shows an example of painting strokes rendered as an object. Note the selection marquee around each of the painting strokes.

FIGURE 7-4   A few brush strokes rendered as an object

Other Ways to Create Objects

The preceding techniques outline just a few of the many ways that you can create objects in PhotoImpact. Here are some other ways to create objects:

- Anything you draw with the path drawing tools becomes a path object.

- Any text you create with the Text tool becomes a text object.

- When you use the Stamp tool, you deposit objects on your image.

- When you use the Component Designer to create buttons and other Web components, the results are also objects.

> **NOTE** *In the case of Web components, you can elect to add your new component to your image document as individual objects (a path object for the button shape, a text object for the title, and so on) or to merge all of the individual Web component elements into one object. See Chapters 10 through 12 for details on creating Web components.*

Edit Objects

The whole point of creating an object is to manipulate it in some way. You may be selecting a portion of an existing image for special treatment of some kind. Perhaps you're creating new image elements that you need to define and then adjust and position to incorporate them into your image document. Either way, the important characteristic of all objects is that you can select and edit the object separately from the base image, background, or other objects in your image.

Objects can be cut, copied, pasted, moved, resized, reshaped, and distorted. You can overlap objects to provide special merge effects. You can also add special-effect filters and color correction to objects. Objects can be aligned and grouped as well.

Working with objects enables you to do all sorts of things with your images. For example, with careful selection work, you can create a composite image of a family member standing in front of Big Ben or the Eiffel Tower.

Resize Objects Manually

To resize an object manually, do the following:

1. Click the Transform tool in the Tool panel and click the object you want to resize. PhotoImpact displays a bounding box around the object.

2. Click the Transform button at the left end of the Attribute toolbar and choose Resize from the menu that appears.

3. Drag one of the sizing handles (small, black squares) on the corners or sides of the bounding box to resize the object:

- Drag a side to stretch or compress the object along that axis.

- Drag a corner to resize the horizontal and vertical axes simultaneously.

- Press the SHIFT key as you drag to maintain the object proportions as you resize it.

Resize Objects Numerically

The Position & Size tab of Object Properties dialog box, shown in Figure 7-5, allows you to resize an object by specifying Width and/or Height values. To open this dialog box, right-click an object and choose Properties; then click the Position & Size tab.

You can resize the image according to a percentage rather than pixel count by clicking the Unit drop-down menu and choosing Percent. To maintain the original proportions, click the Keep Aspect Ratio checkbox.

Move Objects

To position an object, you can simply drag it with the Pick tool or Standard Selection tool. Alternatively, you can position it numerically by specifying Left and Top values in the Position & Size tab of the Object Properties dialog box (see Figure 7-5). Right-click the object and choose Properties to open this dialog box. Numerical positioning works by indicating the number of pixels the object should be from the

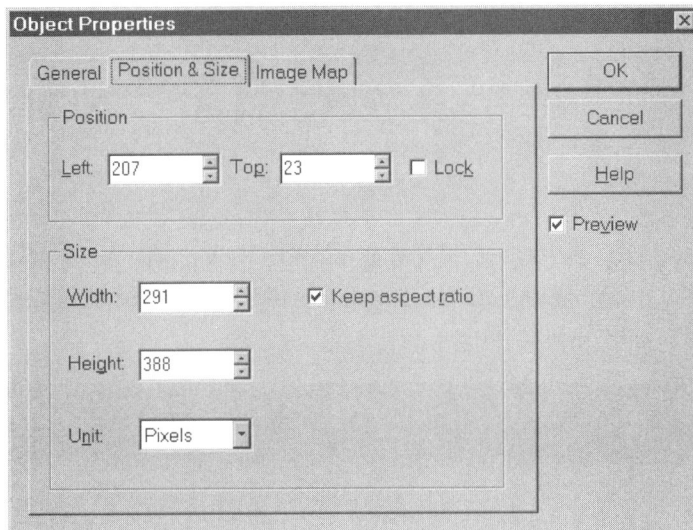

FIGURE 7-5   The Position & Size tab of the Object Properties dialog box

indicated edge. For example, type **50** into the Left field, and the object's left border will be positioned 50 pixels from the left edge of the image. Checking the Lock checkbox enables you to lock the object's position to prevent accidental movement.

Rotate and Flip Objects

To rotate an object, you can use the Transform tool on the Tool panel. Click the object with the Transform tool and then you can use the Attribute toolbar as follows to rotate and flip the object (corresponding commands are also available on the Edit menu):

- To rotate an object numerically, type a rotate amount in the Rotate by Degree field or use the drop-down slider, then click the Rotate Clockwise or Rotate Counterclockwise buttons on either side of the Rotate by Degree box. The object rotates by the degrees you indicate.

- To rotate an object in 90-degree increments, click the Rotate & Flip drop-down menu, and choose a rotation direction. You can rotate left or right 90 degrees or a full 180 degrees.


```
⟲  ▼    ⟲  45.00 ⟳ ≡
🔄 Rotate Left 90°
🔄 Rotate Right 90°
🔄 Rotate 180°
🔄 Flip Horizontally
🔄 Flip Vertically
```

- To rotate an object visually, click the Transform drop-down menu on the Attribute toolbar and choose Rotate Freely. Drag a corner of the bounding box to rotate the object.

- To flip an object, choose Flip Horizontally or Flip Vertically from the Rotate & Flip drop-down menu. (Mirroring an object is the same as flipping it horizontally.)

TIP *You can resize and rotate several objects at once. Just press the* CTRL *key as you click each object with the Transform tool to select it. With multiple objects selected, you can manipulate all of them together.*

Align Objects

When you add multiple objects to an image—for example, a few rows of small thumbnail pictures—you'll want to align them mathematically, not just drag them into place and hope you get it right. To align objects, use the Pick tool to select all of the objects you want to align. You can select multiple objects by clicking each object while holding down the SHIFT key or by dragging a rectangle around them. Then click the Attribute toolbar button for the Align option you want to apply or choose the corresponding command from the Object menu.

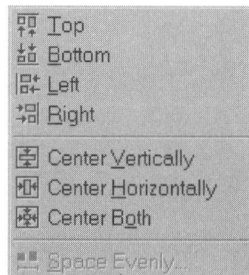

```
🔲 Top
🔲 Bottom
🔲 Left
🔲 Right
🔲 Center Vertically
🔲 Center Horizontally
🔲 Center Both
🔲 Space Evenly...
```

The Align options work as follows:

- To align all selected objects to the leftmost edge of all the objects, choose Object | Align | Left.

- To align all selected objects to the rightmost edge of all selected objects, choose Object | Align | Right.

- To align all selected objects to the top edge of the object nearest the top, choose Object | Align | Top.

- To align all selected objects to the bottom edge of the object nearest the bottom, choose Object | Align | Bottom.

- To center all objects at the objects' common vertical center, choose Object | Align | Center Vertically.

- To center all objects at the objects' common horizontal center, choose Object | Align | Center Horizontally.

- To align all selected objects to the point at the exact center of all selected objects, choose Object | Align | Center Both.

- To create an even amount of horizontal space between all objects, choose Object | Align | Space Evenly. When the Space Evenly dialog box appears, click the Horizontally radio box and click OK.

- To create an even amount of vertical space between all objects, choose Object | Align | Space Evenly. When the Space Evenly dialog box appears, click the Vertically radio box and click OK.

NOTE *If you select a single object for alignment, the document itself will be used as the reference point. For example, click Align Center, and the object will be aligned to the center of the document.*

Group Objects

You can select multiple objects and manipulate them together. However, as soon as you select another object or click the image background, your objects are unselected. If you find yourself repeatedly selecting the same collection of objects so you can manipulate them together, you can save yourself some clicking by creating a group. For example, you might have a drawing of a boat or a logo that is composed of several objects. These objects would be a good candidate for grouping.

To group objects, first select the objects you want to be in the group. Just press and hold down the SHIFT or CTRL keys as you click each object in turn with the Pick tool. Then, with the objects selected, choose Object | Group or press CTRL-ALT-G.

After you define a collection of objects as a group, the group behaves as a single object. Clicking any object in the group selects all the objects in the entire group. Drag one object to move it, and all of the objects in the group move. Grouped objects will stay in their same relative position as you move the group. You can also rotate, resize, and otherwise manipulate the group as a unit. The entire group appears as a single entry in the Layer Manager. (See the "Work with Layers" section later in this chapter for more information about objects and layers.)

If you ever need to edit one of the objects in a group independently of the other grouped objects, you first need to dissolve the group connection so you can access the component objects separately. To dissolve the group, select the group and choose Object | Ungroup or press CTRL-ALT-U.

Merge Several Objects into One

At times, you may want to join several objects together permanently by merging them into a single object. Do this if you want to work with all the objects together as a group, but you want to make the change permanent so that the component elements can't be accessed and changed individually.

Merging several objects together into a single object is a drastic step, because you can't unmerge them later to access the individual component objects. On the other hand, that's the strength of the merging technique: It protects the individual elements of the object from accidental changes. You can move, resize, and distort the merged object as a whole, but the relationship of the component elements of a merged object are forever locked together in relationship to each other. You might want to use this technique on a corporate logo or other graphic that you want to protect from changes.

To merge objects as a single object, select all of the objects you want to merge. Press and hold down the SHIFT or CTRL key as you click each object with the Pick tool. Then choose Object | Merge As Single Object.

Merge Objects into the Base Image

The whole point of an object is that it's a separate entity that you can select and edit without affecting the base image or other objects. However, at some point, you may want an object to become part of the base image or background. The most likely reason for merging an object into the base image is when you need to manipulate the base image and the object together as a single unit.

For example, you might create a composite image composed of a base image of a sunset sky to which you add some foreground trees that you imported as image objects. Now you want to apply a natural painting effect filter to the entire image, and then use it as a background for some text. In order to apply the filter to the sky and trees seamlessly, you need to combine them into a single unit.

To merge an object into the base image, select the object to be merged and choose Object | Merge or press SHIFT-M. The object loses its identity as a separate entity and blends into the base image, replacing the image data from the base image with image data from the object where the two overlap. If you want to merge all the objects in an image document into the base image in one step, you can choose Object | Merge All or press CTRL-SHIFT-M.

CAUTION   *Once you merge an object into the base image, the base image is permanently changed. You can't extract the object from the base image later and restore the portion of the base image that was changed by the addition of the image data from the object.*

7

Transform Objects

Along with resizing and rotating objects, the Transform tool can also bend and twist and manipulate your objects in all kinds of ways. To reshape an object, click it with the Transform tool, and then click the Transform drop-down menu on the upper-left side of the Attribute toolbar. The options on this menu works as follows:

■   Click the Slant button to slant an object. Then drag the mouse along any edge of the object to slant it in the direction you are dragging, as illustrated below.

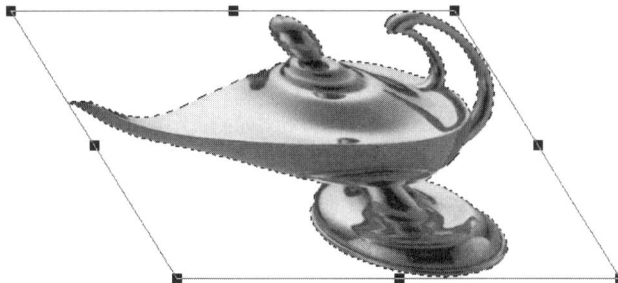

■ Click the Distort button to distort an object. Then drag in any direction on any corner to distort the image accordingly.

■ To add perspective to an object, click the Perspective button. Then drag a corner toward or away from the center of a side to distort the object in a way that simulates perspective, as illustrated below.

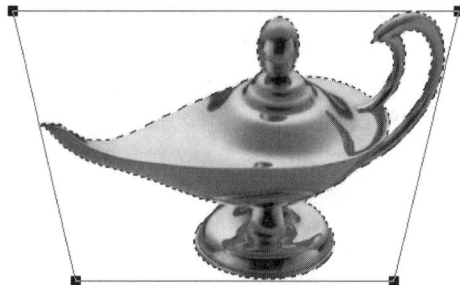

TIP   *You can also distort and twist a shape using the Deform Gallery in the EasyPalette panel.*

Work with Selections

Chapter 2 covered the basics of how to create selections. This section describes some ways you can put the selection tools to good use.

Create Selections

One very common use of selections is to copy sections from other images and paste them against a background, creating a collage. You can isolate sections of images, copying only those portions that will enhance the project.

For simple selections that conform to a basic shape, you may want to use the Standard Selection tool. The Attribute toolbar for the Standard Selection tool includes a Shape drop-down menu offering four shapes: Rectangle, Square, Ellipse, and Circle.

At times, you'll want to create a very precise selection that conforms to a shape defined in the image. This is often done to select only a single clearly identifiable item and cleanly eliminate the background. For irregular shapes, the Lasso tool or Bezier Curve Selection tool is best. Figure 7-6 shows an example of an irregularly shaped selection outline created with the Lasso tool.

To create a precise selection, follow these steps:

1. Draw a rough contour with the Lasso tool.

2. Zoom in on a small section of the edge of the selection.

3. Use the buttons on the Attribute toolbar to switch into Addition or Subtraction mode to refine your selection by adding or deleting small areas to or from the larger selection.

4. Use the scrollbars on the document window to work your way around the selection outline, refining the selection a small section at a time.

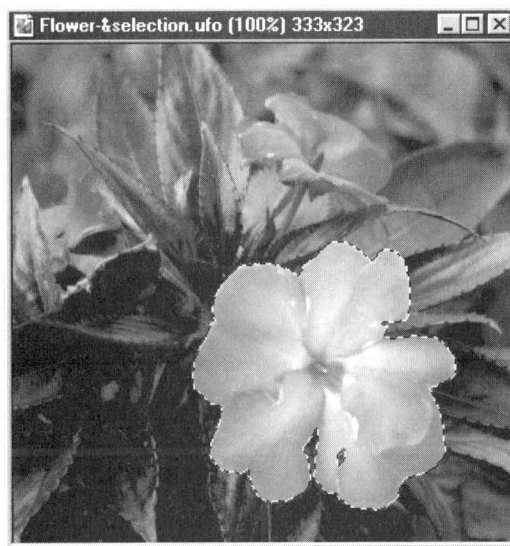

FIGURE 7-6   An irregularly shaped selection outline created with the Lasso tool.

Use Selections for Selective Editing

Selection tools are not only used to copy and move pixel data. There are times you'll want to perform an edit on a portion of an image without affecting the surrounding area. Using selections for selective editing can come in handy when using filters.

For example, Figure 7-7 shows the result of using a filter effect to blur the background around a flower, while keeping the flower sharp. First, an precise selection was created around the flower. Then we chose Selection | Invert to select the rest of the image and exempt the flower from the effect. Finally, we applied the Gaussian Blur effect filter to the selection. (See Chapter 6 for more information about the Gaussian Blur effect and other filters.)

Work with Masks

Selections are closely related to another PhotoImpact feature: *masks*. In fact, a mask is a selection that boasts special transparent properties.

FIGURE 7-7 Selections enable you to apply filter effects to selected areas only.

When you create a selection, you are creating a boundary. You are indicating an area of an image that will be edited. The image area inside the selection will be edited, and the outside will not. For example, if you create a selection and fill it with green, the entire selected area will be filled with green to the boundaries of the selection. Areas of the image outside the selection are unaffected by the green fill.

A mask is a variable selection, one in which the boundaries are often blurred and selected areas can be partially selected. It's the same partial transparency effect you see in the feathered edges of a soft-edged selection, except that the transparency effect can be anywhere in the mask.

A mask is created by drawing with a grayscale palette, using white, gray, and black. Image areas that are white are part of the selection. Image areas that are black are completely unselected; gray areas are partially selected. So, for example, if you fill a mask with green, the white areas of your mask will be completely green, and the gray areas will be tinted partially green. Black areas will not be green at all.

When creating a mask, the darker the gray used, the more transparent, or unselected, the area is. Use lighter gray, and the area will show more of your image manipulations; the mask will be more opaque. In white areas of your mask, all your editing will be full strength.

You can apply a mask to an image and then manipulate the portions of the image selected by the mask, just as you would any other selection. Image manipulations you apply will be partially visible in some areas and completely visible in others. For example, apply a blur filter on a mask, and the amount of blur seen on the underlying image will vary according to the mask's semi-transparent properties.

Applying a PhotoImpact Preset Mask

PhotoImpact comes with an assortment of preset masks, available in the EasyPalette panel's Mask Library, as shown in Figure 7-8. When you apply a preset mask, you can add any fill you like, use any drawing tool inside the mask, or even paste an image inside the mask boundary.

As an example of using a preset mask, the following procedure applies a mask to a blank page and then adds a solid black fill. In this example, you'll see that the color fills only the Mask. Follow these steps:

1. Create a new, blank image, preferably with a background color of white.

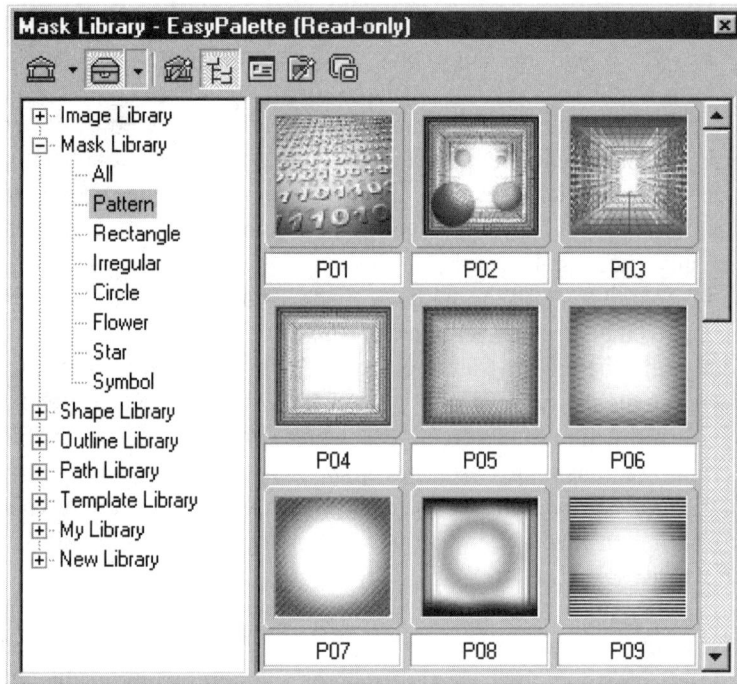

FIGURE 7-8 The EasyPalette showing the Mask Library

2. Open the Easy Palette (choose View | Toolbars & Panels | Easy Palette) and select the Mask Library (see Figure 7-8).

3. Drag a mask thumbnail from the EasyPalette and drop it on your image document. The mask appears as a selection marquee. Depending on the mask you choose, the selection may look quite complicated. The next illustration shows the results of choosing the P02 thumbnail from the Pattern category.

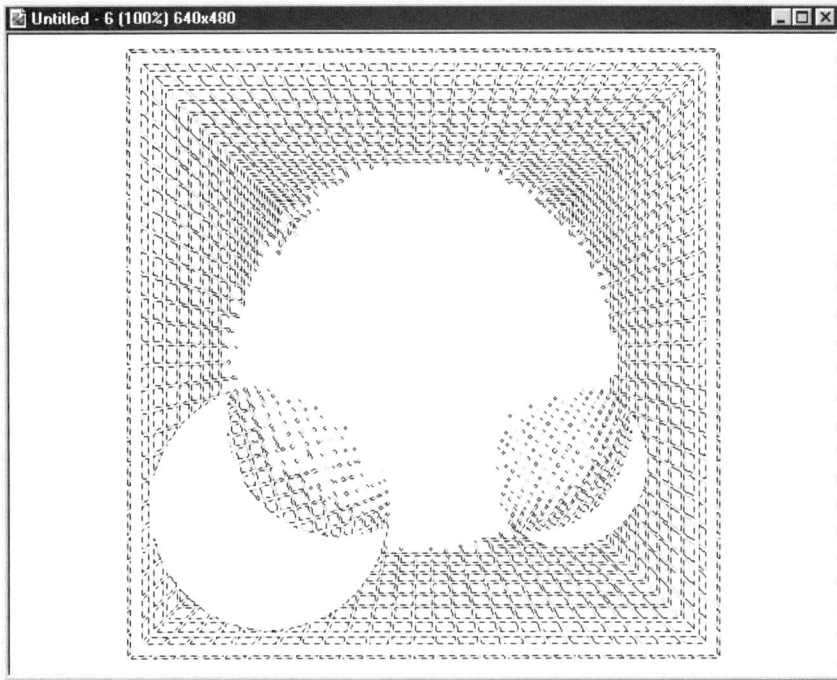

Untitled - 6 (100%) 640x480

4. Select a Fill tool from the Tool panel and set the fill attributes in the Attribute toolbar.

5. Apply the fill to the selection created by the mask. PhotoImpact fills the selection with the fill color. Notice that the fill color isn't applied uniformly. Instead, the fill color is stronger in some areas and weaker in others, depending on the densities in the mask. The next illustration shows the Pattern P02 mask filled with a solid-black fill. All the shades of gray are a result of variations in the mask density.

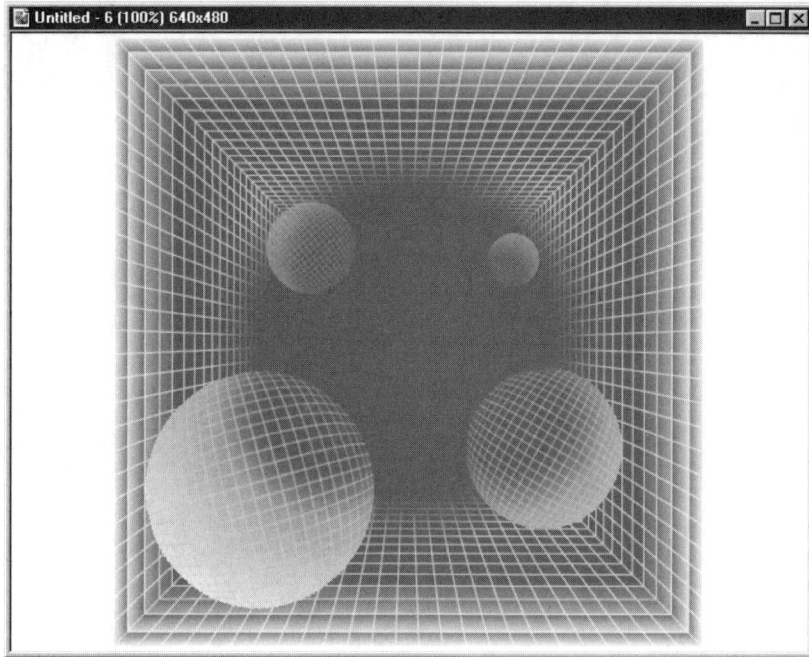

Create a Mask

To create your own mask in PhotoImpact, you work in Mask mode and draw or use fills with shades of gray to control the transparency of the mask. First, click the Mask Mode icon on the Tool panel. Two changes will occur:

Your existing image will be covered by a semi-transparent layer of white, which indicates an opaque mask, as shown in Figure 7-9.

Your color palette will now be grayscale. Everything you create on the canvas will be shades of gray, from white to black.

Now you can define the mask with the PhotoImpact drawing and painting tools. You can paint with any painting tool, draw path objects, and type text objects. You can create a selection with a selection tool and fill it with any Fill tool. You can even import images and objects to become part of the mask.

Draw or paint with white to define areas that will allow the underlying image to show through. Areas that you make black will obscure the underlying image. Define semi-transparent areas of the mask with various shades of gray. As you draw and paint in mask mode, you'll see the underlying image show through the mask overlay to varying degrees. Figure 7-10 shows an example of an image with a mask defined.

FIGURE 7-9   An image in Mask mode

To leave Mask mode, click the Mask Mode icon again. Your mask will appear as a selection in your image. When you apply a fill or edit of some sort, you'll notice the mask's semi-transparent nature.

> **TIP** *When working in Mask mode, it's nearly impossible to see what you're doing to a white mask overlay if it appears on an image composed of a plain, white background. Try changing the background color or opening an existing image before invoking Mask mode. Alternatively, you can change the mask color from white to another color in the PhotoImpact preferences. For details, see Chapter 17, which is available online on the Osborne Web site (www.osborne.com).*

Add a Mask to the EasyPalette

You can save a mask and apply it to another image or to the current image at a later time. For example, you might want to save a mask that conforms to a particular shape, such as a company logo or design. When you save a mask, you are saving

FIGURE 7-10   An image with a mask defined

the transparency values of your mask, not the image data from the image or background the mask is currently sitting on. To save a mask, do the following:

1. Create a mask.

2. Make sure you are no longer in Mask mode and that you do not have the base image selected. You should see the selection marquee on the image.

3. Choose Selection | Copy Selection to Object Library. The Add to EasyPalette dialog box will appear.

4. Fill in the Sample Name, and select appropriate settings in the Gallery/ Library, and Tab Group boxes.

5. Click the OK button to close the Add to EasyPalette dialog box. PhotoImpact adds the selection mask to the specified library in the EasyPalette.

TIP	*You can use this same technique to add a regular selection to the EasyPalette.*

Work with Paths

Path objects can be outlines, filled shapes, or lines and arrows. The path itself is a line or outline, and it is very editable. You can alter a single-line segment within a complex path at any time, even after you've already filled it with a texture or color.

There are three tools for creating paths and one tool for editing paths. Chapter 2 covered the basics of how to access and use the Path Drawing tool, Outline Drawing tool, Line and Arrow tool, and Path Edit tool. This section explains when you might create paths, the Material option for paths, and how to transform a path into a selection.

7

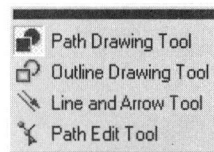

Uses of Paths

Selections are outlines that define an area of the image and select it for editing. However, the path objects you create with PhotoImpact's path-drawing tools can also be considered outlines. So how are selections and paths different, and when would you choose one over the other?

Remember that a path object is a vector graphic rather than a bitmap image. As such, the path object is composed of precise lines and curves that can be resized and manipulated without loss of quality. When bitmaps are enlarged, jagged edges become apparent, and the image is less distinct. Path objects, on the other hand, look sharp even when enlarged several times their original size.

Use paths to create precise shapes with texture that seem to jump off the page. Path objects can have bevels, bumps, and angles. When you apply lighting to a textured or beveled shape, the three-dimensional quality is enhanced. Figure 7-11 shows how a simple shape can be transformed into a three-dimensional object.

For example, you can use path objects to create company logos or designs that will be used in a number of instances. Because shapes based on paths can be resized without loss of quality, it's easy to use the same basic path object for a large version of a logo, which is can be printed at 300 dpi, as well as a small Web version of a logo, sized for rapid download and display. Path objects accommodate this usage much better than bitmap images.

When you save or export your PhotoImpact image as an image file, the path objects are merged into the base image and become part of the bitmapped image along with everything else. However, path objects retain their status as independent entities that can be resized without losing quality only while you work in PhotoImpact or save the image in one of a select few file formats (such as the native PhotoImpact file format, UFO) that support objects.

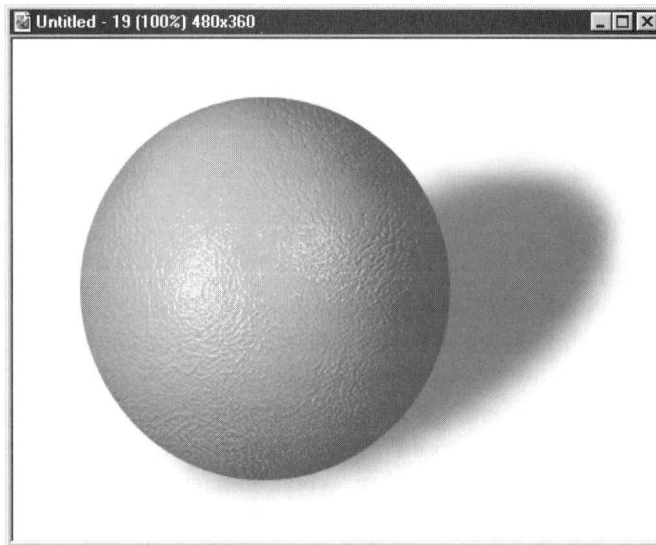

FIGURE 7-11   A path objrect with 3D effects

Use the Material Options

In addition to the obvious color attribute of a path object, the Material options allow you to select 3D effects and set bevel size and height, texture, reflection, bump, and many other parameters to be applied to a new or existing path object, as shown in Figure 7-12.

To access these options, click the Material button on the Attribute toolbar while creating a path object. The Material dialog box appears, as shown in Figure 7-13.

The Material dialog box includes nine tabs with options that affect the surface of your path object. The options on each tab are described in the following sections. If your path is a thin outline, the adjustments you make in the Material dialog box may not be very dramatic. If your path is a filled shape or thicker outline, you'll notice dramatic effects. The preview box on the right side of the Material dialog box displays a generic shape that shows an approximation of the results of your selections in the dialog box.

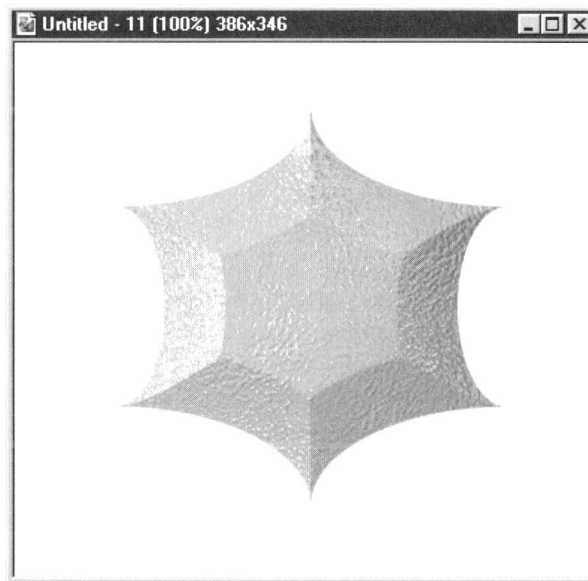

7

Untitled - 11 (100%) 386x346

FIGURE 7-12   Filled shape with surface effect

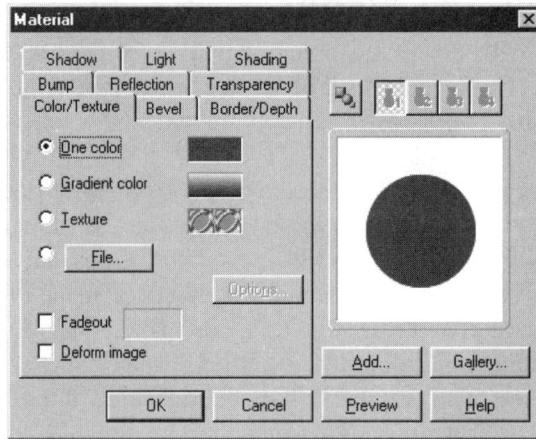

The Material dialog box

Color/Texture Tab

On the Color/Texture tab (see Figure 7-13) you can choose a color, gradient, texture, or image for your path object surface. If your path object is a solid-filled shape, this choice determines the surface appearance for the entire shape.

The One Color, Gradient Color, Texture, and File options provide access to the fill options that are equivalent to their counterparts in the Fill dialog box. (See Chapter 9 for details on working with the Fill dialog box options.) Perhaps the most interesting of these options is the Texture fill. Click the Texture box to access the two Texture libraries: Magic Texture or Natural Texture. The Magic Texture Library is a collection of patterns and designs, such as stone masonry, weaving, and fractals. The Natural Texture Library is largely a collection of patterns found in nature, such as water, grass, and flower fields. However, you'll also find household patterns such as wallpaper and brick. When a library appears, click one of the thumbnail textures, and it will be applied to your path object.

Bevel Tab

On the Bevel tab, you can choose from several bevel types. 3D Round, which creates a smooth, rounded surface, and 3D Chisel, which creates a bevel with a sharper edge, are the most common types of bevels applied to path objects. When you apply a spotlight (through the Light tab), it is the bevel angle that catches the light and adds realism to your path object's surface.

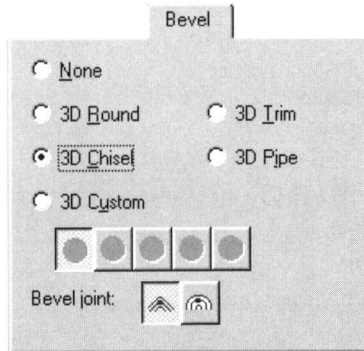

You can also choose a Bevel Joint option, which will be apparent only if your path has sharp corners.

Border/Depth Tab

The Border/Depth tab includes Border and Depth settings, which determine the size and depth of your outline's border and bevel.

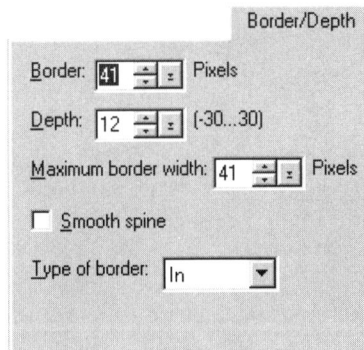

The Maximum Border Width setting applies when using a gradient fill, since gradient fill extents are determined by border amounts.

Bump Tab

On the Bump tab, you can select the Bump Map option and choose an image file as a "bump" (surface) texture. The image you choose will appear embossed across the surface of the path object. See Chapter 9 for more information on Bump Maps.

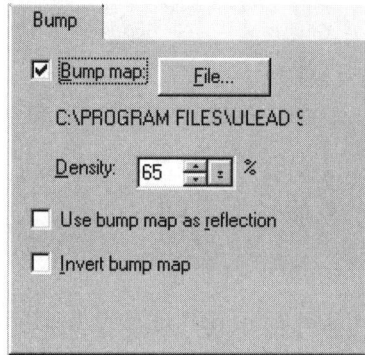

Reflection Tab

On the Reflection tab, you can select the Reflection Map option and choose an image file that will appear to be reflected off the surface of the path object. See Chapter 9 for more information on using the Reflection Map feature.

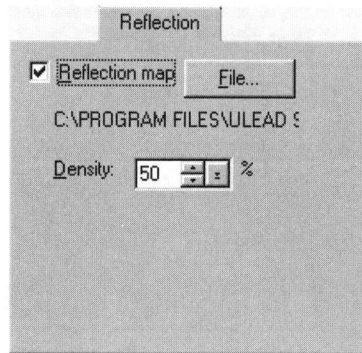

Transparency Tab

If you check the Transparency option on the Transparency tab, you can specify the transparency for the 3D portions of the object. This effect alters the transparency amount of your path object's bevel if you have used a 3D setting; it is separate from (and additive to) the general object transparency that you set in the Object Properties dialog box or the Layer Manager. Since 3D surfaces have variable visibility levels, PhotoImpact also lets you choose a Minimum Transparency amount, so that portions of your path shape don't disappear altogether.

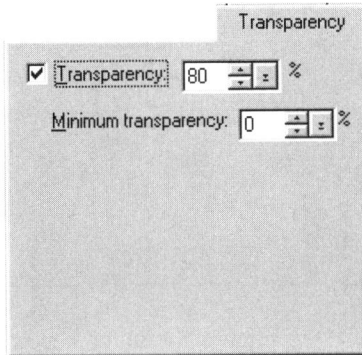

Shadow Tab

Using the Shadow tab, you can add a shadow to the entire object and specify shadow settings. To adjust the shadow settings, click the Options button to open the Shadow dialog box, described in Chapter 6.

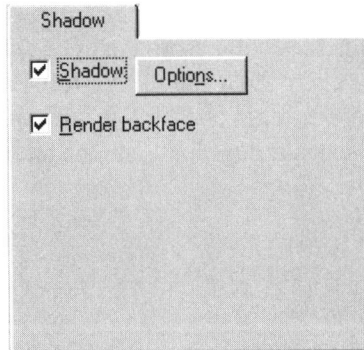

Light Tab

The shading effects that define the 3D surfaces of an object are created by the interaction of the 3D planes with a virtual "light source." You can add more lights using the Light tab. Specify the number and type of lights (Spot or Direct) that create highlights and shading in 3D effects. To dramatize the effect of the direct or spot lighting, reduce the ambient light using the Ambient slider.

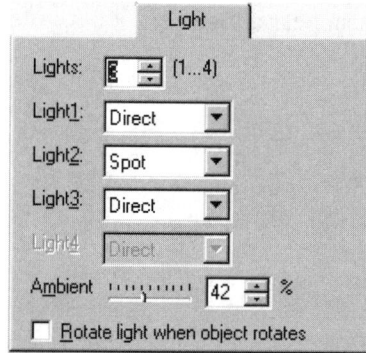

After adding a light, you'll see a new light button become available in the preview area (in all of the Material dialog box tabs), above the image box. You can manually move each light. Click a light button and then drag inside the preview area to move that light. The light's beam will follow your mouse movements.

Shading Tab

The options on the Shading tab determine how dramatically the light reflects off the surface of your path object. Metallic surfaces will reflect light, displaying less of their own color. Phong surfaces will absorb the light, and retain more of the color value of your fill or surface color. You can further refine those basic surface types with the Shininess and Strength settings. The Specular and Ambient color boxes let you set the color of the specular highlight and the ambient light.

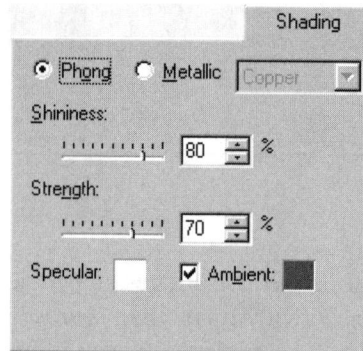

Transform a Path into a Selection

After you create a path object, you can transform it into a selection. If the path object's Attribute toolbar is visible, all you need to do is choose Selection from the Mode list box in the Attribute toolbar. You'll see the path object lines changes to the selection marquee lines.

TIP	*To display the Attribute toolbar for an existing path object, select the object with the Pick tool; then right-click the object and choose Edit Attributes from the pop-up menu that appears.*

If you are doing precise and detailed selection work, there is one huge advantage to creating paths and converting them to selections: using the path-drawing tools, it's easier to create and edit multiple objects than it is to work with a selection composed of several selection areas.

As you may have discovered just by tinkering around, creating a selection automatically deselects any previous selection in the image. You can use the Addition mode to draw additional selection areas, but all it takes is one slip to lose your work defining the selection. However, you can create as many path objects in an image as you like and freely edit each one individually as you see fit. Then, when you're ready to transform the path objects to a selection, follow these steps:

1. Select the path objects you want to convert to a selection. CTRL-click each object with the Pick tool.

2. Choose Object | Merge As Single Object to make the selected objects one entity.

3. Right-click the merged object and choose Edit Attributes from the pop-up menu that appears. PhotoImpact displays the Attribute toolbar for the object.

4. Choose Selection from the Mode list box on the Attribute toolbar. The outline or fill disappears from the path object, and it becomes a selection, marked by a selection marquee.

Work with Layers

One of the interesting facts about objects is that they can overlap. Objects can overlap each other, and they can overlap the base image or background. They can overlap totally or partially.

When an object overlaps the base image or another object, it is stacked on top of the other objects and the base image. The object that is on top of the stack is the one you see, but the other objects and the base image still exist. The object on top may obscure the other objects from view, but it doesn't alter or erase any of the objects below it. If you move the top object, any previously obscured objects will again be fully visible.

This stacked characteristic of objects in layers is in stark contrast to the way PhotoImpact and other image editors work when you use the regular pixel-editing paint mode. When you paint on the base image, you replace pixels of one color with pixels of another color. The image data that was there before is no longer there. If you paint on an image and then go back and select the area you painted and move it, you'll create a hole in the image, because there is only one layer to the base image.

When you work with objects, it may be helpful to visualize a stack of transparent acetate overlays stacked up over your base image — like the overlays used by graphic artists and architects to show alternative versions of a base drawing. Each object resides on a separate overlay, or *layer*. The layers of acetate keep all the various objects neatly arranged and separate. You can select, move, remove, or edit the object on a given layer, without affecting any of the other objects. As you create each new object, it is added to the top of the stack as part of a new layer. Therefore, the last object to be created is normally on top. However, you can rearrange the layers, similar to shuffling a stack of cards, to bring one object closer to the top or bottom of the stack.

Control Object Transparency and Merge Effects

When an object on top of the stack overlaps an object lower in the stack, the top object normally hides the lower object from view. However, PhotoImpact allows you to adjust the transparency of objects, so other results are also possible. When one object overlaps another, three things can happen:

- The top object obscures the lower object. You can't see the lower object at all.

- If the top object is partially transparent, a lower object will be partially visible through the top object.

- Rather than obscure the bottom layer, the top layer's color or saturation values are used to determine the appearance of the lower layer. This occurs if you have applied a merge rule to the upper layer. The lower layer will look different in a number of ways when a Merge setting is applied to the upper layer.

These overlapping effects—opacity, transparency, or merge—are determined by the object properties of each object and their stacking order. You can adjust properties for an object in the Object Properties dialog box (right-click the object and choose Properties from the pop-up menu that appears). You can adjust stacking order by selecting an object with the Pick tool and then clicking one of the Arrange buttons in the Attribute toolbar. However, the easiest way to control object-stacking order, transparency, and Merge mode is by using PhotoImpact's new Layer Manager.

Use the Layer Manager

New to
PhotoImpact 7

The Layer Manager, shown in Figure 7-14, lets you view object-stacking order and an object's Transparency and Merge settings. To open the Layer Manager, choose View | Toolbars & Panels | Access Panel, and click the Layer Manager icon on the upper left.

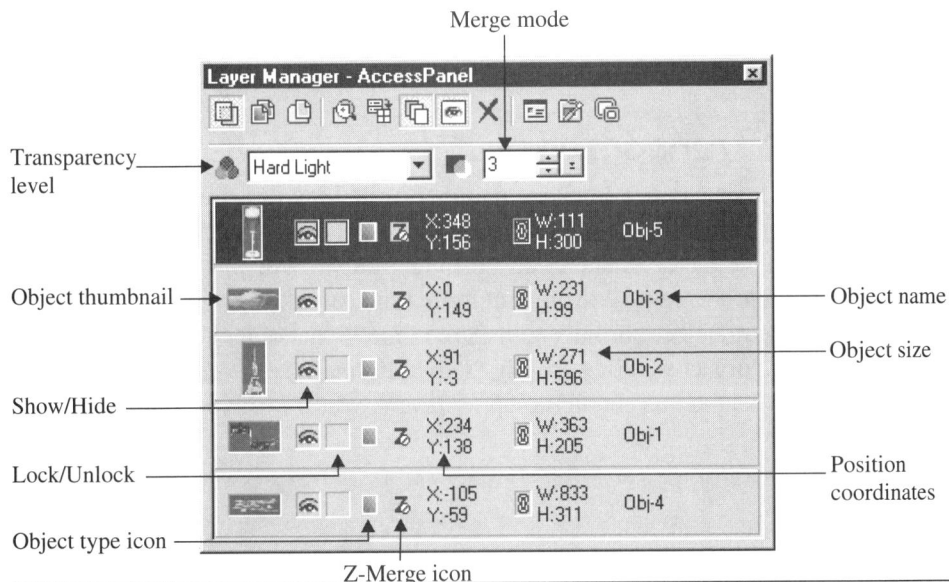

FIGURE 7-14 The Layer Manager

In the Layer Manager, each object in your image appears as a separate row of information. Each row represents a separate layer. A small thumbnail of the object appears at the left end of the row, followed by buttons that allow you to show/hide the layer or lock/unlock its position The other icons and readings are informational.

Layers are displayed according to stacking order. The top object in the Layer Manager is the top object in your image.

> **NOTE** *Normally, each object resides on its own layer. However, if you group objects, the group appears in the Layer Manager as a single layer. When you ungroup objects, they again show up in the Layer Manager as separate layers.*

You can click and drag a layer up or down in the Layer Manager to change the stack order of the layers. Click the eyeball icon on a layer to show or hide that object. The Transparency and Merge list boxes at the top of the Layer Manager enable you to adjust the transparency and merge properties of the selected object. Double-click a layer in the Layer Manager to open the Object Properties dialog box for that object.

When you select a layer in the Layer Manager, the corresponding object is selected in your image. This makes the Layer Manager a convenient way to select objects that are hidden behind other objects and therefore difficult to click with the Pick tool.

Set Object Transparency

You can set the Transparency level for an object, allowing the objects on layers beneath to show through to the degree you specify. To change an object's transparency, on the Layer Manager or Attribute toolbar, type in a Transparency amount. Higher numbers make the object more transparent.

After making an object partially transparent, move that object over another object. The lower object will be partially visible. If you have several layers and high Transparency amounts set on the upper layers, you'll be able to partially see those lower layers.

Set Merge Modes

Merge modes change the basic rules of object visibility. When you change the Merge mode of a layer, you are specifying that the color, saturation, and lightness values of the object on that layer will be used to determine how the overlapping areas of the object should display their colors. Merge modes determine which pixels will show through from a lower layer and which will be blocked.

You can set the Merge mode for an object by using the Merge drop-down menu at the top of the Layer Manager or the corresponding option in the Object Properties dialog box. The default setting is "Always."

The following are the most commonly used Merge modes:

- **Always**   The top object always takes precedence over the lower layers.

- **Multiply**   Treats all layers as if each were semi-transparent and allows each layer's colors to darken the previous layer's colors accordingly.

- **Overlay**   Multiplies the dark pixels of the upper layer and emphasizes the light pixels of the lower layers. This mode often creates a pleasant effect.

- **Lighten**   Applies only the colors in the upper layer that are lighter than the colors in the lower layer. Use this to display the brighter contents of an image against the darker contents of an image below it.

- **Darken**   Applies only the colors in the upper layer that are darker than the colors in the lower layer. Use this to display darker contents of an image against the lighter contents of an image below it.

- **Saturation Only**   Uses the Saturation values of the upper layer to determine how saturated the colors in the lower layer should be. In other words, the S value of the upper layer replaces the S value of the lower layer's HSL (Hue, Saturation, Luminosity) amount.

- **Luminosity Only**   Uses the Luminosity values of the upper layer to determine how light the colors in the lower layer should appear. The L value of the upper layer replaces the L value of the lower layer's HSL value.

- **Difference**   Inverts the colors of the lower layers according to the Brightness value in the upper layer. For example, if the lower layer is red, then areas of white in the upper layer will turn the corresponding lower layer segment green. Areas of black in the upper layer will leave the corresponding lower layer segment unaffected.

7

Stitching Together Panoramas

Have you ever tried to take a picture of a scenic panorama and found that you simply couldn't get it all in one shot with your camera, even on the widest zoom setting? Perhaps you needed to take a picture in a small room and you just couldn't back up far enough to get every thing into the picture that you wanted. Unless you have access to a special panorama camera or ultra-wide angle lens, you'll just have to settle for taking a series of pictures as you pan the camera around to take in the whole scene. Taking multiple pictures records all the information, but it just doesn't have the same visual effect as one panoramic image.

You're in luck. PhotoImpact includes a special feature that facilitates joining multiple images to create one somewhat seamless panorama. This effect depends on the availability of overlapping photographs of a subject. Once you have such photos scanned or copied from your digital camera and in a folder location where PhotoImpact can open them, you are ready to stitch them together.

TIP	*The images used in a panorama should be the same height, but not necessarily the same width. When shooting images for your panorama view, use a tripod and shoot all images on the same horizontal plane for best results.*

You begin by stitching two images together, then build from there. Here are the steps for stitching two images:

1. Open both images you want to stitch together. The image that will appear farthest to the left in your panorama should be the active window.

2. Choose Edit | Stitch. The Stitch dialog box appears. The image you selected will appear in the preview window on the right.

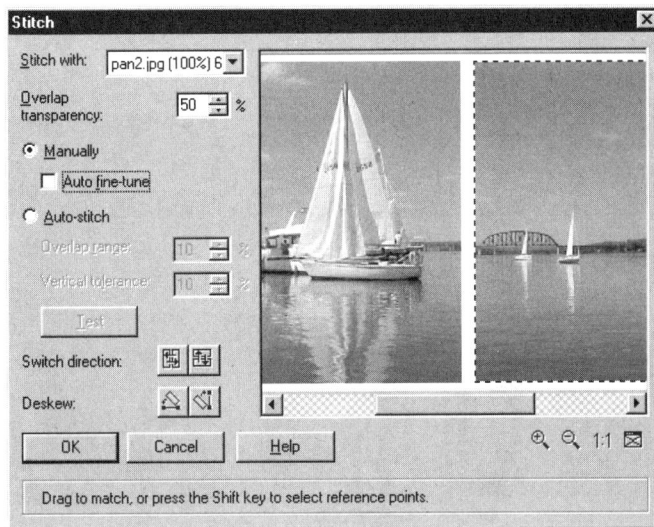

3. Select the next image file from the Stitch With list box at the upper-left side of the dialog box. PhotoImpact adds the new image to the preview window.

4. Click the Manually radio button and deselect the Auto Fine-Tune option.

5. Use the scrollbars and/or the zoom buttons under the preview box to locate the joint between the two images.

6. Click and drag the image on the right in the preview window so that it overlaps and aligns with the image on the left. Position the images so that overlapping is not apparent. Generally, you can align the top or bottom edge of the image, but you may get a better result by aligning a horizontal line or other prominent feature in the middle of the images.

7. Click OK, and the two images will be stitched, appearing as a new file, named Untitled-1, as shown in Figure 7-15.

After you start a panorama by stitching together the first two images, you can simply repeat the procedure to add more images. If you have enough images, you can build a full 360-degree panorama.

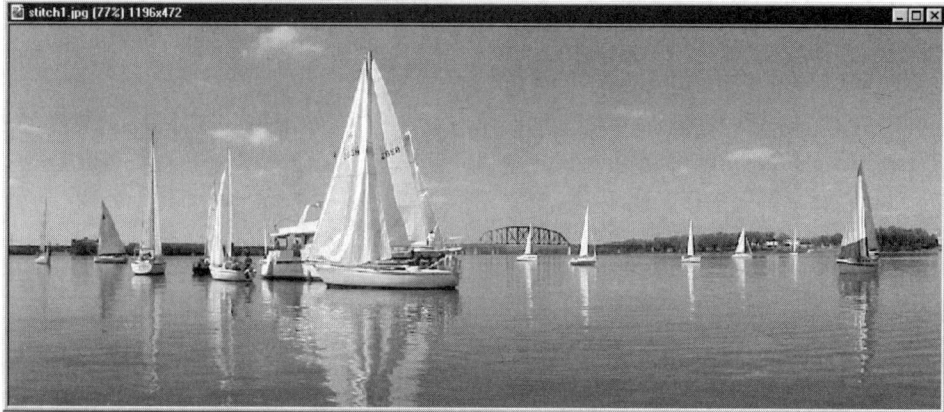

stitch1.jpg (77%) 1196x472

FIGURE 7-15   The new image that results from the initial stitching

CHAPTER 8

Work with Text

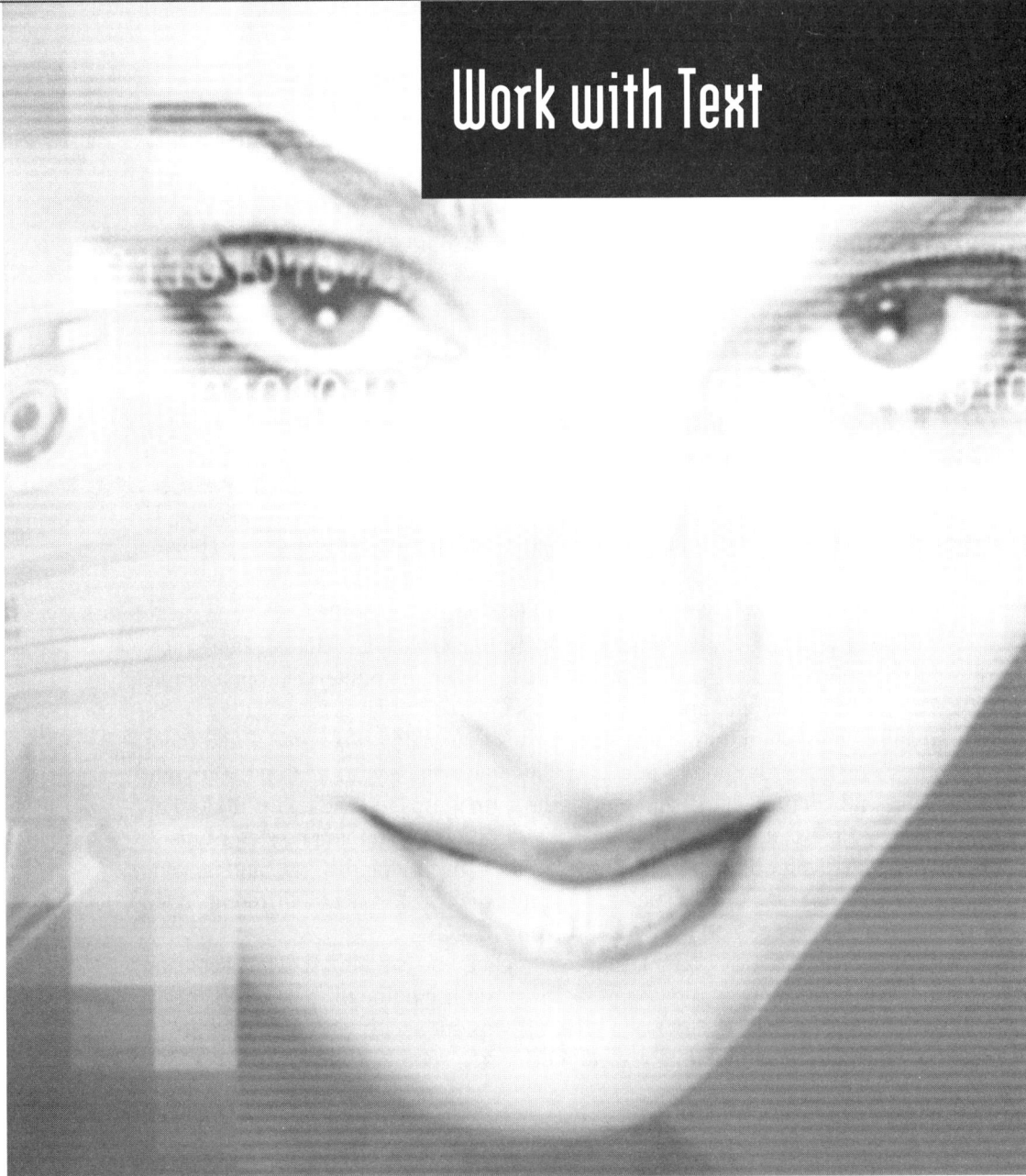

It's tempting to think of text as the forte of word processors and not something you need in an image-editing program. However, the reality is that many of the images and graphics that you work on with PhotoImpact will involve at least some text elements.

Text-editing power is one of PhotoImpact's most compelling features. In PhotoImpact, you can add text to an existing image or to a blank canvas. You can then color the text, move it around, resize it, or add a shadow. You can fill text with textures and patterns; change the font, size, and other attributes; and give it a 3D effect. You can even rotate and distort text. Still, after all that manipulation, you can select and edit the text with the Text tool.

Text Versus Bitmaps

Text and computerized photographs are rooted in different technologies. When you choose a font for your text, you are specifying an alphabet designed with finely honed curves and angles, each letter a work of art in itself. Modern computer text starts out as vector objects, like PhotoImpact's path objects. The lines and curves that define each letter are recorded as mathematical formulas that can be scaled up or down without compromising the precision of the letter shape.

Computerized photographs, on the other hand, are bitmaps. They are composed of rows of colored pixels, which combine to approximate what an original photograph looked like. Upon close inspection, images displayed in computerized photographs have very jagged edges and are far from precise.

In many image-editing programs, text begins as a dialog box entry. From there, it becomes a temporarily mobile selection. Once you place your text on the image background, it becomes an integral part of the bitmap image. The text is no longer a separately editable object; it's just a pattern of pixels. When you resize or twist bitmap text, the quality of the type degrades rapidly, becoming distorted and jagged around the edges. You can't go back and change the text to select a different font or correct a misspelling. You need to start from scratch.

Text in PhotoImpact is different. In PhotoImpact, you can almost always change your original text entry to correct a misspelling, replace a line of text, adjust the text size, or select a different font or style—all without needing to undo or redo other text attributes and even many special effects.

PhotoImpact Text Features

PhotoImpact treats text as a separate object that retains all the precision and editability of vector graphics (like path objects). You can create a text object with the Text tool and position it on your image. The text object remains separate from the background image, which means that you can select and edit it at a later time, even after working with other painting and drawing tools.

A PhotoImpact text object is a vector graphic object, which means that its quality doesn't degrade with changes in size or repeated manipulations. This means that you can create a text object, resize it, add a rainbow-colored fill, and bend it into an arc. Then, if you decide that you would prefer a different font or you need to edit the text to change the wording, you can make those changes easily, without losing any of the effects and manipulations.

Text can also be transformed into a selection, a path object, or an image object. Each object type has a unique affect on how your text appears. For example, after converting a text object to a path object, you can edit the path nodes to alter individual letter shapes. After converting a text object to an image object, you can apply effect filters that work on only pixel-based images or alter the object with painting tools. You can even convert a text object to a selection that you can use as a stencil, carving a cutout into a background bitmap.

8

Create Text

As you create images and graphics in PhotoImpact, you'll undoubtedly find many situations in which you need to create text objects. For example, here are just a few of the many uses of text:

- Create logos
- Create product labels and descriptions
- Add captions and labels to images
- Add paragraphs of text to images
- Create button graphics for web pages
- Create text-based graphics for newsletters and web pages
- Produce business cards
- Design invitations and greeting cards

Creating a text object and adding it to your image is a relatively simple process. The basic procedure for creating text in PhotoImpact is outlined in Chapter 2. The short version is as follows: Select the Text tool and then click the image to open the Text Entry Box. Adjust the text attributes and then type the text. You can enter a single word or phrase, a single line of type, several lines, or a block of multiple paragraphs. Just press ENTER to start a new line. (There is no word wrap feature active in the Text Entry Box.) After you enter the text, click OK to close the Text Entry Box and display the new text object on your image. The text object appears at the location where you clicked the Text tool.

> **TIP** *You can copy text from a word processor or other program and paste it into the Text Entry Box in PhotoImpact. Just select the text you want to copy, press CTRL-C, click in PhotoImpact's Text Entry Box to start entering text, and press CTRL-V to paste the text.*

When your text appears in the document window, it is surrounded by a selection marquee, showing that it is selected for further editing. The selection marquee traces the outline of each letter in the text object, as shown in Figure 8-1. However, the entire text block is one object (unless and until you break it apart into individual lines or letters).

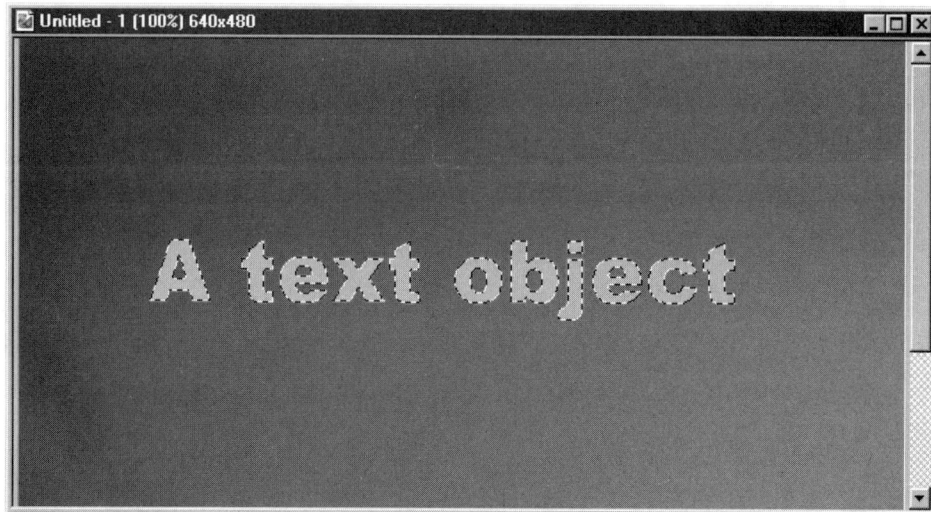

FIGURE 8-1   A newly created text object is surrounded by a selection marquee, showing that it is ready for more editing.

After your text object appears in the document window, you can click and drag it with the Text tool to move it to a new location.

Modify Text Attributes

You can change text attributes by adjusting settings in the Attribute toolbar, Text Entry Box, or Text panel. Text attributes range from basic choices, such as font and style, to more advanced features, such as vertical orientation and baseline shift.

Select Text

When your text object first appears in the document, it is automatically selected for further editing. That's fairly obvious. What isn't so obvious is that the text object retains its identity as a separate entity, even after you use other tools or select and edit other objects. As mentioned earlier in the chapter, a text object doesn't automatically merge into the base image in PhotoImpact, as it does in some other image-editing programs. (You can, however, merge a text object into the base image manually by selecting the object and choosing Object | Merge.)

Since the text object normally remains a separate object, you can reselect the text object at any time and edit it. You select a text object in the same way that you select any other PhotoImpact object. However, the selection tool and technique you use will influence what editing you can do on the text object. Here is a summary of selection techniques for text objects:

- Click the text object with the Pick tool. This selects the object and allows you to move the text object, to adjust alignment and other attributes from the Pick tool's Attribute toolbar and to apply filters and other commands.

- Click the text object with the Standard Selection tool. This also selects the object for routine manipulation.

- Click the text object with the Text tool. This enables more text-editing options because of the text-specific settings available in the Attribute toolbar when the Text tool is in use.

- Open the Layer Manager (click the Layer Manager button in the Panel Manager or press F10 to open the Access Panel and then click the Layer Manager button) and then click the list item corresponding to the text object you want to select. This highlights the row in the Layer Manager and selects the object in the document window.

8

When selecting text with the Text tool, you need to be careful that you are selecting existing text and not creating a new text object. When you point to an existing text object with the Text tool, the I-beam text cursor beside the arrow disappears, indicating that a click will select the text under the pointer. If the I-beam is present, a click will start a new text object. Selecting large, thick text is easy, but you may need a steady hand to select a text object composed of small, thin type, because you need to click on one of the letters, not just anywhere within the outer perimeter of a word or phrase.

> **TIP**   *To select text objects composed of small, thin type, use the Pick tool and drag a rectangle around the text object. PhotoImpact selects the object or objects within the rectangle. Then right-click and choose Edit Attributes from the pop-up menu that appears to display the Text Attributes toolbar, just as if you had selected the text object with the Text tool.*

Change Text Attributes with the Attribute Toolbar

One of the fastest and easiest ways to adjust the attributes of a text object is to use the settings on the Attribute toolbar, as described in Chapter 2. The text attributes are available any time the Text tool is active. You can change the font, size, style, and color of the selected text object using Attribute toolbar settings. You can also change the mode (apply 3D effects and distortions or change the text object to a selection) of a text object, just as you can change these attributes for a path object.

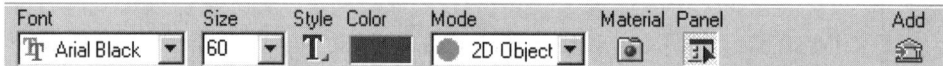

The Attribute toolbar also gives you access to the Material dialog box, where you can define fill textures, shadows, and much more (see Chapter 7 for details on using the Material dialog box). Changes you make in the Attribute toolbar apply to the entire text object.

Change Text Attributes in the Text Entry Box

In addition to being able to change the text attributes with the Attribute toolbar settings, you can also adjust most of those same attributes (and a few extras to boot) in the Text Entry Box. But one of the most useful features of the Text Entry Box is that it allows you to select and modify portions of the text object separately from the rest. For example, you can select a word from the middle of a sentence to make it bold or italic or a different color from the rest of that line of text. You can even select individual letters and change their attributes if you want.

To edit a text object, just double-click the text object with the Text tool, and it will appear inside the Text Entry box, ready for editing. You can also open the Text Entry box by selecting the text object and choosing Object | Edit Text, right-clicking the text object and choosing Edit Text or pressing SHIFT-E.

Select Text in the Text Entry Box

In the Text Entry Box, you can select the text you want to edit, just as you would in a most Windows applications. Here are just a few of the standard techniques you can use to select text in the Text Entry Box:

- Drag across it with the mouse.

- Click at one end of a selection and SHIFT-click the other end.

- Double-click a word to select it.

- Click anywhere in the text and press CTRL-A to select all the text.

The selected text will appear highlighted, as shown in Figure 8-2. After you select the text you want to change, you can adjust any of the text attributes and settings in the Text Entry Box. The changes affect only the highlighted text.

Adjust Settings in the Text Entry Box

In the Text Entry Box, you can adjust the following settings for your text:

- **Font**   To select a new font, click the Font drop-down menu. As you scroll through font choices, a sample of the fonts appears to the right. All True Type fonts installed on your computer will be available to PhotoImpact.

- **Script**   If you have multiple scripts (languages or character sets) installed on your computer, you can click the Script drop-down menu and choose an alternative script.

- **Size**   Type a new font size or use the drop-down menu to choose one.

- **Rotate**   Enter or select a number to rotate each character around its own center, as in the example shown at the bottom of the next page. Positive numbers rotate clockwise. Negative numbers rotate counterclockwise. (To

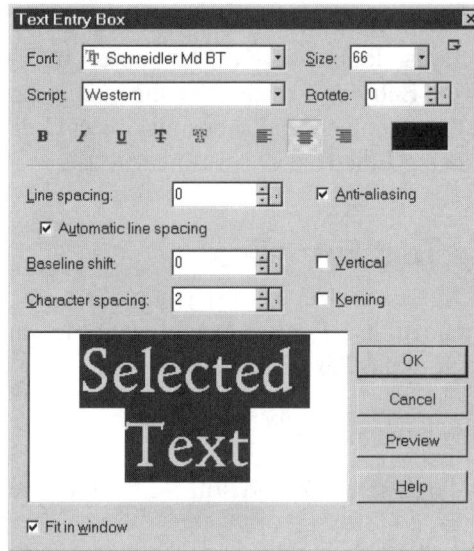

Text Entry Box

Font: ᴛᴛ Schneidler Md BT   Size: 66

Script: Western   Rotate: 0

B *I* U T̲ T̲ ≡ ≡ ≡

Line spacing: 0   ☑ Anti-aliasing

☑ Automatic line spacing

Baseline shift: 0   ☐ Vertical

Character spacing: 2   ☐ Kerning

Selected Text

OK
Cancel
Preview
Help

☑ Fit in window

FIGURE 8-2 Selecting text in the Text Entry Box

rotate the entire text object as a unit instead of rotating individual characters, use the Transform tool.)

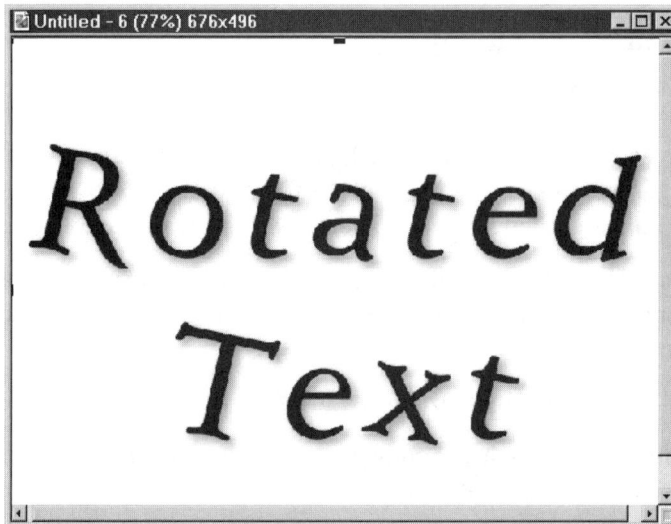

Rotated Text

- **Style**   Click the Bold, Italic, Underline, or Strike-through buttons to apply the corresponding style.

- **Selection**   Click the Selection button (the outlined T) to display your text as a selection only. This is equivalent to choosing Selection in the Mode box on the Attribute toolbar.

- **Justification**   Choose Left, Center, or Right Justification. This option applies to all text in the Text Entry Box, whether it is selected or not.

- **Color**   Click the color swatch to display the Color pop-up menu with its full assortment of color-selection options, including gradient and texture fills.

- **Line Spacing**   Set a value to specify the space between each line of text. Increase the Line Spacing setting to increase the space from the baseline of one line of type to the baseline of the next line of type. This option affects all text in the Text Entry Box, whether it is selected or not.

- **Anti-aliasing**   Check this box to blend the edges of text in order to hide the "jaggies" that appear when curves and diagonal lines are rendered as square pixels.

- **Automatic Line Spacing**   Check this box to change the behavior of the Line Spacing setting. When this option is selected, zero line spacing represents the normal line spacing for the current text size, and changes in the line spacing setting increase or decrease from that norm. You can enter negative numbers in the Line Spacing setting to reduce line spacing below the norm. When this option is *not* selected, the Line Spacing setting sets the actual measurement (in points) from baseline to baseline, and negative numbers are not allowed.

- **Baseline Shift**   Enter a value to raise or lower the selected text above or below the baseline of the surrounding text. Use this option for superscript and subscript, such as chemical symbols and stock quotes, as shown in the following example.

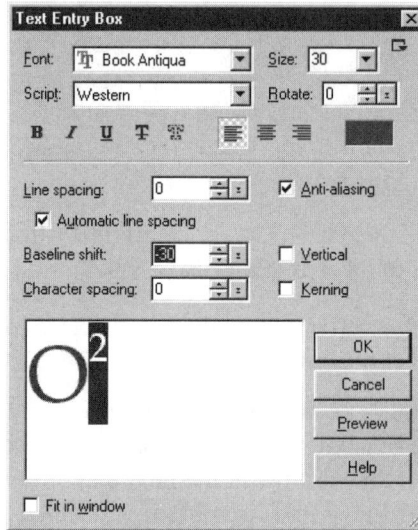

- **Vertical**   Select this option to rotate the entire text block 90 degrees clockwise, like the title on the spine of a book.

> **TIP**   *To create vertical rows of text characters (Chinese writing style), check the Vertical option, rotate the text –90 degrees, and increase the character spacing by an amount equal to about half the text size.*

- **Character Spacing**   Enter a value to specify the space between selected characters. A zero value represents normal character spacing. Positive numbers increase space between characters. Negative numbers reduce space, allowing characters to overlap.

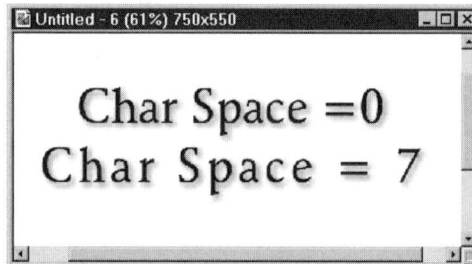

- **Kerning**   Check this box to automatically reduce the space between certain letter pairs to improve the appearance of the line of type.

Use the Text Panel

PhotoImpact's third text-editing tool is the Text panel. By default, the Text panel appears any time the Text tool is active, but you can always show or hide it by clicking the Panel button in the Attribute toolbar. With the exception of the Split Text feature, the settings available in the Text panel are duplicated elsewhere; the Text panel simply provides convenient access to those settings while you work with text objects.

The Text panel has four tabs. The following sections describe the options available on the Text panel tabs. The availability of these options depends on what changes have already been made to your text.

3D Tab

The settings on the 3D tab provide quick access to the adjustments that you're most likely to use to refine the look of a 3D effect applied to a text object. The Border, Depth, and Lighting settings duplicate those found in the Material dialog box.

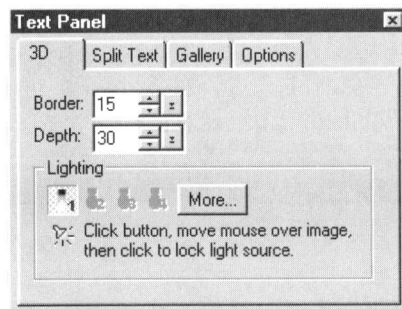

Split Text Tab

You may have a block of text in which you want to manipulate some portions of the text separately from others. Although you can change text attributes such as the font, size, and color of selected portions of a text object in the Text Entry Box, other characteristics, such as 3D attributes, apply to the entire text object. For example, you can't apply a 3D effect to only one portion of a text object without making the rest of the text object 3D as well.

Fortunately, there is no need to re-create the text as a series of smaller text objects. You can break any existing text object apart into smaller component pieces. You do so by using the options on the Split Text tab of the Text panel.

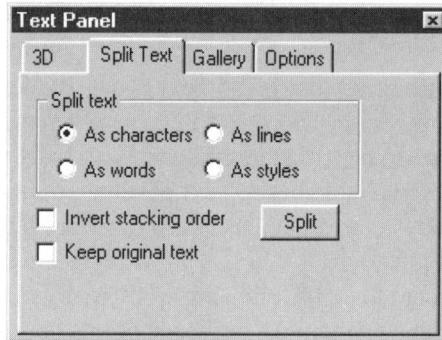

To split a text object, start by selecting the object and displaying the Text panel. Then click the Split Text tab, choose the split options, and then click the Split button. PhotoImpact immediately divides the text object into multiple, smaller text objects according to your instructions. You can split a text object by style (bold, italic, or underscore), line, word, or character. After the split, you can select and manipulate the separate text objects individually.

Gallery Tab

The Gallery tab of the Text panel is divided into two segments. The top segment contains links to four EasyPalette galleries that pertain to editing text objects:

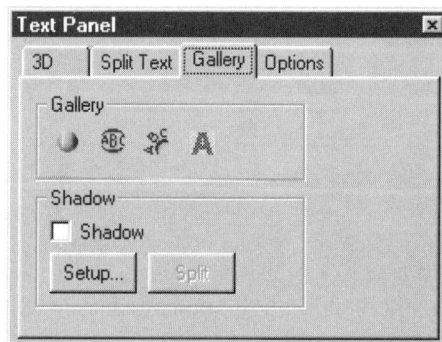

- **Material Gallery**   Lets you drop a texture onto your text. Each texture has a surface quality, reflectivity amount, and so forth. Your text will adopt the "material" you apply by dragging the thumbnail. These are the same settings you'll find by clicking the Material button on the Attribute toolbar.

- **Deform Gallery**   Lets you apply preset distortions to your text object. You can make your text bulge in the middle, taper at the edges, or appear pulled about in any number of ways. These effects are produced by the Transform tool and the Horizontal Distort and Vertical Distort modes. For more details, see the "Reshape Text" section later in this chapter.

- **Wrap Gallery**   Like the Deform Gallery, lets you apply preset distortions to your text object. The difference is that the Wrap Gallery effects cause the text to wrap along a curved path. The text-wrap effects are produced using the techniques outlined in the "Create Text on a Path" section later in this chapter.

- **Type Gallery**   Gives you access to another assortment of preset effects that you can apply to your text object. The effects in the Type Gallery are produced by type effect filters. These type effects are discussed in the "Apply Type Gallery Effects" section later in this chapter.

Just click an icon in the Gallery area to open the EasyPalette panel with the corresponding effects gallery displayed. This gives you easy access to dozens of drag-and-drop controls and effects for your text.

The lower segment of the Gallery tab gives you convenient access to shadow effects for your text object. To apply a shadow to your text object, just check the Shadow option. If you need to adjust the shadow effect, click the Setup button to open the Shadow dialog box, which is the same one you use to create and apply shadows to other objects. (See Chapter 6 for more information about adding shadows.) You can also click the Split button to split the shadow into a separate object so you can manipulate it separately from the text object.

Options Tab

The Options tab of the Text panel is primarily there for consistency with its counterparts, such as the Brush panel. Most of the options are grayed out when working with text. The only option that really applies to text is Anti-aliasing. This duplicates the Anti-aliasing option in the Text Entry Box.

Apply Color, Fills, and Effects to Text

Sometimes, color seems to be the most distinctive characteristic of a text object. Perhaps that is because we're so accustomed to seeing black type on a white page that text of any other color stands out and commands attention.

When you create a text object in PhotoImpact, you can select any color for the type. The full range of colors and color-selection options are at your disposal. Clicking the color box in the Attribute toolbar or the Text Entry Box displays the standard Color pop-up menu, which gives you access to all the same color-selection options you have with any other PhotoImpact object. That includes an assortment of standard colors, the Ulead Color Picker, the Windows Color Picker, and the Eyedropper dialog box, which allows you to match any color in a PhotoImpact document window.

You can also choose gradient fills, magic texture fills, natural texture fills, and fadeout effects for your text, as illustrated below. See Chapter 9 for more information on using gradient fills, magic texture fills, natural texture fills, and image file fills.

TEXT FILLS   TEXT FILLS
TEXT FILLS   TEXT FILLS
TEXT FILLS   TEXT FILLS
TEXT FILLS   TEXT FILLS
TEXT FILLS   TEXT FILLS

In addition to the standard colors, gradients, and fills available from the Color pop-up menu, you also have access to all the effects in the Material dialog box for use with your text objects. The Material dialog box, which is covered in Chapter 7, lets you apply a texture or other bitmap image as a fill for your text. You can also simulate surface textures, reflections, and 3D effects, complete with adjustable depth, highlights, shading, and shadows. The following section discusses some of the Material dialog box options that work well with 3D text effects.

The range of fill effects you can apply to text objects is truly impressive. Although it's true that all the same fill effects are available for use on path objects, that doesn't diminish the fact that some of those effects are particularly striking when applied to text objects.

Work with 3D Text

One of the color-fill treatments that is particularly effective for text objects is the simulated 3D effect. With just a couple of mouse clicks, you can give a flat, two-dimensional text object the illusion of depth, as illustrated below. You can combine the 3D effect with a texture fill to create text objects that have the look of carved wood or chiseled stone.

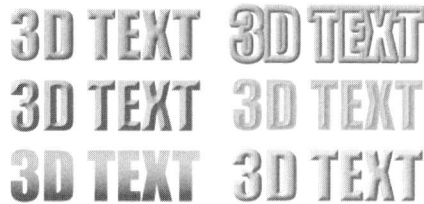

3D TEXT   3D TEXT
3D TEXT   3D TEXT
3D TEXT   3D TEXT

PhotoImpact achieves the 3D effect by making the fill color lighter in some places and darker in others, to simulate the highlights and shading of a rounded shape instead of the uniform color of a flat, cutout shape.

Add a 3D Effect

To add a 3D effect to your text object, select the object with the Text tool and then do one of the following:

■ Select one of the 3D options from the Mode list box in the Attribute toolbar (3D Round and 3D Chisel work best on most text).

■ Open the Material dialog box (click the Material button on the Attribute toolbar) and choose a 3D option from the Bevel tab.

Fine-Tune a 3D Effect

After you apply a 3D effect to your text object, you can fine-tune the effect by adjusting the settings on other tabs of the Material dialog box, as follows:

■ On the Color/Texture tab, select a color, gradient, or texture fill for your text.

- On the Bevel tab, select the 3D mode and choose round or mitered joints to control the appearance of intersecting letter strokes.

- On the Border/Depth tab, set the depth of the 3D effect and the size of the slope that reaches that depth. In the Depth setting, positive numbers make the 3D effect appear to protrude toward the viewer and negative numbers simulate an indentation. Check Smooth Spine to smooth out hard edges in the effect.

- On the Light tab, you can specify up to four light sources and an ambient light level for your text object. You'll usually want to set the lights to match other objects in your image.

- On the Shading tab, you can control the apparent reflectivity of the 3D text object.

- On the Shadow tab, you can add a shadow to your text object and access the Shadow dialog box to set the shadow options.

| NOTE | *The 3D effect only simulates three-dimensional text. It does not transform the text object into a true three-dimensional model that you can rotate and view from different angles. As a result, you can't use the Transform tool's Rotate in Virtual 3D tool with an object that has a 3D effect applied. However, the 3D effect does work reasonably well with the Transform tool's Perspective option.* |

Apply Type Effect Filters

You can apply many of PhotoImpact's inventory of effect filters to a text object. Some of those filters are not very effective when applied to the relatively small areas inside the text characters in a text object, but there's nothing stopping you from experimenting with the full range of effect filters. However, one set of effect filters is intended especially for text: the Type Effects. These filters are designed to produce animation effects, but you can also use them to create still images that incorporate the same effects. (See Chapter 13 for details on using PhotoImpact effect filters for animation effects.) The Fire, Gradient-Light, and Reverse Emboss effects, as shown in the following illustration, are just a few of the effects available in the Type Effects dialog box.

TYPE EFFECTS

TYPE EFFECTS

TYPE EFFECTS

CAUTION *Applying a Type Effect filter to a text object transforms the text object into an image object, which means that you can no longer edit the text characters, font, and so on. Make sure that all your text edits are complete before applying the Type effect filter.*

8

To apply a Type effect filter to a text object, follow these steps:

1. Select the text object.

2. Choose Effect | Creative | Type Effect to open the Type Effect dialog box.

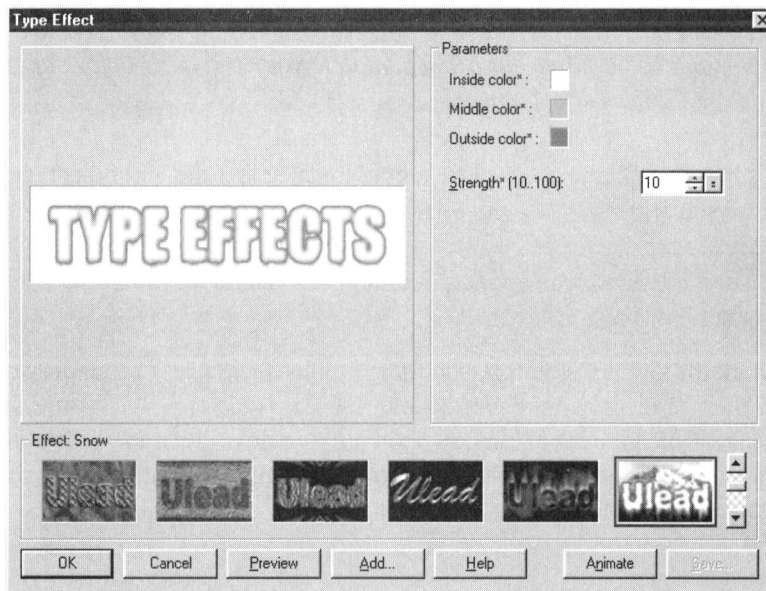

3. Click the Still button at the bottom of the dialog box.

4. Scroll through the thumbnails at the bottom of the dialog box and select the desired effect by clicking its thumbnail. A preview of the effect appears on the left side of the dialog box.

5. Adjust the parameters on the right side of the dialog box as needed. The specific parameters depend on the effect you select.

6. Click OK to close the Type Effect dialog box and apply the effect to your text.

> **TIP** *Most of the Type Effect filters and Type Gallery effects work best on very small quantities of large type, such as a short word or a radio station call letters, set in 72-point type or larger. Many of the Type Gallery effects will render smaller text illegible.*

Apply Type Gallery Effects

If you're looking for still more special type treatments, check out the Type Gallery in the EasyPalette panel. The Type Gallery provides dozens of special effects that you can apply to your text objects with drag-and-drop ease.

> **CAUTION** *Applying a Type Gallery effect to a text object transforms the text object into an image object, which means that you can no longer edit the text, font, and so on. Make sure you complete your text edits before applying a Type Gallery effect.*

To apply a Type Gallery effect to a text object, select the text object and then follow these steps:

1. Open the EasyPalette panel (click the EasyPalette button in the Panel Manager or press F2).

2. Click the Galleries button, and then double-click the Type Gallery category in the tree display on the left side of the EasyPalette panel. You'll see the list of Type Gallery effects, as shown in the next illustration. Select one of the subcategories to display the corresponding thumbnails on the right side of the EasyPalette panel.

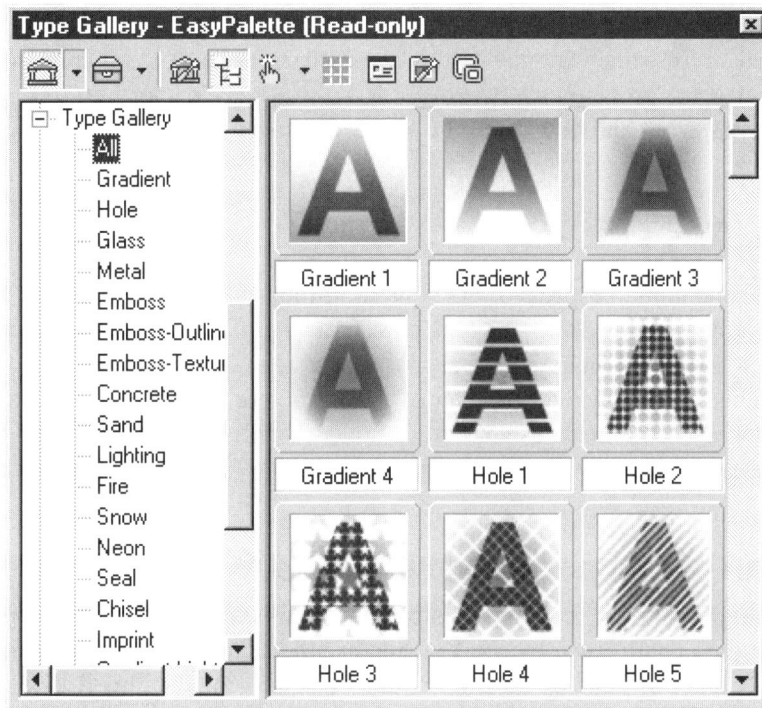

3. Double-click a thumbnail or drag and drop a thumbnail onto your image to apply the effect to your text.

That's all there is to it. Your text object is instantly transformed into an image object with the type treatment applied.

TIP *You can use the same technique to apply other gallery effects to your text object.*

Overlap Transparent Text

Text objects, like all PhotoImpact objects, can overlap other objects and be overlapped by other objects. You can also control the Transparency amount and Merge mode for text objects, just as you can for path objects and image objects. This means that you can create text objects that allow the background to show through to create special effects, such as making the text appear to be made of colored glass.

You work with transparency, Merge mode, and stack order (overlapping) of text objects in the same way you control these characteristics of other objects. The Layer Manager is probably the best tool for the job. See Chapter 7 for information on how layers work and how to use the Layer Manager.

Reshape Text

One of the uncommon aspects of the way PhotoImpact handles text is that you can reshape and distort a text object. You can push, pull, bend, twist, stretch, and compress a text object in any number of different ways. You can curve text around a circle to make it follow the perimeter of a medallion or bend it so that it looks like the text is wrapped around a can or bottle. You can stretch and deform a text object as if it were made of elastic.

Use the Transform Tool to Distort Text

It's probably no surprise that the Transform tool works on text objects just as it does on path objects and image objects. You can use the Transform tool to manipulate text in the same way that you transform other objects, using the Flip, Rotate, Resize, Slant, Distort, Perspective, and Rotate in Virtual 3D options.

Chapter 7 describes how to use the Transform tool on objects. This section describes some transformations that are particularly well suited for use with text objects.

Copy Rotate

The Copy Rotate feature copies your text and rotates it by the degree specified in the Rotate by Degree field. This is great for making "spinning" text, as illustrated on the next page.

Here's how to create something similar to what you see in the illustration:

1. Select the text object you want to spin and then click the Transform tool in the Tool panel.

2. Click the arrow beside the Rotate & Flip button on the Attribute toolbar and choose Rotate 180° from the menu. This positions the text object for the start of the spin.

3. Enter a number in the Rotate by Degrees box to set the rotation for each step of the spin. For example, to create a 180-degree spin in 12 steps, enter **15** in the Rotate by Degrees box.

4. Click the Copy Rotate drop-down menu and choose Clockwise. PhotoImpact makes a copy of your text object, rotated clockwise by the amount you specified.

5. Click the Copy Rotate button (not the drop-down menu) again for each copy of the text that you need in the spin. For example, for a 12-step spin, click the Copy Rotate button 11 times. PhotoImpact creates a new copy of the text object for each click of the button. Each new object is rotated clockwise from the previous copy.

Perspective

Another transformation that is especially useful for text is the Perspective option. You can use the Perspective distortion to make the sides of an object appear to converge, and thus achieve some feeling of depth, as illustrated below. The effect is incomplete because the compression of the text object occurs in only one dimension

and doesn't include any significant size change as the text characters get farther
from the viewer. Still, the effect can be useful if you don't push it to extremes. For
example, you could use the Perspective effect to make text on a sign look like you're
viewing it from an angle instead of straight on. Just don't make the angle too acute.

Here's how to create Perspective text:

1. Select the text object and then click the Transform tool in the Tool panel.

2. Click the Transform button at the left end of the Attribute toolbar and
   choose Perspective from the menu that appears. A bounding box with
   handles at each corner appears around the text object.

3. Click and drag one corner of the bounding box. To create the angled effect
   illustrated above, drag one of the top corners toward the middle of the top
   side. As you drag one corner, PhotoImpact automatically moves the adjacent
   corner to make opposite sides of the bounding box converge.

Rotate in Virtual 3D

PhotoImpact borrows a technique from the fancy 3D modeling programs and
makes it available for use in your images. The Rotate in Virtual 3D option lets you
to create more realistic perspective effects by allowing you to perform three-axis
rotation on any two-dimensional object. This effect works particularly well on text
objects, enabling you to create effects that mimic the classic "Star Wars" title crawl
shown next.

The perspective effect uses converging lines to create an illusion of perspective. But the Rotate in Virtual 3D tool produces more realistic perspective effects.

This effect makes a block of text look like it's laying on a horizontal surface with the top lines receding into the distance. You could use the same tool to distort the text for a sign so that it matches the perspective of the front of a building.

In addition to converging lines, the Rotate in Virtual 3D tool creates foreshortening effects and reduces the size of text characters that are supposed to be farther away from the viewer.

CAUTION *The Rotate in Virtual 3D feature is available only for objects with two-dimensional fill effects. You can't perform a 3D rotation on an object with a 3D fill effect, and you can't apply a 3D fill effect to an object on which you performed a 3D rotation. It is possible to work around the inability to add a 3D fill effect to a rotated object by converting a text object to a path object and then applying the 3D fill to the converted object, but the resulting effect probably won't be as realistic as you would like it to be.*

To use the Rotate in Virtual 3D feature, follow these steps:

1. Select the text object and then click the Transform tool in the Tool panel.

2. Click the Transform button at the left end of the Attribute toolbar and choose Rotate in Virtual 3D from the menu that appears. Instead of a bounding box with handles at each corner, a circle appears around the text object, and the pointer takes the shape of a globe.

3D Rotate

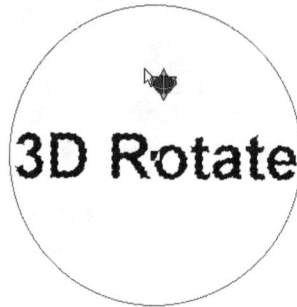

3. Click and drag the pointer around in the circle to achieve the desired effect. To tilt the top of the object back away from the viewer, drag up from the center of the circle. To rotate the object clockwise, drag from the center toward the left.

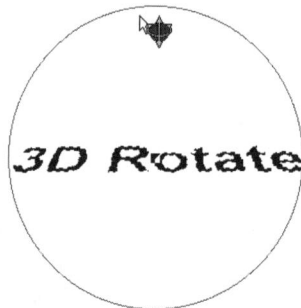

3D Rotate

Deform Text with Horizontal and Vertical Deform Modes

The Transform tool isn't the only way you can distort and reshape a text object. You can also use the Horizontal Deform and Vertical Deform modes to stretch and squeeze a text object. The deform modes are useful for making text look like it bulges out as it wraps around a can or bottle, among other things.

The Horizontal Deform mode and the Vertical Deform mode work the same way. They both create a box around your object and then allow you to distort that box by dragging nodes and control handles. The text within the box is distorted to conform to the contours of the box. The difference between the two modes is that the Horizontal Deform mode allows you to distort the horizontal sides of the box as curves and keeps the vertical sides as straight lines. The Vertical Deform mode treats the vertical sides as curves and the horizontal sides as straight lines.

NOTE *Selecting Vertical Deform mode cancels any previous distortions created with the Horizontal Deform mode and vice versa. You can't combine the two effects.*

To distort a text object with the Horizontal Deform mode, follow these steps:

1. Select the text object with the Text tool.

2. Select Horizontal Deform in the Mode box in the Attribute toolbar. The fill color temporarily disappears from the text, leaving only a wireframe outline. A box appears around the text object with nodes at each corner and control handles (like the ones you use to draw and edit Bezier curves) on the horizontal sides.

8

3. Click and drag a corner node or control handle to change the shape of the box surrounding the text object. As you distort the box, the text inside the box also changes shape. Continue dragging nodes and control handles to achieve the desired effect.

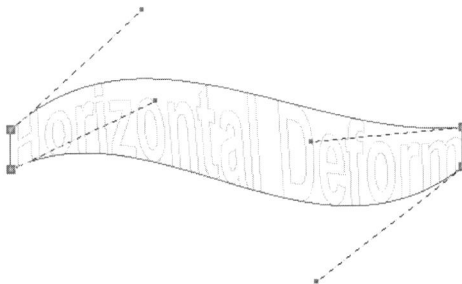

4. Select the normal 2D or 3D fill mode in the Mode box in the Attribute toolbar. The deform box disappears, and the normal text object fill reappears in the newly distorted text object.

Create Text on a Path

From time to time, you may need to arrange text characters to follow an arch or other curve instead of the usual straight baseline. You might be creating artwork for a medallion or shield with text around the perimeter, or you may be adding an inscription along the curve of an arched doorway. One way to achieve the effect is to split a text object into separate objects for each character and then position each character individually, but PhotoImpact provides a better way by allowing you to wrap text to follow a predefined path.

Apply Text to a Path

This text-on-a-path feature is commonly available in most sophisticated illustration and image-editing programs these days, but applying text to a path is easier in PhotoImpact than in most other programs. Here's how:

1. Create a path using the Line and Arrow tool (not the Bezier Curve selection tool). You can use the spline, Bezier, or freeform line shapes. (You can also use the straight-line shape, but there would be no point in that.) See Chapter 2 for details on using the Line and Arrow tool.

2. Right-click the path and choose Wrap | Add Text to Active Path. The Text Entry Box appears, ready for you to type the text as it should appear along your path.

3. Enter your text into the Text Entry Box. Set the size, font, and other attributes as needed.

4. Click OK, and the text will appear on the path, the baseline of each character aligned with the path line. The line disappears. The text will repeat as needed, filling the entire path, as in the example shown next.

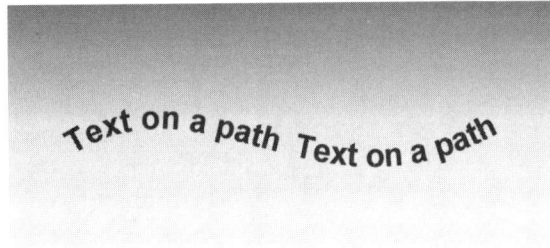

The text created with this technique is a text object, just like any text object you create with the Text tool. You can edit the text, adjust the attributes, and manipulate it in the same ways that you can modify any other text object. In addition, it is linked to an invisible path object—the curved line—that you can edit and reshape.

Edit the Text's Path Line

To edit the line that the text follows, click the text with the Path Edit tool. The text changes to an outline, and the line appears in its "nodes only" editing mode. You can use the Path Edit tool to add, remove, and move nodes on the line, just as you would any other path object. (See Chapter 2 for details on using the Path Edit tool.) Click another tool to make the path line disappear and the text reappear.

Adjust the Text Flow on a Path

You can also edit how the text flows along the path using the Wrap dialog box, shown in Figure 8-3. To open this dialog box, right-click the text object and choose Wrap | Properties.

In the dialog box, adjust the settings as needed to determine the text alignment along the path. You can control the following items:

- **Repeat**   Select Automatic to repeat the text as needed to fill the path line. Select Count and enter a number to specify a fixed number of text repetitions. You can also enter a number to specify spacing between repeated text. The Stretch to Fit option expands the text to fit the line.

- **Position/Size**   The Start Height setting determines the size of the text at the start, and the End Height setting determines the ending size. Sizes are in percent of the normal text size, and the size tapers gradually from one end to the other. Use negative numbers to flip the text upside down. The Start

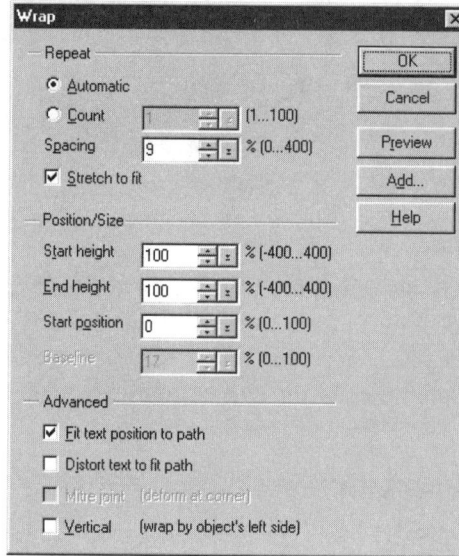

The Wrap dialog box

Position setting specifies an offset from the left end of the line to the starting point for the text. The Baseline setting determines the position of the text baseline relative to the path line. (It's usually grayed out.)

- **Fit Text Position to Path**   Select this option to rotate each text character to orient it perpendicular to the path line.

- **Distort Text to Fit Path**   Select this option to distort text characters to mirror the curves of the path line.

- **Vertical**   Select this option to align the left side of the text object with the path line instead of the baseline. This option is useful only for text objects that contain several lines of text or are oriented vertically.

Convert Text Objects to Other Object Types

One of the main strengths of PhotoImpact's text features is that text objects retain their identity as text, so you can edit the text attributes and the text itself at any time. However, there may be times when you want or need the particular strengths of another object type. You may want to change the shape of individual text characters, merge a text object with another object, or apply a filter effect that is only possible with a pixel-based image. When you need to do something that just isn't possible with a text object, you can convert the text object to another object type. You can even convert a text object to a selection.

> **CAUTION** *Converting a text object to another object type is a one-way street. After the conversion to a path object or an image object, you can't convert the object back to a text object and edit the text and text attributes.*

Convert Text to a Path Object

When you convert a text object to a path object, the resulting path object is a collection of Bezier curves and polygons in the shape of the text characters. You can then edit those paths to alter the shape of individual letters, as in the next illustration. You may want to do this to create some customized lettering for a logo, or to add your own individual touch to an otherwise common-looking font.

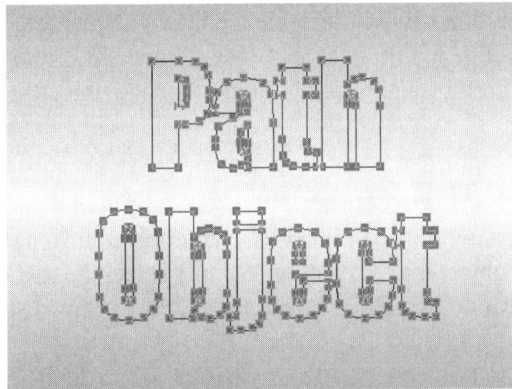

To convert a text object to a path object, select the text object and choose Object | Convert Object Type | From Text/Image to Path. The conversion takes place immediately. You won't see any obvious change, but you won't be able to select and edit the object with the Text tool. Instead, now that it is a path object, you will be able to select and edit the object with the Path Edit tool. This gives you complete access to every node and control handle that defines the shape of the letters.

Path objects and text objects share many of the same characteristics. After you convert a text object to a path object, you still have access to all the same fill and texture options from the Material dialog box, and you can resize and reshape the object without any loss of quality, because both text objects and path objects are vector graphics.

Convert Text to an Image Object

You can also convert a text object to a pixel-based image object. This is a more drastic step than converting it to a path object, because not only do you lose the ability to edit the text, but you also lose the ability to resize and reshape the object while retaining optimum image quality. However, there are times when you may want to manipulate text in a way that is only possible as a pixel-based image. For example, you might want to apply an effect filter, exercise precise control over a gradient fill, or use the painting tools to hand-paint a custom fill for the text characters.

If you apply an effect filter (including effects from the Type Gallery in the EasyPalette panel) to a text object, PhotoImpact automatically changes your text object into an image object. If you want to apply a Fill tool or Paint tool to some text, you'll need to do the conversion manually. To do so, select the text and choose Object | Convert Object Type | From Text/Path to Image. After the conversion to an image object, your text looks the same, but it is just a picture of text rather than a text object. You won't be able to select and edit it with the Text or Path Edit tool. On the other hand, all the painting tools (Paint, Clone, and Retouch tools) and Fill tools will be available for manipulating the new image object.

Convert Text to a Selection

In addition to changing your text object to a path object or image object, you can also change the text object into a selection. Simply select the text object and choose Selection from the Mode list in the Attribute toolbar to convert the text object into a selection.

Converting text to a selection enables you to select a "text-shaped" portion of an image and manipulate it. You can cut, copy, paste, or move the selection. You can add a fill or apply an effect filter. In other words, you can do anything you can do with any other selection, but after you use the selection to select and manipulate your image, you can no longer change the selection back into a text object and edit the type.

One useful application of converting text to a selection is to use the text selection to create a cutout in an image. The image then becomes a stencil—a picture containing a hole where the text once was, as illustrated next.

The stencil effect is easy to produce. You need to start with two image documents of the same size:

- A background image that will show through the stencil cutout

- The image in which you want to cut a text-shaped hole, which will overlay the background image

Here's how to create the stencil effect:

1. Open or create an image document to serve as the background image—the image that will show through the stencil cutout.

2. Open or create another image document to serve as the stencil—the image in which you want to cut a text-shaped hole. Make sure the two images are the same size.

3. Create a text object on the stencil image. Use a large, bold font that provides enough thickness to the type so that the background image will be clearly visible through the stencil cutout.

4. With the text object still selected, choose Selection from the Mode list in the Attribute toolbar. This converts the text object into a selection. You'll see the distinctive selection marquee surrounding the text characters.

5. Choose Selection I Invert to deselect the text shape and select the rest of the image outside the text characters. The result is that the entire image is selected, *except* the space inside the text-character shapes.

6. Choose Edit I Copy or press CTRL-C to copy the selection to the clipboard.

7. Click the other document window to make the background image the active document.

8. Choose Edit | Paste | As Object or press CTRL-V to paste the selection into the active document as an image object.

The result is an image object on top of the background image. The background image shows through the text-shaped hole in the image object.

One interesting effect you can create with the stencil effect is an Insert Shadow. After importing your stencil, apply a shadow to the stencil cutout (not the background behind it). The shadow will appear to be "inside" the text.

CHAPTER 9

Work with Fills and Creative Effects

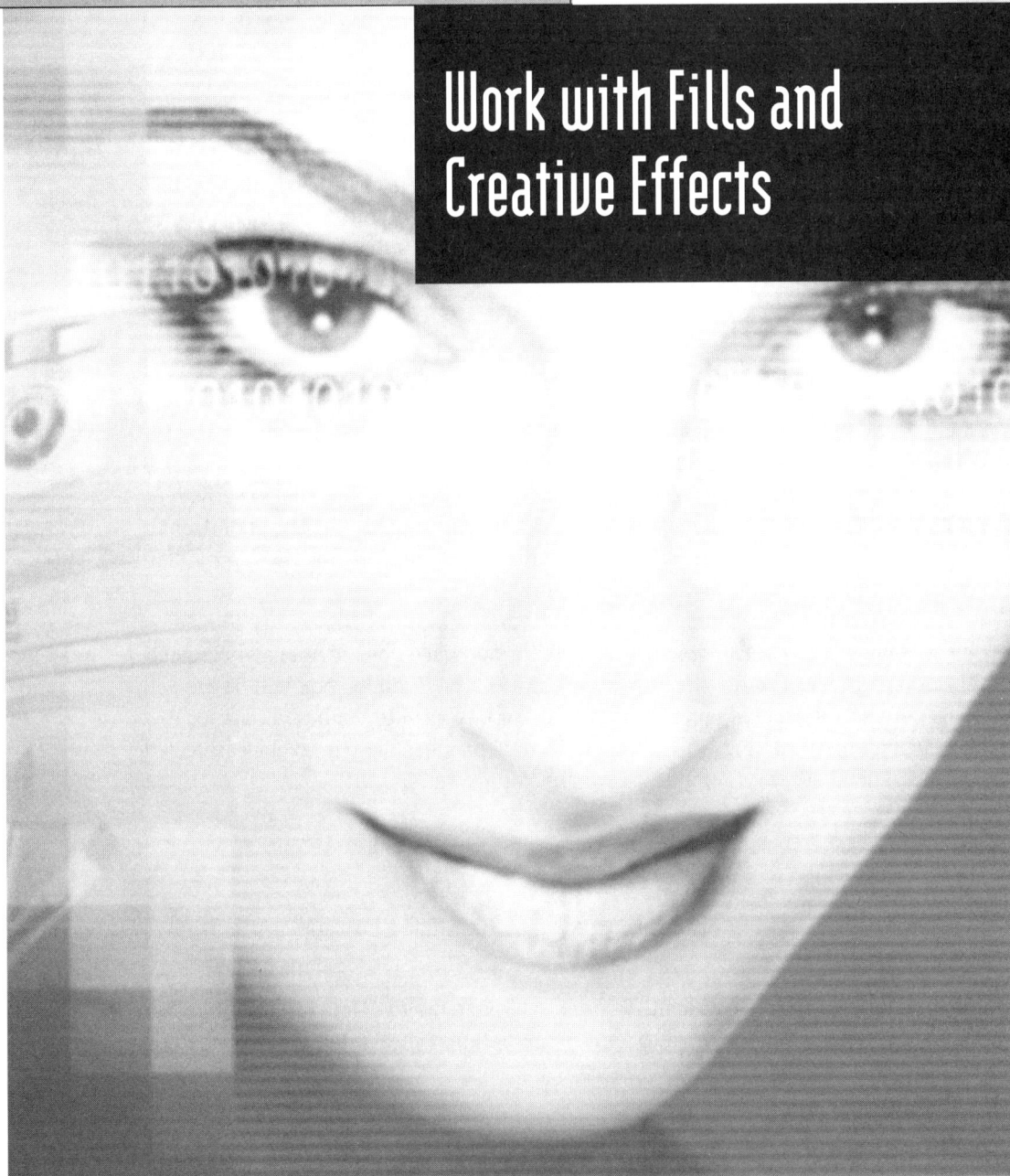

PhotoImpact has a broad selection of color-fill types, and you can apply them very precisely. You can create one-of-a-kind color fills that are splashy and loud, or you can produce subtle fills that gradually fade from one color to the next. You can use fills to simulate a gradually darkening sky, a Day-Glo art poster, or even the various shades of color in human skin.

Previous chapters covered how to add fills to objects as you create them. This chapter covers some alternative ways to apply fills to objects in PhotoImpact, including using the Fill dialog box and applying bump and reflection maps. It also covers an assortment of special-purpose effect filters that PhotoImpact calls Creative effects and Magic effects.

Apply Fills to Objects and Images

One of the most basic characteristics of any object is its fill color. Even an empty canvas starts out with a background color.

Color-fill selection is part of the process of creating any object and is covered in the discussions of path and text objects in earlier chapters. However, PhotoImpact also enables you to work with fills apart from the object-creation process by providing a separate Fill dialog box, as shown in Figure 9-1.

You can use the Fill dialog box to apply various kinds of fills to any selected object—whether it's a path object, a text object, an image object, or a newly created selection marquee. The fill settings you specify in the Fill dialog box will be applied to the currently selected object. You can even apply a fill to the base image or to a blank canvas by specifying a fill in the Fill dialog box when there is no object selected.

The general steps for applying a fill are as follows:

1. Select the object to be filled (if you don't make a selection, the background will be filled).

2. Choose Edit | Fill or press CTRL-F. The Fill dialog box appears (see Figure 9-1).

3. Click the Color, Gradient, Texture, or Image tab to display the settings for the type of fill you want to apply. The options on each tab are described in the following sections.

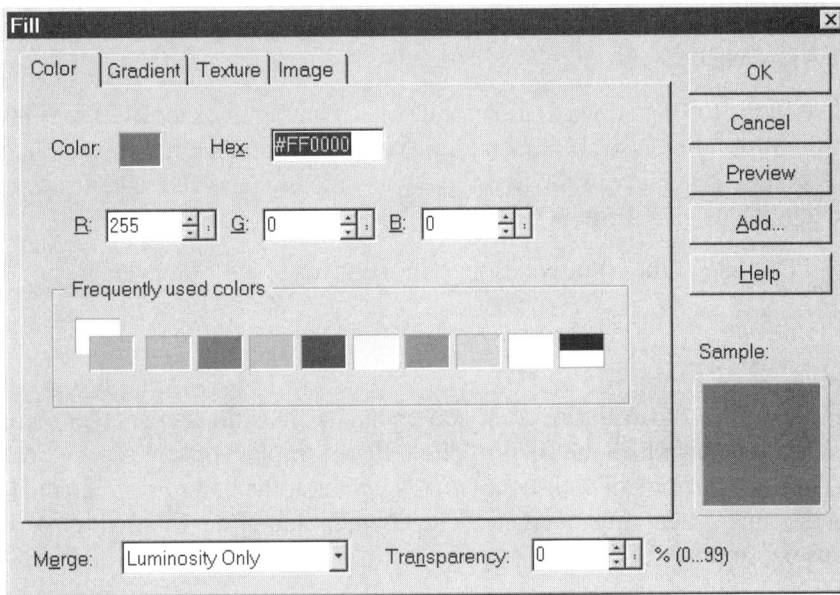

FIGURE 9-1   The Fill dialog box

4. If desired, adjust the settings in the Merge and Transparency boxes at the bottom of the Fill dialog box. These work the same as corresponding settings in the Object Properties dialog box or Layer Manager.

5. Click OK. PhotoImpact applies the fill to your object or selection.

Apply a Solid-Color Fill

The most common fill for most any object is a simple, solid color. The Color tab of the Fill dialog box (see Figure 9-1) contains the settings for solid-color fills. Select or enter a color for the fill. There are four ways to choose a color:

■ Click the Color box and choose a color from the Ulead Color Picker that appears. You can also right-click the Color box to access the additional choices on the Color pop-up menu.

- Type in a hexadecimal color value in the Hex box. (Notice that as you choose colors using other methods in this dialog box, the hexadecimal value changes also.)

- Use the RGB settings to indicate a color. Dialing in exact RGB settings is helpful for precise color matching. You may need this if, for example, you are designing artwork to accompany a company logo and have strict color guidelines to adhere to.

- Click one of the color boxes in the Frequently Used Colors area.

Apply a Gradient Fill

The gradient fill starts with one color and gradually transitions to another color across the object to which the fill is applied. For example, you can use a gradient fill to re-create the look of a clear sky that is lighter at the horizon and gradually gets darker and deeper blue overhead. The Gradient tab of the Fill dialog box contains the settings for defining a gradient fill.

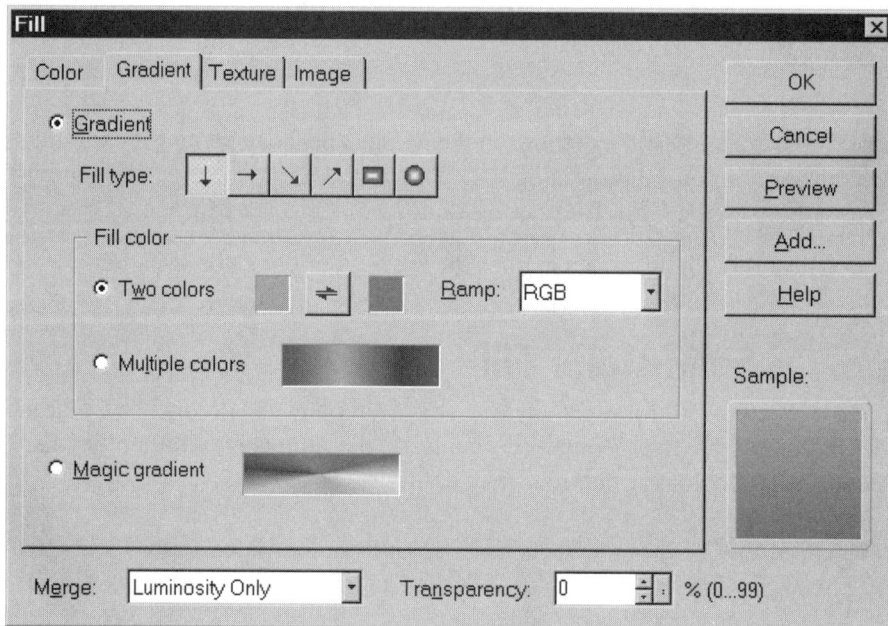

To define the gradient, adjust the following settings:

■ Click one of the Fill Type buttons to specify the pattern for the gradient. You can choose an elliptical gradient, a rectangular gradient, or one of four directions for a linear gradient.

■ Choose a two-color or multiple-color fill. Click the color boxes to specify colors.

■ Use the Swap Color button to change the order in which your colors appear.

■ Use the Ramp drop-down menu to select the color model PhotoImpact uses to make the transition from one color to the next. Choose RGB for a simple blend transition; choose one of the HSB options to move through the entire color wheel before arriving at your second chosen color.

■ To create a Magic gradient, click the Magic Gradient radio button at the bottom of the dialog box. To choose a new Magic gradient, click inside the Magic Gradient rectangle next to the radio button. The Magic Gradient dialog box will appear. Creating Magic gradients is discussed in the "Work with Magic Effects" section later in this chapter.

Apply a Texture Fill

PhotoImpact provides a rich assortment of textures that you can apply as fills for your objects and images. Texture fills can simulate cloth, brick, grass, water, and all sorts of other natural and abstract patterns. The textures are actually small bitmap images that are specially designed to blend together seamlessly when tiled to fill an object.

The texture fills that are available in the Fill dialog box are the same ones that you can access from the Color/Texture tab of the Material dialog box, from the Magic Texture Fill and Natural Texture Fill items on the Color pop-up menu, and from the Fill Gallery in the EasyPalette panel. However, the texture fills are not available on the Color pop-up menu when you're selecting colors for image objects and painting tools, and the Material dialog box is available only when you're working with path and text objects. The Fill dialog box and EasyPalette are the only ways to apply a texture fill to an image object or selection.

The Texture tab of the Fill dialog box displays thumbnails of dozens of textures. Use the Tab Group list box to toggle between Natural Textures and Magic Textures.

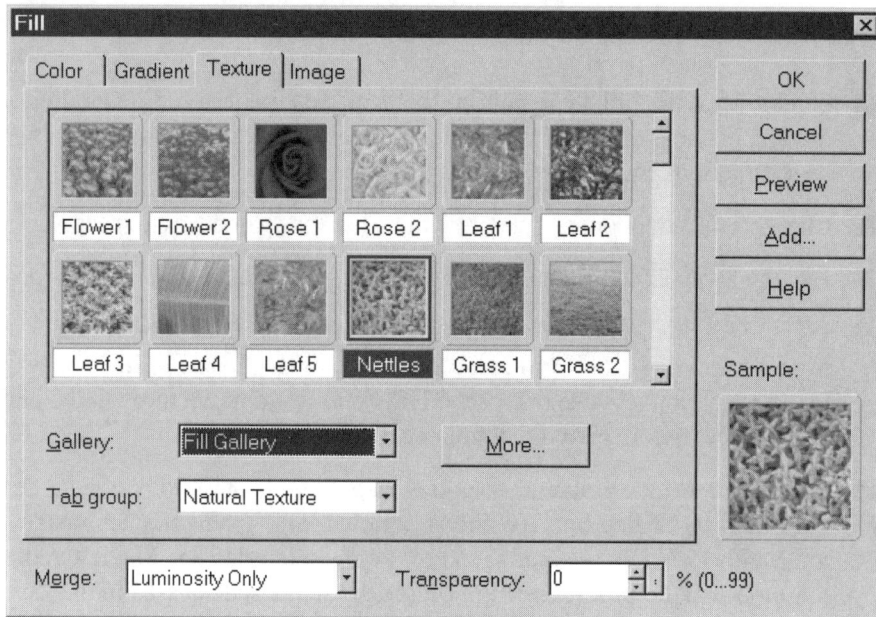

Select a texture by clicking one of the thumbnails. When you click OK to close the dialog box, the texture will fill the selected object, area, or background.

Apply an Image Fill

Just as you can use a small bitmap image to create a texture fill in a PhotoImpact object, you can use a larger bitmap image to fill the object with any image you want. You can use an image fill to replace the view through a window or add a different reflection to a mirror in a photograph. You can also use an image fill to apply your own custom texture to an image. Image fills can be any bitmap, including any type of digital photograph you have on your computer.

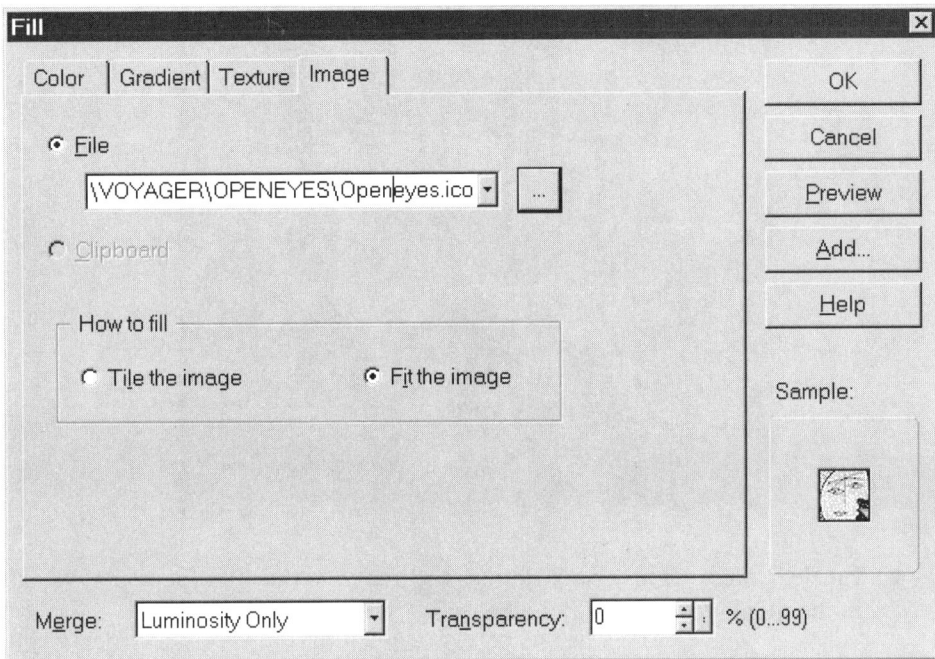

To add an image fill, first select the image source. You can click the File radio button and enter or browse to the location of the image you want to use. Alternatively, you can click the Clipboard button to use an image you had previously copied to the clipboard.

Next, choose how you want the image to fill the area:

■ **Tile the Image**   This option leaves the image sized unchanged, even if it is much smaller or larger than the selection area. If the image is larger than the area to be filled, only a portion of the image will be seen as a fill. If the image is smaller than the filled area, it will repeat as a tile pattern, as illustrated next.

■ **Fit the Image**   This option resizes the image so that all of it displays in the filled area, as illustrated below.

Use Bump and Reflection Maps

PhotoImpact's bump map and reflection map features are special kinds of fill effects that you can add to path objects and text objects to add realistic touches to your images. These features are available through the Material dialog box, which you access by clicking the Material button on the Attribute toolbar while creating or editing a path object or text object. (See Chapter 7 for details on using the Material dialog box.)

Apply a Bump Map

Bump map may seem like a strange name for a fill effect, but it makes sense once you understand what it is. A bump map simulates a three-dimensional surface texture (bumps) with mapping (transferring information from an image onto an object).

A bump map works a lot like the emboss effect filters. It detects edges between dark and light areas in an image, and creates highlights and shadows to make those areas appear slightly raised or depressed. An emboss effect filter works on an entire image and replaces that image with the light/dark-edge effect applied to a solid color. A bump map fill is different in that it works with an external image file and applies the light/dark-edge effect to the fill color of an object. The result is a fairly convincing simulation of a bumpy surface on the object. Figure 9-2 shows an example of an object with a bump map fill.

The bump map effect is available only for path objects and text objects with a 3D mode selected. You apply a bump map to an object with settings on the Bump tab of the Material dialog box, shown in Figure 9-3.

FIGURE 9-2   A bump map simulates surface texture

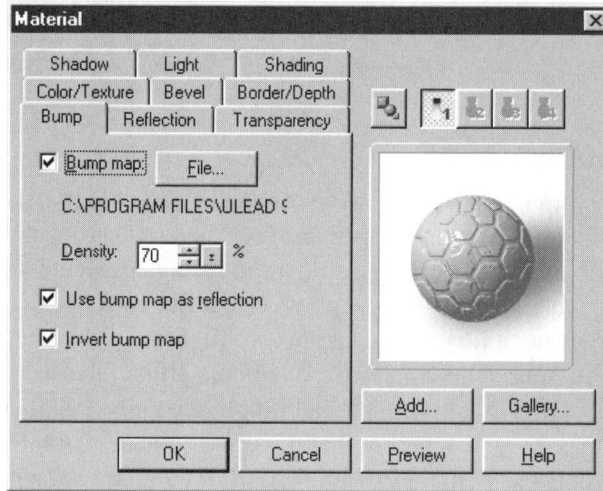

FIGURE 9-3 The Bump tab of the Material dialog box

On the Bump tab, click the File button. The Open dialog box appears. Locate
and select the image file you want to use as the bump map, and then click Open.
A preview of the bump map effect appears in the preview box in the Material dialog
box. Adjust the options on the Bump tab as needed:

- Adjust the Density to control the strength of the bump map effect.

- Check the Use Bump Map As Reflection option to apply the same image
  file as a reflection as well as a bump map. (See the next section for
  information about using reflection maps.)

- Click the Invert Bump Map option to reverse the highlight and shadows
  of the bump map, thus changing the appearance of the bumps from
  protrusions to depressions and vice versa.

Click OK to close the Material dialog box and apply the bump map to the selected
object.

Apply a Reflection Map

The *reflection map* effect is similar to a bump map in that it maps an external image file onto the surface of a path or text object. The difference is that the reflection map simulates the image being reflected off the surface of the object instead of simulating the bumps of a surface texture.

PhotoImpact achieves the reflection effect by applying the reflection image to the object as a transparent overlay. The effect is greatly enhanced by the distortions PhotoImpact applies to make it look like the reflection follows the curves of the 3D object surface.

You can use the reflection map effect to simulate reflections on objects that are supposed to look like glass or polished metal, as shown in Figure 9-4. The reflection map effect can also be used in conjunction with the bump map effect to enrich the look of a surface texture.

Like the bump map effect, reflection maps are available only for use on path objects and text objects with a 3D mode selected. You apply a reflection map to an object with settings in the Reflection tab of the Material dialog box, shown in Figure 9-5.

9

FIGURE 9-4   A reflection map creates the appearance of a reflection on a shiny surface.

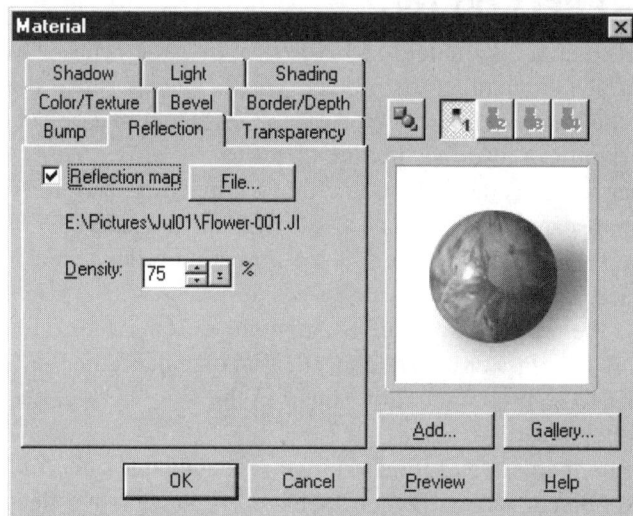

FIGURE 9-5   The Reflection tab of the Material dialog box

On the Reflection tab, click the File button. The Open dialog box appears. Locate and select the image file you want to use as the reflection map and click Open. A preview of the reflection map effect appears in the preview box in the Material dialog box. You can adjust the Density setting to control the strength of the reflection map effect. Click OK to close the Material dialog box and apply the reflection map to the selected object.

Add Creative and Magic Effects to Images and Objects

The Creative and Magic effect filters are a group of specialized filters that behave in a different way from the standard effect filters covered in Chapter 6. Most of the Creative effects are not so much effect filters as they are utility programs that automate the process of applying combinations of standard effect filters and other manipulations to a selected object in order to achieve a certain visual effect. The Magic effect filters each have their own unique characteristics that set them apart from the standard effects.

Work with Creative Effects

Each of the Creative effects is actually a collection of several different visual effects grouped together in one dialog box. Some of the individual effects are similar to some of the standard effect filters that are available individually on the Effect menu. Others are completely new and unique. Many of the Creative effects include the capability of creating animation effects. (See Chapter 13 for details on how to use these effects to build animations.) However, you can also apply the effects to a selected object in a still image. Like all PhotoImpact filters and effects, Creative effects will be applied to any active selection, active object, or, if nothing is selected, to the entire image.

To access the Creative Effects, choose Effect | Creative. You will see a submenu with the following choices:

- Animation Studio
- Artistic Texture
- Creative Warp
- Crystal
- Lighting
- Painting
- Particle
- Transform
- Type Effect

Some effects in this collection have more practical applications than others. For example, the colorful but impractical Artistic Texture effects generate interesting designs, but they wipe out your current image content in the process. Others, like the Painting effects, can help you produce an attractive and interesting image.

Apply a Creative Effect Filter

The basic technique for using most of the Creative effect filters is the same. You select the image or object to which you want to apply the effect, select the effect category from the Creative Effects submenu, and then choose the specific effect you want to produce from the dialog box that appears. You can adjust some settings

9

to fine-tune the effect and click OK to apply it to your object. Figure 9-6 shows the Animation Studio dialog box, which is fairly typical of the Creative effects that offer an assortment of different visual effects in one dialog box.

You use the following features and controls to select the specific effect, adjust its parameters, and then apply the effect to your object:

- **Preview box** The upper-left area of the screen shows a preview of the effect and will update as you add or change effect choices. This way, you don't need to click OK and close the dialog box to see the effect rendered, then open it again and try something new.

- **Effect thumbnails** The row of thumbnails across the bottom of the dialog box shows samples of the available effects. As soon as you open the dialog box, the default effect (indicated by the blue border around the thumbnail) is displayed in the preview area. Click another thumbnail to select it instead.

FIGURE 9-6 The Animation Studio dialog box

- **Parameter settings**   The upper-right quadrant of the dialog box is devoted to the parameter settings for the selected effect. The specific parameters that appear vary, depending on the selected effect. In some cases, there will be more than one tab in the parameters area to make room for additional settings. Adjust the settings to control various aspects of the effect. The preview box shows the results of your parameter settings.

- **Key frame control**   The various buttons, sliders, and boxes in the Key Frame Control area are used to define and control animation effects. Their use is covered in Chapter 13. You don't need the key frame control to apply an effect to a still image. In fact, in some Creative effect dialog boxes, you can click a Still button to hide the key frame control from view and make more room for the effect thumbnails.

- **OK button**   Click OK to apply the effect shown in the preview box to your image. In some cases, you may need to choose Apply Current Frame Effect to Image from the pop-up menu that appears when you click OK.

- **Preview button**   Click Preview to minimize the dialog box to the lower-right corner of the screen. You'll see your effect rendered on the actual image. If you want to try a new setting, click Continue in the minimized dialog box, and the full dialog box will reappear. If you are satisfied with the effect and want to render it permanently, click OK.

- **Add button**   Click Add to save the current customized effect setting to the EasyPalette. You can then apply that customized effect to any image by retrieving it from the EasyPalette.

- **Save button**   Click Save to save the effect in a separate file as an animated GIF. See Chapter 13 for information about animated GIFs.

Apply Animation Studio Effects

The Animation Studio is home to a selection of filters that add water ripples, swirl effects, progressive blurs, and other effects. Most of the individual effects in the Animation Studio are also available as standard effect filters, but the Animation Studio brings them together in one dialog box.

As the name implies, the Animation Studio allows you to create an animation from these effects by making the effect progress from frame to frame through the animation. However, the controls that make it easy to create a sequence of frames for an animation also make it easy to experiment with variations of the effect on a single frame. Because of this ease of use, many PhotoImpact users prefer the Animation Studio dialog box to the normal dialog boxes for the standard effect filters.

To open the Animation Studio dialog box, choose Effects | Creative Effects | Animation Studio. The Animation Studio dialog box (see Figure 9-6) provides 11 effects, each fully editable. See Chapter 13 for descriptions of each of these effects, or simply click the thumbnails to see the effects first hand.

Apply Crystal Effects

The Crystal effect renders transparent shapes in your image, as illustrated in Figure 9-7. The effect simulates the refraction effects that result from looking through a crystal ball, drop of water, faceted glass, and other transparent shapes.

To create a Crystal effect in your image, choose Effects | Creative Effects | Crystal. The Crystal dialog box appears, offering a choice of 10 different transparent shapes ranging from a simple sphere to a polyhedron to a stemmed glass. Scroll

FIGURE 9-7 A Crystal effect example

through the effect thumbnails to see the available shapes, or see Chapter 13 for descriptions.

The Crystal dialog box has two tabs of parameters, Model and Lighting, as shown in Figure 9-8. The Model settings affect the size and surface quality of the crystal object itself. The Lighting tab lets you adjust the light distance, intensity, color, and so forth. You can also adjust the overall lighting amount (ambient light), as opposed to the direct spotlight on the affected area.

The Elements box below the parameter tabs displays the instances of the effect that currently appear in the preview box. You can add several instances of an effect. For example, an image using the Crystal effect can include both a Sphere and a Diamond, or several of each. To add a new element to the image, click the plus sign at the right of the Element list. Whatever effect thumbnail is highlighted will appear in the preview image. Each instance has its own parameter settings, so when you click an item in the Elements list, the parameter tabs will change.

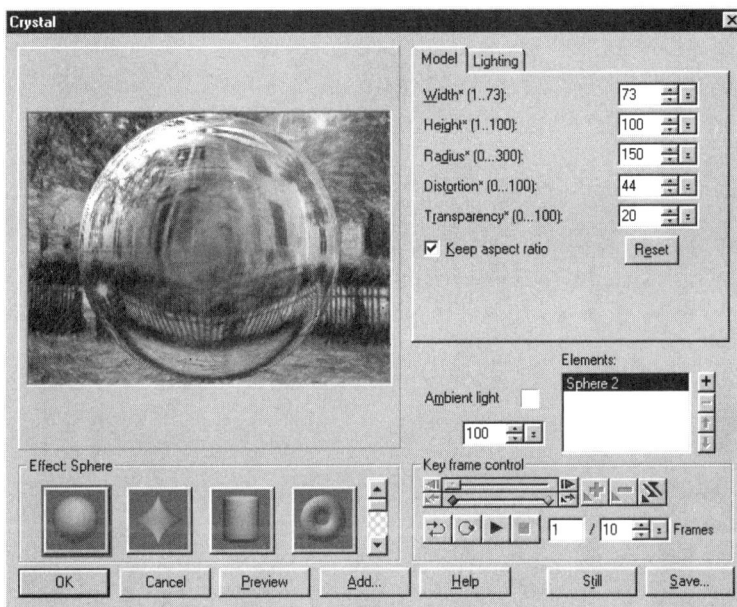

FIGURE 9-8   The Crystal dialog box

Apply Lighting Effects

The Lighting dialog box contains a collection of 10 special effect lighting filters, such as spotlight, meteor, fireworks, and lightning. Scroll through the effect thumbnails to see the available effects, or see Chapter 13 for descriptions. Figure 9-9 shows an example of the Lighting effect filter at work.

To open the Lighting dialog box, choose Effect | Creative | Lighting. The options available in the Lighting dialog box, shown in Figure 9-10, are similar to those in the Crystal dialog box, including the ability to add multiple instances of lighting effects to your image with the Elements box. Since lighting effects need a dark background to show up, PhotoImpact normally darkens your existing image when you apply a Lighting effect. You can control how much your base image is obscured by the darkening effect by adjusting the Ambient Light setting.

Apply Painting Effects

The Painting option on the Creative submenu offers a collection of filters that move the pixels around your image as if by brush strokes, as shown in Figure 9-11. These filters "paint" your image, using brush techniques that try to approximate what an

FIGURE 9-9   An example of an image with a Lighting effect

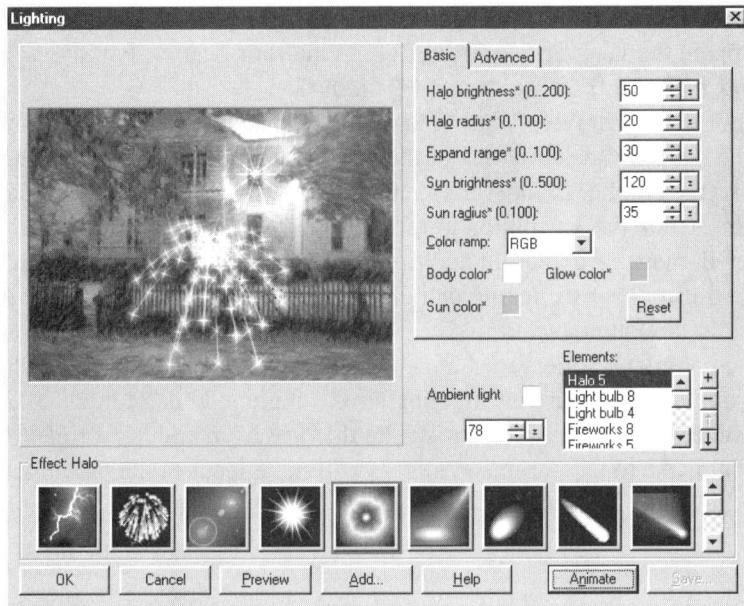

FIGURE 9-10   The Lighting dialog box

FIGURE 9-11   An image "painted" with the Creative Effects Painting effect

artist might do. This is a large collection of filters, and each instance of a filter is
fully editable. There are 49 instant painting techniques you can apply with a mouse-
click. Compare the versatility of this effect to the four Natural Painting effects
covered in Chapter 6 (Effects | Natural Painting).

Select Effect | Creative | Painting to open the Painting dialog box, shown in
Figure 9-12. Start by selecting one of the paint templates by clicking a thumbnail.
Note that some templates render the image in grayscale while others create full
color effects. Click the Try button to replace the default thumbnail image with
your selected image or object. In addition to selecting a template, you can also
change the brush type by clicking one of the thumbnails on the right side of the
dialog box, in the Pattern section.

Use the parameter sliders to change, for example, how dense the brush strokes
should be applied, transparency amount, stroke angle, and paint thickness. You
can also control how much each stroke should vary from another stroke. Note that
changes you make to the parameter sliders will not appear in the preview box until
you click the Apply button.

FIGURE 9-12   The Painting dialog box

Apply Particle Effects

The Particle effect filter is a collection of eight semi-transparent effects such as bubbles, clouds, snow, stars, fire, and mist. Choose Effect | Creative | Particle to open the Particle dialog box, shown in Figure 9-13. The dialog box does not include animation options, but the rest of the options are essentially the same as the other Creative effect filters. You select a specific effect by clicking a thumbnail in the lower-left corner, adjust the parameters on the right side of the dialog box, and preview the effect on the left. Click OK to apply the effect.

Some filters, such as Firefly and Snow, provide a Random button. Click it, and the disbursement of the effect changes randomly. For example, the snow will appear thicker in certain segments, or the firefly lights will vary more in color.

One nice feature of the Particle filters is that you can manually move individual particles—you can grab a star, bubble, of flume of smoke and just drag it out of the way. Let's say you've rendered an interesting effect, but the bulk of it is right on somebody's face. Click on the particle instance that you want to move in the preview box, and the mouse will change to a four-way arrow, indicating that you've

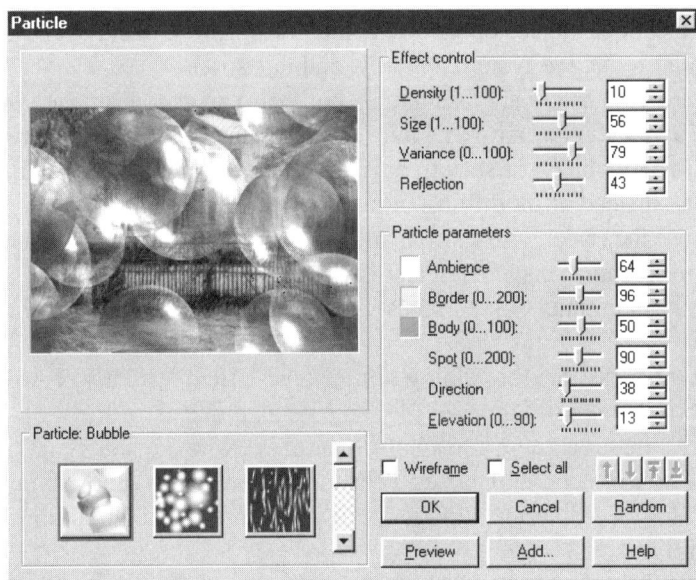

FIGURE 9-13   The Particle dialog box

clicked on something mobile. Then just drag the mouse to move the particle elsewhere.

To move all the particles in one particular direction, click the Select All option. All particles will be selected with rectangular boxes. Then, drag with your mouse in the intended direction.

Apply Type Effects

The Type Effect filter is a collection of 20 preset borders, shadow, and emboss settings that you can automatically apply to any selected text object. Actually, although the effects are called Type Effects, you're not restricted to using them only on text objects. You can apply effects from the Type Effect dialog box to path objects and selections as well.

Whether you apply a Type Effect to text or to another object in a still image, you use the same procedure. It's described in Chapter 8. Like most of the Creative effects, The Type Effect filter can also produce animations. See Chapter 13 for details

Apply Artist Texture Effects

The Artist Texture filter provides elaborate color patterns and embroidery-like textures. You can use this effect to create a colorful image background or exotic patterns similar to Native American quilts and tapestries.

The patterns and colors are fascinating, but their garish contrasts tend to restrict the practical application of Artist Texture effects. When you apply an Artist Texture effect to an image, object, or selection, it completely replaces the existing color fill or image data, instead of modifying or overlaying the current selection. As a result, you need to use the effect with caution and apply it to small selections and separate objects, not to an entire image. With careful attention to the color palette and pattern selection, you can produce some interesting texture effects, but this filter is difficult to control.

To open the Artist Texture dialog box, choose Effect | Creative | Artist Texture. The dialog box, shown in Figure 9-14, contains a unique assortment of settings. There are no animation key frame controls or preview box, as there are in most of the other Creative effect dialog boxes. (The Advanced button enables you to access controls for storyboard-style animation, but you don't need that option to apply the effect to a still image.)

Chapter 13 describes how to use the Artist Texture effect to create a storyboard animation. To apply the effect to a still image, you use the same techniques to select the colors and patterns. Then, instead of dragging a pattern to the storyboard, you

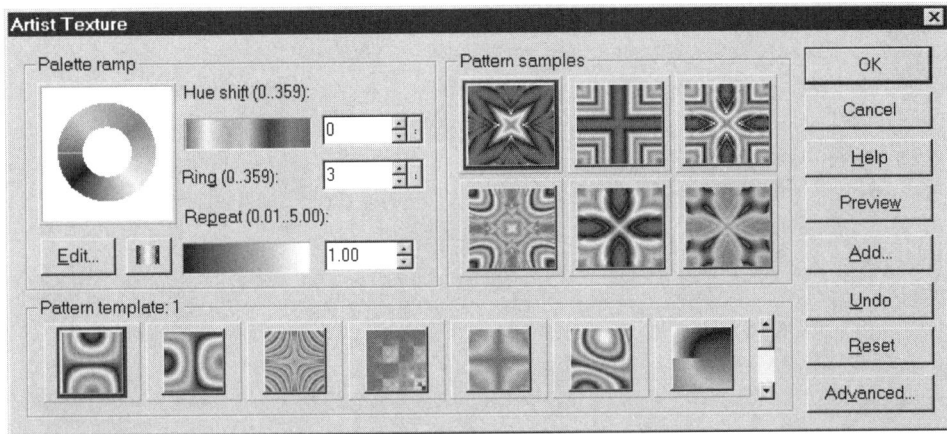

FIGURE 9-14   The Artist Texture dialog box

simply click a pattern sample thumbnail and then click OK (or Preview) to apply it to your object or selection.

Apply Creative Warp Effects

The Creative Warp effect filter provides a collection of kaleidoscope-like patterns that interact with the existing image to produce geometric, repeating effects. This filter uses patterns in a way that is similar to the Artist Texture filter, but the Creative Warp filter uses the colors existing in the object or selection instead of introducing its own palette of colors.

To open the Creative Warp dialog box, choose Effect | Creative | Creative Warp. The dialog box, shown in Figure 9-15, is simpler than the Artist Texture dialog box because there is no color palette to worry about. It's basically just a pair of Before and After thumbnails and a row of pattern template thumbnails. Click a pattern template thumbnail and observe the effect on the preview thumbnail. Again, like Artistic Texture, each time you apply a template thumbnail, the effect is cumulative. The Undo and Reset buttons let you back up a step or start over.

Apply Transform Effects

The Transform effect filter is a collection of deformation filters that punch, squeeze, pull, and distort your image. The Transform filter offers a baker's dozen effects.

FIGURE 9-15 The Creative Warp dialog box

Some of these effects are similar to the standard effect filters on the 2D and 3D submenus, which are covered in Chapter 6.

To open the Transform dialog box, choose Effect | Creative | Transform. The dialog box, shown in Figure 9-16, features a large preview box on the left and a group of transformation template thumbnails on the right. The Storyboard area at the bottom of the dialog box is for building animations, so you can ignore it when working with still images and objects.

Only the last two transformations (Horizontal Squeeze and Vertical Squeeze) take effect immediately when you click a transformation template thumbnail. To use the other transformations, click the transformation template thumbnail and drag the pointer in the preview box to apply the effect to the preview image. To facilitate working on the image, the preview box displays a full-sized image with scrollbars to move about, instead of the more common reduced-size thumbnail. Click the Reset button to restore the preview image to its original condition. When you're pleased with the effect, click OK to apply it to your object or image.

Work with Magic Effects

PhotoImpact Magic effects are similar to Creative effects in some ways, but they tend to offer fewer editable parameters, and they don't offer the option to generate

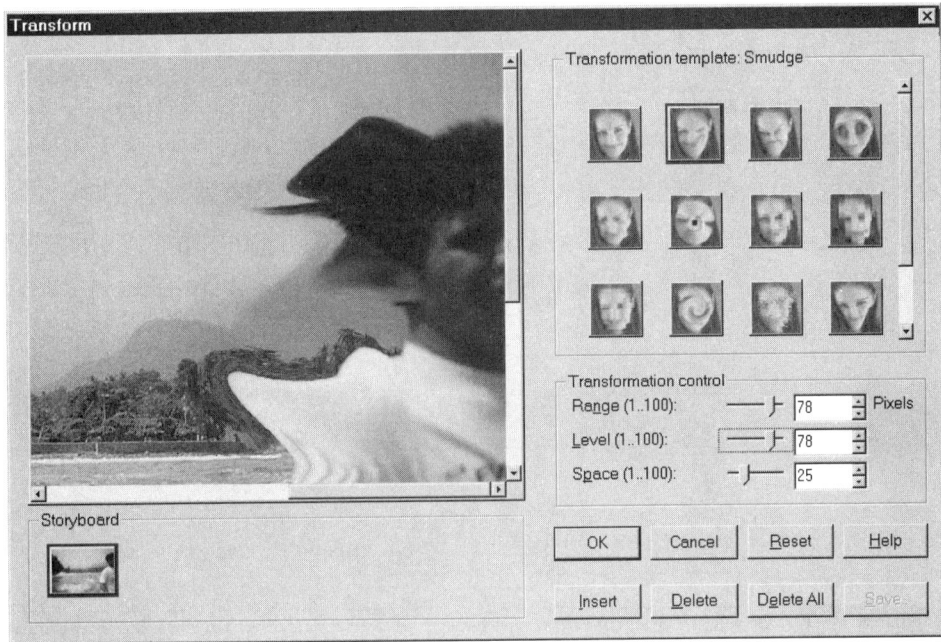

FIGURE 9-16   The Transform dialog box

animation sequences. To access the Magic effects, choose Effects | Magic Effects. You will see a submenu with the choices Kaleidoscope, Light, Magic Gradient, and Turnpage.

Apply Kaleidoscope Effects

True to its name, the Kaleidoscope effect repeats and mirrors segments of your image at various angles, which simulates viewing the image through a kaleidoscope. It's an interesting effect that is fun to play with, but it probably doesn't have a lot of practical applications, unless you need to transform a regular image into a "house of mirrors" view.

To use the Kaleidoscope effect, choose Effect | Magic Effects | Kaleidoscope. The first dialog box that appears displays an array of nine thumbnails representing preset effect settings. To use one of the presets, click the thumbnail and click OK. Otherwise, click the Options button to display the full Kaleidoscope dialog box, as shown in Figure 9-17.

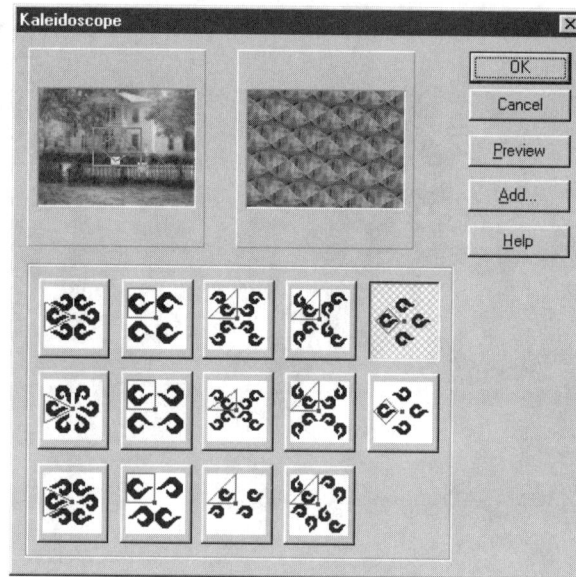

FIGURE 9-17   The Kaleidoscope dialog box

Click a thumbnail to select one of the 14 patterns. Click and drag the boxes on the left (Before) preview image to move or resize the Kaleidoscope focus area. Doing so shifts or expands the area used by the filter to generate the effect. Changing this area greatly affects the filter's results, as shown in the preview image on the right.

Apply Light Effects

The Light effect filter simulates a beam of light focused on your image, object, or selection. You can use this effect to create the look of a spotlight illuminating the subject in your image. This light can be of any color, and you can change the spread of the beam and how light or dark the image outside the beam appears.

To open the Light dialog box, shown in Figure 9-18, choose Effect | Magic Effects | Light.

You can adjust the settings as follows:

- Drag the Exposure slider or click the spin box to change the brightness of the light.

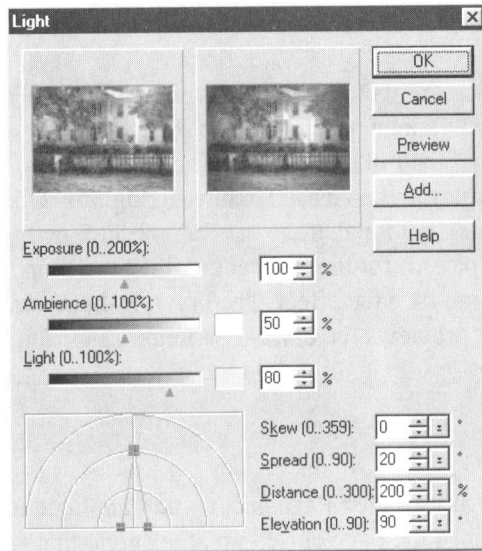

FIGURE 9-18 The Light dialog box

- Drag the Ambience slider or click the spin box to change the brightness of the area outside the focused beam of the light. Click the color box to change the color of the ambient light.

- Drag the Light slider or click the spin box to change the intensity of the light beam. Click the color box to change the color of the light.

- Adjust the size and spread of the light by dragging the control points on the diagram in the lower-left corner of the dialog box, or you can control the light by entering numbers into the Skew, Spread, Distance, and Elevation boxes.

Add Magic Gradient Effects

The Magic Gradient effect filter is similar to the Artist Texture filter found on the Effect | Creative submenu. Like the Artist Texture filter, the Magic Gradient filter produces fills that you can apply to images, objects, and selections. The major differences are that the Magic Gradient patterns are simpler, and the dialog box does not provide the option to generate animation sequences. As a result of the simpler patterns, the Magic Gradient fills look more like color blends than embroidery or textures. The Magic Gradient effect is a good way to create and apply the multiple gradient fills that simulate reflective surfaces such as metal, as illustrated in Figure 9-19.

To open the Magic Gradient dialog box, shown in Figure 9-20, choose Effect | Magic Effects | Magic Gradient. (You can also access the Magic Gradient dialog box from the Gradient tab of the Fill dialog box.) The Palette Ramp area in the upper-left works like its counterpart in the Artist Texture dialog box. Click the Edit button to select and edit a different color palette in the Ramp Editor dialog box. Click a Mode thumbnail to select a pattern for the gradient. Adjust the Slope, Frequency, and Amplitude sliders to fine-tune the effect. The preview thumbnail on the upper-right side of the dialog box previews the current settings. Click and drag the preview thumbnail to move the gradient around on the object.

Apply Turnpage Effects

The Turnpage effect (often called Pagecurl in other applications) creates the appearance of a corner of the page curled up at an angle that reflects light. This popular effect, illustrated in Figure 9-21, can create the turning-page appearance from any corner of the page. You can adjust the curl width, depth, color, and other appearance factors.

> **NOTE** *The Effects | Creative Effects | Animation Studio | Page Turn effect provides an animated version of the Turnpage effect (the page gradually curls and turns).*

FIGURE 9-19   A Magic Gradient fill example

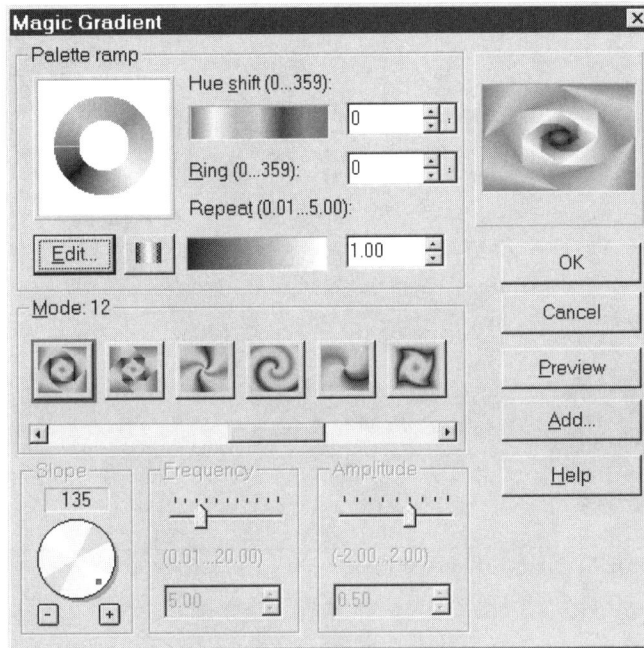

FIGURE 9-20   The Magic Gradient dialog box

To open the Turnpage dialog box, choose Effect | Magic Effects | Turnpage. The dialog box, shown in Figure 9-22, contains Before and After preview thumbnails and an assortment of buttons and other controls to let you adjust the effect.

You can adjust the settings as follows:

- Click a Type icon to select a rounded or corner page effect.

- Click a Corner option to specify which corner of the image should be affected.

- Click a Mode option to specify the appearance of the back side of the turning page.

- Click the Background Color box to choose the color that should appear behind the curl.

- Drag the Angle dial to control how much the page should curl.

A Turnpage effect example

■ Drag the Lighting Direction handle to specify the direction of the light
source that illuminates the turning page. This affects the highlight on the
curl and the shadow it casts.

■ Drag the line on the Before thumbnail to control the angle of the page curl
on the selected corner.

Using these controls, you can quickly choose basic settings such as the corner that
is turning, curl transparency amount, and corner angle and lighting.

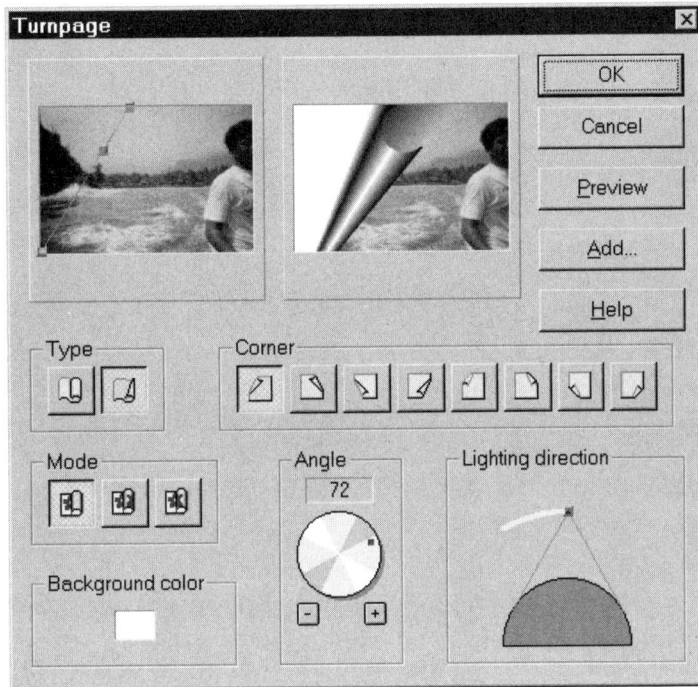

FIGURE 9-22 The Turnpage dialog box

PART IV

Create Web Components and Pages

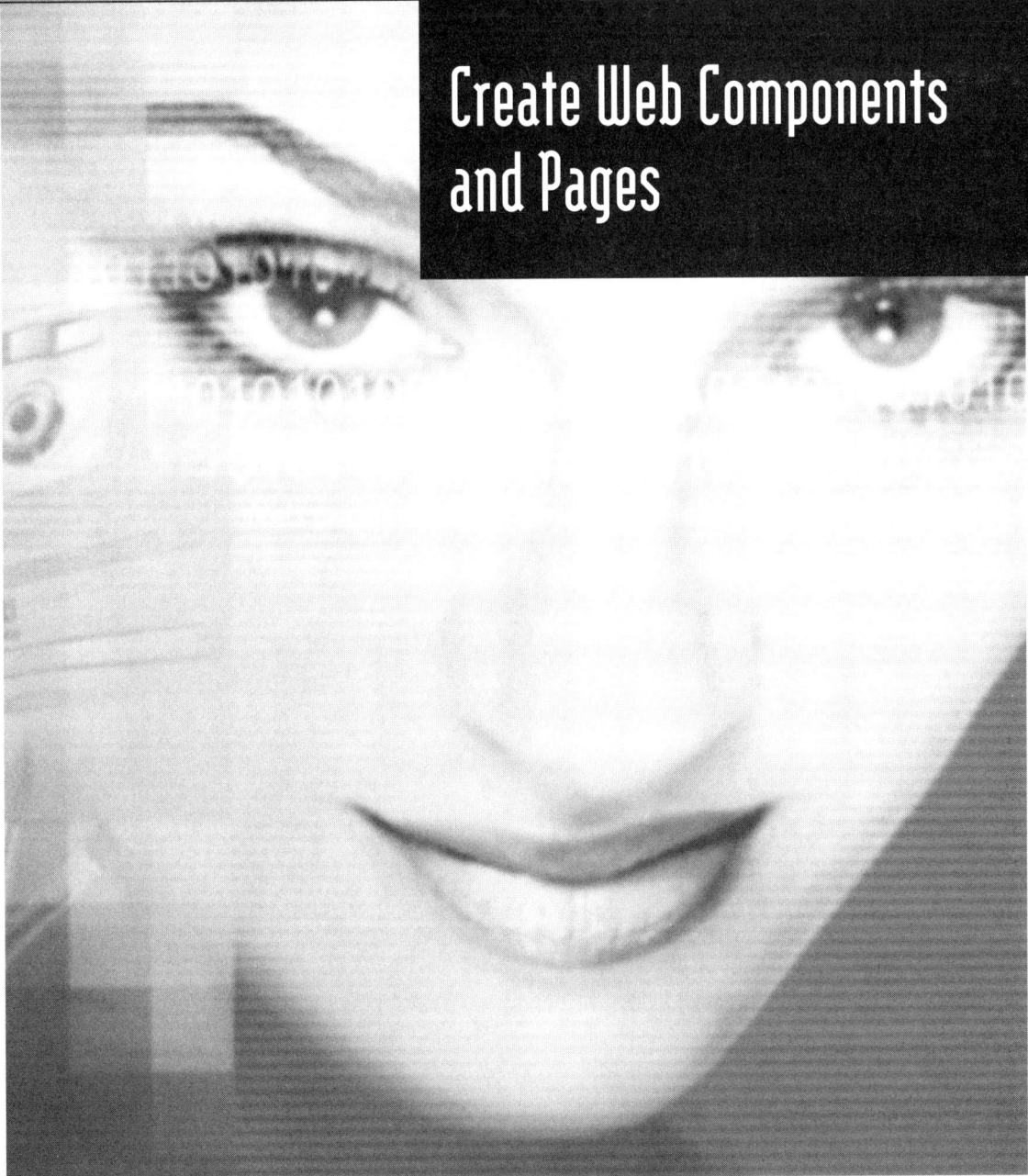

CHAPTER 10

Create Web Components

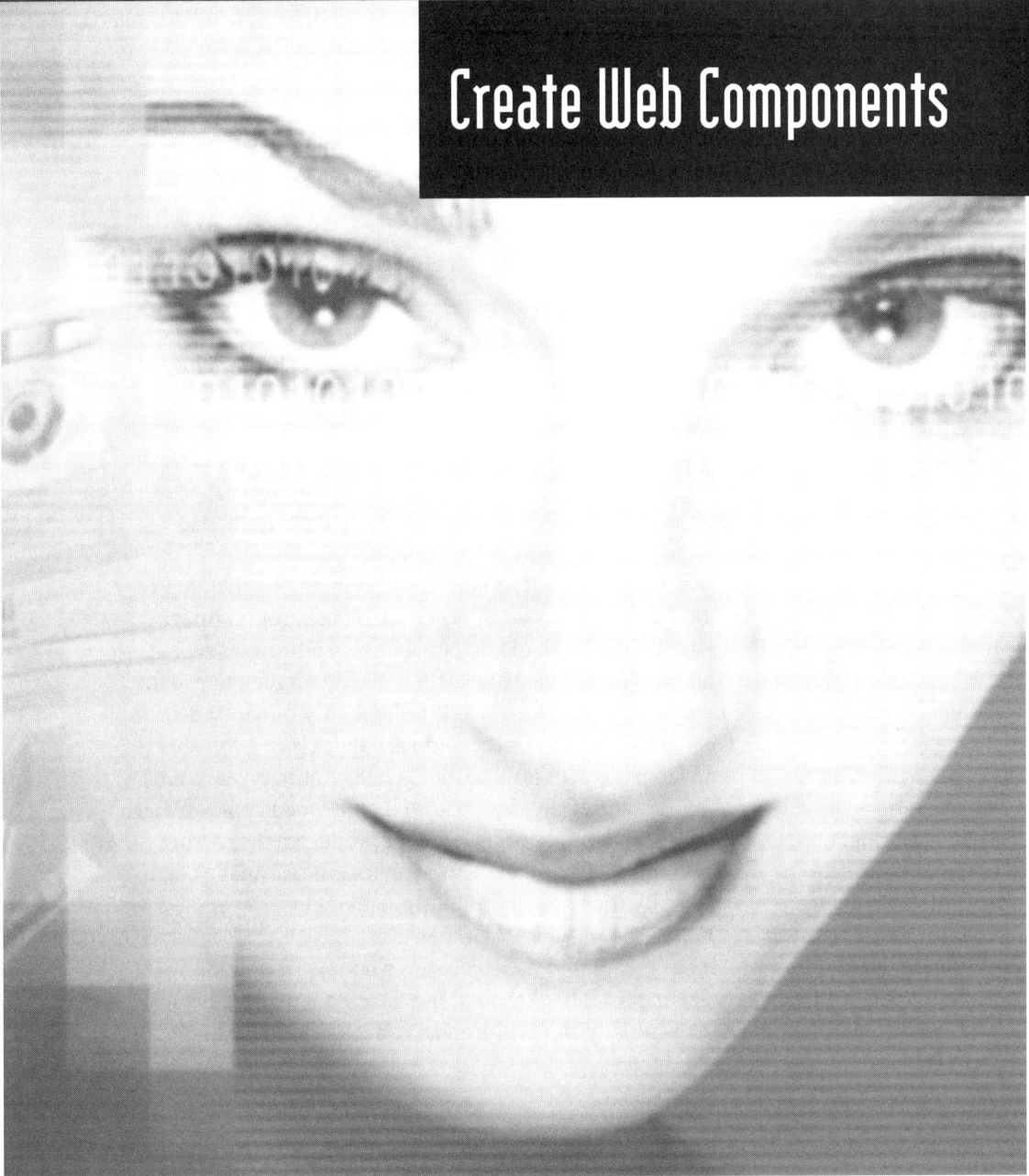

The days of plain-text web pages are ancient history. Modern web pages normally contain multiple graphical components, including buttons, backgrounds, images, and banners. These web graphics give each web page much of its distinctive appearance. Creating web graphics can be fun and challenging.

PhotoImpact's designer wizards make it easy to create various web components and backgrounds that will make your web page fun and interesting to view. In this chapter, you'll learn how to create web page backgrounds, buttons, navigator bars, banners, and separators.

Design a Web Background

One of the many ways to personalize a web page is to replace the solid-color background with an image. The image might be a texture, a pattern, or a corporate logo.

Creating an image big enough to fill the entire page is impractical because such a large image would take too long to load and display. Fortunately, you don't need to create such a monster background image. Instead, you can let the web browser automatically repeat a smaller image as many times as necessary to fill the page background.

Web backgrounds are usually small images that tile out to form one image. For example, a display area of 800 by 600 pixels could use a tiled background image that is only 80 by 80 pixels small. To fill the display area, the web browser repeats the background image 10 times across the page, and 7.5 times down the page. This technique makes the page load faster, because it needs to load only one instance of the image. Once the image is loaded, it can be repeated very quickly.

To create an illusion of a web page background that is one continuous texture, the small background image must be carefully designed so that the tiled copies blend seamlessly together. Otherwise, repeating the image would produce a distracting checkerboard pattern as a background. Creating seamless background images can be quite a challenge to do manually. Fortunately, PhotoImpact includes special features that greatly simplify the process.

When deciding on which background to use, there are a couple of options available to you. You can select a preset background that is already seamless, or you can design your own background with PhotoImpact's Background Designer.

Create a Simple Background Tile

A background tile is simply a small image that is repeated to fill the entire area of a page, table cell, or button. These images are generally very small and consist of a simple texture or a subtle pattern.

To design a background tile, do the following:

1. Create a new image document for your background tile. (See Chapter 1 for details.) The standard size for a background tile is 80 by 80 pixels.

2. Fill the image with a pattern or texture. The simplest way to fill the image with a texture is to use the EasyPalette. Press F2 to open the EasyPalette panel if it's not already open. Select the Fill Gallery in the EasyPalette, and then drag a fill from the EasyPalette and drop it onto your image.

3. Save the image for the web. (See the next section for details.)

Save an Image As a Web Graphic

After you create a background tile or other web graphic, you need to save it in the proper file format for use on a web page. PhotoImpact includes a special command to facilitate saving images for the web. This is how it works:

1. Choose File | Save for Web | Entire Image. PhotoImpact opens the Image Optimizer dialog box, shown in Figure 10-1.

2. Adjust the JPEG compression settings and other options as needed, and then click Save As. PhotoImpact opens the Save As dialog box.

3. Locate the directory where you want to save the file, give the file a name, and then click Save. PhotoImpact closes the Save As dialog box and creates the file containing your background tile.

In addition to saving the entire image for the web, you can select a portion of an image and save the selection or object as a web graphic. Just choose File | Save for Web | As Single Object, and then complete steps 2 and 3 above for saving a web graphic. PhotoImpact saves the selected object as a separate file, using the format and settings appropriate for web graphics.

10

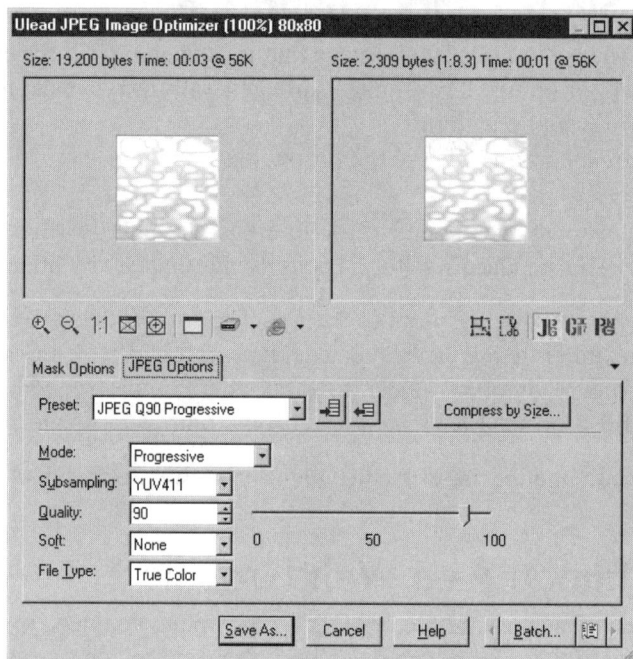

FIGURE 10-1 The Image Optimizer dialog box

Design a Seamless Tile

Although you can save any image as a background tile, you can significantly improve the overall effect by making the background tile seamless. Seamless tiles are a lot less obvious because they are blended together to soften the edges, as shown in the following illustration.

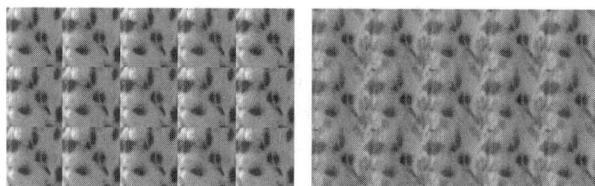

Nonseamless   Seamless

To create a seamless background tile, do the following:

1. Create a new image document or open an existing image you want to use as a pattern or texture for your background tile.

2. Using the Standard Selection tool, create an 80 by 80 pixel square around the area you want to include in your tile.

> **TIP** *To create a perfect square, hold down the* SHIFT *key while selecting the area.*

3. Choose Web | Create Seamless Tile. PhotoImpact opens the Create Seamless Image dialog box.

4. Adjust the settings in the Create Seamless Image dialog box as necessary. The Merge Size value determines the overlap of the tiles. You can enter a higher value to increase the overlap of the image tiles or enter a lower value to decrease the overlap. The Merge Ratio value adjusts the edge blending level between tiles. A higher value blends the edges more and creates a smoother look.

5. To find the settings that are best for your tile, start with the defaults and click the Preview button to view the results (a full screen of the tiled background). To return to the dialog box, click the tiled background. In most cases, PhotoImpact will set the correct values for you.

6. Click OK. PhotoImpact closes the Create Seamless Image dialog box and creates the tile for you. The tile appears in a new, untitled document window.

7. Save the image for the web (choose File | Save for Web | Entire Image).

Use the Background Designer

The PhotoImpact Background Designer is a fun tool. You can use it to create a web background tile by selecting from several templates. By adjusting various settings, you can produce an almost infinite variety of textures and patterns.

To access this tool, choose Web | Background Designer or press SHIFT-B. PhotoImpact opens the Background Designer dialog box, as shown in Figure 10-2. In this dialog box, adjust the various settings and options to achieve the desired effect.

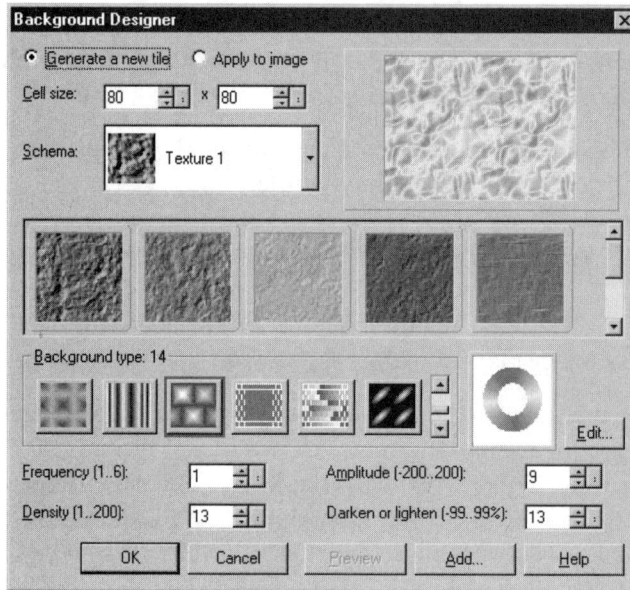

FIGURE 10-2   The Background Designer dialog box

- **Generate a New File**   Select this option if you want to create a new background tile. This background tile can be saved as a JPEG and used for several applications, such as table or button backgrounds.

- **Apply to Image**   Select this option if you want to apply the tile to a background or selected area. If you have an area selected, such as a button or banner, the Apply to Image option will apply the tile to the selected area only. This option is available only if you have a file open.

- **Cell Size**   By default, this value is set to 80 × 80 pixels. This is because most web pages are designed for a screen set to 800 × 600 dots per inch (dpi). This is generally the smallest screen size at which anyone will be viewing your screen.

> **TIP**   *As a rule, you should take the width of your display area and divide that number by ten. This will give you the optimal tile size that should be used to fill that area. For example, if you want to fill the first row of a table with a background tile, and the table width is set to 500 pixels, you want to create a tile that is 50 × 50 pixels.*

- **Schema**   This is where the fun begins. Click the down arrow to view a variety of schemas and textures. Select one that basically suits your needs. With the following options, you can alter the look and feel of that schema.

- **Background Type**   Click a background type and notice how the schema changes in the preview pane. Try them all and see how they transform the selected schema. Find a selection that is close to what you want. You can continue to make adjustments with the other settings in the dialog box.

- **Palette Ramp Editor (Edit)**   Click the Edit button to change the color and light source. To start, select a color ring that closely meets your needs. From there, you can adjust the Hue shift and Ring settings to achieve the desired light source and color variation. If you want to save this design, click the Add button. This creates a new color ring in the designer. If you simply want to apply your selections to the current file, click OK.

- **Frequency**   Raising the Frequency value will tighten your pattern. Lowering this value will make the pattern loose and look softer.

- **Density**   Raising this value will make your image seem more defined, and in some instances, darker. Lowering this value will make the image appear flatter and less defined.

- **Amplitude**   This value acts as a contrast adjustment. Raise this value to increase contrast. Lower this value to soften, or decrease, the contrast.

- **Darken or Lighten**   This value acts as a brightness adjustment. Raise this value to increase brightness. Lower this value to darken the image.

- **Preview**   This button is available only if the Apply to Image option is selected. Click this button to preview your selections. In this mode, you'll see your preview and a panel with five choices: OK (accepts your changes and closes the Background Designer dialog box), Cancel (cancels your changes and closes the dialog box), Undo/Redo, Continue (returns to the dialog box), and Add (adds the background tile to the EasyPalette).

When you click OK in the Background Designer dialog box, PhotoImpact closes the dialog box and creates the background tile image in a new document window. To save the background tile as a separate image, choose File | Save for Web | Entire Image.

Assemble Buttons

Buttons are another common web graphic component. Computer users are accustomed to clicking on-screen buttons to make the computer do something, so buttons naturally become an important part of the design of web pages. They are particularly useful as navigational tools when the viewer needs to click to move from one page to another. A button can be a simple text graphic or a shaped button with text that indicates the page to which it links. The following illustration shows a few web-button variations.

Like most other web components, buttons are really small graphic images that you create with an image editor such as PhotoImpact and then add to your web page. You could use the various PhotoImpact drawing tools to create button graphics from scratch, but PhotoImpact includes the Button Designer and the Component Designer, two tools that make the job faster and easier. First, we'll cover how to use the Button Designer, which is specifically designed for creating buttons. Then we'll explore the Component Designer, which guides you through the steps for creating buttons and other web page components.

Use the Button Designer

The simplest buttons do not contain text. They are usually simple shapes, such as a rectangle or an ellipse, and are commonly used as bullets or companions to linked text on a page. The button graphics normally have a beveled-edge effect that gives them the distinctive identification as a button. Depending on the edge effect, the button can look raised or depressed, rounded or sharply beveled. The Button Designer enables you to convert any image (or selection) into a button with ease.

Create a Rectangular Button

To design a simple button with the Button Designer, first create a new document for your button. Then color your image or apply a background color or texture. Choose Web | Button Designer | Rectangular to open the Button Designer dialog box, shown in Figure 10-3.

Select one of the preset button templates below the preview thumbnail in the upper-right corner or select your own combinations of settings from the left side of the dialog box. You can set the following options:

■ **Style**   Click the style that best suits your needs.

■ **Direction**   Select Outward to expand the size of the image. Select Inward to constrain the size of the button to the selection dimensions.

■ **Options**   There are three possible selections. The Mirror option synchronizes the top and left edges and the right and bottom edges as you adjust the bevel width. The Mirror All option synchronizes all four edges as you adjust the bevel width. The Individual Sides option allows you to adjust the bevel width of each side separately.

10

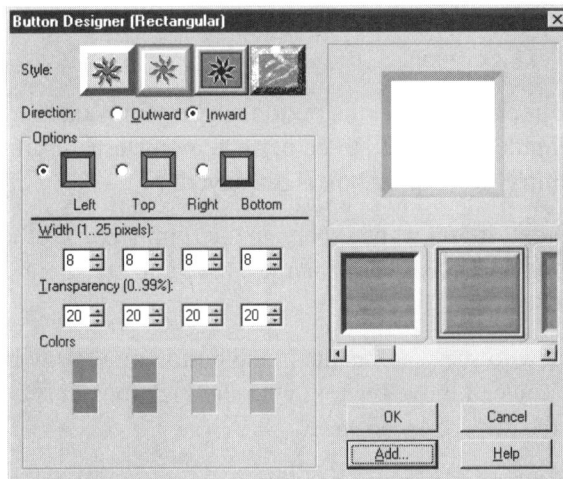

FIGURE 10-3   The Button Designer (Rectangular) dialog box

- ■ **Width**   Use this option to set the width of the left, top, right, and bottom bevel edges.

- ■ **Transparency**   This option is available only when the Inward direction is selected. Select the value that determines how much the base image should show through the button border.

- ■ **Colors**   Select the colors you want to use for the button.

When you're finished, click OK to close the Button Designer dialog box. PhotoImpact applies the beveled edge effect to your image. To save the image for the web, choose File | Save for Web | Entire Image.

> TIP   *If you like with the look and feel of your button, be sure to save it as a native PhotoImpact (UFO) file, so you can edit and add to it if necessary.*

Add Text to Your Button

Adding text to your buttons makes them a bit more intuitive to your users and requires less real estate on your page, because there is no need for separate text describing the button option. With PhotoImpact, you can easily add text to an existing button image by using the Text tool. To add text to an existing button, open the button image, and then do the following:

1. Click the Text tool icon.

2. Position your cursor inside the button where you want the text to appear. This position does not need to be perfect. You can adjust the location later. The Text Entry Box dialog box is displayed.

3. Type your text. If you want to change the font, size, or other attributes, select the text and make your changes. (See Chapter 2 for details on using the Text tool.)

4. Click Preview to see your results in the button on your work page. If necessary, you can move the text with the Pick tool. Just click and drag the text to the desired location.

5. When you are satisfied with the look of your text, click OK in the Text Entry Box. PhotoImpact closes the Text Entry Box.

Using the EasyPalette, you can add texture and other effects to your text.

6. Save the image for the web (choose File | Save for Web | Entire Image).

Create Irregular Buttons

Buttons don't need to be rectangles. You can also use ellipses, circles, diamonds, stars, pentagons, and other shapes as buttons. PhotoImpact calls these "any shape" buttons, as you can see in the version of the Button Designer dialog box shown in Figure 10-4. Irregular buttons can help to add character to your web page. You may need to use the shape of a logo or simply want something to draw the eye of your viewers.

To create an irregular button with the Button Designer, first create a new image document for your button or open an existing image file. Then create an object of an irregular shape with the Path Drawing tool. Alternatively, you could select a

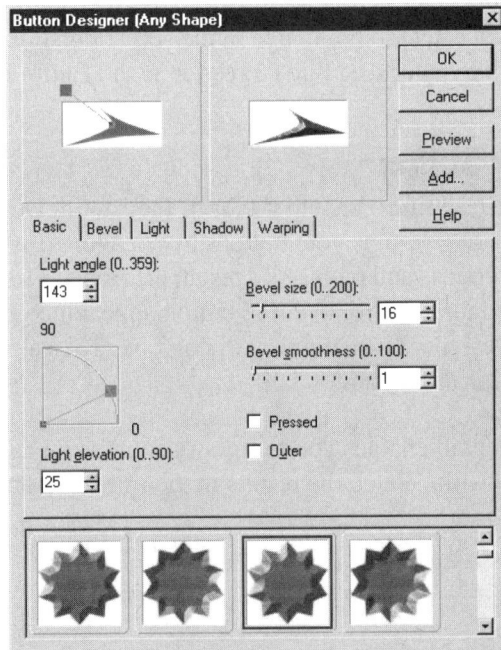

10

FIGURE 10-4   The Button Designer (Any Shape) dialog box

shape from the Shape Library in the EasyPalette or define a selection with one of the Selection tools. Make sure the object is the active selection.

Choose Web | Button Designer | Any Shape to open the Button Designer dialog box (see Figure 10-4). From the thumbnail images in the Basic tab, select the style you want to use. If it is not exactly what you want, you can adjust it in multiple ways.

To adjust the size of the bevel, use the Bevel Size slider. The lower the number, the flatter the image. For a smoother bevel, adjust the Bevel Smoothness slider up to a higher value.

Once you have made the desired bevel adjustments, adjust the light source to match the other objects you have on your page. You can do this in one or two ways:

- The left thumbnail pane at the top of the dialog has a red square. Click and drag this square to where you want the light source. When you release your mouse button, see the effects of your change in the right preview pane.

- Adjust the Light Angle and Light Elevation settings separately. The higher the elevation, the more ambient the light becomes.

When you're finished, click OK. PhotoImpact closes the Button Designer dialog box and adds the bevel effect to the image in the active document window. Save the image for the web by choosing File | Save for Web | Entire Image.

Fine-Tune Your Button

In addition to the basic settings, the other tabs of the Button Designer (Any Shape) dialog box enable you to fine-tune your buttons by changing the shape of the bevel, adjusting the lighting effects, and more. As a result, the Button Designer (Any Shape) dialog box gives you more control over the button appearance than you get with the simpler Button Designer (Rectangular) dialog box. Take a moment to explore the other options in this dialog box.

Bevel Tab   The Bevel tab enables you to fine-tune the bevel adjustments. These are rather fun to play with. Watch the results in the preview pane until you find the right look.

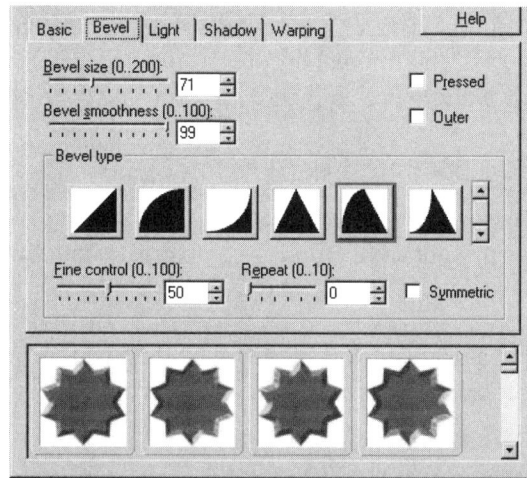

The Bevel Size and Bevel Smoothness settings control the amplitude and definition of the bevel. For a more defined bevel, raise the Bevel Size value and lower the Bevel Smoothness value.

Light Tab   The Light tab enables you to add additional light sources and fine-tune your light settings. For fun, add another light source by increasing the Lights value. Select that light source and change the color. Play with the various settings to see how each one affects the object.

10

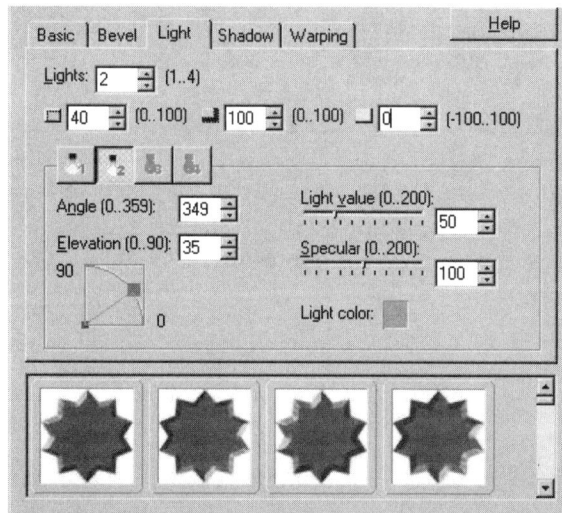

The three value settings beneath the Lights value enable you to control the intensity of the shadows. The first value controls the upper-left corner, the center value controls the lower-right corner, and the third value controls the surface light.

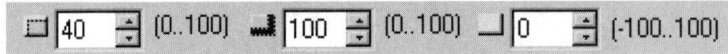

You can adjust each light source separately to create unusual effects. Select the light source and change its values. The results are shown in the preview pane.

Shadow Tab   To add a drop-shadow effect, click the Shadow tab. Select the drop shadow that best matches your light source, and then adjust it as necessary.

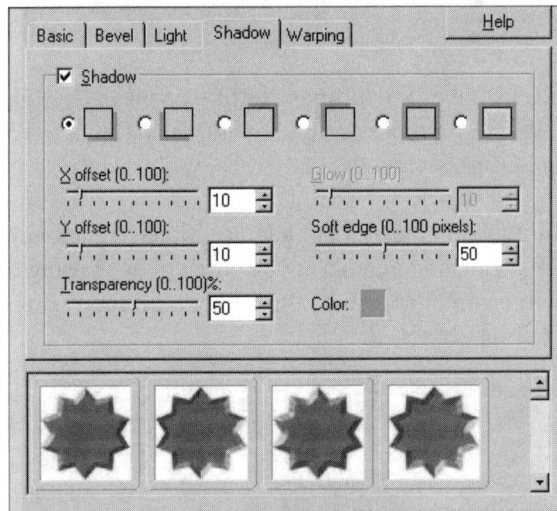

Warping Tab   The Warping tab lets you add chrome characteristics to your button. This type of effect does not look good with all shapes of objects. You may need to adjust your light source to get the desired results.

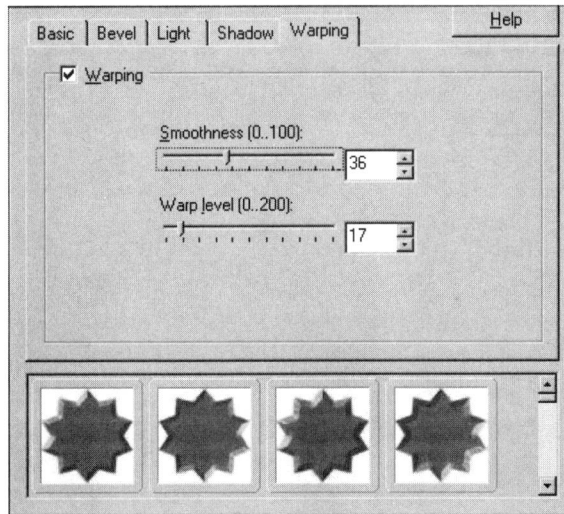

Use the Component Designer to Create Buttons

The Component Designer is a wizard-based tool that guides you though the process of creating components for your web page. The web graphics you can create with the Component Designer include buttons, bullets, banners, icons, and separators, as you can see in Figure 10-5.

The Component Designer is very simple to use; however, it does not enable you to perform as many customizations as the other techniques do. If you just want to create some quick and simple buttons, this is a good tool to use. It's also a good way to quickly create the button variations needed for button bars and rollover effects. If you want to customize the look of the buttons in ways that the Component Designer doesn't allow, you can save them as a native PhotoImpact file and edit them as necessary.

Create a Button with the Component Designer

You do not need to open a file before you create a button with the Component Designer. Follow these steps to begin:

1. Choose Web | Component Designer. PhotoImpact displays the Component Designer dialog box (see Figure 10-5).

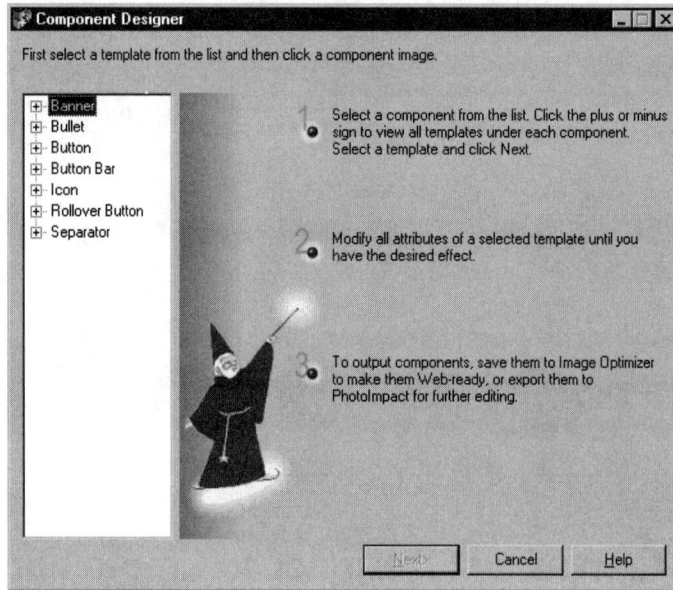

The opening page of the Component Designer

2. Double-click the Button category in the list box on the left side of the dialog box to expand the list of button shapes.

3. Select the shape of button you want to create. A set of thumbnails appear in the preview pane on the right.

4. Select a button design; then click Next.

5. Select Button in the list box in the lower-left portion of the dialog box.

When you select a button design, PhotoImpact changes the Component Designer dialog box to show a large preview of the button at the top and settings to control the details of the button appearance in the tabs below the preview, as shown in Figure 10-6. You can adjust the size, shadow, and hyperlink settings for the button. You can also add text and adjust the shape of the button. Finally, you can export your button. These options are described in the following sections.

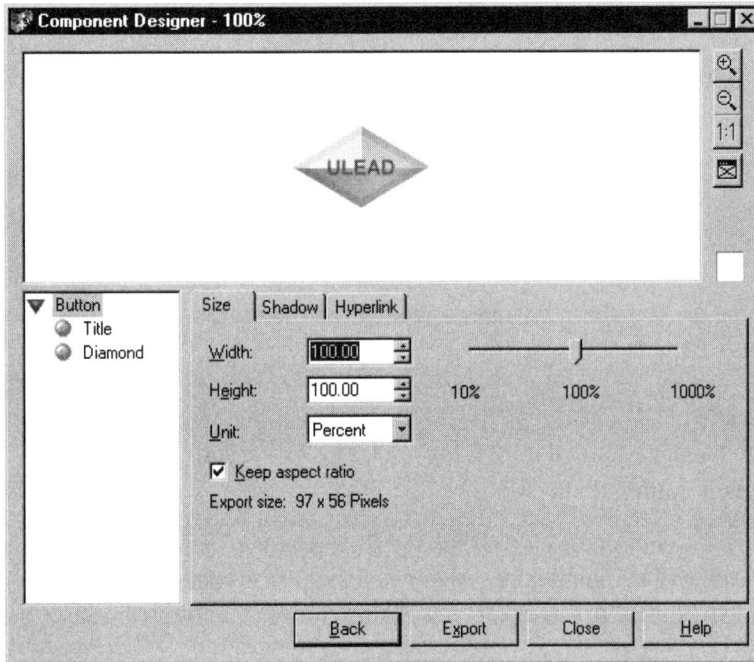

FIGURE 10-6   The Component Designer options for buttons

Set Size, Shadow, and Hyperlink Options   Adjust the size of the image in the Size tab. If you want to change the width and height separately from one another, uncheck the Keep Aspect Ratio option by clicking the checkbox.

If you want to add a shadow to the button, click the Shadow tab. Then check the Shadow option and adjust the settings as needed.

If you plan to add your button directly to a web page you are creating in PhotoImpact, click the Hyperlink tab. You can skip this step if you're creating button graphics that you plan to add to a web page manually using another web page editor. Enter the required information:

■ For the URL, enter the page or link you want the button to launch.

■ If you leave the target field blank, _self is assumed, meaning the URL will be launched in the same window.

■ If users have graphics disabled on their browser, or cannot view your button image, the text they will see in its place is what you enter for Alt text.

■ The Status Bar text displays in the status bar when the button is selected. If left blank, the URL is displayed.

Add Text   Click the Title option to display two new tabs where you can change the text and color of the title text on the button. Enter text and adjust the settings as follows:

■ Type the text that you want to appear on the button into the Text box on the Text tab.

■ Pick a font from the Font list box.

■ Click a checkbox in the Style area to apply a style, such as bold or italic, to your button text.

■ If you do not uncheck the Change Shape When Text Changes option, the button will automatically resize when the text is changed. You may not want this to happen if you are trying to make several buttons the same size.

■ Click the Color tab and select a color for the text using the color swatches on the Color tab. You can also apply gradient fills and textures to your button text.

Adjust Button Elements   Click each of the other options describing the shape of the button to change that element's attributes. The elements that make up the button will vary depending on the button design. Typical button elements might be Panel, Frame, and Plate. You can usually set the color for each element, and you can sometimes set other element attributes.

Export Your Button   Click Export to save the button in the format you need. A pop-up menu appears that enables you to select from three export options:

■ To jump directly to the Image Optimizer dialog box, choose the To Image Optimizer option.

■ To create a new document for the button containing separate component objects, choose the As Individual Objects option.

■ To paste the button into the current document as a single object, choose the As Component option.

Create a Rollover Button

Rollover effects enable you to create buttons that interact with viewers when they view your web page in their web browser. A rollover button can change its appearance when viewers point their mouse at the button or click it.

A rollover effect causes a button to change its appearance based on the state of the mouse button. For example, your button is normally purple, but when the user moves the cursor over the button, it changes to red. When clicked, the button changes to green.

You can define up to three rollover events:

■ **Normal state**   How the button appears when first displayed to the user.

■ **Mouseover state**   How the button appears when the user moves the cursor over the button.

■ **Mousedown state**   How the button appears when the user clicks on it.

Normally, you create a different variation of the basic button graphic for each mouse state, so you need three separate button images to create a rollover effect.

The rollover effect uses JavaScript to determine the state of the mouse and to display the appropriate image. All three images are preloaded when the page is accessed, but only the normal image is visible until a mouse event occurs, such as mouseover or mousedown event.

The Component Designer offers a quick and easy way for creating a rollover effect and all the images needed to make it work, as shown in Figure 10-7. The three buttons in the Java Rollover preview pane represent the different states of the button: The left button represents the normal state, the center button represents the mouseover state, and the right button represents the mousedown state.

To create a rollover effect with the Component Designer, follow these steps:

1. Choose Web | Component Designer to open the Component Designer dialog box.

2. Click the Rollover Button category, and then select a rollover theme. The preview pane shows an assortment of button sets. Each button set consists of three buttons—one for each mouse state.

10

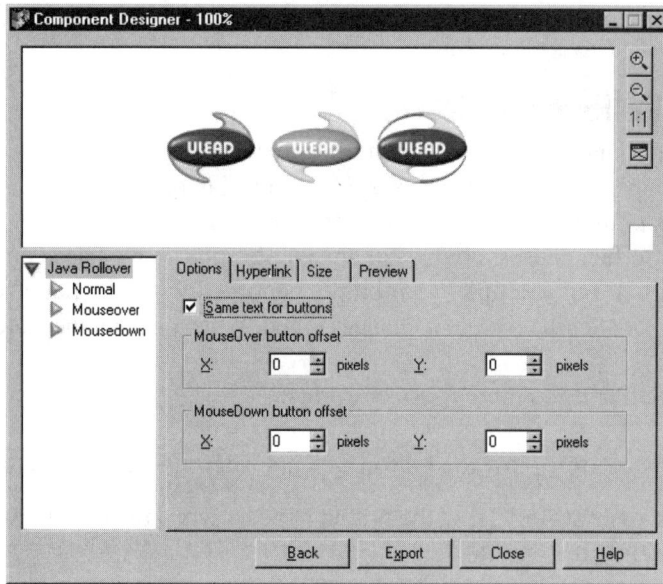

FIGURE 10-7   The Component Designer options for rollover effects

3. Select a button set that best suits your needs and then click Next.

4. To change the appearance of each state, select the state from the list, then change its attributes with the various tab pages.

5. The option settings vary, depending on which theme and button set you choose. Make your changes as necessary using the provided tabs for each button. If you select the Same Text for Buttons option, all of the button states will display the same text.

6. To view your results, click the Java Rollover category and then click the Preview tab. Notice how only the normal button is visible. When you move your mouse over the image in the preview pane, the mouse changes to the mouseover image. When you click your mouse down, the mouse changes to the mousedown image.

7. Click the Hyperlink tab to enter the link information. These instructions are executed when the button is clicked.

When you are satisfied with your rollovers, click Export to specify a save operation. PhotoImpact displays a pop-up menu with four export options:

- To create the HTML code that displays the button, select the To HTML option. This code includes the JavaScript that is used to control the various states. The buttons are exported as three separate images and placed in an Images folder, where the HTML file is stored.

- To save each button state as a separate image, select the To Image Optimizer option.

- To create individual objects in the document you have open, select the As Individual Objects option.

- To save the rollover buttons as one object that can later be modified, select the As Component Object.

Construct Navigation Bars

A *navigation bar* is a common feature of many web pages. The navigation bar consists of a column or row of buttons that the viewer can click to access other web pages. Typically, the navigation bar appears in the same location on each page of a web site to provide a consistent way for the viewers to navigate the site. However, you can also create groups of buttons for other purposes, such as links to other web sites or links to anchors within a single page of text. These button bars can be simple or fairly complex, depending on your needs and the design of your page.

The Component Designer provides a comprehensive wizard that guides you through the process of creating a simple, yet very effective navigation bar for your web page. Figure 10-8 shows the Component Designer options for a button bar.

10

Create a Navigation Bar

To create a simple navigation bar with the Component Designer, follow these steps:

1. Choose Web | Component Designer. PhotoImpact displays the Component Designer dialog box.

2. Click the Button Bar category and select a theme from the samples in the preview pane on the right.

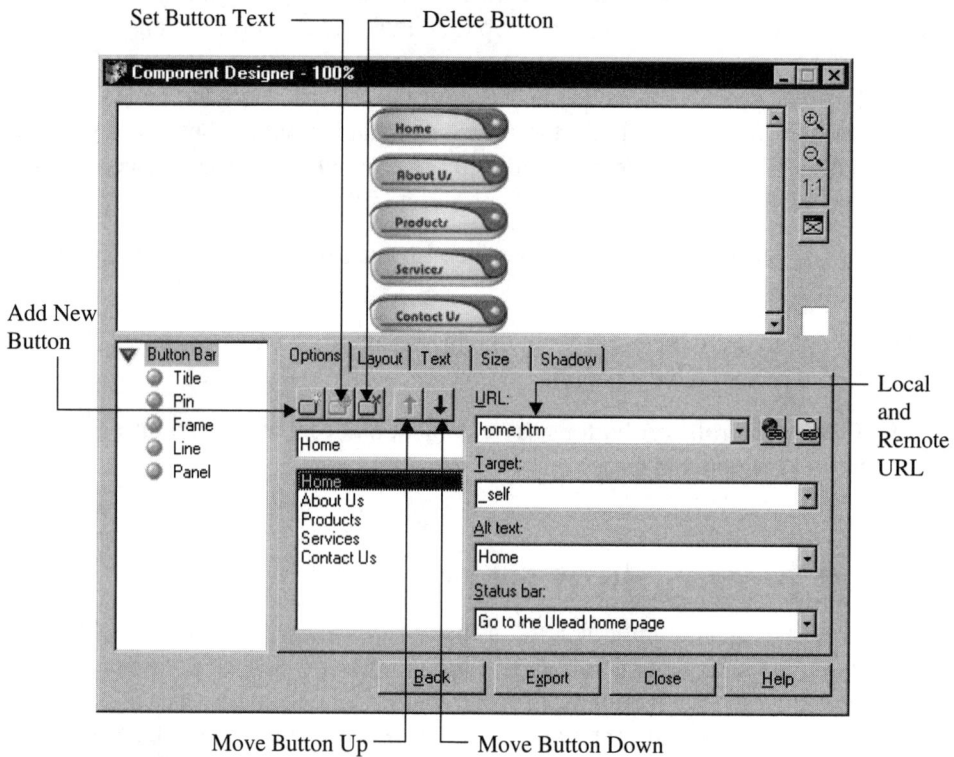

FIGURE 10-8   The Component Designer options for button bars

3. Select a navigation bar that best suits your needs, and then click Next. The Component Designer dialog box displays the options that enable you to define a group of matching buttons (see Figure 10-8).

4. Click Add New Button for each additional button you require. PhotoImpact adds an entry to the list box on the Options tab and also adds a button to the viewing area at the top of the dialog box.

5. If you want to remove a button, select the name of the button you want to remove in the list box and click Delete Button.

6. To change the button text, click the text you want to change and type the new text in the text box just above the button list box. Click Set Button Text to save your change. Repeat this step for each of the remaining buttons.

7. To change the position of the buttons, select the button you want to move, and then click either Move Button Up or Move Button Down.

8. To assign a link to a button, select the button text, then click either Remote URL or Local URL to navigate to the desired link or file. If you know the address of the link, you can simply type it into the URL text box.

Fine-Tune Your Navigation Bar

Experiment with some of the tab settings to change the look and feel of your navigation bar. Each button in the button bar shares the same attributes, with the exception of the title. There are five tabs of settings for a button bar:

- The Options tab options determine the number of buttons in the bar, their order, the text displayed in each button, and the link attributes for each button.

- The Layout tab options set the spacing and alignment for the buttons.

- The Text tab options specify the font and style of your text.

- The Shadow tab applies a shadow to the button bar component.

- The Color tab lets you assign a color to the selected object.

Export Your Navigation Bar

When you're finished building your navigation bar, click Export in the Component Designer dialog box to save it to the desired file format. The pop-up menu that appears contains the same four options that are available for rollover buttons, as described in the "Create a Rollover Button" section earlier in this chapter.

Build Banners

Banners are the largest of the common web graphics components. They are usually horizontal rectangles that extend most of the way across a web page and are composed of a line or two of text on a graphical background. Banners can serve a variety of purposes on your web page, ranging from a letterhead to an advertisement. Banners can be static or animated, and they can be simple graphics or clickable links, like big buttons.

The Component Designer offers a convenient wizard that guides you through the process of creating a static banner based on a variety of designs. Figure 10-9 shows the Component Designer options for a banner.

To create a static banner with the Component Designer, follow these steps:

1. Choose Web | Component Designer to open the Component Designer dialog box.

2. Click the Banner category and select a theme. Thumbnail samples of banner designs appear in the preview pane on the right side of the dialog box.

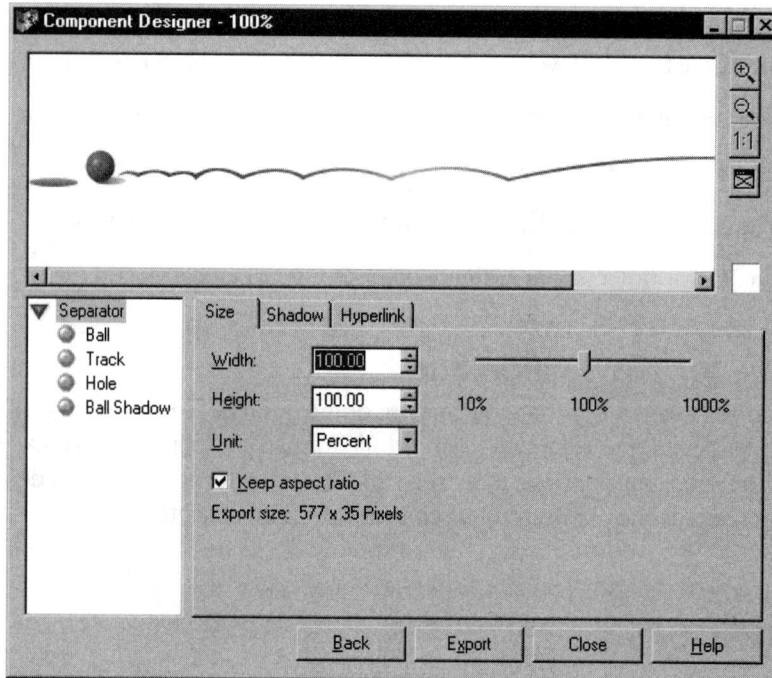

FIGURE 10-9   The Component Designer options for banners

3. Select a banner that best suits your needs and click Next. The Component Designer dialog box displays the selected banner in the viewing area at the top of the dialog box and the options for the selected banner at the bottom (see Figure 10-9).

4. If necessary, change the size of the banner.

5. To change the text, click Title in the element list on the left and then make the appropriate changes to the text, font, and font color.

6. To enter a link, click the Banner element in the list on the left and click the Hypertext tab. Enter the URL and other settings as needed.

7. Experiment with the options on the other tabs to achieve the look you are after. The tabs for a banner are similar to those for creating a button (described in the "Create a Button with the Component Designer" section earlier in this chapter).

8. When you are satisfied with your banner, click Export to save the file in an appropriate format. The pop-up menu that appears contains the same four options that are available for rollover buttons (described in the "Create a Rollover Button" section earlier in this chapter).

10

Create Separators

Separators are the horizontal lines used to separate tables, navigation bars, and other elements in your web page. You can create plain, horizontal rules using HTML code, but graphical separators are much more attractive and can help add a creative flair to your page. Many web designers like to create a unified graphical theme for their web pages by creating separators, buttons, and other graphical elements that share the same color scheme and design.

As with the other web page components described in the previous sections, the Component Designer provides an easy way to create graphical separators. Figure 10-10 shows the options for a separator.

To create a separator with the Component Designer, follow these steps:

1. Choose Web | Component Designer to open the Component Designer dialog box.

2. Click the Separator category and select a theme. Thumbnails of various sample separators appear in the preview pane on the right.

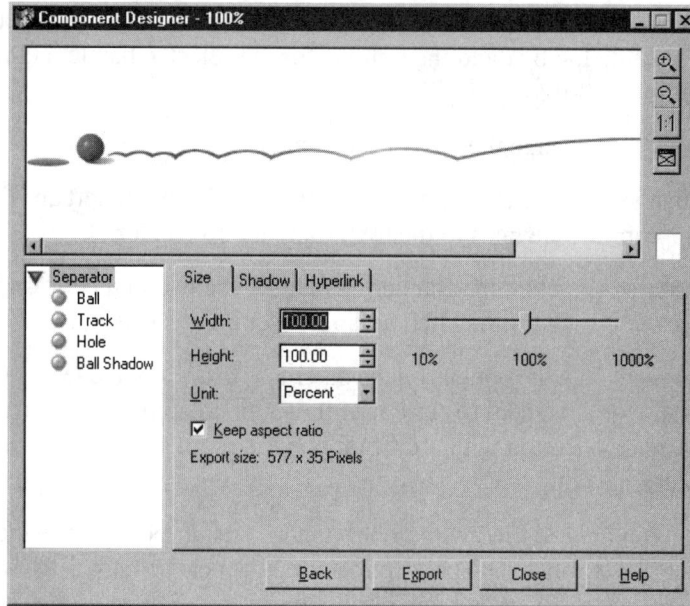

FIGURE 10-10   The Component Designer options for separators

3. Select a separator and click Next. The separator appears in the viewing area at the top of the dialog box, and the options for modifying the appearance of the separator appear below (see Figure 10-10).

4. Experiment with the options to achieve the look you desire. The tabs for a separator are similar to those for creating a button (described in the "Create a Button with the Component Designer" section earlier in this chapter).

5. When you are satisfied with your separator, click Export to save the file in an appropriate format. The pop-up menu that appears contains the same four options that are available for rollover buttons (described in the "Create a Rollover Button" section earlier in this chapter).

The Component Designer can also create icons and bullets. They work in much the same way as buttons and separators, so experiment and have fun. The next two chapters explain how to save your files efficiently and put them all together in a web page.

CHAPTER 11

Optimize and Slice Images

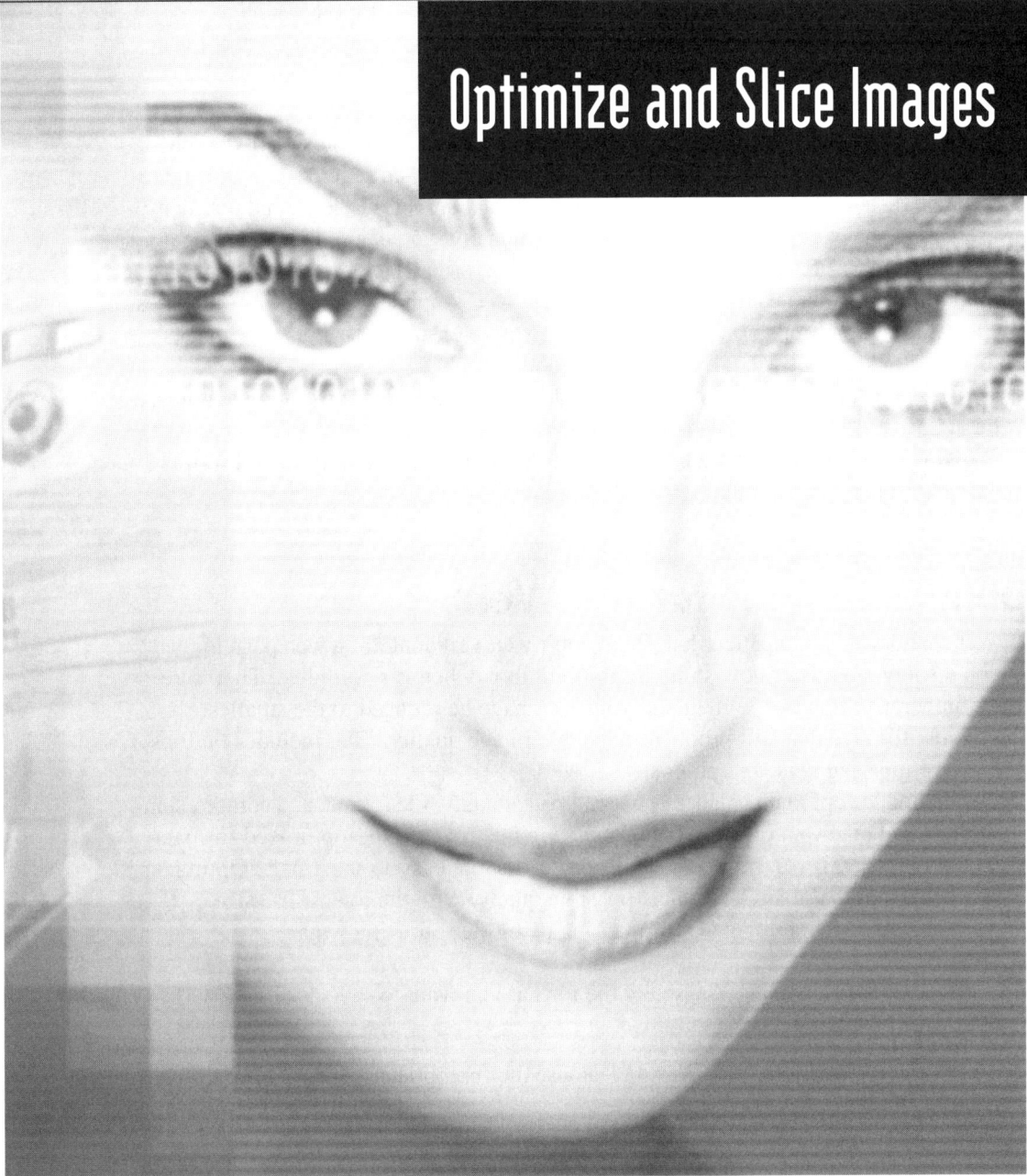

Nothing is less inviting than a web page full of plain text. Images intrigue your viewers and attract their attention. Charts and photographs can convey important information, as well as add visual interest. Web graphics, such as buttons, not only serve as design elements, but are also an important part of the user interface of your web site.

Unfortunately, there is a price to pay for using graphics and photos on a web page. Compared to simple text, image files can be quite large and require a lot of time to load and display. As a result, your web page can take minutes to load, and not many users have the patience to wait that long. Fortunately, you can reduce the impact of large graphic files by carefully selecting the file format and compression options to minimize file size when you create and edit web graphics. PhotoImpact includes special image-optimization tools that enable you to ensure that your web images load as quickly as possible and still look good.

This chapter shows you how to use PhotoImpact's image-optimization features, but it doesn't stop there. It also covers how to slice images and how to create image maps. The chapter also includes coverage of PhotoImpact's ability to add script effects, such as pop-up menus, to web graphics.

Optimize Images for the Web

Web visitors are an impatient lot. They won't wait very long for a web page to load and display, no matter how stunning it might look when it's complete. Therefore, it's imperative that every image on your web page be reduced to the smallest possible file size that still produces adequate image quality. That includes buttons, backgrounds, banners, and photos.

Finding the optimum balance between image quality, file format, and compression settings and other options is called *optimizing* the image. Web-optimized formats include JPEG, GIF, and PNG. PhotoImpact offers an easy-to-use Image Optimizer that helps you maintain the highest possible quality with the lowest file size.

You can open the Image Optimizer in one of the following ways:

■ Choose File | Save As, select the format you want to save as (JPEG, GIF, or PNG), and click Options.

■ Choose File | Save for Web and choose the appropriate submenu option.

■ Right-click a selected object and choose Image Optimizer.

■ Choose Web | Image Optimizer or press F4.

The options and available features can vary in the Image Optimizer, depending on how the dialog box is opened.

The Image Optimizer dialog box, shown in Figure 11-1, displays before and after preview images side by side in the upper half of the dialog box. By default, the original image is shown in the left preview pane, and the optimized image is shown in the right preview pane. This enables you to see how your settings affect the image quality and size. You want to achieve the highest quality with the lowest file size. You want your image to load quickly, but you do not want to compromise

11

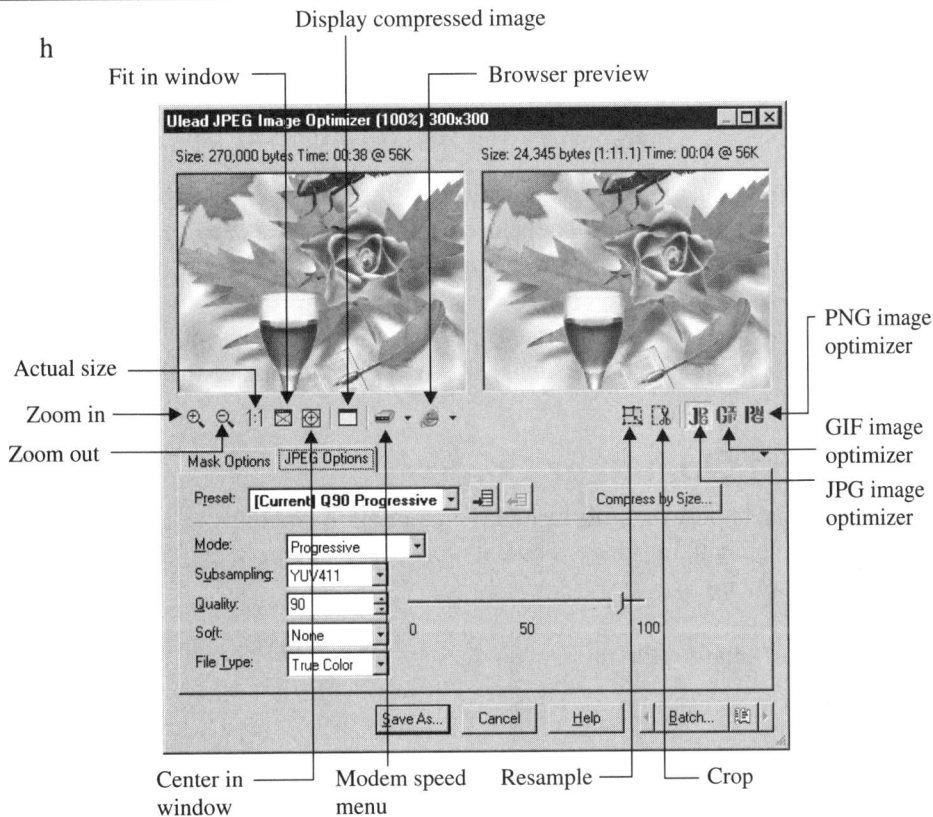

FIGURE 11-1   The Image Optimizer dialog box

the image quality too much. When you change the optimization settings in the lower half of the dialog box, the file size and download time are displayed above the preview panes.

To optimize an image, following these general steps:

1. Open the image you want to optimize.

2. Choose Web | Image Optimizer. If you have an object selected, you are prompted to make a choice between saving the entire image or saving selected objects.

3. Click the appropriate button beneath the right preview pane—JPEG, GIF, or PNG— if it isn't already selected.

4. Adjust the settings in the dialog box to achieve the best results for your application.

5. Click the Mask Options tab and adjust the mask settings as needed.

6. Click Save As. PhotoImpact opens the Save dialog box for the file format.

7. Select the folder where you want to save the image, enter a filename, and then click Save. PhotoImpact closes both dialog boxes and saves the image file according to your specifications.

The following sections describe the controls in the Image Optimizer dialog box, the masking options, and the options available for each of the image file formats.

Use Image Optimizer Controls

The controls that appear in the Image Optimizer dialog box depend on the type of image you are trying to optimize. The buttons beneath the preview images may include the following:

- Zoom In enlarges the preview images.
- Zoom Out reduces the preview images.

- Show Actual Size displays the images in the preview panes at their normal size.

- Fit in Window adjusts the images to fit in the preview panes.

- Center in Window centers the images in the preview panes.

- Display Original/Compressed Images toggles between displaying both the original and compressed images and only the compressed image.

- Modem Speed Menu enables you to select a speed for calculating Internet download times.

- Browser Preview displays the image in a browser window.

- Resample resamples the pixels to resize the image. Use caution when using this feature, since it could deteriorate the image quality.

- Crop removes unwanted portions of the image.

- JPEG optimizes the image in a JPEG format.

- GIF optimizes the image in a GIF format.

- PNG optimizes the image in a PNG format.

- Show/Hide Preview Panes displays or hides the preview panes.

11

Set Matte and Mask Options

The Mask Options tab of the Image Optimizer dialog box contains Matte and Mask options. A *matte* fills in transparent image or gaps in the image being optimized. A *mask* performs the inverse function of a matte: It creates transparent areas within the optimized image. When displayed in the web page, the background will show through transparent areas of a GIF or PNG images, if the Transparency checkbox is selected before saving the file.

The Matte setting is white by default. Click the color square to select another color or click the down arrow for other options. The Image File option fills transparent areas with an image of your choice. The selected color or image will fill transparent areas or gaps in the image being optimized. Enter the name of the file or click Browse to search for the file.

> **TIP** *In many cases, it may be beneficial to select None as Matte. Otherwise, it will be necessary create a new version of the semi-transparent image if it is used in a new environment. This is especially important if the transparent areas lie around the perimeter of the image—no matter where the image is positioned, it will not interfere with the background.*

The Mask setting enables you to select a mask option. Click the down arrow to select from a list of options. Select None if you do not want to apply a mask. If you choose the Pick Color option, you can use the tools below to select which colors you want to use as a mask. To specify an image to use as a mask, click Import. Enter the filename you want to use as your mask or click Browse to search for the file.

Optimizing in JPEG Format

The Joint Photographic Experts Group (JPEG) created a lossy compressed 24-bit format to store photorealistic color images. This process tends to produce smaller file sizes than GIF. The lossy format, however, means that the more the file is compressed, the more image data is lost. To get the desired results, you can control exactly how much compression is applied to the image.

> **NOTE** *The JPEG file format does not support transparent backgrounds.*

The following settings are available for optimizing an image as a JPEG:

- **Preset** Offers common settings for this format. Using the Add or Delete buttons to the right of this setting, you can add your own presets or delete ones that you do not use.

- **Mode** Enables you to select the mode in which the image loads in the browser. Progressive causes the image to fade in as it downloads and produces the smallest file size. The Progressive mode is more efficient than the Standard mode, but it is not compatible with all browsers. The Standard Optimized choice creates an image that is compatible with most browsers, producing the smallest file size using a nonprogressive compression technique.

- **Subsampling** Enables you to try other sampling techniques that may reduce the file size. The results vary, depending on the image you are optimizing.

■ **Quality**   Enables you to decrease the file quality to reduce the file size and load time. You can enter a value in the text box or use the slider to adjust this setting. If you have a particular file size you are trying to achieve, click the Compress By Size button.

■ **Soft**   Blurs the image to hide flaws. This can be useful when you have decreased the image quality and want to make the image appear smoother.

■ **File Type**   Saves the file as color or grayscale. Grayscale images are considerably smaller in size.

Optimizing in GIF Format

The Graphics Interchange Format (GIF) supports a maximum of 256 (8-bit) colors, making it perfect for line art or text. It features good compression for small file sizes, but unlike the JPEG format, the standard compression is not lossy and doesn't reduce image quality. (Lossy compression is available as an option for those times when you're willing to sacrifice some image quality for further reductions in file size.)

The main option you adjust when optimizing files in the GIF format is the color palette. Reducing the number of colors in the palette reduces file size. This format also supports the transparency option.

The following settings are available for optimizing an image as a GIF:

■ **Preset**   Offers common settings for this format. Using the Add or Delete buttons to the right of this setting, you can add your own presets or delete ones you do not use.

■ **Color**   Sets the maximum number of colors that your file contains.

■ **Weight**   Enables you to specify the color channel that you want to emphasize. This causes the program to emphasize certain color channels (Red, Green, or Blue) when building the color palette.

■ **Palette**   Specifies the default palette type you want to use. Select one of the standard palettes or choose User Defined to open the Load Color Table dialog box, where you can specify a palette file (*.PAL) to load.

11

- **Soft**   Determines the amount of blur to apply to the image. The higher the number, the smoother your image appears. This facilitates compression and compensates for any dithering you've previously applied to your image.

- **File Type**   Defines your file as indexed or grayscale.

- **Lossy**   Selects lossy compression mode, which removes pixels from the image, based on the specified value. The higher the value, the more pixels removed, and the smaller the resulting file size.

- **Dither**   Applies dithering to your image. This mixes existing colors from the palette in different patterns in order to mimic the missing color.

- **Interlaced**   Gradually loads the image into the web browser.

- **Transparency**   Makes the image background transparent.

Optimizing in PNG Format

The Portable Network Graphics (PNG) format offers 24-bit images and supports gamma information and transparency. The advantage of using this format over JPEG is that it uses a lossless compression method while supporting True-Color images. A disadvantage is that not all browsers support this format yet.

The settings available for optimizing an image as a PNG are the same as those for a GIF (described in the previous section), except that instead of a Lossy option, there is a Filter option. Filter applies a filter to your image to further reduce its size.

Testing Your Images with Batch

Trying different image optimization settings in order to find the best balance of file size and image quality is basically a trial-and-error process, which can be tedious. To help speed the process, the Image Optimizer dialog box offers a Batch utility that automates the process of experimenting with the file format variables that affect the image the most. The Batch command button at the bottom of the dialog box enables you to try out different compression settings on your file before actually saving it.

For GIF and PNG formats, the number of colors is tested. For JPEG formats, the extent of compression is tested. At the completion of the test, PhotoImpact displays the results in a dialog box so you can compare the results and select the best combination of settings.

To perform a batch test, do the following:

1. Open the image you want to optimize; choose Web | Image Optimizer to open the Image Optimizer dialog box; and then click the JPEG, GIF, or PNG button to select the file format.

2. Click the Batch button in the Image Optimizer dialog box. The Batch dialog box appears.

3. For JPEG formats, enter a percentage of compression for the lowest quality and the highest quality.

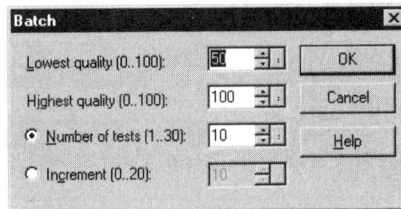

Batch	✕
Lowest quality (0..100): 80	OK
Highest quality (0..100): 100	Cancel
⦿ Number of tests (1..30): 10	Help
○ Increment (0..20): 10	

4. For the GIF format, enter the fewest and most colors to test.

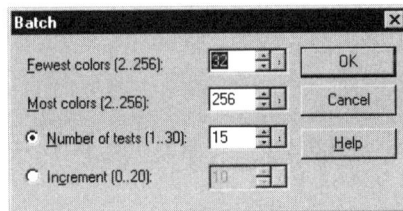

Batch	✕
Fewest colors (2..256): 32	OK
Most colors (2..256): 256	Cancel
⦿ Number of tests (1..30): 15	Help
○ Increment (0..20): 10	

5. Select either a number of tests to perform or increment. If you select increment, the lower the number will result in the most number of tests.

6. Click OK to close the Batch dialog box and begin the test. PhotoImpact displays a message box showing the progress of the test. When the tests complete, the Batch Results dialog appears, as shown in Figure 11-2.

7. Scroll through the test results to find the best combination of image quality and file size. Click a file size to view the corresponding image in the viewing area of the dialog box.

11

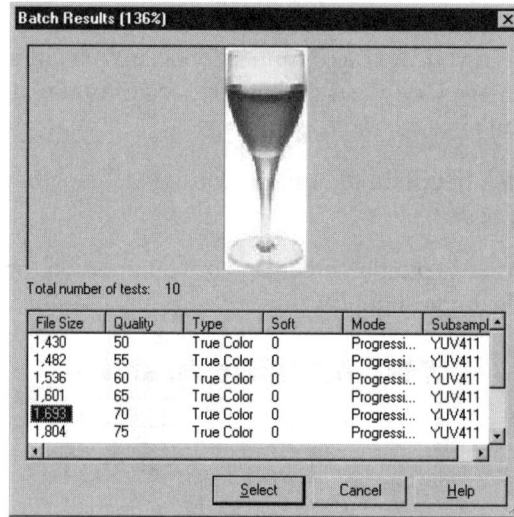

FIGURE 11-2   The Batch Results dialog box

8. Select the setting you want and click Select. PhotoImpact closes the Batch Results dialog box and transfers the selected settings to the Image Optimizer dialog box.

With the settings in the Image Optimizer dialog box, you can make further adjustments if desired, or just save the file.

Slice Images

One of the perpetual problems web designers face is how to handle large images that take significant time to load. Even when optimized, these images cause a noticeable delay as the web page loads. Since many viewers often won't wait for more than a few seconds without seeing visible progress, such delays can cause viewers to get frustrated and abandon the web page.

One solution is to break a large image into smaller chunks that each take a fraction of the time to load. The small component images are then reassembled on the web page like pieces of a jigsaw puzzle, so that the full image appears a piece at a time. By optimizing each small image individually, the total image size and load time is often reduced. Even if there is no net reduction in the time it takes for the whole image to appear, the viewers are able to see progress as each chunk is added to the image in the web browser, and so they are more likely to stick around long enough to see the whole page.

The process of cutting a large image into smaller pieces is called *slicing*. To reassemble the image, the slices (smaller images) are loaded into table cells. Each table cell can have a hyperlink, target frame, and script effects assigned to it. When you slice a large image, the end result is a series of smaller component images, each stored in a separate image file, and an HTML table to position all the slices on the web page.

New to PhotoImpact 7 PhotoImpact provides the Slice tool for creating slices and gives you the option of slicing the image automatically or manually. Objects that have slicing disabled are combined with the background. You may want to do this before using the automatic slicing tool. This basically tells the application that you do not want to create a separate slice for the disabled objects.

Slicing your image gives you the flexibility of optimizing each image appropriately. For example, if a slice contains one simple color or text, it is best optimized as a GIF. Cells that contain more complex objects can be saved in JPEG format.

Set Slice Tool Attributes

When you access the Slice tool in the Tool panel, a set of slice-related tools and options are displayed on the Attribute toolbar.

The Slice tool's Attribute toolbar offers the following options:

- **Auto Slice**   Automatically slices around objects in your document.

- **Pick**   Selects a cell. The cell must be selected to customize its properties. Using this tool also allows you to move and combine slice lines.

- **Method**   Enables you to add a horizontal or vertical slice line or resize a cell. It also enables you to define a new rectangular cell.

- **Erase**   Removes slice lines individually.

- **Protect Web Objects**   Prevents web objects from being sliced. This feature is overridden when Erase All or Slice Evenly is used.

- **Slice Evenly**   Creates cells of the same size.

- **Erase All**   Removes all slice lines.

- **Slice Data**   Applies a Ulead Slice Table file (.USS) to the current image. This is used to apply the same slicing method to several images.

- **Calculate Size**   Calculates the download speed based on a specified bandwidth.

- **Panel**   Shows or hides the Slice panel.

- **Add**   Adds slice settings to the EasyPalette.

Specify Slice Information

By default, the Slice panel, shown in Figure 11-3, is displayed when you you access the Slice tool. This panel has three tabs: Cell Properties, Optimizer, and Script Effects.

On the Cell Properties tab, you can specify the following information:

- **Cell Name**   Specifies a unique name for the slice.

- **URL**   Defines a link for the slice.

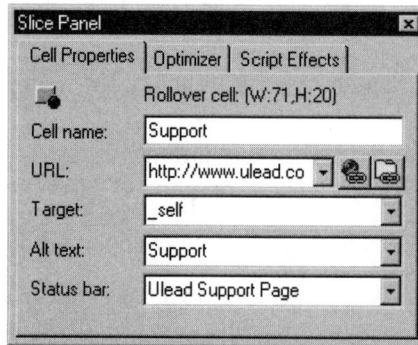

FIGURE 11-3   The Slice panel

- **Target**   Specifies a frame target for the above link.
- **Alt Text**   Defines the text that is displayed when if the image cannot load.
- **Status Bar**   Specifies what to display in the status bar when the mouse is placed over the slice.

On the Optimizer tab, you can specify which optimization method to use. On the Script Effect tab, you can add script effects that are triggered by either the page or slice cell. For more information about using script effects, see the "Add Script Effects" section later in this chapter.

Slice Images Automatically

When you slice images automatically, PhotoImpact assumes that you want to have each object in its own cell. When an object has slicing disabled, it is treated as part of the background. If you want the entire image to be sliced in even slices, you can enable the Slice Evenly option in the Slice tool's Attribute toolbar. This offers a quick way to slice your page. Then you can adjust each cell to fit your needs.

You can slice images automatically in two ways:

- To slice your entire page with the same size cell, select the Slice Evenly option in the Attribute toolbar. You can adjust these slice cells manually once the action completes.

- Select the Auto Slice option in the Attribute toolbar if you want PhotoImpact to slice the page as it sees fit. Separate objects will be contained in their own slice cell. This enables you to apply scripts to these objects without needing to manually specify the slice cell.

Slice Images Manually

If you have a complex layout or simply want the images to load in a specific way, you can choose to slice your image manually. You can also use the manual slice options to edit and refine slices that were originally created with the Auto Slice or Slice Evenly options.

To slice your image manually, follow these steps:

1. Open the image you want to slice.

11

2. Click the Slice tool in the Tool panel.

3. Select the type of cell or slice line you want to create by clicking the down arrow next to the Method tool and selecting Rectangle, Horizontal Line, or Vertical Line.

4. Click and drag to position a slice line or rectangular cell on the image to define a slice. Drag the tool to create a slice using the method you've chosen. To create a rectangle, you can drag diagonally or right-click an object and choose Slice Around Object from the pop-up menu to automatically create a rectangular slice around the object.

> **TIP** *When creating horizontal or vertical lines, you can toggle between the two methods by pressing and holding the* CTRL *key as you drag the Slice tool.*

5. Repeat as needed to define additional slices. If an object in the image is sliced inappropriately, you can protect that object by drawing a new slice around it.

6. Reposition slice lines with the Pick Slice tool. Click the Pick Slice option in the Attribute toolbar and then position your cursor over the line you want to adjust. The cursor changes to a double-arrow. Click and drag the line to where you want it. To release the line, release your mouse button.

7. Define properties for each slice. Click a slice with the Pick Slice tool to select it and then define its properties in the Slice panel. Repeat for each slice in the image.

Save the Sliced Images

When you are finished creating your slices and defining their properties, you are ready to save your work. Choose File | Save for Web | As HTML. The file that is created is an HTML file with several table cells. The slice cells that you have applied scripts to will be linked to the JavaScript embedded in the HTML file.

Each slice cell is saved as a separate image file in the Image directory. This directory is automatically created in the same location as the saved HTML file. These image files are saved with the name you specified when creating the slice.

Create Image Maps

It's common for an image on a web page to have a hyperlink associated with it, so when the viewer clicks the image, the web browser opens the linked web page. After all, that's what makes buttons work.

An image map takes the idea of hyperlinked images a step further by allowing multiple hyperlinks from one image. An image map contains one or more *hotspots*. Each hotspot is a defined area of the image that is associated with a hyperlink or script effect. The hotspot is invisible to the viewer, but it usually corresponds to an identifiable area of the underlying image, such as a logo or other symbol. When viewers click a hotspot, their web browser loads the page linked to that hotspot. Clicking a different hotspot loads a different page.

For example, you could have an image map that is a map of the United States, with each state defined as a separate hotspot. When users click a state, they are taken to the appropriate page for that state.

PhotoImpact includes tools that enable you to create image map hotspots. In fact, there are two different ways to produce image map hotspots with PhotoImpact: You can create object-based hotspots or manually created hotspots. You can mix and match the two techniques to define the hotspots for an image map.

Save Your Image Map

11

In order to use an image map on your web page, you need a web-optimized copy of the base image and the HTML code that defines the hotspot areas and their hyperlinks. PhotoImpact can create both image map components for you. Simply choose File | Save for Web | As HTML. The file that is created is an HTML file with several table cells. The slice cells that you have applied scripts to will be linked to the JavaScript embedded into the HTML file.

Each slice cell is saved as a separate image file in the Image directory. This directory is automatically created in the same location as the saved HTML file. These image files are saved with the name you specified when creating the slice.

Create Manual Image Maps

New to
PhotoImpact 7

What makes an image map work is the hotspots—the clickable areas of the image that are linked to hyperlinks. To transform a regular image into an image map, you must define those hotspots and their associated hyperlinks. The Image

Map tool enables you to define areas of your image as hotspots and then assign hyperlinks to those areas.

Set Image Map Tool Attributes

When you access the Image Map tool in the Tool panel, a set of hotspot-related tools and options are displayed on the Attribute toolbar.

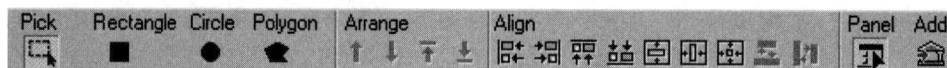

The Image Map tool's Attribute toolbar offers the following options:

- **Pick**   Selects a hotspot. Once you've selected a hotspot, you can assign or edit its properties in the Image Map panel.

- **Rectangle**   Creates a rectangular hotspot.

- **Circle**   Creates a circular hotspot.

- **Polygon**   Enables you to create multisided hotspot shapes. To complete the shape, double-click your mouse button.

- **Arrange**   Changes the stack location (overlap order) of the selected hotspot. Click the up arrow to move the hotspot up one position. Click the up arrow with the bar above it to move the hotspot to the top of the stack. By default, newer hotspots are placed on top of the stack.

> **NOTE**   *If two hotspots overlap each other, the web browser uses the hyperlink from the hotspot that is on top when a viewer clicks in the overlapping area. Normally, the hotspot that was created last is on top and will take precedence over the older hotspot unless you rearrange their order.*

- **Align**   Aligns the selected hotspots. To select more than one hotspot, hold down the CTRL key while making your selections

- **Panel**   Shows or hides the Image Map panel.

- **Add**   Adds your configuration to the EasyPalette.

Specify Image Map Information

By default, the Image Map panel is displayed when the Image Map tool is accessed, as shown in Figure 11-4. On the Properties tab, you can define a URL line for the hotspot, a frame target for the link, alt text to display if the image cannot load, and the text that appears in the status bar when the mouse is over the hotspot.

On the Script Effects tab, you can add script effects that are triggered by either the page or image map. For example, you can add a script that causes an image to change when the user moves their cursor over it. Script effects are discussed in detail in the "Add Script Effects" section later in this chapter.

Using the HTML tab options, you can modify the area defining the map or copy the parameters to the clipboard to be used in your HTML page.

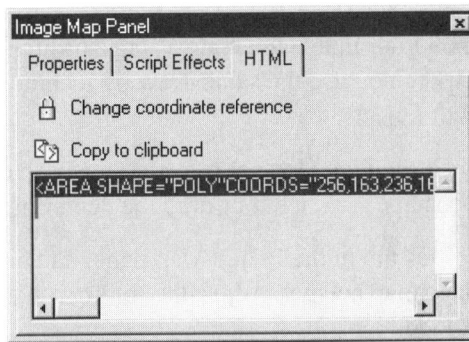

For example, you may have an HTML file with an image. Now you want to create an image map of this image so that the user can view various pages,

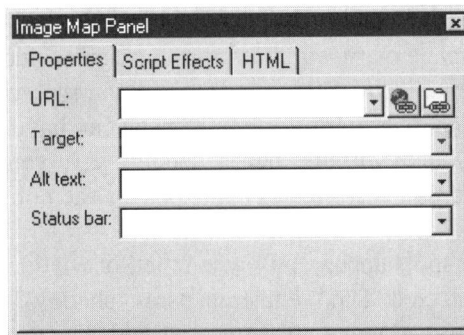

FIGURE 11-4   The Image Map Panel

depending on which area is clicked within that image. You can adjust the coordinates if necessary and copy the resulting text to the clipboard. Now, you can open your HTML file for editing and add the copied text to your file. This text will replace the old <IMG> tag text.

Create an Image Map Manually

To create a manual image map, follow these steps:

1. Open the image file.

2. Click one of the shape options in the Attribute toolbar (Rectangle, Circle, or Polygon).

3. Click and drag on your image to create a shape around the area you want to define as a hotspot. You use the same drawing techniques you use to define selections or path objects.

4. If necessary, click the Pick Hotspot tool and drag one of the handles on the perimeter of the shape to resize it or drag the center of the shape to move it.

5. Click the Properties tab in the Image Map panel and enter the properties for the selected image map hotspot. Adjust the settings on the other Image Map panel tabs if needed.

6. Repeat steps 2 through 5 to create other hotspots as needed.

7. Choose File | Save for Web | As HTML to save your image map.

Create Object-Based Image Maps

To facilitate creating image maps, all PhotoImpact objects—including path objects, text objects, and image objects—can have image map properties assigned to them. In other words, each and every object in your image can have a hyperlink, target, and alternate text associated with it. Then, when you save your image as an image map, PhotoImpact automatically creates a hotspot for each object that includes image map properties.

The image map hotspots appear only when the Show/Hide Image Map button on the Tool panel is selected. The "semi-transparent shadow" appears around only those objects that have image map properties defined. The shadow is dark red, and it's hard to see. The dark-red rectangle around the object is more obvious. The manually created hotspots show up as transparent shapes of an ugly, dirty yellowish color.

To create an object-based image map, follow these steps:

1. Open or create the image file from which you want to create the image map. The image should contain objects that you want to use as hotspots in your image map. Make sure the objects have not been merged into the base image.

2. Right-click an object with the Pick tool and choose Properties from the pop-up menu. PhotoImpact opens the Object Properties dialog box.

3. Click the Image Map tab to display the options shown in Figure 11-5.

4. Enter the image map properties for the selected object. The Shape setting defines the shape that best fits the shape of the object you are mapping. If the object is an unusual size that does not fit into the round or rectangle category, click the odd-shaped button on the right. The other settings are the same as those on the Image Map panel's Properties tab.

5. Click OK. PhotoImpact assigns the image map properties to the selected object.

11

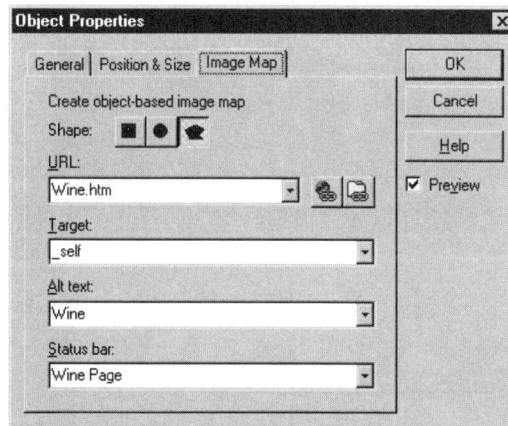

FIGURE 11-5   The Image Map tab of the Object Properties dialog box

6. Repeat steps 2 through 5 for each object that you want to define as an image map hotspot.

7. Choose File | Save for Web | As HTML to save the PhotoImpact image as an image map.

Add Script Effects

New to
PhotoImpact 7

When you slice images and create image maps, you can define a hyperlink for each slice and hotspot. However, you're not restricted to simple links to web pages and other URLs; you can also define script effects for most slices and hotspots. Script effects link JavaScript code to your slices and hotspots to make then more dynamic and eye-catching. With script effects, you can create pop-up menus, status bar messages, and image swaps. In addition, you can use script effects to add a variety of text effects to slices.

CAUTION

Not all browsers support JavaScript. Therefore, your script effects may not appear as intended.

You add script effects through the Script Effects tab of the Image Map panel or Slice panel. The tab contains three control buttons for adding, deleting, and modifying script effects.

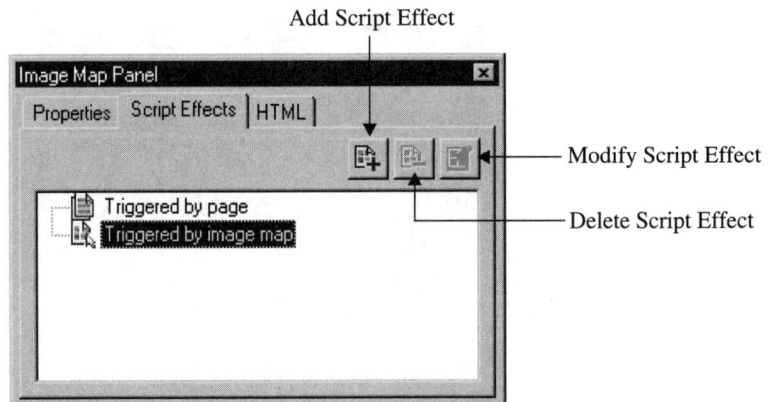

Add Script Effect

Image Map Panel

Properties   Script Effects | HTML |

Triggered by page
Triggered by image map

Modify Script Effect

Delete Script Effect

The Script Effects tab offers two options for how your script effect will be executed:

- **Triggered by Page**   Executes the script when the page is loaded in the browser window.

- **Triggered by Image Map/Cell**   Executes the script when specific events take place, such as mouseover and mousedown.

To add a script effect to a slice or an image map hotspot, follow these steps:

1. Open the image that has been sliced or contains one or more image map hotspots.

2. If you're working with a sliced image, click the Slice tool in the Tool panel. If you want to add a script effect to an image map hotspot, click the Image Map tool.

3. Click the Pick Slice or Pick Hotspot tool in the Attribute toolbar and select the slice cell or image map hotspot to which you want to add a script effect.

4. Click the Script Effects tab in either the Slice or Image Map panel.

5. Select either the Triggered by Page or Triggered by Image Map (or Cell) option.

6. Click the Add Script Effect button and choose the effect from the pop-up menu that appears. PhotoImpact opens a dialog box where you can specify the settings and options for the effect you want to add. The following sections describe some of the specific effects.

11

| NOTE | *Only available script effects for the selected object will be active. For example, if the slice cell does not contain HTML text, none of the text options will be available.* |

7. Adjust the settings in the dialog box and click OK. PhotoImpact adds the code required to execute the effect to the selected object.

When you save the sliced image or image map, PhotoImpact adds the JavaScript code necessary to produce the script effect to the HTML file it creates. You can then copy and paste the code from the HTML file into your own web page.

After you add a script effect to a slice or an image map hotspot, PhotoImpact lists it on the Script Effects tab. To update an existing script attached to a slice or hotspot, select that script on the Script Effects tab of the Slice panel or Image Map panel and click the Modify Script Effect button. PhotoImpact opens the dialog box containing the settings for that effect. To delete an effect, select that effect and click the Delete Script Effect button.

Create a Pop-up Menu

A pop-up menu lets you associate more than one hyperlink with a single slice cell or image map hotspot. When a viewer points to a slice or hotspot with a pop-up menu script effect attached, the web browser displays the pop-up menu, and the viewer can choose from the options that appear on that menu. PhotoImpact's pop-up menu script effect lets you define your own custom pop-up menu for any slice cell or image map hotspot.

To add a pop-up menu, perform steps 1 through 6 of the procedure for adding a script effect, choosing the Pop-up Menu option from the menu that appears when you click the Add Script Effect button. PhotoImpact opens the Pop-up Menu dialog box, shown in Figure 11-6.

Add Menu Items

Enter the information for the first menu item in the pop-up menu you want to create:

- In the Text box, enter the text that you want to appear in the pop-up menu.

- In the URL box, specify the hyperlink that you want to activate when users click their mouse button on this menu item.

- In the Alt Text box, enter the alternate text that you want to appear when users point to the menu item.

- In the Status Bar box, enter the text that you want users to see in the status bar when they place their cursor over this menu item.

Click the Add button to add the menu item you have just defined to the box in the middle of the dialog box. Then repeat this procedure as needed to define other menu items.

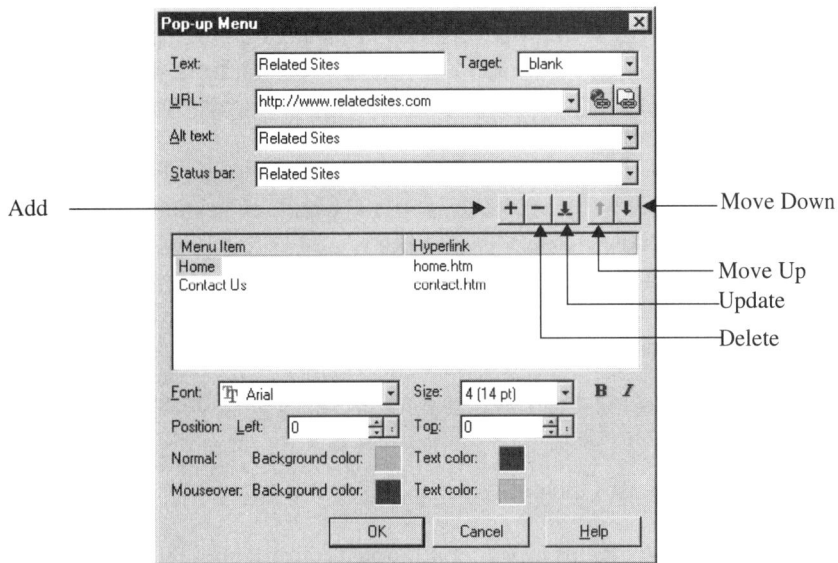

FIGURE 11-6 The Pop-up Menu dialog box

Fine-Tune Your Menu

You can adjust the settings in the lower portion of the Pop-up Menu dialog box to control the font, color, and position of the pop-up menu. The font, size, and color settings are common text controls.

To modify the properties of a specific menu item, click that item, change the required information, and click the Update button. The positioning coordinates apply to the whole menu and start at the upper-left corner of the image map hotspot or slice cell.

When you're finished, click OK. PhotoImpact closes the Pop-up Menu dialog box and adds the script effect to the selected slice cell or image map hotspot.

Create a Status Bar Script

Normally, when a viewer points to a hyperlinked item on a web page, the linked URL appears in the web browser's status bar, but it doesn't have to be that way. You can create a script effect that displays the text of your choice in the status bar when the viewer points to the selected slice cell or image map hotspot. To catch the attention of your viewers, you can even make the status bar text scroll and repeat or use some other effect.

To add a status bar script, perform steps 1 through 6 of the procedure for adding a script effect, choosing the Status Bar Message option from the menu that appears when you click the Add Script Effect button. PhotoImpact opens the Status Bar dialog box, shown in Figure 11-7.

Select a mouse event from the Event list box, click the Display Effect on Event checkbox to activate the effect for the selected event, and enter the text you want to appear in the status bar in the Message box.

The Type options specify how the message will be displayed:

■ Normal causes the string to appear character-by-character from left to right.

■ Shrink scrolling causes the text string to slide from right to left, exposing one character at a time.

■ Marquee causes the entire string to scroll from right to left.

If you want the message to repeat continuously throughout the duration of the event, check the Repeat checkbox.

You can repeat this procedure as needed to define actions for other events. Typically, you define only the onMouseOver event for when the viewer points the mouse to the slice or hotspot. However, you can also define separate actions for onMouseOut, onMouseMove, onMouseUp, and onMouseDown.

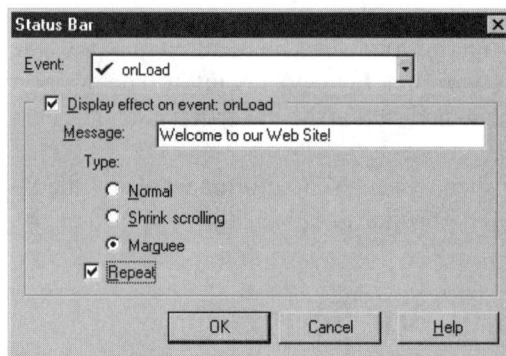

FIGURE 11-7   The Status Bar dialog box

When you're finished, click OK. PhotoImpact closes the Status Bar dialog box and adds the script effect to the selected slice cell or image map hotspot.

Create a Swap Image Script

The swap image effect causes the viewer's web browser to replace one image with another. For example, if the user moves the mouse over an image map or slice cell, this script effect will cause another image to appear in place of the original image. It's the same basic technique that creates a rollover effect by replacing one button image with a variation of that button image. You can use a swap image script to make the item under the viewer's mouse pointer glow or change color. Of course, for this technique to work, you'll also need to create another image to swap in to replace the original image, but that's easy to do with PhotoImpact.

NOTE	*If you are using an image map for this effect, make certain you have it sliced so you have a destination cell for the swapped image.*

To add a swap image script, perform steps 1 through 6 of the procedure for adding a script effect, choosing the Swap Image option from the menu that appears when you click the Add Script Effect button. PhotoImpact opens the Swap Image dialog box, shown in Figure 11-8.

Select a mouse event from the Event list box, click the Display Effect on Event checkbox to activate the effect for the selected event, and then adjust the settings to define the action:

- In the Cell to Display Swap Effect preview, choose the cell in which the swap image will be displayed.

- In the Swap Image field, enter the name of the image to swap into the selected cell name (type the full name or browse to locate it).

- If you want the swapped image to fit in the selected cell, check the Resize Image to Fit in Cell checkbox. If you do not check this option, the image may be cut off if it is too large for the cell.

- If you want the original image to return to the cell when the mouse event is not active, check the Restore After Rollover checkbox.

11

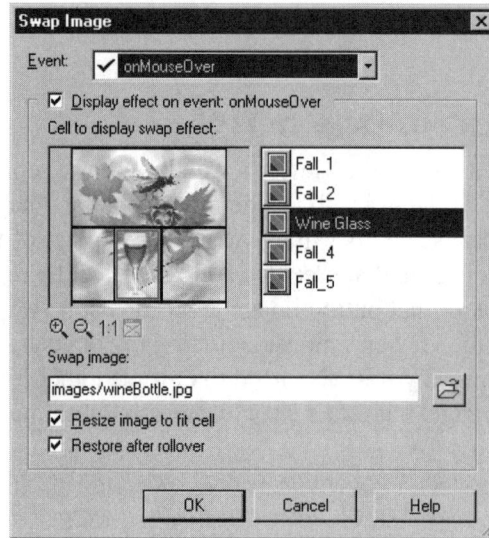

FIGURE 11-8   The Swap Image dialog box

If you want to, you can repeat this procedure to define actions for other events. Typically, you define only the onMouseOver event for when the viewer points the mouse to the slice or hotspot. However, you can also define separate actions for onMouseOut, onMouseMove, onMouseUp, and onMouseDown.

Click OK when you're finished. PhotoImpact closes the Swap Image dialog box and adds the script effect to the selected slice cell or image map hotspot.

Create a Vertical Scroll Script

A vertical scroll script is used to roll text or images up in a designated cell. This effect works only with slice cells; it does not apply to image map hotspots.

A vertical scroll script is a variation on the pop-up menu effect. Instead of a list of menu items appearing when you point to a slice cell, the scroll items are superimposed on the slice and appear immediately after the page loads. Scroll items scroll into view one at a time. Viewers can click a scroll item to go to the associated link, just as they can click menu items in a pop-up menu. Since the vertical scroll script effect supports images as well as text, you can set it up to show button graphics or icons instead of plain text as the scroll items.

To add a vertical text script, perform steps 1 through 6 of the procedure for adding a script effect (with the Slice tool activated, not the Image Map tool), choosing the Vertical Scroll option from the menu that appears when you click the Add Script Effect button. PhotoImpact opens the Vertical Scroll dialog box, shown in Figure 11-9.

Add Scroll Items

Enter the information for the first scroll item you want to create:

- For the Type option, check either Text or Image.

- If you selected Text, enter the text for the scroll item in the Text box. If you choose Image, specify the image file to scroll in the Image box.

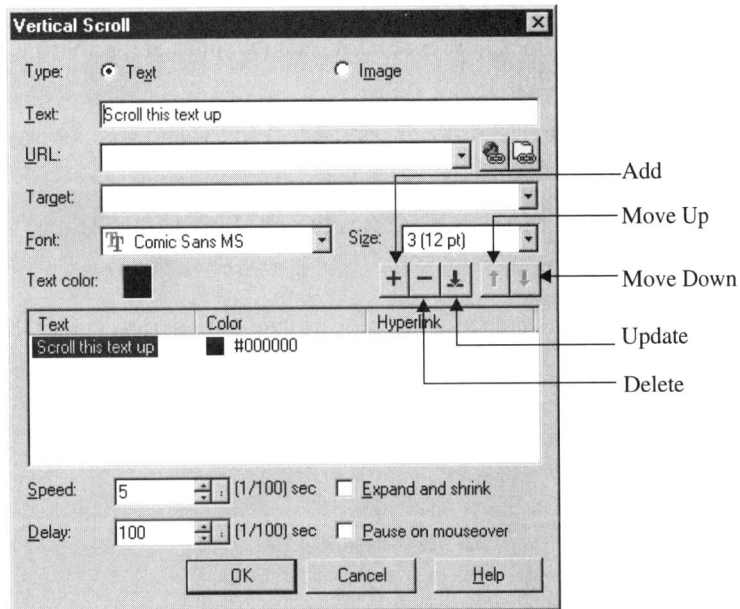

11

FIGURE 11-9   The Vertical Scroll dialog box

- In the URL box, specify a hyperlink. This link occurs when users click their mouse button on this cell.

- In the Target box, specify where to load the text or image.

- For the Font, Size, and Font Color options, choose these characteristics for the menu item's text.

Click the Add button to add the menu item you have just defined to the box in the middle of the dialog box. Then repeat this procedure to define your other scroll items.

Fine-Tune the Vertical Scroll

You can adjust the settings in the lower portion of the Vertical Scroll dialog box to control the way the items scroll up over the slice cell:

- Speed defines how fast you want the image or text to move up in the cell.

- Delay defines how much time you want to elapse before beginning the scroll again.

- Expand and Shrink causes the text to expand and contract as it scrolls upward.

- Pause on Mouseover causes the scrolling to stop when the user moves the mouse over the cell.

When you're finished creating the vertical scroll script, click OK. PhotoImpact closes the Vertical Scroll dialog box and adds the script effect to the selected slice cell.

CHAPTER 12

Create Web Pages

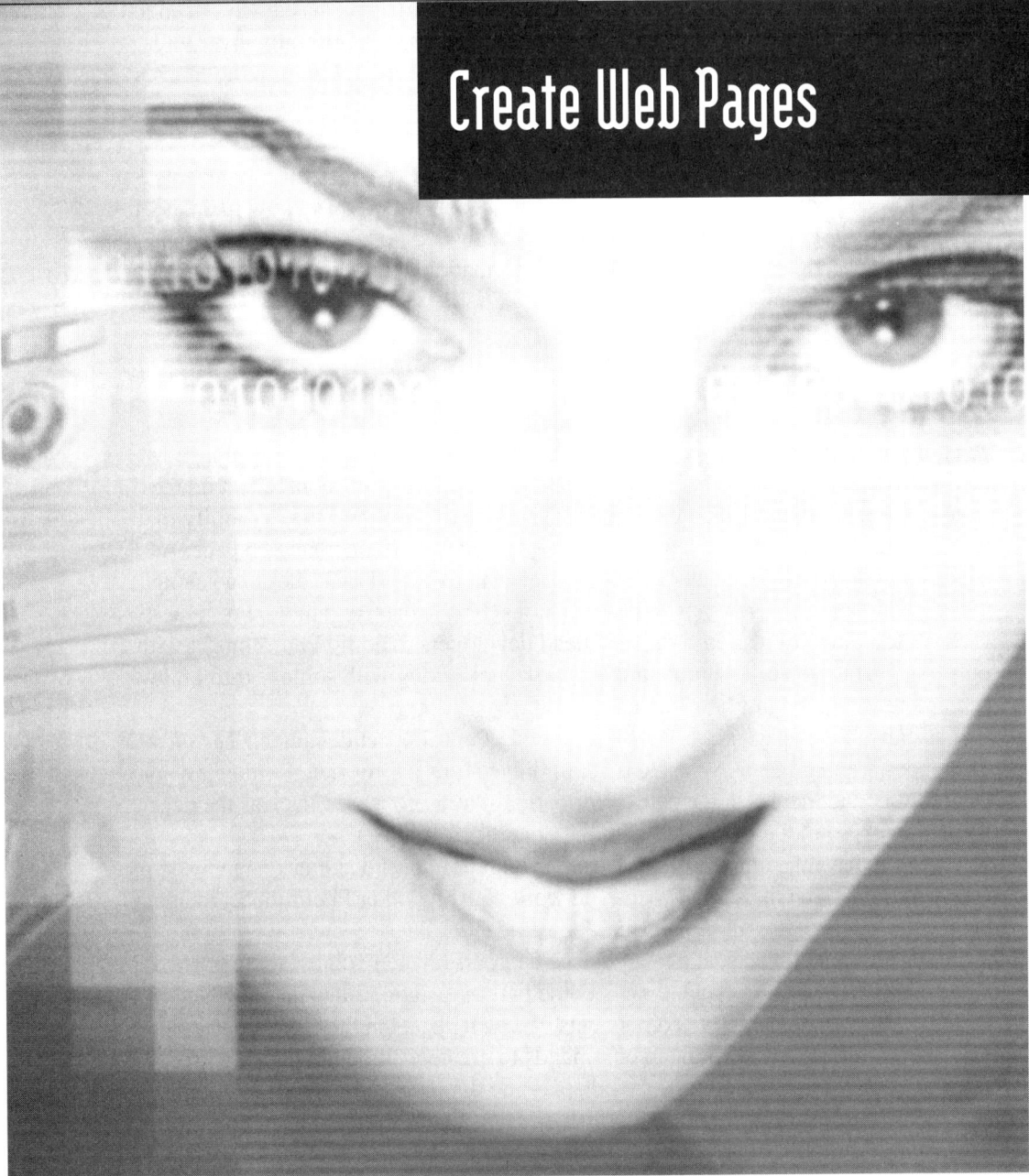

Photolmpact is, first and foremost, an image-editing program, and you don't normally use an image-editing program to create web pages. On the other hand, modern web pages do include a lot of images, and PhotoImpact has always been a good tool for preparing those images. In fact, PhotoImpact is brimming over with features designed specifically for creating web components and optimizing images for use on the Web.

The previous chapters in this part discuss, in detail, how to create web components. This chapter explains how to put it all together. The chapter covers how to create web pages from scratch, including how to work with web text and how to assemble web components on a page. You'll also find information about how to preview web pages in a browser and save web pages.

PhotoImpact Tools for Creating Web Pages

When it comes to creating web components, PhotoImpact is no ordinary image-editing program. PhotoImpact not only creates and optimizes the component images for use on the Web, the Ulead developers also gave the program the capability to generate the HTML code needed to make those images work on your web page. As explained in the previous chapters, PhotoImpact can produce HTML files to go along with sliced images, image maps, rollover buttons, button bars, and more. From there, it wasn't too much of a stretch for the Ulead developers to equip PhotoImpact with tools that enable you to assemble those components along with some text to build a complete web page in PhotoImpact.

Basically, a web page starts out like any other PhotoImpact document. The only differences are that the canvas size is set to dimensions appropriate for display in a web browser and there is some extra information—web properties, such as the page title and background—associated with the document.

Once you have the future web page open in a PhotoImpact document window, you work with it in much the same way as you work with any other PhotoImpact image document. You can use all the normal PhotoImpact tools to create and manipulate image objects, path objects, and text objects. Of course, when you use these normal image elements on a web page, they become part of a static image that appears on the page rather than interactive components of a web page. On the other hand, when you use PhotoImpact's Web menu commands to create web components (buttons, banners, HTML text, and so on), they display the distinctive characteristics of web page elements, such as hyperlinks, scripts, and text that reflows to fit within the web browser window.

Finally, when your document is complete, you can export that document for use as a web page. PhotoImpact automatically generates the HTML code and the component images needed to display the web page.

Web Page Components

Web pages are nothing more than a composition of plain text and images placed within a framework of Hypertext Markup Language (HTML) codes. HTML contains tag elements that are easily understood by browsers such as Microsoft Internet Explorer and Netscape Navigator. This markup language tells the browsers how to display the information on the screen.

Common web pages contain the following elements:

- Images are used to make the page look interesting and fun.

- Hyperlinked text enables the user to jump to another page.

- Buttons provide a graphical link to another page.

- HTML text offers the user something to read.

- Banners are used for titles, advertisements, and special announcements.

Figure 12-1 illustrates these elements on a web page.

12

Create a Web Page Document

The characteristic of a web page document that distinguishes it from a normal PhotoImpact image document is the web properties information associated with the document. Web properties include information such as the page title and background.

In order to work with a web page in PhotoImpact, you *must* start with a PhotoImpact document. You can't open an existing HTML file for a web page and edit it in PhotoImpact.

Create a New Web Page Document

You can add web properties to any PhotoImpact image document. However, since you'll usually want to create a new document specifically for your web page, PhotoImpact includes a separate New Web Page command for this purpose. As

Image   Banner

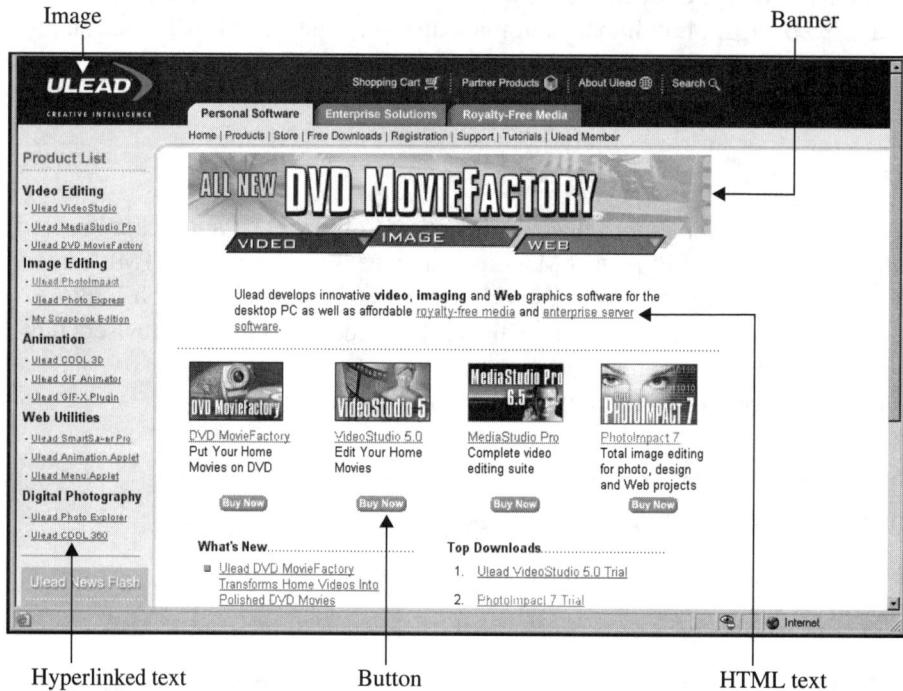

Hyperlinked text   Button   HTML text

FIGURE 12-1   Common web page elements

shown in Figure 12-2, the New Web Page dialog box enables you to choose an appropriate canvas size and set the essential web properties for the new document.

To create a web page document from scratch, follow these steps:

1. Choose File | New | New Web Page, click the New Web Page button on the toolbar, or press SHIFT-A. PhotoImpact displays the New Web Page dialog box (see Figure 12-2).

2. Enter a title for your web page. This is the title text that appears in the browser's title bar when the page is viewed. You can also set the encoding if you need your page to have support for foreign-language characters.

3. Check the Generate Background option. Then check the Color option and select a background color by clicking the color box. It's a good idea to define a background color, even if you intend to add a background image that will

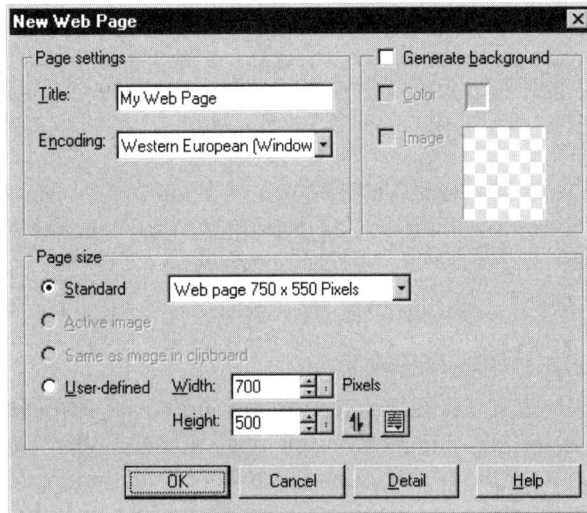

FIGURE 12-2   The New Web Page dialog box

cover it up. You can also specify a background image by checking the Image option and then clicking the image sample box to select background options. However, it's usually easier to set the background options in the Web Properties dialog box (described in the next section).

4. Select the page size. The standard web page is 750×550 pixels, which is designed for 800×600 screen resolution. You can select from several other common sizes or specify a user-defined size.

5. Click OK. PhotoImpact closes the New Web Page dialog box and opens a new document window to display your web page. The document window is untitled; it doesn't pick up the page title from the web properties.

NOTE   *If you defined a background for your web page, that background appears in the document window. Otherwise, the document window background displays the gray-and-white checkerboard pattern that normally indicates transparency in PhotoImpact. However, on a web page background, the checkerboard indicates that the browser's default background color (usually light gray or white) will be used.*

12

The New Web Page dialog box allows you to set the bare minimum web properties —just the page title and background. There are several other web property settings available, which are covered in the next section. If you want to set those options while creating the new document, you can open the Web Properties dialog box by clicking the Detail button in the New Web Page dialog box.

> **CAUTION**   *Although you can create a web page with PhotoImpact, you can't open and edit an existing HTML file. This means that you can't use PhotoImpact to edit web pages created with other programs.*

Set the Web Properties

There are more web properties for a web page than just the page title and background. The web properties information includes the page title and other data that goes into the <HEAD> section of the HTML file for the web page, options for specifying a web page background, and a number of default settings that PhotoImpact uses when it generates the HTML and image files for your web page.

You can easily set the web properties for any PhotoImpact document, whether it was originally created as a web page document or not. Simply choose Web | Web Properties to open the Web Properties dialog box, shown in Figure 12-3. Adjust the dialog box settings as needed and click OK to close the dialog box. PhotoImpact applies the web properties to the document.

> **TIP**   *You can also open the Web Properties dialog box by pressing SHIFT-ENTER or by right-clicking a document and choosing Web Properties from the pop-up menu that appears.*

PhotoImpact organizes the many settings and options in the Web Properties dialog box by distributing them onto five tabs: General, Background, Image File, Slice, and HTML. The properties on each of these pages are described in the following sections.

General Web Properties

The General tab includes an assortment of settings that record information about your web page. This information is stored in the <HEAD> section of the HTML file and does not appear on the web page itself. You can set the following properties on the General tab:

■ **Title** Specifies a title that describes the page content. This title will be displayed in the title bar of the browser window.

■ **Author** Identifies the person who is creating the page. This content is embedded into a meta tag in the HTML code and is not displayed in the browser window.

■ **Keywords** Describes the content on the page. Keywords are used by Internet search engines to help find your web page. All words must be separated by a comma. For example, if your page describes construction in the Renton, Washington area, your keywords may look like this: *construction, Renton, Washington, WA, cabinets, remodeling.*

■ **Description** Specifies the information that displays when a search engine is used to find your site. When the user moves the cursor over the link to your web site, this is the information that appears.

12

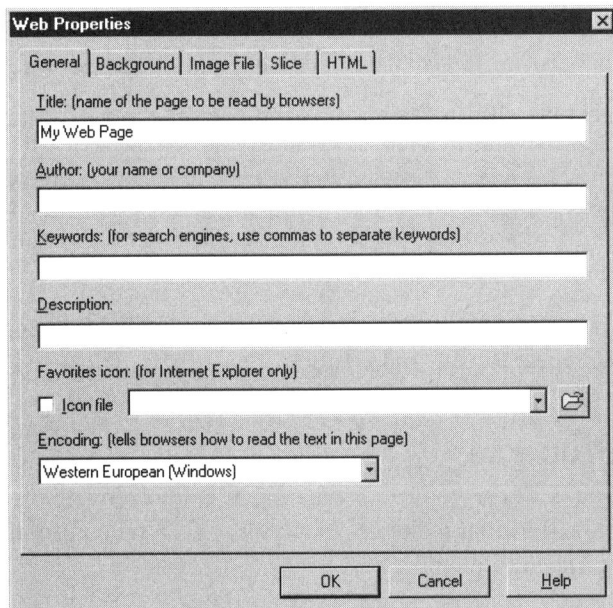

FIGURE 12-3 The Web Properties dialog box

- **Favorites Icon**   Enables you to select an icon file for your web site. This icon is stored in the Favorites menu when your page is added as a favorite in Internet Explorer.

- **Encoding**   Specifies the character set you want to use in the browser window.

Background Properties

The Background tab enables you to define the background color and/or a background image for your web page. You can set the following properties on the Background tab:

- **Color**   Sets the background color of the HTML document.

- **Image**   Uses an image in the background of the HTML document.

- **Preset Texture**   Enables you to select from a predefined texture image to use as the background.

- **Background Designer Texture**   Opens the Background Designer dialog box to help you create your own background.

- **File**   Enables you to specify a file to use as the background.

- **Transparency**   Shifts the background from the image to the specified color.

- **Shift Image Offset**   Repositions the background image so the tiling starts from a specified position. This is enabled only when an image is used as the background.

New to
PhotoImpact 7

- **Using CSS**   Enables you to specify three types of Cascading Style Sheet attributes: repeat, scroll, and position.

Image File Properties

The Image File tab is where you can set the defaults PhotoImpact uses when it generates the image files that make up your web page. You can set the following properties on the Image File tab:

- **Optimizer Setting**   Enables you to select the file format and quality of the saved background or cell image.

- **File Naming Pattern**   Specifies the naming pattern and compatibility with Macintosh and Unix platforms.

- **Put Images In Subfolder**   Copies all images to a predefined image subfolder.

- **Copy Background Image to Subfolder**   Copies all images used as backgrounds to a predefined image subfolder.

- **Copy Linked Files to Subfolder**   Copies all images that are referenced link objects to a predefined image subfolder.

Slice Properties

The settings on the Slice tab enable you to tell PhotoImpact how to slice the image document into smaller pieces. You can set the following properties on the Slice tab:

- **Enable Slicing**   Activates the slice features.

- **Generate by Table**   Places each slice cell into its own table cell.

- **Empty Cell**   Determines how empty cells are treated. They can appear in the browser as spacer images or blank cells.

- **Generate by CSS**   Places each slice cell between <DIV> tags with the specified attributes.

- **Bind With**   Specifies the output format of the generated CSS.

- **Slice Naming Pattern**   Sets the naming pattern for slices.

HTML Properties

The settings on the HTML tab let you exercise some control over the formatting of the HTML code that PhotoImpact generates when you save your web page as an HTML file. You can set the following properties on the HTML tab:

- **Case for Tags**   Sets the case you want to use for HTML tags.

- **Case for Attributes**   Sets the case you want to use for attribute tags.

- **Line Break**   Places a line break at the insertion point.

- **Indent Type**   Sets the type of indentation you want to use for the HTML code. If you select space, define the character width of the space you want to use.

- **Quote Attributes**   Encloses your attribute values within quotation marks.

- **Generate Relative URL for Reference**   Points all references to the directory where the HTML code is stored unless specified otherwise. For example, if the directory where your code is stored has an Image folder, you would need to include that path (Images/) in your statement.

New to
PhotoImpact 7

- **Conform to XHTML Specification**   Outputs the file as an XHTML document.

TIP   *We strongly recommend that you check the Conform to XHTML Specification option. Doing so ensures that PhotoImpact generates HTML code that is standard-compliant, which means that it should work in any current or future web browser.*

Add Text to Your Web Page

Text may not be the most glamorous part of a web page, but it's an essential element. Text is the primary medium you use to communicate with visitors to your web site. Pictures may speak a thousand words, but it's difficult to predict how your users perceive those words. Text, on the other hand, is much more reliable. As a result, the bulk of the content on most web pages is presented as text.

Since the Web was originally conceived as a way to share text-based documents, web browsers include built-in text handling capabilities:

- The browser can display text in different fonts and sizes and with attributes such as bold and italic.

- The browser automatically wraps text as needed to fit within the browser window, so the web text displays properly, regardless of the user's screen resolution and web browser window size.

- Web text is stored in the web page's HTML file, along with the HTML codes that describe the page.

Unlike images, plain text takes up very little space in a file, so HTML text doesn't add the kind of overhead to your web page that makes the page slow to load and display.

HMTL Text Versus Text Tool Text

It's important to understand that web page text—the kind stored in the HTML file—is fundamentally different from the regular text you create with the Text tool in PhotoImpact's Tool panel.

PhotoImpact includes a special HTML Text Object command for creating text in the page's HTML file. HTML text downloads quickly, takes very little storage space, and automatically wraps to fit the browser window. However, there are some limitations on HTML text. Specifically, HTML text is available in a very limited range of sizes and fonts. Also, the automatic text wrapping to fit within different browser window sizes can be problem instead of an advantage when you need to exercise precise control over the line breaks in a text layout.

If you create text with the Text tool on PhotoImpact's Tool panel and use it in a web page document, that text does *not* become part of the HTML file for the web page. Instead, when you export the web page as HTML, the text object is converted to an image, which is a bitmapped picture of the text. The image file is relatively large, slow to load, and can't adapt to fit in different size web browser windows. Also, because the text is displayed as a bitmap image, it isn't as sharp and crisp as HTML text, which is displayed using the system's own fonts. However, such text is free of the limitations of HTML text. You can use any font, size, color, fill, or special effect that you want, as long as you're willing to pay the price in download time. Using this type of text on your web page is described in the "Work with Text Images" section later in this chapter.

HTML text is, by far, the most efficient way to place text on a web page. Whenever possible, it is a good idea to use HTML text rather than text images. Of course, you may not be able to create some of the fancy effects that you're accustomed to creating with PhotoImpact's regular Text tool, but in most cases, the efficiency of HTML text far outweighs its limitations. Using HTML text is described in the following sections.

Add HTML Text

Using the HTML Text Object is similar to using the regular PhotoImpact Text tool, as you can see in its text-entry dialog box, shown in Figure 12-4. However, you do need to be careful with your font selections for HTML text. Otherwise, your web site visitors may not see the results you intended when they view your web page in a browser.

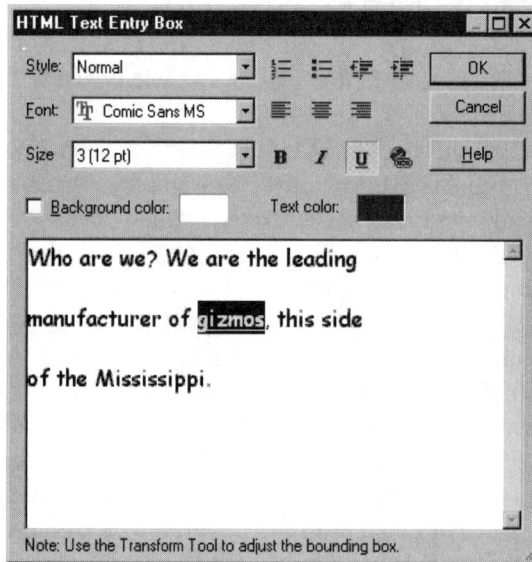

FIGURE 12-4   The HTML Text Entry Box

The problem is that HTML text relies on the fonts on the viewer's system to display the text in the browser window. Therefore, the trick to achieving predictable results when using HTML text is selecting a common font that is standard on most systems and easy to read on the screen. You may have many attractive fonts installed on your system, but if you select one that is not available on the user's system, the browser will substitute a different font, which may not produce the look you were after when designing the page.

Unfortunately, the list of almost universally available fonts is very short. Safe font choices include the following:

- Arial

- Times New Roman

- Courier

In addition, the standard installation of Internet Explorer includes a few select fonts. Given the popularity of Internet Explorer as a web browser, you can assume that many (but not all) of your web site visitors will also have the following fonts:

■ Comic Sans

■ Georgia

■ Tahoma

■ Trebuchet

■ Verdana

To add HTML text to a web page, follow these steps:

1. Choose Web | HTML Text Object or press SHIFT-T. PhotoImpact opens the HTML Text Entry Box (see Figure 12-4).

2. Select the style, font, size, and color for the text. The Style selection uses HTML paragraph tags to apply preset formatting to the text.

3. Optionally, use the buttons in the HTML Text Entry Box to make the text a numbered or bulleted list; change the indent; set alignment; or add bold, italic, or underscore attributes to the text.

4. In the text box, type the text you want to display. As in the regular Text Entry Box, you can enter multiple lines of text.

5. Click OK to close the HTML Text Entry Box dialog box. The text appears in the document window, surrounded by a bounding box.

12

Edit and Position HTML Text

After you create a block of HTML text, you can move and resize it to position it properly on your web page. You can also reopen the HTML Text Entry Box to edit or add to the text. To manipulate HTML text, use the following techniques:

■ To move the text block, drag the text box with the Pick tool.

■ To resize the boundary box, click the Transform tool and then drag a corner handle.

■ To edit the HTML text, select the text block, then press SHIFT-E or right-click the text and choose Edit HTML Text Object from the pop-up menu that appears. PhotoImpact opens the HTML Text Entry Box with the text displayed. Drag across the text in the text-entry box to select the portion of the text you want to edit or change.

Add a Hyperlink to HTML Text

One of the most important characteristics of HTML text is that any portion of the text can have a hyperlink attached. When your site visitor clicks the linked text, the browser loads the web page referenced in the hyperlink. This capability is at the core of what makes the Web function.

To add a hyperlink to your HTML text, follow these steps:

1. Select the HTML text object and press SHIFT-E to open the HTML Text Entry Box.

2. Select the text you want to link and click the Hyperlink button to open the Hyperlink dialog box.

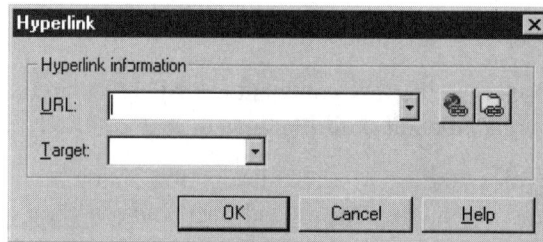

3. Enter the URL to which you want to link and select the target browser window. Then click OK to close the Hyperlink dialog box.

4. Click OK to close the HTML Text Entry Box.

Work with Text Images

If you absolutely cannot achieve the desired effect with HTML text, you can use the Text tool from the PhotoImpact Tool panel to create a regular text object and place it on the web page. With regular text, you can use a nonstandard font or add some colorful effects to your text. See Chapter 8 for information about creating and working with text objects.

Just remember that the text object will be converted to an image when you save the document as a web page. After the text object is converted to an image and displayed in the web browser, it probably won't be as sharp as HTML text. Also, the text image will take much longer to download and display than HTML text. Image optimization can help reduce the file size, but image compression can cause serious problems with text sharpness. Typically, text image files end up being larger than photographic image files of comparable dimensions.

CAUTION | *Carefully consider the impact of adding large text image files to your web page. Use regular text objects on a web page only as a last resort.*

Add Images to Your Web Page

The Web may have started as a primarily text-based medium, but today's web pages use a lot of images. Images draw the eye of your viewers and add some pizzazz to your page. Images can be an important part of the page content or simply decoration. Images can give your web page its distinctive look and feel, and images of buttons and banners add interactive components that help viewers navigate your web site.

There are various types of graphics you can place on a web page. These include static images that simply look nice, animated graphics that move and make people smile, and rollover images that change when the mouse pointer passes over the image.

No matter what kind of images you add to your web page, PhotoImpact saves the image files in an subfolder in the project directory when you export your web page as HTML. For example, if you save your HTML files in a directory called MyWebPage, PhotoImpact creates a subfolder in that directory called Images and saves all the image files from the web page there. You can change the name of the images subfolder on the Image Files tab of the Web Properties dialog box.

12

Add Static and Animated Images

A static image is simply that—static. It does not move or change in any way. Common applications for static images include company logos, photos, graphs, illustrations, simple buttons, separators, and most other web graphics.

Animated images, on the other hand, are comprised of several individual images (called *frames*) that are displayed in a sequence to create motion effects. Examples of animated images include logos that rotate, objects that appear to move across an image, and text that sparkles and changes color. When an animated image is saved in the GIF file format, you can add it to your web page in the same way that you add any other image. To create and edit an animated image, you need to use PhotoImpact's special animation tools or an animation editor such as GIF Animator (see Chapters 13 through 15). Note that Chapter 15 is on the Osborne web site (www.osborne.com).

> **NOTE**   *Along with animated GIFs, there are other media file formats that can produce animation effects as well as video and sound. See the "Add Media Objects to Your Web Page" section later in this chapter for information about adding those items to your web page.*

The procedure for adding static images and animated GIF images to your web page is the same. In both cases, you do the following:

1. Choose Web | Link Object | File. PhotoImpact displays the Open dialog box.

2. Select the file you want to insert and click Open. PhotoImpact closes the dialog box and displays the image in the document window with a selection marquee around it.

3. Use the Pick tool to move the image to the desired location. Use the Transform tool to resize the image, if necessary.

Add an Image from the Web

One of the interesting aspects of web page design is that you're not restricted to using only the images and other elements that are available on your own system or web server. You can reach out to the entire Web and pull elements into your web page. Any image for which you have the correct URL can be incorporated into your web page. PhotoImpact includes a special command that helps you pull images from other web sites and add them to your page. Using the Open Image from Web Page dialog box, shown in Figure 12-5, you can easily specify a web image for your web page.

> **CAUTION**   *Just because it's technically possible to pull images from other web sites doesn't mean that it's legal to do so. You need permission from the image owner before you can use an image on your web site. The feature is primarily intended to make it convenient for you to pull images from web resources that you own, not for pilfering other web designers' work.*

To add an image from the Web, do the following:

1. Choose Web | Link Object | Web. PhotoImpact displays the Open Image from Web dialog box, which includes a mini-browser (see Figure 12-5).

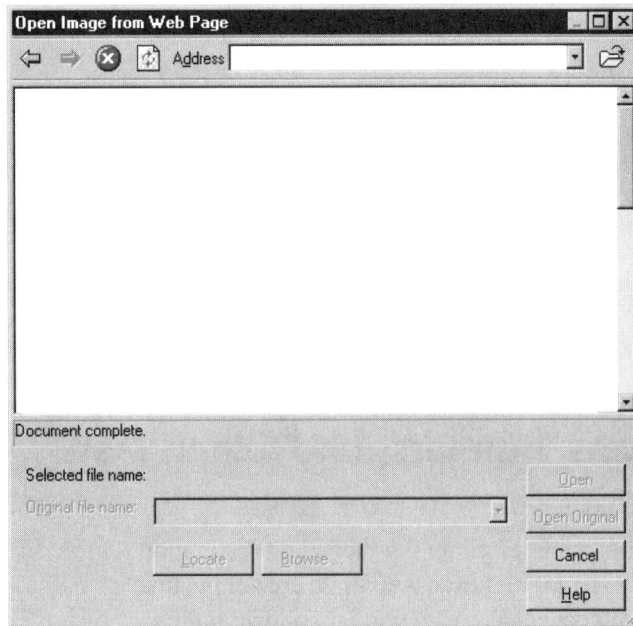

FIGURE 12-5   The Open Image from Web Page dialog box

12

2. Browse to the web page containing the image you want to add to your page. Enter a URL into the Address box at the top of the dialog box. When the page appears, you can click hyperlinks on the page and/or use the forward and back buttons to navigate the site, just as you would in a normal web browser.

3. Select the image you want to use by clicking it in the mini-browser box, and then click Open. PhotoImpact closes the Open Image from Web dialog box and adds the image to the document window with a selection marquee around it.

4. Use the Pick tool to move the image to the desired location. Use the Transform tool to resize the image, if necessary.

Add a Hyperlink to an Image

You can add hyperlinks to images just as you can add hyperlinks to HTML text. Then, when viewers click the image in their web browser, the browser goes to the

URL referenced in the hyperlinks. This is the concept that makes buttons on web pages work, but the same principle applies to any image.

To add a hyperlink to an image, follow these steps:

1. Right-click the image with the Pick tool and choose Properties from the pop-up menu that appears. PhotoImpact opens the Object Properties dialog box.

2. Click the Hyperlink tab and enter the URL for the hyperlink. Adjust the other settings as needed.

3. Click OK. PhotoImpact closes the Object Properties dialog box and adds the hyperlink to the image.

Add Buttons, Banners, and Other Web Components

Web components include banners, bullets, buttons, button bars, icons, rollover buttons, and separators. In most cases, these are simple images that may or may not have hyperlinks attached. The exception is rollover buttons, which are composed of multiple images controlled by JavaScript code, so that the button changes appearance when the viewer points to or clicks the button image. Creating web components is covered in detail in Chapter 10.

If you've already created an image for a web component, such as a simple button or separator, and want to add it to your web page, you can treat it like any other image. Just use the techniques outlined in the previous section to insert the image and define its hyperlink.

If you want to create a new button, banner, or other component, you can use PhotoImpact's Component Designer to build the component you need. See Chapter 10 for details on how to use the Component Designer wizard to produce the various web components. The instructions in Chapter 10 explain how to create various web components and save them to separate files. To add the component to the current document instead of saving it to a separate file, follow the procedure summarized in the following steps:

1. Choose Web | Component Designer. PhotoImpact opens the Component Designer wizard.

2. Select the desired component category (Banner, Button, and so on) and template and click Next to display the detail settings and options for that component.

3. Adjust the settings as necessary to define the web component. (See Chapter 10 for detailed instructions.)

4. Click Export and choose As Component Object from the pop-up menu. The component appears as a floating selection in the document window.

5. Move the component to the desired position and click to fix its position. PhotoImpact adds the component to your document. That includes both the image(s) and any necessary HTML code for hyperlinks and rollover effects.

When you export a web component from the Component Designer wizard as a component object, the Component Designer window remains open, with all the current component settings intact. Therefore, you can easily export the same component to another web page by opening the new page document in PhotoImpact, clicking the Component Designer window to make it active and repeating the export procedure to export the component to the new web page document.

Add Media Objects to Your Web Page

When you link a web object, the browser can open, read, and run the source file embedded in the HTML document, even if it is written in a format the browser normally does not recognize. Objects can be linked from a local file, a web page, a plug-in, an applet, Flash, and Shockwave files.

To link web object, follow these steps:

1. Select Web| Link Object. Select the type of object you want to link.

2. From the browse list, select the file you want to insert and click Open.

3. Position the object in your workspace. Make certain it does not overlap other objects.

4. Select the Slice tool. Right-click the object and select Slice Around Object. This will ensure that the slice cell includes the entire object.

5. Assign the appropriate attributes and behaviors to the web object in the Slice panel. (See Chapter 11 for details on using the Slice panel.)

6. Save the document.

7. To view the results, select File | Preview in Browser.

12

Slice Your Page

PhotoImpact lets you position images, text, web components, and other elements freely anywhere on your web page document. However, web browsers can't display elements in those positions without some help. Consequently, unless your web page is very simple, you need to slice your web page into cells to provide the positioning information the browser needs to place everything properly.

Basically, a web page document is one big image that needs to be sliced so that each text block, image, and web component is in a separate slice cell, interspersed with empty cells for spacing. Usually, you can use the Slice tool's Auto Slice option to slice your web page documents. Slicing the page is normally the last step you take before previewing or saving your web page. The techniques for slicing images are covered in Chapter 11.

Preview Your Web Page

When you work with a web page document in PhotoImpact, most of the elements appear in the document window looking pretty much the way they will look when viewed in a web browser. Still, there's no substitute for a preview in a real web browser, and PhotoImpact makes this easy to do.

Open the Page in Your Browser

For a quick preview, simply choose File | Preview in Browser and select the desired browser from the list. PhotoImpact opens a browser window and displays the page as the viewer will see it, including the links and any script effects you applied. Behind the scenes, PhotoImpact creates a bunch of temporary files for the HTML code and all the image files and other components that make up your page. This all happens automatically so you don't need to be concerned with those details.

If you have potential errors on your page, PhotoImpact displays an error dialog box, describing the problems and suggested solutions, as shown in Figure 12-6. Apply the solutions and click the Refresh button to check for additional errors.

Add a Browser to PhotoImpact's List

PhotoImpact automatically detects your default web browser during program installation and adds it to the list of browsers that appears when you choose File |

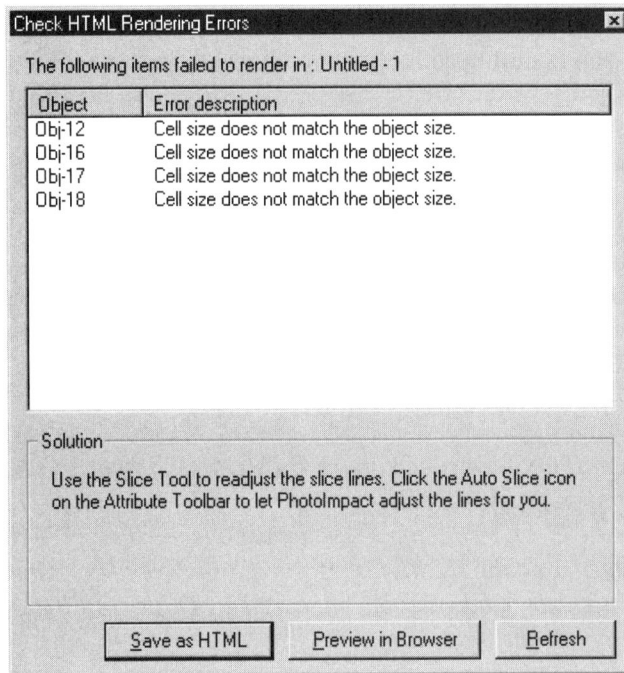

When you preview your web page in a browser, PhotoImpact informs you about any errors and offers solutions.

Preview in Browser. If you have other browsers that you want to use to preview web documents, you can add them to the list. Here's how:

1. Choose File | Preview in Browser | Edit Browser List. PhotoImpact opens the Edit Browser List dialog box.

2. Click Add to open the Add Browser dialog box.

3. Type the browser name as you want it to appear in the PhotoImpact menu.

4. Enter the command that launches the browser or click Browse to display the Open dialog box, where you can locate and select the browser's executable file.

5. Click OK to close the Add Browser dialog box and return to the Edit Browser List dialog box. The new browser appears in the Browsers list box.

12

6. Click OK. PhotoImpact closes the Edit Browser List dialog box and updates the list on the menu. The new browser is now available for previewing web pages from PhotoImpact.

Save Web Pages

Finally, when your document is complete, it's time to save your work. Saving a web page is a two-part procedure. First, you need to save your work as a native PhotoImpact file (.UFO). After you have done that, you can save your page for the Web. You'll need the PhotoImpact file available if you ever want to edit your web page, because PhotoImpact can't load and edit the HTML file that is created when you save your web page as HTML.

| CAUTION | *Although PhotoImpact can create HTML files for web pages, the program cannot open or edit HTML files. Therefore, if you want to edit a web page you created with PhotoImpact, you must open and edit the UFO file, and then regenerate the HTML file. If you didn't save the original document from which you made the web page as a UFO file, you'll need to start over and re-create the page from scratch.* |

When you export the document as a web page, PhotoImpact does the following:

- Merges all the usual image components (image objects, path objects, and text objects) into a base image file

- Slices everything into smaller pieces

- Saves separate image files for the web components and other pieces

- Generates an HTML file containing the HTML text and all the HTML code needed to instruct a web browser how to display the web page

To save your web page, perform the following steps:

1. Choose File | Save As. PhotoImpact displays the Save As dialog box.

2. Navigate to the desired location where you want to save the file.

3. Enter a name for the file and select the UFO format in the Save As Type box.

4. Click Save. PhotoImpact closes the dialog box and saves the document as a PhotoImpact image file. All the web components and other objects are saved as separate objects. You can reopen and edit this file later.

5. Choose File | Save for Web | As HTML. PhotoImpact opens a slightly different version of the Save As dialog box.

6. Navigate to the location where you want to save the HTML file.

7. Enter a filename for the web page.

8. Click Save. PhotoImpact closes the dialog box and generates an HTML file containing the web text and all the HTML code needed to display your web page. PhotoImpact also creates separate image files for the slice images, web components, and other image elements on the page and saves them in a subfolder of the folder designated for the HTML file.

After you save your web page as HTML, you can publish it on a web server for the world to see. You can use a web-publishing tool, such as the Windows Web Publishing Wizard, to publish your web page. Alternatively, you can use your favorite FTP utility to copy the HTML file and all the supporting image files to the web server. Just be sure to check with the system administrators for the web server where you're posting the site and follow their instructions regarding the directories where you should place your files and how to access those directories on the server.

12

PART V

Build Animations

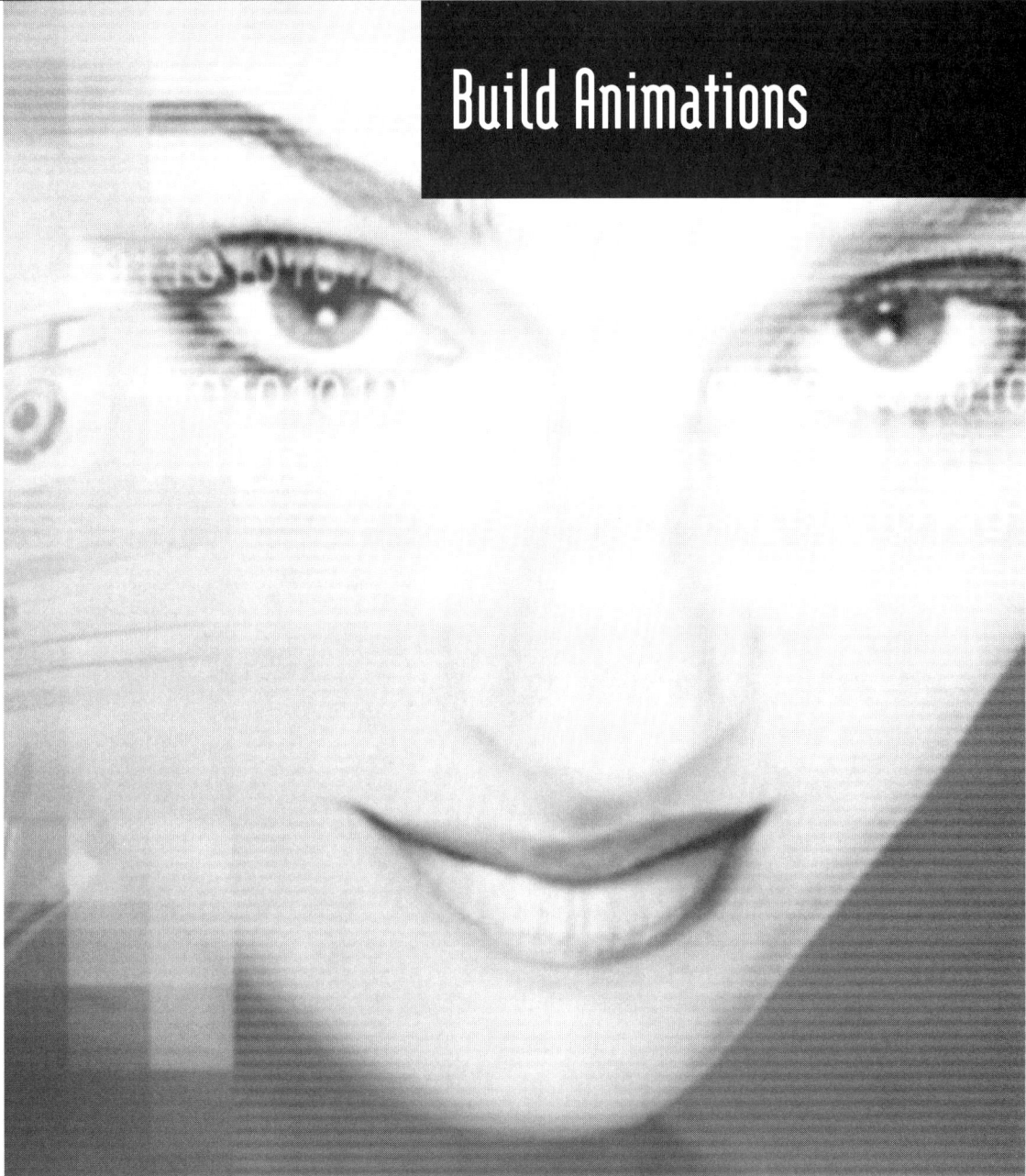

CHAPTER 13

Create Animation and Special Effects in PhotoImpact

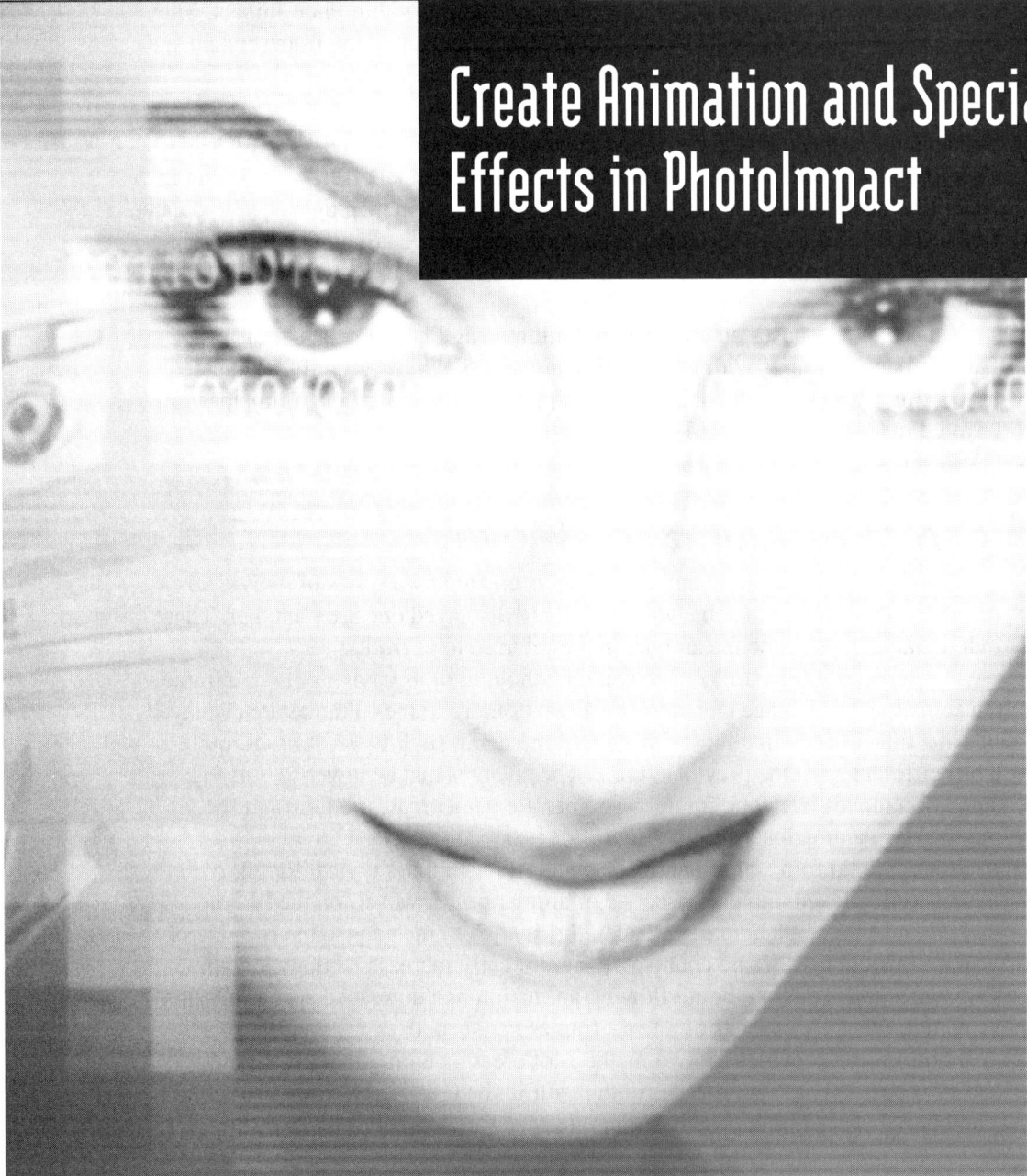

Ulead PhotoImpact was the first image editor to ship with the built-in ability to create special effects and animation. These effects, which are often referred to as *plugins* or *filters*, operate like miniature programs within PhotoImpact. They enable you to add special effects to a still image, create animation from scratch, and add animation to an already existing image such as a photograph.

The animation and special effects tradition continues with the release of Ulead PhotoImpact 7, which contains every animation and special effect plugin found in previous versions of PhotoImpact, plus an impressive new plugin used to create still and animated Crystal effects. In this chapter, you'll learn how to use these plugins to create attention-grabbing animations that will set your web site apart from the crowd.

This chapter focuses on creating animation using PhotoImpact's tools. PhotoImpact also ships with Ulead GIF Animator 5, which is a utility dedicated to working with animated GIF files. Creating animation with GIF Animator is covered in Chapters 14 and 15.

What Makes Animation Move?

The illusion of movement in any animation is created by a series of individual images, each different in some way, which are displayed one after another. These individual images inside the animation are referred to as *frames*.

In a sense, a static (still) image could be thought of as having only one frame. An animation is an image that consists of two or more frames. Frames are displayed one at a time in an animation, with each frame being slightly (or at times, quite a bit) different from the previous frame. The changes that a viewer sees as the animation moves from one frame to another are what create the look and feel of motion in an animation.

In traditional forms of animation such as television, it's typical for 24 to 30 frames to be packed into every second of animation. However, on the Internet, frame counts this high are not practical. Since each frame adds to the file size of your animation, high frame counts will significantly increase its download time. To balance the need for smooth flowing animation and download speed, Internet animation typically consists of 8 to 12 frames per second.

PhotoImpact provides for two methods of creating animation: key frame and storyboard. These approaches both result in the creation of frames for your animation, but they provide a different interface for creating those frames.

Key Frame Animation

Key frame animation uses a technique borrowed from professional television, film, and video animation. A *key frame* is a frame in which you tell PhotoImpact what you want the animation to look like, using the controls in the PhotoImpact filter's interface. Every key frame animation must have at least two key frames: The first frame in the animation must be a key frame, to control how you want the animation to look when it begins, and another frame in the animation must be a key frame, to control how you want the animation to look when it ends.

If you were creating an animation manually, you would not only need to produce the key frames with the main visual changes, but also all of the frames in between those key frames, This is where the true power of key frame animation in PhotoImpact comes into the picture. You just set up the key frames, and PhotoImpact fills in the in-between frames for you.

For example, suppose you have an eight-frame animation of fireworks. All you need to do is set what you would like the animation to look like in the first and last frames. Then, PhotoImpact examines the key frames, determines what the fireworks should look like in the six in-between frames, and creates each of those in-between frames for you. Clearly, key frames are a powerful tool, not only for creating impressive animation, but also for significantly enhancing productivity.

In PhotoImpact, you create key frame animation using the key frame control, which enables you to manipulate effects in key frames and preview your animation. Using the key frame control, you can add and remove frames and set the total number of frames for your animation.

Storyboard Animation

Storyboard animation uses a computer version of the traditional storyboard, which is a series of drawings representing important changes in the look of an animation. In a traditional storyboard designed for print, television, or film, an artist draws the storyboard frames for the purpose of demonstrating what the animation would look like to a writer or director. The artist then goes on to draw all of the frames in between storyboard frames—obviously, an extremely time-consuming task.

In a PhotoImpact storyboard animation, you place thumbnail images of the important changes on the storyboard line. Once the storyboard thumbnails (or frames) are in place, PhotoImpact will create the in-between frames for your animation, just as with key frame animation.

13

Use PhotoImpact's Animation Effects

PhotoImpact ships with a wide assortment of effects filters that are specifically designed for use in creating animation. PhotoImpact's animation filters are accessed through the Effects menu. You can also drag and drop many effects (such as a bolt of lightning) onto an image by using the EasyPalette. The form of animation used—key frame or storyboard—depends on the interface for the effect you've selected.

When you add a special effect to a key frame or storyboard thumbnail, it becomes part of your animation. You can adjust the settings for each effect, so that it appears differently in each key frame or storyboard thumbnail. (Of course, you can also apply these special effects to static images in PhotoImpact.)

Prepare Images for Animation

One you've selected an image to animate (photographs are often excellent choices when working with PhotoImpact's animation filters), you should assess the image's dimensions to see if downsizing is needed. Typically, the largest image size you would want to work with for an animation is in the area of about 300 by 200 pixels, or at the most, about 320 by 240 pixels. Of course, larger dimensions are possible, but they will add significantly to your final file size. If you need to downsize your image, you can do so by clicking Format | Image Size in PhotoImpact 7.

| NOTE | *Although an image's dimensions can add significantly to its file size, contrary to what is sometimes claimed, resolution, or dots per inch (dpi), is irrelevant. Setting an image's resolution in PhotoImpact (or any other image editor) affects the print process, not the display process. Although printers can change their resolution (typically in the area of 72 dpi to 1200 dpi) according to the value you specify through Format | Resolution, monitors can display only a preset resolution (typically 96 dpi).* |

Animate with Key Frames

PhotoImpact 7 includes four sets of unique effects that allow you to use the key frame method of animation:

- ■ Animation Studio adds animation to traditionally static filters such as Whirlpool Swirl, Page Turn, and Water Droplets.

Finding Photos and Objects for Animation

In most cases, you'll probably be adding animation to designs that you've created in PhotoImpact or to photographs that you've scanned into PhotoImpact or downloaded into PhotoImpact from a digital camera. However, for those occasions when you're seeking something different, the /Samples/Images folder on your PhotoImpact 7 CD and the /Samples/Images folder on this book's companion CD both contain professional photographs that you may use in your projects royalty-free.

As you may already know, there are a wealth of resources available on the Internet for obtaining free photographs. A search for "free" and "photo" in your favorite search engine will reveal an abundance of such resources. When you need a large selection of images on CD-ROM, you may want to consider a collection such as Ulead's Pick a Photo (http://www.ulead.com/pap/), Hemera's Photo Objects (http://www.hemera.com), Kodak's Photo CDs (http://www.kodak.com), or Corbis' CD collections (http://www.corbis.com/).

- Crystal, the newest addition to the PhotoImpact animated filter library, is used to create the illusion of looking at a portion of your image through animated crystal shapes, such as spheres, diamonds, and polyhedrons.

- Lighting adds spectacular animated lighting changes to your image, such as fireworks, lightning, and comets.

- Type lets you add a wide variety of special effects to text, such as Fire, Ice, and Concrete.

You use the same basic technique to apply each of these effects to your key frames, as explained in the following sections.

Create Animation in the Animation Studio

The PhotoImpact Animation Studio creates eye-catching animation based on filters that are traditionally used for applying effects to static images. PhotoImpact transforms these static effects into animations by increasing or decreasing the intensity of the effects as you move from frame to frame through the animation. You can change the appearance of the animation by controlling the strength of the effect at the key frames within the animation.

13

When you've decided on an image, and downsized its dimensions if needed, select Effect I Animation Studio to access the Animation Studio. Figure 13-1 shows the Animation Studio dialog box.

Pick an Effect

Icons representing each available effect are located near the lower-left side of the dialog box. The Animation Studio contains 11 effects:

- **Ripple**   Creates a wave-like effect. In Radial mode, the effect originates from the center and spreads outward, similar to the effect you would see when throwing a stone into a body of water. In Linear mode, the effect resembles that of wind on a body of water.

- **Diffuse**   Applies pixel diffusion to your image, an effect that breaks up blocks of pixels and scatters them. The effect is similar to looking at your image through a translucent glass, such as a shower door.

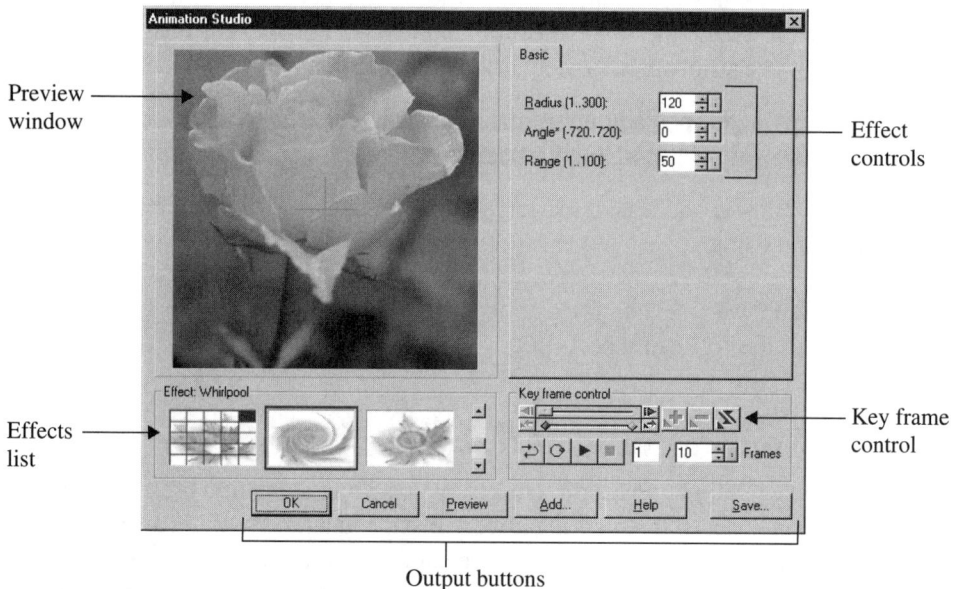

FIGURE 13-1   The Animation Studio dialog box

- **Gaussian Blur**   Applies a blur effect to your image. A Gaussian blur differs slightly from a traditional blur effect, in that it is applied in a slightly random manner. Traditional blurs are applied in a uniform manner across an entire image.

- **Signature**   Uses a pen tool to write a message or a signature across an image. The animation typically begins with no writing on the image, and then the message is displayed one or two pen strokes at a time, as though handwriting is being applied to the image.

- **Wave**   Creates a waving effect, similar to that of a flag waving in the wind.

- **Jump**   Applies a slight perspective-like distortion to the top and left side or bottom and right side of an image, to make it look as though the image is jumping from one position to another.

- **Puzzle**   Divides your image into rows and columns, and then moves the pieces to different locations.

- **Whirlpool**   Creates a swirling pattern emerging from a center point. The pattern can move clockwise or counterclockwise, and the center point can be moved to anywhere on the image by dragging and dropping a crosshair.

- **Droplet**   Simulates the effect of a water being slowly dropped onto your image. A circular distortion appears in the middle of the image and then flows outward toward the edges.

- **Motion Blur**   Simulates the effect of a motion blur filter being applied in increasing or decreasing intensity. Three motions are available: Linear, which is similar to a zoom blur; Whirlpool, which moves the blur in a swirling pattern; and Wave, which moves the blur along a waving vertical to horizontal pattern.

- **Page Turn**   Simulates the classic page-turn effect, with an important difference: Since the effect appears to be moving, the page actually appears to turn, beginning with a slight curl and eventually completely disappearing. Two different curl patterns are available: a classic curl and a triangular-shaped curl called Corn. The page can be curled from any of its four corners, and the back of the curling page can show a traditional opaque pattern, a reverse pattern, or a transparent pattern.

Click an effect icon to select the effect to apply to your image.

13

Set Key Frames

The key frame control, located to the right of the effect icons, contains everything you need to set the key frames for your animation. You can add and remove key frames, access individual frames, and play a preview of your animation. When you begin, by default, the key frame control will be set to the first frame of the animation.

Navigate the Animation's Frames   On the upper-left side of the key frame control are two sliders: the preview slider and the key frame slider. These sliders allow you to navigate through the frames in your animation. The components of the sliders are shown in the following illustration.

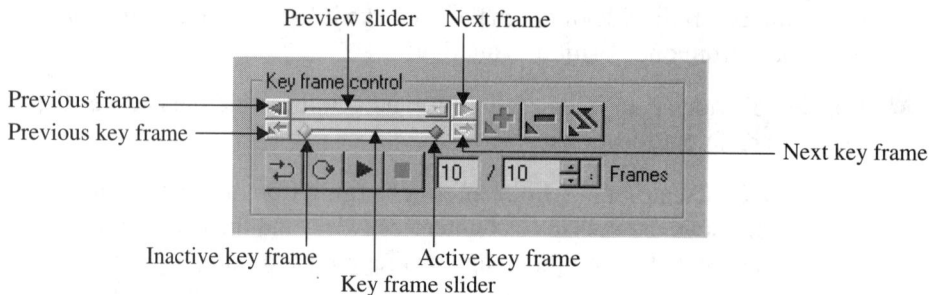

The top slider, called the preview slider, allows you to move back and forth between all of the frames in your animation. Click the small button on the left or right side of the preview slider to move backward or forward, respectively, one frame at a time. You can also use the small rectangular button on the preview slider to navigate back and forth.

The slider below the preview slider is used to navigate through key frames. The small diamond shapes on the key frame slider indicate the location of your animation's key frames. The *active* key frame—the key frame that can be manipulated via the control tab and is displayed in the preview window—is highlighted by a colored diamond; the inactive key frame(s) remain gray. Click the small buttons located on the left and right side of the key frame slider to move backward and forward between key frames.

TIP *When an animation preview plays, occasionally you'll notice that one frame doesn't look quite as you expected it to look. When this happens, the preview slider's buttons provide a convenient method of examining your animation preview one frame at a time.*

You can also navigate to any frame in your animation by entering a number in the first Frames text box, in the middle of the key frame control. That box shows the frame that's currently being displayed in the preview window. When you type in another number, you move directly to that frame.

Add, Remove, and Reverse Key Frames   To the right of the preview and key frame sliders, you'll see a set of three larger buttons, as shown here.

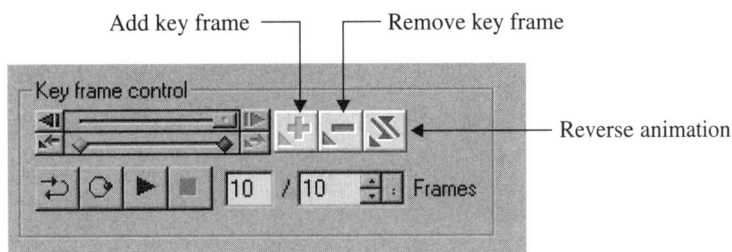

Add key frame ———   ——— Remove key frame

Key frame control

——— Reverse animation

10 / 10   Frames

Use these buttons to add, remove, and reverse key frames in your animation, as follows:

- To add a key frame, use the preview slider or the preview slider's buttons to navigate to the frame where you would like to add the key frame and click the plus (+) button. Note that the button is grayed out if the current frame is already a key frame.

- To remove a key frame, navigate to the desired key frame using the key frame slider or the key frame slider's buttons or click the key frame's small diamond icon and click the minus (–) button. Note that since the first frame is always a key frame, it cannot be removed.

- Occasionally, you may want to reverse the play direction of an animation (begin with the last key frame and move to the first one). To accomplish this in a single step, click the button to the right of the minus button.

13

Control the Number of Frames The two Frames text boxes show the current frame and the total number of frames in your animation.

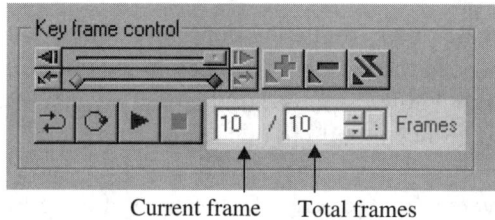

Current frame   Total frames

As noted earlier, you can enter another number in the current frame box to move to that frame. To change the total number of frames in your animation, enter a different number in the second Frames text box.

NOTE *Each frame you add increases the file size of your animation, so use caution when increasing frame count. Ten frames is generally a good starting point for a GIF animation.*

Set Effects for Key Frames You control the animation for each key frame by selecting that key frame and then setting the options for the effect you selected. These options appear on the tab to the right of the preview window. This tab contains each effect's unique set of controls. Some PhotoImpact animation effects will have a second tab, which is used for setting advanced controls.

TIP *Click the Help button to see detailed pop-up help regarding the currently selected effect's controls.*

Setting the effect controls here is essentially the same process as setting the controls in any other dialog box in PhotoImpact. The only difference is that when you set these controls for an animation, you adjust them for each of the animation's key frames. The change in settings as your animation moves from key frame to key frame is what creates the look and feel of motion in your animation, as you will see in the examples throughout this chapter. Just continue to select key frames and set effects to create your animation.

When an effect requires that you set coordinates, you can use the preview window to visually accomplish this task. For example, when you choose the

Whirlpool effect, a crosshair will appear in the preview window. You can drag and drop this crosshair to set the center point for the whirlpool's swirls.

Preview Your Animation   To preview your animation, simply click the play button (with the right-pointing arrow) in the set of buttons beneath the key frame slider. Your animation will play once and then stop. You can stop the preview anytime by clicking the stop button (with the square icon), located next to the play button.

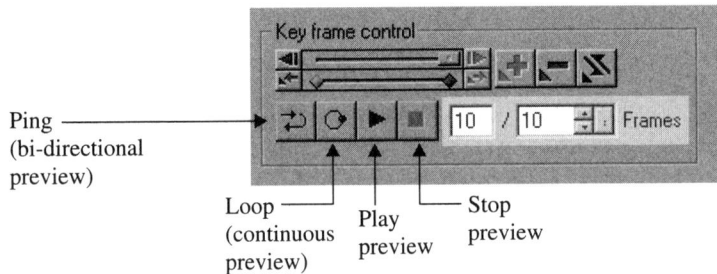

Ping (bi-directional preview)

Loop (continuous preview)   Play preview   Stop preview

The two buttons to the left of the play button let you control the playback, as follows:

- If you enable the ping (bi-directional preview) button, when you click play, the preview will play forward (from first frame to last frame) and then backward (from last frame to first frame) until you click stop.

- If you enable the loop (continuous preview) button, when you click play, the preview will play forward (from first frame to last frame), until you click stop.

13

NOTE   *Previewing your animation continuously versus playing it forward and then backward does not affect the playback of your final animation file. These are merely preview controls, which are used to see if you like the effect of continuous play and/or forward-and-then backward play.*

The Preview button in the dialog box previews the effect that is currently seen in the preview window to your active image in PhotoImpact. This is not an animation preview; it just previews changes to the static image in PhotoImpact.

Apply Your Frame Effects When you click the OK button, a pop-up menu appears with a still frame option and an animation option.

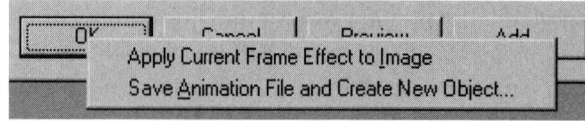

These options work as follows:

- The Apply Current Frame Effect to Image option applies the effect currently shown in the preview window to your active image in PhotoImpact.

- The Save Animation File and Create New Object option applies the effect currently shown in the preview window as a new object in your image (thus preserving your original image) and then opens the Save Animation dialog box, which is discussed in the next section.

Save Your Key Frame Settings To add your key frame effects to the EasyPalette, click the Add button in the Animation Studio dialog box. Like the OK button, the Add button offers a pop-up menu with two choices.

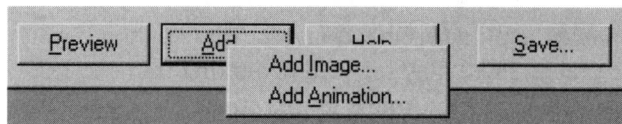

These options work as follows:

- The Add Image option adds a single animation effect to the EasyPalette, based on the frame currently being previewed.

- The Add Animation option adds all of your key frame information to the EasyPalette, and even creates an animated preview for the EasyPalette.

If you choose the Add Animation option, you can access the key frame effect later by right-clicking it in the EasyPalette and then clicking Modify Properties and Apply. You can use this procedure to edit an animation by changing the key frame settings and then resaving the animation, or you can apply the key frame effects to another background image, creating a new animation.

Save Your Animation

When you're ready to save your animation, click the Save button in the Animation Studio dialog box. You can choose between two file types: Animated GIF Files (*.GIF) or Sequence BMP Files (*BMP). If you simply want to create an animation in as few steps as possible, saving your file as an animated GIF is the way to go. If you want to do more work on your animation in the Ulead GIF Animator program, saving the animation as a sequence of bitmaps is the best choice.

Create Animated GIFs By default, your file is saved as an animated GIF. When you use this setting, the GIF Animation Options settings at the bottom of the Save As dialog box are available, as shown in Figure 13-2.

The GIF Animation Options work as follows:

■ The Colors option sets the number of colors used in your animation. The default (and maximum) is 256.

13

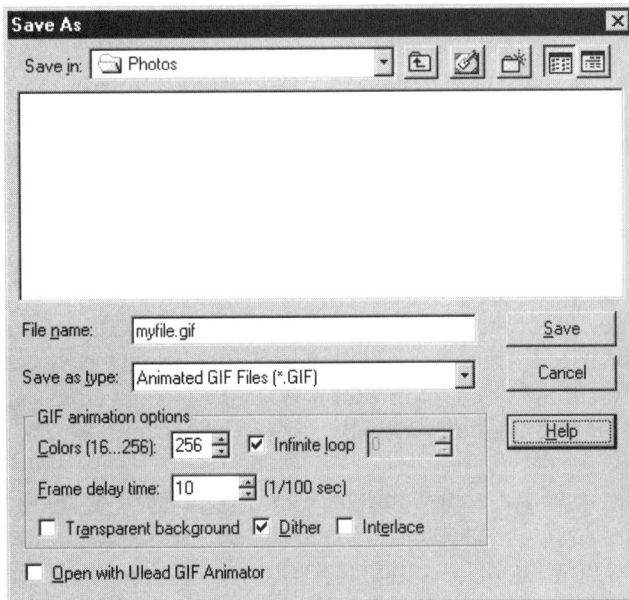

FIGURE 13-2 Saving a GIF animation in PhotoImpact

- The Infinite Loop checkbox determines whether your animation will play repeatedly until manually stopped. If this checkbox is not selected, you can enter the number of times to repeat the animation in the text box to its right.

- The Frame Delay Time option sets the amount of time that each frame remains displayed, in hundredth second increments. The default is 10/100 second.

- The Transparent Background checkbox makes the background of your animation transparent, so that the page beneath it shows through.

- The Dither checkbox tells PhotoImpact to dither the animation images. *Dithering* simulates the appearance of additional colors that don't exist in your palette.

- The Interlace checkbox causes the image to come into focus gradually.

- The Open with Ulead GIF Animator checkbox tells PhotoImpact to open the saved file in GIF Animator.

TIP

GIF animations permit only 256 colors per frame, which is seldom enough color to accurately reproduce a real-life image, such as a photograph or a gradient color scheme. Therefore, dithering is an extremely powerful option when using high-color images in GIF animations. However, dithering can increase file size. If you're not using a high-color image, it's a good idea to uncheck the Dithering option.

For now, I suggest that you use the settings shown in the Save As dialog box in Figure 13-2. If you want to experiment with these options, it's a good idea to use Ulead GIF Animator 5, which is discussed in the next two chapters. This tool is designed specifically for manipulating the more advanced GIF animation options (and can even be used to export your animation to video or the Macromedia Flash file format). GIF Animator's Optimization Wizard enables you to experiment with the animation's settings, without actually saving the file until you're completely satisfied with the results.

For example, consider what would happen if you changed your animation's Colors setting to 128 colors, in an effort to reduce file size. It sounds like a good idea, but you may end up with a very minimal savings in file size and a GIF animation that's lost far too much quality. If you make this change in PhotoImpact's Save As dialog box, and then open the animation in GIF Animator, that program would have no accurate method of restoring these colors. For this reason, it's usually best to save your GIF file with the suggested options and then make any adjustments in GIF Animator, as described in the next chapter.

Now suppose that you want to preserve all the colors in your animation—you don't want to reduce every frame to 256 colors. Reducing to 256 colors is necessary for animated GIFs, but it isn't necessary if you ultimately plan on exporting your animation to video or to the Macromedia Flash format. If you want to go this route, use the other file type option in the Save As dialog box, described next.

Save in Bitmap Format   If you want to use the powerful features of Ulead GIF Animator 5, such as its Optimization Wizard or its Flash export, PhotoImpact provides a method of saving your animation in a completely lossless file format. There is absolutely no color loss, and you do not have any options to be concerned about.

PhotoImpact accomplishes this by enabling you to save each frame of your animation as a bitmap file, by selecting Sequence BMP Files from the Save As Type drop-down list. When you choose this file type, the GIF Animation Options become unavailable.

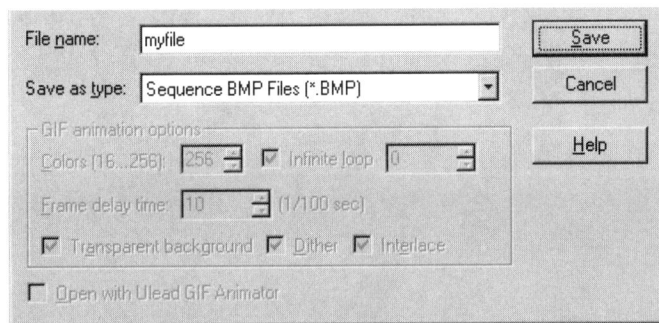

You only need to click Save once and provide a single filename. PhotoImpact will then save each frame of your animation and append a frame number to the filename, so that there's absolutely no confusion as to which file represents which frame of your animation. You can then open all of the files at the same time from GIF Animator by choosing File | Add Images and selecting the images. Each image will be inserted into its proper frame, reconstructing your PhotoImpact animation with absolutely no loss of quality or color. See Chapter 14 for details on using GIF Animator.

An Animation Studio Example

Now that you've read about how the Animation Studio and key frame animation work, let's try it out. In this example, you'll create an animation that starts out with a minimal effect and gradually increases to a much stronger effect. Open the image that you wish to animate and follow these steps:

1. Select Effect | Animation Studio to open the Animation Studio dialog box.

2. Click the Ripple icon (the first icon) in the Animation Studio's effects list.

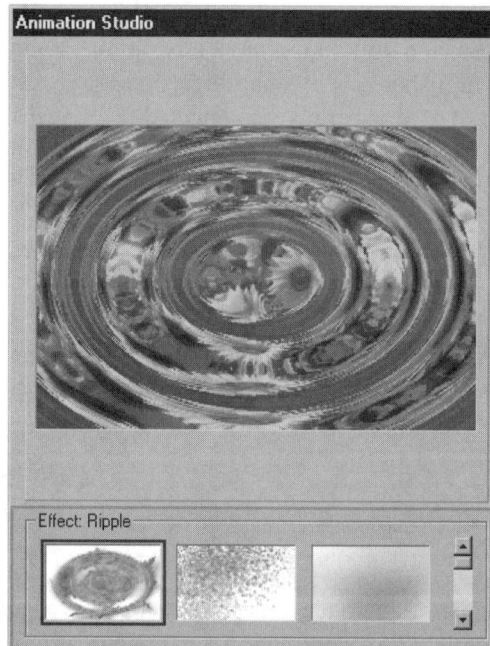

3. In the key frame control, set the total number of frames to 6 (by entering **6** in the text box directly to the left of Frames).

4. In the Basic tab, change only one of the effect's default settings for the first key frame of the animation (selected by default). Set the Angle option to –45, which will make the effect a bit more subtle than it is at its default setting of –90.

5. Move to the last key frame by clicking its small diamond icon. In the Basic tab, set the Angle option to 45 (instead of the default of 90), again to create a more subtle effect.

6. Click the play button to preview the animation. The effect will decrease in intensity as the angle moves from –45 (in the first key frame) toward 0 (near the middle of the animation) and increase in intensity as the angle moves up to +45 (in the last frame).

7. Click the loop button (to the left of the play button) and preview the animation again. You'll notice that the animation has a somewhat abrupt effect when it ends and then begins playing again. This is because when the animation loops, the last frame (set at +45) is followed suddenly by the first frame (set at –45). After the angle effect reaches +45, it would be nice to have the effect slowly return to the level of –45 seen in the first frame. Let's make this modification.

8. Change the setting in the total frames text box to 12.

9. Click the key frame icon (the small diamond) for the twelfth frame, and drag it to the left, until it's in position as the sixth frame.

10. Drag the button in the preview slider to the twelfth frame (or enter the **12** in the current frame text entry box) so that you can set the way the animation will look when it ends.

11. To set controls for the frame, make it a key frame by clicking the plus (+) button.

12. Make the last frame look identical to the first frame by setting Angle to –45.

13. Click the preview button (with the loop button enabled), and you'll see that you have an animation that loops smoothly from beginning to end (and back to beginning). However, you'll notice a slight pause as it ends and then begins. This is because the last and first frames are identical. When the animation plays, the image gives the effect of being paused when these two identical frames display one after the other.

14. To remove this pause, select the last frame and reduce the Angle setting a bit. A setting of –37 should work well.

15. Click the preview button (with the loop button enabled) again. Since the last frame is set at –37 and the first frame is set at –45, an illusion

13

of movement will be created even as the animation stops and then starts again, making for an animation that loops perfectly. Here is a frame-by-frame view of the animation.

16. Click the Add button and click the Add Animation item in the pop-up menu to add your key frame settings to the EasyPalette.

17. Click the Save button. Enter a filename for the animation. Then you can click the Save button to accept the defaults (or optionally, change the settings) and save the animation as an animated GIF file. If you want to save the animation as a series of bitmaps to work with in GIF Animator, choose Sequence BMP Files in the Save As Type drop-down list and click the Save button.

<table>
<tr><td>New to
PhotoImpact 7</td></tr>
</table>

Create Crystal Animations

What color is crystal? Crystal is more of a reflection than it is a particular color, making it difficult to duplicate on a computer screen. Ulead PhotoImpact 7 solves this problem with a new filter called Crystal. In addition to being able to apply the filter effect to a single image, you can also use the Crystal effect to create beautiful crystal animations.

Use a Crystal Effect

To use a Crystal effect, select Effect | Creative | Crystal to open the Crystal dialog box, shown in Figure 13-3. Like the Animation Studio dialog box, the Crystal dialog box contains a preview window, a list of effects on the lower-left side, and a key frame control. It also includes a few more effect settings and options.

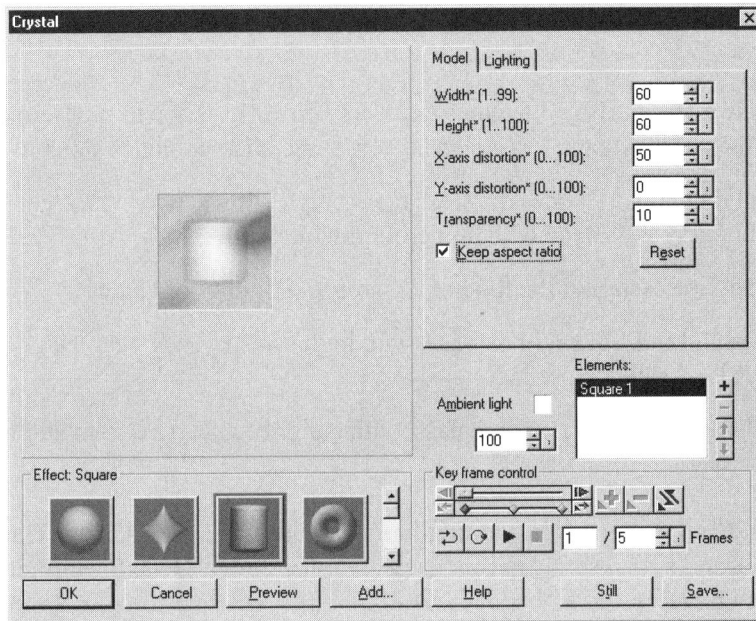

FIGURE 13-3   The Crystal dialog box

Choose a Crystal Shape   The Crystal dialog box effects list offers ten unique filter shapes:

■ **Sphere**   Creates a round effect that can be either a perfect circle or an ellipse.

■ **Rhombus**   Creates a diamond-shaped effect.

■ **Square**   Creates an effect that almost looks cylindrical due to its lighting, although it's actually a square with a slightly beveled (raised) middle and tapered edges.

■ **Donut**   Creates the classic donut shape—a highly reflective, semi-transparent circular shape, with a small inner diameter and larger outer diameter.

13

- **Diamond**   Creates an effect similar to that of a diamond ring. Color is intensified in the center and distributed more widely along the edges of the effect.

- **Star and Pudding**   Creates an effect similar in shape to the Diamond effect, except that it has a circular center and sharper angles along its edges.

- **Polyhedron**   Creates the classic 3D polyhedron shape, which consists of a broad round shape with numerous angular patterns on its surface.

- **Drop**   Resembles the look of a teardrop or a drop of water.

- **Vase**   Looks like a glass vase, with high transparency near the middle and less transparency around the edges.

- **Glass**   Looks like a wine glass, with a highly reflective stem and highly transparent glass area.

Set Crystal Effect Options   In addition to its unique shape, each Crystal filter uses 3D lighting and strong semi-transparency and reflection effects. Each filter has two control tabs:

- The Model tab contains settings for fine-tuning the effect's size and shape.

- The Lighting tab contains settings to control the 3D lighting effects.

The element controls, below the Model (or Lighting) tab, provide additional settings for the Crystal effect. The Ambient Light text box and color box control the general lighting in your image. You can use these controls to change the color of the lighting in your image or reduce the general brightness of your image. For example, if your effect isn't showing up well against a bright background image, you can try lowering the Ambient Light level.

Next to the Ambient Light controls are the Element list box and control buttons. These are available when you want to use two or more Crystal effects in the same image, as described in the "Create a Multiple Crystal Animation" section, a bit later in this chapter.

NOTE

The Crystal dialog box, as well as the dialog boxes for other effects accessed through Effect | Creative, includes a Still button next to the Save button. This button removes the key frame control, which creates more room for displaying effect icons. When you do this, the Still button turns into an Animate button. To return the key frame control to the dialog box, click the Animate button.

Animate a Crystal Button

One area where Crystal animations are likely to become popular is in the creation of web interfaces. For example, a pulsating web button can be created with just a few mouse clicks.

To create a Crystal button, first create a background in PhotoImpact. The background can be just about anything—a solid color (except solid black, since the Crystal filters require at least a little bit of light to create their effect), a gradient fill, a magic texture, a natural texture, or a background created in the Background Designer are a few examples. The button's dimensions can be whatever you would like to use, but you should keep in mind the Crystal effect needs some room in order to display properly; dimensions of under 60 percent by 60 percent may not create the desired result.

Once you have a background image selected, follow these steps to create the Crystal button:

1. Select Effect | Creative | Crystal to open the Crystal dialog box.

2. Select the Square effect in the effects list.

3. The Square's dimensions of 79 percent by 80 percent are a little larger than what's needed in this case, so set the Width option to 60 in the Model tab. Since the Keep Aspect Ratio checkbox is checked by default, when you change the width to 60, the height will automatically change to 60 (as soon as the cursor leaves the Width text box).

4. Since this effect will require only a few frames, set the total frames text box in the key frame control to 5 frames.

5. Click the diamond representing the second key frame and change the second key frame's width to 60. The height will again change to 60 automatically.

13

6. Now all that needs to be done is to add a key frame with different values than the first and last key frames, to create movement in the animation. Use the preview slider to move to frame 3, and then click the plus (+) button to add a key frame.

7. Set the width and height for this middle key frame to 95.

8. Click the play button to confirm that everything works as expected. The button will now pulsate from a medium size of 60×60, up to a larger size of 95×95 and then back down to the medium size of 60×60.

When using a button such as this on a web site, you may want to add interactivity to the site by using a still frame version of the button for when there is no user activity, and then add the animated version as a rollover that animates when the user hovers the mouse over the button.

To create a set of still and animated buttons, use the key frame control to move to the first frame of the animation, click OK, select Save Animation File and Create New Object, and save the file as an animated GIF. Your rollover animation will be created and saved, and the first frame of the animation will be applied to your background image in PhotoImpact, which you can then save by using the Web Image Optimizer. The still and animated image may then be added to your web site using PhotoImpact's extensive set of web design tools.

Create Moving Crystal Effects

A Crystal effect can appear to move from one point to another point on your background image. As an example, here are the steps for animating a drop of wax sliding down the side of a candle:

1. Select Effect | Creative | Crystal to open the Crystal dialog box.

2. Select the Drop effect in the effects list.

3. The Drop effect's default size is far too large for this particular image, so change its size to about 8 percent by 8 percent by entering 8 in the Width text box in the Model tab.

4. Position the drop near the top of the image by placing your mouse over the drop in the preview window and then dragging and dropping it to the chosen location.

5. Since you'll want the Drop effect to slowly move down the candle, this animation will need a few extra frames. Change the total frame setting from 10 to 12. When you move to the last key frame in the animation, you'll notice that the drop once again takes on huge dimensions. You could change this by using the Width and Height settings, but there is another method available.

6. Delete the last key frame by clicking the minus (–) button. The last frame in the animation will now take on the effect of the closest key frame, which already has the correct dimensions. Click the plus (+) button, and the correct dimensions will be added as a new key frame.

7. Drag and drop the Drop effect in the preview window to the bottom of the image, so that it's completely off screen. Note that as you near any of the edges of a preview window, the selection area for the effect gets smaller, so you may need to try a couple times to get the drop completely off screen. Even though it can't be seen, make certain you placed the drop in the last key frame directly below the drop in the first key frame, so that the drop appears to move in a straight line as it travels down the candle.

8. Click the play button to preview the animation. Notice that the shape of the drop is identical throughout the animation. In reality, a drop moving down a candle would probably change its shape some as it moved.

9. To simulate a change in the drop's shape, you can use a lighting effect. Many of the lighting effects will not make a noticeable change on a crystal this small, but one that will is the Slant setting, which sets the angle of light hitting the drop. Click the first key frame, and click the Lighting tab.

10. Change the Slant setting to 20 for the first key frame and leave it at its default of 90 in the last key frame.

11. Click the play button to preview the animation again. The drop will now appear more flat in the first key frame, and it will slowly change shape and

13

take on a more drop-like appearance as it moves down the candle. This is a subtle change, but it can be used to mimic what would happen in real life— a drop of wax slowly taking shape as it moves down the candle. Here is a frame-by-frame look at the animation.

Create a Multiple Crystal Animation

You can create some interesting animations by using multiple Crystal effects. To add a new effect to your image, click the plus (+) button next to the Elements list box (beneath the Model tab in the Crystal dialog box) and click the effect's icon. To remove an effect, click the effect name in the Elements list box and click the minus (–) button.

When adding an effect, be sure to click the plus button first and then click the effect icon. If you click the effect icon first, you will change your current effect into the new effect instead of adding an effect. As a result of changing to the new effect, any custom changes you made to the original effect's key frame settings will be lost. When you click the plus button and then click the new effect's icon, no changes are made to your original effect's key frame settings.

The up and down arrows under the Element list box's plus and minus buttons are used to control effect placement. Although all effects are created on a single background layer, you can use these arrows to place an effect in front of or behind another effect, as shown in Figures 13-4 and 13-5. In Figure 13-4, the polyhedron is placed *in front of* the donut, obstructing the view of the hole in the center of the donut. In Figure 13-5, the polyhedron is placed *behind* the donut, resulting in some distortion in the face of the polyhedron as it's being viewed through the semi-transparent surface of the donut.

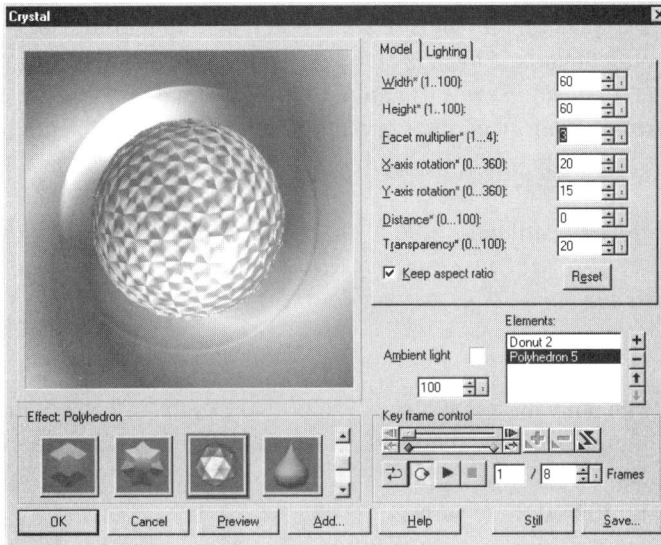

FIGURE 13-4   A polyhedron in front of a donut

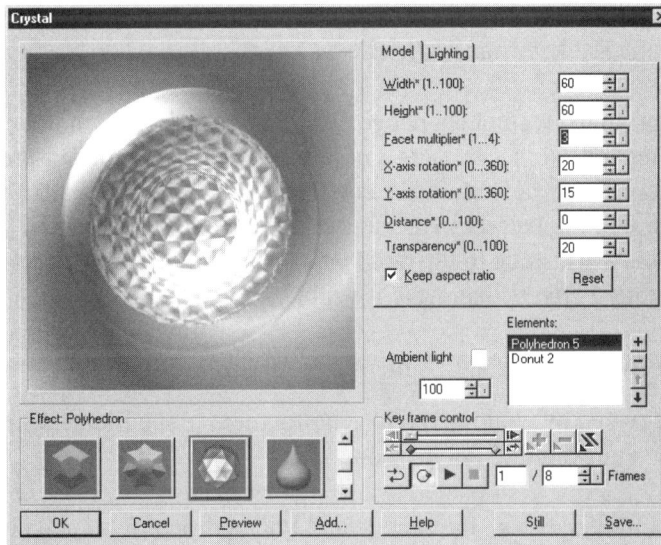

FIGURE 13-5   A donut in front of a polyhedron

13

When you look at Figures 13-4 and 13-5, notice in the Element list boxes that the name of the Crystal effect that is in front is at the *bottom* of the list, and the name of the Crystal effect that is in back is at the *top* of the list. Thus, the up arrow button is used to move a crystal *in back of* another crystal. The down arrow button is used to move a crystal *in front of* another crystal. Since this is the opposite of the way layering controls usually work, it may seem a bit unusual at first.

> **NOTE**   *In Ulead GIF Animator, and even in PhotoImpact (except in the key frame dialog boxes), moving an object with an up arrow moves the object to the top, and moving an object with a down arrow moves the object to the bottom, just as you might expect.*

Let's create an animation that makes use of two Crystal effects. In the following example, you'll create a Crystal animation in which one Crystal effect disappears and a new Crystal effect appears in its place. Start out with a background image in PhotoImpact and follow these steps:

1. Select Effect | Creative | Crystal to open the Crystal dialog box.

2. Set the total frames for the animation to 8.

3. By default, the Sphere effect will be selected, along with its default dimensions. You will use the Sphere for the beginning of this animation. Move the last key frame to frame 5.

This creates an interesting challenge: The Sphere will be seen in only the first half of the animation. However, there's no off switch to turn it off for the second half of the animation. Fortunately, there's a convenient (and undocumented) workaround. By reducing any Crystal effect to the size of 1 percent by 1 percent, it will be too small to be seen. This is due to the fact that such a small Crystal effect cannot process the lighting effects that make it visible.

1. Set the Width and Height dimensions for frame 5 to 1.

2. Add a crystal by clicking the plus button next to the Element list box and then clicking the Polyhedron icon.

Notice that although both the Sphere and Polyhedron effects exist in the same animation, only the key frames for the Crystal effect that you're working with (in this case, the Polyhedron) are visible. By hiding key frames that aren't associated with the current effect, PhotoImpact makes it easy to avoid accidentally setting key frames for the wrong effect. No matter how many effects you choose to add to your animation, you can always access the one you want to work with by clicking its name in the Elements list box.

1. Just as the Sphere is only going to be visible in the first half of this animation, the Polyhedron is only going to be visible in the second half of the animation. To make the Polyhedron invisible for the beginning of the animation, set this effect's first key frame to 1 percent by 1 percent. The last key frame should remain set at its default dimensions of 80 percent by 80 percent.

2. Move to the third frame of the animation, and you'll see another interesting challenge. One of the goals here is to keep the Polyhedron invisible until the middle of the animation. However, even at frame 3, it has reached dimensions of 24×24. Fortunately, there's a solution for this problem as well.

3. Move to frame 4 of the animation and set the Polyhedron's dimensions to 1×1. By doing this, you've set the Polyhedron to dimensions of 1×1 from frame 1 to frame 4, effectively rendering it invisible for all four of these frames.

4. Preview your animation by clicking the play button. You'll see that the Sphere is visible from frames 1 to 4, and the Polyhedron is visible in frames 5 to 8.

13

Create Animated Text Effects

The PhotoImpact 7 Type effects are a unique set of filters designed specifically for adding special effects and animation to text. These powerful effects can also be added to selections and objects, but you'll probably find yourself using them mainly for creating impressive text effects. For more information on effects, see Chapter 8.

As you learned in Chapter 8, the PhotoImpact Type effects are accessed by selecting Effect | Creative | Type. There are a total of 20 Type effects, such as Gradient, Emboss, Fire, Ice, Neon, and many more. Here, we will focus on how to use these effects in your animations.

Even if you had never heard of key frames before picking up this book, by now, you're probably getting comfortable with the concepts involved in using these powerful tools. The key frame control for the Type effects is the same as the one in the Animation Studio and effects dialog boxes you've seen so far in this chapter. Figure 13-6 shows the Type dialog box.

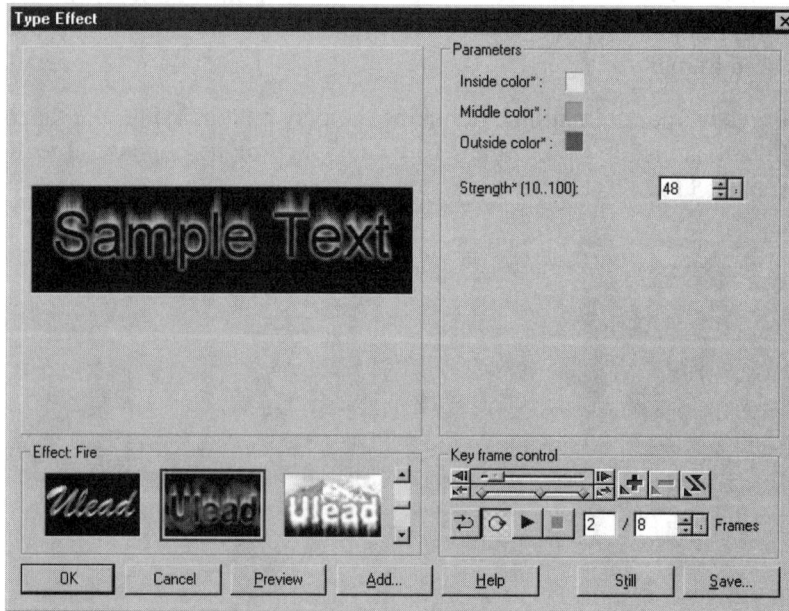

FIGURE 13-6   The Type dialog box

To create an animation with a Type effect, use the same techniques as described for creating key frame animation in the previous sections: Add text to an image with the PhotoImpact Text Tool, open the Type dialog box, select the effect you wish to use, and apply that effect to key frames, setting the various effect controls as desired.

Let's work through a short example using the Fire effect. The default Fire animation uses a value of 30 in the first key frame and 50 in the last key frame. For the sake of adding a little more variety to this animation, you'll add some key frames and change some settings. Select your text object and follow these steps:

1. Select Effect | Creative | Type to open the Type dialog box.

2. Click the Fire effect in the effects list.

3. To shorten the length of this animation, enter **8** in the total frames text box. This should be more than sufficient to display the effect.

4. Leave the first key frame set to 30. Add a key frame near the middle of the image and set its value to 100, and then set the value of the last key frame to 40.

5. Click the play button to preview the animation. As you can see in the following illustration, the animation appears to moves "full circle"—in this case, from low intensity to high intensity and then back to low intensity. The animation moves smoothly when it reaches its last frame and then begins playing its first frame again.

13

> **TIP** *If you're creating an animated banner for a web page, keep in mind that you should use a background color in your image that's similar (or even better, identical to) the background color of your web page. This will enhance how well the (often sharp) edges of text are able to blend into the web page's background.*

If you want to save your key frame settings, click the Add button in the Type dialog box, and then click Add Animation. If you've created this image on a solid-color background, as shown in this example, and you want to save the animation as a GIF file (instead of as a sequence of bitmaps), try turning off the Dithering option. The Dithering option is recommended when your background image is a photograph, but on a solid-color background, it should not be needed. Click the Save button to export your GIF file (or your bitmap sequence if you chose the BMP option).

Animate with Lighting Effects

PhotoImpact's Lighting filters are among the most spectacular plugin sets that you'll find on the market. The Lighting filters are used to create digital versions of real-world lighting spotlights and fireworks. Perhaps the most impressive feature of these very realistic effects is that they can be animated. Instead of simply showing a bolt of lightning on a background image, your animation can show lightning as it emerges from a cloud, branches out as it reaches its target, hits its target, and then disappears back into the clouds.

Use a Lighting Effect

To create a Lighting animation, select a photograph or other image, downsize it if necessary, and select Effect | Creative | Lighting. You'll notice that the Lighting dialog box, shown in Figure 13-7 looks similar to the Crystal dialog box.

Choose a Lighting Effect   In the Lighting effects list, you can choose from ten effects:

- ■ **Lightning**   Creates lightning bolts, complete with realistic branching and forking patterns.

- ■ **Fireworks**   Creates completely customizable animated fireworks, beginning with the fireworks bursting open in the sky, and ending with the fireworks leaving a faint light trail as they disappears into the darkness.

- ■ **Lens Flare**   Creates an effect similar to that caused by a bright light, such as a flash bulb or the sun, being captured by a camera.

- ■ **Light Bulb**   Creates a brilliant light with spikes emanating from the light's center (perhaps this filter should have been named star burst).

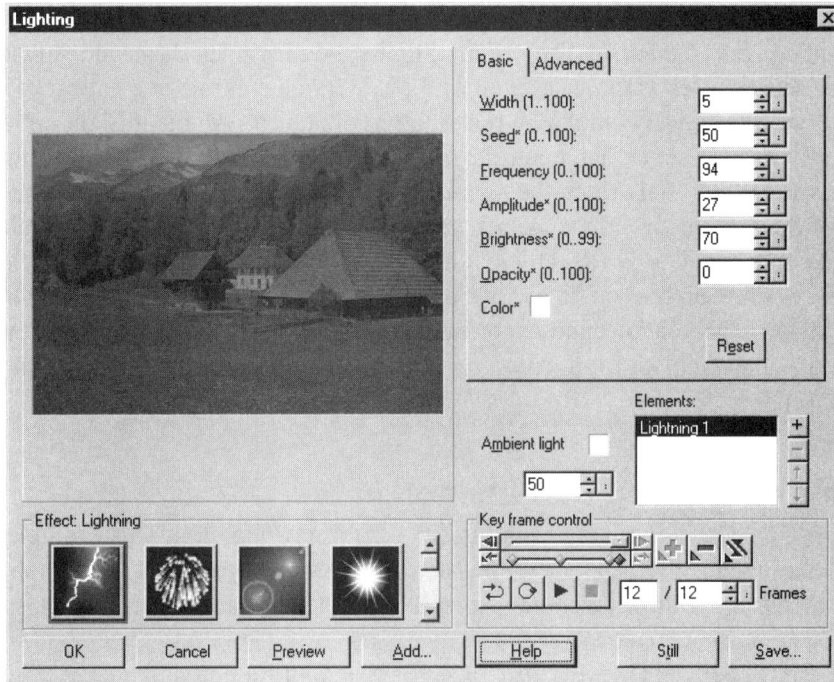

FIGURE 13-7   The Lighting dialog box

■ **Halo**   Creates a halo, with a light appearing in the center of the effect and a halo-like ring surrounding the center. The brightness and radius of both the sun (the center) and the halo can be adjusted independently of each other.

■ **Spotlight**   Creates a spotlight when the base of the effect is located at the top of the image and aiming downward. It can also be used to create a searchlight effect, when the base of the effect is located at the bottom of an image and the light is aiming upward.

■ **Flashlight**   Creates an intense lighting effect, with light decreasing at an angle, just as light does when its source is a flashlight bulb.

■ **Meteor**   Creates a thin, brightly lit line with diffused edges.

■ **Comet**   Creates a bright comet head with a wide, highly diffused tail. An Ionic Deviate option creates the look of gases off the comet's tail.

13

■ **Laser**   Uses a gradient color pattern to create a linear or spiral laser effect.

Set Lighting Effect Options   The Lighting dialog box includes Basic and Advanced tabs for setting effect options, as well as the key frame control for creating your animation. Like the Crystal dialog box, it also contains an Ambient Light option and an Elements list box and controls, for working with multiple Lighting effects.

As with the Crystal effect, the Ambient Light controls allow you to change the color of the lighting or reduce the general brightness of your image. By default, the Lighting effects will lower the ambient lighting in your image to a value of 50, since the effects show up best on darker backgrounds. You can adjust this level by using the Ambient Light text box and Ambient Light color box. A value of 100, with white selected as the Ambient Light color, causes no changes to be made to your image's ambient lighting.

Create a Lightning Bolt Animation

As an example, you'll use the Lightning effect for an animation. This example uses a photograph with a countryside estate, but you can open any photograph in PhotoImpact. Folllow these steps to add lightning to your image:

1. Select Effect | Creative | Lighting to open the Lighting dialog box.

2. Click the Lightning effect in the effects list. PhotoImpact places the lightning bolt fairly close to the center of your image.

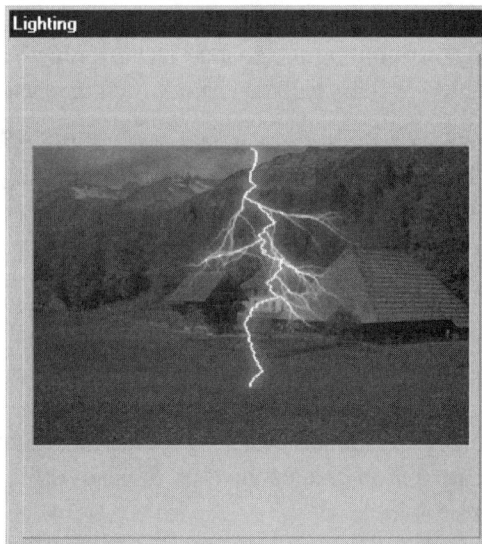

3. Set the total frames to 12.

4. Drag and drop the top part of the lightning bolt to a new location, near the top of the image. Then drag and drop the bottom of the bolt so that it's fairly close to the top of the bolt. This will set the way that the lightning bolt looks as it begins to emerge from the clouds.

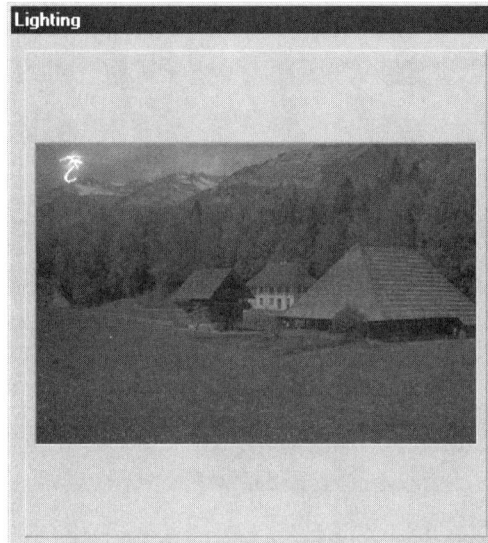

5. Remove the last key frame (the one with the lightning bolt in the middle of the screen). If you left it in, the lightning bolt would look very unnatural. It would appear to hop across the screen from left to right, instead of following a natural downward path.

6. Add two key frames: one at the middle of the animation (in frame 6) and one at the end of the animation (in frame 12). The second key frame will be used to define the lightning bolt at the point when it's closest to the ground, and the third key frame will define the lightning bolt as it disappears back into the clouds.

You could drag and drop the lightning bolt in all thee key frames into its correct position. However, by setting the position in the first key frame, and then deleting and adding key frames, you automatically set the bolt in the same position for all three key frames. Although you will be manipulating the position of the bottom of the lightning bolt, you won't be manipulating the position of the top of the lightning

13

bolt. Removing and then adding key frames in the manner described here ensures that the top of the lightning bolt will always be in the exact same place, so you won't need to be concerned with dropping the lightning bolt in all three key frames into exactly the same place, since it already is in the same spot.

1. Move to the second key frame, and drag and drop the bottom of the lightning bolt to the position where you want it to strike.

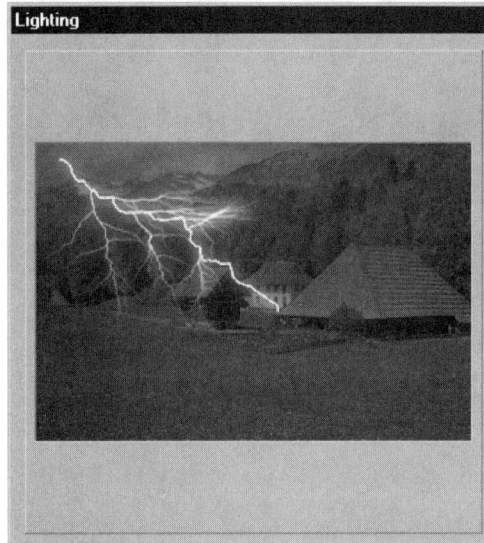

2. Click the play button to preview your animation. You'll see that you have a realistic bolt of lightning, with one exception: It never disappears. An adjustment needs to be made so that the lightning maintains its brightness in its second-to-last frame, but then disappears entirely in its last frame.

3. Move to the last key frame, which is also the last frame in the animation. Drag the key frame to the left one frame, so that it is now located in the second-to-last frame (the eleventh frame).

4. Add a key frame to the last framc. Set the lightning's Opacity to 0. This will have the effect of making the lightning transparent, and thus turned off in the animation's last frame.

You'll continue with this example in the next section, which describes how to use multiple Lighting effects in an animation.

Create a Multiple Lighting Effect Animation

By using multiple Lighting effects, you can enhance the realism of your animation or produce other special effects. Using multiple Lighting effects works the same as using multiple Crystal effects, as described earlier in this chapter. Just click the plus button next to the Elements list box and click the effect you wish to add. Remember that clicking the down arrow places the effect *in front of* the other effect.

To experiment with multiple lighting effects, you can continue with the lightening bolt example. When lightning hits a target, it usually emits a bright flash of light. The Light Bulb effect is excellent for creating such a flash. The Light Bulb effect settings include Range and Strength options, which you can use to adjust the strength of the bulb. The Range control affects the width of the light bulb flash. The Strength control affects the brightness of the middle of the flash.

Add the Light Bulb effect as follows:

1. In the Lighting dialog box, click the plus button next to the Element list box and click the Light Bulb icon in the effects list.

2. Move to the sixth frame of the animation, which is the animation where the lightning strikes, and drag and drop the Light Bulb effect to the exact same location.

3. Change the Range setting from its default of 20 to 35. Change the Strength control from its default of 100 to 150. You'll now have a very bright flash for when the lightning strikes its target.

13

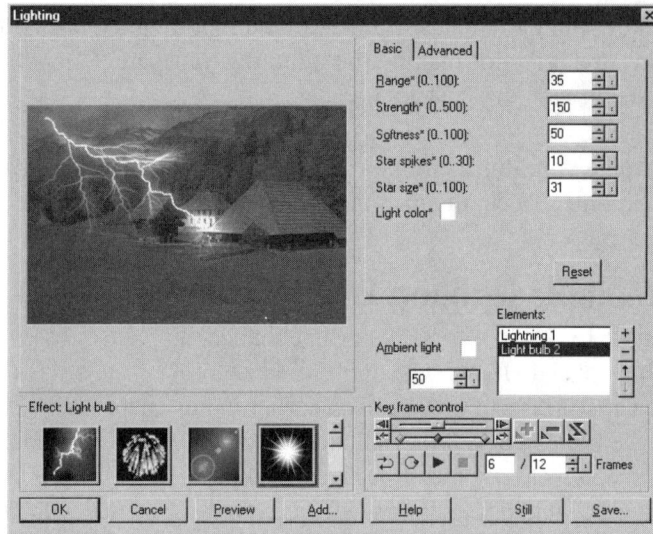

4. Click the play button to preview your animation. You'll see that there's only one problem here: The light bulb flash is present throughout the animation. You must find a way to turn off the light bulb until the lightning strike.

5. Move to the first frame of the animation, and set the light bulb's Strength to 0.

6. Move to the frame right before the lightning strike (frame 5), and again set the Strength to 0. (Note that when you make a change to a non-key frame, it automatically becomes a key frame, so you can skip the step of clicking the plus button to add it.)

The two changes just described will essentially create a pause in the light bulb, from the first frame until just before the lightning strikes, it will be completely invisible. Then, when the lightning strikes, the light bulb will suddenly turn on at the exact same moment. Since the flash would disappear almost immediately in real life, that effect should now be added to the animation.

7. The lightning strikes and light bulb turns on in frame 6, so move to frame 8, and turn the light bulb off again by setting its Strength to 0.

8. Move to the last frame (frame 12) and confirm that this key frame also uses a Strength of 0.

9. Click the play button to preview your animation. You'll likely find that the Light Bulb effect adds an impressive touch of realism to the bolt of lightning. By taking these extra steps, you've added another pause to the bulb effect. The light bulb will now be turned off in frames 1 through 5, bright in frame 6, dim in frame 7, and then turned off again for frames 8 through 12.

This has been the most complex animation you've created thus far, because it contains nine key frames. Four key frames are used to define the bolt of lightning, and five are used to define the flash from the light bulb. You're now ready to save the key frame settings by clicking the Add button and to export the animation using the Save button. If you're concerned about the lightning being turned off for too short a period of time at the end of the animation, you can adjust the amount of time that the last frame is displayed by opening the animation (or sequence of bitmap images) in Ulead GIF Animator, which will be discussed in the next two chapters.

Now let's take our experimentation one step further with a more complex combination of Lighting effects.

Create a Complex Key Frame Animation

Now that you have been introduced to the various effects useful for key frame animation, you're ready to try your hand at creating a more complex animation. In this example, you will use a combination of Lighting effects to create animated fireworks, including Fireworks, Meteor, and Lens Flare effects. Find or create an image to use as the background for the animation and downsize it if needed. This example uses a photograph of a ship at night.

Use the Fireworks Effect   You'll begin by adding fireworks to your background. On the Basic tab for the Fireworks effect, you'll find a setting labeled Completeness, which you'll use in this exercise. Completeness sets the amount that the fireworks have completed in their cycle. You can set your fireworks to look as though they've just appeared in the sky (by setting Completeness to 0), somewhere in the process of going off (with a Completeness setting of more than 0 and less than 100), or complete with the light they created fading away (with a Completeness setting of 100). Follow these steps:

1. Select Effect | Creative | Lighting. Click the Fireworks effect.

2. Click the first key frame icon. To set the point in the background image where you would like the fireworks to begin displaying, drag and drop the fireworks in the preview window.

3. Set Completeness to 0 for the first key frame of the animation.

4. If you would like to make changes to the sun and star colors of the fireworks, this is the best time to do so, because all of the following key frames will adopt your new colors automatically.

5. Once you're satisfied with the colors, click on the last key frame to delete it.

6. Add a new key frame in the last frame of your animation. This process will enable the last key frame to take on the position and colors of the first key frame.

7. Set the Completeness option for the last key frame to 100.

8. Preview the initial animation by clicking the play button.

Add the Meteor Effect   To add realism to the animation, it would be nice to create the effect of the fireworks being launched into the sky. You can accomplish this with the Meteor effect.

1. In the Lighting dialog box, click the plus (+) button next to the Element list box and then click the Meteor icon.

2. Set the Brightness option for the meteor to at least 50, so that you can see it well.

3. Delete the last key frame.

4. The meteor will now appear at an angle. To adjust the meteor so that it appears as though it's being launched from the ground into the sky, set the Angle option on the Basic tab to 270.

5. Move the meteor so that it's directly under the fireworks and the tip of the meteor is actually below the preview window, as shown in Figure 13-8.

6. The meteor will be used to create the effect of the fireworks launching, but since the fireworks are already visible, they'll need to be turned off for the first few frames of this animation.

7. Click Fireworks in the Elements list box and change the Brightness option to 0 in both the first and third frame of the animation.

8. Set the Brightness option to its default of 288 for the fourth frame. Set the Completeness option for the fourth frame to 0.

9. This will create a three-frame pause before the fireworks begin to animate. You'll use this pause area to create the effect of the fireworks being launched.

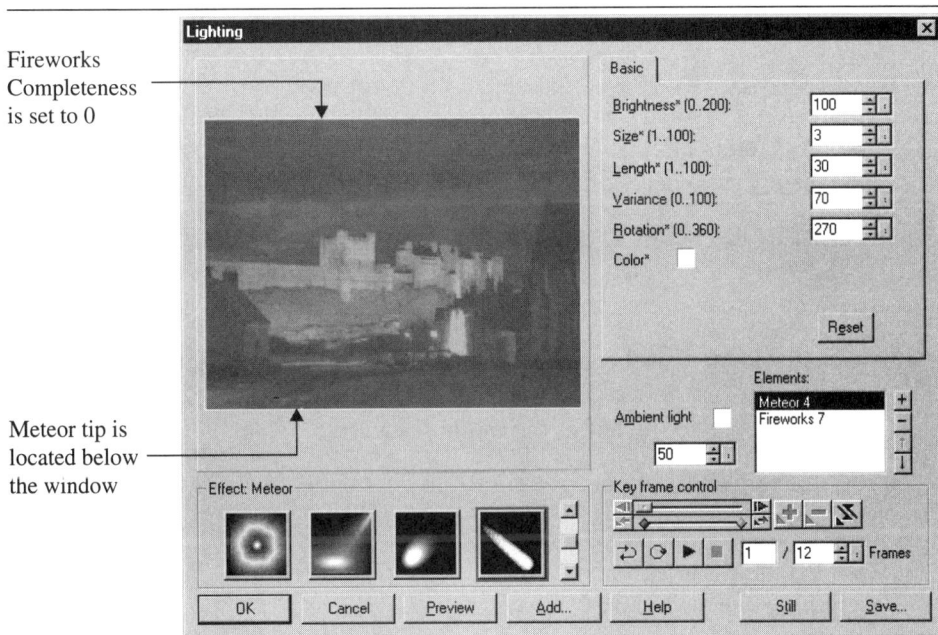

Fireworks Completeness is set to 0

Meteor tip is located below the window

13

FIGURE 13-8   The first frame of the animation, with both the Fireworks and Meteor effects invisible

10. Click Meteor in the Elements list box. Move to the fourth frame of the animation and drag and drop the meteor so that it's directly under the fireworks.

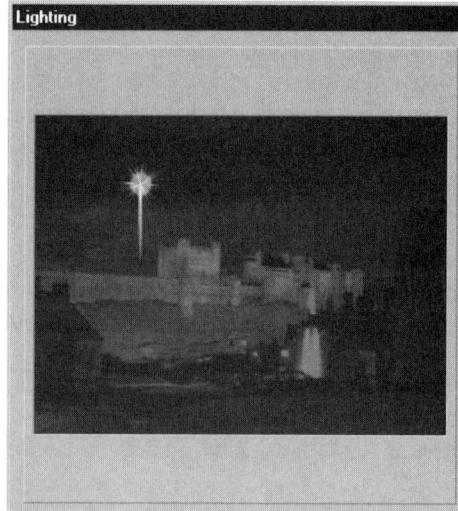

11. Set the Meteor effect's Brightness to 0 in the fifth and last frames so that the meteor disappears after the fireworks begin to display.

12. Click the play button to preview the animation. You'll see that in frames 1 through 4, the fireworks appear to be launching, and then in frames 4 through 12, the fireworks are being displayed.

13. Move to frame 5 of the animation and add two additional sets of Fireworks effects: one just below and to the right of the initial fireworks and another just below and to the left of the initial fireworks.

14. For the Fireworks effects, set the Brightness option to 0 for frames 1 through 4.

15. Set Brightness to 228 and Completeness to 0 for frame 5. This frame will have a triple burst of fireworks.

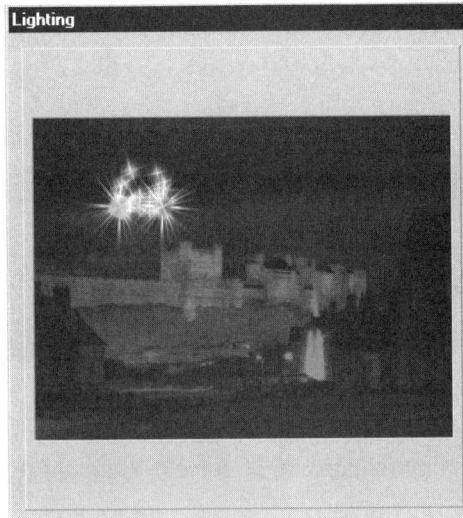

16. To balance the animation's appearance, add a fireworks and meteor set to the right side of the image, using the same settings as you did for the first fireworks and meteor set.

17. To add color variation to this set of fireworks, set the Hue Change option on the Basic tab to 90 for frame 4. This will cause a variety of firework colors to appear, regardless of the colors you have set in the Firework effect's color boxes. Your frame should look something like this one.

13

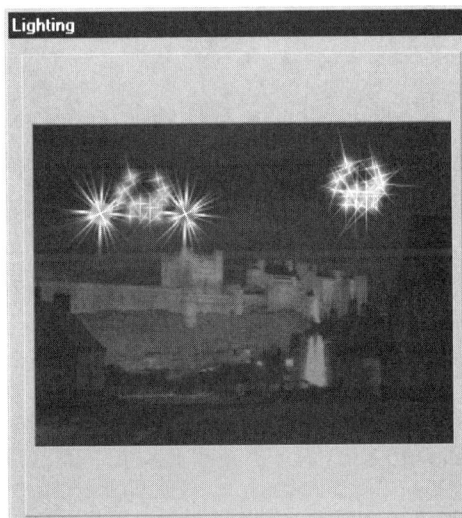

Add the Finishing Touches with the Lens Flare Effect   You can use the Lens Flare effect to add a nice finishing touch to the fireworks that you just added to this animation.

1. Click the plus (+) button next to the Elements list box and click the Lens Flare icon.

2. Set the Intensity option to 0 for frames 1 and 3, to turn off the lens flare while the fireworks are launching.

3. Drag and drop the lens flare to place it directly behind the new set of fireworks for frame 4 of the animation.

4. Delete the last key frame, and then add a new key frame in the last frame so that the lens flare remains in the same position throughout the animation.

5. Set the Intensity and Strength options to 50 for frame 4 of the animation. The lens flare will appear to be part of the fireworks, since it will "light up" at exactly the same time as the fireworks begin to display.

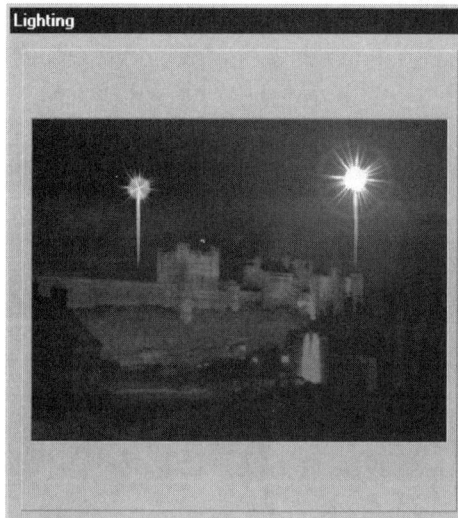

6. Move to frame 8 and set both Size and Intensity to 0.

7. Confirm that Size and Intensity are both set to 0 in the last frame. This will cause the lens flare to appear as though it were a natural part of the explosion

that begins the display of fireworks and then quickly disappears, so that it does not distract attention from the fireworks display.

8. Click the Advanced tab for the Lens Flare effect. Be sure that the Extra Strength option is set to 0 throughout the animation. Extra Strength can create a nice reflection effect, but it won't look realistic when the lens flare is used with a fireworks effect.

9. Click the play button to preview your fireworks animation. A frame-by-frame look is shown next.

You should now have a thorough knowledge of how key frames work and how to use them effectively. In the next section, you'll learn to create storyboard animations.

Create Storyboard Animations

The concept behind storyboard animation is similar to that of key frame animation: You set certain frames of the animation to look a certain way, and PhotoImpact fills in the "in-between" frames. However, in storyboard animation, instead of setting key frames, you drag and drop image thumbnails onto a storyboard. These thumbnails perform the same function as key frames.

In a PhotoImpact storyboard animation, the animation filter enables you to create the special effect that will be in each storyboard image, simply by setting controls in the filter's interface. Just as with key frame animation, storyboard animation requires at least two storyboard frames: one at the beginning and one at the end of the animation. When you use a storyboard filter, the number of frames is selected when you save the file.

PhotoImpact 7 offers three sets of effects that allow you to use the storyboard method of animation:

- Creative Warp creates animated kaleidoscope patterns from any still image.

- Transform is used to paint various distortion effects onto your image, such as diffusion, smear, and squeeze.

- Artist Texture, sometimes referred to as "digital tie dye," is used to create striking patterns of moving colors.

Create a Creative Warp Animation

The Creative Warp filter essentially works as a morphing filter, changing an image from its original appearance to a completely new, highly distorted appearance. It offers 21 pattern templates that may be used to apply changes to an image. As you add more thumbnails, more morphing is applied to the animation. In order to avoid distorting your image so much that it becomes unrecognizable, it's a good idea to use only two or three thumbnails per animation.

To begin using the Creative Warp filter, select an image in PhotoImpact and choose Effect | Creative | Creative Warp. Click the Advanced button to access the storyboard, as shown in Figure 13-9.

> **NOTE** *When in Advanced mode (animation mode), the Advanced button becomes the Normal button. To close the storyboard and select a pattern to apply to a single image (instead of creating an animation), click the Normal button.*

The image on the left displays the original image from PhotoImpact. The image on the right shows a preview of the image after one of the template effects has been applied. Directly under these images you'll find the pattern template list. You can experiment with the templates by clicking a template icon and examining the preview image.

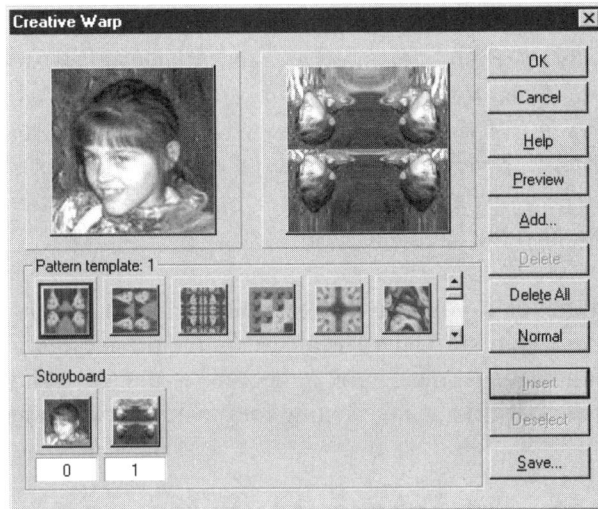

FIGURE 13-9   The Creative Warp dialog box

To add a thumbnail to the storyboard, double-click the preview image. Then drag and drop the preview image into the storyboard or click the Insert button.

NOTE   *You cannot add thumbnails while another thumbnail is selected. If you are experiencing problems adding thumbnails to the storyboard, make certain that none of the storyboard thumbnails are selected by clicking the Deselect button.*

13

If you want to delete the currently selected storyboard thumbnail, click the Delete button. The Delete All button is used to remove all thumbnails from the storyboard.

To add the original image to the animation, click the Delete All button and double-click the preview window. Since the Delete All button must be clicked first, the original image may be added only as the first frame in the animation.

| TIP | *Since the original image cannot be added as the final thumbnail image, this may seem to make a "full circle" animation impossible. Fortunately, there is a workaround. When saving your image, check the Open with Ulead GIF Animator box at the bottom of the Save As dialog box. Select the images in GIF Animator and choose Frame | Duplicate Frames. Then select Frame | Reverse Frame Order | Reverse the Order of the Selected Frames. The animation will appear to go from no distortion, to full distortion, then back to no distortion every time it loops.* |

Click the Add button if you want to save your current storyboard settings to the EasyPalette. To save your storyboard as a GIF animation or bitmap sequence, click the Save button. The Save As dialog box is the same as the one for saving key frame animation, except that it contains the setting for the number of frames.

Animate with the Transform Filter

The Transform filter is a morphing-based filter that enables you to gradually move images from one distortion effect to another. To create a Transform animation, select an image in PhotoImpact and click Effect | Creative | Transform. This opens the Transform dialog box, shown in Figure 13-10.

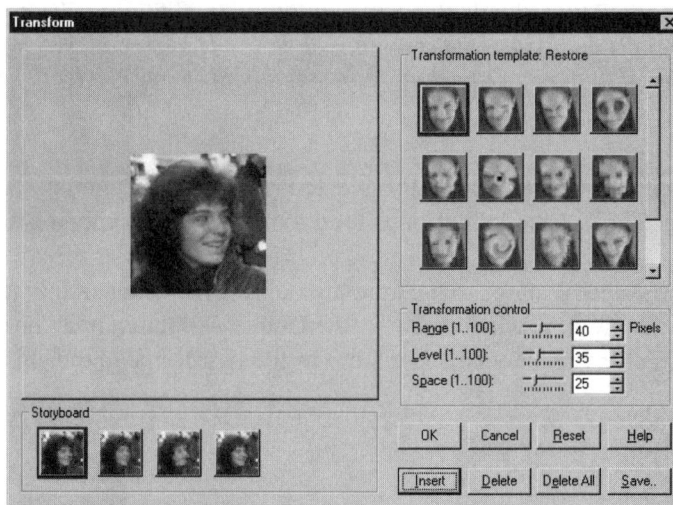

FIGURE 13-10   The Transform dialog box

Choose a Transformation Template

Next to the preview window is the transformation template list. You can choose from 12 transformation template effects:

- **Smudge**   Scatters pixels into a wider area than they would normally occupy. The effect is similar to running your finger over wet paint or wet ink.

- **Pinch**   Squeezes pixels closer together. This transformation gets its name from the fact that it resembles the effect seen on a piece of paper if you were to pinch it: the ink in the pinched area would be pulled into a smaller area than it originally occupied.

- **Punch**   Spreads pixels further apart. This is essentially the opposite of the Pinch template.

- **Ripple**   Creates the appearance of looking at an image through a rippled surface such as water.

- **Stone**   Creates the appearance of flattening bumps in an image, as though they were crushed by a stone.

- **Mirror**   Creates a mild mosaic effect, somewhat like looking at a highly reflective surface.

- **Horizontal Mirror**   A variation on the mirror effect, which adds a mild horizontal pinch as it moves pixels closer together.

- **Vertical Mirror**   Similar to the horizontal mirror effect, except that it adds a mild vertical pinch instead of horizontal pinch effect.

- **Whirlpool**   Applies a swirl effect to your image, where pixels appear to move toward a center point.

- **Diffuse**   Applies a scattering effect, as though looking at an image through translucent glass, such as a shower door.

- **Horizontal Squeeze**   Applies a strong pinch effect, as though the sides of the image were being squeezed closer together.

- **Vertical Squeeze**   Similar to the Horizontal Squeeze effect, except that the image appears as though its top and bottom are being squeezed closer together.

13

When using the Transform filter, all of the effects, except for Horizontal Squeeze and Vertical Squeeze, are painted on the image using a paintbrush tool.

Set Transformation Controls

Underneath the template icons are a group of settings that control how each effect is applied:

- Range is used to control how much of the image is painted with each brush stroke.

- Level controls the intensity of each brush stroke.

- Space controls the distance between the center of each stroke.

The controls are slightly different when using the Vertical Squeeze and Horizontal Squeeze templates, since these effects are applied to the entire image, instead of being painted on the image. Both of these tools have two settings: Level, which controls the strength of the effect, and Effect, which controls the angle of the effect.

Add Thumbnails to the Storyboard

To add thumbnails to the storyboard, click the thumbnail and then click Insert. Since the Transform effects are not quite as intense as the Creative Warp effects, you can usually add from three to five thumbnails without causing excessive distortion. To finish your animation without an effect, click the Reset button and then click the Insert button. The Delete button deletes the currently selected thumbnail, and the Delete All button deletes all of the thumbnails.

Here is a frame-by-frame view of the Transform filter's Diffuse and Ripple effects in action.

Create an Artist Texture Animation

The Artist Texture filter is used to create spectacular color animation. The colors in the Artist Texture fill start out as gradient patterns similar to those found in the Magic Gradient effect. The colors are then applied to one of 21 templates, which blend the gradient colors in kaleidoscope-like designs. From each template, six color patterns are created, any (or all) which may be added to the storyboard as a thumbnail. These thumbnails are then used to create a bitmap sequence and/or GIF animation.

Artist texture animation is sometimes used on its own, and can also be used as an animated fill for objects such as buttons or text and can also be used to create animated backgrounds.

> **NOTE** *If you choose to create an animated background, it's best to do so for a small area of your site, such as a navigation frame. Heavy use of animated backgrounds can be distracting to your audience.*

To access the Artist Texture filter, select Effect | Creative | Artist Texture. The Artist Texture dialog box is shown in Figure 13-11.

Select Colors and Patterns

To select colors, click the Edit button underneath the Palette Ramp on the left side of the dialog box. The Edit button opens the Palette Ramp Editor, which contains more than 100 preset gradient color patterns, as shown in Figure 13-12.

You can choose from any of the preset patterns or create your own by right-clicking a color block in the Palette Ramp Editor and selecting Change Color.

13

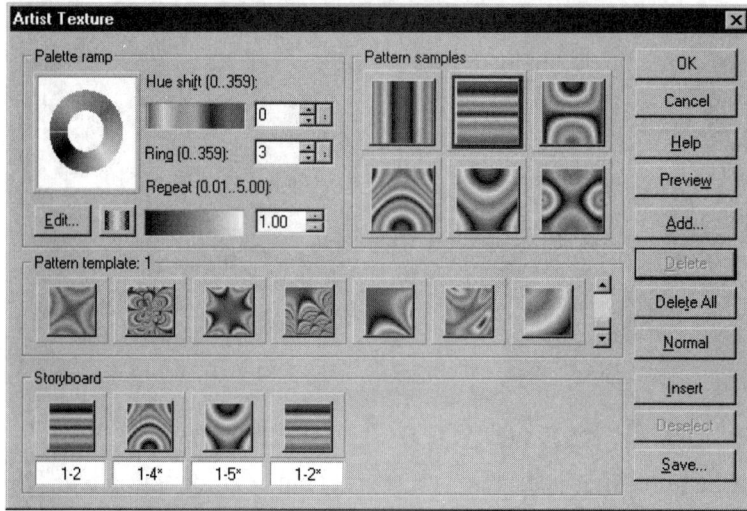

FIGURE 13-11   The Artist Texture dialog box

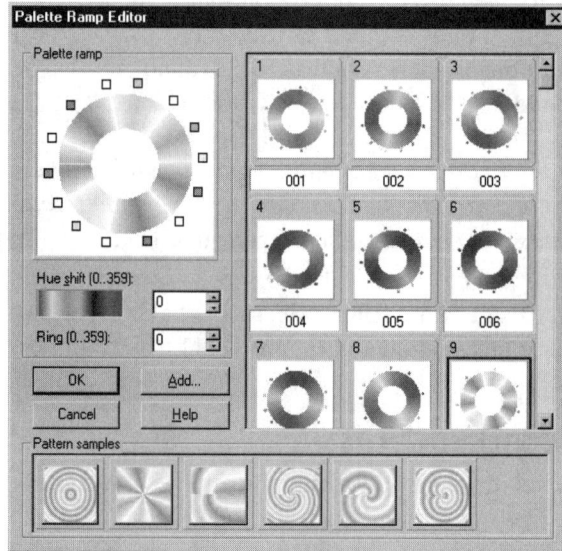

FIGURE 13-12   The Palette Ramp Editor dialog box

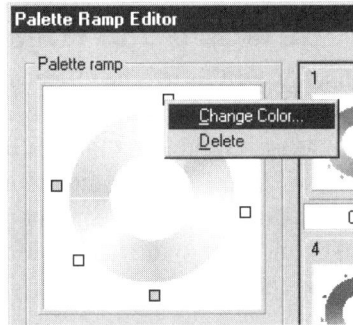

To add a newly created color pattern to the presets, click the Add button in the Palette Ramp Editor. When you've chosen a color gradient that you're satisfied with, click OK to return to the main Artist Texture dialog box.

Adjust Colors

From the Artist Texture dialog box, you can make additional changes to your selected colors, as follows:

- You can change the hue in the colors by dragging the Hue Shift slider in the Palette Ramp section or by setting a numerical hue value in the text box next to the slider.

- You can rotate the Palette Ramp by entering a new value in the Ring text box. Note that this does not change the colors, just the order in which they appear.

- You can set the number of times that the colors in the Palette Ramp are repeated by clicking the arrows next to the Repeat text box. For example, if you increase the repeat value from 1 to 2, the same colors will appear in your image, but the color pattern will be repeated twice. To make room for the twice as many color changes, colors will be squeezed closer together.

The grayscale display to the left of the Repeat box can give you a visual guide as to how closely together you're squeezing your colors.

NOTE *For values under 1 repeat, the grayscale display cannot accurately display your changes, although you'll still be able to see them in the sample patterns to the right of the Palette Ramp controls.*

13

Control How Colors Are Applied to Patterns

To the left of the grayscale display, you'll find the reflect control button. This button controls how colors are applied to the sample patterns. When the button is not pressed, colors are applied in a linear pattern (similar to that of a linear fill), from the first position on the color ramp to the last position on the color ramp. When the button is enabled, colors are applied in a circular pattern (similar to that of an elliptical fill), from the first position on the color ramp to the last position on the color ramp, and then back to the first position on the color ramp.

> **NOTE** *Applying color in a circular pattern while the repeat control is set to 1 is very similar to applying color in a linear pattern while the control is set to 2. Both have the effect of doubling the amount of times colors are displayed in the Palette Ramp.*

Choose a Pattern Template

The row of pattern templates below the Palette Ramp are the kaleidoscope-like designs that control how the colors of your Palette Ramp are displayed. Above the template display and to the right of the Palette Ramp, you'll find the six patterns that are created each time the colors of a Palette Ramp are applied to the design in a template. This Sample Pattern area is where you'll choose images to drag and drop into the storyboard.

Add Thumbnails to the Storyboard

Once you've selected a Palette Ramp, click the Advanced button to open the storyboard section of the interface. Click the default thumbnail in the storyboard and click Delete (it's usually best to start out with a clean slate instead of using the default thumbnail). When you delete the default thumbnail, the six sample patterns change considerably, from abstract kaleidoscope-like patterns to basic lines and curves. This is an what the Palette Ramp colors look like before being blended with any of the 21 templates.

> **TIP** *The ability to use Palette Ramp colors without using the templates is an undocumented feature of the Artist Texture filter. The result is more basic color patterns than the abstract and wildly colorful patterns usually created in the Artist Texture filter. When you require a color image that's a little more conservative than the Artist Texture filter generally allows, consider using this feature.*

Experiment with applying the various templates until you see a pattern in the Pattern Samples that you would like to use in your image. To add the pattern to the storyboard, click it, and then click Insert or drag and drop it into the storyboard. This first thumbnail image essentially acts as the first key frame of your storyboard animation.

Continue experimenting with templates until you find another pattern that you would like to use in your image, and then add the pattern to the storyboard. When you add patterns, you'll notice that each has a unique name, such as 1-3. The first number in this naming convention tells you which template was used to create the sample, and the second number tells you which of the six individual samples you selected.

When you're adding thumbnails, keep in mind the concept of animations going full circle for smooth looping. If you were to start with one pattern and end with another pattern, when the animation loops, it will not move smoothly from the last frame to the first frame. To achieve a full-circle effect, consider using identical first and last thumbnails.

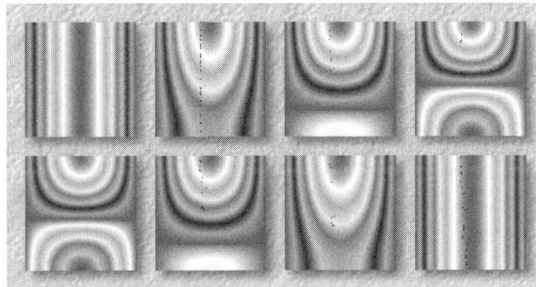

Animate a Text Fill

The Artist Texture filter quickly creates spectacular color patterns, but applying those color patterns to an animation is a bit more complicated than creating them. Perhaps the best way to make use of the Artist Texture colors is to use them as a fill for objects such as text, a technique which you'll learn more about in this section. Follow these steps to create a sequence of bitmaps to use as fills for text:

1. Create a text object in PhotoImpact. Since you're going to be filling the text with color patterns, it's best to use a font that has wide borders, so that there's plenty of room for displaying the fill. A font such as Arial Black

will generally work out well. In the example shown here, Arial Black size 48 is used.

2. Center the text object in your background image by selecting Object | Align | Center Both.

3. Open the Artist Texture dialog box by choosing Effect | Creative | Artist Texture.

4. Create an Artist Texture animation, using four storyboard thumbnails.

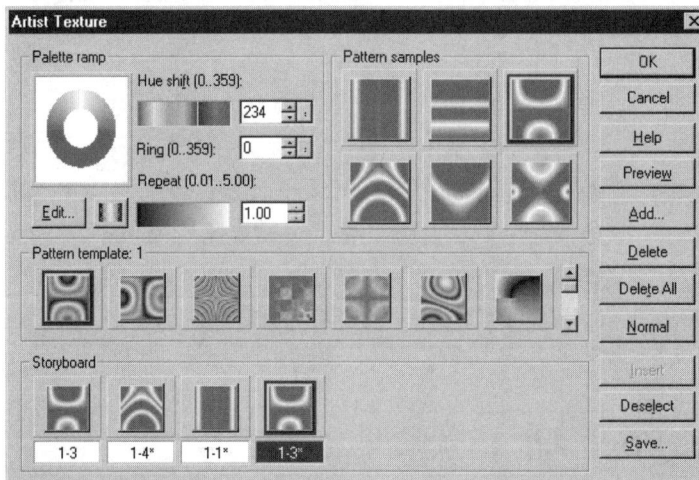

5. Click Add to add the storyboard to the EasyPalette and click Save. Specify 10 frames for this animation. Instead of exporting the frames as a GIF animation, save them as a sequence of bitmaps.

6. Open the ten bitmap images that you just created by choosing File | Open or File | Visual Open. Find the filename *.00001.bmp. The 00001 in the filename identifies it as the first frame of your animation.

7. Copy this file and click your text image. Select Edit | Paste | Fit into Selection to paste the bitmap into the text object. Save this file with a filename that identifies the frame number as frame 1 (such as File01.bmp).

8. The next part gets a little tedious, as sometimes happens when creating animation. Take each of the bitmap images, in numerical order, paste them into the text object and save the file. There will be a total of ten copy, paste, and save operations. Your final ten bitmaps should look like the ones shown here.

The frames are now ready to be opened in GIF Animator and saved as a GIF, Video, or Macromedia Flash file. In GIF Animator, you can open a sequence of bitmaps by clicking File | Add Images, selecting the images and clicking Insert as New Frames in the Add Image dialog box. Note that if the default frame size is different from the frame size of the images you added, you can correct this by clicking Edit | Resize Image. Delete the default blank frame that GIF Animator opened, and you're ready to convert your bitmap sequence into an animation.

13

As you've seen in this chapter, PhotoImpact's computer-driven key frame and storyboard animation methods offer significant productivity enhancement. They make the task of creating an animation less tedious and more enjoyable. In the next two chapters, you'll learn how to work with GIF animations using the impressive features of Ulead GIF Animator 5.

CHAPTER 14

Build Animation with GIF Animator

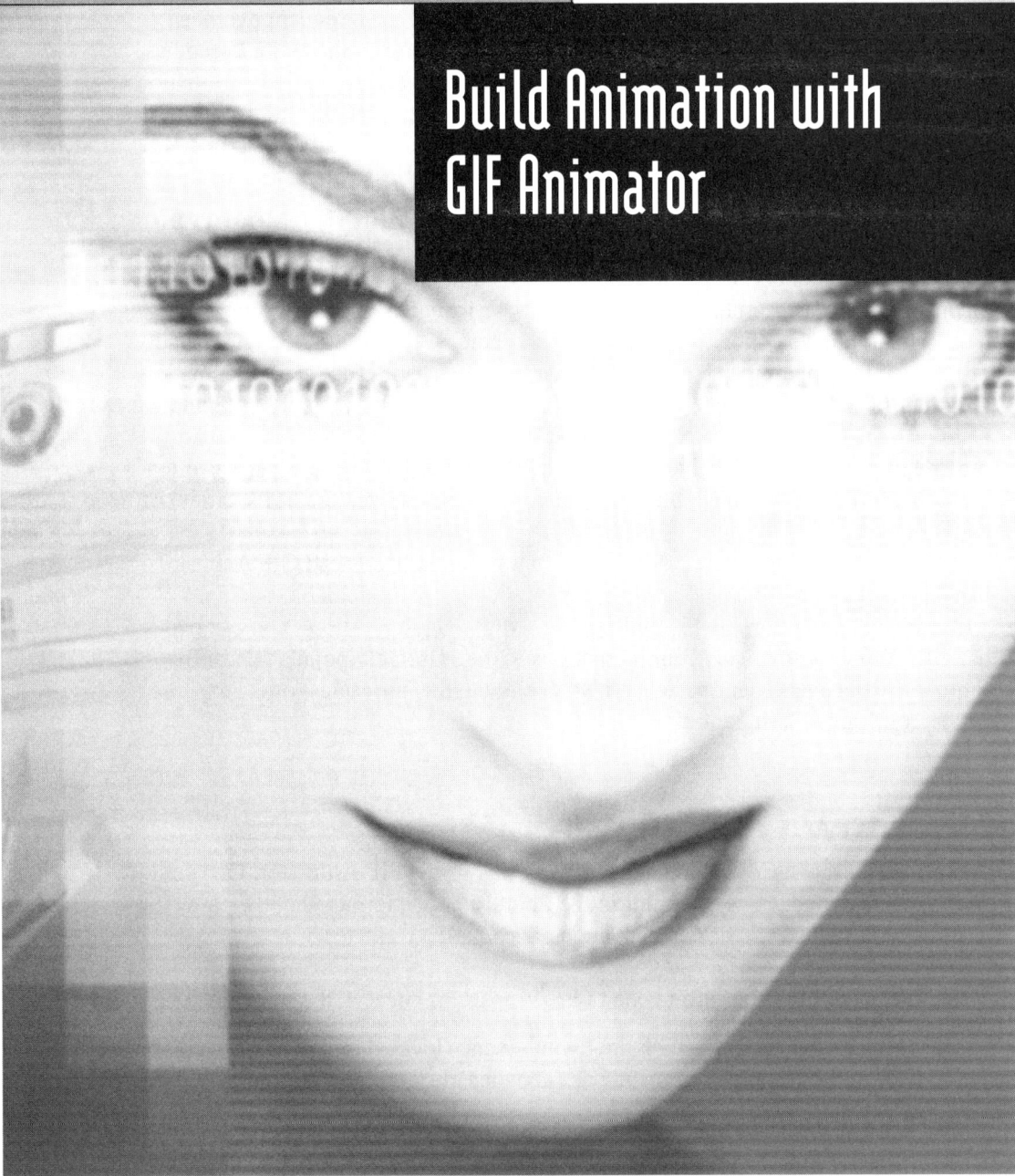

G IF animations are popular with animators because they offer a compact and convenient file format for storing multiple image frames in a single file, without resorting to a full-fledged movie format with all the attendant overhead. Since the time when GIF animations first began appearing on the Web, Ulead has lead the way in providing software for creating, editing, and saving GIF animation files with an emphasis on high quality and small file size. The tradition continues with the release of the industry-standard GIF animation tool, Ulead GIF Animator 5. GIF Animator ships with PhotoImpact, as a utility specifically designed to handle the unique task of working with animated GIF files.

Ulead's GIF Animator 5 is also available as a stand-alone product, making it popular among a broad spectrum of designers, even those who don't use PhotoImpact as their primary image editor. It's common for a dedicated fan of Adobe Photoshop or Jasc Paint Shop Pro to use Ulead's GIF Animator as their primary GIF animation program. In addition, complex 3D rendering programs such as Corel Bryce and Curious Labs Poser do an exceptional job of creating animated files, but do not provide tools for editing or fine-tuning animations. Users of those programs often bring their GIF animations into GIF Animator 5 to take advantage of its variety of editing tools.

In addition to being a state-of-the-art GIF animation utility, Ulead GIF Animator 5 handles other motion-based file types as well. GIF Animator can be used with a wide range of video formats, including AVI, MOV, QT, and MPG. You can even use GIF Animator to export your animations to the extremely popular Flash file format, without ever having to concern yourself with the intricacies (or the expense) of Macromedia's Flash editor.

Get to Know GIF Animator

PhotoImpact users have a unique advantage when using GIF Animator: GIF Animator's interface is very similar to the PhotoImpact interface that they are already comfortable using. You can launch Ulead GIF Animator 5 in several ways:

- Select Start | Programs | Ulead PhotoImpact 7 | Ulead GIF Animator 5.

- From PhotoImpact 7, click the Switch menu (located on the upper-right side of the PhotoImpact menu bar), and then click Ulead GIF Animator 5.0.

- From one of the PhotoImpact animation effects dialog boxes (Animation Studio, Artist Texture, Creative Warp, Lighting, Transform, and Type), click Save, and then click Open in GIF Animator in the Save As dialog box.

The Startup Wizard

The first time you open GIF Animator, you'll see the Startup Wizard, which assists you in beginning the process of creating or editing an animation, as shown in Figure 14-1. From here, you can choose to create a new animation, open existing files, or go to the online tutorial.

You can choose to create a GIF animation by using the Animation Wizard or by starting from scratch with a blank animation. The Animation Wizard provides step-by-step assistance with the process of creating a new animation. If you choose the Blank Animation option, you go directly to the GIF Animator interface. By default, a single-frame animation will open. You can then begin the process of adding frames to create an animation.

The Open section of the Startup Wizard dialog box offers choices for opening an existing image file (such as a BMP or JPEG file or an animated GIF file), an existing video file, or one of the sample animations that ship with GIF Animator. The Online Tutorial option takes you directly to the GIF Animator page on Ulead's Web based Learning Center, where you'll find a series of online tutorials.

If you don't want to use the Startup Wizard with GIF Animator, select the "Do not show this dialog box next time" checkbox at the bottom of the Startup Wizard dialog box. If you decide later that you want to return to using the Startup Wizard, choose File | Preferences | General and select Enable Startup Wizard.

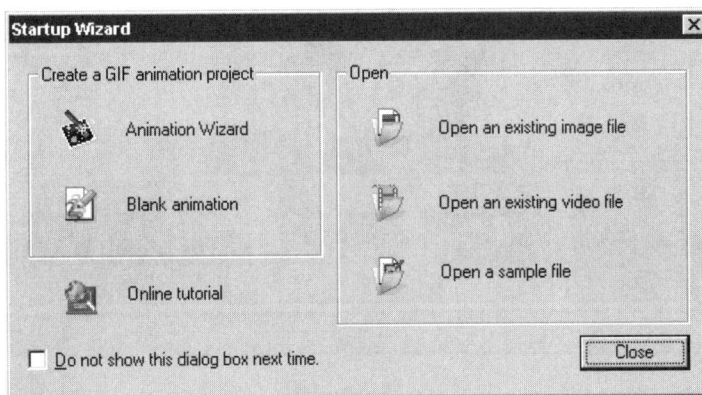

FIGURE 14-1   The GIF Animation Startup Wizard

The GIF Animator Window

Your animation images appear in the GIF Animator window, shown in Figure 14-2. This window has many of the same features as the PhotoImpact window.

Just as in PhotoImpact, the top area of the window contains a menu bar, a Standard toolbar, and an Attribute toolbar, and a Tool panel is located on the left side of the screen. The main work area, in the middle of the screen, is where you'll create and edit your animations. To the right of the work area is the Object Manager panel, which provides information on any objects that you add to your animation. The Frame panel, located near the bottom of the screen, provides information on the frames in your animation. (The Object Manager and Frame panels are both movable.) The status bar, located at the bottom of the screen, provides general status information, just as it does in PhotoImpact.

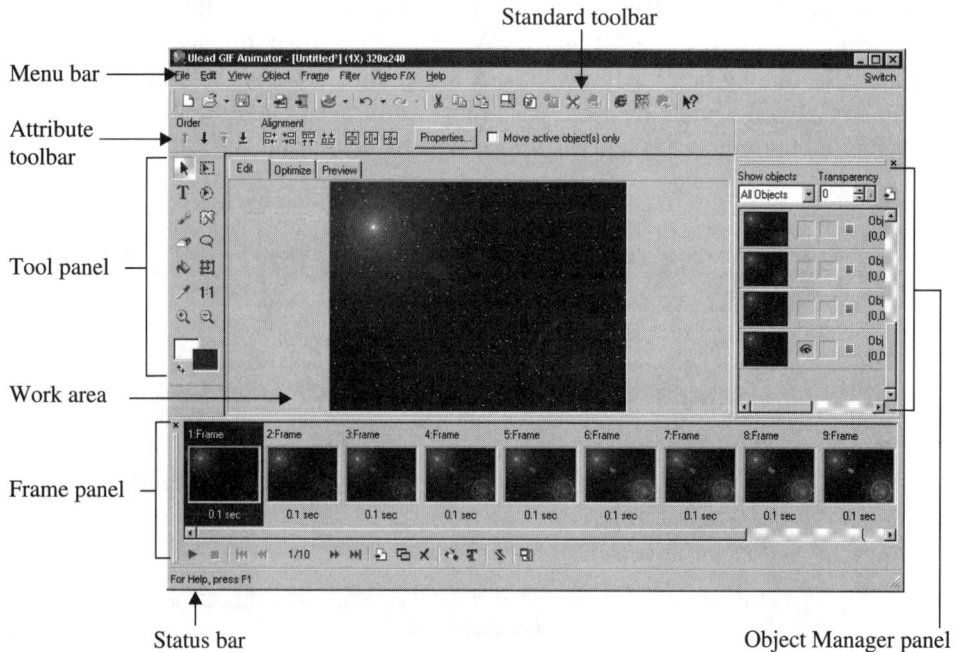

FIGURE 14-2   The GIF Animator window

NOTE   *If you don't see the toolbar or panel you're looking for, open the View menu, and make sure that the toolbar or panel is set to be visible. A visible toolbar or panel will have a checkmark to the left of its name.*

Notice that the GIF Animator work area has three tabs: Edit, Optimize, and Preview, which provide different views for working with your animation:

■ The Edit tab (see Figure 14-2) is used during the process of creating and editing an animation.

■ The Optimize tab is used to optimize your animation for use on the Web. Optimizing your animation is covered later in this chapter.

■ The Preview tab, shown in Figure 14-3, displays a preview of your animation. In this mode, most panels are hidden, so that more screen space is available for the preview.

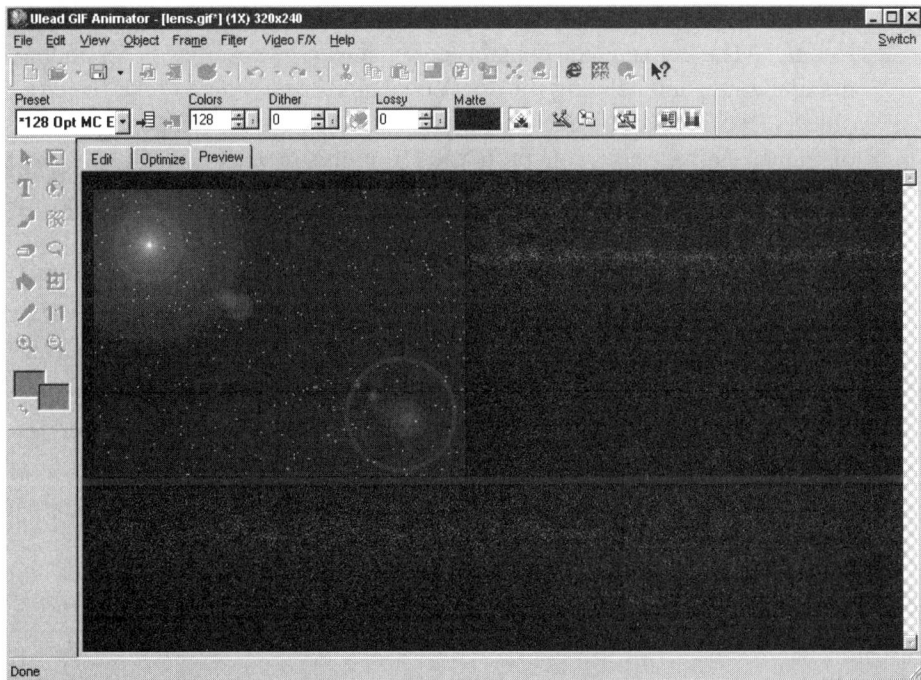

FIGURE 14-3   GIF Animator in Preview mode

The GIF Animator Menus

GIF Animator's menu structure is similar to the menu structure of PhotoImpact. The following menus are found in GIF Animator:

■ **File**   The File menu contains the usual commands for creating a new file, opening files, and saving files. You can also access GIF Animator program preferences, and the Animation and Optimization wizards from this menu.

■ **Edit**   The Edit menu contains undo, redo, cut, copy and paste commands, plus commands used for resizing and cropping animation files, and for using your favorite image editor with GIF Animator.

■ **View**   The View menu is used to access commands for previewing your animation, such as zoom and play, and for showing and hiding GIF Animator's toolbars and panels.

■ **Object**   The Object menu can be used to add, duplicate, trim, and delete objects. You can also access object properties and manipulate text objects from this menu.

■ **Frame**   The Frame menu contains commands used specifically for adding, manipulating, and deleting frames. You can also add banner text, tween objects, synchronize objects across frames, reverse and change the order of frames, and access frame properties from this menu.

■ **Filter**   The Filter menu is used to access third party filters (such as Kai's Power Tools) from within GIF Animator. Note that before you can access third party filters, you must tell GIF Animator where your third party filters are stored by clicking File | Preferences | Plug In Filters, and then shut down and reopen GIF Animator. Most of the popular "Photoshop Filters" (which use the *.8BF file format) will work quite well in both PhotoImpact and GIF Animator.

■ **Video F\X**   This menu is used to access GIF Animator's unique animation based effects filters. You'll learn more about using these powerful filters in Chapter 15, which is available online at www.osborne.com.

- **Help**   The Help Menu contains GIF Animators help tools, and enables access to the Startup Wizard, online tutorials and Ulead's Web site.

The GIF Animator Standard Toolbar

As you might expect, the GIF Animator standard toolbar is similar to the standard toolbar found in PhotoImpact. The standard toolbar contains buttons for frequently used commands such as creating a new file, opening and saving files, and adding images and videos to a file. See Figure 14-3.

The GIF Animator Attribute Toolbar

Just as it does in PhotoImpact, the GIF Animator attribute toolbar changes in accordance with the tool currently selected. The attribute toolbar, as it appears when you open GIF Animator (and when you have the Pick Tool selected) is shown in Figure 14-3.

The GIF Animator Tool Panel

The GIF Animator tool panel also bears resemblance to the PhotoImpact tool panel. The GIF Animator tool panel contains 17 tools:

- **Pick Tool**   Use to select and move objects.

- **Selection Tool, Rectangle**   Use to create rectangular selections, and to add or remove a rectangular shape from an already existing selection.

- **Text Tool**   Use to create and edit GIF Animator text.

- **Selection Tool, Ellipse**   Works in the same way as the rectangular selection tool, except that it uses an ellipse shape to create, add, or remove areas from selections.

- **Paintbrush Tool**   Use to add paint to an active object. Note that if an active object contains a selection, paint can only be added to the selection area.

- **Selection Tool, Magic Wand**   Use to create, add, or remove an area from a selection, based on color similarity.

14

- **Eraser Tool** Use to remove paint from an active object or selection. As with the paintbrush tool, if an active object contains a selection, only pixels within the selection area may be erased.

- **Selection Tool, Lasso** Use to create, add, or remove an area from a selection, using an irregular (non rectangular or non elliptical) shape.

- **Fill Tool** Use to fill selections with color.

- **Transform Tool** Enables you to rotate and resize objects by dragging and dropping them.

- **Eyedropper Tool** Use to select a color from an image and make it the GIF Animator foreground color.

- **Actual View** Use to view your image without any zoom applied.

- **Zoom In and Zoom Out** Use these two tools to alter your view of the image by zooming in or zooming out.

- **Background Color and Foreground Color** Clicking on either of these color boxes opens the Ulead Color Pickers, which can be used to set background and foreground colors.

- **Swap Color** This button is used to interchange foreground and background colors.

The GIF Animator Object Manager Panel

Objects are similar to what are commonly called *layers* in other image-editing programs, such as Adobe Photoshop and Jasc Paint Shop Pro. An object (or layer) floats above a background image and can be manipulated separately from it. Thus, an effect can be applied to objects without affecting the underlying background image; objects can be moved to any location or stacked on top of each other; and objects can possess a transparency level that reveals the background image. Although similar to layers, objects have a very clear advantage: Layers must be rectangles, but objects can take on any shape you desire.

In GIF Animator, use the Object Manager panel to work with the objects in your animations. This panel is discussed in the "Manipulate Objects" section later in this chapter.

The GIF Animator Frame Panel

As explained in Chapter 13, *frames* are the individual images which, when displayed one after another, create your animation. A static (still) image could be thought of as having only one frame, while an animation consists of two or more frames.

In GIF Animator, frames appear in the Frame panel along the bottom of the window. You can work with frames using the Frame panel buttons beneath the frames. Working with the Frame panel is covered later in this chapter, in the "Manipulate Frames" section.

Open Files in GIF Animator

Since Ulead GIF Animator 5 opens both static and animated images, you can use it to add animation to a static image or to edit a previously created animation file. For example, you may want to take a picture of a cityscape stored in JPEG format and add animated fireworks to it. Or, you may want to take an animation you created in another program and fine-tune it using GIF Animator's powerful optimization tools.

NOTE	*Most file formats are designed either to hold static images or to contain animation. The GIF format is an exception to this general rule, since GIF files can contain either a single image or an animation.*

Open Static Images

In addition to static GIFs, Ulead GIF Animator 5 opens files stored in a variety of other commonly used static file formats. These formats include the following:

- **BMP** (the default Windows graphics format)
- **JPEG/JPG** (a commonly used full-color Web format)
- **PCD** (Kodak's Photo Compact Disk format)
- **PNG** (a newer Web format, and Macromedia Firework's default format)
- **PSD** (Adobe Photoshop's default format)
- **PSP** (Jasc Paint Shop Pro's default format)
- **TGA** (a commonly used Windows and Macintosh format)
- **UFO** (Ulead PhotoImpact's default format)

14

The decision as to which image format to use when you're exporting an image from another program and plan on opening it in GIF Animator is actually much easier than it sounds. As a general rule, you should use your image editor's default file format (such as UFO for Ulead PhotoImpact, PSP for Jasc Paint Shop Pro, PSD for Adobe Photoshop, and PNG for Macromedia Fireworks). When you're using an image editor other than those listed above (such as Corel Bryce or Curious Labs Poser), BMP is generally the best format to use, since it's the default format for Windows. If you're familiar with the PNG format, you may want to use PNG instead of BMP, since PNGs take less storage space than BMPs.

> **TIP** *When working with Photo CD collections, Kodak's PCD format is the obvious choice for Kodak's impressive line of CD products. However, TGA is the best choice for the increasingly popular Hemera Photo Objects CDs.*

To open a static image in Ulead GIF Animator 5, select File | Open Image or press CTRL-O. You can also click Open an Existing Image File in the Startup Wizard dialog box that appears when you first open GIF Animator.

Open Animated Images

In addition to animated GIFs, Ulead GIF Animator 5 also opens a variety of other commonly used animation file formats, including the following:

- **AVI** (Audio Video Interleave, the default video format for Windows)
- **FLC, FLI,** and **FLX** (Autodesk animation formats)
- **MOV** and **QT** (default Macintosh video formats)
- **MPG** (a commonly used format on Windows and the Internet)

As a general rule, if you're working with a video format in another program and plan on exporting the video so that you can open it in Ulead GIF Animator, AVI is the best format to choose for your file, since this is Window's default video format.

> **NOTE** *Since it is used for image-based editing, GIF Animator does not support audio. If you require a video editor that includes audio support, you may want to check out Ulead's Video Studio (http://www.ulead.com/vs/) and Ulead's Media Studio Pro (http://www.ulead.com/msp/).*

To open a video in Ulead GIF Animator 5, select File | Open Video. You can also click Open an Existing Video File in the Startup Wizard dialog box.

Build Animations from Scratch

In this section, you'll learn animation from scratch, including the factors you should consider beforehand, so that your final animation is as small as possible, while still displaying the quality that you (and your audience) will expect.

Plan Your Animation

The most important decision that you'll make as you plan your animation is the selection of the animation's dimensions. You also need to consider the background and color for your animation.

Animation Size

Size is an important issue not only because of the slow speed of most Internet connections, but also because of the very nature of animations: They contain multiple images. A single image on your web site that's slightly bigger than it needs to be probably won't present much of a problem. However, when an animation is larger than it needs to be, every frame in the animation is affected. In a 20-frame animation, an image that's too big, multiplied by a factor of 20, goes from being a minor inconvenience to being a significant issue.

Over the last few years, some typical sizes have emerged for various types of animation. You may use these sizes as a guideline in determining the dimensions of your own animations:

14

- For web banners, 468 pixels wide by 60 pixels high (468×60) is a common size.

- For animations designed to display a logo or a photograph in the background, 160×120 has become popular, although dimensions up to 320×240 are commonly seen.

- Icons typically use dimensions of 16×16, 32×32, and 48×48.

■ Sizes for buttons vary quite a bit, but they generally have either square dimensions, such as 60×60, or are two to four times wider than they are high (for example, 60×30 or 120×30).

Of course, these are just general guidelines; your own artistic judgment is likely to serve you best in making size decisions.

Animation Backgrounds

In some animations, such as those where special effects are added to a photograph, a background image (the photograph) obviously must be used. However, if your animation doesn't really *require* a background design, you can reduce file size by using a solid color instead of a pattern.

In the illustration below, three background images are shown side by side for comparison. The image on the left is a simple black background, the image in the middle is a blue to black gradient, and the image on the right is a somewhat busy fractal pattern.

203 bytes   2,488 bytes   14,799 bytes

When converted to GIF format, the image on the left is just 203 bytes. The image in the middle is quite a bit larger at 2,488 bytes, but still small enough to download in less than 1 second on a 56Kbps connection. The image on the right weighs in at 14,799 bytes, even though its dimensions are the same as those of the other images. This doesn't mean that you couldn't use the image on the right in an animation. There's a technique called "removing redundant pixels" (which you'll learn more about later in this chapter, in the "Optimize Animations for the Web" section) that would help to minimize the size increase caused by this background. However, avoiding high-color backgrounds is something to consider whenever practical.

Choose a background color that's similar to your web page's background color. This will prevent the appearance of GIF *halos*, which occur when a GIF is created on one background color and displayed on another background color. Here are examples of a GIF image with a halo (on the left) and without a halo (on the right).

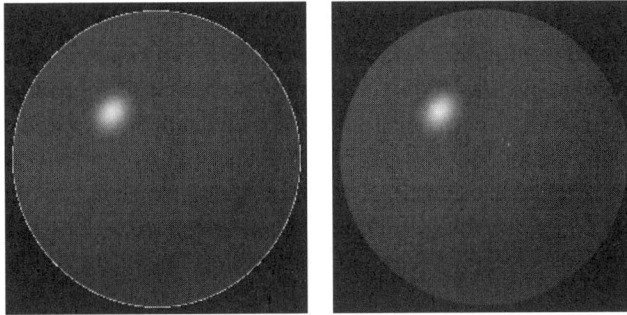

Create a New Animation

To begin building an animation from scratch, open Ulead GIF Animator 5 (from the Windows Start menu or the PhotoImpact Switch menu) and, if you're presented with the Startup Wizard, click Blank Animation. Next, select File | New or click the new icon on the far-left side of the Standard toolbar. The New File dialog box opens, as shown in Figure 14-4. Select the dimensions and background color for your animation, and then click OK.

The GIF Animator window appears in Edit mode, with the main work area set for the dimensions you selected. From here, you can create your new animation using GIF Animator's tools and menu options, as described in the "The GIF Animator Window" section earlier in this chapter.

Create a Banner Animation

Given the popularity of banner animation, Ulead has added a special banner animation module to GIF Animator 5 to simplify the process of building an animated banner. To create a banner animation, select Frame | Add Banner Text, click the Add Banner Text icon at the bottom of the Frame panel, or press CONTROL-ALT- B. You will see the Add Banner Text dialog box, as shown in Figure 14-5.

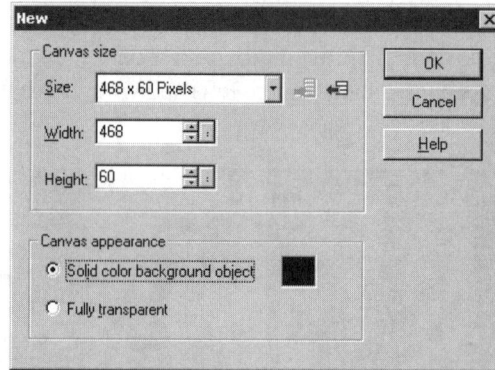

FIGURE 14-4   The New dialog box

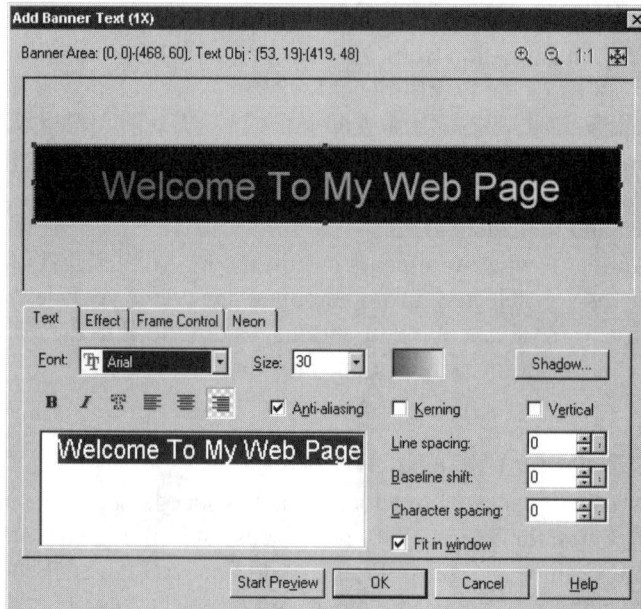

FIGURE 14-5   The Add Banner Text dialog box

What About Using Web-Safe Colors?

A great deal has been written about *web-safe colors* and why it's important to use them in GIF animations. Unfortunately for the readers of such material, the information is seriously outdated.

Web-safe colors refers to a palette of 216 colors that could be displayed accurately using the 8-bit (256 color) monitors and video cards that were common in the late 1980s and early 1990s. (The static GIF format was invented in 1987, and animation was added in 1989.) At the time, a serious problem existed: Most web site viewers had 8-bit monitors and video cards, but many designers were willing to pay top dollar for high-end 16-bit (65,536 color) monitors and video cards. As a result, designers weren't seeing the same thing that their viewers were seeing.

When an 8-bit system came across one of the over 65,000 colors that it couldn't display, it substituted the color with the closest match from its 256-color palette. Sometimes, a designer would get lucky: The colors he or she used would be so close a match to the standard 256 colors, that viewers wouldn't notice the difference. Other times, the results were disastrous: Colors that the designer carefully selected would get replaced with a neutral color such as white or gray.

As a result, designers started using only the web-safe colors. By doing this, designers severely limited the number of colors available when creating an image, but they were able to ensure that the colors seen on their monitors would be the same colors seen on their viewers' monitors. When this approach was created, it made sense. However, now that most of the web-surfing public can see (at least) 65,536 colors, the web-safe colors approach is quite outdated.

Sometimes, the terms *Microsoft Internet Explorer palette* and *Netscape palette* are used instead of the term *web-safe palette*. Microsoft and Netscape haven't agreed on a lot of things over the years, and the issue of color is no exception. While Microsoft chose to number their web-safe colors starting with black and ending with white, Netscape chose to start with white and end with black. What effect does this have on you and your audience? None. It's the same 216 colors, displayed in exactly the same way.

14

The Add Banner Text dialog box has four tabs with settings for creating your banner text:

- The Text tab is used to add text to the banner and to format the appearance of the text.

- The Effect tab lets you apply special transition effects to your text.

- The Frame Control tab is used to set the speed of your animation.

- The Neon tab enables you to add the effect of a neon glow surrounding the text.

Each tab includes a preview window at the top and a Start Preview button at the bottom. When you click the Start Preview button, your text appears in the preview window with the settings you have applied so far, and the Start Preview button turns into a Stop Preview button. Click the Stop Preview button to turn off the preview and continue to adjust settings for your banner.

Add and Format Text   To add the text to your animated banner, enter it in the text-entry box (the large white box) on the Text tab (see Figure 14-5). Then use the options and controls in the dialog box to format your text.

These options and controls work in the same way as they do in PhotoImpact, with the exception of the color box, which is set up a bit differently in GIF Animator. To select text color, you must *left* click on the color box, since right clicking is not enabled. You'll see a pop-up menu with color choices, as shown here.

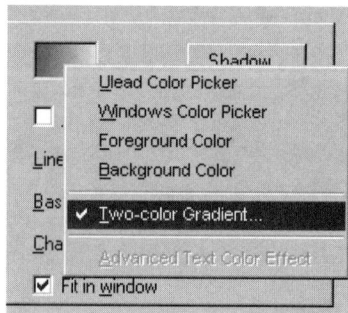

The Two-Color Gradient option enables you to select two colors that will slowly blend into each other. However, there's an undocumented trick you can use to add more than two colors using this option. Pick any two colors, and then choose HSB Clockwise or HSB Counterclockwise for the Color Mode option. Regardless of which two colors you choose, or even if you choose the same color as the starting and ending color, one of these modes will create a multi-colored rainbow effect, and the rainbow will begin and end with the colors you selected.

The Anti-aliasing option helps your text blend smoothly into the background. So, in most cases, you'll want to leave this option selected. However, if you're using very small text or outlined text, and you notice that your text has blurry edges, try selecting the text in the text-entry box and then deselecting Anti-aliasing. In most cases, this will fix the problem.

Note that once you've added text and then decide you want to change something (such as the font face or size), you must first select the text that you want to change in the text-entry box. Select the text by dragging over it (press the left mouse button, run your mouse over the text you want to edit, and then release the mouse button).

To change the placement of your text on your banner, run your mouse over the text in the preview window until the cursor changes to a small black arrow, as shown below. Then drag and drop the text into your desired location.

Apply Text Effects   From the Effect tab, shown in Figure 14-6, you can apply transition effects to your text. Choose the Enter Scene option to animate the process of your text entering the banner, the Exit Scene option to animate the process of your text exiting the banner, or both to apply both entrance and exit effects.

Next, choose an effect from the list boxes for the entrance and exit effects. There are a total of 12 effects available:

- **Scroll Left**   Text moves from the right side of the banner to the left side of the banner.

14

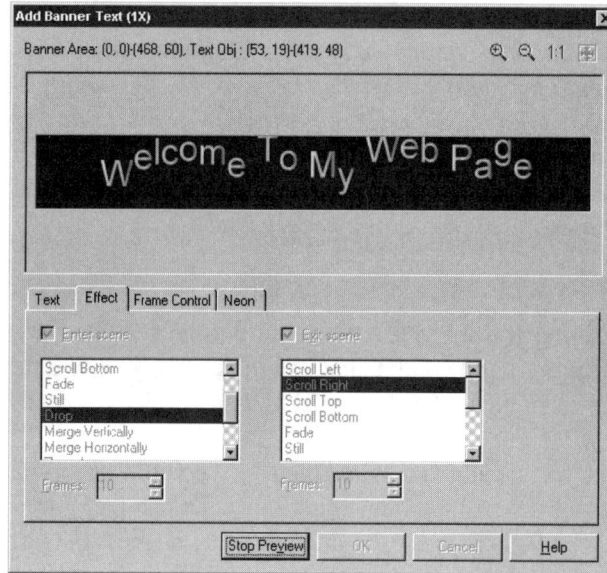

FIGURE 14-6 The Effect tab of the Add Banner Text dialog box

- **Scroll Right** Text moves from the left side of the banner to the right side of the banner.

- **Scroll Top** Text scrolls upward from the bottom of the banner.

- **Scroll Bottom** Text scrolls downward from the top of the banner.

- **Fade** Text fades into existence (when used on entrance) or out of existence (when used at exit).

- **Drop** In the entrance effect, text drops into place with different letters traveling at different speeds (see Figure 14-6). In the exit effect, text drops toward the bottom of the banner, again with different letters traveling at different speeds.

- **Merge Vertically** In the entrance effect, odd-numbered characters move into place from the top of the banner, while even-numbered characters move into place from the bottom of the banner. (GIF Animator essentially numbers the characters in your text; you don't actually see the numbers, but they're used by GIF Animator to create the animation.) In the exit effect, the characters start out in their original position, and then the odd-numbered characters move toward the bottom of the banner, while the even-numbered characters move toward the top of the banner.

- **Merge Horizontally** Using the odd-numbered/even-numbered characters approach described for Merge Vertically, in the entrance effect, the odd-numbered characters move into place from the left side of the banner, and the even-numbered characters move into place from the right side of the banner. In the exit effect, the odd-numbered characters move toward the right of the banner, while the even-numbered characters move toward the left of the banner.

- **Zoom In** In the entrance effect, the text starts out almost invisible and slowly moves into place. In the exit effect, the text starts out normal, and appears to move toward the screen with the letters becoming bigger as they move "closer" to you.

- **Zoom Out** In the entrance effect, the text starts out large and slowly zooms into place. In the exit effect, the text starts normal, and then slowly zooms out until it's so small it can't be seen.

- **Zoom In Rotate** This works the same as the Zoom In effect, but with an added feature: In addition to zooming, the text rotates as it moves into or out of place.

- **Zoom Out Rotate** As you might expect, this is the opposite of the Zoom In Rotate effect. In addition to zooming, the text rotates as it zooms into or out of place.

NOTE *There is also a Still effect available, which simply freezes the text in place on entrance or on exit.*

14

When you apply an entrance effect, GIF Animator will start the effect with the text almost entirely off the screen and slowly move the text into the position where you put it when you dragged and dropped it into place. For example, if you positioned the text in the middle of the banner and selected the Scroll Left entrance effect, the text would start on the right side of the screen, move (or scroll) left, and stop at the point where you positioned the text originally.

When you apply an exit effect, the effect *starts* at the point where you dropped it into place. For example, if you choose the Scroll Right exit effect, the exit effect will *start* with the text appearing exactly where you dropped it, and the text will then slowly scroll to the right until it moves off the screen.

You can mix and match entrance and exit effects in any manner you desire. For example, you may want to use Zoom In as an entrance effect and Merge Vertically as an exit effect, so that there are two different effects in the same animation. When mixing and matching effects in this way, there are well over 100 different combinations.

You can also set the amount of frames that you would like devoted to both your entrance and exit effect, using the Frames control beneath the list boxes. More frames means a more detailed animation, but also a larger animation (in terms of file size). As a general rule, if you're going to use both an entrance and an exit effect, it's a good idea to start out by using 10 frames for each effect, and then click the Start Preview button to see if you're pleased with the results. If you would like a more detailed effect, consider using 20 frames for either an entrance or an exit effect, but instead of applying both entrance and exit effects, apply only one of these effects.

Set Frame Speed   The Frame Control tab, shown in Figure 14-7, is used to set the speed of your animation. When working with GIF animations, the frame speed is measured in hundreths of a second. You may find the following chart helpful in translating GIF time delays to real time.

GIF Delay Time	Actual Time
1	1/100 second
10	1/10 second
100	1 second
200	2 seconds
500	5 seconds

In the Delay Time box, set the speed for most of the frames in your animation. A setting of 10 is a good starting point, particularly if you chose to use a 10-frame entrance effect and a 10-frame exit effect. This will cause the entrance to occur over a period of 1 second, and the exit to appear over a period of 1 second.

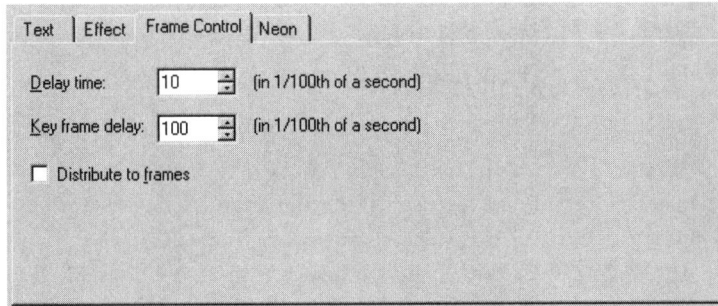

FIGURE 14-7   The Frame Control tab of the Add Banner Text dialog box

Whenever you create an entrance effect only, GIF Animator will add a special frame to the end of the animation where no transition occurs. When you create an exit effect only, this special frame will be added to the beginning of the animation. If you use both an entrance effect and an exit effect, GIF Animator will add this special frame to the middle of the animation. This special frame is referred to by the Animated Banner module as the Key Frame. In the Key Frame Delay box, you set the speed for this special frame. When working with text, you'll usually want to use a Key Frame Delay setting of at least 100 to 200 (1 to 2 seconds). This gives your audience sufficient time to read the text, without the distraction that can be caused by excessive movement.

The last setting in the Frame Control tab is the Distribute to Frames checkbox. If you have an existing animation that you want to add text animation to, you'll find this checkbox to be extremely powerful. To use this option, first load your existing animation into GIF Animator. Next, follow the usual procedure to create a banner animation, paying extra attention to placing the text precisely where you want it to appear on top of your existing animation. When you're finished creating your banner animation, the text will be added to your existing animation using a transparent background, so that the banner text blends in perfectly with your existing animation. This powerful ability to combine text and a background animation is the kind of feature you would normally see in only a very complicated (and very expensive) video editor.

14

Individual Frame Speed— A GIF Animation Bonus

The ability to change the rate of speed at which each frame is displayed is a unique quality of GIF animation. In video animation, there is no such control. The only speed that can be set in video animation is the speed for the entire animation (for example, 10 frames per second).

Suppose you were using a speed of 10 frames per second in a video. If you wanted the animation to stay motionless for 2 seconds after a transition, the only way to accomplish this would be to add 20 copies of the same frame at the point where you wanted the video to appear to pause. This padding technique obviously adds significantly to the file size of a video.

The ability to avoid padding, by being able to set a unique speed for each frame in an animation, is one of the factors that has made GIF animation such an exceptional format for use on the Web.

Add a Neon Effect   If you want to add another impressive special effect to your animation, click the Neon tab in the Add Banner Text Effects dialog box. This tab lets you add a neon glow surrounding the text, as shown in Figure 14-8.

You can set the following options for the neon effect:

- The Direction drop-down box offers options for adding the neon effect to the inside of your text, the outside of your text, or both the inside and outside of your text. For the most realistic neon effect, you'll usually want to use the Outside setting.

- The Width box sets the width of the neon glow.

- The Color box sets the color of the glow.

- The Glow checkbox makes the neon effect slowly fade on and off during your animation. In most cases, you'll want to leave this box unchecked, since adding too much activity to a text animation can be distracting.

- The Transparency checkbox makes your text transparent, but surrounded by a neon glow.

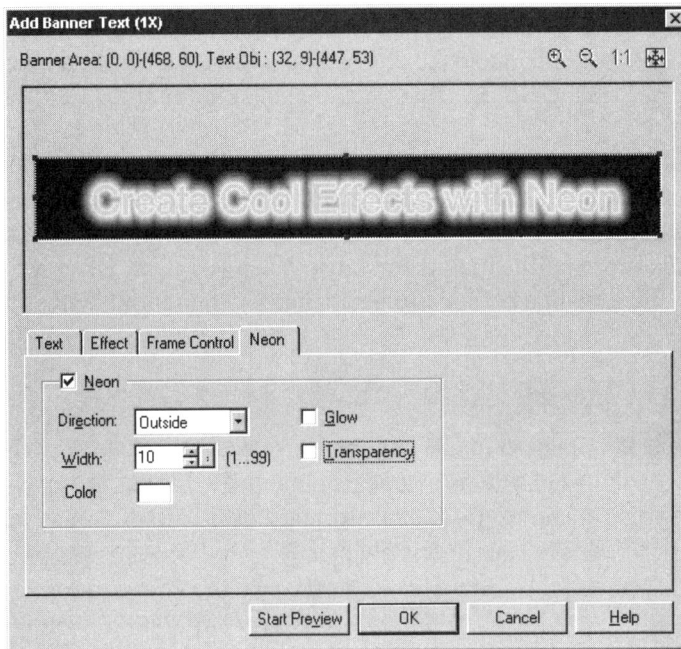

FIGURE 14-8   The Neon tab of the Add Banner Text dialog box

If you're seeing jagged edges between your neon and your text, try deselecting Anti-aliasing on the Text tab.

> **TIP** *You can create pulsating neon text from the Add Banner Text dialog box without using transition effects. Set both the entrance and exit effects to Still, and check the Glow box on the Neon tab. Your text will remain perfectly still, but the Neon light surrounding it will pulsate on and off.*

Finish the Animated Banner Creation   When you are satisfied with your animated banner settings, click OK in the Add Banner Text box to create it. GIF Animator will give you two options:

- The Create As Individual Objects option creates your text as objects on a transparent background. This is a powerful option for when you plan on adding the text animation to another animation that you haven't yet created.

14

- The Create As Banner Text option creates your animation using a series of GIF Animator Text Objects. The advantage in using these special text objects is that you can make changes to a banner animation by selecting the text object in the Object Panel and then clicking Frame | Edit Banner Text.

Edit Your Banner Animation   After you close the Add Banner Text dialog box, you can return to it if you want to make changes to your animated banner. To do so, select Frame | Edit Animated Banner. Then you can modify the animated banner settings in any of the dialog box tabs. When you click OK after making your changes, they will automatically be applied to your entire banner animation.

Save Your Work

To save your new animation in GIF Animator, select File | Save As. Ulead GIF Animator 5 uses the UGA file format as its default file format. Along with the UGA option, you can choose from other formats, as described in the "Export Your Animation" section later in this chapter.

| TIP | *It's a good idea to save your work using GIF Animator's default file format, even if you export the image to a format such as GIF, JPEG, or PNG. This way, you will have a copy of the animation that retains all of sthe GIF Animator information. When you export an image to another format, you usually lose some image information that may be useful if you choose to edit the image at a later time.* |

When you choose the UGA format, GIF Animator presents you with an options dialog box. These three options deal only with compression:

- The None option uses no compression. On a *very* slow computer, the None option might save your file a bit faster than the other options.

- The RLE option uses RLE compression, which is *lossless*. This means it compresses the animation without losing any image information.

- The JPEG option should be avoided unless you're on the edge of running out of hard disk space. Although JPEG compression will result in the smallest possible UGA file, it accomplishes this by using *lossy* compression, meaning that some image data could be lost during the compression process.

Usually, it's a good idea to use RLE as your compression option.

Use GIF Animator's Editing Power

After you create a GIF animation—in GIF Animator, PhotoImpact, or another image editor such as Adobe Photoshop or Corel Bryce—you can take advantage of GIF Animator's powerful editing features to fine-tune your animation. You'll learn about using GIF Animator's editing features in the following section.

Add Images to GIF Animator

One way to work with GIF Animator is to open a group of previously saved images and put them together as an animation using GIF Animator's tools. For example, if you saved an animation you created with one of PhotoImpact's animation effects as a series of bitmap images, as explained in Chapter 13, you can open these files in GIF Animator.

To add one or more images to an animation in GIF Animator, select File | Add Images or press the INSERT key. The Add Image dialog box opens, as shown in Figure 14-9.

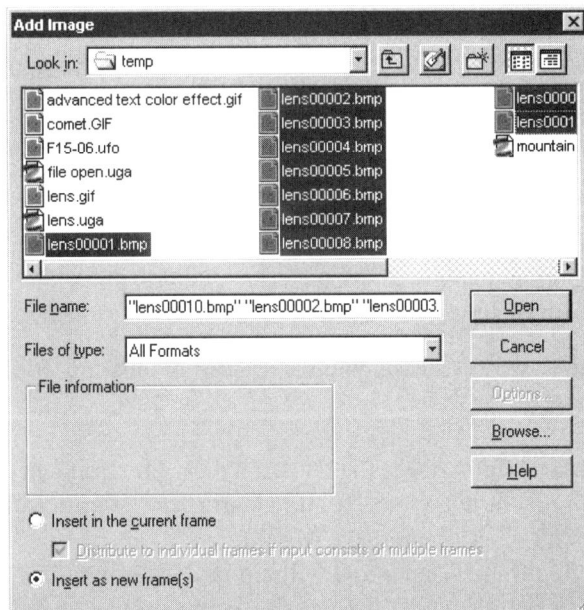

FIGURE 14-9 Adding a series of images to an animation in GIF Animator

You can select multiple image files to add at the same time, using standard Windows techniques. To select a group of consecutively listed image files (a series of images that are in alphabetical order; PhotoImpact's animation filters name images in this way), SHIFT-click (click the first desired image, then while pressing the SHIFT key, click the last desired image). To choose image files that are not consecutively listed, CTRL-click (click while pressing the CTRL key) each image. When you're finished selecting images, be sure that the Insert As New Frame(s) radio button is selected at the bottom of the dialog box. Then click OK. The images will each be added to GIF Animator, in alphabetical order.

> **NOTE**   *If you're starting out with a blank animation in GIF Animator and assembling frames created in PhotoImpact (or another editor), the blank animation should be the same dimensions as the animation that you're adding. If the blank animation is not the same dimensions, choose File | New, enter the correct dimensions, and click OK.*

Add Video or Animated GIFs to GIF Animator

To add a video (or a previously created animated GIF) to GIF Animator, choose File | Add Video. The Add Video dialog box opens, as shown in Figure 14-10.

You'll notice that the Add Video dialog box has a few more features than the Add Images dialog box. These options work as follows:

- The play button, near the bottom of the dialog box, shows a preview of the file before opening it. When the Auto Play checkbox is selected, the preview will play automatically whenever you click a new animated GIF or video file.

- The Info button displays a property sheet that displays file information such as compression type, frames per second, and file size.

- The Duration button allows you want to bring only a portion of the file into GIF Animator.

Clicking the Duration button opens the Duration dialog box, shown in Figure 14-11. Here, you set the point at which you want to start copying frames from the video and placing them in GIF Animator (the Mark In point) and the point at which you want to stop copying frames and opening them in GIF Animator (the Mark Out point). Use the four buttons under the left side of the preview window to advance backward and forward in the video. When you reach the point where you want to start copying frames, click the Mark In button, which is the one with the left-

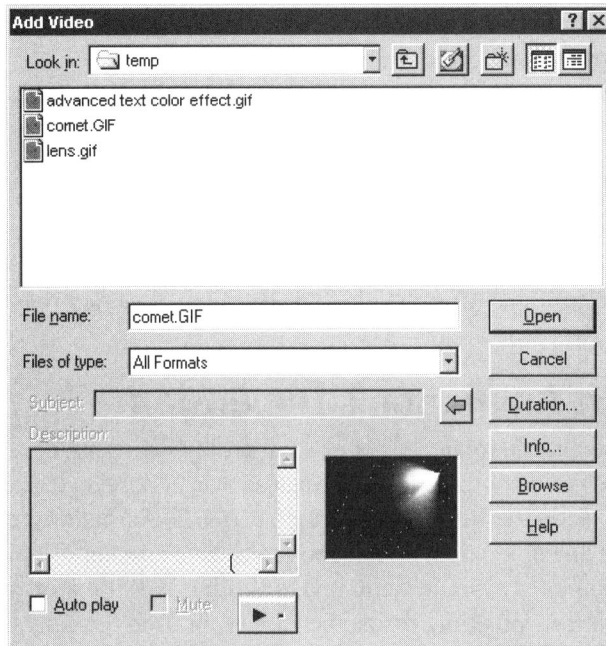

FIGURE 14-10   The Add Video dialog box

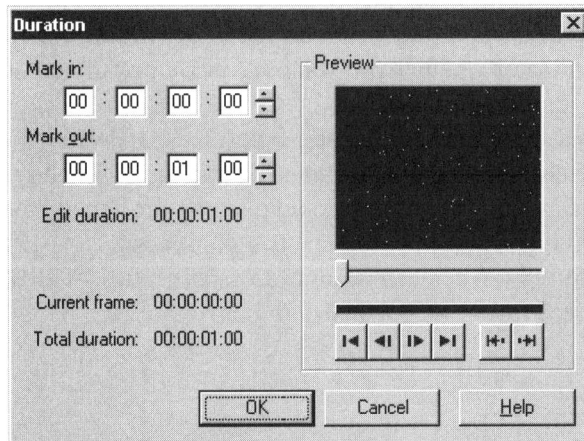

FIGURE 14-11   The Duration dialog box

pointing arrow in the pair of buttons under the right side of the preview window. To set the point where you want to stop copying frames, click the Mark Out button, which is to the right of the Mark In button.

The Mark In and Mark Out edit boxes on the left side of the Duration dialog box may also be used to enter the Mark In and Mark Out times. When using these edit boxes, time is measured in the format HH:MM:SS:FF (Hours, Minutes, Seconds, Frames). Note that the last number is not measuring the total number of frames in the video; it's only measuring frames since the last time the seconds value changed. For example, the frame that exists at 00:00:02:01 is not the first frame of the video. Rather, it's the first frame after the video reached the 2-second point.

Change an Animation's Dimensions

It's easy to make a static image larger or smaller, but changing the size of an animation can be more complex. This is because every frame in the animation must be changed in exactly the same way. Fortunately, GIF Animator provides tools to make changes to an entire animation in about the same amount of time it would take you to make changes to a single static image. With GIF Animator, you can change the size of the entire animation, resize the canvas, or crop the canvas.

Resize Your Animation

To change the size of your entire animation in a single step, select Edit | Resize Image. The Resize Image dialog box opens, as shown in Figure 14-12.

Set the new dimensions in the Width and Height boxes. Use the Unit drop-down list to tell GIF Animator whether you want to calculate your new image size using pixels or percentages.

Selecting the Keep Aspect Ratio checkbox forces GIF Animator to keep your animation's current proportions. Maintaining the aspect ratio will prevent you from accidentally entering dimensions that could distort your image. For example, if your image is 200 pixels wide by 100 pixels high, it has a 2:1 aspect ratio (width is always measured first when determining an aspect ratio). A 200×100 image can easily be resized to 100×50, since both image sizes use the same aspect ratio.

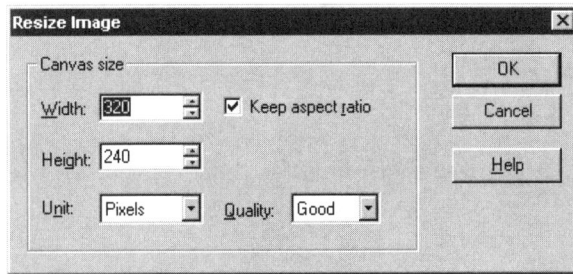

FIGURE 14-12   The Resize Image dialog box

However, if you were to change your 200×100 image's dimensions to 100×100, you would change the aspect ratio to 1:1, resulting in quite a bit of distortion.

The Quality drop-down list offers options to tell GIF Animator how much detail to put into calculating the change in dimensions. Your choices are Fair, Good, and Best. Although your computer may be able to tell the difference between the Quality settings Good and Best, the differences are likely to be undetectable to the human eye. So, in most cases, a setting of Good will be sufficient.

Resize the Canvas

GIF Animator allows you to resize your canvas without resizing the image that's currently on your canvas. For example, suppose you have an image of a landscape and you want to make room to add banner text above the landscape, without changing the size of the landscape image. By enlarging the canvas, you can add space for the text, without making the landscape any bigger, as shown here.

14

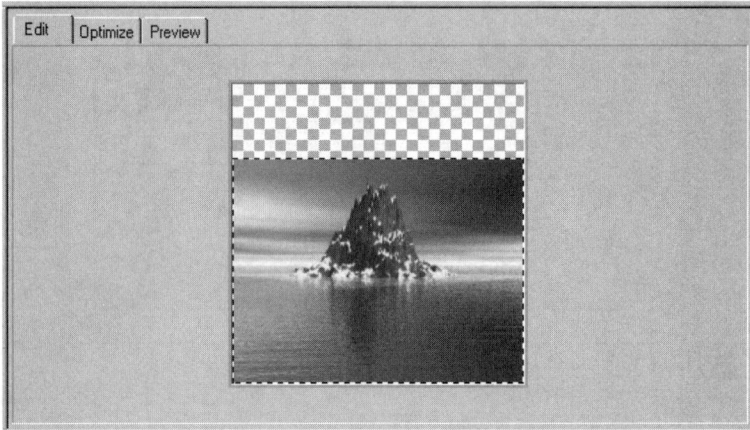

To change the size of the canvas, select Edit | Resize Canvas or press CTRL-G. GIF Animator displays the Canvas Size dialog box, as shown in Figure 14-13.

Like the Resize Image dialog box, the Canvas Size dialog box includes Keep Aspect Ratio, Width, Height, and Unit options. When you resize your canvas, you can allow the aspect ratio to be changed without causing distortion, because no changes are made to your image.

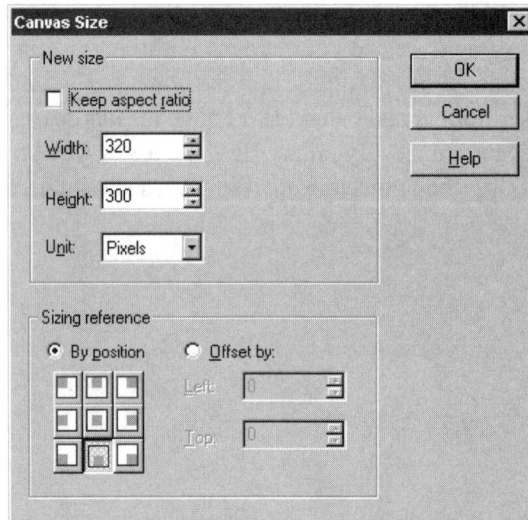

FIGURE 14-13 The Canvas Size dialog box

The Canvas Size dialog box also includes a Sizing Reference section, which enables you to decide where you would like your current image to be placed on your new canvas. You can click any of the nine squares to tell GIF Animator where to position your current image in relation to your new canvas, or use the Offset By option to enter exact coordinates for your current image.

Crop the Canvas

As in an image editor, GIF Animator allows you to crop your images. First, use one of the selection tools in the Tool panel to select the image area that you want to keep. Then select Edit | Crop Canvas or press CTRL-R to remove any part of your image that is outside the selection area.

> **TIP** *An undocumented feature in GIF Animator enables you to use the selection tools found in the tool panel to add to or subtract from a selection, in addition to using them to create the original selection. To add to a selection area, hold down the SHIFT key while using the selection tool. To subtract from a selection area, hold down the ALT key while using the selection tool.*

Undo and Redo Changes

Like Photompact, GIF Animator tracks changes that you make and provides extremely useful undo and redo capabilities. To undo in GIF Animator, click the Undo button on the Standard toolbar. To redo something you've undone, click the Redo button on the Standard toolbar. If you would like to undo or redo more than one change, click the small arrow to the right of the undo or redo button for a list of items that you may undo or redo. By default, GIF Animator stores nine levels of undo and redo. However, you may increase this to up to 50 levels. To access the undo/redo properties, select File | Preferences | General.

14

> **TIP** *It's a good idea to set the undo and redo levels to the maximum of 50, just in case you ever need to undo or redo major changes to an image. However, if your machine has limited resources, an undo/redo level of 20 may be more reasonable.*

Manipulate Objects

Each frame in GIF Animator contains at least one object (unless the frame is completely transparent). Of course, you can add more than one object to a frame, and make the same object visible across as many frames as you like (this is a process that can be used in object animation).

To work with an object, you must first select it to make it the active object. To do so, click the object using the Pick tool or click it in the Object Manager panel, as shown here.

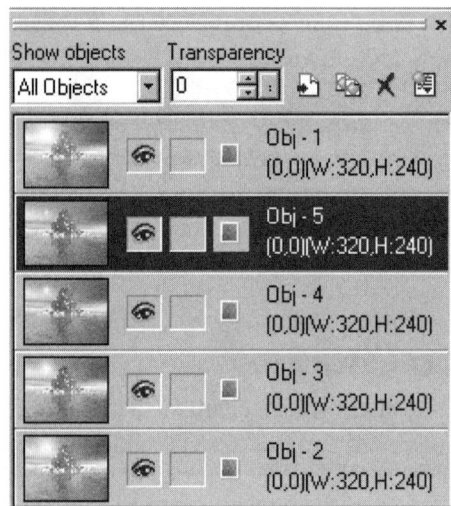

In the Object Manager panel, notice the eye icons. When an eye icon appears next to an object, that means that the object is visible. If an object shows as visible, but you still can't see it, move it to the front of all other objects by clicking the Pick tool and then clicking the Bring to Front tool (the third tool from the left) on the Pick tool's Attribute panel.

As you can also see in the Object Manager panel, GIF Animator gives each object you create a default name, such as Obj-1. If you have a large collection of objects, you may find it convenient to give your objects descriptive names, such as Background or Floating Sphere. You can rename an object in the Name edit box in the Object Properties dialog box, shown in Figure 14-14. This dialog box also offers a convenient way to change various object properties, such as size, location, shadow, and transparency.

You can work with objects as follows:

- **Delete an object**   To delete an object, select it and choose Object | Delete Object or press the DELETE key.

- **Add an object**   To add an object, select Object | New Blank Object or press CTRL-ALT-D. New blank objects automatically use the size of your canvas as their default size. Once a new object is created, you may fill it with color, paint on it, or manipulate as you would any other object. You may also add a rectangular object from any image editor by copying it into the clipboard and then pasting it into GIF Animator (this offers a convenient way to add objects into GIF Animator which were created in other image editors).

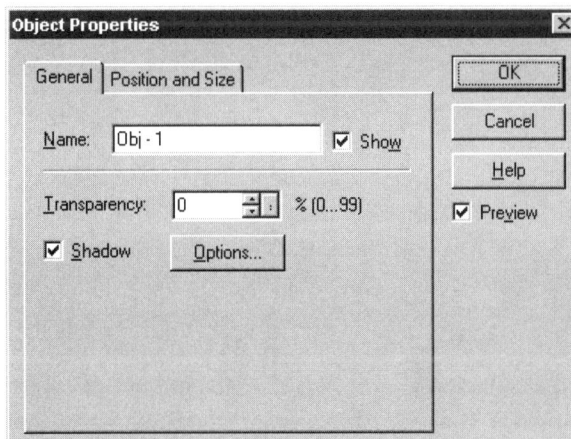

FIGURE 14-14   The Object Properties dialog box

- **Duplicate an object**   To duplicate an object, select it and choose Object |
  Duplicate Object. You can then use the Pick tool to place the object exactly
  where you want it to be located.

- **Trim an object**   Trimming enables you to convert a selection in GIF
  Animator into an object with a transparent background. To do this, create
  a selection and then choose Object | Trim Object. Note that since the
  background will be transparent, you can use nonrectangular selections.

- **Add a shadow**   To add a shadow to an object, select Object | Shadow.
  This opens the Shadow dialog box, as shown in Figure 14-15. The dialog
  box works in the same way as the Shadow dialog box in PhotoImpact and
  in GIF Animator's Banner Text module. You can separate a shadow from
  an object, so that it can be manipulated independently of its parent object,
  by choosing Object | Shadow | Split Shadow.

TIP *You can use the Shadow dialog box to create a glow effect around an
object. To accomplish this, change the shadow color from black to a light
color or white. Then click the fifth shadow type button from the left (see
Figure 14-15).*

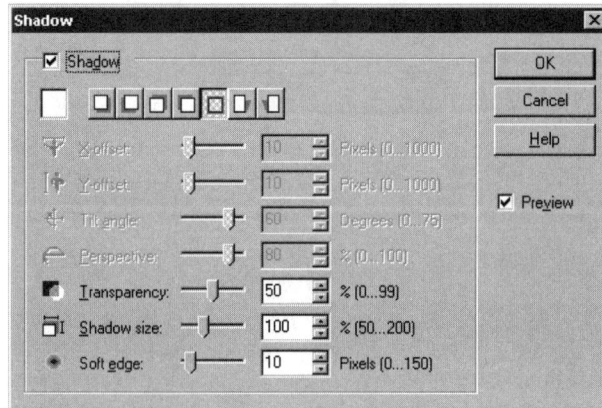

FIGURE 14-15   Using the Object Shadow dialog box to create a glow effect

- **Fill an object with color**   To fill part or all of a transparent object with color, first make a selection (if desired), then click the Fill tool. Make sure that the Allow Painting on Transparent Areas option in the Fill tool's Attribute toolbar is checked, and then use the Fill tool to color the object.

- **Split text objects**   When you create text in GIF Animator, it's created as a single text object. However, if you want to treat each letter of text as an individual object (for example, to create a custom text animation effect), select the text and choose Object | Text | Split Text. GIF Animator converts each letter of your text into an object, complete with a transparent background.

Manipulate Frames

As you learned earlier, a frame is a single image contained in an animation file. There may be times when you'll want to make changes to frames, just as you make changes to the objects that frames contain.

> **TIP**   *You can select two or more frames at the same time by holding down the* SHIFT *or* CTRL *key while left-clicking. Then, whatever action you take next will be taken on all of the selected frames.*

Add, Duplicate, and Remove Frames

You can add, copy, and delete frames as follows:

- **Add a frame**   To add a blank frame to you animation, choose Frame | Add Frame or press CTRL-ALT-F. Of course, a blank frame isn't all that useful without an object to put in it. If you've already created your object in your image editor, copy it into the clipboard and paste it into the frame in GIF Animator.

- **Duplicate a frame**   To duplicate a frame, select the frame by clicking it with the Pick tool, and then choose Frame | Duplicate Frame(s) or press CTRL-F. If objects were visible in the original frame, the same objects will visible in the newly created frame.

- **Delete a frame**   To delete a frame, select the frame and choose Frame | Delete Frame(s).

14

Adjust Frame Movement

When you press the play button under the left side of the Frame panel, you'll get a preview of what your animation will look like (you can also preview at any time by clicking the Preview tab). If you feel that the movement from one frame to the next is not smooth, adjust the frame removal method.

To accomplish this, select all your frames, right-click, and click Frame Properties. Try changing the frame removal method from Smart to Web Browser Decides. This will resolve almost all issues, but if you're still not pleased with the results, experiment with the other frame removal methods.

Add Adobe Photoshop Filters to GIF Animator

One of the many things that sets Ulead GIF Animator 5 apart from other GIF animation programs is its ability to handle Adobe Photoshop plugins. Adobe Photoshop plugins are used to add additional features to a program, such as color correction, texture creation, and image sharpening. Most such plugins aren't actually made by Adobe, but since they comply with a plugin format that was originally developed by Adobe for use in Photoshop, the term *Adobe Photoshop plugins* is used to describe them.

Almost every Adobe Photoshop plugin on the market will work in both Ulead PhotoImpact 7 and Ulead GIF Animator 5 (there are a few minor exceptions, such as plugins that are used to change the Abode Photoshop interface). If you have Adobe Photoshop plugins on your hard drive and would like to make them available in GIF Animator, select File | Preferences | Plug-In Filters and use the browse button to locate the filters. After you add the filters, you will need to close and reopen GIF Animator for the filters to become available. To access your new filters, open the Filter menu.

> **NOTE** *Most filters work on only 16-bit (or higher) full-color images, so you'll need to use them before compressing your files to the 8-bit GIF file format.*

Edit in Another Image Editor

Ulead GIF Animator 5 has an exhaustive selection of editing tools. Still, there will be times when you'll want to use your favorite image editor, such as Ulead PhotoImpact, to perform editing that can only be done outside GIF Animator. For example, you may want to use PhotoImpact to create a 3D sphere with a reflection map for use in a GIF Animation, or use PhotoImpact's photo editing tools to touch up a photograph. When such an occasion arises, GIF Animator has the unique ability to work in real time with your image editor, through its Favorite Image Editor feature.

Set Up Favorite Image Editors

The only requirement for making your image editor a Favorite Image Editor is that it be able to use either Ulead's UFO format or Adobe's PSD format. Since Adobe's PSD format was one of the first layer/object-oriented file formats to be used in Windows, it's available in every major image editor on the market, including Adobe Photoshop, Corel Photo-Paint, Jasc Paint Shop Pro, and Macromedia Fireworks. Although PhotoImpact supports Adobe's PSD file format, the preferred UFO format is used when you select PhotoImpact as your Favorite Image Editor.

To set up a list of Favorite Image Editors, choose Edit | Favorite Image Editor | Organize Favorite Image Editor. Click the Add button and then use the browse button to search for your image editors on your hard drive (they'll usually be located in C:\Program Files). Type a name for the image editor in the Program Name dialog box, and then click OK.

Edit in Your Favorite Image Editor

To edit the frames of your animation in one of your Favorite Image Editors, select Edit | Favorite Image Editor and click its name. Your animation file will be saved as a PSD or UFO file, with each frame in the animation saved as a unique layer/ object in the PSD or UFO file. The file will then be opened in the image editor you selected.

You can proceed to edit the image just as you would any other image using the image editor. When you would like to update the image in GIF Animator, choose to save the file in your image editor. A dialog box will automatically pop up and offer to update the image in GIF Animator. When you're finished editing, close the image in your image editor and return to GIF Animator. A dialog box will open, asking if you're ready to close the session and delete the temporary file. Click Yes to accept the option. The image will then update in GIF Animator, complete with any changes you made to it in your image editor.

14

Optimize Animations for the Web

Optimization is a process made necessary by the speed limitations of most Internet connections. When you're working with print images, optimization isn't a factor. As long as you have enough room on your hard drive to store the image, there's no need to risk making changes to the image just to make its file size smaller.

On the Web, it's a different story. The larger your image is, the longer it will take your web site's viewers to download it. Given the vast resources of the Web, most web surfers don't feel the need to waste time waiting for a slow loading page to display. If your page doesn't load quick enough, visitors will simply click the stop button on their browser, and then visit another site. For this reason, it's important to keep your animations as small as possible.

Optimizing images for use on the Web is a concept that Ulead practically invented with its original GIF Animator. Since then, GIF Animator's compression tools have continued to improve with every release. The tools in GIF Animator 5 will enable you to create images with the best combination of high quality and small file size.

GIF Animator's Optimization tab and Optimization Wizard both make the same suite of powerful compression tools available to you. The only difference is that the Wizard guides you through the use of these tools step by step, while the Optimization tab enables you to set options in any order you desire.

Compare Optimizations on the Optimization Tab

GIF Animator's Optimize tab, shown in Figure 14-16, provides tools for optimizing your animations. On this tab, the work area display two windows side by side. The window on the left displays a frame from your image without optimization applied; the window on the right shows the same frame with optimization applied. Above the left window, you'll see your animation's file size and download time estimate before optimization. Above the right window, you'll see your animation's file size and download time estimate after optimization.

By comparing the frames in the left and right windows, and their respective file size and download time estimates, you'll be able to find the best combination of file size and image quality. In terms of how you arrive at this best combination, there's no single recipe that works with every animation—the optimization process is more of an art than it is a science. However, by learning optimization methods that have the most impact on file size and the least impact on quality, you can quickly master this art and apply it to your animations.

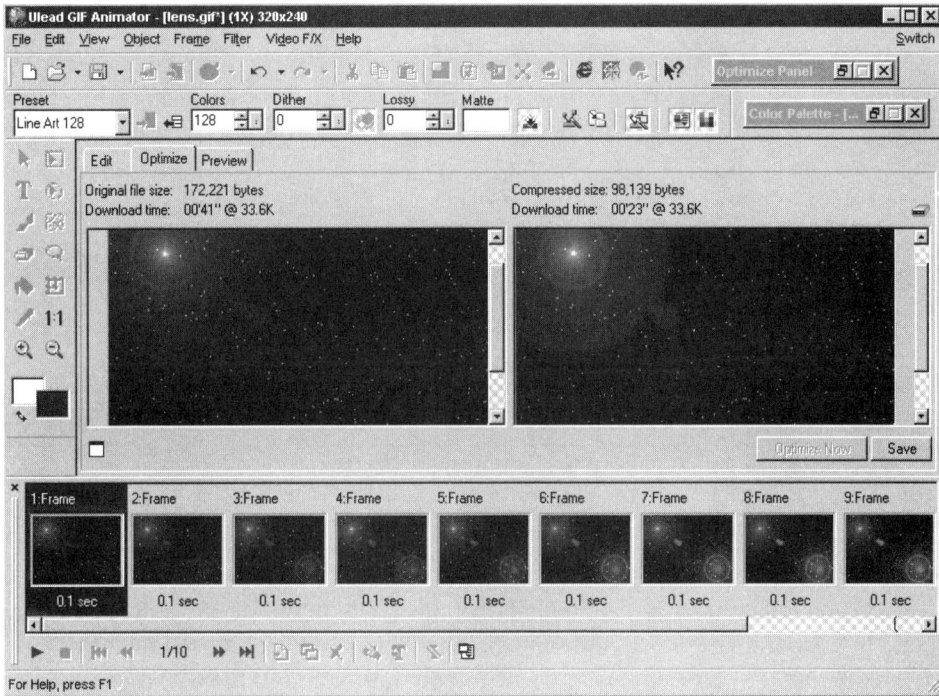

FIGURE 14-16   The Optimize tab

As noted earlier, you can use the settings on the Optimization tab to apply optimizations to your animation. The next section details the optimization options and processes.

Use the Optimization Wizard

The Optimization Wizard provides step-by-step assistance in optimizing your animations. However, keep in mind that whether you prefer to use the Optimization Wizard or the settings on the Optimization tab, the results are identical.

To access the Optimization Wizard, select File | Optimization Wizard or press F11. The first page of the Wizard opens, as shown in Figure 14-17. Although you could just select the Optimize Using a Preset option, choose a preset, and click Finish, it's best for the learning process to see how each page of the Wizard works.

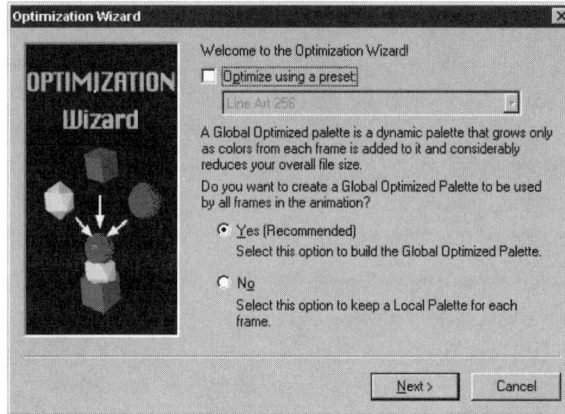

FIGURE 14-17   The first page of the Optimization Wizard

Global Palette versus Local Palettes

Every GIF animation has a palette that contains a maximum of 256 colors. If every frame in your animation uses the same palette, this palette is referred to as the *global palette*. If you permit each frame in your animation to have its own palette, these palettes are referred to as *local palettes*.

As for which type of palette is better to use in your animations, the answer is almost always the global palette. This is because a single global palette takes up less space than a series of local palettes. How much less space is directly related to the number of frames in your animation.

In addition to the room needed to store your animation's frames, the GIF format needs exactly 768 extra bytes of file space for every 256-color palette that it contains. In a 3-frame animation using local palettes, this would total 2,304 bytes dedicated to palette storage, a fairly insignificant number that wouldn't really affect your download time. On the other hand, you don't see many 3-frame GIF animations. In a 20-frame GIF animation, you would need 15,360 extra bytes to store 20 local palettes. This is where the benefit of using the global palette becomes apparent.

As a general rule, you should always use a global palette. And, as with any general rule, there is an exception to this one: If your animation contains significant color changes as it moves from frame to frame, you may want to use local palettes to preserve those extra colors. But always try the global palette first. When you're finished setting options in the Optimization Wizard, you'll have the opportunity to preview your results. If you aren't happy with them, you can make changes to your optimization choices. The Optimization Wizard even contains a Try Again button that you can use to return to the first page of the Wizard.

Color Count and Dither Value

The next page of the Wizard, shown in Figure 14-18, lets you set color count and dithering. As you know, GIF animations contain a maximum of 256 colors per frame. However, GIFs can contain fewer colors if you want them to. In most cases, you'll want to take advantage of having 256 colors available in your GIF. But if you find that you file size is too large, and you're already using a global palette, you may be able to trim some additional file size by lowering your animation's color count.

If you're considering reducing the number of colors, it's a good idea to cut your color count in half, and then check your results. So, if you're not happy with the results you get using 256 colors, try 128 colors, then 64 colors, then 32 colors. Although GIF Animator is capable of using as few as 2 colors, results using under 32 colors are seldom acceptable.

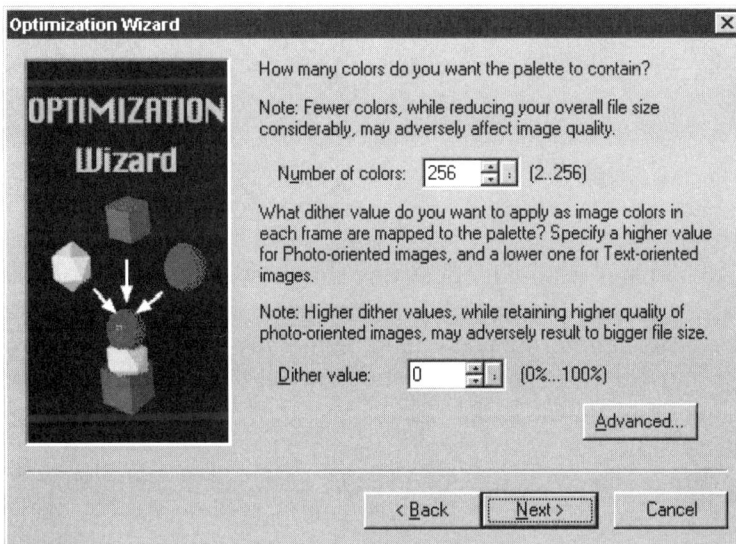

FIGURE 14-18   Setting color count and dithering in the Optimization Wizard

A common problem in some GIF animation programs is that they use 256 colors even if they don't need to. GIF Animator will not make this mistake. If, for example, your image contains only 128 colors, GIF Animator is programmed to realize this, and it will not use more than 128 colors when compressing the image.

The next value that you'll set is dithering. Dithering is the process of using two colors that are available in your palette to simulate the presence of a third color that's not available in your palette. Consider the images shown below. The image on the left basically looks like a block of gray, but it's not a block of gray at all. It's actually a series of black and white dots placed closely together to simulate the color gray. The image on the right shows the same image magnified by a factor of 4, which makes it clear that the image contains plenty of black and white, but no gray.

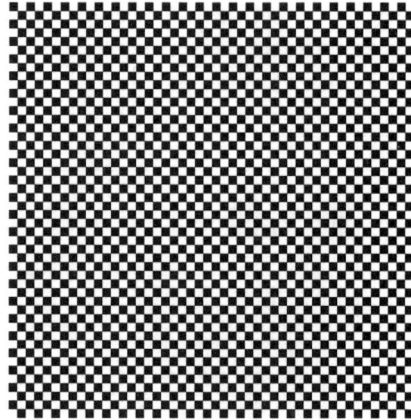

This is dithering in action. It effectively simulates the existence of colors that really aren't there. Unfortunately, there is a negative side to dithering: The GIF format has a difficult time compressing the constantly changing dots of color that dithering creates. So, when should you use dithering? Sometimes, a high-color image, such as a GIF animation that uses a photograph as a background, will require dithering. That aside, you usually won't need it.

In the Optimization Wizard, you can apply a level of dithering from 0 (no dithering) to 100 percent (full dithering). If you find that 100 percent dithering increases the file size too much, try reducing the dithering setting to 50 percent and examine the results.

Set Advanced Options

The second page of the Optimization Wizard has an Advanced button that gives you control over even more GIF Animator options. Click this button to open the Advanced Options dialog box, shown in Figure 14-19.

Lossy GIF Optimization   The first option in the Advanced Options dialog box is Lossy GIF Optimization. *Lossy optimization* improves compression by discarding some image data. This is a trick that the JPEG format can get away with, since it's not very detectable on the high-color images used in JPEG compression. In GIF compression, it doesn't work out quite as well. If you're working with a photograph, and dithering increased your file size way too much, you might try lossy GIF at 10 percent, just to see what happens. In any case, lossy GIF settings of over 20 percent are best avoided entirely.

Palette   The Palette option offers three choices: Optimized, Web 216, and user-defined. Optimized is usually the best choice since it creates a palette based on the colors already found in your image. Web 216 is the web-safe palette that was discussed earlier in this chapter. User-defined is available in case you want to create your own palette, which is rarely (if ever) necessary, since GIF Animator does such an excellent job of choosing the best colors for your palette.

Method   Next you have a chance to tell GIF Animator how you want to create your optimized palette. Of the two options, Minimum Variance almost always produces the color palette that more closely represents the colors in your original image. On the other hand, the Median Cut option usually results in a slightly

14

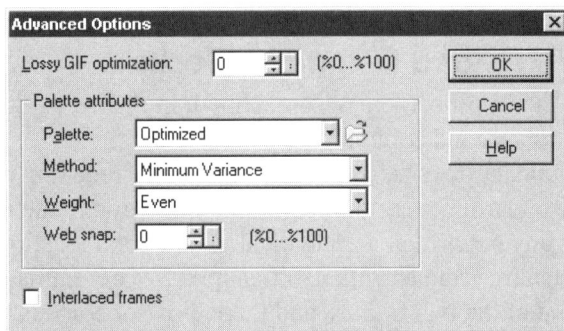

FIGURE 14-19   Setting Advanced Options in the Optimization Wizard

smaller file size. Try Minimum Variance as your first option. If the file size of your end result is too large, try switching to Median Cut. If the file size improves and you're pleased with color reproduction, you can go with this method.

Weight   The Weight option enables you to tell GIF Animator if it should favor a particular color channel when creating your palette. This option is usually best set at Even. However, if you find that a particular color isn't reproducing well, try favoring a specific color channel to see if it improves color reproduction. This option has a very minimal effect on file size, so it should be a concern only when a color reproduction issue arises.

Web Snap   Web Snap lets you add a percentage of the Web 216 colors to your image. Since Web Safe colors are not recommended, you'll probably never need to change this setting from 0.

Interlaced Frames   Checking the Interlaced Frames checkbox in the Advanced Options dialog box causes each frame to be saved with the GIF Interlace option. In the case of static GIFs, this can be a nice effect, since it causes the image to gradually come into focus. However, since animations are designed to quickly move from image to image, and since this option can increase file size, you'll usually avoid using interlacing. If you have a particular animation that just isn't playing the way you want it to, you can try interlacing to see if it creates the effect that you're trying to achieve.

Redundant Pixels and Comment Blocks

The third page of the Optimization Wizard, shown in Figure 14-20, allows you to remove redundant pixels and comment blocks.

Removing redundant pixels is a powerful option for reducing file size. The option works by comparing every frame of your animation to the next frame and seeing if there are any pixels that are identical in color and location. If there are, for example, consecutive frames with identical pixels, GIF animator removes the pixels in the second of the two frames, and then allows the pixels from the first frame to continue displaying while rest of the second frame is being displayed.

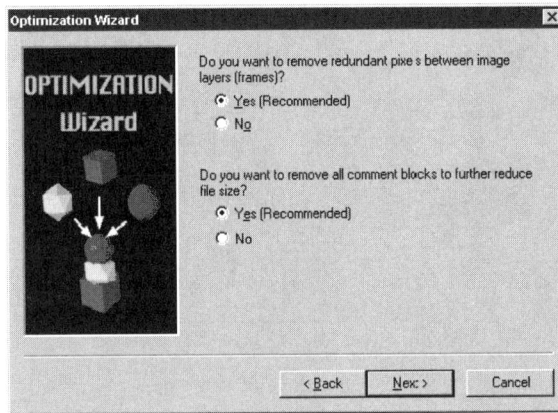

FIGURE 14-20   Removing redundant pixels and comment blocks in the Optimization Wizard

It may sound awkward, but the effect is undetectable to the human eye, and it can often result in a significant improvement in file size.

Removing the comment blocks that some image editors add to GIF animation files is another method of reducing file size without affecting quality. However, since the comments are limited in size, the effect is minimal.

Save Your Optimized Animation as a GIF File

When you click Finish in the Optimization Wizard, you'll be taken to a summary dialog box that shows you exactly how well the compression process worked out, as shown in Figure 14-21. If you're happy with the results, click Save As to save your file.

In the Save As dialog box, there's an Open in Index Editor option. The Index Editor, shown in Figure 14-22, lets you set a transparent background color and gives you an opportunity to make any final changes to your animation.

To set a transparency color, check the Transparent Index option, click the color in the color palette that you want to be transparent, and then click the Apply Transparent Index to All Images icon (at the bottom of the Index Editor). Click Save As to save any changes.

14

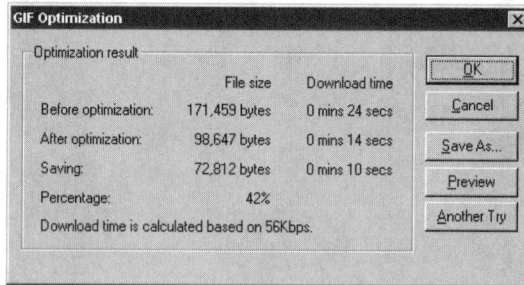

FIGURE 14-21 The GIF Optimization dialog box

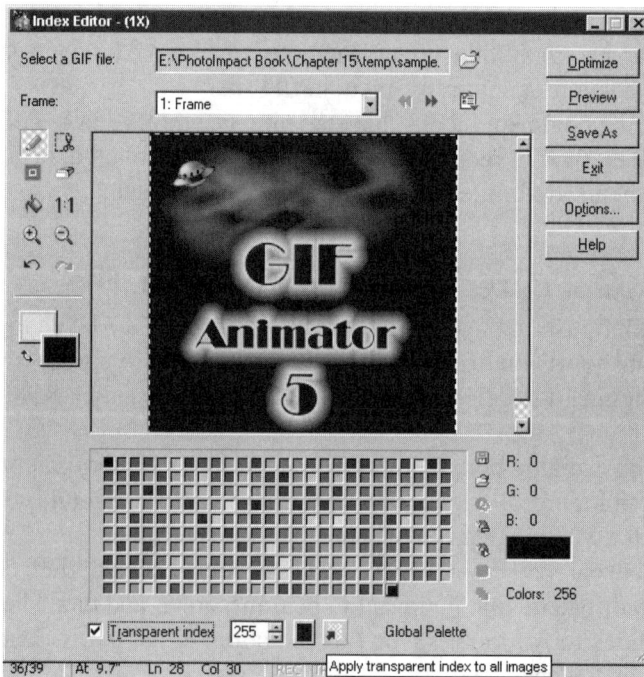

FIGURE 14-22 The Index Editor

Some Final Words on Optimization

Each of the figures showing an Optimization Wizard page (Figures 14-17 through
14-20) shows my personal recommendations for optimization. You may want to
use these recommendations as a guide in setting options the first few times that you
use the Optimization Wizard. Table 14-1 provides a summary of the optimization
settings, the values I recommend, and when you might use other settings.

As you become more comfortable with the optimization process, you may want
to start using the Optimization tab instead of the Optimization Wizard. You're less

Option	Recommended Start Value	When to Change
Global vs local palette	Global palette	Use local palette when the animation needs significant color changes from frame to frame.
Color count	256	Try fewer colors when you need to reduce file size (but try changing to the Median Cut method first).
Dithering	0	Set a dither percentage if you need to correct poor color reproduction in photos (which will often require 100% dithering).
Lossy compression	0	Set a lossy compression percentage if you need to reduce file size (this is usually a last-resort method).
Palette	Optimized	Changing this setting is not recommended.
Method	Minimum Variance	If you need to reduce file size, switching this to Median Cut is a good place to start.
Weight	Even	Try changing the weight to favor a particular color channel if a color or group of similar colors is not reproducing accurately.
Web Snap	0	Changing this setting is not recommended.
Interlacing	Off	In some rare cases, interlacing results in better playback.
Remove redundant pixels	On	Changing this setting is not recommended.
Remove Comment Block	On	Turn this off if you want to include a text comment in your file.

TABLE 14-1   Recommended Optimization Settings

14

likely to miss trying an optimization method in the Wizard, given its page-by-page walk-through of the optimization process. However, as you gain more experience, you may find the "everything on one page" approach of the Optimization tab to be more convenient.

Export Your Animation

As you learned in the previous section, when you complete the optimization process, you can save your animation in GIF format. You can also export your animation as an animated GIF file from the File | Save As dialog box. However, unless you choose to open the Index Editor from the Save As dialog box, and then choose to open the Optimization Wizard from within the Index Editor, you'll be missing the opportunity to use GIF Animator's powerful optimization features. Using the Optimization Wizard (by selecting File | Optimization Wizard or pressing F11) is the preferred option for exporting GIF animations.

In addition to the GIF animation format, GIF Animator provides additional export options. Regardless of which export options you choose, it's a good idea to also save a copy of your file in the UGA (Ulead GIF Animation) format by selecting File | Save As | UGA. Since this is GIF Animator's proprietary format, it's the best way to ensure that you'll be able to edit your file in the future, should you choose to make changes.

Export Images

To export a series of individual images from GIF Animator, such as two or more frames, click File | Save As | Image Frames or press CTRL-E. Be certain that you click the Export All Frames box (unless you only want to export the currently selected frame).

The PNG format is the best option, since it uses lossless compression. However, PNG compression can be a bit slow, particularly on older computers, and PNG images will take up more file space than JPEG images. If either of these issues presents a problem, choose JPEG as your compression format, and set the quality to 90 for best results.

You can also export your animation as a single UFO or PSD file containing all of your animation's frames. The frames will be saved as objects (when using UFO) or layers (when using PSD). To export using either of these formats, select File | Save As and click UFO or PSD.

Export Videos

Video is becoming increasingly popular as a full-color alternative to GIF animation. The following video formats can be exported from GIF Animator:

- AVI

- FLC, FLI, and FLX

- MOV and QT

- MPG

To export your animation as a video file, select File | Save As | Video File. AVI is generally the best format to use, since this is the default video format for Windows. Since the recent rise in popularity of Windows Media Player 7 the Microsoft MPEG 4 Video Codec for AVI has become the compression method of choice for the best combination of quality and file size.

CAUTION   *Although the new Div-X codecs often provide better quality and compression than the Microsoft codecs, the Div-X codecs are not yet widely distributed among end users, so you should use the Div-X codecs with quite a bit of caution. If you compress using a Div-X codec, and your audience does not have the Div-X codec installed, your video will not be playable.*

Export Flash Animations

The ability to export Ulead GIF animation files as bitmap-based Macromedia Flash animations is a very welcome new feature. Macromedia reports that its Flash player is present on nearly all Web-connected computers. Flash animation supports 24-bit true color, so there's no need to be concerned with losing colors (as can happen when you compress your images to the GIF format). But, perhaps the best news of all is that Flash enjoys this full-color support in files that are often half the size of comparable GIF animations.

Exporting to the Flash format from within GIF Animator takes just a few seconds. Select File | Save As | Macromedia Flash and then choose With BMP or With JPEG. JPEG is the preferred compression method, since bitmaps will often result in unnecessarily large Flash files. GIF Animator sets the default JPEG compression quality at 90 and the default subsampling at YUV411. Note that 90 may be a bit

14

excessive. You can usually lower the compression quality setting to 80, as shown below, and end up with a smaller Flash file and no noticeable quality loss.

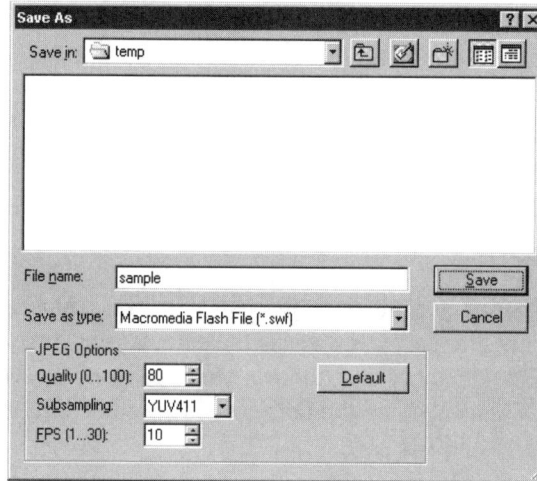

You won't need to be concerned about the FPS (Frames Per Second) setting, since GIF Animator will calculate this automatically based on the speed used by the frames in your GIF animation.

TIP	*JPEG-based compression is known for creating artifacts in files that contain text. If you run into this problem when using JPEG-based Flash animation, set the Quality option to 80 and the Subsampling option to None. This should prevent JPEG text artifacts from forming in your Flash file.*

Export an HTML File

Exporting your animation as an HTML file has GIF Animator save an HTML file along with your animation. (This option saves both an HTML file and your GIF file.) Choose File | Export | Export as HTML File to use this option. You can then open the HTML code in a text editor (such as Notepad), copy the HTML code, and paste it into your HTML editor. The <IMG SRC> tag is the HTML tag that you're looking for. In the example below, this tag is highlighted in bold type.

```
<HTML>
<HEAD>
```

```
<TITLE>Ulead GIF Animator</TITLE>
<META http-equiv="Content-Type" content="text/html">
</HEAD>
<BODY bgcolor = "ffffff">
<IMG SRC="banner.gif" WIDTH=468 HEIGHT=60 BORDER=0 ALT="banner.gif">
</BODY>
</HTML>
```

Note that you should use this option with caution, as the GIF file is saved with the same name that you give the HTML file. For example, saving banner.htm will result in a GIF file called banner.gif. The risk is that if you already have a file in the folder you're using with the name banner.gif, that file will be overwritten without warning, with a new file called banner.gif.

Export an Active Desktop Item

To play an animated GIF file on your desktop, you normally need to display your desktop using the Microsoft Active Desktop feature, include your animation in a web page, and then set this web page as your Active Desktop background. Choosing File | Export | Export As Active Desktop Item performs all of these steps in a single action.

When you choose Export As Active Desktop Item, GIF Animator produces the export and automatically replaces your current desktop. If you aren't happy with the results, you can change your Windows desktop to remove the animation (Windows desktop settings are accessed by right-clicking the Windows desktop and then clicking Properties).

Export an Animated Package

14

The File | Export | Export As Animated Package option is a unique choice that you won't usually find in a GIF animation program. It enables you to add music to your animation, in the form of a WAV or MIDI file, and then export the entire package as an .exe (executable) file that can be e-mailed to friends or business associates. When using this option, MIDI music files will result in much smaller file sizes than WAV files.

The file can then be played on any computer using Windows, even if your recipients don't have GIF animation software installed on their computers.

> **TIP** *The Page Turn effect in the PhotoImpact Animation Studio can be used to create a virtual greeting card similar to those often seen on greeting card web sites, complete with music and animation.*

This is a nice option for sending an animated greeting card for birthdays and holidays, but it's something that's obviously useful only if your recipient knows and trusts you. Since the .exe file format could be used by a malicious user to store a virus, most recipients won't open the file unless they know you can be trusted.

Index

INTERNATIONAL CONTACT INFORMATION

AUSTRALIA
McGraw-Hill Book Company Australia Pty. Ltd.
TEL +61-2-9417-9899
FAX +61-2-9417-5687
http://www.mcgraw-hill.com.au
books-it_sydney@mcgraw-hill.com

CANADA
McGraw-Hill Ryerson Ltd.
TEL +905-430-5000
FAX +905-430-5020
http://www.mcgrawhill.ca

GREECE, MIDDLE EAST,
NORTHERN AFRICA
McGraw-Hill Hellas
TEL +30-1-656-0990-3-4
FAX +30-1-654-5525

MEXICO (Also serving Latin America)
McGraw-Hill Interamericana Editores S.A. de C.V.
TEL +525-117-1583
FAX +525-117-1589
http://www.mcgraw-hill.com.mx
fernando_castellanos@mcgraw-hill.com

SINGAPORE (Serving Asia)
McGraw-Hill Book Company
TEL +65-863-1580
FAX +65-862-3354
http://www.mcgraw-hill.com.sg
mghasia@mcgraw-hill.com

SOUTH AFRICA
McGraw-Hill South Africa
TEL +27-11-622-7512
FAX +27-11-622-9045
robyn_swanepoel@mcgraw-hill.com

UNITED KINGDOM & EUROPE
(Excluding Southern Europe)
McGraw-Hill Education Europe
TEL +44-1-628-502500
FAX +44-1-628-770224
http://www.mcgraw-hill.co.uk
computing_neurope@mcgraw-hill.com

ALL OTHER INQUIRIES Contact:
Osborne/McGraw-Hill
TEL +1-510-549-6600
FAX +1-510-883-7600
http://www.osborne.com
omg_international@mcgraw-hill.com

OTHER COOL TOOLS
from Ulead

About the CD

The CD includes a free demo version of PhotoImpact 7, including the Ulead companion program GIF Animator. You get these two programs, and several other Ulead products to try out, plus an assortment of sample images from the book's chapters that you can use to get started experimenting with PhotoImpact and its capabilities. The software is fully functional, but it will expire after a 30-day trial period. You can convert the trial software to unlimited use by purchasing a license from the Ulead web site at http://www.ulead.com. (See the installation instructions and license agreement on the CD for full details.)

Also on the CD, you will find color versions of many of the figures and illustrations that appear in the book. That way, you can open the images to see what the images really look like instead of relying solely on the black-and-white illustrations on the book pages. The images are located on the CD in a folder called PhotoImpact Official Guide and are organized into subfolders according to chapter.